PROVERBS-ECCLESIASTES

Smyth & Helwys Bible Commentary: Proverbs-Ecclesiastes

Publication Staff

President & CEO
Cecil P. Staton

Publisher & Executive Vice-President
David Cassady

Vice-President, Editorial
Lex Horton

Senior Editor
Mark K. McElroy

Book Editor
P. Keith Gammons

Art Director
Jim Burt

Assistant Editors
Kelley Land, Laura Shuman

Smyth & Helwys Publishing, Inc.
6316 Peake Road
Macon, Georgia 31210-3960
1-800-747-3016

The paper used in this publication meets the minimum
requirements of American National Standard for Information
Sciences—Permanence of Paper for Printed Library Materials.
ANSI Z39.48–1984 (alk. paper)

Library of Congress Cataloging-in-Publication Data

Horne, Milton P.
Proverbs-Ecclesiastes / Milton P. Horne
p. cm. — (Smyth & Helwys Bible commentary, 12)
Includes bibliographical references and indexes.
ISBN 1-57312-069-3
1. Bible. O.T. Proverbs – Commentaries.
2. Bible. O.T. Ecclesiastes – Commentaries.
I. Title. II. Series.

BS1465.53 H67 2003
223'.707—dc22

2003014881

SMYTH & HELWYS BIBLE COMMENTARY

PROVERBS-ECCLESIASTES

MILTON P. HORNE

SMYTH&HELWYS
PUBLISHING INCORPORATED · MACON, GEORGIA

PROJECT EDITOR
R. SCOTT NASH
Mercer University
Macon, Georgia

OLD TESTAMENT
GENERAL EDITOR
SAMUEL E. BALENTINE
Baptist Theological Seminary
at Richmond, Virginia

NEW TESTAMENT
GENERAL EDITOR
R. ALAN CULPEPPER
McAfee School of Theology
Mercer University
Atlanta, Georgia

AREA
OLD TESTAMENT EDITORS
MARK E. BIDDLE
Baptist Theological Seminary
at Richmond, Virginia

AREA
NEW TESTAMENT EDITORS
R. SCOTT NASH
Mercer University
Macon, Georgia

KANDY QUEEN-SUTHERLAND
Stetson University
Deland, Florida

RICHARD B. VINSON
Baptist Theological Seminary
at Richmond, Virginia

KENNETH G. HOGLUND
Wake Forest University
Winston-Salem, North Carolina

ART EDITOR
FRED WHITEHURST
Georgia State University
Atlanta, Georgia

ADVANCE PRAISE

This commentary on Proverbs and Ecclesiastes provides a balanced examination of two of the primary collections of wisdom from ancient Israel and early Judaism. What are especially helpful are the succinct introductions to each of these two books that examines the various options for viewing them within the sapiential and historical contexts of the larger Israelite and Jewish communities. Thus, Horne avoids the pitfall of simply providing a literary treatment that points to ideas and the peculiarities of the moral understandings and language of these two books. In addition, his work demonstrates the theological richness of wisdom in general and these two books in particular. This commentary undoubtedly will earn a place among the best treatments of Proverbs and Ecclesiasties in recent scholarship.

Leo G. Perdue
Gast Professor of Old Testament
Heidelberg University

As the most recent addition to the Smyth & Helwys Bible Commentary Series, *Proverbs/Ecclesiastes* is informative and well-written, crafted for both the biblical scholar and the interested layperson. Horne tackles the contentious aspects of Proverbs and Ecclesiastes with keen sensitivity. He carefully interprets a voluminous body of scholarship without overwhelming the reader. A grand reward awaits those who enter within.

Wayne Ballard
Associate Professor of Religion
Carson-Newman College

ADVANCE PRAISE

Milton Horne's introduction to Proverbs and Ecclesiastes is truly remarkable. He transforms the best of contemporary Wisdom scholarship into a language and format that is accessible for general readers. The writing is clear and enjoyable, while his interpretive insights are sensitive and compelling. The book truly shines, though, as a point of entry into academic approaches to the Bible. Horne demonstrates how the questions and methods employed by scholars can strengthen and enrich faithful exegesis in the church. For teachers and students in church and university settings, this introduction will provide a firm basis for learning, and serve as an inspiring model for serious inquiry into the Bible's meaning.

Bryan Bibb
Department of Religion
Furman University

The books of Proverbs and Ecclesiastes are wondrous reflections on wisdom and the life of faith, and Milton Horne, in the new Smyth & Helwys commentary on Proverbs and Ecclesiastes, has brought these books alive for the reader. Professor Horne's introductory essays provide readers with the background and information to thoroughly read and study these two very different wisdom writings. The commentary on the text of books is lively and engaging. The illustrations, sidebars, and tools are, as has become the standard in the Smyth & Helwys commentary series, outstanding. With this commentary, I believe that readers will come to a new appreciation of the importance of the books of Proverbs and Ecclesiastes to the life of faith.

Nancy L. deClaissé-Walford
Associate Professor of Old Testament and Biblical Languages
McAfee School of Theology

CONTENTS

PROVERBS

ECCLESIASTES

ABBREVIATIONS USED IN THIS COMMENTARY

Books of the Old Testament, Apocrypha, and New Testament are generally abbreviated in the Sidebars, parenthetical references, and notes according to the following system.

The Old Testament

Genesis	Gen
Exodus	Exod
Leviticus	Lev
Numbers	Num
Deuteronomy	Deut
Joshua	Josh
Judges	Judg
Ruth	Ruth
1–2 Samuel	1–2 Sam
1–2 Kings	1–2 Kgs
1–2 Chronicles	1–2 Chr
Ezra	Ezra
Nehemiah	Neh
Esther	Esth
Job	Job
Psalm (Psalms)	Ps (Pss)
Proverbs	Prov
Ecclesiastes	Eccl
or Qoheleth	Qoh
Song of Solomon	Song
or Song of Songs	Song
or Canticles	Cant
Isaiah	Isa
Jeremiah	Jer
Lamentations	Lam
Ezekiel	Ezek
Daniel	Dan
Hosea	Hos
Joel	Joel
Amos	Amos
Obadiah	Obad
Jonah	Jonah
Micah	Mic

Nahum	Nah
Habakkuk	Hab
Zephaniah	Zeph
Haggai	Hag
Zechariah	Zech
Malachi	Mal

The Apocrypha

1–2 Esdras	1–2 Esdr
Tobit	Tob
Judith	Jdt
Additions to Esther	Add Esth
Wisdom of Solomon	Wis
Ecclesiasticus or the Wisdom of Jesus Son of Sirach	Sir
Baruch	Bar
Epistle (or Letter) of Jeremiah	Ep Jer
Prayer of Azariah and the Song of the Three	Pr Azar
Daniel and Susanna	Sus
Daniel, Bel, and the Dragon	Bel
Prayer of Manasseh	Pr Man
1–4 Maccabees	1–4 Macc

The New Testament

Matthew	Matt
Mark	Mark
Luke	Luke
John	John
Acts	Acts
Romans	Rom
1–2 Corinthians	1–2 Cor
Galatians	Gal
Ephesians	Eph
Philippians	Phil
Colossians	Col
1–2 Thessalonians	1–2 Thess
1–2 Timothy	1–2 Tim
Titus	Titus
Philemon	Phlm
Hebrews	Heb
James	Jas
1–2 Peter	1–2 Pet
1–2–3 John	1–2–3 John
Jude	Jude
Revelation	Rev

Other commonly used abbreviations include:

BC	Before Christ
(also commonly referred to as BCE = Before the Common Era)	
AD	*Anno Domini* ("in the year of the Lord")
(also commonly referred to as CE = the Common Era)	
v.	verse
vv.	verses
C.	century
c.	*circa* (around "that time")
cf.	*confer* (compare)
ch.	chapter
chs.	chapters
d.	died
ed.	edition or edited by or editor
eds.	editors
e.g.	*exempli gratia* (for example)
et al.	*et alii* (and others)
f./ff.	and the following one(s)
gen. ed.	general editor
ibid.	*ibidem* (in the same place)
i.e.	*id est* (that is)
LCL	Loeb Classical Library
lit.	literally
n.d.	no date
rev. and exp. ed.	revised and expanded edition
sg.	singular
trans.	translated by or translator(s)
vol(s).	volume(s)

Selected additional written works cited by abbreviations include:

AB	Anchor Bible
ABD	*Anchor Bible Dictionary*
ANET	*Ancient NearEastern Texts*
AJSL	*American Journal of Semitic Languages and Literature*
BA	*Biblical Archaeologist*
BETL	Bibliotheca ephemeridum theologi carum lovaniensium
Bib	*Biblica*
BKAT	Biblischer Kommentar: Altes Testament
CBQ	*Catholic Biblical Quarterly*

CBQMS	Catholic Biblical Quarterly — Monograph Series
CJT	*Canadian Journal of Theology*
COT	Commentary on the Old Testament
CUP	Cambridge University Press
HBD	*Harper's Bible Dictionary*
HTR	Harvard Theological Review
HSM	Harvard Semitic Monographs
HUCA	*Hebrew Union College Annual*
IBC	Interpretation: A Bible Commentary for Teaching and Preaching
IDB	*Interpreter's Dictionary of the Bible*
JAOS	*Journal of the American Oriental Society*
JBL	*Journal of Biblical Literature*
JSOT	*Journal for the Study of the Old Testament*
JSOTSup	Journal for the Study of the Old Testament — Supplement Series
MT	Masoretic Text
MDB	*Mercer Dictionary of the Bible*
MMM	*Man, Myth & Magic*
NAC	New American Commentary
NIB	*New Interpreter's Bible*
OBT	Overtures to Biblical Theology
REP	Routledge Encyclopedia of Philosophy
RHP	Routledge History of Philosophy
SA	Scientific American
TDOT	*Theological Dictionary of the Old Testament*
UCOP	University of Cambridge Oriental Publications
VT	*Vetus Testamentum*
WBC	Word Biblical Commentary

AUTHOR'S PREFACE

It is with both thanksgiving and reluctance that I complete this commentary on Proverbs and Ecclesiastes. Cause for thanksgiving is obvious; reluctance stems from now having the experience of writing such a work and retrospectively imagining how I might have done things differently. Humility remains. So much of this work is indebted to the expansive learning of so many other scholars whose works I have read. The process of reflection on Proverbs and Ecclesiastes has truly been a journey of learning. Of course, the weaknesses of this volume may only be attributed to my limitations as a student, certainly not to any shortcoming of my teachers.

I must offer gratitude to William Jewell College for granting me leave to begin the project back in 1994. My colleagues at the college who have patiently listened to me go on and on about these biblical books deserve much more than mere mention in a preface. I also fondly remember friends at the Second Baptist Church, Liberty, Missouri, who read portions of the manuscript and offered both encouragement and caution. I have deeply appreciated the help of Jared Horne and Julia Kennedy in preparing indices. Finally, my colleagues in the religion department at William Jewell — Dr. David Nelson Duke, until his death in 2000, Dr. J. Bradley Chance, and most recently Dr. Sally Holt — have been models of disciplined scholarship, deep devotion to the classroom, and faith that does not shrink from or gloss over questions that lack clear answers.

Milton Horne

SERIES PREFACE

The *Smyth & Helwys Bible Commentary* is a visually stimulating and user-friendly series that is as close to multimedia in print as possible. Written by accomplished scholars with all students of Scripture in mind, the primary goal of the *Smyth & Helwys Bible Commentary* is to make available serious, credible biblical scholarship in an accessible and less intimidating format.

Far too many Bible commentaries fall short of bridging the gap between the insights of biblical scholars and the needs of students of God's written word. In an unprecedented way, the *Smyth & Helwys Bible Commentary* brings insightful commentary to bear on the lives of contemporary Christians. Using a multimedia format, the volumes employ a stunning array of art, photographs, maps, and drawings to illustrate the truths of the Bible for a visual generation of believers.

The *Smyth & Helwys Bible Commentary* is built upon the idea that meaningful Bible study can occur when the insights of contemporary biblical scholars blend with sensitivity to the needs of lifelong students of Scripture. Some persons within local faith communities, however, struggle with potentially informative biblical scholarship for several reasons. Oftentimes, such scholarship is cast in technical language easily grasped by other scholars, but not by the general reader. For example, lengthy, technical discussions on every detail of a particular scriptural text can hinder the quest for a clear grasp of the whole. Also, the format for presenting scholarly insights has often been confusing to the general reader, rendering the work less than helpful. Unfortunately, responses to the hurdles of reading extensive commentaries have led some publishers to produce works for a general readership that merely skim the surface of the rich resources of biblical scholarship. This commentary series incorporates works of fine art in an accurate and scholarly manner, yet the format remains "user-friendly." An important facet is the presentation and explanation of images of art, which interpret the biblical material or illustrate how the biblical material has been understood and interpreted in the past. A visual generation of believers deserves a commentary series that contains not only the all-important textual commentary on Scripture, but images, photographs, maps, works of fine art, and drawings that bring the text to life.

The *Smyth & Helwys Bible Commentary* makes serious, credible biblical scholarship more accessible to a wider audience. Writers and editors alike present information in ways that encourage readers to gain a better understanding of the Bible. The editorial board has worked to develop a format that is useful and usable, informative and pleasing to the eye. Our writers are reputable scholars who participate in the community of faith and sense a calling to communicate the results of their scholarship to their faith community.

The *Smyth & Helwys Bible Commentary* addresses Christians and the larger church. While both respect for and sensitivity to the needs and contributions of other faith communities are reflected in the work of the series authors, the authors speak primarily to Christians. Thus the reader can note a confessional tone throughout the volumes. No particular "confession of faith" guides the authors, and diverse perspectives are observed in the various volumes. Each writer, though, brings to the biblical text the best scholarly tools available and expresses the results of their studies in commentary and visuals that assist readers seeking a word from the Lord for the church.

To accomplish this goal, writers in this series have drawn from numerous streams in the rich tradition of biblical interpretation. The basic focus is the biblical text itself, and considerable attention is given to the wording and structure of texts. Each particular text, however, is also considered in the light of the entire canon of Christian Scriptures. Beyond this, attention is given to the cultural context of the biblical writings. Information from archaeology, ancient history, geography, comparative literature, history of religions, politics, sociology, and even economics is used to illuminate the culture of the people who produced the Bible. In addition, the writers have drawn from the history of interpretation, not only as it is found in traditional commentary on the Bible but also in literature, theater, church history, and the visual arts. Finally, the *Commentary* on Scripture is joined with *Connections* to the world of the contemporary church. Here again, the writers draw on scholarship in many fields as well as relevant issues in the popular culture.

This wealth of information might easily overwhelm a reader if not presented in a "user-friendly" format. Thus the heavier discussions of detail and the treatments of other helpful topics are presented in special-interest boxes, or Sidebars, clearly connected to the passages under discussion so as not to interrupt the flow of the basic interpretation. The result is a commentary on Scripture that focuses on the theological significance of a text while also offering the reader a rich array of additional information related to the text and its interpretation.

An accompanying CD-ROM offers powerful searching and research tools. The commentary text, Sidebars, and visuals are all reproduced on a CD that is fully indexed and searchable. Pairing a text version with a digital resource is a distinctive feature of the *Smyth & Helwys Bible Commentary.*

Combining credible biblical scholarship, user-friendly study features, and sensitivity to the needs of a visually oriented generation of believers creates a unique and unprecedented type of commentary series. With insight from many of today's finest biblical scholars and a stunning visual format, it is our hope that the *Smyth & Helwys Bible Commentary* will be a welcome addition to the personal libraries of all students of Scripture.

The Editors

HOW TO USE
THIS COMMENTARY

The *Smyth & Helwys Bible Commentary* is written by accomplished biblical scholars with a wide array of readers in mind. Whether engaged in the study of Scripture in a church setting or in a college or seminary classroom, all students of the Bible will find a number of useful features throughout the commentary that are helpful for interpreting the Bible.

Basic Design of the Volumes

Each volume features an Introduction to a particular book of the Bible, providing a brief guide to information that is necessary for reading and interpreting the text: the historical setting, literary design, and theological significance. Each Introduction also includes a comprehensive outline of the particular book under study.

Each chapter of the commentary investigates the text according to logical divisions in a particular book of the Bible. Sometimes these divisions follow the traditional chapter segmentation, while at other times the textual units consist of sections of chapters or portions of more than one chapter. The divisions reflect the literary structure of a book and offer a guide for selecting passages that are useful in preaching and teaching.

An accompanying CD-ROM offers powerful searching and research tools. The commentary text, Sidebars, and visuals are all reproduced on a CD that is fully indexed and searchable. Pairing a text version with a digital resource also allows unprecedented flexibility and freedom for the reader. Carry the text version to locations you most enjoy doing research while knowing that the CD offers a portable alternative for travel from the office, church, classroom, and your home.

Commentary and Connections

As each chapter explores a textual unit, the discussion centers around two basic sections: *Commentary* and *Connections*. The analysis of a passage, including the details of its language, the history reflected in the text, and the literary forms found in the text, are the main focus of the *Commentary* section. The primary concern of the *Commentary* section is to explore the theological issues presented by the Scripture passage. *Connections* presents potential applications of the insights provided in the *Commentary* section. The *Connections* portion of each chapter considers what issues are relevant for teaching and suggests useful methods and resources. *Connections* also identifies themes suitable for sermon planning and suggests helpful approaches for preaching on the Scripture text.

Sidebars

The *Smyth & Helwys Bible Commentary* provides a unique hyperlink format that quickly guides the reader to additional insights. Since other more technical or supplementary information is vital for understanding a text and its implications, the volumes feature distinctive Sidebars, or special-interest boxes, that provide a wealth of information on such matters as:

• Historical information (such as chronological charts, lists of kings or rulers, maps, descriptions of monetary systems, descriptions of special groups, descriptions of archaeological sites or geographical settings).

• Graphic outlines of literary structure (including such items as poetry, chiasm, repetition, epistolary form).

• Definition or brief discussions of technical or theological terms and issues.

• Insightful quotations that are not integrated into the running text but are relevant to the passage under discussion.

• Notes on the history of interpretation (Augustine on the Good Samaritan, Luther on James, Stendahl on Romans, etc.).

• Line drawings, photographs, and other illustrations relevant for understanding the historical context or interpretive significance of the text.

• Presentation and discussion of works of fine art that have interpreted a Scripture passage.

Each Sidebar is printed in color and is referenced at the appropriate place in the *Commentary* or *Connections* section with a color-coded title that directs the reader to the relevant Sidebar. In addition, helpful icons appear in the Sidebars, which provide the reader with visual cues to the type of material that is explained in each Sidebar. Throughout the commentary, these four distinct hyperlinks provide useful links in an easily recognizable design.

Alpha & Omega Language

This icon identifies the information as a language-based tool that offers further exploration of the Scripture selection. This could include syntactical information, word studies, popular or additional uses of the word(s) in question, additional contexts in which the term appears, and the history of the term's translation. All non-English terms are transliterated into the appropriate English characters.

Culture/Context

This icon introduces further comment on contextual or cultural details that shed light on the Scripture selection. Describing the place and time to which a Scripture passage refers is often vital to the task of biblical interpretation. Sidebar items introduced with this icon could include geographical, historical, political, social, topographical, or economic information. Here, the reader may find an excerpt of an ancient text or inscription that sheds light on the text. Or one may find a description of some element of ancient religion such as Baalism in Canaan or the Hero cult in the Mystery Religions of the Greco-Roman world.

Interpretation

Sidebars that appear under this icon serve a general interpretive function in terms of both historical and contemporary renderings. Under this heading, the reader might find a selection from classic or contemporary literature that illuminates the Scripture text or a significant quotation from a famous sermon that addresses the passage. Insights are drawn from various sources, including literature, worship, theater, church history, and sociology.

Additional Resources Study

Here, the reader finds a convenient list of useful resources for further investigation of the selected Scripture text, including books, journals, websites, special collections, organizations, and societies. Specialized discussions of works not often associated with biblical studies may also appear here.

Additional Features

Each volume also includes a basic Bibliography on the biblical book under study. Other bibliographies on selected issues are often included that point the reader to other helpful resources.

Notes at the end of each chapter provide full documentation of sources used and contain additional discussions of related matters.

Abbreviations used in each volume are explained in a list of abbreviations found after the Table of Contents.

Readers of the *Smyth & Helwys Bible Commentary* can regularly visit the Internet support site for news, information, updates, and enhancements to the series at <**www.helwys.com/commentary**>.

Several thorough indexes enable the reader to locate information quickly. These indexes include:

• An *Index of Sidebars* groups content from the special-interest boxes by category (maps, fine art, photographs, drawings, etc.).

• An *Index of Scriptures* lists citations to particular biblical texts.

• An *Index of Topics* lists alphabetically the major subjects, names, topics, and locations referenced or discussed in the volume.

• An *Index of Modern Authors* organizes contemporary authors whose works are cited in the volume.

INTRODUCTION TO PROVERBS AND ECCLESIASTES

The purpose of a biblical commentary is to help readers interpret a biblical text more meaningfully. While different commentaries have different audiences and make various assumptions about what a meaningful reading of the Bible might be, all readers would agree that meaning is the goal.

One Hellenistic Jewish sage provides readers with a fairly accurate idea of what might be involved in reading ancient Israel's wisdom literature. He states that devoting oneself to the study of the law means one has to seek out the "hidden meanings of proverbs" and be "at home with the obscurities of parables" (Sir 39:3). Indeed, reading Proverbs and Ecclesiastes will leave readers with a new appreciation for hiddenness. Yet, the uncovering of what is hidden within these books will provide not only a fulfilling challenge in reading ancient Scripture, but will also require that readers begin by actually reflecting upon how to go about it.

This introduction is concerned with some of the questions that help readers understand the processes involved in interpreting these books. To begin, a good rule of thumb is that most questions about reading the Bible can be categorized under one of three categories. Most questions modern readers bring to the Bible are literary, historical, or theological in nature.

Literary questions concern the conventions of writing, collecting, and transmitting the books that now make up the Bible; our concern, first, is with Proverbs and Ecclesiastes and their literary dimensions. Historical questions concern the ancient contexts—historical, cultural, sociological, ideological, and theological—that shaped the performance, writing, collecting, and transmission of the materials contained within our biblical books. Theological questions, a special category of historical questions, concern the sense in which these documents and their contents give expression and guidance to the faith and practice of various communities that worshiped and continue to worship the God of the Bible.

Readers should not think of these three categories as unrelated, however. It is not possible to investigate literary questions, as readers shall see, without also noting historical contexts and theological influences behind the literature. One may not, therefore, simply ask theological questions—under the influence of modern theological interests—without also investigating the ancient theological motivations. Rather, readers should think of these three categories, and the many related subcategories of questions, as forming an interpretive matrix—a kind of three-dimensional grid. Every theological question has a corresponding historical and literary point of contact that informs the theological question. And, to the extent that the relevant historical and literary information is available, readers should use them in formulating meanings of a passage.

Literary Dimensions of Proverbs and Ecclesiastes

The most logical place to begin describing our interpretive matrix seems to be with literary questions. Those who read Proverbs and Ecclesiastes for the first time begin with the text itself and thus begin to make distinctions of various types of materials contained within both books.

Literary Forms

Readers will encounter a diversity of rhetorical forms before completing chapter 1 of Proverbs. The *parental instruction* (Prov 1:8-19) is characterized by a parent's exhortation (1:8-10, 15) and contains a short *saying* (*māšāl*) (1:17), which makes an observation for reflection. A *wisdom poem* (Prov 1:20-33) reflects upon the nature of wisdom. Likewise, the first chapter of the book of Ecclesiastes confronts readers with a *didactic poem* (1:4-11), which opens with a *rhetorical question* (1:3) and leads into a *confession* or *testament* (1:12–2:26). Other forms readers will encounter include *example stories* (Prov 7:6-20; Eccl 4:13-16; 9:13-15), where a short narrative is offered by the instructor to illustrate a point or a conclusion; *better-than* sayings (Prov 17:1; 19:1; Eccl 4:6; 7:2), sayings that make explicit claims about the comparative value of various things by introducing the comparison with the word "better"; and *numerical sayings* (Prov 6:16-19; 30:18-19), where numbers provide an ordinal basis for comparing various phenomena.[1]

This is not an exhaustive list of rhetorical forms readers will encounter. We will address refinements as they arise in the commentary. But there are enough listed in the opening chapters of Proverbs and Ecclesiastes alone to illustrate the kind of attention readers must invest in reading. To read these books meaningfully readers must take note of the subtle distinctions in rhetorical forms within the various collections. It will not suffice to read material that is deliberately shaped as parental instruction, with its explicit imperatives and authoritative reasons, in the same way one would read a saying that makes no explicit attempt to be instructional, or didactic.

Literary Art

In a number of respects, the various forms indicate a level of artistry of which readers may not be aware. Beneath the various *genres* or rhetorical forms is the impulse to express convictions, beliefs, even worldviews in an artistic form. Readers encounter this immediately in the most important and basic poetic convention that defines this literature: parallelism. In Proverbs and Ecclesiastes (and other places in the Hebrew Bible) a single poetic line (or verse) consists of at least two statements placed in relationship to each other. The initial statement makes an observation or a description; its partner(s) qualifies or develops that opening statement in some way. The key to understanding the saying or particular line of poetry is in recognizing the logical relationship(s) between the constituent statements.[2]

For instance, Proverbs 20:5 reads: "The purposes in the human mind are like deep water, but the intelligent will draw them out." The initial statement juxtaposes the "purposes within the human mind" and "deep water." In Hebrew the simile (i.e., use of "like") is *not* there. So the second phrase defines only one possible implication of the first statement with the statement that the "intelligent [i.e., the person of understanding] draws [meaning] out." The word for "draw" is used in reference to the drawing of water elsewhere in the Bible (e.g., Exod 2:19). With the implications of the simile defining the inner "purposes" as water in this saying, it suggests that the intelligent person penetrates beneath the various human facades to understand what cannot be seen on the surface. The sage would be quick to add, were it a lecture format, that only an understanding person has the ability to do this. The double statements therefore stand in a close relationship. The first half-line, or stichos, as we will call them in this commentary, creates the metaphor; the second stichos makes a statement that both assumes the preceding metaphor and advances to at least one possible implication of the statement. While there are several different types of proverbs and sayings—*similes, numerical sayings, imperatives, instructions*—they all have in common this phenomenon of doubling or parallelism. It remains for readers of Proverbs and Ecclesiastes to ponder how the artifice of doubling conveys meaning in each case.

A deeper appreciation of the technique of doubling requires attention to yet other kinds of rhetorical devices. In addition to defining reality through observations that make explicit comparisons and contrasts, techniques of alliteration, paronomasia, and rhyme function to create irony, parody, and humor. Alliteration, for instance, is the repetition of initial identical consonantal sounds in succession, as in "Peter Piper picked a peck of pickled peppers." Readers with knowledge of biblical Hebrew will recognize this in Proverbs 26:1, which accomplishes a similar effect through the repetition of hard gutturals, transliterated as "k" and "q." Paronomasia, or punning, is a play on words based on the similarity of their sounds, even though they have different meanings, as in "They went and told the Sexton and the Sexton tolled the bell."[3] Again, readers of biblical Hebrew see the same effect in Proverbs 6:27. The examples are extensive, and we will consider the remainder as they arise in the text.

Such conventions of creating artistic expression are further accompanied by the proverbs' refined application of metaphor. For instance, some of the proverbs are mere observations that do not purport to have meaning at any level other than the literal. In 18:16-17, for instance, the statements "A gift opens doors; it gives access to the great" or "The one who first states a case seems right, until the other comes and cross-examines" have meaning at only the literal level. Usually scholars refer to these as aphorisms or sayings. Other proverbs have significance beyond the literal level (see [Sayings and Proverbs]). In 18:4 there are two contrasting metaphors: "The words of the mouth are deep waters; the fountain of wisdom is a gushing stream." Metaphor is effective when it implies that two dissimilar things or notions are similar. In 18:4a, words are deep waters; in v. 4b wisdom is a gushing stream. Obviously, the intention is to communicate figuratively, to attribute the qualities of natural phenomena to words and wisdom. The statements invite readers to think at a new level beyond the literal.

Literary Collections

It is clear that within the book of Proverbs there are a variety of different forms of speech. At another level readers quickly discover there are a variety of collections that make up the book. These collections of individual sayings, proverbs, instructions, and poems may exist within larger collections themselves. For instance, a cluster of sayings in 10:1-5 seems to open the larger collection of sayings called "Proverbs of Solomon" in 10:1–22:16. It is not clear that this smaller cluster ever existed independently, but readers have a deeper appreciation of the art that exists at the level of various collections if they are able to recognize it. This larger collection, 10:1–22:16, is itself composed of at least three different collections or sub-collections: 10:1–15:33; 16:1-33; and 17:1–22:16. Even at this level it is not clear that such collections ever existed independently. Readers soon discover that there are at least eight different collections of sayings, instructions, and proverbs that comprise the book of Proverbs, each designated with its own heading: "Sayings of Solomon, Son of David" (*mišlê šělōmōh ben Dāwid*), 1:1–9:18; "Sayings of Solomon" (*mišlê šělōmōh*), 10:1–22:16; "Words of the Wise" (*dibrê ḥăkāmîm*), 22:17–24:22; "These also are of the Wise" (*gam-ʾēlleh laḥăkāmîm*), 24:23-34; "These are other proverbs of Solomon that the officials of King Hezekiah of Judah copied" (*gam-ʾēlleh mišlê šělōmōh ʾăšer heʿtîqû ʾanšê ḥizqiyyâ melek yěhûdâ*), 25–29; "The Words of Agur" (*dibrê ʾagûr*), 30:1-33; "The Words of King Lemuel" (*dibrê lěmûʾēl melek maśśāʾ*), 31:1-9; and 31:10-31. Readers of Proverbs are not merely reading a book, but rather a collection of collections of sayings.

The same cannot be said of Ecclesiastes, however. While some would argue that the editorial process reflects the gradual accretion of materials,[4] a broader consensus exists that there was a single author who created a framework, a persona, and explored contradictory ideas throughout the book.[5] Nevertheless, the author still demands that readers be attentive to the various rhetorical forms of speech used throughout.

Literary Transmission

Readers are acquainted with the challenges posed by multiple English translations available in modern settings of worship and study. Investigation gets more challenging when readers seek explanations for why the NRSV (New Revised Standard Version), the translation used in this commentary, translates Proverbs 22:17a as "Incline your ear and hear my words," while the REB (Revised English Bible) translates the same half-line as "Pay heed and listen to the sayings of the wise." Setting aside the idiomatic renderings, one stichos speaks of "my words" while the other speaks of the "sayings [or words] of the wise." Whose words are they? The answer has to do with the various ancient translations of Proverbs that are now in existence and therefore available for translation. In the preceding example, the NRSV bases its translation upon the Septuagint (LXX in this commentary), the Greek translation of the Hebrew Bible, and the REB bases its translation of that verse upon the Masoretic Text (MT in this commentary). While accounting for the difference, the divergence between Greek and Hebrew traditions makes readers aware of yet another aspect of the matrix of interpretation. Not only were Proverbs and Ecclesiastes written and/or collected, but they were transmitted in ways that included translation into other languages.

The original manuscripts of Proverbs and Ecclesiastes do not survive. The oldest manuscript of Proverbs comes from Qumran, a village in the Judean desert from around 150 BC to AD 70. That village was home to Zadokite priests who had fled what they felt was a perverted and impure temple cult in Jerusalem. They sought to live a life of purity in the desert. The two Hebrew fragments of Proverbs, 4QProv^a and 4QProv^b, date from around 30–31 BC and AD 50 respectively.

Long before the writing of the scrolls at Qumran, however, a project to translate the Hebrew Bible into Greek had been initiated in Alexandria, Egypt. The translation is called the Septuagint, or "Seventy," due largely to the legend that there were seventy-two scholars who translated the entire Hebrew Bible into Greek. More likely the Pentateuch alone was actually translated during the reign of Ptolemy Philadelphus (285–246 BC) in Alexandria. This began a trend in translation that eventually saw all of the Jewish Scripture translated. This commentary will refer frequently to the Septuagint (LXX) for comparative analysis of sayings.

As noted above, we do not have the manuscripts that the LXX scholars had when they were translating Proverbs and Ecclesiastes. Translators base modern-day translations upon the so-called "Masoretic Text" (see [The Masoretes]) a text established, not created, by Jewish scholars after the destruction of the temple in 70 BC. The work of these people involved vocalizing a traditional consonantal text, and thus moving in the direction of standardizing the many and divergent Hebrew manuscripts. By the second century AD the divergencies between texts evident among the manuscripts at Qumran no longer existed as extensively. Yet even this movement to standardize the text had to overcome divergencies between Jewish scribal schools in Babylon and Palestine. By the tenth century AD, a family of texts—the ben Asher text—began to take priority over all others. So, while we compare our English translations with the Masoretic Text (MT) and the LXX, we must be aware that these are not themselves original texts, but stand in a process of transmission that involved translation.[6]

This commentary will only refer to other versions of Proverbs and Ecclesiastes as secondary resources do. Those other versions might include the Targums, which is a literal translation of the MT into Aramaic; the Peshitta (S), which is a translation into Syriac, produced mainly for Syriac-speaking Christians in the second century AD; and the Vulgate (V), a Fourth-century AD translation from Hebrew into Latin.

It is important to discuss the literary transmission of Proverbs and Ecclesiastes because it is relevant to the origins of the texts and translations, and also because the process of transmission and translation leads readers into another relevant aspect of the interpretive matrix. Clearly, readers can see that the book of Proverbs, indeed the Bible, is a product of human processes. This does not necessarily detract from notions of inspiration; but it does require that readers, who take seriously the literary processes set out above, now take seriously the role that historical context plays in our reading.

Historical Dimensions of Proverbs and Ecclesiastes

The questions readers may ask take them beyond the mere consideration of the text. Nothing makes this more clear than the array of ancient translations of the Hebrew Bible that now exist and are available for our reading. Each translation invites readers to consider the events, particular circumstances, the audience, and the people who caused them to happen. The question "why translate" is ultimately one that is contextual, not textual. And if context is relevant in matters of transmission of text, it might also be relevant in reference to the collection of the text or the very production of the text. One might also ask whether the context also contributes to the various rhetorical distinctions represented by the text itself. Ultimately, modern readers are able to apply to biblical texts the same kinds of commonsense principles they apply to other kinds of written texts; social and historical context influence the shape and meaning of the text.

Authorship
The book of Proverbs is attributed to Solomon (e.g., 1:1; 10:1), and the book of Ecclesiastes implies the same (1:1, 12). We shall focus here on Proverbs and treat Ecclesiastes in the introduction to that book. That Solomon alone is the author of the entirety of Proverbs seems impossible given the ascriptions to others, such as one named "Agur" (30:1) and "Lemuel" (31:1). Further, in order to maintain Solomonic authorship in a literal sense as we know it today, readers would have to include Solomon in the guild of "the wise," sages to whom other collections of the proverbs are

attributed (e.g., 22:17; 24:23). Of course, it is not impossible that the very large collections of materials might preserve sayings coined by Solomon. It seems unlikely however, even if Solomon were involved somewhat in the authorship of the Proverbs, that he alone put the book together. Given the work of kings as administrators, it seems equally unlikely that Solomon, or any king, might have been a member of a group of sages. The reference to "Hezekiah's officials," who collected and perhaps arranged the materials in Proverbs 25–29 (25:1), suggests that kings patronized the arts and education in antiquity. It was not the kings themselves, however, but their officials at court who actually did the work.

Several aspects of the sayings within the book of Proverbs suggest that there may be multiple sources of origins. That some of the collections were attributed to non-Israelite kings, for instance (e.g., 30:1; 31:1), implies that there may have been a non-Israelite influence on the sayings. The extensive parallels between the collection in Proverbs 22:17–23:24 and the Egyptian collection attributed to Amenemopet reinforces the relevance of comparing the biblical wisdom with non-Israelite wisdom collections as a means of determining origins. Further, since there is a strong tradition that Israelite kings were involved in passing on the wisdom tradition (e.g., 1 Kgs 4:29-34; Prov 25:1), it is reasonable to examine the royal courts of ancient Judah and Israel as contexts in which wisdom might have been preserved. Yet, since the sayings themselves concern matters of family and community, readers are not off track by supposing a family setting for the preservation of wisdom. In fact, the first nine chapters of the book of Proverbs give the impression that these sayings were remembered as having been passed on by parents to their children.[7] In none of these cases, though, is there hard and fast evidence of any particular setting. At most, readers can only draw inferences from parallels with other non-biblical literatures and the claims of the biblical literature itself.

Date

Finding a historical date for the materials within the book is even more complicated than the question of authorship. As noted above, there are fragments of the book at Qumran, allowing one terminus for dating the book sometime in the first century BC. Most scholars would agree that the final editing of the book is no later than Qumran. The ascriptions that head various collections in the book, however, would place some of the materials in the ninth century BC (Solomon) and the late eighth century BC (Hezekiah). Given the

Qumran
The desolate cliffs lining the western edge of the Dead Sea contain many caves, including these near Qumran. In these caves were hidden several clay jars containing what we know as the Dead Sea Scrolls.

need of the court for scribes, and the preservation of materials important to the state, it is not unreasonable to assume that by the time of Hezekiah (715–687 BC) there was a thoroughgoing literary tradition in existence as might be inferred from the superscription in Proverbs 25:1.[8] It is further probable that this tradition preserved wisdom materials that originated in rural, family settings from periods long before the late 8th century. So the materials being collected by Hezekiah's men had been around for some time, perhaps collected in early royal scribal settings. The difficulty is determining how long they had been around.[9]

Linguistic analysis does not yield definitive results, either. The assumption is that materials may be dated according to hypothetical linguistic characteristics of ancient Hebrew. But the process of transmission means that copyists who are passing materials on to subsequent generations are constantly updating, making very ancient writing conventions more accessible to contemporary readers. Such a process, though, wipes out the evidence of antiquity, making linguistics an unreliable way of dating. As it stands, most scholars think the materials in Proverbs 10:1–22:16 and 25–29 are pre-exilic (older than the sixth century BC) and the instructions in Proverbs 1–9 are post-exilic (after sixth century BC).[10]

Social Context

By social context we refer to a phenomenon different from, although related to, the historical context. The guiding assumption is that there had to be socially legitimate institutions within ancient Israel that preserved such materials as proverbs and sayings or we would never have them today. For example, one might think of the way the modern church preserves Scripture; analogously, judicial institutions preserve law and priestly institutions preserve the rituals and liturgies of worship. Since we do not really know what kinds of ancient institutions might have been available to preserve the materials in wisdom, we must draw inferences and form hypotheses. The question is, what social institution stands behind modes of speech that are contained in sayings, aphorisms, proverbs, and instructions?

While the literary stage of the biblical text surely reflects a setting that valued knowledge, certain normative behaviors, and the written transmission of these, it is perfectly plausible that the preservation of such existed long before they were written. The universal character of proverbial traditions[11] makes Israelite wisdom's setting within family contexts entirely plausible. Many of these short sayings and observations about ways of life that saved time, that took advantage of technology, that sought out a better way, reflect the ethos of the home environment with its emphasis upon survival, prosperity, and common sense. The instructions opening with "my child" in Proverbs 1–9 certainly betray that familial ethos. Likewise, sayings that suggest the importance of the authority of parents, and heeding their instruction, also suggest the concerns of the family and tribe (e.g., Prov 10:1; 15:20; 20:20; 23:22; 30:11, 17). Sayings that are concerned with disciplining children (e.g., 19:18; 22:6) and caring for family and land (e.g., 5:10; 6:31; 24:27; 28:19) indicate the concern with continuity and security. The recurring theme of proper marriage partners recognizes that concern for community matters begins at home (e.g., 12:4; 14:1; 18:22).

Scholars disagree about the existence of schools in ancient Israel largely because of the lack of direct evidence.[12] However, it is not difficult to infer the need for schools due to the existence of institutions that needed to pass knowledge on to succeeding generations. The existence of the ancient monarchy, with its need for a scribal community to maintain record-keeping and to teach writing, allows the inference of such educational endeavors. The temple institution likewise would have had to educate succeeding generations of priests in matters of ritual and ceremonial cleanliness, not to mention proper interpretations of cultic inquiry. The importance of institutional self-perpetuation makes education, especially in the context of the royal court, almost unavoidable.[13] Such headings as that in Proverbs 25:1, "These are other proverbs of Solomon that the officials of King Hezekiah of Judah copied," make clear that by the eighth century at least some process of collecting and copying these sayings was sponsored by the royal court. The concluding epilogue of the book of Ecclesiastes suggests that the sage whose wisdom is contained in the book was one

Scribe

This sculpture of an Egyptian scribe attests to the institution of education and the preservation of knowledge in ancient Egypt. It is uncertain whether such institutions existed in pre-exilic Israel.

Egyptian Scribe from Saqqara, Egypt. Old Kingdom. 5th Dynasty. c. 2400 BC. Limestone, alabaster, and rock crystal. Musée du Louvre. Paris.

who "taught the people knowledge, weighing and studying and arranging many proverbs." What is more, the verbal, formal, and conceptual correspondences between biblical wisdom texts and ancient Near Eastern wisdom texts allow one to assume the connection between court and schools.

Ancient Near Eastern Context

The past two centuries of biblical studies have increasingly been influenced by the ability to reconstruct the ancient world of Egypt and the civilizations of Mesopotamia. Greater awareness of the vast influence of these cultures makes biblical readers realize that ancient Israel, as significant as it has come to be for Western religion, was but a small part of the ancient world.[14] Ancient Israel was naturally influenced by the worldview, the cultural heritage, and the events it shared with neighbors to the south and east.

Readers wishing to understand the historical matrix behind Proverbs and Ecclesiastes must reckon the influence of these more ancient and widely influential wisdom traditions. The discovery in Egypt of "The Instructions of Amenemopet" (see Prov 22:17–23:24) has provided new illumination, not only for biblical proverbs, but for such references to non-Israelite wisdom as contained, for example, in 1 Kings 4:30: "Solomon's wisdom surpassed the wisdom of all the people of the east, and all wisdom of Egypt." The Aramean wise man Ahiqar is remembered as one of the influential sages of the ancient Near East. The collection of proverbs in his name, dating from the fifth century BC but perhaps as old as the seventh, further illuminate the biblical practice of collecting sayings and instructions.[15] The similarity of theological content between the biblical book of Job and Mesopotamian works such as *Ludlul bel nemeqi*, "I Will Praise the Lord of Wisdom," makes clear that long before the composition of the Israelite poem about an Edomite righteous man, the Mesopotamian poets were reflecting upon the problem of the suffering of innocent people.[16] Most striking are the affinities between the Babylonian *Gilgamesh Epic* and the book of Ecclesiastes. Both works grapple with the problems of mortality and humanity's response to its limitations.[17]

One need not argue for any kind of direct literary dependence upon these more ancient works in the production of the biblical materials. However, it is clear that such works helped to define the larger intellectual context in which the biblical materials were produced. The literary forms and theological themes were common to the intelligentsia from the fertile crescent to the first cataract of the Nile. Granting such an assumption, understanding the biblical wisdom literature requires a close comparison with the very similar literature from across the Near East. Such comparative study further provides a wealth of evidence that helps scholars reconstruct both the theological and sociological contexts out of which various wisdom traditions emerged.

Theological Dimensions of Proverbs and Ecclesiastes

When we speak of theology we refer to the way that we comprehend God. So in asking about wisdom theology, or the theology behind Proverbs and Ecclesiastes, we are seeking to understand how the collections of sayings and instructions comprehend God. Of course, the sayings do not necessarily aim to offer explicit theological statements as we wish they did, so the reader's task is to draw inferences about the theology of the sages based upon what statements are made about matters that might betray theological assumptions.

Theology functioned in the ancient world, as for many people today, as a frame of reference providing a basis for interpreting and understanding the events of life. It explains who God is, how one knows the deity, the nature of humanity and its dilemmas. As the Deuteronomist insists that God is revealed through Israel's escape from Egypt, the sages thought God to be revealed in a still more immediate way. Wisdom itself is one of the ways of knowing God.

Absence of the Story of Yahweh's Revelation

Readers soon recognize a profound silence in Proverbs and Ecclesiastes (Job, too) regarding the story of Yahweh's self-revelation through specific historical events and through individuals. The idea of God's entering into covenant with a specific nation of people, a covenant defined by stipulations of social and moral behavior, is likewise absent. The readers and performers of ancient wisdom traditions, the guild of scribes and court teachers, clearly found an alternative system of thinking about the way of knowing God.

Some scholars have defined this absence as a deliberate abandonment of the nationalistic, or particularistic, features of Yahwism for more universalistic features.[18] Wisdom accommodated a need for more universalistic (less particularistic) theology because of the international relations promoted at court in the pre-exilic setting,[19] or perhaps more significantly, because of the absence of the political support structure to make it meaningful in the post-exilic period of transition.[20] The point is that readers familiar with the stories of Abraham, Isaac, Jacob, Moses, Joshua, and David will not hear references to them as they do in the Pentateuch. The sages offer alternative ways of asserting the nature of God's relationship with God's people.

Wisdom's Anthropocentrism

The sayings and instructions in Proverbs and Ecclesiastes, while assuming a God who has created an orderly and reliable cosmos, are distinctive in their consciousness of the signal importance of the human perspective. Although the sages ultimately attribute wisdom's origins to the deity, wisdom is described and fleshed out as human skills of intellection, reflection, speech, and timely action (e.g., Prov 1:1-3). The human experiences gained through such skills are passed on authoritatively to succeeding generations.

Behind such skills there seems to exist a "self-righting" universe that is bound to principles of equity, justice, and piety.[21] Of course, the sayings and instructions name Yahweh as the one who has established that universe, but, again, the perspective is that of humanity (e.g., 16:4). Individuals perceive this order that, according to the sages, makes sense only if one figures it out by bringing oneself into harmony with its order. For human society and its individuals the universe fragments itself into the need for discovery, understanding, and cooperation. Individuals have ever before them the choice between "two ways:" one that accords with this ordered universe, the other that does not (e.g., 2:20; 4:18; 12:26; 13:15; 25:26); one that accords with righteousness, for instance, and one that does not (e.g., 11:10, 23; 12:21); one that accords with the traditions as passed on through parents and teachers (e.g., 15:31, 32, 33), and one that does not (e.g., 13:1, 13; 16:5).

Revelation through Creation

The link between human observation of an ordered universe and the affirmation that the deity stands behind it rests in the frequent affirmations of creation. This order has been established in creation and is evident in the natural world all around. Thus several poems in the Proverbs assert the interrelationship between Yahweh's creation and the order of human civilization (e.g., Prov 3:19-20; 8:22-31; Eccl 1:4-10; 11:5–12:7). Readers are not surprised that the cycles of nature and agriculture stand behind many observations (Eccl 1:4-11; Prov 6:6-11; 11:22; 12:10; 14:4; 18:4) or humanity's interaction with natural aspects of its own being (Prov 12:25; 14:13; 16:31; 17:14; 20:13).

The link between the creator, nature, and the human realm is wisdom, both in the forms of instructions passed on by parents and teachers, and in the human form of a woman who stands with Yahweh as creation and world-maintenance take place (e.g., Prov 1:20-33; 4:1-12). Woman Wisdom is a mediator, and by embracing her and her teaching, the uneducated may come to understand the deity's creation.

Over against this confident assertion of Yahweh's revelation through the created order are various assertions that order is not as readily evident as the confident sayings of the sages would imply. Thus, the sages are quick to point out human limitations and finitude that establish humanity's role over against the natural order, which Yahweh alone understands (e.g., Prov 16:1-2, 33; 19:21, 23). This does not preclude the human expression of bewilderment when life does not coincide with faith. Ample testimony of the refrain-like reminder of human inferiority permeates Proverbs and Ecclesiastes (e.g., Prov 30:1-4).

Human inferiority leads to a new level of reflection in the book of Ecclesiastes, though. Qoheleth, the sage behind the book of Ecclesiastes, seems to reverse values through his observations. Unlike Proverbs, whose reflections on nature are introduced with the confident affirmation of the "fear of Yahweh" in chapters 1–9, Ecclesiastes begins with observations of nature and its cycles (Eccl 1:4-11). There can be no question of order in these verses. But, is this order something ultimately that assures humans of the deity's concern, or of the deity's absence (e.g., Eccl 3:1-11)? If one did not already affirm and celebrate a beneficent deity, would Qoheleth's observations from nature be convincing that there was one at all?

Does Qoheleth's emphasis upon nature represent an ancient "natural theology"? Natural theology is simply defined as those insights that humanity can have about God without God's special revelation (e.g., through individuals such as prophets and through events such as the exodus and Sinai). Such conclusions are certainly implied by an emphasis upon humanity's perspective and the created, natural order. If the biblical wisdom literature does not put forward a true natural theology,[22] it is at least an expression of a theological perspective that takes seriously the natural world.

Humanity still must submit, recognizing its limitations over against God's created order. Humans still seek to understand the workings of the created order, and to bring their lives into a harmonic relationship with it. But the language and imagery of direct relationship between human and deity, of a particular history that defines who the people of God are, is not present in the same sense as it is in other biblical books.

NOTES

[1] For fuller treatments of rhetorical forms in Proverbs and Ecclesiastes, see James L. Crenshaw, *Old Testament Wisdom: An Introduction* (Atlanta: John Knox Press, 1981), 36-41; idem, "Wisdom," in *Old Testament Form Criticism*, ed. J. H. Hayes (San Antonio: Trinity University Press, 1974), 225-64; G. von Rad, *Wisdom in Israel* (Nashville and New York: Abingdon, 1972).

[2] Several helpful works are available on this point. See Robert Alter, *The Art of Biblical Poetry* (New York: Basic Books, 1985), 3-26; James Kugel, *The Idea of Biblical Poetry* (New Haven CT: Yale University Press, 1983); Luis Alonso Schökel, *A Manual of Hebrew Poetics* (Rome: Editrice Pontificio Istituto Biblico, 1988).

[3] Quoted in C. Hugh Holman, *A Handbook to Literature* (3rd ed.; Indianapolis and New York: The Odyssey Press, 1972), 425.

[4] See James L. Crenshaw, *Ecclesiastes* (OTL; Philadelphia: Westminster, 1987), 34-49 for a discussion of many possibilities.

[5] Michael V. Fox, *A Time to Tear Down & A Time to Build Up* (Grand Rapids MI: Eerdmans, 1999), 147-53; Choon L. Seow, *Ecclesiastes* (AB 18C; New York, Toronto, London, Sydney, Auckland: Doubleday, 1997), 38-43.

[6] For a fuller discussion, see Richard Clifford, "Observations on the Texts and Versions of Proverbs," in *Wisdom, You are My Sister*, FS Roland E. Murphy, ed. M. L. Barré (Washington, DC: Catholic Biblical Association, 1997), 47-61.

[7] See the discussions of R. N. Whybray, *The Book of Proverbs: A Survey of Modern Study*, History of Biblical Interpretation Series 1 (Leiden: Brill, 1995), 1-33; and Michael V. Fox, "The Social Location of the Book of Proverbs," in *Texts, Temples, and Traditions*, FS M. Haran, ed. M. V. Fox et al. (Winona Lake IN: Eisenbrauns, 1996), 227-39.

[8] See Richard J. Clifford, *Proverbs* (OTL; Louisville: Westminster John Knox Press, 1999), 3-6, for an excellent and brief discussion of dating and various criteria for dating.

[9] Joseph Blenkinsopp, *Sage, Priest, Prophet* (Louisville: Westminster John Knox Press, 1995) 32-41.

[10] Clifford, "Observation on the Texts and Versions of Proverbs," 4.

[11] Claus Westermann, *Roots of Wisdom,* trans. J. Daryl Charles (Louisville: Westminster John Knox Press, 1995).

[12] See the opening remarks of G. I. Davies's "Were there schools in ancient Israel?" in *Wisdom in Ancient Israel*, FS J. A. Emerton, ed. John Day, Robert P. Gordon, and H. G. M. Williamson (Cambridge: Cambridge Univ. Press, 1995), 199.

[13] Numerous scholars share this view in varying degrees from G. Von Rad, *Wisdom in Israel*, trans. James D. Martin (London: SCM Press Ltd., 1970), 17-18, to Carole R. Fontaine, "Wisdom in Proverbs," in *In Search of Wisdom*, ed. Leo G. Perdue, Bernard B. Scott, William J. Wiseman (Louisville: Westminster John Knox Press, 1993), 104-108.

[14] H .W. F. Saggs, *Civilization Before Greece and Rome* (New York and London: Yale University Press, 1989).

[15] Jonas Greenfield, "The Wisdom of Ahiqar," in Day, Gordon, and Williamson, 43-54.

[16] John Gray, "The Book of Job in the Context of Near Eastern Literature," ZAW 82 (1970): 251-69.

[17] B. W. Jones, "From Gilgamesh to Qoheleth," in *The Bible in the Light of Cuneiform Literature*, ed. W. W. Hallo, B. W. Jones, and G. L. Mattingley (Lewiston: Edwin Mellen Press, 1990), 349-79.

[18] E.g., James L. Crenshaw, "The Concept of God in Old Testament Wisdom," in *In Search of Wisdom*, ed. Leo G. Perdue, Bernard B. Scott, and William J. Wiseman (Louisville: Westminster John Knox Press, 1993), 1-18; R. E. Clements, *Wisdom in Theology* (Grand Rapids MI: Eerdmans, 1989), 13-39.

[19] Thus William McKane, *Proverbs* (London: SCM Press, 1970).

[20] Thus Clements, *Wisdom in Theology,* 13-39.

[21] This brief section owes much to Richard J. Clifford, *Proverbs*, 19-23.

[22] James Barr, *Biblical Faith and Natural Theology* (Oxford: Clarendon, 1993), 91.

PROVERBS

PROVERBS WITH PURPOSE

Proverbs 1:1-7

A Testament of Instruction, Proverbs 1–9

The book of Proverbs opens in chapters 1–9 with materials scholars identify as "instruction." Unlike the short sayings that follow in Proverbs 10:1–22:16, the instructions are explicitly didactic. [Structure at a Glance: Proverbs 1–9] They are formulated to imply a setting in which knowledge is deliberately imparted by an authority figure, either a parent or some kind of teacher. The frequent imperatives to "hear" (1:8), "listen" (4:1), "be attentive" (5:1), "keep my words" (7:1), etc., along with language implying that the audience is a child or student, are unambiguously intended to inculcate the values of wisdom.

Instructions are not the only features of this introductory collection. Interspersed throughout are four wisdom poems and one miscellaneous collection (1:20-33; 3:13-20; 6:12-19; 8:1-36; 9:1-18). These poetic compositions aim to elevate and celebrate wisdom. A most striking feature is their personification of wisdom as a successful woman, a device that functions elsewhere in Israel's Scripture (e.g., Gen 3:1-7). The fact that such a wisdom poem occurs at the beginning and end of the collection is no accident. The sages sought to package their instructions in ways that ensured the reader's (or listener's) careful attention. [Inclusio with Two Women] This woman who calls

Structure at a Glance: Proverbs 1–9

In general readers will recognize the recurring formula of introduction, instruction, and observation throughout chs. 1–9. These formula help to delineate the sections within the collection as well as to distinguish the collection from those that follow in chs. 10–31 (see [Inclusio with Two Women]). The instructions and reflections established throughout Prov 1–9 are isolated as follows:

I.   1:8-19 Prosperity from Greed
     1:20-33 Wisdom's Security
II. 2:1-22 The Teacher's Syllabus
III. 3:1-12 Wisdom's Absolute Surrender
     3:13-20 Wisdom's Incomparability
IV. 3:12-35 Wisdom for Community Life
V.   4:1-9 The Wisdom of Experience
VI. 4:10-19 The Wisdom Way of Life
VII. 4:20-27 The Heart of Wisdom
VIII. 5:1-23 The Seduction of An "Other"
     6:12-19 Thoughts on Foolishness
IX. 6:20-35 The Foolishness of Adultery
X.   7:1-27 The Parent's Final Admonition on Adultery
     8:1-36 Woman Wisdom Comes Calling
     9:1-18 Feasting at Wisdom's Table

For further reading, see R. N. Whybray, *Wisdom in Proverbs* (SBT 41; London: SCM Press, 1965); idem, *The Composition of the Book of Proverbs* (JSOTSup 68; Sheffield: Sheffield Academic Press, 1994); and Michael V. Fox, "Ideas of Wisdom in Proverbs 1-9," JBL 116/4 (Winter, 1997): 601-12.

Inclusio with Two Women

AΩ Readers will notice throughout the book of Proverbs several devices for organizing information that are different from modern conventions of chapter headings, verse markers, and page numbers. Much more common is the use of repetition of words, phrases, themes, etc., to provide framing structures that function like bookends to mark the boundaries of units of material. Such a boundary convention is referred to as an *inclusio*. When readers recognize such a device, they immediately begin to ask how the unit of material functions together to make a particular kind of meaning. Some examples of various kinds of inclusios might include Ps 8:1 and 9; Job 1–2 and 42; Eccl 1:1-11 and 11:1-9. An important inclusio framing Prov 1–9 is thus formed by the location of references to two women: Woman Wisdom and Woman Folly, the one a personification of wisdom, the other a personification of folly.

Readers encounter Woman Wisdom in 1:20-33 and again in 8:1-36 and 9:1-6. Woman Folly is also met along the way in 9:13-18.

I.	1:8-19 Prosperity from Greed
	1:20-33 (Woman) Wisdom's Security
II.	2:1-22 The Teacher's Syllabus
III.	3:1-12 Wisdom's Absolute Surrender
	3:13-20 Wisdom's Incomparability
IV.	3:12-35 Wisdom for Community Life
V.	4:1-9 The Wisdom of Experience
VI.	4:10-19 The Wisdom Way of Life
VII.	4:20-27 The Heart of Wisdom
VIII.	5:1-23 The Seduction of An "Other"
	6:1-19 Thoughts on Foolishness
IX.	6:20-35 The Foolishness of Adultery
X.	7:1-27 The Parent's Final Admonition on Adultery
	8:1-36 Woman Wisdom Comes Calling
	9:1-18 Feasting at (Woman) Wisdom's Table

These two women, both personifying opposing values of wisdom instruction, provide a framework for the instructions that are within Prov 2–7. By arranging these two poems in this way, the sages could use the images of these two women to exemplify the competing values of wisdom instruction. That they used such images in this fashion suggests their remarkable ambivalence toward women's roles in their own society. On the one hand, Woman Folly is antithetical to wisdom values, associated as she is with activities that threaten a patriarchal society. On the other hand, Woman Wisdom stands as an opponent to the foolish and validates a feminine attribute to wisdom.

For further reading, see Claudia Camp, *Wisdom and the Feminine in the Book of Proverbs* (Sheffield: JSOT/Almond Press, 1985); Roland E. Murphy, "Wisdom's Song: Proverbs 1:20-33," *CBQ* 48 (1986): 456-60; and Carol Newsom, "Women and the Discourse of Patriarchal Wisdom: A Study of Proverbs 1-9," in *Gender and Difference in Ancient Israel,* ed. Peggy L. Day (Minneapolis: Fortress, 1989), 142-60.

---

implicitly presents herself as an opponent of other women who also call to young men.

While there is a general consensus that Proverbs 1–9 are written later than the materials contained in Proverbs 10–30 (probably post-exilic times), there is no definitive proof of the dating of any of the materials.[1] It is highly unlikely that there is any historical validity to the claim of Solomonic authorship (e.g., Prov 1:1). It is helpful to remember that as proverbs became "popular," authorship ceased to matter.[2] The purpose of the instruction poems is manifested in their theological content. The pragmatic aims of wisdom simultaneously maintain a high theology that is illustrated in their view of creation.[3] The cosmos is like a well-planned city wherein Woman Wisdom walks about and teaches young men who would become citizens. Wisdom speaks for God. Her words and images convey an ongoing process to maintain creation order.[4] The implications for young men include surrendering to the Lord as well as to the instructions of Woman Wisdom. Thus, Proverbs 1–9 provide a theological introduction to the remainder of the sayings contained in the present form of the book. These opening nine chapters inspire readers that wisdom comes from Yahweh alone, and that it is therefore grounded in the framework of the very creation. Thus, wisdom's worldview and value system may be asserted authoritatively as the only valid alternative for the young.

Proverbs with Purpose, 1:1-7

The opening verse of the book of Proverbs catapults readers immediately into the story world of ancient Israel. The traditional view was that Solomon, son of David, was himself among the wise ones. If Solomon himself was therefore known for his great wisdom and understanding (1 Kgs 4:29-34), the king's reputation carried great weight with readers. Whatever humble folk origins wisdom may have had (see Introduction), wisdom was important in the court of one of the most important kings in Israel. By reminding readers of this, the opening statement offers implicit legitimization and authentication for the collection of instructions and sayings that follow. They become the legacy, or testament, of Solomon, Israel's great king.

These first seven verses of the book set out the overall aims of the accompanying collections of admonitions and sayings. Several questions should guide readers as they begin to reflect upon these verses. First, how does the phrase "proverbs of Solomon" inform the reading of this biblical book? Second, how is the purpose of this book elaborated and clarified by the many terms that are compounded in vv. 2-6? Third, what is "the fear of the LORD," and how does it connect with the concerns of wisdom as set out in vv. 2-6 and the following collections of materials?

COMMENTARY

The Superscription, "The Proverbs of Solomon," 1:1

Superscriptions similar to this are also attached to other collections within the book (e.g., 10:1; 25:1; 22:17; 24:23; 30:1; 31:1), and two of these also attribute origins to Solomon (10:1; 25:1). The figure of Solomon is offered in part to gain the weight of authority. That authority comes both because he is a character out of Israel's distinguished past and because his story provides readers a point of origin for thinking about wisdom. Wisdom in these collections is therefore the testimony of that ancient king, Solomon.

Solomon is not the author, however. External literary evidence from ancient Egyptian and Babylonian wisdom collections gives us some indication as to why. In those settings royalty certainly patronized the work of wise men, but did not themselves participate in composition and collection. Further evidence from within the Bible itself attests to the phenomenon of attributing writings to great figures long after such figures lived. One should consider, for instance, the first century BC date for "The Wisdom of Solomon," an apocryphal book that also attributes its authorship to this same king. The superscription to another pre-exilic collection of proverbs contained within biblical Proverbs (25:1) admits both a process of

---

Pre-exilic

AΩ This is a term readers will encounter throughout the commentary. The term, along with its counterpart "post-exilic," is a historical reference that is also a watershed in understanding the development of ancient Israelite religion and theology. Pre-exilic refers to the period before the Babylonian exile, conventionally dated to 587 BC. This moment in history witnessed the destruction of the city of Jerusalem, the deportation of its citizens, and, most importantly, the destruction of the Solomonic temple. The destruction of Jerusalem marks the end of the old order, as it were.

When Babylon fell to Persia, the Persian court embarked upon a new policy toward captive nations by allowing them to return to and resettle their homelands under the aegis of the Persian court. With the return of some of the exiles to Jerusalem after 538 BC (see Ezra and Nehemiah), the absence of real political independence, as well as the institutional loss of the Davidic monarchy, nevertheless required radical rethinking of ancient Israelite traditions. Many scholars believe that wisdom takes on a greater significance in this post-exilic period than in the pre-exilic period as Jewish refugees sought to redefine their lives under Persian domination.

For further reading, see Robert P. Carroll, "Israel, History of (Post-Monarchic Period)," *ABD* 3:567-76; and M. A. Knibb, "The Exile in the Literature of the Intertestamental Period," *HeyJ* 17 (1976): 253-72.

Pre-exilic Timeline

1486 BC: Canaanite army defeated at Megiddo by Egyptian pharaoh Thutmose, consolidating Egyptian rule over Canaan

1300 BC: Moses leads the Jews out of Egypt

c. 1200 BC: Philistines arrive by ship and give the name "Palestine" to the area; Jews start to arrive in Land of Israel

990 BC: Jerusalem captured by King David and Israel unified as one nation

950 BC: First Temple built by King Solomon

928 BC: After a fight over taxation, Israel splits into two nations: "Judah" in the south and "Israel" in the north

597 BC: Babylonians send army to put down a rebellion and take prominent Jews into exile

586 BC: Babylonians arrive to put down another rebellion, destroy the First Temple, and remove more Jews into exile

transmission and more than one person involved. [Pre-exilic] One should not necessarily conclude that the final collectors of these materials aimed to exploit readers' credulity with fraudulent statements. Rather, the attribution of literary works to great characters of the past was a widely practiced convention in antiquity. Finally, the sages also appeal to "the LORD" as the giver of wisdom (1:7; 2:5; 3:5-6; 9:10) or to wisdom personified as a female teacher of wisdom (1:20-33; 8:22-36; 9:1-6).

Perhaps more important for readers of this superscription is the meaning of the term the NRSV translates as "proverbs." The word is a plural form of the Hebrew word *māšāl* (also v. 6). A linguistic definition offers not one but two relevant insights on the meaning of the term. It may mean (1) "to rule" or "to reign" (e.g., Gen 37:8; Judg 8:22; Isa 63:19), thus reinforcing a proverb's authority; and (2) "to represent, or be like," (e.g., Ps 49:12, 20; Isa 46:5; Job 30:19), thus wisdom's way of describing and defining the world. More precision in meaning is certainly necessary for an understanding and appreciation of the entire collection. Yet this may only be derived as one gains experience in reading. For instance, the intuitive understanding of proverbs as short, catchy sayings that convey multiple levels of meaning and truth must either be modified or abandoned in the opening section of the book.

Proverbs 1–9 (also compare Prov 22:17–24:22; 24:23-34; 31:1-9). In these chapters readers encounter much lengthier forms, characterized by motivated instruction and admonition rather than by short, catchy sayings. And yet, both broad literary types are included in a book of *mešālîm*. If readers look beyond this book to the entire Hebrew Bible, they find yet more extensive poetic and contextual variation in the use of the term *māšāl*. Form criticism allows readers to recognize so-called sayings (1 Sam 24:13; 1 Kgs 20:11), taunts (Mic 2:4; Hab 2:6-8), similes (Gen 10:9; 1 Sam 10:11), and other such short aphoristic sayings that are not at all like the much more stylized poetic proverbs we encounter in the book of Proverbs. [Form Criticism]

Form Criticism

Form criticism is a mode of reading the Bible that attends closely to linguistic patterns within a text for the purpose of classifying them according to type or *genre*. The implicit assumption is that the structure of language or patterns of speech reflect the social contexts in which those patterns functioned. For instance, in much the same way as one hypothesizes the background of a hymn of praise to be congregational worship on a high holy day, one might similarly place a proverb within a certain instructional setting.

The form critic further hypothesizes that as the social setting changes and develops, the speech patterns reflect this change as well. This hypothesis theoretically allows a later reader to trace the development over time of certain patterns of speech associated with the developments of certain social settings. While there is not enough evidence to trace definitively the history of wisdom genres, it is possible to delineate several different wisdom genres and sub-genres within the biblical corpus. These would include the proverb, the riddle, the numerical saying, the instruction, the allegory, the fable, the autobiographical discourse, the dialogue, and lists.

For further reading, see John Barton, *Reading the Old Testament* (London: Darton, Longman, and Todd, 1985); James L. Crenshaw, *Old Testament Wisdom* (Atlanta: John Knox Press, 1981); and Gene M. Tucker, "Form Criticism, O.T.," *IDBSup*, 342-45.

The Purpose in the Prologue, 1:2-7

The first six verses after the superscription set out the several purposes of these collections of proverbs and instructions in a series of "purpose" clauses. They conclude with a thematic statement locating the "fear of the LORD" at the center of the pursuit of wisdom (v. 7). For Hebrew readers, orthographic features, word repetition, and syntax combine to indicate both the unity and the poetic nature of this series of verses. [Hebrew Orthography and Transliteration] Our English translations of the Bible are not nearly so elegant, but nevertheless convey the purposive function of these verses in the translations, "for learning" (v. 2a), "for understanding" (v 2b), "for gaining instruction" (v. 3a), "to teach" (v. 4a), and "to understand" (v. 6a). The repetition of the Hebrew words for "wisdom" and "instruction" (*ḥokmâ* and *mûsār*) in vv. 2a and 7c create a poetic "inclusio," or boundary, thematically marking off the beginning and ending of this particular unit. Within this inclusio (see [Inclusio with Two Women]) readers encounter similar repetition in vv. 2b and 6a and b with the Hebrew words *lĕhābîn ʾimrê bînâ*, "for understanding words of insight" (v. 2b) and *lĕhābîn dibrê ḥakāmîm*, "to understand the words of the wise" (vv. 6a and b).

Hebrew Orthography and Transliteration

AΩ Orthography generally concerns the spelling of words in ancient Hebrew. Transliteration concerns the representation of those ancient Hebrew spellings in English script. Paleographers, scholars who study the development of ancient language, attend to matters of orthography as indications of how ancient languages may have changed over time.

The spelling of Hebrew words offers poets the potential of using words and letters to create meaningful structure. Like most poetry, concision of expression is one of the underlying aims of the poet. In the opening unit, Prov 1:1-7, the repetition of the Hebrew letter *lamed* creates a distinctive orthographic pattern evident in vv. 2, 3, 4, and 6. What is more, since the *lamed* functions as a preposition and is followed by the respective infinitival purpose clauses, 1:1-7 has the introductory function of specifying the purpose of the instructions that follow. Therefore readers must be alert to how the ancient poets might be communicating through orthography, or spelling.

For further reading, see Frank M. Cross, "The Development of the Jewish Scripts," in *The Bible in the Ancient Near East*, ed. G. Ernest Wright (Garden City NY: Doubleday; reprint, Winona Lake IN, 1979); and Mark L. McLean, "Hebrew Scripts," *ABD* 3:96-97.

Samples of Semitic alphabets: (1) Samaria Ostraca, (2) Lachish Ostraca, (3) Elephantine Papyri.

Recognizing such deliberate organization of the text invites a deeper appreciation of the poetic aspects of this kind of instruction.

The opening passage indicates the purpose of the wisdom instruction that follows. The compounding of terminology indicates the defining intellectual, moral, and aesthetic characteristics of the wisdom tradition in general. Furthermore, in these wisdom terms readers encounter some of the most frequently recurring vocabulary of the book of Proverbs as a whole. While the list of wisdom terminology is not exhaustive, it is worthwhile to define the terms for them briefly.[5]

Words denoting intellectual processes: For the following discussion readers should consult the table below.

The Language of Wisdom

Intellectual Processes	*Aesthetic Processes*	*Moral Processes*
v. 2 wisdom (*ḥokmâ*)	v.1 saying (*māšāl*)	v.3 righteousness (*ṣedeq*)
instruction (*mûsār*)		justice (*mišpāṭ*)
understanding (*bînâ*)	v.6 figure (*mělîṣâ*)	equity (*mêšārîm*)
	riddle (*ḥîdâ*)	
v. 4 shrewdness (*'ormâ*)		
knowledge (*da'at*)		
skill (*taḥbūlôt*)		
prudence (*mězimmâ*)		
v. 5 learning (*leqaḥ*)		
v.7 fear of LORD (*yir'at yhwh*)		

Words concerning various processes of intellection and cognition include "wisdom" (*ḥokmâ*), "instruction" (*mûsār*), and "understanding" (*bînâ*), all occurring in v. 2; "shrewdness" (*'ormâ*), "knowledge" (*da'at*), and "prudence" (*mězimmâ*) in v. 4; "learning" (*leqaḥ*) and "skill" (*taḥbulôt*) in v. 5. The first of these—*ḥokmâ*—is always translated as "wisdom" and occurs more frequently in the Proverbs than any of the others, forty-one times. *Ḥokmâ* is one of the central concepts of the wisdom literature generally, and is coupled with the term "knowledge" (*da'at*), which occurs thirty-seven times in Proverbs. This latter term, *da'at*, is always translated as "knowledge" (v. 4b) and forms along with "wisdom" the broad conceptual parameters within which the remaining terms fall. The two terms in v. 2 that further qualify wisdom, "instruction" (*mûsār*) and "understanding" (*bînâ*), aim much more precisely at activities that contribute to one's gaining of wisdom. The former, "instruction," occurs thirty times in Proverbs and clearly implies an educational context. It carries with it the idea of discipline. The latter term in v. 2, "understanding" or "insight," occurs only fourteen times in Proverbs and denotes an activity or faculty of intellectual discernment. Thus, becoming wise is a process of receiving instruction that leads one to understand the sayings of intellectuals.

Verse 4 continues with two words in addition to "knowledge:" these are "shrewdness" (*'ormâ*) and "prudence" (*mĕzimmâ*). In v. 4 these two faculties are offered to the naive (*liptayim*) and the inexperienced youth (*lĕna'ar*). Both terms may convey activities that are morally questionable. Thus the serpent of Genesis 3:1 is said to have this characteristic of shrewdness or cleverness. The Gibeonites of Joshua 9:4 are likewise shrewd. But shrewdness, occurring three times in Proverbs, also has a legitimate meaning as a practical faculty that facilitates the accomplishment of one's tasks. The term occurs eight times in Proverbs and is translated in these verses (v. 4) as "prudence" but is probably better captured by the terms "scheming" or "devising." It is another potentially morally questionable term that is co-opted by the sages. Readers have but to recall the scheming of Job's friends (e.g., 21:27-28) to recognize the scope of the term's possible application. But in the writings of the sages such intellectual machinations are legitimate and fall under the governance of an accompanying morality. In a word, v. 4 suggests that wisdom offers to the uninitiated some practical intellectual skills for survival in the world.

Verse 5 concludes the list of wisdom terms with two very infrequent words, "learning" (*leqaḥ*) and "skill" (*taḥbulôt*). The former term, occurring only five times in Proverbs, is a derivative of the verb "to take," *lāqaḥ*, and thus denotes the activity of learning. The second term, also occurring only five times in Proverbs, is probably better rendered "guidance" or "steering" and has affinities with the idea of "counsel" or "advise" (e.g., Prov 11:14; 12:5; 20:18; 24:6). What is perhaps more significant in v. 5 is that even those already wise may benefit from these proverbs.

Aesthetic Features. Linguistic and literary sensitivity are also required for appreciating wisdom's process of intellection and cognition. Put briefly, *how* the sages communicate is at least as important as *what* they communicate. We have already spoken of the "proverb" (*māšāl*) in v. 1, and made reference to the "words of the wise" (*dibrê ḥăkāmîm*), but v. 6 mentions two other concepts that students must master through the study of this collection. These are the "figure of speech" (*mĕlîṣâ*) and the "riddle" (*ḥîdâ*). Both riddles and figures of speech call to mind Jesus Ben Sirach's (second century BC) conviction that reckoning with "hidden meanings," *apokrypha paroimion* (Sir 39:3), was part of the sage's task.

Fear of the Lord

AΩ The concept "fear of the LORD," translating the Hebrew phrase *yir'at yhwh*, frames the introductory collection of instructions (1:7 and 9:10), the entire book of Proverbs (1:7 and 31:30), and the combined books of Proverbs and Ecclesiastes (1:7 and Eccl 12:13). The repetition of the phrase throughout the Proverbs indicates its centrality to the sages' thinking about the relationship between wisdom and piety (e.g., 2:5; 8:13; 10:27; 14:27; 15:33; 19:23; 22:4; Job 28:28).

The idea of fear in the sense of terror is part of the larger background for its function in Proverbs. Readers of the Scripture will recall the people's response to the Lord at Sinai (Exod 20:18), Joshua's obeisance before the Lord's commander of hosts (Josh 5:14), and Isaiah's sense of woe in the presence of the Lord (Isa 6:5) as examples of the emotional and behavioral responses to the terror of the deity. The Deuteronomist admonished that fear of the Lord was required of the covenant people, only in this case there was more than mere terror. The Deuteronomist's admonition parallels "fear of Yahweh" with "walk[ing] in all his ways," "lov[ing] him," and "serv[ing] the LORD your God with all your heart and with all your soul" (Deut 10:12). The implication in Deuteronomy is that fear of the Lord is realized in a lifestyle, thus functioning as a term for morality. The concept moves beyond mere terror of the presence of the deity to a concern for one's society. This is probably the understanding most widely applicable in Proverbs.

That lifestyle begins by recognizing the Lord as creator, and therefore also as the one who enforces the cosmic connections between human deeds and their consequences. The universe is designed to reflect a moral order that must be obeyed by every individual. Not to recognize this moral order, or worse, not to obey it, is foolishness—the opposite of wisdom. Thus in Prov 10:27 it is the Lord who distinguishes between the rewards for the righteous and the wicked: "The fear of the LORD prolongs life, but the years of the wicked will be short." Because the creator of the moral order is righteous, prosperity gained by wickedness could not endure; therefore, the value of poverty with the Lord's blessing could be affirmed as in Prov 15:16: "Better is a little with the fear of the LORD than great treasure and trouble with it." Fearing Yahweh, with its many implications for lifestyle, simply becomes a way of avoiding evil, Prov 16:6. Interestingly, in the later wisdom materials that comprise Prov 1–9, the fear of the Lord becomes knowledge itself (1:29; 2:5; 9:10).

For further reading, see B. Bamburger, "Fear and Love of God in the Old Testament," *HUCA* 7 (1929): 39-54; H. Bloche, "The Fear of the Lord as the 'principle' of Wisdom," *TynBul* 28 (1977): 3-28; Dermit Cox, "Fear or Conscience? *Yir'at YHWH* in Proverbs 1–9," *Studia Hierosolymitana* 3 (1982): 83-90; H. Fuhs, "*yare*," *TDOT* 6:290-315; and Roland E. Murphy, "Excursus on the Fear of the Lord," in *Proverbs* (WBC 22; Nashville: Thomas Nelson, 1998), 254-58.

The riddle clearly has to do with language's capacity for the artful concealment of knowledge. Knowledge, the sages believed, is only available for those who are willing to search it out. If one may take the *mĕlîṣâ* as "figure of speech,"[6] one wishing to be wise must master a mode of symbolic and metaphorical reflection upon reality. This skill will furthermore be critical for reading this collection of sayings and instructions. So modern readers must themselves learn the sages' manner of wisdom in addition to its matter.

Moral Values. Wisdom is further characterized by its concern with a moral consistency to all of reality. Students should also embrace the concepts denoted by the terms "righteousness" (*ṣedeq*), "justice" (*mišpāṭ*), and "equity" (*mêšārîm*; v. 3). These concepts betray the sages' assumption of the principles on which all meaningful human activity hinges. The close connection between a moral order and wisdom's processes of understanding is further indication that those who fail to live by moral principles are not only immoral, but are fools as well. The concluding verse of the passage (v. 7), a thematic statement on the "fear of the LORD," emphasizes the origins of this moral order. [Fear of the Lord] By associating wisdom with the Lord, the moral order obtains cosmic significance: the Lord, the sages believe, is the one who created and maintains a universe that turns on righteousness, justice, and equity. The fear of the Lord as the "beginning" of wisdom, then, is not simply a first step beyond which one eventually moves. Rather, the fear of the Lord is the "beginning" in the sense of the foundational, most important, principle that permeates the entire scope of one's search for wisdom. From this grounding assumption readers may search for connections between wisdom and other features of ancient Israel's confession of faith (e.g., Exod 3:6; Deut 5:5; Ps 111:10).

CONNECTIONS

The Beginning of Wisdom

The instructions open by echoing another great "beginning" in Genesis 1:1. Readers are left to wonder what exactly the beginning of wisdom might be. Should readers interpret this in some subjective sense where they are themselves subjectively related to wisdom's beginning? In that case readers would ask of these verses where wisdom begins for them, personally. How do they obtain it? What must they do to get on the path? Alternatively, readers might interpret this beginning in some objective sense, quite apart from wisdom's possible relevance to their desires or needs. In that case, readers must ponder on that beginning point for wisdom. What are its origins? From whence does it come? How does it relate to the traditions that have been handed down as revealed of the Lord? Such questions are not unique to contemporary readers.

Inquiring about the beginning of wisdom has another significance that may derive from thinking about the subjective and the objective, the personal and the public significance of wisdom's beginnings. This significance is illustrated, perhaps, in readers' recollection that wisdom comes from the Lord as well as from that ancient king of such great fame. The affirmation of Solomonic beginnings, and thus of very particular and even personal origins, was of such import in antiquity it is invoked again in the book of Ecclesiastes. So wisdom comes both from the Lord and from Solomon. It comes from the Lord and is remembered through sages stemming back to Solomon.

Arthur Miller's autobiography begins with a provocative image of geologic formation that might help readers to reflect upon the role memory plays in such activities of composition.[7] [Timebends] Geological formation of the earth's crust is not simply a matter of sedimentation, where layers and layers of dust, mud, detrital material, etc., neatly settle on top of old layers. Forces over time such as erosion, heat, pressure, stress, and emanations from the earth all combine to cause folding, faulting, shifting, and landsliding. The result is a stratification that does not provide a convenient depiction of the origins of those strata. Faulting and shifting displace parts of some strata alongside other strata. Older layers of sediment now appear on top of much younger layers of sediment, making it difficult to know where anything really begins or ends. Such is memory, for Miller, in his reconstruction of his own story. One's point of view at any given moment is always providing a different way of reconstructing the past. Similarly, the origins of wisdom succumb to the same effects of many different forces of use and reinterpretation, editing and reediting over the passage of time.

Timebends

Memory keeps folding in upon itself like geological layers of rock, the deeper strata sometimes appearing on top before they slope downward into the depths again.

Arthur Miller, *Timebends* (New York: Grove Press, 1987), 586.

The sages of ancient Israel surely knew that time bends and refracts one's point of view. Framing these ever-changing points of view by appealing both to the wisdom of a great king and their confession that the Lord was the ultimate beginning point, the sages in effect abandon any search for a historical beginning. They choose confession instead of historicality. Such a confession confronts readers with the challenge to let wisdom begin with the sages' understanding that the Lord has no real beginning or end. The book of wisdom in Proverbs only begins for the reader. Wisdom itself has no beginning since it ultimately was with the Lord before the beginning (Prov 8:22-31).

NOTES

[1] Roland Murphy, *Proverbs* (WBC 22; Nashville: Thomas Nelson, 1998), xix-xx; Carol Fontaine, "Wisdom in Proverbs," in *In Search of Wisdom: Essays in Memory of John Gammie*, ed. Leo Perdue, Bernard B. Scott, and William Wiseman (Louisville: Westminster John Knox Press, 1993), 99-114. For an older source consulted frequently in this commentary, see William McKane, *Proverbs* (London: SCM Press Ltd., 1970), 1-9.

[2] Ibid., 170.

[3] Leo Perdue, *Wisdom and Creation: The Theology of Wisdom Literature* (Nashville: Abingdon, 1994), 70-80.

[4] Ibid., 80-81.

[5] The discussion that follows relies heavily upon Michael V. Fox, "Words for Wisdom," *ZAH* 6/2 (1993): 149-69; other useful sources would include, R. N. Whybray, *The Intellectual Tradition in the Old Testament* (Berlin & New York: Walter de Gruyter, 1974), 131-49; and William McKane, *Prophets and Wise Men* (London: SCM Press, 1965, 1983).

[6] With only two occurrences in the Hebrew Bible (Hab 2:6 and Prov 1:6), comparative evidence is simply unavailable for discernment of its meaning. Note that LXX translates as "dark word," *skoteinon logon.*

[7] Arthur Miller, *Timebends* (New York: Grove Press, 1987), 586.

PROSPERITY FROM GREED

Proverbs 1:8-19

COMMENTARY

Of the three units in the opening chapter of Proverbs (1:1-7, 8-19, 20-33), 1:8-19 comprises the first instruction of the collection. Ancient teachers, whether professional or parental, were concerned about the benefits, or outcomes, of their wisdom instructions (see especially 10:1–22:16). Ecclesiastes will ask explicitly about the "profitability" of human wisdom and toil (e.g., Eccl 1:3; 3:9). The opening instruction of Proverbs offers a negative example of such prosperity, establishing unambiguously the way not to achieve such benefit. Ultimately, seeking to prosper through crime is self-defeating (1:19). This would be a concern of one in a school setting who sought to reinforce the values of the community. It would be of special import to parents who sought success in the community—marriage, work, child rearing, inheritance—for their children.

It is tempting to speculate about the particular social location envisioned by the author of these words. We might imagine that the temptation to join the ancient equivalent of our "street gangs" was poverty. As today, crime in antiquity paid well. Robbing from the rich to satisfy legitimate needs, however inadvisable, may find its own social legitimation. However, since the people portrayed in this instruction do their dirty work "for nothing," (*ḥinnām*, v. 11), the evil deed is not even a socially motivated crime.[1] The topic here is not violence for defense or survival, but simply gratuitous violence.

Verses 8-9 open with the frequently recurring introductory appeal, "Hear, my child , . . ." one of those patterns that remind readers of structural boundaries that are essential to understand this literature (see [Inclusio with Two Women]). The appeal occurs several times throughout the instructions in Proverbs 1–9 and is a defining characteristic of instruction generally (e.g. 2:1; 3:1-4, 21-22; 4:1-2, 10-12; 5:1-2; 6:20-22; 7:1-3). The appeal is equally an assertion of authority, using the stereotypical language of teachers (see comments on 1:1-7). In this instance both discipline (*mûsār*) and instruction (*tôrat*) stand parallel with one another. Readers will recognize in v. 9 a motive clause, typically introduced with the particle "for" (*kî*) that accompanies the call to "hear." The implicit message is that instruction brings rewards that lead to the good life.

Verses 10-19 form the body of the instruction, which provides a fictional example of temptation (vv. 10-14) followed by an admonition (vv. 15-19). At a glance readers may readily discern the movement of the sage's thought. Verses 11 and 18 form an inclusio (see [Inclusio with Two Women]) around the contents through the repeated use of the same pair of verbs for "lie in wait" (*'ārab*) and "ambush" (*ṣāpan*). The fictional example in vv. 10-14 is introduced with a condition; the conditional particle "if" opens and conveys the rhetorical idea that the teacher is offering a hypothetical

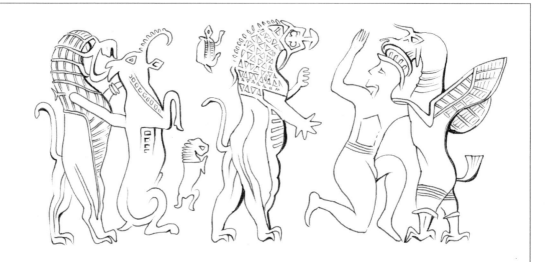

The Jaws of Death

Readers shall see throughout the Proverbs many examples of how ancient Israel used the imagery of the surrounding civilizations to give expression to that generation's own understanding of reality. The idea of death having jaws is likely an allusion from Canaanite mythology. The function of such imagery was not so different from our use of figures such as "an Achilles heel" or "the Sirens' song," both originating in Homer's *Iliad* and *Odyssey*.

The Canaanite religion conceived of deities that represented different aspects of nature. Death, of course, was just such a natural process to ancient peoples. In Canaanite myth, death, or *Mot*, was the son of the ruling god, *el*. *Mot* ruled the underworld. To pass into the under-

Cylinder seal from the first Babylonian Dynasty depicts an individual being swallowed by a representation of death.

world, or the realm of the dead, one had to pass through his throat. Obviously, the personification of death's appetite would use references to the human appetite, the mouth and the jaws. It would further give expression to the view that death was a voracious eater. The deity consumed people, feeding on them as an ordinary human dined at table.

For further reading, see John Gray, *Near Eastern Mythology* (New York: Peter Bedrick Books, 1988), 64-102; William McKane, *Proverbs* (London: SCM Press, 1970), 269-70; and Jonathan N. Tubb, *Canaanites* (Norman: University of Oklahoma Press, 1998), 74.

example: "if sinners entice you," "if they say to you." The teacher elaborates, though, by helping his charge to imagine the reasoning of sinners: their appeal to Sheol, the Pit, and other mythological images as allies (v. 12),[2] their enticement to gain hordes of wealth (v. 13), and their command to join a fellowship of crime (v. 14). [The Jaws of Death] The very development of ideas—from mythology, to wealth, to the imperative to join the band of criminals—suggests the seduction of the sinners' processes of reasoning.

Verse 15 introduces the admonitions of the teacher with a negative imperative, "do not walk in their way." The teacher's appeal is to show that the rationale offered by sinners makes no sense at all. Verse 17 is a traditional saying, or proverb, used here to illustrate the inevitability of justice. As the verse is translated by NRSV, it pictures a net baited to attract birds. Even though the quarry can see the net in advance and can see that it is baited, the bird's appetite draws it to its own capture and ultimate death.

The saying in v. 17 functions as a metaphor for the fate of the highwaymen, but readers wonder how the metaphor works in reference to v. 18. Do the birds stand for the innocent people who are attacked by the highwaymen? Or do the birds represent the highwaymen who, even though they see a trap being baited to their inevitable demise, nevertheless fall into it themselves?

One of the key terms in understanding the meaning is translated "in vain" (*ḥinnām*). Readers have already encountered it in v. 11, translated by NRSV as "wantonly." It denotes an absence of rationality or abandonment of conventional practices based upon such rationality. In the same way that there is no reason for highwaymen to attack innocent travelers, there should be no way for birds, who see the trap being baited for them, to fall into it. But, birds inevitably do fall into such traps. So do criminals. Even though they can see the eventual and inevitable outcome of their actions, they fall into their own trap and receive punishment.

The teacher's concluding observation, v. 19, asserts the principle of retribution. The teacher's confident assertion of this retributive universe recurs repeatedly throughout most of the Proverbs, especially in the view that ultimately right prospers and evil fails. This confidence stems from the assurance, evident in the created order, that Yahweh himself enforces justice for the righteous and the wicked. For the Deuteronomist, retribution is the principle upon which he bases the benefits of covenanting with Yahweh (Deut 8:1; 10:12-22); for the Chronicler, retribution is the turning point of history (2 Chr 25:20-27); for the sages, retribution makes life meaningful and predictable (Prov 11:5-6, 23; 12:2, 7, 13; 13:2;

Birds Caught in Net

This wallpainting is only one of several in the tomb of the ancient Egyptian scribe Nakht depicting life in the Nile delta.

Servants Netting Wild Geese. Detail of a wallpainting in the tomb of Nakht, scribe and priest under the Pharaoh Thutmosis IV. 18th Dynasty. 16th–14th C. BC. Sheikh Abd el-Qurna. Tombs of the Nobles. Thebes, Egypt.

15:27, 29; 29:23), thus facilitating their perception of divine control.

The teacher who stands behind the book of Ecclesiastes is not so confident, however, since he has seen evidence to the contrary. There are "righteous people who perish in their righteousness, and there are wicked people who prolong their life in their evil-doing" (Eccl 7:15). There are the "righteous people who are treated according to the conduct of the wicked . . ." (Eccl 8:14). Readers must know in advance that in exploring the words of the sages, they are tracking many sides of the ancient struggles with the idea of a just universe. In a sense, readers are exploring how these ancient sages came to terms with the reality of their world.

CONNECTIONS

The Inevitability that Justice Prevails

Flannery O'Connor's short story, "A Good Man Is Hard to Find," ultimately raises the question of the costliness of grace. The narrative about a family senselessly murdered along the highway by escaped convicts confronts readers with the chilling reality that the innocent are not always spared, and sociopaths are not always punished in this world. For there to be grace, there must be a high price to pay in suffering. The grandmother—who (more than any of the family members) lives in a world of sentimental values and false consciousness—only comes to recognize the fragility of her convictions when she is confronted with her imminent and unavoidable death at the hands of the Misfit, the leader of the escaped convicts. The Misfit's final remark before he shoots her in cold blood, "she would've been a good woman, if there had been someone there to shoot her every minute of her life," jolts readers into their own repressed awareness of the tissue-thin veneer of success, assurance, confidence, and even justice. We wonder if it could actually be true that suffering is the only phenomenon that actually gives us clarity on life's meaning. Such is the consciousness of our time: it is possible for all of us to identify with the grandmother. The awareness of the suffering of millions of people is part of our everyday routine. On the front pages of daily newspapers around the world is the ceaseless reminder that human suffering and pain is inescapable. The photos printed in newspapers and flashed across television and computer screens grow more and more explicit. Undoubtedly, this is due to our dullness toward pain brought on by the numbing bombardment of reports. People displaced as refugees or children slaughtered in drive-by shootings while in recess at school increasingly persuade us that the absence of suffering is the abnormal phenomenon. The world of order and meaning constantly teeters on the verge of chaos, and the boundaries between the two are blurry.

For such reasons, readers remark the theological exuberance and confidence of the ancient sage. Why were the sages so confident that justice would prevail, that retribution would not fail? It makes us attend even more to the point of view of the innocent: the traveler waylaid by the highwaymen, the struggling family set back even more by the financial burden of illness, the business person who unexpectedly is out of a job. If retribution does not fail, why is there such suffering?

O'Connor on Grace

For Flannery O'Connor, sentimentality is antithetical to honesty about suffering. What she means by sentimentality is a trivialization of suffering by idealizing its purpose or place. The idealization is a process of denial, or a false consciousness of reality, that ultimately can only be shattered through one's own experience of pain. She says:

> We lost our innocence in the Fall, and our return to it is through the Redemption which was brought about by Christ's death and by our slow participation in it. Sentimentality is a skipping of this process in its concrete reality and an early arrival at a mock state of innocence, which strongly suggests its opposite.

Flannery O'Connor, *Mystery and Manners,* ed. Sally and Robert Fitzgerald (New York]: Farrar, Straus, Giroux, 1969), 148.

Finally, people who seek meaning and order in their Christian faith may find it useful to strive for social justice as an expression of some tangible sense of order. But, no matter how tangible justice may seem, it, too, leaves much to be desired. The desire for social justice in fact may be analogous to the ancient notion of retribution: it cannot exist unless a society also accepts the accompanying notion of the great price that must be paid in suffering. In other words, we may not be able to agree that justice wins out unless we are also willing to agree that there is a price to be paid. That price is our own slow and personal participation in the suffering of Jesus the Nazarene. [O'Connor on Grace]

But there is the difficulty. If one operates in a worldview like that of the sages, then there is a reason for everything. Embracing suffering so that someone else might experience justice is about the farthest thing from the kind of personal justice that most people come to associate with their faith, and indeed, with their own worldviews. And yet, this may be the heart and soul of the call of Jesus of Nazareth: to embrace suffering so that someone else might experience justice.

NOTES

[1] R. N. Whybray, *Wealth and Poverty in the Book of Proverbs* (Sheffield: JSOT Press, 1990), 102-103. Given the social conditions of the post-exilic period prior to the reforms of Ezra–Nehemiah, it is tempting to read this as a reflection of the malaise during the period. See also R. E. Clements's description of the period as "liminal" in *Wisdom in Theology* (Grand Rapids MI: Eerdmans, 1992), 26-31.

[2] Roland Murphy, *Proverbs* (WBC 22; Nashville: Thomas Nelson, 1998), 9.

WISDOM'S SECURITY

Proverbs 1:20-33

In contrast to the preceding instruction on the enticement of sinners and the course one's life takes by heeding that temptation, Woman Wisdom now calls. In vv. 20-33 we encounter the first of four wisdom poems, all of which "personify" wisdom as a woman (1:20-33; 3:13-20; 8:1-36; 9:1-6).[1] [Women and Wisdom] One of the immediate effects of picturing wisdom as a character is to disallow the view that wisdom is something to be possessed. It is more likely that Wisdom, the woman who calls in the streets of the city, is one who herself possesses those who come to learn from her. [Structure at a Glance: Proverbs 1:20-33]

Women and Wisdom

One of the framing devices for the collection of Proverbs is the image of wisdom as a woman (see [Inclusio with Two Women]). By bringing together these two notions, the ancient sages created a metaphor whereby each part of the metaphor illuminated the other. The reader's task is to ask about ancient social roles of women that might illuminate the sage's understanding of wisdom. And vice versa, one must ask what is known about ancient Israelite wisdom that helps to appreciate ancient concepts of the feminine.

We know that Israel's was a patriarchal society. This means that the family name, land, and inheritance—in other words, power—passed through the male members of a family. Women gained status as wives and mothers; but outside the special context of a family unit, they were second-class citizens. What is remarkable about the portrayal of wisdom as a woman is that these traditional female roles of wives and mothers are not used explicitly in reference to Woman Wisdom. She, by contrast, is equal to a male without appealing to her role as a mother. Thus, she goes about in the public places of the city as a male would. She calls to young men in order to provide instruction for them. She values her product according to the currency of exchange in the male-dominated marketplace.

Nevertheless, Woman Wisdom's activities are those that recall the activities of other important women in the biblical tradition. She, like the matriarchs (e.g., Sarah, Rebekah, Leah, and Rachel), has control over the household and her children. Like women who are remembered as giving advice to their husbands (e.g., Manoah's wife, Judg 13:23; and Bathsheba, 1 Kgs 1:15-21), so Woman Wisdom gives advice to those who would come and receive it from her. As a wife and mother, she is also a lover. She is both seductive to young males and also absolutely loyal in her relationship with her husband. As such, she sets a standard against which her counterpart, Woman Folly, is depicted as an adulteress and liar (see Camp).

For further reading, see Carol R Fontaine, "The Personification of Wisdom," in *HBC*, 501-503; Carol R. Fontaine and Sharon H. Ringe, eds., *Woman's Bible Commentary* (Louisville: Westminster John Knox Press, 1998), 154; Roland E Murphy, "Excursus on Woman Wisdom and Woman Folly," in *Proverbs* (WBC 22; Nashville: Thomas Nelson Publishers, 1998), 278-87; and idem, "The Personification of Wisdom," in *Wisdom in Ancient Israel: Essays in Honour of J. A. Emerton*, ed. John Day et al. (Cambridge: CUP, 1995), 222-33.

Claudia Camp, *Wisdom and the Feminine in the Book of Proverbs* (Sheffield: JSOT/Almond Press, 1985), 71-147.

Structure at a Glance: Proverbs 1:20-33

AΩ The structure of the poem is chiastic, and recognizing this helps readers understand the central thrust of the poem. The word *chiasm* stems from the Greek letter "chi." The letter looks like the English letter "X": two lines that cross in the middle. By analogy, the word *chiasm* is used to describe a pattern of arranging lines of poetry or words within a line of poetry. For instance, if a line of Hebrew poetry consists of four words, where the outer two words are similar and the inner two words are similar, one has a pattern that might be described this way: A, B, B′, A′. Other patterns might include A, B, C, B′, A′. Such patterns can apply to words as well as lines of poetry, and also to clusters of poetic lines. It is much easier to spot a chiastic structure in Hebrew than in English unless the chiasm also applies to the arranging of themes.

In the case of this poem some scholars identify the chiastic arrangement as follows (quoted in Garrett):

A. Introduction: an appeal for listeners (vv. 20-21)
  B. Address to the untutored, scoffers, and fools (v. 22)
    C. Declaration of disclosure (v. 23)
      D. Reasons for the announcement (vv. 24-25)
        E. Announcement of derisive judgment (vv. 26-28)
      D′. Reason for the announcement (vv. 29-30)
    C′. Declaration of retribution (v. 31)
  B′. Fate of the untutored and fools (v. 32)
A′. Conclusion: an appeal for a hearer (v. 33)

There are obvious problems with such an approach to reading. The symmetrical correspondences are seldom exact, requiring the reader to bend the criteria somewhat. That notwithstanding, why arrange instruction in this way? The most obvious answer has to do with the artfulness of such wisdom instructions. Art invites readers and listeners to pause, reflect, and use imagination. But, such arrangements may also serve a rhetorical purpose. Chiasm is a device that influences *how* a statement means as much as *what* it means. Repetition in the middle of the line invites the readers' perceptions of an emphatic statement, perhaps as a way of focusing the attention of the reader/listener. (For further reading, see James L. Kugel, "Poetry," *HBD*, 804-806; idem, *The Idea of Biblical Poetry* [Cambridge: Yale University Press, 1982]; and Luis Alonso Schökel, *A Manual of Hebrew Poetics* [Rome: Editrice Pontificio Istituto Biblico, 1988], 23, 55, 59.)

The task of the reader, then, is not only one of reading the linear movement of the poem, but also of noting the ideas created through the opposing parts of the poem. For instance, vv. 20-21, Wisdom's opening call, has its counterpart in v. 33, Wisdom's closing appeal. Likewise, her address to the simple, the scoffers, and the fools in v. 22 has its counterpart in her assertion of the fate of these same characters in v. 32.

Duane A. Garrett, *Proverbs and Ecclesiastes* (NAC 14; Nashville: Broadman Press, 1994), 71; Garrett cites P. Trible, "Wisdom Builds a Poem: The Architecture of Proverbs 1:20-33," JBL 94 [1975]: 509-18.

COMMENTARY

Wisdom's Call, 1:20-21

The poem opens with a third-person depiction of Wisdom's call to her students. She is pictured as extending her services to the simple ones, the scoffers, and the fools. This latter group reminds readers of the stated purpose of the entire collection in 1:4. What is more, her work is in the most public of places, the "streets," and "squares," at the entrance to the "city gates." [The Ancient City Gate]

The style of Wisdom's address has similarities with a prophetic style characterized by "appeal, denunciation, threat, and promise."[2] The poet's intention may well be one of conveying a similar intensity and urgency about Wisdom's—a teacher's, not a prophet's—message. Certainly the phrase "how long" (*'ad mātay,* v. 22) occurs frequently in the prophets as an indication of utter confusion regarding the Lord's will. (e.g., Jer 4:14, 21; 12:4; 23:26; see also Hos 8:5; Isa 6:11; Hab 2:6). Here the phrase expresses an ironic bewilderment of the teacher with the apparent reluctance of those in need of wisdom. Verse 33, opposed by vv. 20-22, offers Wisdom's appeal based upon the promise of security.

Wisdom's Message, 1:22-33

Wisdom's instruction builds in a series of stages to the central image of judgment contained in vv. 26-28. Those who have failed to follow Wisdom's instruction will find that in the midst of their calamity it is too late to call on her. Against the inevitable judgment in the preceding instruction, pronounced upon those who are "greedy for gain" and who "wantonly ambush the innocent" (vv. 11, 19), Wisdom's laugh has a peculiarly eerie effect. With the tenor of prophetic doom, Wisdom's message is simply that time runs out. In stark contrast to what some ancient ears had surely grown accustomed to hearing, Wisdom offers no sense of the possibility to "return," as the Deuteronomist does (e.g.,

The Ancient City Gate

ΑΩ The image of Woman Wisdom calling to people as they pass through the city gate is quite realistic given present understanding of this ancient feature. The architecture of the walled city illustrates the city gate to be one of the most important structures. It was the only opening in the city's surrounding casemate wall (two parallel walls with perpendicular walls placed in intervals) by which to obtain passage in and out of the city. The city gate was the most vulnerable part of an ancient city's defenses. Therefore, it was reinforced with towers flanking each side and its passageway was a series of chambers. These chambers were likely used as guardhouses, as meeting places for the city's residents, and also as a marketplace for city commerce. Since it was the entry and exit into and out of the city, people were constantly coming and going. As such, the city gate complex was one of the most important public structures of the entire city.

For further reading, see A. Biran, "Dan, Tel," *Encyclopedia of Archaeological Excavations in the Holy Land* ed. Michael Avi-Yonah (English) (Englewood Cliffs NJ: Prentice Hall, Inc., 1975), 313-21; and Amnon Ben-Tor, *The Archaeology of Ancient Israel*, trans. R. Greenberg (Tel-Aviv: The Open University of Israel, 1992), 175-77.

Deut 4:29-30). To those who have rejected her, Wisdom becomes a scornful enemy in the midst of distress.

On either side of this central image of Wisdom's rejection of those who reject her are the assertion of the possibilities for the youth, v. 23, and the reality of life's situation, v. 31. The simple ones could have had the benefits of Wisdom's thoughts and words; instead "they shall eat the fruit of their way, and be sated with their own devices." Twice Wisdom asserts that she called and was rejected, vv. 24-25 and vv. 29-30. In v.29, furthermore, the association between Wisdom's instruction and the fear of the Lord is made unambiguous. Rejecting Wisdom is tantamount to rejecting piety and devotion to Yahweh.

In v. 29 readers see the equation between knowledge and the fear of the Lord. In v. 7, the programmatic introductory statement, the fear of the Lord is the beginning of knowledge. Here in v. 29, to reject knowledge is to reject the fear of the Lord. This suggests that Wisdom speaks with greater authority than any mere wisdom teacher. The instruction that she proposes carries with it both the authority and therefore the urgency of the most deeply held religious values. Her words have significance deriving from the creator of the cosmos.

The concluding verse, v. 33, counterpoises the ones who "listen" with those who, in v. 32, are wayward and complacent. This reminds readers of Wisdom's opening call to all in the street (v. 20). Further, the wayward and complacent evoke readers' recollection of the young highwaymen in the preceding instruction (1:8-19). Ultimately, the concluding verse is an assertion of the fundamental order of the universe (see 1:1-7). The natural result of one's attentive response to Wisdom is the assurance that disaster shall not strike. This retributionary order of all creation will give back in relationship to one's behavior.

The Latin roots of this English word, "retribution," provide a clue to its meaning: *re* means "back," and *tribuere* means "to pay." Thus, in its basic sense it means to pay back. As an ancient theological concept it denotes one important feature of wisdom's worldview. The universe operates on a principle of "pay-backs," as it were. Every act is either rewarded or punished depending upon whether it is good or evil.

The sages reflected upon what is good and what is the order of the universe that allows one to know and do that good. Generally speaking, the entire wisdom enterprise attempted to develop and provide an intellectual apparatus for realizing the good. Such a notion facilitated the idea that the universe itself was therefore just;

justice was the guiding principle of the created order as it derived from the creator who presided over creation.[3]

CONNECTIONS

Is It Ever Too Late?

Woman Wisdom's compelling case for embracing the discipline of knowledge is intensified by her view that there comes a point in time when there are no more second chances. Disaster strikes and there is no one there to give assistance or aid. One of ancient Judah's greatest historians, the so-called "Deuteronomistic Historian" saw a recurring pattern throughout his people's story. It was one of God's grace, the people's sin, national disaster, repentance, and God's grace and restoration. For this historian, the pattern came to have theological significance. [The Deuteronomistic Pattern] The pattern was so important to telling Israel's story that it became a tacit assumption for establishing the need to return to Yahweh in the midst of disaster, especially in the second temple period (e.g., Neh 9:6-37). But one wonders whether, as a strategy, it potentially feeds complacency by harboring the bad-faith notion that there is always a second chance, that Yahweh always forgives; therefore everyone may ultimately escape the consequences of their actions.

It is interesting to speculate on how future generations will remember the final few years of the twentieth century. Will they be able to reconstruct and understand the global "Y2K" computer compatibility questions that were put forward as a kind of eschaton? How will they judge those who, in fear of the potential chaos of a massive multi-system computer failure around the world, stockpiled food, built shelters, stored arms, formed survivalist communities, established survival protocols, and much more? Or, more interestingly, how will future generations judge those who rather glibly continued on and did nothing

The Deuteronomistic Pattern

The editors of the biblical books of Joshua, Judges, Samuel, and Kings have conventionally been referred to as the Deuteronomistic Historian as though there were a single editor/historian who imposed his theology and ideology upon the more ancient stories within these books. While there is ongoing debate about who that person or those people were, the literary, theological, and structural characteristics of the work are more certain. One of the defining characteristics of the final form of the history is the perspective that ancient Israel's history was shaped by the ongoing process of retribution. This process is given expression in a recognizable pattern of grace, national sin, punishment, repentance, and restoration. The pattern is especially pronounced in the Deuteronomistic passages such as Judg 2:6-23 and in later rereadings of such theology such as that in Neh 9:6-37. The pattern functions to convey both the waywardness of the ancient Israelite nation and the grace of Yahweh who initiated a relationship with the people.

For further reading, see Terence E. Fretheim, *The Deuteronomic History* (Nashville: Abingdon Press, 1983); Steven McKenzie, "Deuteronomistic History," *ABD* 2:160-68; and Ernest W. Nicholson, *Deuteronomy and Tradition* (Oxford: Basil Blackwell, 1967), 107-24.

despite the fact that they had no technical knowledge providing a rationale for their choices? Will there be proverbs written about the final few years of the twentieth century? Will the present-day generation be the future's negative examples on the subject of facing uncertain futures?

One can only wonder what it would be like to live life as though there were no second chances. Heeding Woman Wisdom's call, it seems, is embracing life with a level of seriousness that obtains because one only gets one crack at things. It is a sobering thought that the forgiveness, patience, and mercy extended to us by others might too often be taken as a matter of course, as though they would always be there. What if there were no grace? Or what if we had a deeper appreciation for the costliness of grace? The possibility of a second chance to take a teacher's words seriously, or a spouse's love as rare and precious, would not be so deeply entrenched into our psyches that we would take such liberties with our thoughts and actions.

NOTES

[1] Roland Murphy, *Proverbs* (WBC 22; Nashville: Thomas Nelson, 1998), 278, notes that there are three other kinds of women in Proverbs: Woman Folly (9:13-18), one's wife (5:15-19), and the "Stranger" (2:16-19; 5:1-14, 20; 6:24-35; 7:25-27).

[2] R. B. Y. Scott, *Proverbs and Ecclesiastes* (AB 18; Garden City NY: Doubleday, 1965), 39.

[3] Klaus Koch, "Is There a Doctrine of Retribution in the Old Testament" in *Theodicy in the Old Testament*, ed. James L. Crenshaw (Philadelphia: Fortress, 1983), 57-87; W. S. Towner, "Retribution," *IDB*, 865-66.

THE TEACHER'S SYLLABUS

Proverbs 2:1-22

All of the contents of chapter 2 are devoted to a single poem on the most important subject matter of wisdom's instruction.[1] The chief difficulty for readers is in grasping all twenty-two verses as a whole. That is because in the MT the poem is one long conditional sentence. A conditional sentence is one whose rhetorical function is to create a condition or some contingency. The grammatical features are easy to recognize. There are two parts. First, there is the condition itself, or the protasis. It is typically introduced with some conditional particles, most commonly "if." The second part is the result that eventuates when the particular condition is in effect, called the apodosis. It is usually introduced by a particle implying a contingent circumstance, such as "then."

The rhetoric of the condition governs one's reading of the poem in 2:1-22. The protasis, or the condition itself, is set out in vv. 1-4. The remainder of the poem serves as the apodosis, or the results that ensue from meeting the conditions in vv. 1-4. The apodosis may be further broken into four sections with a final admonition. Verses 5-8 and vv. 9-11 both assert the result that wisdom shall be obtained by the diligent seeker. Verses 12-15 and vv. 16-19 further develop the implications of obtaining wisdom by offering examples of deliverance from two types of people: the perverse man (*ʾîš mĕdabbēr tahpukôt*), and the foreign woman (*ʾiššâ zārâ*). The closing admonition in vv. 20-22 appears to be in the form of instruction. An overall unity of the poem is further reinforced by alluding to an acrostic structure. [Structure at a Glance: Proverbs 2]

The poem admonishes the pupil to obey proper instruction while describing the contents of that instruction. This also makes readers sensitive to allusions to other biblical instructions. The admonitory style of the poem in Proverbs 2 is the most distinctive feature and reminds readers of the Mosaic sermons in Deuteronomy (e.g., Deut 5–11). It is, however, difficult to conclude whether such evidence of inner-biblical cross-fertilization implies that the sages were influenced by the Deuteronomists (see [The Deuteronomistic Pattern]), or vice versa.[2]

Structure at a Glance: Proverbs 2

AΩ The structural layout of the poem facilitates reading in that there is a clear organization and movement of ideas (see diagram below). However, the overall unity of the poem is also facilitated by the poem's affinities with what is known as an "acrostic poem."

I. The Introduction (vv. 1-11)
   A. The Call (vv. 1-4)
   B. The Results of the Search (vv. 5-8)
   C. The Results of the Search (vv. 9-11)
II. Pragmatic Outcomes (vv. 12-22)
   A. Salvation from the perverted (vv. 12-15)
   B. Salvation from the "other" woman (vv. 16-19)
   C. Final Admonition (vv. 20-22)

Two main features characterize the acrostic in Hebrew. First, the poem is twenty-two verses long, the exact number of lines for every letter of the Hebrew alphabet. Second, there is a correspondence between the beginning of each line of poetry and each letter of the Hebrew alphabet. Such a device is thought to be a deliberate artistic means of communicating wholeness and completeness. One of the classic biblical examples of an acrostic poem is Ps 119.

In the case of Ps 119, a "Torah Psalm," the connotation is that Torah comprehends all of reality. There may also be some pedagogical value in the use of such a device in that an alphabetic sequence provides a convenient mnemonic aid. The concluding poem in the book of Proverbs is an acrostic on the valorous or excellent woman, Wisdom herself. Keeping in mind the rhetorical purpose of such an acrostic only helps readers to infer the elevated status of this woman being described. Other acrostic poems in the Bible include Pss 9–10; 25; 37; 111; 112; and Prov 31:10-31.

While Prov 2:1-22 does not strictly adhere to the formal features of an acrostic, the first 11 verses (the first half of the poem) have the first letter of the Hebrew alphabet, "aleph" (') occurring at key locations: v. 1 (after the opening "my son") and v. 4, vv. 5 and 9. The Hebrew letter "lamed" (l), which begins the second half of the Hebrew alphabet, begins verses 12, 16, and 20 of the second half of the poem (see Roland Murphy quoting P. W. Skehan). Skehan has noted that there is furthermore a strophic symmetry in this poem. Strophes are like stanzas in a song, and readers may subdivide the lines of the poem into a pattern of strophes as follows: 4, 4, 3; 4, 4, 3. Thus, vv. 1-4; 5-8; 9-11; and vv. 12-15; 16-19; 20-22.

For further reading, see D. N. Freedman, "Acrostics and Metrics in Hebrew Poetry," *HTR* 65 (1972): 367-92; W. Soll, "Acrostic," *ABD* 1:58-60; L. Alonso-Schökel, *A Manual of Hebrew Poetics* (Roma: Editrice Pontificio Istituto Biblico, 1988), 190-91; and Richard L. Clifford, *Proverbs* (OTL; Louisville: Westminster John Knox Press, 1999), 45-46.

Roland Murphy, *Proverbs* (WBC 22; Nashville: Thomas Nelson, 1998), 14.

P. W. Skehan, *Studies in Israelite Poetry and Wisdom*, CBQMS (Washington D.C.: Catholic Biblical Association, 1971), 9-10, 16.

COMMENTARY

The Condition, 2:1-4

The section opens with the common address to "my child," establishing a parental voice as instructor. Following the preceding wisdom poem in chapter 1, however, readers may also hear the residual voice of Woman Wisdom calling to the simple and the foolish who in a childlike way stubbornly resist her calls (1:22-23). Interestingly, when readers reach Proverbs 31:1-31, they encounter the final poem in the book, which is about a remarkable and valorous woman strongly identifying with Woman Wisdom. Readers may then retrospectively decide that the parental voice of instruction is as much a mother's voice as it is a father's. The call in

Proverbs 2 in any event is for the child to receive instructive words. As Woman Wisdom, the challenge to "treasure up my command-ments" heightens the significance by alluding to the Mosaic commandments, *miṣwôt* (occurring some thirty times in the Deuteronomistic History; it occurs also in Prov 3:1; 4:4; 6:20; 7:1; 10:8). The piling up of references to wisdom in vv. 2-4 reminds readers of the introduction to the entire collection, where all of the synonyms for wisdom were first set out (see 1:1-7). Here again readers encounter "wisdom" (*ḥokmâ*), "understanding" (*bînâ*), and "insight" (*tĕbûnâ*), the key features of the sages' concept of intellection and cognition.

The accompanying verbs are noteworthy. The student is to "be attentive" and "incline the heart," instructions frequently encountered in the admonitions of the prophets (e.g., Hos 5:1; Isa 10:30; Mic 1:2; Jer 18:19). Further, the instructions to "cry out" (*tiqrâ*) and "lift one's voice" (*tittēn qôlekā*) describe activities frequently used for supplication before deity in times of trouble (e.g., Pss 18:4; 50:15; 86:5-6; Hos 7:11). In Proverbs 2:3 this language conveys both an attitude of supplication and urgency as the student considers what must be done in order to obtain wisdom.

The Results of the Search, 2:5-11

Diligent seeking for wisdom conditionally leads to two results: first, a knowledge of God (vv. 5-8); second, an understanding of an ethical lifestyle befitting such knowledge of God (vv. 9-11). Both of these results are clearly introduced by two "then" clauses. The Hebrew word "then" (*ʾāz*) stands at the beginning of, thus introducing, each section.

The sage is confident that the end result is "understanding the fear of the LORD" and "finding the knowledge of God" (v. 5). It may be that the main purpose of the sage is simply to assert that the true source of wisdom is the Lord, countering any notion of one's finding wisdom on one's own. Readers do not read too far in the wisdom tradition, however, before encountering harsh polemic against the notion that one can really find the knowledge of God. Job 28, a poem written during the same historical (post-exilic) time frame, certainly acknowledges that wisdom is with God, but also affirms wisdom's ultimate hiddenness from humans (28:20-22). The student's final decision must be made while also weighing the still less enthusiastic realism of Qoheleth, the sage behind the book of Ecclesiastes. Qoheleth is certain that one cannot ultimately know the mind of God (Eccl 3:11; 8:16-17).

Not only does finding wisdom provide security and protection for the righteous and upright (vv. 7-8), but it leads to an understanding of the morals and ethics of righteousness (vv. 9-11). Verse 8 alludes to the motif of the two paths mentioned both in the wisdom poem and in the opening instruction (1:8-19; see also [Hebrew Orthography and Transliteration]). This image provides transition into the second result clause. The second result clause provides a helpful transition from the promise of finding wisdom with its accompanying lifestyle to the assertion of deliverance and protection from those who do not have it, especially the perverse man and the foreign woman.

Wisdom's Salvation, 2:12-19

The process of learning, if mastered, has some eventual advantages. First, learning will deliver the novice from the way of the perverted man (vv. 12-15). This implies that a proper education will keep a young person from choosing to follow in the paths of such a one. Even though no specific sin or crime is mentioned in these verses, the behavior of such wicked people is characterized by their speech; it is crooked and deceptive. The implication is that knowledge enables people to recognize such twisted and deceptive speech.

The "Strange" Woman

AΩ We have already mentioned the metaphorical function of the feminine in the book of Proverbs (see [Inclusio with Two Women] and Introduction). Here we encounter a negative application of feminine imagery in the invocation of the "loose woman." NRSV footnotes this translation with an alternate of "strange woman." In this commentary we shall keep in mind that readers might also think of her as the "other" woman since she is an opponent of a young man's wife (chs. 5, 6, and 7) and is symbolically in competition with Woman Wisdom. The translation of "loose" would seem to foreshadow her sexually profligate behavior, which readers encounter in later instructions. The question is, in what sense is she "strange?"

The Hebrew term *'iššâ zārâ* simply means "strange woman." Paralleled as it is with the Hebrew term *nokrîyyâ*, "foreign, or alien," the idea of otherness and foreignness comes to the fore but does not explain in what sense she is understood to be foreign. If the instruction could be placed with certainty in the second-temple period, then correspondences with Ezra–Nehemiah would suggest that, indeed, the parental concern is for intermarriage with people of non-Jewish descent. The practical problem for residents of the Persian province of Yehud of that historical period has to do with inheritance of the land. Taking "strange" in a more metaphorical sense, however, this woman is considered strange because her sexual mores are antithetical to the community's sexual standards. In this sense she becomes a foreigner. It could be that her sexual mores are different precisely because she is ethnically foreign and thus brings with her cultic practices that include sacred prostitution. In this case, not only does she become one who subverts marital fidelity, but inculcates non-Yahwistic cultic practices as well.

For further reading, see J. Blenkinsopp, "The Social Context of the 'Outsider Woman' in Proverbs 1-9," *Bib* 72 (1991): 457-73; Harold C. Washington, "The Strange Woman (אשה זרה נכריה) of Proverbs 19 and Post-exilic Judean Society," in *Second Temple Studies 2: Temple and Community in the Persian Period*, ed. T. C. Eskenazi and K. Richards (JSOTSup 175; Sheffield: JSOT, 1994), 217-42; and Gail Yee, "'I have perfumed my bed with myrrh,': The Foreign Woman (*'iššâ zārâ*) in Proverbs 1-9," JSOT 43 (1989): 53-68.

Similarly, education provides the wisdom to steer clear of the "loose" (thus NRSV) or "strange/other" woman (*'iššâ zārâ*). Verse 16b parallels the adjective "strange" with the word for "foreign" (*nokrîyyâ*), implying that this woman is in some sense an outsider to the community. One immediately wonders who this "other" woman was thought to symbolize within the community. [The "Strange" Woman] Readers will see that this figure recurs several times throughout the opening collection (e.g., 5:20; 6:24; 7:5). She, like the perverted or twisted man, is also recognizable through her "smooth" words (v. 16b). The language that describes the fate of her followers heightens her significance even more. The figure of "death" (*māwet*), itself an allusion to the Canaanite god of the dead (*môt*, see [The Jaws of Death]), gives her a certain mythological dimension.[3] Intercourse with the "strange woman" ensnares young men in ways from which there can be no escape.

To Inherit the Land, 2:20-22

The conclusion of the poem makes an unambiguous connection between wisdom and righteousness. The now familiar contrast between the two ways—that of the righteous and that of the wicked—serves as the overriding metaphor of the choice that stands before the young learner. Verses 20 and 21 use an accumulation of epithets for those who are morally just: they are the "good" (*ṭôbîm*), the "righteous" (*ṣaddîqîm*), the "upright" (*yĕšārîm*), and the "innocent" (*tĕmîmîm*). These stand in contrast with the "wicked" (*rĕšā'îm*) and the "treacherous" (*bôgĕdîm*).

Even more important is the allusion to inheritance of the land in the closing three verses of the poem. The imagery of land ownership is familiar from the literature of worship. Psalm 37:3, 9, 11, 22, for instance, picture land ownership as signs of God's pleasure and bestowal of blessing. Loss of the land, however, results from God's displeasure and punishment. Gaining wisdom becomes a way to possess the land in these verses. The language concerning land in Proverbs 2:20-22 may also be evidence of a late reinterpretation of Israel's theological land traditions. [Deuteronomic Land Tradition] Given the second-temple period as the most likely time for the editing of the book of Proverbs, the problem of inheriting the land was of paramount importance.[4] Remaining independent of foreign marriages and the entangling religious connections would ensure that land inheritance remained within Jewish families. From such sociological analysis it is clear that the notion of land inheritance as it existed prior to the Babylonian exile has been reinterpreted; no

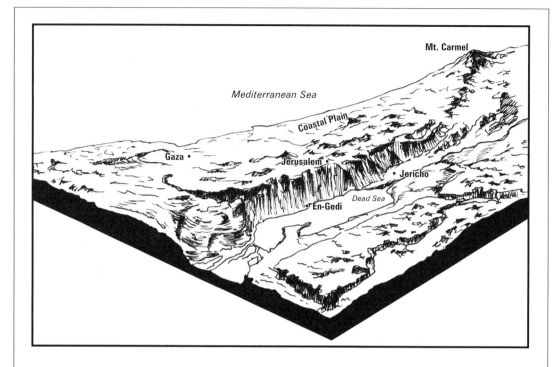

Deuteronomic Land Tradition

Readers familiar with the biblical story will recognize this as an echo of the Deuteronomic land tradition. We have used the term *Deuteronomistic* in reference to the great history compiled in the sixth century BC that scholars believe to consist of the biblical books of Deuteronomy, Joshua, Judges, Samuel (1 and 2), and Kings (1 and 2). The term *Deuteronomic*, though related, is used differently. It speaks of a much earlier, formative stage of this distinctive school of thought, responsible for assembling the law code that is contained in what is now the book of Deuteronomy. The Deuteronomic law had a profound influence upon later Deuteronomistic theologians who gave expression to their views by retelling the story of ancient Israel's rise and eventual fall to Babylon. It was one of the central ideas of that earlier theological school that the land was Yahweh's conditional gift to Yahweh's people. The condition was that the people keep covenant requirements (e.g., Deut 4:1; 6:1-3; Jer 23:5-6).

The great Deuteronomistic History, incorporating the more ancient Deuteronomic ethos that celebrated the theological significance of the land, evaluated Israel's performance in the land. This historian's negative assessment of the kings' obedience to the covenant laws provides an explanation for why Israel went into captivity to Babylon and thus lost the blessing of land.

For further reading, see Walter Brueggemann, *The Land: Place as Gift, Promise and Challenge in Biblical Faith* (OBT; Philadelphia: Fortress Press, 1977); W. Janzen, "Land," *ABD* 3; Roland Murphy, *Proverbs* (WBC 22; Nashville: Thomas Nelson, 1998), 17; and Steven L. McKenzie, "Deuteronomistic History," *ABD* 2:160-68.

longer did ownership of the land have a nationalistic significance (Judah at this time was a province of the Persian empire). The goal of the preaching of Woman Wisdom, the teacher, and all instruction, was securing the ownership of land on a much more individualized basis. The many commercial terms and references of Ecclesiastes, if also written during the Persian period (see introduction to Ecclesiastes), might further reflect this reinterpretation of the significance of land.

CONNECTIONS

How Learning Takes Place

One scholar argues that Proverbs 2 represents more than a mere outline of the importance of education. Rather, it attempts to encourage the young learner "by leading him through the logic of the educational process."[5] That logical process, according to the author, is one that has been recognized since the time of medieval rabbinic scholars. In other words, as important as inheritance of the land may be, one's understanding of the process of learning is even more important.

The process is in three parts: First comes the parent's teaching and the child's "rote incorporation," followed by the child's own "thought and inquiry." Then, God responds and grants wisdom, since God alone is the source of all wisdom. Paraphrasing Sa'adia Gaon, a medieval Jewish commentator, Fox writes, "God's grant of wisdom, . . . has an earthly precondition, namely, the labor invested in study, just as God's giving bread (Ps 136:25) responds to the human labor of farming." Education is thus a cooperative effort of child, parents, and God.[6]

The recognition that learning takes place in stages, beginning with very concrete activities and only then moving to more abstract activities, is axiomatic in modern education. Benjamin Bloom's taxonomy of educational objectives helps modern educators understand that the exchange of knowledge is only the most basic of educational processes. What is now referred to in common educational parlance as "Bloom's Taxonomy" is more fully known as the "Taxonomy of Educational Objectives." Written in 1956, this scheme of six educational processes is thought to be one of the most influential models for educational evaluation. The categories represent processes of learning that move from the most basic to the most complex. They are Knowledge, Comprehension, Application, Analysis, Synthesis, and Evaluation. One of the main contributions of this taxonomy is its fundamental assertion that the mere exchange of knowledge is only the most basic process of learning and thus, teaching is more properly a task of enabling much higher levels of reflective process.[7] Clearly, learning in its

Schools in Israel

Raphael. 1483–1520. *The School of Athens*. Stanza della Segnatura. Vatican Palace, Vatican State. Italy.

The language of this chapter also provokes questions about schools in ancient Israel (see Introduction), especially since Wisdom is herself portrayed as having a clear teaching agenda. While there is no end to evidence of an educated people who could write (Isa 8:16; Job 31:35-37; Deut 24:1, 3) and who could therefore read, there is little clear evidence where or how that education was obtained.

Jesus ben Sirach, written around 185 BC, speaks of a school; however, this was only for those who could pay for it (Sir 51:23 and 28). Still earlier, the author of Ecclesiastes speaks of his mentor as a teacher of the people (12:9). Perhaps earlier still there were trade or guild schools in which the practitioners passed on the skills and knowledge of their profession. But 2 Chr 17:7-9 leaves readers the impression that Levites moved beyond the confines of their own guild, teaching ordinary people the law. Still, even with these references, there is not clear evidence of any school system, nor is there evidence of a court school for courtiers. Readers must therefore be cautious in inferring too much about schools from such a paucity of data. (An excellent review of the research is that of James L. Crenshaw.)

For further reading, see Walter Brueggemann, *The Creative Word: Canon as a Model for Biblical Education* (Philadelphia: Fortress, 1982); James L. Crenshaw, *Education in Ancient Israel: Across the Deadening Silence* (New York: Doubleday, 1998); André Lemaire, "Education (Israel)," *ABD* 2:301-12; and A. R. Millard, "An Assessment of the Evidence of Writing in Ancient Israel," in *Biblical Archaeology Today* (Jerusalem, 1985).

James L. Crenshaw, "Education in Ancient Israel," JBL 104 (1985): 601-15.

most mature sense is a far more complicated process of reflection and analysis.

Young teachers immediately out of graduate school too frequently conceive their task as one of making daily deposits of knowledge in the memory banks of the students. Unfortunately, too many teachers continue this notion unreflectively well into their more established professorial careers. It is likely that such teaching causes misunderstanding of the teaching profession. Aside from the fact that there is simply too much knowledge to share fully with students, students become passive receptors of the points of view of others, never venturing to take responsibility for their own learning. For students to become responsible learners, the teacher must move students into the higher processes of reflection, making them independent learners with the self-motivation to hear Wisdom's voice. These higher processes ultimately define what it means to be an effective learner. They also define what it means to be an effective teacher. [Schools in Israel]

NOTES

[1] R. B. Y. Scott, *Proverbs and Ecclesiastes* (Garden City NY: Doubleday, 1965), 42-43.

[2] See William McKane, *Proverbs* (London: SCM Press, 1970), 278-80, who acknowledges a "hortatory style" and allows that there may be some debt to Deuteronomists, but also sees as significant an extra-Israelite influence on the "instruction form."

[3] Both McKane, 287-88, and Scott, 43, note the allusive imagery to the underworld in ancient Near Eastern mythology. Roland Murphy, *Proverbs* (WBC 22; Nashville: Thomas Nelson, 1998), 17, doubts the reference to Canaanite mythology contributes anything to the general understanding of this passage.

[4] See Claudia Camp's discussion of "The Ethos of Post-Exilic Israel," in *Wisdom and the Feminine in the Book of Proverbs* (Sheffield: Almond, 1985), 239-54.

[5] Michael V. Fox, "the Pedagogy of Proverbs 2," *JBL* 113/2 (1994): 233-43.

[6] Ibid., 242.

[7] Lorin W. Anderson and Lauren A. Sosinak, *Bloom's Taxonomy: A Forty Year Retrospective* (Chicago: NSSE, 1994).

WISDOM'S ABSOLUTE SURRENDER

Proverbs 3:1-12

The opening twelve verses (vv. 1-12) are set apart from what follows largely because vv. 13-20 do not contain the characteristic instruction language and appear to be another short poem on Woman Wisdom. Instruction resumes again in v. 21 with the parent's familiar call for his child's attention and the characteristic language of admonition. [The Meaning of the Hebrew "Son"] Chapter 3 thus contains two instructions, vv. 1-12 and vv. 21-35, and a wisdom poem, vv. 13-20.[1] [Structure at a Glance: Proverbs 3:1-12]

The Meaning of the Hebrew "Son"

AΩ As noted already, the recurrence of "my son" functions to help readers isolate individual instructions throughout chs. 1–9 (e.g., 1:8, 10, 15; 2:1; 3:1, 11, 21; 4:10, 20; 6:1, 3, 20; 7:1). It further implies that the context of instruction is familial rather than academic, although there is no material evidence that either was actually real. The phrase also raises the question whether males only or both males and females received education. The question is important since the NRSV translates the Hebrew word for "son" as "child" throughout chs. 1–9. This translation implies that, in that ancient context, both males and females were the recipients of instruction.

Even though the figure of Woman Wisdom subverts to certain degrees the patriarchalism of antiquity, it cannot be doubted that education was directed toward males of the society. Without doubt, the use of the word "son" may refer to a female child in a generic sense (e.g., Gen 15:3; Exod 21:5). Yet the images of the feminine within the larger context of Proverbs, in which the feminine figures Woman Folly (9:13-18) and the "other" woman (5:1-23; 6:20-35; 7:1-27) are offered as negative examples, could only succeed if the audience was male. Hence, readers should understand that the use of the word "son" meant a male child in its originating context. The translation of the NRSV as "child" and "children" grows from a desire to render the Scriptures for a social context that embraces the notion of male and female equality under God. Both young men and young women must receive Wisdom's call.

For further reading, see Paul J. Achtemeier, ed., "The Bible, Theology, and Feminist Approaches," *Int* 42 (1988); Carol A. Newsom, "Woman and the Discourse of Patriarchal Wisdom: A Study of Proverbs 1–9," in *Gender and Difference in Ancient Israel*, ed. Peggy L. Day (Minneapolis: Fortress, 1989), 142-68; Sharon H. Ringe, "When Women Interpret the Bible," in *Women's Bible Commentary*, expanded ed., ed. Carol A. Newsom and Sharon H. Ringe (Louisville: Westminster John Knox Press, 1998), 1-9; and Phyllis Trible, *God and the Rhetoric of Sexuality*, (OBT; Philadelphia: Fortress Press, 1984).

Structure at a Glance: Proverbs 3:1-12

AΩ Internally the opening instruction's shape (vv. 1-12) is determined by the now recognizable call to the child or student to be receptive to the father's commands. The body of the poem is clearly marked by the recurrence of imperatives accompanied by motive clauses. Three of the four admonitions within vv. 5-12 open with an imperative (vv. 5, 7, and 9). While there is a negative imperative within the final two verses that parallels the same construction in v. 7 (see vv. 11-12), such negative advice is a variant from the preceding positive rhetoric. These admonitions and accompanying motive clauses create a series of six doublets within the poem (vv. 1-2, 3-4, 5-6, 7-8, 9-10, and 11-12). Readers should note in these verses the recurring appeal to religious themes as both topics for reflection and motives for action. Ultimately, surrender to Wisdom is grounded in the sacred heavens.

COMMENTARY

The Promise of Total Surrender, 3:1-4

The language of the parent's call to the child is easily recognizable in these opening four verses. Holding up the parent's commandments before the child is reminiscent of the previous instruction (2:1) and echoes the Deuteronomist's presentation of the Mosaic Law (Deut 6:7-8; 11:18-19). Whether there was ever any historical affinity between the sages and the Deuteronomic legal specialists is debatable. [Deuteronomy and Wisdom]

The image of writing the instruction upon the heart (v. 3) especially recalls the promise of a new covenant stemming from the disciples of Jeremiah (Jer 31:33). With this covenant allusion close to hand, the motive clauses contained in the opening exhortation stand out with even greater relief. The motive clauses in vv. 2-4 are remarkable in that they appeal to "length of days" and "good repute," both in the eyes of "God" and "people." Not only is strong legitimization offered by such promises, but the breadth of wisdom's scope becomes thereby evident. These are promises of the good life, which may only be obtained through diligent obedience to parental instruction. The good life is defined in both social and religious terms: favor in the eyes of both God and community. Readers connect such promises with the notion of covenant, that is, the view that God and God's people have promised to remain loyal to each other. The idea of covenant relationship is prevalent in the nationalistic histories of Israel that dominate the Pentateuch and the Deuteronomistic History.[2] While readers do not find the imagery of covenant associated with Wisdom, it is nevertheless the covenant God of Israel who assures the outcomes of the student's attention to parental instruction.

The Program of Total Surrender, 3:5-12

These verses comprise the body of the poem's instruction. Each verse refers to some form of surrender or submission to the Lord. The first two verses, vv. 5-6, are imperatives, and relate to each other in their concern for the surrender of one's own reason. The second two verses, vv. 7-8, comment on the first by reinforcing the importance of an attitude of self-surrender. The third imperative, vv. 9-10, concerns proper offerings. These verses are the only ones in the entire book of Proverbs that command individuals to have a vital role in public worship.[3] Following the admonitions in vv. 5-8 to surrender one's own reason, participation in the official cult of the state provides a palpable way of determining one's surrender. In vv. 11-12 the parent elaborates the surrender of reason to the point that one even endures suffering as coming from the Lord's hand. In retrospect, we can see a progression of thought that begins with the surrender of one's own reason. This surrender is measured by one's participation in the religious rituals of the cult. Finally, the climactic measure of surrender is the embrace of suffering as an expression of the Lord's love.

It is at this point that we see most clearly the clash between one's own capacity for reason and one's faith in Yahweh. In other collections in the book of Proverbs reliance upon one's own insights is encouraged. Still, one's own wisdom is held in check by faith in Yahweh (e.g., Prov 26:12; Jer 9:23-24). One influential scholar, William McKane, is especially known for the view that the apparent contradiction between piety and rationality within these instructions and sayings represents at least two separate stages of wisdom interpretation. According to this view, Israelite wisdom

Deuteronomy and Wisdom

Readers will recognize language and conventions throughout the book of Proverbs that echo the book of Deuteronomy or the larger Deuteronomistic History. One scholar in particular, Moshe Weinfeld, is known for his view that sages were a part of the scribal circles that contributed to the creation of Deuteronomy. As evidence he cites the affinities between the book of Deuteronomy and the wisdom books, especially Proverbs. There are verbal and conceptual relationships, such as the "abomination" formula (*tô'ăbat yhwh*, "abomination of the LORD"); there are instructions that seem to be reformulated as law (e.g., Prov 20:10 and Deut 25:13-16); there are laws that have no parallel in other legal codes that have parallels in Proverbs and the wisdom literature (e.g., Deut 4:2; 13:1-3; and Prov 30:5-6; or Deut 19:14 and Prov 22:28; or Deut 25:14-16 and Prov 11:1); the book of Deuteronomy depicts Moses as equating the obedience of the commandments with wisdom (Deut 4:6; the Deuteronomistic Historian is sympathetic with wisdom [1 Kgs 3:4-28]). Under such influence, readers may begin to formulate connections between the two.

For further reading, see G. Buccelatti, "Wisdom and Not: The Case of Mesopotamia," *JAOS* 101 (1981): 35-47; James L. Crenshaw, "Method in Determining Wisdom Influences upon 'Historical' Literature," *JBL* 88 (1969): 129-42; and R. Yaron, "The Climactic Tricolon," *JJS* 37 (1985): 153-59.

See an abridged summary of this position in Moshe Weinfeld's more recent *Deuteronomy* 1-11 (New York: Doubleday, 1991), 62-64.

achieved its earliest expression in a secular form. It focused upon human capacities to reason and to speak. The original setting for wisdom's emergence was the royal court as a means of providing political analysis and advice for the king. The pedagogical aims of this "old wisdom" centered on providing the individual with the cognitive tools necessary for a successful life and effective service in the court.

The emphasis on Yahwistic piety that especially distinguishes Proverbs 1–9 from other parts of Proverbs is accordingly a later stage of interpretation. In this stage of interpretation the assumptions of Yahwism are incorporated into the assertions of human skill. The reader encounters the explicit moralization of the antithesis between the righteous and the unrighteous. Moreover, the understanding of the ordered universe is now subsumed under Yahweh's direct control over all things.[4]

In v. 6 one is not to rely upon one's own insight. Rather, true insight comes from the Lord, and it is the Lord who will make one's path straight. Literally the Hebrew root for straight derives from the root *yāšar*. This word denotes the physical quality of being straight, level, or flat. Thus it may indicate a direction without any deviation (e.g., Isa 40:3); or when modifying a surface, it may indicate flatness (*mîšōr*, e.g., Deut 3:10; 4:43; Josh 13:9). It may also have a more metaphorical meaning that conveys the idea of moral uprightness. Proverbs 21:18 especially indicates this significance through the juxtaposition of opposites. Counterposed with *yĕšārîm*, translated "the upright ones" is *rāšāʿ*, the wicked.

Verses 7-8 of Proverbs 3 tighten the focus by making clear that trusting in the Lord means not being wise in one's own eyes. It gives expression to a view that human wisdom was not as efficacious as might be thought. Readers will encounter other expressions of a lack of confidence in human wisdom intermingled with the sayings in 10:1–22:16 (e.g., 16:9; 19:21; 20:24; 21:30). In Proverbs 3:7-8, the unambiguous statement that one is not to rely upon oneself shapes the way readers understand the sayings that follow (e.g., 26:5, 12, 16; 28:11). It is especially interesting that v. 8 sees such surrender as a kind of therapy. Allowing one's faith to have priority over one's reason is "a refreshment for your body."

The surrender to the Lord is not simply one of the processes of intellection. It takes on a very concrete form of expression in the offering of gifts in the context of worship. This is not the only reference to such offering of sacrifice in the Proverbs (e.g., 7:14; 15:8; 21:3, 27), but it is the only place in the book where such activity is admonished. Readers should bear in mind similar such admonitions in Ecclesiastes 5 and Sirach 7:27-31. The reference to the offering of the "first fruits" in v. 9 would seems to indicate an awareness and affirmation of the stipulations in Exodus 23:19; Numbers 28:26-27; and Deuteronomy 26:1-2. Not only is an individual's trust in the Lord a matter of action, it is a matter of action within the framework of community worship.

The final imperative in vv. 11-12, which may not be original to the poem,[5] takes the idea of trust one step beyond the subjection of reason to faith. In vv. 11-12 readers see the abandonment of rationality altogether. These verses address the problem of suffering by drawing parallels between a parent's punishment of his child (e.g., 13:24) and Yahweh's discipline of those Yahweh loves. The verse therefore implicitly acknowledges that suffering does indeed accompany the life of the faithful. It is an eerie response to the exuberant confidence of the opening verses. Of course, this suffering is well disguised as discipline using the traditional wisdom concept, *mûsar*, the same word for "instruction." However, as the closing reflection upon the call to be faithful to Yahweh, vv. 11-12 command and echo the words of Job's friend Eliphaz (Job 5:17-21).

If one reads the phrase from the perspective of the necessity of "reproof" for good education (as in the cases of 19:18 and 29:17), then the Lord becomes an effective instructor through the use of pain and suffering. Alternatively, if one reads this with Eliphaz's facile theodicy in mind, one begins to see the possibility that surrender of one's rationality can go too far. All suffering need not as a matter of necessity be considered a result of the Lord's teaching. Some suffering is simply unexplainable, unjustifiable pain, which the faithful are called to endure.

CONNECTIONS

On Surrendering All

The hymns of Christian faith give expression to the theology by which the faithful live their daily lives. One could easily argue that theology exists in the hymns sung in worship long before it finds expression in systematic treatises. In fact, for most worshiping people, formal theological training never happens. One hymn that has been popular among evangelicals is "I Surrender All." [All to Jesus I Surrender] It surely shaped and continues to shape the way that

All to Jesus I Surrender

The title of a popular evangelical hymn written by Judson W. Van DeVenter, first published in 1896. Van DeVenter has noted that the hymn was written "in memory of the time when, after a long struggle, I had surrendered and dedicated my life to active Christian service.

The first verse is as follows:

"All to Jesus I surrender, All to Him I freely give; Let me feel Thy Holy Spirit, Truly know that Thou art mine."

Van DeVenter, quoted from William J. Reynolds, *Hymns of Our Faith* (Nashville: Broadman Press, 1967), 12.

many Christians understand the nature of relationship to God and God's church. The opening line of the text makes clear that such surrender is not taken by God, but is to be freely offered: "All to Jesus I surrender, All to Him I freely give." It goes on to define that surrender in terms of love and trust in God's presence: "I will ever love and trust Him, In His presence daily live."

If readers take seriously the confession of which the hymn sings, then they may ask themselves whether there are boundaries for that "all." Are there aspects of their selves, their lives, their identities that they would not, indeed could not, give up—even for God? What is more, are there implications for Christian theology if the faithful served a deity who would demand or even take some of those things? More specifically, most people who sing the song might well remember its function especially at the conclusion to worship services focusing upon giving of money, time, special abilities, etc. Judson W. Van DeVenter wrote the hymn after he himself had "surrendered" to "active Christian service." Can readers remember its being used, however, as an affirmation to surrender their ability to reason, to think, to ask questions? Does surrender to Christ require the automatic disconnection of mental processes?

Any attempt to hold simultaneously to wisdom and to Christian faith must also attempt to hold in balance reason and piety. Surrender to wisdom depicted in this passage includes such affirmation of personal piety, but it implicitly affirms reason also. Readers of these passages must construct a new model for what it means to be a thinking Christian. While surrender is important, Christians must actively recognize that the "all" does not mean that reason vanishes under sincere practice of the discipline of piety. In his *Evangelical Theology: An Introduction*, Karl Barth asserts a helpful relationship between study and prayer. He writes, "Theological study can only be done in the indissoluable unity of prayer and study. Prayer without study would be empty. Study without prayer would be blind."[6]

NOTES

[1] R. N. Whybray, *The Composition of the Book of Proverbs*, (JSOTsup 168; Sheffield: JSOT, 1994), 18-20, treats vv. 1-12 as the third instruction, followed by a short wisdom poem; likewise Michael Fox, "The Pedagogy of Proverbs 2," *JBL* 113/2 (1994): 235. William McKane, *Proverbs* (London: SCM Press, 1970), 289-90, allows the possibility that 3:21 may simply be a resumptive device, thus treating chapter 3 as a unity; Duane A. Garrett, *Proverbs, Ecclesiastes, Song of Songs* (NAC 14; Nashville: Broadman Press, 1993), 79-84, analyzes similarly.

[2] See George Mendenhall and Gary Herion, "Covenant," *ABD* 1:1179-1202.

[3] Richard J. Clifford, *Proverbs* (OTL; Louisville: Westminster John Knox Press, 1999), 52.

[4] McKane, *Proverbs*, 10-22. For further reading, see James Barr, *Biblical Faith and Natural Theology* (Oxford: Clarendon Press, 1993); John J. Collins, "Proverbial Wisdom and the Yahwist Vision," in *Gnomic Wisdom*, ed. J. E. Crossan (Chico, CA: Scholars Press, 1980); R. N. Whybray, "Yahweh Sayings and their Contexts in Proverbs 10:1–22:16," in *La Sagesse de l'Ancien Testament*, ed. M. Gilbert (BETL 51; Leuven: University Press, 1979), 153-65.

[5] Whybray, *The Composition of the Book of Proverbs*, 18-20.

[6] Karl Barth, *Evangelical Theology: An Introduction* (Grand Rapids: William B. Eerdmans, 1979), 171.

WISDOM'S INCOMPARABILITY

Proverbs 3:13-20

Verses 13-20 consist of a short hymn to wisdom that has probably been editorially inserted between the two instructions contained in vv. 1-12 and 21-35. A quick reading reveals that wisdom is still personified as a powerful woman (note references to her "right hand" and "left hand," v. 16). Unlike the wisdom poem in 1:20-33, here Wisdom is not herself the speaker. Rather, the poem intones her glories in the third person. Why the poem is inserted provides reason for pause. Readers remember that the wisdom poem in 1:20-33 also came between instructions, so the precedent for such insertion is already established. By elevating woman wisdom through assertions of her incomparability, surrender to her is unavoidable. Readers may respond, however, by questioning whether such surrender is necessarily positive. Considering this poem against the final two verses of the previous instruction, vv. 11-12, the question of whether surrender is truly worth it is even starker. There we read the rather frank admission that suffering accompanies wisdom (see above). The poem in vv. 13-20 may offer a word of balance by insisting that surrender to wisdom, and thus to Yahweh, is not necessarily as grim as previously implied. The internal structure is provided in [Structure at a Glance: Proverbs 3:13-20]

Structure at a Glance: Proverbs 3:13-20

ΑΩ Readers have already seen in preceding sections the importance of organizing the poetic ideas into structural units. Again, recognizing structural arrangement assists recognition of both the ideas of submission to wisdom and wisdom's submission to Yahweh. The units might be considered as follows:

Vv. 13-18 Wisdom and Happiness
Vv. 19-20 Wisdom's Surrender to Yahweh

The poem is arranged in two clear sections. Verses 13-18 are clearly marked as a unit by the inclusio using two words, both of which are translated "happy" 'ašrê (v. 13) and mě'uššār (v. 18). Leo Perdue further subdivides these sections into four "couplets or strophes": vv. 13-14 on the joy of discovering wisdom; vv. 15-16 on wisdom's incomparability;

vv. 17-18 depicting wisdom as a goddess; and vv. 19-20 reflecting upon wisdom's role in creation. It may well be that at one time v. 18 was the original extent of the poem, with vv. 19-20 being added after its composition (see Whybray, for instance. Also see discussions in Clifford; Murphy). The idea is reinforced by the change in presentation of wisdom in the concluding verses. In vv. 19-20 she is no longer independent, but a subject of Yahweh. She alone is no longer the giver of life, but Yahweh is. She is one who must practice submission, too; in submitting to the Lord, she becomes a model of both independence and submission.

Richard Clifford, *Proverbs* (OTL; Louisville: Westminster John Knox Press, 1999), 53-55.

Roland Murphy, *Proverbs* (WBC 22; Nashville: Thomas Nelson, 1998), 22.

Leo Perdue, *Proverbs* (IBC; Louisville: Westminster John Knox Press, 2000), 101-102.

R. N. Whybray, *The Composition of the Book of Proverbs* (JSOTSup 168; Sheffield: JSOT, 1994), 35-36.

Readers should also look to the ways this short poem on wisdom anticipates the description of wisdom in Proverbs 31:10-31, the conclusion of the book. Is it possible that the poem to the "able wife" in chapter 31 is really a *double entendre* for Woman Wisdom herself? Consider that both poems assert her value as being above that of jewels (3:14-15 and 31:10); both make reference to the work and benefits of her hands (3:16 and 31:19-20); those who have her are happy and her children call her happy (3:18 and 31:28). Indeed the final poem of the book offers a far more detailed description of a woman's ways with her household, but the parallels between these two poems are suggestive.

By reading the two poems against each other, one notices a clear application of wisdom to everyday life and work as well as an elevation of those who submit to the rigors and tedious activities of such everyday life and work. Wisdom makes its mark on life by facilitating the operation of a family and home. Such successes parallel the creativeness, inventiveness, and diligence of wisdom in founding the universe.

COMMENTARY

Happy Are They Who Find Her, 3:13-18

The hymn opens with the familiar word "happy," or "blessed" (*'ašrê*). Readers encounter such language in the psalms, especially Psalms 1 and 119. However, the notion of happiness and blessedness is not foreign to the proverbs as readers shall see (e.g., 8:34; 14:21; 16:20; 28:14; 29:18). The verbal form of the Hebrew word *'ašrê* means to make someone happy (Gen 30:13; Mal 3:12; Job 29:11; Cant 6:9; Pss 41:3; 72:17). It is not difficult to understand how the word might be used to introduce an assertion of blessing or happiness. Its frequent occurrence in psalmic passages implies that the blessing was a liturgical cry, likely related to some cultic act through which worshipers were seeking happiness. Happiness, therefore, belongs to those who participate fully in relationship to God (Prov 16:20), who have compassion on the oppressed (14:21), and who walk in integrity (20:7).[1]

While the description of wisdom in this passage resembles those already found in previous instructions, the movement of this description follows an interesting sequence. After the opening statement of "happiness," there follow two lines on wisdom's incomparability (vv. 14-15), after which follows an assertion of her actual benefits to humankind (vv. 16-18).[2] Those relative benefits are calculated in terms of profit from silver and gold.

The incomparability of wisdom is the first reason for an individual's search for wisdom. The verb "to find" (*māṣāʾ*) implies that one is to search. Other wisdom literatures will state explicitly the difficulty of finding wisdom, however (Job 28:12, 20). Qoheleth will state explicitly that happiness is something that comes from God, so finding it is tantamount to God's giving it (e.g., Eccl 3:11-13; 5:18-19). Whether it is treasure, pearls, or any conceivable delight, there is no comparison with wisdom (e.g., Prov 2:4). The appeal is in her ability to guarantee long life and riches. But the implication is that learners must forsake any materialistic motivation that might initially be a basis for embarking upon the search for wisdom. In v. 18 the poet includes an allusion to "the tree of life," language readers may have encountered through their reading in the Pentateuch (Gen 2:9; 3:22), the Prophets (Ezek 47:12), and the New Testament Apocalypse (Rev 2:7). The image recurs throughout the book of Proverbs, too (e.g., 11:30; 13:12; 15:4). The image of the tree of life in the ancient Near East was one of fertility and fecundity and may well function to reassert the divine status of wisdom here.[3] [Tree of Life]

Tree of Life

In Gen 2–3 there are two trees in the primordial garden: the tree of knowledge (of good and evil) and the tree of life. The tree of life bestows everlasting life on those who eat its fruit. By having such a life-giving plant, the biblical story is at one with the ancient Near Eastern myths that also had life-giving plants. Asherah, the Canaanite fertility goddess, is herself portrayed as a living tree. In the biblical context the ancient mythological implications of a plurality of gods are of course abandoned. The only deity the Old Testament knows is Yahweh, and thus the possibility of rival deities is eliminated. The "tree of life" is a metaphor for happiness alone.

Yet, in one more well-known ancient myth shared by multiple Mesopotamian civilizations of the 3rd millennium BC, "The Gilgamesh Epic," the hero, Gilgamesh, goes in search of eternal life as a result of the death of his friend, Enkidu. Failing to find it, he obtains temporarily a life-giving plant, only to lose it to a serpent. In losing the plant, he also loses immortality, thus having to embrace death forever as a part of mortal life.

For further reading, see James Barr, *The Garden of Eden and the Hope of Immortality* (Philadelphia: Augsburg/Fortress Press, 1993); John Gray, *Near Eastern Mythology* (New York: Peter Bedrick Books, 1988), 26-52; R. Marcus, "The Tree of Life in the Book of Proverbs," *JBL* 62 (1943): 117-20; and H. N. Wallace, "Tree of Knowledge and Tree of Life," *ABD* 6:658-60.

Different designs of sacred trees from ancient Nippur and Assur

Wisdom of Yahweh, 3:19-20

Scholars do not agree on the origins of these final two verses. These concluding two lines of the poem shift abruptly the emphasis from wisdom the woman to wisdom the intellectual agency of the Lord. Verse 19 asserts that the Lord used wisdom in founding earth and heavens. To maintain the personification of "wisdom" in 19a, one would have to maintain it for the parallel term in 19b, "understanding" (*tĕbûnâ*). So, it seems the poet abandons the strategy of personification at this point. However, readers cannot escape the connections already established between wisdom as agent and wisdom as woman. Is this an elevation of wisdom as woman or a subjugation of wisdom to Yahweh? The question must wait until the theme is taken up again in Proverbs 8.

CONNECTIONS

Retaining Dignity in Surrender

With the overall effect of the poem raising the question of the relationship between wisdom (as woman) to Yahweh the creator, perhaps it also gives readers pause to reflect further on the extent and meaning of their own religious surrender. Woman Wisdom, to whom humankind is invited to surrender for the sake of instruction, is indeed a model of surrender to Yahweh. Surrender raises questions about the possibility of losing one's own identity and worth, especially in extreme cases. Yet, Woman Wisdom retains her dignity as an agent of the Lord because that agency is an act of relational surrender. What I mean by "relational surrender" is perhaps illustrated through film.

The film *Rapture* explores the question of extreme surrender to God in a graphically sexual and violent way. It is the story of a young woman whose life, consisting of meaningless tedium and promiscuous sex, is radically transformed when she has a Christian conversion experience. She joins a group of Christian worshipers who are waiting for the imminent return of Christ. Their message and defining community feature is one of total surrender to God. The main character's conversion experience is so compelling that she takes her practice of surrender to an incredible extreme, most evident in her desire to die and be with her Lord.

It is perhaps impertinent, if not impious, to ask whether there are not limits to individuals' surrender when it comes to reason and rationality. Perhaps the limits of rationality are reached when one must surrender one's own self worth, or perhaps the value and worth of someone else. Should one surrender all rationality when it comes to religious observance? The film raises that horrible prospect by the woman's inevitable despair about the delay of the Lord's return. In a crazed state, brought on partly by hunger and exhaustion, she feels moved to take her life and that of her young daughter. This, she thinks, will hasten entry into heaven. However, she realizes that, if she takes her own life, she will be barred from following her daughter to heaven. So she kills her daughter, instead. When she has finished the horrific act, she then realizes the implications of the murder as well as the irrationality that stands behind her religious surrender: to get to heaven, one must obey God no matter what horrific things one is driven to do in the name of that obedience. Ultimately, it is such extreme surrender that the woman grows unwilling to offer any longer.

Such extreme surrender provides an informative touchstone for understanding the counsel of Job's friends. Their case rests upon the assumption of human worthlessness and sinfulness: "What are mortals that they can be clean, Or those born of woman, that they can be righteous" (Job 15:14). Such an assumption leads them to counsel Job simply to embrace his inferiority and worthlessness and to confess his sins: "Is it for your piety that he [God] reproves you, and enters into judgment with you? Is not your wickedness great? There is no end to your iniquities" (Job 22:4-5). Throughout the course of his laments, Job realizes that such extreme surrender denies his dignity and self-worth and ultimately is dishonest. He responds to his friends: "My foot has held fast to his steps; I have kept his way and have not turned aside. . . . But he stands alone and who can dissuade him? What he desires, that he does" (Job 23:11, 13). [Job's Calculus of Surrender] Job's complaints are not therefore only to a silent deity or to an unjust universe, but concern the ultimate outcome that humans must continue to live in a world of denial unless Godself is honest. Woman Wisdom provides here a model of surrender to Yahweh wherein she retains her dignity and self-worth.

Job's Calculus of Surrender

James L. Crenshaw argues in his *Theodicy in the Old Testament* that "Self-abnegation lies at the heart of all theodicy. Only as the individual fades into nothingness can the deity achieve absolute pardon." Surrender, so vital and affirmative in Wisdom's relationship to God, takes an extreme form in cases of suffering. The book of Job is illustrative. Compare the passages in Job 4:17-21; 15:14-16; and 25:4-6 on their assumptions of human inferiority to God. Notice how that inferiority intensifies as humans are described successively as "houses of clay," thus ephemeral, "abominable and corrupt," thus sinful, and finally, "maggots and worms," thus subhuman. Since these images are asserted by Job's friends in their attempts to explain the cause of Job's suffering without holding God responsible, readers conclude that religious surrender can make extreme demands upon humanity. Job's reasoning, rationality, observations, indeed his common sense, are established as a counter-proposal to the (revealed?) theology of Job's friends.

William Blake's illustrations of the book of Job portray Job and his wife submitting to God.

William Blake. 1757–1827. *The Vision of Christ.* Illustrations of the Book of Job. III, 45, pl.17. Watercolor. The Pierpont Morgan Library. New York, USA.

Interestingly, the narrative movement of the poem about Job's suffering resolves the question to some degree in Yahweh's condemnation of Job's friends. Not only does God condemn the friends' theological counsel (42:8b), but God accepts Job's prayer on their behalf (42:8a). While such a conclusion is open to many interpretations, at the very least one may surmise that the friends' move to spare the deity at the cost of their friend's dignity and worth was overridden.

For further reading, see James Barr, *Biblical Faith and Natural Theology* (Oxford: Clarendon Press, 1993); James L. Crenshaw, ed., *Theodicy in the Old Testament* (Philadelphia: Fortress, 1983); Ernest W. Nicholson, "The Limits of Theodicy as a Theme of the Book of Job," in *Wisdom in Ancient Israel*, ed. John Day et al. (Cambridge: Cambridge University Press, 1995), 71-82.

James L. Crenshaw, ed. *Theodicy in the Old Testament* (Philadelphia: Fortress Press, 1983), 6.

NOTES

[1] For further reading, see G. Bertram, *"makarios," TDNT* 4:364-67; H. Cazelles, *"ashre," TDOT* 1:445-48; W. Janzen, *"Ashre* in the Old Testament," *HTR* 58 (1965): 215-26; and Claus Westermann, *Blessing in the Bible and the Life of the Church,* trans. Keith Crim (OBT; Philadelphia: Fortress, 1968).

[2] Otto Plöger, *Sprüche Salomos (Proverbia)* (BKAT 17; Neukirchen: Neukirchener Verlag, 1984), 36.

[3] Leo Perdue, *Proverbs* (IBC; Louisville: Westminster John Knox Press, 2000), 103.

WISDOM FOR COMMUNITY LIFE

Proverbs 3:21-35

The concluding section of chapter 3 comprises the fourth instruction of the overall collection within Proverbs 1–9. Readers encounter great variation of style within the boundaries of vv. 21-35. The unit opens with the usual address to "my child" and proceeds to discuss the importance of wisdom for one's life and security. The body of the instruction consists of negative admonitions on topics that concern community living. On the assumption that people wish to contribute positively to the society in which they live, these verses set out those behaviors that should be avoided. There is no appeal in vv. 27-30 to Yahwistic motivation. Rather, the benefits of community-mindedness appear to be self-evident. The instruction seems to appeal more to common sense than to religious piety. [Structure at a Glance: Proverbs 3:21-35]

Structure at a Glance: Proverbs 3:21-35

AΩ The structure for reading the passage may be considered in three parts: an introductory call, a fourfold admonition, and concluding curses.

Vv. 21-26: Call to Wisdom
Vv. 27-30: A Fourfold Admonition
Vv. 31-35: Curses on the Violent

There is a clear distinction between the introductory call in vv. 21-26 and the negative admonitions that follow in vv. 27-30. Further subdivision of each section is also possible: the introductory call has a couplet asserting wisdom's benefits concluded by an appeal to Yahweh as guarantor (vv. 24-26). Readers should observe that the four negative admonitions in vv. 27-30 are surrounded by negative admonitions that have Yahwistic motive clauses (e.g., vv. 25-26 and vv. 31-32) (Perdue). What is here called a "Yahwistic motive clause" is recognizable by two features. First, its rhetorical function in relationship to preceding statements is to offer a reason for taking an admonition seriously. Typically such motive clauses are introduced with the preposition "for," or in Hebrew, *kî*. Secondly, the motivation is the Lord's assurance of wisdom's reliability. The association with deity, in other words, raises wisdom's significance to that of a cosmic level. Putting trust in wisdom (i.e., by obeying instruction) is tantamount to putting one's trust in the Lord.

Leo Perdue, *Proverbs* (IBC; Louisville: Westminster John Knox Press, 2000), 106.

COMMENTARY

Call to Wisdom, 3:21-26

The call is not to obedience to the commands of the parent as in previous introductory admonitions (e.g., 2:1; 3:1-2). Rather, the parents instruct their child not to let "sound wisdom" (*tušîyâ*) and "prudence" (*mĕzimmâ*) out of his sight. These are wisdom terms designating processes of intellection and decision-making (see Prov 1:1-7). Interestingly, they are not necessarily attributes of piety, nor do they necessarily lead to the fear of Yahweh. But the same attributes of long life (v. 22) and security (v. 23) accompany those who possess such abilities.

Verses 25-26 may seem somewhat redundant since vv. 23-24 also assert the motive of security. However, vv. 25-26 articulate the idea of security as a negative admonition: "Do not be afraid." The threat is left unspecified. Readers may recall both the threat of the wicked (Prov 1:11-12) and the dread that comes upon those who fail to heed Wisdom's voice (1:26). Further, as a conclusion to the introductory call to wisdom, these verses appeal to the motive of Yahweh's watch-care. Readers are again confronted with the difference between confidence in one's faith over against confidence in one's own wits (see 3:7-10). In the present form of the passage, confidence in one's own wits is clearly to take a secondary place to one's confidence in Yahweh. Additionally, as a conclusion to the introductory admonition to wisdom and prudence, the rhetorical form of vv. 25-26 as a negative admonition provides a transition into the next section, which consists of four such negative admonitions.

A Fourfold Admonition, 3:27-30

The four negative admonitions in vv. 27-30 provide the instruction's central focus. They concern proper behavior toward neighbors. They may be read in thematic pairs of couplets. Verses 27 and 28 concern ways of withholding the good that is due a neighbor. Verses 29 and 30 concern unnecessary and unwarranted harm one might inflict upon one's neighbor.

Commentators envision vv. 27 and 28 as being especially concerned with those people who are in power. People who have positions of public authority might withhold what is due a person unjustly. Likewise, such individuals might be portrayed as quick with an excuse such as "come back tomorrow." Verse 28 provides a

concrete example of how such power might be abused under the
guise of administrative necessity. Nevertheless, such advice is just as
applicable in community relationships. In this case the issue is that
of offering goodness only when it is "due."

Verses 29 and 30 change the thematic polarity, so to speak, and
warn against inflicting evil. While all four negative admonitions
urge behaviors that are *not* to be done, v. 29 seems a subtle intensification. By observing that neighbors live trustingly within their
community, the admonition not to plan harm stands out as a
special violation of trust. In other words, evil hurts the community
at a personal level of individual relationship; therefore, the phrase
"violation of trust" has meaning at both the public and the private
levels.

The dynamic equivalence offered in v. 29 by the NRSV for the
particular negative behavior envisioned—"planning harm"—hides
the colorful image that is created by the use of the Hebrew word
ḥāraš, "to plow." The word occurs in varying contexts throughout
the Hebrew Bible where it may denote plowing (1 Kgs 19:19; Deut
22:10) or engraving (1 Kgs 7:14; Gen 4:22). Related to this verbal
idea is the noun "engraver," "artificer," or one who is an idol-maker
(Isa 45:16; 2 Kgs 24:14, 16).

The image in Proverbs 3:29 is of those who cultivate evil, or
"plan harm," against neighbors. But the terminology evokes the
image of people shaping evil as though they were making a statue.
The image is therefore one of planning, calculating, and effecting
unrighteousness with great skill and care. The negative admonition
in v. 29 is not merely referring to an individual's occasional lapse in
community responsibility. Rather, it is imagining people who are
devoted to the subversion of the entire social order.

Verse 30 envisions the unwarranted behavior of a community
member. The word translated "quarrel" comes from the legal
sphere, implying the action of taking one to court.[1] Within this
verse is another colorful word that provides some insight into the
rationality of the worldview of the sage, *ḥinnām*, translated
"without cause" (see discussion of 1:17). We have already encountered this term in Proverbs 1:11 and 17 where it depicts a situation
of unjustifiable activity. The term *ḥinnām* conveys the idea of gra-
tuitousness or activity that has no conceivable purpose. (See Prov
23:29 and Job 2:3.) To hate someone without a reason or cause is a
particularly negative judgment, as in Psalms 35:19 and 69:4. Such
behavior is irrational, purposeless, groundless, and arbitrary. Such
descriptions convey the chaotic nature of those acts that cannot be
placed within some meaningful framework. Thus, taking a person

to court without justification, *ḥinnām*, betrays a much more unsettling reality of evil that motivates such activity.

Curses on the Man of Violence, 3:31-35

Readers have already encountered in 2:12-19 an extended reference to evil people, whose words are perverse and whose actions are twisted and subversive. There have been admonitions against following those who participate in criminal activity (e.g., 1:18-19). Even though the reference here is to the "man of violence" (*ʾîš ḥāmās*), readers may make connections with these previous images. The concluding section begins with a negative admonition against envy of such evil people. It continues with an extended motive clause asserting the conviction that Yahweh blesses the upright and curses the wicked.

A series of oppositional statements comprise vv. 32-35. Verse 32 contrasts the "perverse" (*nālôz*), with the "upright" (*yěšārîm*). The assertion of "abomination" (*tôʿabat*) is a cultic term describing cultic impurity, or ritual uncleanness. ["Abomination of the Lord"] Even more striking is the assertion that the "upright" are in Yahweh's "counsel" (*sôdô*). This idea has affinity with the belief that prophets receive the word of Yahweh by standing in Yahweh's presence (e.g., Amos 3:7). Three more contrasts follow in vv. 33-35. First, Yahweh brings curses upon the house of the wicked and blessings upon the dwelling of the righteous. Secondly, Yahweh scoffs at scoffers but shows favor to the lowly. Finally, the concluding statement of the instruction opposes the wise with fools. The wise ones inherit glory; fools heighten disgrace. To the wise, there is honor in

---

"Abomination of the Lord"

AΩ This phrase occurs in this passage and ten times more in Prov 10:1–22:16 (11:1; 11:20; 12:22; 15:8; 15:9; 15:26; 16:5; 17:15; 20:10; and 20:23). The same meaning is implied in a slightly different syntactical arrangement in 6:16 (following the *qěrē'* tradition rather than the *kětîb*). The term translated "abomination" conveys the idea of impurity, as that which is ritually unclean (see Deut 13:14; 14:3; 17:4; Ezek 16:50). Thus by attributing such ritual significance to behavior that has nothing to do with the ritual of worship, the sages are overlaying these behaviors with an important religious significance (as in 11:1; 12:22; 17:15). Unjust scales are not only a serious violation of community relationships, but render an individual unclean before God's presence, too. Likewise, telling a lie, especially in court, is harmful to the community, but also renders one unclean before the Lord. The fact that this particular combination of words only occurs in Proverbs and Deuteronomy may provide further basis for considering the affinities between the sages and the Deuteronomists.

For further reading, see R. E. Clements, "Abomination in the Book of Proverbs," in *Texts, Temples, and Traditions*, ed. M. V. Fox et al. (Winona Lake IN: Eisenbrauns, 1996), 211-25; and L. L. Morris, "Abomination," *NBD³*, 4.

uprightness and moral purity; this is honor that exists within the framework of community. Any behavior that falls short of such uprightness and moral purity not only hurts the community, but brings shame upon the individual members of that community.

CONNECTIONS

Community Values

Maintaining one's obligations to the community seems simple enough to those who do not have to decide what is right and wrong, or which people deserve good and not. The question is intensified in the post-Enlightenment western world, where radical individualism stands as the ultimate authority over against the values of the community. What is viewed as liberation resting upon the individual's ability to reason often stands in stark contrast to those guidelines that have been passed on for millennia by religious and state sanction. Albert Camus's "The Guest"[2] is an important reflection upon the dilemma that individuals face when they have within their power to make decisions concerning community values. [Albert Camus and the Modern World (1913–1960)]

The story is set just after World War II, before the outbreak of civil war between Algerian nationals and French colonists. An old gendarme brings an Arab prisoner to a French schoolhouse. The French schoolmaster is given the responsibility of turning the prisoner over for prosecution under French law for the crime of murder. The schoolmaster clearly sees the Arab prisoner differently than the gendarme. He is much more sympathetic to the plight of the nationals, and the reader also begins to see the conflict of interests that underlies the plot. Does Daru, the schoolmaster, have an obligation to do what is right according to French law—the laws of the occupying nation—or should he be more sympathetic to the cultural circumstances and their possible mitigating effects of any so-called crime committed under French law? In the end, Daru takes the prisoner to a place where the prisoner himself can decide by which set of laws he will be bound, thus whether to go to a certain prison-term (under French law) or turn to flee. The prisoner chooses, in his freedom, to go to prison, thus abiding by the laws of the occupying nation. The story concludes with a scene in which Daru is on the porch of his empty school. The accusatory

Albert Camus and the Modern World (1913–1960)

Camus was a French novelist and playwright known especially for his atheistic existentialism. He is widely known for his novel *The Stranger* (*L'Étranger*, 1942) in which he illustrates the irrationality of existence by appealing to the myth of Sisyphus. In Greek mythology, Sisyphus was condemned by the gods to futile labor in the underworld. His sin varies in different traditions, but it was his impiety toward the gods that resulted in his punishment. His futile labor was that of ceaselessly rolling a rock up a mountain; the weight of the rock would then cause it to roll down the mountain. This repetitive activity that accomplished nothing was the punishment Sisyphus had to endure forever.

But for Camus there was a victory in even this meaningless and endless toil. It came through Sisyphus's consciousness of his situation. He *knows* its futility, but in such knowledge he gains victory over futility through his conscious scorn. It is during the moments of Sisyphus's descent from the mountain that this consciousness is most lucid, and of this period of reflection Camus says, "The lucidity that was to constitute his torture at the same time crowns his victory. There is no fate that cannot be surmounted by scorn." This attitude characterizes Camus's modern people. They are people caught between the controlled confidence of the enlightenment and the unbridled confidence of post-modernity. Camus's modern people are disillusioned but find joy in their disillusionment, which is at the heart of absurdity.

For further reading, see D. R. Ellison, *Understanding Albert Camus* (Columbia: University of South Carolina Press, 1990); and H. R. Lottman, *Albert Camus: A Biography* (Garden City NY: Doubleday, 1979).

Albert Camus, *The Myth of Sisyphus & Other Essays* (New York: Vintage Books, 1955), 90.

Michael Bergt. *Sisyphus Sleeping.* 1993. 12"x9". Egg tempera.

words are written on the blackboard, "You handed over our brother. You will pay for this."

Community is quite messy. It is easy to speak of abiding by the community's guidelines, but then we all live in many communities at once. We live and serve within the community of faith; we also live and make our livelihoods within secular communities. Our problem is in deciding which guidelines are most authoritative and binding and which communities have priority over other communities. Perhaps the most difficult question is *how* one makes such decisions. The wisdom of Yahweh does not shirk such ethical dilemmas by choosing the convenient answers. Wisdom for the community is the practice of allowing equally valid though competing values to stand.

NOTES

[1] Roland Murphy, *Proverbs* (WBC 22; Nashville: Thomas Nelson, 1998), 23.

[2] Included in *Exile and the Kingdom*, trans. Justin O'Brien (Alfred A. Knopf, 1957).

THE WISDOM OF EXPERIENCE

Proverbs 4:1-9

The fifth instruction in the collection begins chapter 4 (4:1-9) and two further instructions follow within that chapter (4:10-19 and 4:20-27).[1] The familiar language of the introductory appeal, "my child," provides defining criteria for delineating the instructions within the overall chapter. The instruction in vv. 1-9 comprises a parent's reminiscence, which, if heeded by the child, will lead to wisdom's bestowal of great honor. [Structure at a Glance: Proverbs 4:1-9]

COMMENTARY

Reminiscence of a Father, 4:1-5

The opening two verses vary from the typical introductory appeal (e.g., 2:1; 3:1; 5:1) in that v. 1 is addressed to "children" (*bānîm*) rather than to "my child" (*běnî*). Nevertheless, the introduction functions as previous appeals have—to convey the role of the parent as teacher and to introduce the instruction that follows. The most

---

Structure at a Glance: Proverbs 4:1-9

AΩ The structure of ch. 4 is recognizable by the formal delineations provided by the parental appeals: 4:1; 4:10; and 4:20. Within the first instruction, 4:1-9, readers encounter two main units of thought.

> Vv. 1-5: Reminiscence of the Parent
> Vv. 6-9: Poem to Wisdom

Verses 1-5 form the personal recollection of the grandfather; vv. 6-9, still a part of the reminiscence, is a poem on wisdom.

This opening instruction has larger structural significance in appealing to parental authority based upon personal experience. Looking ahead, readers may anticipate the final instruction in the collection, 7:1-27, as a final appeal to personal experience (Plöger). Chapters 4–7 seem to have a framework of instructions that derive from personal experi-

ence. With these framing instructions in mind, readers of 4:1-9 and 7:1-27 may find a coherence within the instructions contained thereby. In both introductory and concluding passages the basis for authority is personal experience and reflection of a parental figure. Thus, wisdom and knowledge gained by personal experience, as opposed to tradition or even religious revelation, provides a framework for at least one mode of authority asserted in this central section of instructions. By offering such experience as a mode of authority, readers are confronted with the implications of such experience as means by which all people come to receive wisdom from Yahweh. There is a challenge of holding in constructive tension the appeal to Yahweh's ultimate authority and the authority of personal experience as passed on through both the father and the mother.

Otto Plöger, *Sprüche Salomos (Proverbia)* (BKAT 17; Neukirchen: Neukirchener Verlag, 1984), 45-46.

unique aspect of this instruction comes in vv. 3-5. The father reminisces about his own father's instruction. His instruction consists of another appeal to keep the parent's commandments without forsaking his words (v. 4). There are similarities between v. 4 and many of Deuteronomy's admonitions to keep the commandments (e.g., Deut 5:1; 8:1; 11:8). The evocative language suggests that more than a parent is speaking here; one can hear the voice of Moses through the voice of Woman Wisdom through the voice of parental teaching. Interestingly, the MT text of v. 5 contains the imperatives translated by NRSV as "get wisdom; get insight: do not forget, nor turn away from the words of my mouth." While there is no problem with the translation, when compared with the Septuagint—the Greek translation of the Old Testament (hereafter LXX)—the text does not appear at all. The absence of this verse from the LXX suggests that the Hebrew text was not firmly established at the time of the LXX translation; there may therefore be a possibility that this line in v. 5a was added in order to bridge into the second half of the instruction.[2] [LXX of Proverbs 4:5]

LXX of Proverbs 4:5

AΩ The letters LXX are a shorthand expression for Septuagint, the Greek translation of the Hebrew Bible. The letters are the Roman numerals for "seventy," which in Greek is "*septuaginta*." The number comes from the legend that, during the reign of Philadelphus (Ptolemy) in 285–247 BC, seventy (really seventy-two) Jewish scholars translated the Hebrew text into Greek. Originally, the

Sample page of the Septuagint

subject of their legendary work was only the Pentateuch, but later the legend was applied to the entire Hebrew Bible. Of course, modern-day Septuagints are eclectic texts combining the best of the various later Greek translations.

There is not much certainty in the dating of the Septuagint of Proverbs. Besides the fact that there has not been much research on the question, the process of making such a determination is complex. Scholar Johann Cook believes he can identify within the LXX translation of Proverbs "concentrated endeavours by the translator to warn against the dangers of Hellenistic philosophical ideas." He dates the translation to around the 2d century BC.

Prov 4:5 illustrates the complexity of having various translations and traditions of the same text. The phrase in the Hebrew text translated "Get wisdom; get insight" does not appear in the LXX, and only appears in other places in the various versions of the LXX. This allows modern readers to infer that very likely the Hebrew text itself was not firmly fixed at the time when it first began to be translated into Greek.

For further reading, see R. W. Klein, *Textual Criticism of the Old Testament* (Philadelphia: Fortress, 1974); M. K. H. Peters, "Why Study the Septuagint," *BA* 49 (1986): 174-81; Emmanuel Tov, *The Text Critical Use of the Septuagint in Biblical Research* (Jerusalem, 1982); T. C. Smith, "Septuagint," *MDB*, 808-809; and M. H. Goshen-Gottstein, "Theory and Practice of Textual Criticism: The Text-Critical Use of the Septuagint," *Textus* 3 (1963): 130-58.

Johann Cook, "The Dating of Septuagint Proverbs," *ETL* 69/4 (1993): 398-99.

Poem on Wisdom, 4:6-9

The poem to wisdom in these verses continues as part of the instruction of the grandfather. Notice how in the admonition to get wisdom as the first of one's duties, there is personification. The repetition of the word "get" some four times (vv. 5 and 7), the language of love, all contribute to the elevation of this command to the heights of emotional ecstasy. As in the previous instructions, wisdom is imagined as a woman with great power. She brings honor and recognition to the one who lifts her up. Only here there is an unmistakable erotic quality. She, Woman Wisdom, is responsive. She is to be loved (v. 6) and she will watch over her lover. She is to be exalted and she in turn will "embrace" the one who lifts her up (v. 8). Such sensual language anticipates one of the recurring motifs of Proverbs 4–7. There are several admonitions throughout these chapters against the "other" or "foreign" woman (e.g., 5:1-6; 6:20-35; 7:1-27). The teacher sage suggestively urges that wisdom is herself one's true wife and that a long relationship yields even greater delights.

The language that describes the relationship is significant. Children are admonished to "Prize her highly" (*salsĕlehā*) and to "honor her" (*tĕkabbēdkā*). While the language evokes thoughts of husbands and wives in strong embrace, the imagery of marriage conjures up thoughts of more than passion. Wisdom's response with a "fair garland" reminds readers of the parental teaching in 1:9. Her offering of a "beautiful crown" (*ʿăṭeret tipʾeret*) reminds readers of the use of such imagery in The Song of Solomon (3:11), in which marriage is a more explicit topic.[3] Commitment and responsibility also come to readers' minds. A relationship with wisdom is not just one for the senses, but also for the will. The honor wisdom gives only comes from a life of faithful pursuit of her love.

CONNECTIONS

Beginnings

Beginning points are usually ominous. The occurrence of the very word "beginning" in v. 7 conjures other notable beginnings (Gen 1:1; John 1:1). The wisdom that derives from experience reflects on "the beginning of wisdom" (*rēʾšît ḥokmâ*) in these verses (v. 7). In the present form of this instruction, the first part of wisdom, its beginnings, is to get wisdom. It is difficult to understand such a turn of speech in view of our previous understanding that the beginning of wisdom is the fear of the Lord (e.g., 1:7; 2:6; 3:5). It is as though one must reconcile the incipient human will to be wise with the requirement to surrender to Yahweh. But the notion of "beginning" is worth pausing over here, for it conveys more than a particular temporal point relative to a process. The word for "beginning" is used to convey the idea of importance and value as well. This is readily evident based upon the contexts in which the term occurs in the Hebrew Bible. Examine the following passages in the Bible: Exodus 23:19; Deuteronomy 21:17; 26:2; Amos 6:7; Ecclesiastes 7:8. Within these verses we see, first, that the Hebrew word is translated variously. In Exodus 23:19, NRSV translates the word as "choicest," indicating that this offering of the first fruits is special for reasons other than that they happen to have ripened before others. The parallel passage in Deuteronomy 26:2 does translate the word as "first," but, again, context indicates that the term implies the fruit to be set apart for other reasons. The irony in Amos 6:7 is that the ones who will be "first" to go into exile are those who are the wealthiest; they are set apart as the choicest of the community who cared least for the "ruin of Joseph" (6:6). Ecclesiastes 7:8 makes explicit that simply because a phenomenon occurs first in sequence, it is not necessarily the most important. In this ironic passage, the "end of a thing" has greater value than the beginning.

Beginnings, or the first things, are incomplete and therefore cannot take the pride of place. They are merely potentials full of promises and expectations. The offering to Yahweh of the "first fruits" (Exod 23:19 and Deut 26:2) of one's agricultural produce is an acknowledgment that more is both promised and expected. To live on the edge of faith is to celebrate in advance such beginnings, even though they are only full of potential. Yahweh alone will bring the crop to its fullest fruition. Thus one should sacrifice to him the first of the yield that one has in hand is the supreme virtue.

The best advice is valuable not because it is the first. The best advice wisdom could offer is to "get wisdom." Whatever the cost and however long it takes, obtaining a relationship with this woman is of supreme importance. That is because only in relationship to Woman Wisdom is there the potential for true happiness and prosperity in life.

NOTES

[1] Richard J. Clifford, *Proverbs* (OTL; Louisville: Westminster John Knox Press 1999), 59. Compare Leo Perdue, *Proverbs*, (IBC; Louisville: Westminster John Knox Press, 2000) 115-17, who judges only two instructions to comprise Proverbs 4.

[2] R. N. Whybray, *The Composition of the Book of Proverbs* (JSOTSup 168; Sheffield: JSOT Press, 1994), 21; William McKane, *Proverbs* (OTL; London: SCM, 1970), 303. The same also holds for v. 4a, "keep my commandments, and live."

[3] Roland Murphy, *Proverbs* (WBC 22; Nashville: Word, 1998), 27; also Murphy's "Wisdom and Eros in Proverbs 1-9," *CBQ* 50 (1988): 600-603.

THE WAY OF LIFE

Proverbs 4:10-19

The second of three instructions in chapter 4, the sixth instruction in Proverbs 1–9, begins in v. 10 and is so indicated by the familiar appeal to the child. Readers see for the third time in the chapter similar language in v. 20, contributing to the delineation between the three instructions contained within the chapter.[1] The overall thematic concern returns to the contrast of the ways of the wicked and the righteous, a theme readers have already encountered in 2:12-22. As before, the way of righteousness leads to long life, while the way of wickedness leads to destruction.

In contrast to the instruction in vv. 1-9, vv. 10-19 contain the parent's own instruction. An interesting pattern is implied by the rhetoric in this section. As the father relied upon his own father's advice, so the son must also do the same.[2] There is a connection between the two units that appears immediately in the language of "holding on" (v. 13).

As far as structure is concerned, vv. 10-13 comprise the opening appeal to the child. Here the parent calls for careful attendance to his instruction, *mûsār*, the familiar term encountered in 1:2. The main body of the instruction is contained by vv. 14-19. These verses offer the contrast between the two paths, one that leads to righteousness and the other to unrighteousness. The conclusion to the instruction actually begins with v. 18 by summing up the contrast between the two paths.[3] The section might be read with the following outline in mind:

Vv. 10-13: Wisdom as Instruction
Vv. 14-19: The Way of Life

COMMENTARY

Wisdom as Instruction, 4:10-13

The opening appeal is contained in these first four verses. The parent appeals to the child on the promise that long life results if parental instructions are heeded. The promise of long life as a motivation for embracing wisdom occurs in previous instructions (e.g. 2:19; 3:2, 16) in Proverbs 1–9. The reference occurs twice, however, in vv. 10 and 13, forming an inclusio around the opening instruction. While an inclusio typically functions to delimit rhetorical sections from others in this kind of poetry, readers might also recognize the repetition as an emphasis upon the motivation for obedience.[4] The emphasis upon obeying parental instruction is set in relief by the following instruction which recognizes that youth face considerable choices.

The instruction that follows in vv. 14-19 concerns the contrast between the two paths that the young student might take. The instruction is anticipated by the opening appeal in v. 11. Here the parent recounts his instruction in the "way" (*derek*) of wisdom and the paths of "uprightness." The term translated "uprightness" (*yošer*) is especially appropriate since it may also be translated "straight." Such straight paths lend themselves to easy travel since there are no circuitous routes that must be traversed. Ease of travel is a familiar image in Deutero-Isaiah's vision of restoration and provides an interesting point of reflection here (Isa 40:27-31). In Proverbs 4:12 the children will not find any hindrance in this path, whether they walk or run. The concluding admonition to "keep hold of instruction," *mûsār*, is paralleled in 13b with a feminine pronoun, "guard her." This makes an explicit comparison between instruction, designated by a masculine noun, and Woman Wisdom, designated with a feminine suffixial pronoun, *niṣṣĕrehā*. In this final word readers encounter an interesting echo of the image of the call to embrace wisdom in v. 8 of the preceding section.

Opposing Lifestyles, 4:14-19

Verses 14-17 admonish youths away from the life of wickedness by counseling them to avoid the ways of wicked people. Such wicked people are characterized here as ones who cannot sleep unless they have done evil or caused someone else to commit evil. Their fondness for evil is depicted as an appetite. They eat "the bread of

Bread and Wine

AΩ The text of v. 17 describes the wicked as eating "the bread of wickedness" and drinking "the wine of violence." Bread and wine were two most common staples of Palestinian agricultural production. One could say that bread and wine were rather ordinary, everyday commodities of survival. It should come as no surprise, further, that the word for bread used here occurs some 296 times in the Hebrew Scriptures, indicating its commonality.

Bread therefore may be used as a metaphor for destruction (Num 14:9), for hospitality (Gen 19:3), and even for wisdom itself (Prov 9:5). What is more, the human appetite, which bread satisfies, is an anthropological universal functioning to indicate still further the commonality of wickedness to humankind. With such commonality in view, the effect of the metaphor is to convey the idea that, to the wicked, wickedness is as common as bread. But even more so, it may well be the common lot of all humankind.

For further reading, see John Rogerson and P. Davies, *The Old Testament World* (Englewood Cliffs NJ: Prentice Hall, 1989), 13-44; and Oded Borowski, *Agriculture in Ancient Israel* (Winona Lake IN: Eisenbrauns, 1987).

---

wickedness" and drink the "wine of violence." [Bread and Wine] In a perverted way, these people find wickedness to be their sustenance. We may imagine that they only eat and drink food that they have obtained through dishonest means. They wash down their illegally gotten bread with wine they have stolen. Readers might reflect upon the contrasting natural imagery that characterizes those who do evil and those who seek wisdom in vv. 1-9 and 14-19. In vv. 14-19 people are drawn to wickedness as a result of an appetite; an erotic appetite characterizes the embrace of wisdom in vv. 1-9.

Verses 18-19 conclude the instruction by offering two more opposing images of the righteous and wicked people. The overriding motif of the "path" continues here also. The righteous are portrayed as the light of the dawn, providing light along the path. [Light Imagery] Instead of causing people to stumble in their way, the righteous assist people in keeping their steps. The closing statement returns to the wicked, establishing a closing contrast to the way of the righteous. The wicked way is portrayed as a darkness that causes stumbling along the path.

Light Imagery

AΩ Light is also common in the Hebrew Scriptures. Clearly the term is theologically loaded in the creation story where God makes light before God makes sun, moon, and stars (Gen 1:3, 14). Psalmists confessed that Yahweh was their own light (e.g., Ps 27:1); they affirmed that Yahwehself was clothed in light (e.g., Ps 104:2). In Ecclesiastes light is also a term signifying "life" (e.g., Eccl 11:7) Thus, in speaking of light one is talking about the life-giving cause of all things. Thus to identify the righteous with a phenomenon that could be so singularly identified with Yahweh was to assert the stark difference between the righteous and the wicked.

CONNECTIONS

The Two-dimensional World

The contrast between the ways of wickedness and righteousness are reinforced in the concluding statement with the imagery of light and darkness. The problem for the youthful student, as for anyone, is to recognize the way to take. Edwin Abbot's *Flatland* provides an opportunity for reflection upon the problem. In his allegorical world of geometrical shapes, status is determined by the number of "sides" one has, along with the size of one's angles. Thus, women are straight lines, members of the military are isosceles triangles, the middle class are made up of equilateral triangles, professionals and gentlemen are squares and pentagons, nobility begin with six sides, or are hexagonal, and the priestly class are circles.[5]

One of the difficulties in this society, however, is learning how to recognize one's neighbors. This is because the world is two-dimensional, and to the viewer everything appears to be a straight line. How does one distinguish between an individual who is a woman and a person of another status? Of course, the narrator does suggest ways of recognizing the differences. People in this two-dimensional society must simply develop more refined sensitivities. They develop acute senses of hearing that allow members of that society to differentiate people of status. They feel, allowing them to infer the number of sides and angles of their neighbors. Finally, they develop a more acute sense of sight that differentiates every shadow of light that is cast because of the inclination of an angle.

The sages also seem to have created a two-dimensional world in their contrasts between the righteous and wicked. As different as righteousness and wickedness seem to be conceptually, from the perspective of another member of that two-dimensional society, it is easy to confuse the two. While the image of contrasting ways or paths is a useful beginning point, life does not always fraction itself in such two-dimensional ways. Likewise, people do not always fit into such neat categories of righteous and wicked. Experience teaches us that, often, the people we tend to put in the category of "wicked" surprise us by responding to us with goodness. The problem is then of applying two-dimensional categories to a multi-dimensional experience of reality. In a larger sense, it is a problem of allowing the ideas of tradition (e.g., "the two paths") to continue to speak authoritatively in settings where those ideas seem to have lost their relevance.

The world we live in is not a flatland of two dimensions, just like the world of the sages was not one that could be naively reduced to the righteous and the wicked. If it were, who would need instruction? It is the perspective of the teacher, the educated one, who provides the third dimension. In fact, education always provides the perspective of that third dimension and allows the viewer the perspective of one who has struggled to recognize the two paths. The dimension of the instructor's experience allows a youthful learner awareness of the tricks of recognition, and thus avoidance of the pitfalls of the evil that awaits those who follow down its paths.

NOTES

[1] Compare Leo Perdue, *Proverbs* (IBC; Louisville: Westminster John Knox Press, 2000), 115-17, however, who does not break at v. 19 and determines that the second instruction consists of all of vv. 10-27.

[2] R. Murphy, *Proverbs* (WBC 22; Dallas: Word, 1998), 24.

[3] R. N. Whybray, *The Composition of the Book of Proverbs* (JSOTSup 168; Sheffield: JSOT Press, 1994), 21.

[4] Otto Plöger, *Sprüche Salomos (Proverbia)* (BKAT 17; Neukirchen: Neukirchener Verlag, 1984), 48.

[5] Edwin Abbot, *Flatland* (Oxford: One World, 1994), 19-20.

THE HEART OF WISDOM

Proverbs 4:20-27

The seventh instruction concludes chapter 4 of the book of Proverbs. As is common in all three of these instructions, the appeal is only to the authority of the parent or grandparent, not to any divine or abstract sense of legitimization. For this reason the instruction has affinity with the opening instruction in 1:8-19: parents admonish their children to avoid the way of the wicked on their own authority.[1] At the source of the admonition is the parents' use of the image of the heart, v. 23. The heart stands at the center of decision-making, and thus as the source of life for the educated youth. In fact, the multiple occurrences of body imagery remind readers of the previous two poems and their appeal to various aspects of human nature. In 4:1-9 the appeal is to get wisdom and is offered in a way to suggest a kind of erotic desire for her. Similarly, vv. 10-19 use images of the human appetite to characterize human wickedness. [Structure at a Glance: Proverbs 4:20-27]

Structure at a Glance: Proverbs 4:20-27

AΩ Structurally, the key indicators are language and style. There is an opening appeal to the child to listen to parental instruction. The body of the instruction follows in vv. 23-27 and is marked by the use of imperatives. One scholar has some concern that the instruction does not conclude with the usual motive clauses. Rather, v. 27 continues with imperatives, suggesting that the text is damaged in some sense (see Scott, who transposes 5:21-23 to the position after 4:27). Further evidence of this is that the LXX has inserted two extra verses at the conclusion of v. 27 that provide a more typical conclusion. Most regard the additions in the LXX as late and not tied to the Hebrew text. The motive for the additions may be, moreover, the apparent lack of any appeal to Yahweh, which is supplied by the addition (McKane). Readers might consider the following very broad outline to direct their reading of these verses.

Vv. 20-22: Appeal to the Heart
Vv. 23-27: The Heart Leads the Way

William McKane, *Proverbs* (OTL; London: SCM, 1970), 309.

R. B. Y. Scott, *Proverbs, Ecclesiastes* (AB; New York: Doubleday, 1965), 52.

COMMENTARY

Appeal to the Heart, 4:20-22

The opening appeal calls the child to listen to the parents' words and nothing else. The appeal is for the child to keep parental instruction

The Heart

AΩ In the biblical literature the human heart is the foundation of all human activity. It is the organ thought to be the center not only of mental and spiritual activity, but of physical activity as well. Gen 18:5 tells of Abraham's provision of food for his guests that they might "sustain [their] hearts." Similarly, Judg 19:5 reports another such occurrence where the "the heart" is sustained by the taking of food.

Heaviness of heart is a metaphor for sadness in Prov 25:20; thinking and reflection come from the heart in Prov 22:7. Joy originates in the heart in Ps 4:7 and Isa 66:14. The heart is also the location of one's moral sense in Job 27:6. Jeremiah therefore observes that wickedness comes from the heart. When Saul becomes king, Yahweh gives him a new heart (1 Sam 10:9).

A further significance of heart would fall under the larger category of "theological anthropology" (see Introduction for a discussion of creation and revelation). The category of creation helps readers to realize an important theological shift in ancient wisdom thought. Creation, though the Hebrew God might be behind it, was nevertheless a universal category that all people, whether they covenanted with ancient Israel's God or not, could reflect upon. Creation, including all of life's experiences that could be subsumed under it, was a category that transcended the historical boundaries of Israelite notions of revelation. Nature, a category of the creation, becomes the means by which God may be known. Humanity itself is a category subsumed under that of nature, so that knowing God does not require God's breaking into creation; rather, it requires humans to understand that creation points to God. The human heart becomes the means of apprehension. In a sense, then, theology begins with observation of the human, or the anthropological, realm.

For further reading, see Raymond C. Van Leeuwen, "Excursis: The 'Heart' in the Old Testament," in *Proverbs* (NIB 5; Nashville: Abingdon, 1997), 60-61.

within the "heart." Readers have encountered this image already as the center of human understanding. The opening appeal in chapter 2 invites children to "incline" their hearts toward understanding (v. 2). Likewise, the instruction in chapter 3 has the imagery of the heart as the stone tablets upon which the parents' instructions are to be inscribed (v. 3c). Without implying any opposition between internal thought and external action, the sages frequently invoke the imagery of the heart as a part of the learning process. [The Heart]

In the appeal in 4:21 and 22 the heart is the receptacle of the father's instruction. Learning is to be stored within. Moreover, the parents' wisdom and instruction are sources of life and healing to the one who keeps them (v. 22). In other words, physical well-being results from the parent's instruction. The allusion to physical well-being, and in particular the use of the word "their flesh" (*bĕśārām*), anticipates the remaining body of the instruction. There readers encounter a series of concluding admonitions that also appeal to other parts of the body—the mouth, the eyes, the feet—that are to be marshaled in the quest for the good life.

The Heart Leads the Way, 4:23-27

The opening of the instruction proper asserts that the most important part of obtaining knowledge is keeping watch on the heart. NRSV translates 4:23 as "Keep your heart with all vigilance." The final phrase of this translation, "with all vigilance," derives from the

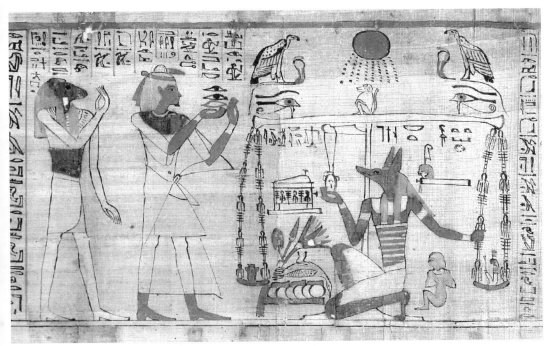

The Heart

Egyptian judgment scene. The heart is weighed against *Maat*, portrayed here by the feather, on a judgment scale. From papyrus of Hu-nefer.

Psychostasis (Weighing of the Souls). The Book of the Dead and the Priest Aaner. Papyrus. New Kingdom. Museo Egizio. Turin, Egypt.

presumed use of the Hebrew preposition *bě*, thus *bikkol.* This translation is based upon the LXX and the Latin Vulgate. The MT actually reads "Above all else, keep your heart." This derives from the presumed original use of the Hebrew preposition *mě*, thus *mikkol.* This latter reading therefore asserts the heart as the singular most important focus of a young person's attention.[2] The heart is the source of life. If one reads "heart" (*lēb*), as denoting the intellect, then the assertion gives an important place to the powers of the intellect. The heart provides the source of words for the mouth (v. 24), sight for the eyes (v. 25), and guidance for the steps of one's feet (v. 26).

Each of the body organs listed in vv. 24-27 is an organ of steerage and control. This instructor knows that the mouth can be a "fountain of life" (e.g. 10:11; 12:14; 15:4). Therefore, he admonishes the young learner to turn away from "crooked speech." One's eyes also provide direction; they must be attuned to one's heart, however (e.g., 2:2). Finally, the youth's feet must remain on the straight path without turning either to the right or to the left. The concluding admonition in v. 27 reiterates the statement in v. 26, thus providing the conclusion to the instruction. The reuse of the verb to "turn" (*sûr*) in the conclusion recalls its use in v. 24 while providing closure on the body of the instruction.

CONNECTIONS

The Center of Virtues and Values

Inculcating values is the clarion call of educators as American society remembers the twentieth century and enters the twentieth-first century. We seem to be as bewildered by it, though, as we might if called upon to reinvent the light bulb. Perhaps reexamining the ancient understanding of heart is a beginning point. It continues to be a powerful metaphor in western thought.

We use the image of the heart most frequently to denote a center. "Get to the heart of the matter," we say, or we direct that a city may be in "the heart of the country." We also use it to distinguish internal from external as in "he played that song by heart" or "her words came from her heart." It is a metaphor for emotion and sincerity when we say, "we offer our heartfelt condolences" or our "wholehearted support." Emotion may be a basis for decision-making as well, as implied in our distinction between heart and head. Often in American society, however, decisions from the heart are considered inferior as in "thinking with his heart and not his head." But we don't like people who are hardhearted, that is, who "have no heart" or are "heartless." What an extreme variation the language must make when we speak of "heart surgery" and "heart bypasses," even "heart transplants." Yet, even in a world that can successfully remove and replace one's heart, the metaphorical power of the heart remains. It is still the center—or at least it should be.

The metaphor of heart forces educators and community leaders to ask what is at the center. Whether the sage had any idea of the physiological significance of the term *heart*, he recognized the difference between those processes of decision-making, of choice, of intellection and reflection that went on within a person and those things that a person apprehends from others. He knew already that it was not what went into a person's mouth that defiled him, but what came out of his mouth, because what came out of the mouth came from the center of one's being, and thus one's deepest commitments. [Jesus and the Heart] He knew that one could not easily separate emotion from intellection. They were inextricably bound up with each other. He knew that to be a mature person, a

Jesus and the Heart

It may seem inappropriate to link ancient Israel's wisdom literature with Christianity's Jesus. However, recent studies would not support this supposition. In fact, it is highly likely that not only did the historical Jesus fall under the influence of first-century Jewish wisdom thought, but that wisdom ideas and logic continued to influence the ones who shaped the story of Jesus through their preaching, teaching, letters, and Gospels (see, for instance, Witherington).

Matthew's Gospel is just one example in that the evangelist presents Jesus as a teacher. The Pharisees and scribes question Jesus about his disciples' failure to wash their hands before they eat (Matt 15:1-9). Jesus rebukes them by calling attention to their hypocritical reading of Scripture, thus offering a new kind of wisdom. He then teaches the crowd that it is not what goes into the mouth that defiles, but rather what comes out of the mouth. The disciples approach him and Peter asks for an explanation. Jesus says, "Do you not see that whatever goes into the mouth enters the stomach, and goes out into the sewer? But what comes out of the mouth proceeds from the heart, and this is what defiles."

For further reading, see G. Bornkamm, G. Barth, and H. Held, *Tradition and Interpretation in Matthew* (London: SCM, 1963), 86-95; F. Murphy, *The Religious World of Jesus* (Nashville: Abingdon, 1991), 75-76; and E. P. Sanders, *The Historical Figure of Jesus* (London: Penguin, 1993), 33-48.

Ben Witherington III, *Jesus the Sage: The Pilgrimage of Wisdom* (Minneapolis: Fortress Press, 1994).

---

successful person, a contributing member of society, one had to have the wherewithal to make the right choices on one's own. Such choices our sage would say come from the heart.

Perhaps we moderns know so much about the heart—its physiology, its chemistry, its biological function—that we have missed the powerful implication of the heart as a metaphor: that of the importance of having a center for our lives. This center is not only one of intellection, but one of feeling and emotion. Decision-making and commitment to ultimate truth therefore require both rational faculties and emotional faculties. To separate the two is to misconstrue the ordered universe and the human response to it.

NOTES

[1] R. N. Whybray, *The Composition of the Book of Proverbs* (JSOTSup 168; Sheffield: JSOT Press, 1994), 14-15.

[2] Roland Murphy, *Proverbs* (WBC 22; Nashville: Word, 1998), 26.

THE SEDUCTION
OF AN "OTHER"

Proverbs 5:1-23

The eighth instruction turns to a parental concern that children learn to practice proper sexual restraint. It is one of those frank parent-son "lectures" that asserts the parent's belief in absolute fidelity within the marriage and unequivocal avoidance of sexual liaisons with other women. The subject of the parent's fear is the "foreign woman" (*zārâ*), or the "other" woman (cf. 2:16). In earlier instructions the emphasis has been on violent and twisted men. Proverbs 6:20-35 and Proverbs 7 will develop the theme of the other woman. The symbolic power of sexuality and love to define both licit and illicit relationships provides ample means for application to a sage's relationship with wisdom itself. In other words, sexual promiscuity symbolizes unfaithfulness to wisdom, herself a woman (4:1-9) and wife (31:10-31). Succumbing to the seduction of ignorance and folly leads an individual ultimately to ruin and death. [Structure at a Glance: Proverbs 5]

Structure at a Glance: Proverbs 5

AΩ The present structure of the instruction takes the shape of three subsections with a coda-like conclusion. It may well be that we have an original poem that has been expanded with reuse and reinterpretation. (R. N. Whybray believes that the original instructions consisted of vv. 3-6, 8. Verse 7, since it is identical with 7:24, is likely an interpolation subsequent to the original composition of the poem.) The coda, or conclusion (vv. 21-23), stands apart from the whole of the poem since it virtually introduces a new perspective to the body of the poem: both a concern with discipline, *mûsār*, and the assertion of Yahweh's judgment upon the wicked, *rāšāʿ*. There are no other explicit references either to wisdom or to Yahweh throughout the chapter. However, in the present three-part form the reader may observe the instructor's pedagogical technique.

In vv. 1-6 there is a general assertion that the other woman leads away from life. Verses 7-14 expand on this theme, elaborating the kind of death to which such liaisons lead. The final instruction, vv. 15-20, moves to a common metaphor for life in a region where water is an essential component for society's survival. This image allows the instructor to leave his pupils with a most vivid recollection of his frank and vitally important instructions. The discussion follows the order set out below.

Vv. 1-6: Her Feet Lead to Death
Vv. 7-14: The "End" for the Adulterer
Vv. 15-20: The Well of Fertility
Vv. 21-23: The Coda: The Constancy of the Lord's Gaze

R. N. Whybray, *The Composition of the Book of Proverbs* (JSOTSup 168 Sheffield: JSOT Press, 1994), 22-24

COMMENTARY

Her Feet Lead to Death, 5:1-6

The first section consists of vv. 1-6 and opens with the familiar introductory appeal in vv. 1-2, calling the child to be attentive to a parent's wisdom. The stock introduction seems a bit irrelevant; readers rightly wonder how "guarding knowledge" and "holding to prudence" possibly prepare one to face the threat that comes from the "other" woman. The body of the instruction, vv. 3-6, shift to a concern with the *zārâ*, whom readers have encountered in earlier instructions. NRSV translates the term as "loose woman," implying a character who has no moral convictions, and from the sage's point of view, cares only for the seduction of young men. Whether she is a prostitute who earns her wages by providing sexual pleasure, a temple prostitute who plies her trade for the service of a foreign deity and the benefit of her own community, or an adulteress, the effect for the young man is the same (e.g., 2:16-19).

The imagery of seduction that follows in v. 3 provides some connection with, and perhaps rationale for, the retention of the image of "lips" in v. 2. In the introduction, one's lips, a metaphor for speech, guard knowledge. It is a statement about the strategic role of the individual's speech. This stands in contrast to the speech, also evoked by the imagery of "lips," of the "other" woman (see [The "Strange" Woman]). Her speech does not guard knowledge; rather, her speech is built upon lies. The images of honey and oil, depicting the sensuality of her words and the bodily fluids that facilitate her sexual acts,[1] raise doubts about the reliability of the woman's claims. Verse 4 stands in a paired relationship with v. 3 and starkly contrasts "sweetness" with "bitterness," and "smoothness" with "sharpness." In vv. 3 and 4 the parent notes the smoothness of the other woman's speech, then urges that she is sharp as a sword. This is a clever irony in that sharpness is the qualitative result of the physical state of smoothness. Adopting the parent's point of view means recognizing this ironic inconsistency and thus acknowledging that the woman's success depends upon her deception of the inexperienced.

Two images of the woman's "end" (*'aḥărît*) follow in vv. 5 and 6. It is of interest that the contrast in vv. 5 and 6 provides analogous contrast to that in vv. 3 and 4. The woman's end refers to the outcome for those who participate with her in wanton sexual pleasure, as opposed to her own personal fate. Both vv. 5 and 6 use the imagery of the path or way to point to the outcomes of her behavior. She places a young man on the path to death and Sheol instead of the path of life.[2] What she fails to understand is that she does not realize the end that awaits herself.

The "End" for the Adulterer, 5:7-14

A decisive shift in the intensity of focus characterizes this part of the instruction. The father explores in greater detail the nature of that fate that follows in the wake of relationships with the other woman. In vv. 3-6 the other woman's activities are characterized with sensual imagery. In this section (vv. 7-14), by contrast, the possible effects of having a liaison with such a woman are set out in full detail. The parental teacher is not interested in understanding the woman's point of view. He only cares about the outcomes for his child.

Verse 7 opens with language resembling an introductory appeal. The adverb "now" (*wĕʿattâ*), functioning as a conjunction, introduces a second appeal to the child.[3] An imperative follows, which, unlike v. 2 above, is much more relevant to the topic at hand: "keep your way far from her [the other woman], and do not go near the door of her house." Verses 9-10 set out explicitly the possible outcomes. Both are introduced with the Hebrew conjunction, *pen*, translated "lest," conveying the idea of fear or concern about the preceding circumstance. Verse 9a and b parallel the ideas of "others" with the "merciless" (*ʾakzārî*). [The *ʾakzārî*] The phrase in v. 10 parallels "strangers" (*zārîm*) with the "alien" (*nokrî*). The plural forms in 9a and 10a leave readers to consider the possibility that interactions with this other woman have consequences that do not stop with her as an individual. One may become involved in paying with one's own blood for being involved with another's wife (e.g., Exod 20:14; Deut 5:18; 22:22-24).

The ʾakzārî

AΩ NRSV translates this word as "the merciless." As it stands, it is in parallel with "others" and likely serves to specify the noun in v. 9a. The word has a lexical meaning of "cruel."

Duane A. Garrett offers five possibilities for the identity of the others mentioned here: (1) If the woman is a prostitute, the other man is her agent; (2) if the woman is a mistress, then the strangers are those who profit from her access to easy money; (3) if she is married, and thus an adulteress, then the other man is her outraged husband; (4) if she is both an adulteress and a foreign woman, then the implication for her partner is that covenant has been breached; (5) if she is a cult prostitute, the strangers are the priests and cult officials.

Duane A. Garrett, *Proverbs, Ecclesiastes, Song of Solomon* (NAC 14; Nashville: Broadman Press, 1993), 92.

Verses 11-14 depict the lamentation of the one whose life has been wrecked by his liaisons with the other woman. Verse 11 portrays the groaning of the youth, now grown old, presumably because of diminished status in the community (loss of honor), diminished wealth possibly, and, perhaps, failing health. ["Groaning" and *nāḥam*] The end of this one's life is full of regrets, not the least of

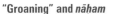

which is the failure to listen to his teachers. In v. 11, by contrast with v. 4, clearly the concern has switched from the "end" to which the woman leads to the "end" that comes to the young man as a result of following the woman. The concluding image is of humiliation in some public setting. The specific language that is used recalls expressions exclusively used to identify the Israelite cultic assembly (*qāhāl*) and congregation (*ʿēdâ*). However, beyond such allusive language, the context does not specifically require readers to conclude that one will be shamed within the context of the worshiping community. Sirach 23:21 envisions public shame for an adulterer (v. 18), but the shaming takes place "in the streets of the city." Sirach 23:22-26 envision the adulteress being dragged before the "assembly" (*eis ekklēsian*).

"Groaning" and *nāḥam*

AΩ An interesting description of results of the liaisons with the other woman is one's groaning due to the consumption of the body and flesh. The word for groaning is more frequently used of the growling of an animal. Hunger brings such a response and here therefore we may speculate that one's poverty, which also causes hunger, brings on such a despairing growling. (Of a lion, Isa 5:30; of the sea, Isa 5:30; but of a king's wrath, Prov 19:12; 20:2.) It is of interest that the LXX translated the Hebrew word *nāḥam* with *metamelethesei*, implying an understanding of *nāḥam*, as the Niphal of the root meaning repent. In this case the groaning is that of the sorrow of repentance.

Sumerian lion figurines from 2d millennium attest to their importance as symbols of strength and terror

Guardian Lion. Terracotta. From the temple at Tell Harmai, Iraq. Isin-Larsa period. 1800 BC. Iraq Museum. Baghdad, Iraq.

The Well of Fertility, 5:15-20

The concluding admonition punctuates the foregoing instruction by shifting away from the foreign woman to one's own wife. The image of the well or cistern may, according to the context in which it occurs, connote sexuality, and thus operate as a metaphor for wife. The larger context to which this conclusion is attached makes such connotations likely. The question is what specifically within marriage the image of the well designates. If we are to take the cistern as an image of fertility, then the wife is a receptacle for her husband's "streams of water" that will yield offspring. In a land where water was scarce, where cisterns were built to store every drop for the sake of irrigation and survival, the image makes a strong equation between marital infidelity on the parts of the husband and the wife[4] and the wastage of the precious natural resource.

Verses 19 and 20 shift the metaphor from fertility to pleasure. The evocation of sexual pleasure is accomplished by the descriptions of the physical aspects of the wife. ["Lovely Deer, a Graceful Doe"] Readers encounter a parental admonition to delight in the "breasts" and the "love" of one's wife. What is more, the use of the verb *tišgeh*, "to be intoxicated," evokes an image of wanton, sensuous delight—between a married couple. It may be appropriate at this point to note that the language sounds like stereotypical male language. This is mainly because the woman is being described as an object. In any event, the language is similar to that in Song of Solomon, a love poem (e.g., Cant 2:7, 9, 17; 3:5; 4:2, 5; 6:6; 8:14). Such beauty and sensuousness, however, is diminished in Proverbs 31:30, where the fear of Yahweh supersedes. The language nevertheless further evokes a reader's recollection of similar implications in 4:8, where the sexuality of wisdom is exploited as a motivation to seek it (her!) out. Readers further note that the same verb, *tišgeh*, is used in v. 20 to admonish the youth against such affairs with the other woman. The overall effect is to suggest that both one's sexual delight and one's offspring should come from within the boundaries of one's own marriage.

"Lovely Deer, a Graceful Doe"

AΩ This is the only place in the Old Testament where woman is compared to an animal as an expression of beauty (Toy). One interesting supposition of the meaning of this phrase is that of Delitzsch who suggests the deer to be the object of comparison for the animal's slenderness and black eyes (Keil and Delitzsch).

However, note that in Jacob's blessing, Naphtali is called "doe who brings forth beautiful fawns." Here the image is of fertility, and perhaps it is the fawns that are particularly graceful (Gen 49:21).

C. F. Keil and F. Delitzsch, *Proverbs*, vol. 1 (COT 6 Grand Rapids: Eerdmans, 1950), 130-31.

C. H. Toy, *The Book of Proverbs* (ICC; Edinburgh: T & T Clark, 1899), 115.

The Coda—The Constancy of Yahweh's Gaze, 5:21-23

Readers have already seen that some scholars regard these concluding three verses to be secondary to the poem itself. Even a cursory reading of these concluding verses in light of the preceding instructions leaves readers feeling that a new topic is here introduced. Suddenly we return to the familiar assertion that Yahweh ultimately rewards or punishes the actions of humankind (e.g., 3:33-34). The idea of Yahweh's watchfulness over one's wanton sexual pleasure, even if it is with one's own wife, and eventuates in the building of one's own family, creates some slightly self-conscious feelings for modern readers.

For this coda to have its effect—which is one of shame in the presence of Yahweh—one must adopt Yahweh's point of view. To put it another way, one must see the Lord as though Yahweh were watching everything that could possibly happen. It is not less than the shame of the man and the woman in the garden, whose eyes having been "opened," had come to see things as Yahweh saw them. Suddenly, they had a new point of view (Gen 3:7). But Yahweh's point of view is that of a third party who stands aloof and watches. This perspective is a kind of subjectivism males are implicitly urged to adopt within the marital relationship. Here in this passage, in contrast to the other woman, the wife is made out to be an object of the husband's gaze. The imagery of physical beauty—slender limbs as a doe or a mountain goat, dark beastly eyes, her breasts—facilitate this objectification and eroticization, and thus, the husband's lust. The other woman, by contrast, only attracts through her seductive words.

CONNECTIONS

Instruction from Eroticism

This instruction requires that the youth reflect upon his own sexuality and its relationship to social power within the confines of a marital relationship. If readers take the rather rough opening appeal—that the youth's lips "guard knowledge"—as a broader allusion to sexuality, then it is all too clear what the parents' instruction is aiming toward. [Knowledge and Sexuality] They want their son to recognize the delicate balance that must be maintained between control over the body and surrender to the body. This balance is exemplified in the split created by the teacher between the objective and the subjective points of view. The objective point of view is that of the one who is the object of one's gaze; the subjective point of view is that of the one gazing upon the object. The subject of the gaze interprets the object of the gaze, construing meaning in whatever way power allows.

The split between subjectivity and objectivity is captured in the film *M. Butterfly*. The film takes its plot from Puccini's famous opera about a Japanese woman whose love is rejected by a British military officer. The plot of the film features a Chinese man, who is a spy in female disguise in order to seduce foreign male officials into providing sensitive government information. The story itself is about her seduction of a British foreign minister, who actually has quite a lengthy affair with her, and never knows until a much later public trial that she is a male spy. In one scene, when the transves-

Knowledge and Sexuality

AΩ It is a peculiar phenomenon that one of the euphemisms for sex in the biblical literature is knowledge. The classic introduction to this usage is in Gen 4:1: "Now the man knew his wife Eve, and she conceived and bore Cain." The word "to know" is an unambiguous reference to sexual intercourse. The classic play on this meaning is in the prophet Hosea's condemnation of Israel's faithlessness to Yahweh's commands. That faithlessness was understood in the imagery of the prophet as the prostitution of Israel with foreign deities (Hos 4:1-6). In other words, they did not *know* Yahweh's commandments.

For further reading, see George W. Buchannan, "The Old Testament Meaning of the Knowledge of Good and Evil," *JBL* 75 (1956): 114-20; and David J. A. Clines, "The Tree of Knowledge and the Law of Yahweh," *VT* 24 (1974): 8-14.

The figure of Amon-Min reminds modern viewers of the importance of sexuality to ancient Egyptian religion.

Fertility and Harvest. God Amon-Min (left) and Pharaoh Hatshepsut and god Amun (right). Reliefs from the Red Chapel of Hatshepsut and Tuthmosis III. Karnak. Thebes, Egypt.

tite spy is in a conversation with her own communist comrades, she observes that it is always males who play the most seductive females, because males know what kinds of sensual titillations and seductions other males want from females. Here is the classic assertion of the power of the subjective point of view. Only the one who is in a subjective position, that is the position of power and of the creation of meaning, understands the seductiveness of the eroticized objective position.

More than a mere warning about the wiles of the other woman, this instruction is an assertion of an ongoing struggle between the control over the body and surrender to the body. The other woman represents what is uncontrolled and uncontrollable. By making her the object of desire, there is the simultaneous attempt to assert control over her. Her threat, however, is not in her beauty, but in her attempt to gain the subjective position through her words. In wisdom, remember, it is through words that meaning is conveyed. She seduces through her honeyed speech. By contrast, the appeal of the "wife of your youth" is physical. She does not assert herself into the subjective, meaning-giving position. She remains the object of her husband's erotic desires.

In reflecting upon the admonition to be drunk upon the beauty of one's own wife, we cannot help inferring that the mechanism for such fidelity is not merely a physical attraction. Rather, attraction to one's own wife must take advantage of a construction of significance within the eyes and mind of the husband that accompanies the physical charms of his wife. Physical beauty, in other words, is as much a construct of one's own mind as it is the body.

NOTES

[1] See Roland Murphy, *Proverbs* (WBC 22; Nashville: Word, 1998), 31, quoting Raymond Van Leeuwen, *The Book of Proverbs* (*NIB* 5; Nashville: Abingdon, 1997).

[2] This is reading *bal* or *lo'* for the word "lest," *pen*, which more characteristically begins a sentence. Murphy, *Proverbs,* 30, doubts the necessity of this, however.

[3] NRSV bases "son" on LXX, which renders the Hebrew "sons" (*bānîm*) with the singular *huie.*

[4] Murphy, *Proverbs*, 32, who notes that the imagery can both designate male unfaithfulness and the neglect of the female, exposing her "to seeking consolation elsewhere."

AN INTERLUDE ON FOOLISHNESS AND WICKEDNESS

Proverbs 6:1-19

The verses contained in this unit reflect a change in thematic content as well as an abandonment of the typical introductory appeal we have seen up to this point in chapters 1–9 of Proverbs. A quick glance back at other introductory appeals reveals a lack in this instance of the parent's extensive commendation of his own instruction (e.g., 4:1-2; 3:1-4). Further, chapters 5–7 are dominated by the theme of maintaining sexual propriety. The verses in chapter 6 turn abruptly to offer examples of various other kinds of foolish social behavior. For these reasons scholars consider the unit to be somewhat intrusive and possibly originating from a different source than that of the preceding instructions.

The variation in style here, whatever the origins and dating of the materials,[1] still allows useful thematic connections with the preceding parental assertion of the foolishness of sexual impropriety in chapter 5. The several examples of foolishness contained in vv. 1-9 are thought by one scholar to be "inner obstacles" to obtaining wisdom. They stand in contrast to the "outer obstacles" to obtaining wisdom created chiefly by the "other" woman.[2] There are indeed vestiges of the formal language of the larger instructional context in chapters 1–9. Readers will still recognize in chapter 6 the imperatives with explanatory and motive clauses evident throughout the entire collection of instructions. [Structure at a Glance: Proverbs 6:1-19]

Structure at a Glance: Proverbs 6:1-19

AΩ The structure of the chapter appears as follows.

Vv. 1-5: Danger of Loans for Strangers
Vv. 6-11: Diligence and Laziness
Vv. 12-15: Fate of the Wicked
Vv. 16-19: Seven Things Yahweh Hates

The sections are set out here in a stair-step fashion to suggest a graphically thematic movement that climaxes in reflections from the deity's perspective. The topic of making loans to outsiders connects with the reason people need loans to begin with: they lack diligence and are lazy. The third section advances to the general topic of wickedness, inviting readers to draw the inference that an absence of work and diligence leads to more than poverty, but to other kinds of wickedness as well. The final statement is that of Yahweh's ultimate displeasure and judgment.

COMMENTARY

Financial Folly, 6:1-5

The instruction anticipates several sayings in the ensuing collections within Proverbs that reflect upon the dangers of providing financial security for people, that is, of intervening with financial help for someone else's debt. This would be a serious risk, especially on behalf of those who are not members of the community (e.g., 11:15; 17:18; 20:16; 27:13). One difficulty of reading, however, is identifying to whom the terms "neighbor" (*rē'ekā*) and "other" (*zār*) refer. Readers may not have the best understanding here if they interpret the two terms as though, in standard parallelistic fashion, they refer to the same person who lives within the community. [Neighbor and Other] Another possibility is understanding that one is in debt to one's neighbor (perhaps a money lender) on behalf of one who is not known within the community. The law codes prohibit charging interest (e.g., Exod 22:25), and offer some indication of the nature of such financial agreements (e.g., Deut 24:6, 10-11), but offer little in the way of legislation or policy about the securing of a loan.[3] The theme of providing financial security also forms an interesting counterpoint to one potential contextual detail for Qoheleth's advice. In the book of Ecclesiastes, the context may well be that of Persian political and economic domination. Taking financial risks, therefore, certainly required borrowing and lending. Providing financial backing for someone outside the community could easily help to define that sage's understanding of "vanity."

The concern about being under the authority of someone outside of the community is not new to this passage. We have already

---

Neighbor and Other

AΩ Although the practice of giving "a pledge" for another is not treated extensively in the law codes, various sayings seem to assume that the practice was common. One difficulty in understanding the practice arises in the parallel words "neighbor" (*rēa'*) and "another" (*zār*). How do the two terms illuminate each other? The word for "another" means foreigner, one who lives outside the confines of the community. It seems unlikely that a foreigner could be considered a neighbor and is therefore difficult to understand how the two terms parallel each other. Is anyone really foolish enough to guarantee a loan to someone outside the community? One solution is add another person into the scheme; to consider the neighbor (*rēa'*) as the creditor for the *zār*, but the one being admonished in this passage, a "neighbor" (*rēa'*) has provided collateral for another neighbor's (*rēa'*) loan to the *zār* (McKane). (Roland E. Murphy considers it "probably" that the neighbor/foreigner is the debtor.)

William McKane, *Proverbs* (OTL; London: SCM, 1970), 321-22.
Roland E. Murphy, *Proverbs* (WBC 22; Nashville: Thomas Nelson, 1998), 39.

encountered this picture in the instruction on sexual propriety (5:10-14). Further, readers have also seen that coming under the influence of another's words may lead to such ensnarement (5:3-6). Here, offering a financial obligation on behalf of an outsider is like being ensnared in one's own words. There is a possible connection therefore between this instruction on financial propriety and the previous instruction on sexual propriety. The two themes reinforce and illuminate each other. Whether it is ensnarement to a community member or to one outside the community, this instruction urges great haste in being free from the commitment.

In v. 3 NRSV translates the Hebrew word *hitrappēs* as "hurry," conveying the sense of urgency. The ensuing imperative also conveys the necessity of such haste. In vv. 4-5 the invocation of nature through the use of these swift-footed or winged animals as models of escape further conveys the sense of danger associated with financial obligations. One who is committed to such financial arrangements is not only like an ensnared wild animal, but there is an implicit accusation as well. The people who are engaged in promoting such transactions are like hunters seeking whomever they may catch in their traps.

Want of Work, 6:6-11

Verses 6-11 form the second section of the whole. The nature imagery in vv. 4-5 forms an effective connection with the word picture in vv. 6-11 concerning the diligence of the ant. The observation of natural order and pattern is a source of authority for these sages. In these verses readers encounter a lighthearted description of the diligence of one of the smallest creatures on the face of the earth (see Prov 30:24-28). Laziness is another of the themes readers will encounter in the following collections of proverbial sayings (e.g., 10:26; 13:4; 15:19; 19:24; 20:4; 21:25; 22:13; 24:30; 26:13-16). The lazy person, *āṣēl,* is itself a class of people analogous to the wise and the foolish. Laziness, however, does not necessarily imply a kind of inescapable foolishness. The opening admonition is for the lazy person to reflect upon the work of the ant and "be wise." The ant is the appropriate model since there is apparently no external force to motivate it. Motivation must come from within. The poetic effect is one already seen in Proverbs 1:1-7, that of compiling descriptive terms. In 6:7 readers find three different terms for leader, none of which stands over the ant for the sake of motivation: "chief" (*qaṣîn*), "officer" (*šoṭēr*), and "ruler" (*mōšēl*). The point is that the ant is its own motivation and does extraordinary work. The image of failing to harvest, and its tragic consequences for individuals and for communities, anticipates treatment in 10:5 and more poignantly in 24:30-34. In this latter passage, the field is grown over with thorns and nettles and the protecting wall is broken down. [LXX Addition of the Bee]

Verses 9-11 return to direct address by appeal to the logic of associating sleep with laziness. The implicit call to wake up works at both a literal and a metaphorical level. Lazy people need to spend more time working than sleeping. They also need to come to their senses, "be wise," and recognize the costliness of present comfort to future security. The same belief in the long-term efficaciousness of work is apparently subverted by the writer of Ecclesiastes (e.g., 4:4), who challenges the profitability of work generally. The saying in Proverbs rests upon the observation of a connection between sleeping and poverty. Poverty comes like a "robber" and like an "armed warrior." The writer of Ecclesiastes has come to the conclusion that "Better is a handful with quiet than two handfuls with toil, and a chasing after wind" (4:6).

The Work of the Wicked, 6:12-15

Verse 12 turns to another type of person: the wicked one. The more common language used to characterize the wicked in the sayings that follow this collection is the *rāšāʿ*. In these verses the text refers to the "scoundrel" (*ʾādām bĕlîyaʿal*). Verse 13 contains a summary of physical activities that characterize this wicked person's behavior. Winking, one of the actions, is mentioned elsewhere, including other Proverbs (e.g., 10:10; Ps 35:19). In those instances it is a signal of malicious intent. With these sayings, the themes have moved from the image of work that is good (i.e., that of the ant) to the image of work that is evil (i.e., that of the scoundrel).

The meaning of these hand, eye, and feet signals is unambiguously addressed in v. 14. The person who practices them is bent upon nothing but wickedness and discord within the community. Perversion is constantly on the minds of such ones. Just as certain as their lives' work is the inevitable disaster that will strike them suddenly, and there will be no deliverance. Disaster is as inevitable to these evildoers as poverty is to laziness (vv. 6-11) and financial servitude is to providing financial security for strangers (vv. 1-5).

Raised to a Higher Power, 6:16-19

These verses contain a numerical saying; it is so called because numbers (sixes and sevens) provide a structure that parallels the instructional content. It is the only such saying in the book outside of chapter 30. [Numerical Sayings] The concluding statement on "sowing discord" (v. 19) picks up the same behavior encountered in v. 14, which is characteristic of the "scoundrel." In the context of vv. 16-19, the appeal is not only to the power of the seventh in the sequence, but is also to Yahweh's hate for these behaviors. This is a Yahweh saying that provides a fitting conclusion to the section.

The behaviors in vv. 17-19 are significant. Not only do these define abominable behavior, but they also serve to anticipate treatments of the same behaviors in the following collections of sayings.

Numerical Sayings

(See [Form Criticism]). Verses 16-19 contain a "numerical saying." The form is a poetic convention that leads the reader through a sequence of phenomena to a climactic point. This climax usually reveals its corresponding phenomenon as being distinct in some sense from the others in the sequence. An examination of some of the other numerical sayings in the book of Proverbs might be helpful in understanding how to read Prov 6:16-19.

Consider Prov 30:18-19, for instance. In this passage four different phenomena are named. Each phenomenon is similar to the other three; each has a "way" to be compared: the way of an eagle, the way of a snake, the way of a ship, the way of a man with a woman. The numbers three and four imply that the fourth is somehow different, and indeed, readers intuitively recognize that the fourth phenomenon

concerns a relational phenomenon rather than a singular phenomenon. Thus readers are invited to consider the similarities of the four while reflecting upon the differences of the fourth from the third. The numbers simply help readers structure the comparison.

In Prov 6:16-19 readers observe that the main distinction between the first six and the seventh is its specific regard for the family. All seven are similar in that the activities are antisocial and thus threaten a community. The seventh seems to provide a climax in that its explicit concern is for a special kind of community: the family. Consider also Prov 30:21-23, 24-28, 29-31; and Sirach 25–26.

For further reading, see Luis Alonso-Schökel, *A Manual of Hebrew Poetics* (Rome: Pontifical Biblical Institute: 1988); and James L. Crenshaw, *Old Testament Wisdom: An Introduction* (Atlanta: John Knox Press, 1981).

For instance, readers have encountered the phrase "haughty eyes" in 6:17 (also Pss 18:27; 131:1; Sir 23:4); they should also compare with 21:24 and 30:13. A "lying tongue" occurs in 12:19; 17:7; 21:6; and 26:28 (also Ps 109:2). Readers have also encountered "bloodshed" in 1:10-11 and 16; consider also 12:6 ("deadly ambush" translates the Hebrew *'ĕrob dām*, "blood"). The deceptive heart is also revisited in 24:2. In having Yahweh pass judgment upon these particular activities (Prov 6:16-19), the sage asserts a position on key behaviors (the opposites of these named) that are implicitly to be taken as normative for the community.

CONNECTIONS

What Is Good for Society?

Gerhard von Rad's classic definition of the ancient sages' understanding of "the good" is a helpful point of departure for our reflection. He says, "'Good' is that which does good; 'evil' is that which causes harm."[4] This statement on its own, while apparently obvious, really does not help readers to understand exactly what kinds of specific behaviors and activities contribute to von Rad's notion of doing good. However, something with this kind of extraordinary specificity appears to be the aim of the sages in these passages in Proverbs 6. The sages offer two reflections on the good for an individual (vv. 1-11) and two reflections on the good for a community (vv. 12-19).

In the book *Common Fire: Lives of Commitment in a Complex World,* Sharon Daloz Parks pursues a contemporary definition of the good. She interviews people across the United States who "had sustained long-term commitments to work on behalf of the common good."[5] The research team summarizes what such people are like, how they become committed to others, and what keeps them going. The story of Bill Wallace, the head of an environmental engineering firm, is summarized as an example of "interbeing." As one Buddhist monk explains, "We cannot just be by ourselves alone. We have to interbe with every other thing."[6] This idea of "interbeing" is an image of the interconnectedness of the individual with every aspect of the community, indeed with every aspect of nature. Perhaps clarifying such interconnectedness is the beginning point for understanding the sage's admonitions about what is good and evil.

In this instructional interlude of Proverbs 6:1-19, readers may pause to think about foolish behaviors in comparison to the preceding instructions concerning behaviors that threaten one's obtaining wisdom: foreign women and wicked men. With the four separate admonitions readers encounter in Proverbs 6:1-19, there is an expression of the importance of an individual's self-awareness as well as a consciousness of the importance of an individual's contributions to community. Financial freedom is essential to community service in the sage's world. People who are weighed down with financial obligations cannot make any significant contribution to the greater good of the community. What is more, the ethos that defines appropriate individual behavior is one that asks what is best for the community. The wicked are those whose behavior threatens not only individuals, but the structure of the society as a whole. In other words, what is good for society seems to rest on the assumption of a kind of "interbeing." The high mark for this connectedness for the sage is trust and obedience to Yahweh, the creator. One's success as an individual rests upon one's contributions to society in such a way that it creates good for all involved. These contributions to society begin with Yahweh.

NOTES

[1] R. N. Whybray, *The Composition of the Book of Proverbs* (JSOTSup 168; Sheffield: JSOT, 1994), 48-50. William McKane, *Proverbs* (OTL; London: SCM, 1970), 320, acknowledges variation in style and form, but is not nearly so certain as Whybray that these verses should be treated as intrusions from a later hand.

[2] Richard Clifford, *Proverbs* (OTL; Louisville: Westminster John Knox Press, 1999), 73.

[3] Roland E. Murphy, *Proverbs* (WBC 22; Nashville: Thomas Nelson, 1998), 37.

[4] Gerhard von Rad, *Wisdom in Israel*, trans. James D. Martin (London: SCM Press, 1972), 77.

[5] Laurent A. Parks Daloz, Cheryl H. Keen, James P. Keen, Sharon Daloz Parks, *Common Fire: Lives of Commitment in a Complex World* (Boston: Beacon Press, 1996), 5.

[6] Ibid., 26; the name is fictitious.

THE FOOLISHNESS
OF ADULTERY

Proverbs 6:20-35

These verses form the ninth instruction in Proverbs 1–9. The opening appeal in v. 20 makes a clear separation with the series of admonitions in 6:1-19, indicating the beginning of a new instruction. Readers recognize in vv. 20-22 the familiar self-commendation of parental instruction. There is also in v. 20 the assertion of the authority of both mother and father as already encountered in 1:8. The appeal to both parents reminds readers that they are to understand that instruction comes from the home and not the academy. The threat of adultery places the home in danger, not only society at large. The implied split between family and larger social community follows closely upon the climactic numerical saying in vv. 16-19, where readers are made aware of Yahweh's disapproval of anything that threatens family stability. What is more, whereas a positive approach to the import of marriage is taken in Proverbs 5:7-23, here the passage takes a frank and negative approach. [Structure at a Glance: Proverbs 6:20-35]

Structure at a Glance: Proverbs 6:20-35

AΩ The passage may be examined in three major sections of thought distinguished, as usual, by rhetoric and specific themes:

Vv. 20-24: Parental Exhortation
[Note that Richard Clifford transposes v. 22 from its present position to Prov 5. Leo Perdue organizes the passage as follows: parental exhortation, v. 20; instruction, vv. 21-24; final instructions, vv. 25-35.]
Vv. 25-29: Adultery and the Prostitute
Vv. 30-35: The Adulterer and the Thief

The three sections are easily recognizable through consideration of familiar rhetorical changes. Verse 20 opens with an imperative; v. 25 opens with a negative admonition ('al); v. 30 opens with a negative (lo'). Two sets of comparisons dominate the thematic concerns of the two instructions in vv. 25-29 and vv. 30-35: the adulteress and the prostitute (vv. 25-29) and the adulterer and the thief (vv. 30-35). Verses 26-35 make a sharp change to third-person language; direct address of parental admonition ceases in v. 25. The concluding reflection in vv. 32-35 lays out a stark image of the shame and public humiliation that result from the cuckolded husband's refusal to be compensated.

Richard Clifford, *Proverbs* (OTL; Louisville: Westminster John Knox Press, 1999), 67 and 78.
Leo Perdue, *Proverbs* (IBC; Louisville: Westminster John Knox Press, 2000), 128.

COMMENTARY

Parental Exhortation, 6:20-23

The opening appeal calls youths to keep the commands of the father and the instruction of the mother. This language has a decided Deuteronomic sound to it (see [Deuteronomic Land Tradition]). It is Deuteronomy 4:45 that refers to the "decrees," "statutes," and "ordinances" as the "torah" given by Moses. What is more, Deuteronomy 6:7 enjoins God's people to teach their children the laws and ordinances of torah. Further, Deuteronomy 6:8 admonishes that the laws and commandments be "bound" upon the hand as a sign. Proverbs 6:21-23 has similar language. Instead of binding to the hand, though, the youth is admonished to "bind" the parental instruction to the heart. This presence of parental instruction will then guide at all times: in one's walking, one's lying down, and one's waking up. Thus, the parents' instruction is to pervade every part of one's life much like the teaching of Moses.[1]

The similarities between the Deuteronomic torah and the parental exhortation are intensified in v. 23. The words "commandment" and "teaching" are no longer specified as merely parental. The metaphorical language that equates law to light and teaching to life has the familiar sound of Psalm 119, a Torah Psalm. [Torah Psalm] In particular, Psalm 119:105 refers to Yahweh's words as light. The instruction in 6:23 refers to the parents' words as light. The allusion to the Mosaic torah requires the tacit analogy between the binding authority of both.

Verse 24 actually begins in the middle of a thought. It provides the purpose clause for v. 23. In the NRSV's translation the theme of v. 24 is unambiguously "the wife of another." The Hebrew text, however, has "evil woman" or "evil wife." The term "foreign woman" in 24b parallels the "evil woman." So, it is only through the translation that we escape the actual ambiguity of the verse. Are we talking about a sexual rendezvous that is illicit because it is outside of marriage, or within marriage? [What Is Adultery?] Verses 29 and 32 make unambiguous references to adultery and therefore contribute to the translation "the wife of another" in v. 24.

Torah Psalm

AΩ During the second-temple period (post-515 BC) the word for instruction, *tôrâ*, came to identify the collection of religious laws that were attributed to Moses. While the word *tôrâ* as instruction indeed occurs in Pss 1, 37, and 40, in two psalms this word refers to its more technical meaning of law code. These psalms, 19:8-15 and 119, are written with the special aim of intoning the glories of Yahweh's laws given through his servant, Moses. They reflect the emerging second-temple piety that centered mainly on the strict adherence to the Mosaic law codes.

For further reading, see D. G. Ashburn, "Creation and the Torah in Psalm 19," *Jewish Bible Quarterly* 22 (1994): 241-48; Duane L. Christensen, "The Book of Psalms Within the Canonical Process in Ancient Israel," *JETS* 39 (1996): 421-32; and Mark S. Smith, "The Theology of the Redaction of the Psalter: Some Observations," *ZAW* 104/3 (1992): 408-12.

What Is Adultery?

To modern readers, adultery is the act of engaging in sexual intercourse, while in the state of marriage, with a partner other than one's spouse. Readers should remember, however, that in the ancient world there is a double standard for men and women due mainly to the different social status held by males and females. Thus, a man who visited a prostitute would not be committing adultery. By contrast, a married woman would be committing adultery any time she had sex with someone other than her husband or betrothed.

Throughout the Bible, there are intriguing variations in the rules for sexual conduct among married people. The covenant code forbids adultery (Exod 20:14). The Deuteronomic code prescribes death for adulterers, both male and female (Deut 22:22-27), as does the Levitical code (Lev 18:20; 20:10). Matthew's Gospel indicates that at least one 1st-century Christian community understood adultery as merely desiring to have sex with a married woman (Matt 5:28; cf. Job 31:1-4). Interestingly, Paul thinks that sexual relations with a prostitute constitute a marriage of sorts (1 Cor 6:15-20).

For further reading, see Jacob Milgrom, "A Husband's Pride, A Mob's Prejudice," *BibRev* 12 (1996): 21; and Raymond Westbrook, "Adultery in Ancient Near Eastern Law," *RB* 97 (1990): 542-80.

Adultery and Foreignness, 6:25-29

It is interesting that the instruction uses more erotic language to describe the woman in v. 25, referring to her beauty, and in particular her eyes. Murphy stresses the assumption of the male's responsibility in the commission of adultery.[2] Recall the comparatively erotic imagery used to describe one's own wife in 5:19, suggesting her objective position relative to both the male speakers. Not only does this clarify the male point of view, but it reinforces the idea that the passage is talking about someone's wife here, and not a mere foreign woman.

The contrast in v. 26 between a prostitute (*zônâ*) and this "other woman" may also suggest that the latter is married.[3] The contrast between the two women consists of the relative costs of having sex with either. From a male's point of view, the former is quite inexpensive, the relative equivalent of subsistence wages only. The latter, by contrast, is quite expensive. The phrase translated in NRSV "a man's very life" (*nepeš yĕqārâ*) conveys the notion of one's own life, while invoking the image of a man who is a person of substance. The rhetorical question that follows, v. 27, invokes the images of one's cloak as an unlikely tool for carrying the coals of a fire, as well as of marriage. This double meaning of "bosom" (*ḥêq*), suggests the possibility that the question originated as a riddle. The implied equation between woman or wife (v. 26b, *ʾēšet*) and fire (v. 27, *ʾēš*) creates a commonsense basis for the admonition, "Stay away from fire/another's wife: they both burn!"

The Adulterer and the Thief, 6:30-35

Verses 30 and 31 invoke another argument, appealing by analogy to the offense of stealing. The analogy between illicit sex and stealing is not uncommon in the Bible. Readers will encounter it again in 9:17. Readers see it also in the biblical narratives about the exploits of David. The ancient historians were unabashed in describing the episode of the king's sexual liaison with Bathsheba (2 Sam 11). Nathan's strategy in indicting the king's behavior is to tell a parable that equates the king's adultery with stealing. The parable describes the rich man's stealing the poor man's beloved family pet, a lamb, to make a tasty stew for a visitor (2 Sam 12:1-15). NRSV translates Proverbs 6:30 as though the mere satisfaction of one's appetite might be a mitigating factor to the crime of stealing. By analogy, sex simply to satisfy one's sexual appetite would also be mitigated in some sense, even though it is not clear to modern readers how such a liaison is less evil (see Matt 5:27-30). Yet, v. 31 implies that restoration of what is stolen is set at seven times the value of the merchandise. Even the Covenant Code only sets the price of restoration for stealing livestock at five times for an oxen and four times for a sheep (e.g., Exod 22:1). The implication may be that a sevenfold recourse is an extraordinary amount. [Covenant Code] Indeed, the penalty for stealing is high, which offers support for reading v. 30 as a rhetorical question, even though there is no interrogative particle: "Are not thieves despised who steal to satisfy their appetite when they are hungry?"[4] Reading v. 30 as a rhetorical question eliminates the possibility that the sage could have been implying a double standard on certain kinds of sexual relationships.

The summary in vv. 32-35 adds force to the argument. If the consequences of stealing are high, how much more costly is adultery. One lacks sense entirely because the price will require one's own life in every respect. Not only does the language of these verses imply physical wounds, but public shame that will not escape society's memory. The jealous husband will not be inclined to show restraint and will not find acceptable any level of compensation.

Legal Documents

This description of a lawsuit found at Hazor is evidence of a thriving practice of jurisprudence in antiquity.

Cuneiform Tablet. Terracotta. Bronze Age. 18th–16th C. BC. Israel Museum. Jerusalem, Israel.

Covenant Code

There are three major codes of law within the Old Testament. The Covenant Code is the first in canonical sequence (Exod 21:1–23:33). The other two law codes are the Deuteronomic code (Deut 12–26), and the Holiness code (Lev 17–26). The Covenant Code is so called since its narrative framework places it in the context of Yahweh's giving of the law to Moses at Sinai (Exod 19–24) According to the narrative, it is on the basis of this law that Yahweh enters into covenant with Yahweh's people.

Scholars believe that this code existed independently of its narrative framework in its inception. Most likely, it is a composite of other kinds of materials that originated in worship and that reflected common law. Further, though there are similarities in structure and content with the other two law codes, the Covenant Code is the oldest. The latter two law codes, scholars believe, are reinterpretations of the older code.

For further reading, see J. H. Sailhamer, "The Mosaic Law and the Theology of the Pentateuch," *WTJ* 53 (1991): 241-61; Dale Patrick, *Old Testament Law* (Atlanta: John Knox Press, 1981); and R. Norman Whybray, *Introduction to the Pentateuch* (Grand Rapids: Eerdmans, 1995), 107-32.

Medieval representation of Moses receiving the Ten Commandments and then giving them to the Israelites in the wilderness.

Moses and the Tablets of Law. Illustration from the Bible of Charles the Bald. 9th C. Ms. Latin 1, Fol. 27 v. Bibliotheque Nationale. Paris, France.

The price of adultery, far more than stealing, is physical pain, public shame, and the unquenchable wrath of the woman's husband. What fool would become so entangled?

CONNECTIONS

On the Problem of Desire

It would seem from the father's admonition that desire is the beginning of adultery. Therefore the instruction rightly admonishes the son not to entertain his desires (v. 25). This admonition, in fact, uses nearly the identical language as the final commandment in the decalogue in Exodus, which is translated "you shall not covet,"

Job's Oath

The passage occurs in the larger context of Job 29–31 comprising Job's concluding oath. It is significant rhetorically only as one understands the way an oath worked in antiquity.

Job 31 climaxes Job's recollection of former days of glory (ch. 29) and compares them to his present-day miseries (ch. 30). The oaths Job invokes are against himself if he has committed any of the sins named. The irony in such a rhetorical strategy is that Yahweh, who has remained silent against the sound of Yahweh's servant's questioning and accusation up to this point in the poem, is the only one who can enforce the oath Job takes. If Yahweh does not appear and enact the curses Job invokes, then Job is innocent by default. If Job is in fact consumed by his curses (thus by Yahweh), then Job is guilty of sin and there is not failure of justice. There is further an explanation for Job's suffering: he has sinned just as his friends have insisted.

For further reading, see James Barr, "The Book of Job and its Modern Interpreters," *BJRL* 54 (1971): 28-46; and James L. Crenshaw, *Old Testament Wisdom* (Atlanta: John Knox Press, 1981), 100-25.

loʾ taḥmōd (Exod 20:17). In other words, simply desiring what is not one's own—an internal thought—quite apart from whether the desire is fulfilled, is itself a sin. One cannot therefore view the laws and instructions of the Old Testament as somehow being only concerned with actions as opposed to thoughts. Job's powerful defense in the face of Yahweh opens with the assertion that he did not even *look* at a virgin, presumably to desire her. For that, he says, would justify the disasters that befall the unrighteous (Job 31:1-3). [Job's Oath]

Readers should recall the comments in the connections concerning the instruction in 5:1-23, which also concern the problem of adultery. There we discussed the relative positions of power depending upon whether one was the subject or the object. The irony of this split as it applies to desire is that one may be seduced by one's own mental construction of beauty. Put another way, one desires what one has created to be erotic, even pornographic. Beauty is a net one casts and then is caught in it. In other words, the admonition not to desire locates the problem of adultery not in the beauty of the other, but in one's internal constructions of one's own.

In the prologue to his book, *Love's Executioner,* Irven D. Yalom, M.D. states that one of the goals of the therapist is to get patients to assume responsibility for their own circumstances. "Every therapist knows that the crucial first step in therapy is the patient's assumption of responsibility for his or her life predicament."[5] The first step in remaining faithful to one's own relationships within marriage is to recognize that desire is not a result of the seductiveness of some other, but the internal eroticizing by oneself.

NOTES

[1] Roland Murphy, *Proverbs* (WBC 22; Nashville: Word, 1998), 39.

[2] Ibid.

[3] William McKane, *Proverbs* (OTL; London: SLM Press, 1970), 329.

[4] Ibid., 330.

[5] Irven D. Yalom, M.D., *Love's Executioner* (New York: Basic Books, 1989), 8.

THE PARENT'S FINAL ADMONITION ON ADULTERY

Proverbs 7:1-27

Proverbs 7 contains the tenth and final instruction in the series within Proverbs 1–9. This is the fourth of the instructions on adultery (cf. 2:16-19; 5:1-14; 6:20-35.) A concluding reflection occurs in the poem in 9:13-18. Of the four instructions, this one certainly offers the most elaborate narrative description of the ways of the adulteress (vv. 6-23). It may be read as the climactic statement of the four admonitions, punctuating the previous warnings with the most provocative detail of the process of seduction.

In addition to the interesting structural arrangement of the chapter, readers may be interested in the narrative strategy used in vv. 6-23, the central descriptive section. [Structure at a Glance: Proverbs 7] There are three stages of discourse: first is the sage's observation (vv. 6-9), followed by the third person narrative frame within the observations of the sage (vv. 10-13), and the first person experiences of the adulteress herself (vv. 14-20). The central section closes with a return to the narrative frame (vv. 21-23), paralleling vv. 10-13.[1]

Structure at a Glance: Proverbs 7

AΩ The section on the seduction of the adulteress invites its own structural box to demonstrate graphically the rhetorical development and the strategies of parallelism within.

Vv. 1-5: The Parents' Commands Bring Life
  Vv. 6-23: The Seduction of the Adulteress
    Vv. 6-9 (Observation of sage)
      Vv. 10-13 (Narrative description)
        Vv. 14-20 (First-person description)
      Vv. 21-23 (Narrative description)
Vv. 24-27: Listen to the Father's Words

As in preceding instructions, the structure of the unit is determined by the most significant rhetorical features. Readers will recognize the typical opening appeal of the parent in vv. 1-5. The central section is made up of the description of the seduction of a young man and takes up the entirety of vv. 6-23. Note the different levels of discourse including the sage, an unknown narrator, and the first person dialogue of the adulteress. The closing verses return to yet a final admonition from the parent, forming a symmetrical frame with vv. 1-5.

COMMENTARY

The Parents' Commands Bring Life, 7:1-5

As in 6:20-24 the parent again calls the child to observe parental commandments. This opening appeal is not generic, however, since its clear aim is to introduce further reflection upon the threat of the "other" woman (7:5). In 7:2 as in 6:23 the appeal is to the hope of obtaining life. These appeals help readers to recall previous descriptions of the ways of the woman that only lead to death (2:18; 5:5). The parents' commands echo the Deuteronomist's appeal to choose life by choosing to keep the Lord's commandments (Deut 30:15-20). The choice of life over death is one of making the parent's instructions an ever-present reality in one's life. The metaphor of writing upon "the tablets of the heart" (v. 3), which we have encountered once in 3:3, implies the internalizing of the instruction.

It is noteworthy that the only reference to wisdom comes in 7:4. The young man is to call wisdom "his sister." The usage reflects a convention of using "sister" as either an image of intimacy or as an epithet for "wife." In the Song of Solomon, for instance, the term "sister" stands in parallel with "bride" and thus functions as a term of both endearment and intimate relationship. This personification of wisdom recalls and anticipates the poems in 1:20-33, 8:1-36, and 9:1-12. The intimate relationship envisioned between the young man and wisdom accomplishes two things rhetorically. First, it reminds readers that adultery is an act of foolishness, the very opposite of wisdom (6:32; 5:12; 2:10). That there is no such speech between the young man and the "other" woman in this narrative[2] leaves the impression that the "other" woman is in some respects less than a person. In a sense she is deliberately dehumanized. Second, the personification of wisdom as a woman creates an opposition and rivalry between the adulteress and Woman Wisdom. This rivalry will be developed further in the concluding poem (9:1-18). These two women, the adulteress and Woman Wisdom, symbolize for the sage at least one choice a young man must make.

The Seduction of the Adulteress, 7:6-23

This section reflects an autobiographical style. It is a narrative couched in terms of the parental instructor's personal experience. One may easily see from the poem's structure how it might have stood on its own apart from the context of instruction provided by 7:1-5 and 24-27.[3]

Verses 6-9 provide an introduction characterized by the instructor's first person point of view. The narrative proper begins in v. 10, and the narrator's third person point of view remains until v. 14. At v. 14 the point of view switches to that of the adulteress, who describes for the unwitting young man her circumstances. In vv. 21-23 the poem returns to the narrator's point of view.

In its present form readers naturally equate the "I" of vv. 6-9 with the parental instructor of vv. 1-5. Some hold that it is the "other" woman herself standing in the window. Such a view seems unlikely, however, based upon the Masoretic Text.[4] Nevertheless, the autobiographical style lends authority to the implications of the poem. It further provokes the reader's own detachment from the scene. We can only envision these events through the eyes of the person looking out of the window, in this case, the instructor, who at this point is offering little interpretation. The inevitable question is whether the young man intends to be there or is simply there through his own lack of forethought. In the latter case, his innocence is one of naivete and lack of experience.

The narrator's voice, which we still associate with the "I" of the preceding verses, moves to a much fuller narrative description of the woman in vv. 10-13. Readers now encounter a woman who is exactly the opposite of every value the sages place upon a good wife. This woman is loud, willful, and will not stay at home. She spends her time in the public places: the street, the squares, and at every corner. Her dress identifies her as a prostitute, perhaps for a religious cult that is foreign to Israelite society. [Prostitution in the Ancient Near East]

One of the most provocative questions has to do with the relationship between this prostitute and the "other" woman who is mentioned in v. 5. It is impossible to be certain that when these

---

Prostitution in the Ancient Near East

Jean Bottero explains that in the Mesopotamian context males were free to pursue sexual liaisons outside of the marriage bond. The husband was required by law only to "support his legal family [his wife and children] and not violate anybody's rights." It was therefore common for married males to add concubines to their principle wives and to visit other women, married or unmarried, outside their households.

In such a context, which is characterized by an attitude of "free love," both sacred (cultic) and secular (business) prostitutes were common. Behind such an attitude was the widely prevalent assumption that fertility and the accompanying emphasis on sexuality contributed to the common good of society.

For further reading, see Frederique Apffel Marglin, "Hierodouleia," *ER* 6:309-13; and Judith Ochshorn, "Ishtar and Her Cult," in *The Book of the Goddess Past and Present* (New York: Crossroad, 1983), 16-28.

Jean Bottero, *Mesopotamia* (Chicago & London: University of Chicago, 1992), 185-98.

Prostitutes

Toulouse-Lautrec shows the "human" side of these ladies of the night. Without seduction or allurement, the ladies are depicted by the artist in an intimate casualness as they bask in the ennui of waiting. The human tragedy may be detected in their demeanor of listlessness — silhouetted props emptied of substance.

Henri de Toulouse-Lautrec. 1864–1901. *In the Salon at Rue des Moulins.* 1894. Charcoal and oil on canvas. 111.5cm x 132.5cm. Musée Toulouse-Lautrec. Albi, France.

poems speak of other, or foreign women, they are only speaking of non-Jewish women. The term may be more metaphorical in nature, referring rather to characteristics of behavior that make them outsiders to the values of the community envisioned by the teachers. The narrator's perspective is that this woman is a predator "lying in wait" for her prey. She is shameless in her public display of sensuality. Sex is here a commodity for the market place. Such sensuality has its place, however (e.g., Song 5:1-8)—just not in the place of public business.

In vv. 14-20 the woman herself now speaks, and the pace of the description slows as the narrative strategy is one of dialogue rather than narration. The character herself discloses the ways of her seduction. By her own words her intention is to have sex with the young man (vv. 16-18). It appears that the youth is entangling in a ritual sex act that is a part of the woman's obligations to the particular religious cult to which she belongs. Her offerings at the sacred place must be fulfilled with the sacred meal and the sacred sex act.

The concluding verses (vv. 19-20) are strategically placed at the end of the woman's seduction as much for the reader as for the young man in the story. The fact that the husband is absent probably matters little to a youth, whose powers of resistance are microscopic anyway next to the overpowering persuasions of this woman. One can hardly believe that in the face of such an aggressive seduction the youth would even remember to think about the woman's husband. However, readers viewing the narrative from outside may remember to think about the husband (especially if they have read Prov 5:9-10 and 6:29-35). In some respects this narrative is an invocation of a new level of significance to this liaison—adultery—as well as an assertion of the ultimate seduction—that of the reader. There is not much chance that the reader will be discovered. Thus the reader is seduced as well—not by the woman's sensual appearance, but by her words.

At this crucial moment, when both the youth and the reader are feeling the heady and titillating delights of the seductress, the narrative voice intrudes in vv. 21-23. He reiterates the power and compelling force of this woman's seduction. The imagery of smooth, slick words reminds readers of similar imagery in 2:16 and 5:3. It is her speech in the end that creates the greatest threat. The sage alludes again to the previous image of the woman as predator, only she has not been lying in wait for any prey that offers much of a challenge. Rather, the animals cited here move rather predictably toward their inevitable deaths. Such is the foolish youth who strays onto her street.

Listen to the Father's Words, 7:24-27

The closing four verses read as another introductory appeal. However, in this location the similar imperative tone and negative admonitions function as a framing conclusion to the poem. Verse 24 appeals to "children" rather than the more common "child." As the conclusion to the final instruction, this perhaps provides a unifying marker in conjunction with the introduction in 4:1, where we saw a similar appeal to "children." The dominant theme of these final instructions is the "other" woman (e.g., 5:1-23; 6:20-35; 7:1-27).

The most compelling reason to attend to the parental instruction that is put forward in this conclusion comes through the invocation of the mythology of death. The woman's house is the way to the underworld, Sheol, and the chambers of death (see [Sheol and Abaddon]). What is more, there are many victims such as those in the narrative who have been led there by her. Thus the parent admonishes the youth not to venture into her way. The reiteration of the imagery of the path or road (v. 25) reminds readers that the youth had ventured onto her street in the beginning (v. 8). The use of the term "heart" (*libbekā*) situates the problem within the realm of individual desire.

CONNECTIONS

Caution, X-rated

The concluding admonition on adultery addresses the voyeurism of the male reader through the phrase "My husband is not at home." Ironically, the condemnation of male lust betrays a deeper antipathy toward females. Male readers happily observe the seduction of the young man in the story (and therefore are themselves also seduced), until suddenly the poet's rope snaps taut and male readers are implicated by the reminder that this seduction has implications beyond the sex act. The woman here serves only as a foil for an understanding of the complexities of social and sexual development of male youths. By the successful seduction of the reader and the assertion of the moral implications, two defining characteristics are established that help us to understand the sages' instructions on sexuality.

Margaret R. Miles introduces her book *Carnal Knowing* by summarizing the roles of women in the Babylonian Gilgamesh Epic. [The Gilgamesh Epic] At three significant places women symbolize the developing male subjectivity as expressed in art. Gilgamesh the great king has a voracious sexual appetite and insists on having sexual intercourse with every bride in his city. Enkidu, the wild man, becomes a champion for the complaining people and defeats Gilgamesh in a battle, thus preventing him from fulfilling his sexual desire. Likewise, a prostitute teaches Enkidu the art of making love and tames him as well. Thus the women in the story represent both the objects of male insatiable lust and the limits imposed by society on that lust.[5] The "other" woman in this final proverbial instruction as well as in the preceding instructions is just such a poetic device with similar symbolic values. She gives

The Gilgamesh Epic

This ancient epic, preserved in Akkadian on twelve clay tablets, may have been written around 2000 BC, although it contains material that is likely much older (Heidel). The poem grew up around the legendary king Gilgamesh of Uruk (biblical Erech). Gilgamesh's quest for fame changes for immortality as he faces the death of his friend, Enkidu. In the end, Gilgamesh finds immortality but then loses it just as quickly and, like all humankind, is forced to face his own mortality.

The Gilgamesh Epic is of special interest to readers of the book of Ecclesiastes since there are remarkable parallels between those two works. Concluding that there is no real gain in any kind of toil in this life, the sage of Ecclesiastes says,

Go, eat your bread with enjoyment, and drink your wine with a merry heart; for God has long ago approved what you do. Let your garments always be white; do not let oil be lacking on your head. Enjoy life with the wife whom you love, all the days of your vain life that are given you under the sun, because that is your portion in life and in your toil at which you toil under the sun. (9:7-9)

It may be that Gilgamesh has not yet discovered life to be vain. At the point where he goes in search of immortality due to the death of his friend, Enkidu, the ale-wife, Siduri, encounters him on his journey and says:

Gilgamesh, wither rovest thou?
The life thou pursuest thou shalt not find,
When the Gods created mankind,
Death for mankind they set aside,
Life in their own hands retaining.
Thou, Gilgamesh, let full be thy belly,
Make thou merry by day and by night.
Of each day make thou a feast of rejoicing,
Day and night dance thou and play!

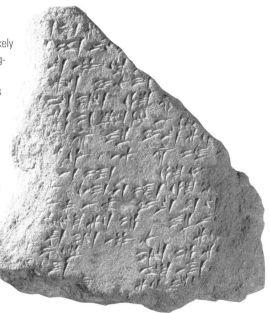

The Babylonian epic of Gilgamesh describes the deeds of the legendary hero who seeks eternal life.

Gilgamesh Cuneiform Tablet. Terracotta. Babylonian from Megiddo. 15th C. BC. Israel Museum. Jerusalem, Israel.

Let thy garments be sparkling fresh,
Thy head be washed; bathe thou in water.
Pay heed to the little one that holds to thy hand,
Let thy spouse delight in thy bosom!
For this is the task of mankind! [*ANET*, 90.]

Readers should note the similarities with the biblical sage.

For further reading, see John Gray, *Near Eastern Mythology* (New York: Peter Bedrick, 1985), 40-52.

Alexander Heidel, *The Gilgamesh Epic and Old Testament Parallels* (Chicago & London: University of Chicago, 1963).

expression to insatiable male sexual appetites and the limitations that are placed upon those appetites through the instruction of the sages.

The problem is, do males who embrace such teaching ever come to appreciate the female's point of view? The sages' instructions assert a certain perspective on women. They are either wives or whores, always foils in some sense to male existence. There does not seem to be any in-between. By embracing the sages' teaching, must there be a general denigration of all women? Putting it in a slightly different way, to adopt these proverbial instructions on relationships with women and male sexuality, one is asked to take a certain view of women generally. It is a view that has not taken into account the female point of view, and it is this costliness to women that is X-rated. One must hold these ancient views with caution.

NOTES

[1] Compare Leo Perdue's treatment of this passage's structure in *Proverbs* (IBC; Louisville: Westminster John Knox Press, 2000), 133-34.

[2] See Richard J. Clifford, *Proverbs* (OTL; Louisville: Westminster John Knox Press, 1999), 87.

[3] R. N. Whybray, *The Composition of the Book of Proverbs* (JSOTSup 168; Sheffield: JSOT, 1994), 25.

[4] In order to maintain such an interpretation, one must rely upon the LXX translation rather than the MT. See the discussion of William McKane, *Proverbs* (OTL; London: SCM, 1970), 334-35. Roland Murphy concurs in *Proverbs* (WBC 22; Nashville: Thomas Nelson, 1998), 42, note 6a.

[5] Margaret R. Miles, *Carnal Knowing; Female Nakedness and Religious Meaning in the Christian West* (New York: Random House, 1989), 3.

WOMAN WISDOM COMES CALLING

Proverbs 8:1-36

There is another voice, as we have already seen (e.g., Introduction; Prov 1:20-33), besides that of the "other" woman. It is Wisdom herself who also takes to the streets, to the heights beside the way. Her voice again calls to young men who, as the reader knows, are pulled in many different directions. In this poem Woman Wisdom is herself shown to be much more enticing. Far different from the threat she posed in 1:20-33—where time runs out for those who delay to heed her call—here Wisdom commends herself. As the seduction in chapter 7 is the most explicit of those in the instructions on adultery, the self-disclosure of wisdom in the poem in chapter 8 is also the most detailed self-revelation of who she is. [Structure at a Glance: Proverbs 8]

Structure at a Glance: Proverbs 8

AΩ The structural scheme below suggests that the poem advances thematically toward a climactic revelation and statement of identity. There seems to be development from ideas of lesser importance to greater importance.

Vv. 1-3: Wisdom in the Streets
  Vv. 4-11: Wisdom's Themes
    Vv. 12-21: Skills for the Public Place
      Vv. 22-31: Wisdom's Identity in Creation
        Vv. 32-36 Wisdom Has Yahweh's Favor

Readers easily recognize the poem to be in five sections: (1) vv. 1-3 set the scene; (2) vv. 4-11 describe Wisdom's audience and the nature of her message; (3) vv. 12-21 shift to a much more narrow form of self-disclosure with the opening words in v. 12, "I, Wisdom"; (4) vv. 22-31 depict Wisdom reaching mythological heights of significance by appealing to her origins before creation; (5) vv. 32-36 contain a final appeal from Wisdom, echoing the appeals of the father to his child throughout the collection.

The final and climactic call to the youth of the land forms a symmetrical balance with the opening call in the first Wisdom poem in Prov 1:20-33. In these final verses, now containing several instructions and warnings about Wisdom's rival, Wisdom calls again. Thus, the poems in 1:20-33 and 8:1-36 form a framework for the various instructions contained within, which elevates those teachings to a level beyond the mundane.

COMMENTARY

Wisdom in the Streets, 8:1-3

The most recognizable difference between the language in vv. 1-3 and that in vv. 4-11 is point of view. Verses 1-3 are in third person narrative, providing the perspective of a sage presumably; vv. 4-11 are in first person speech, providing the perspective of Woman Wisdom herself. In the opening verses the narrator asks the rhetorical question about Wisdom's call, introducing thereby the admonition that will follow in vv. 4-7. Readers observe that Woman Wisdom does her work in the same places as the "other" woman: in the streets, beside the way, at the crossroads, and in the city gates. On the one hand, she is as common as the city market. On the other hand, there are few who take advantage of what she offers.

One scholar observes that these wisdom poems provide a rhetorical framework that characterizes the youth's obtaining wisdom as the result of a response rather than a self-initiated investigation.[1] This suggestion is helpful not only because it reflects the rhetorical situation described in the poem itself, but because it also corresponds to the theological features readers have already observed throughout the collection of instructions. Wisdom comes from Yahweh. One may only find it when Yahweh offers it. This theological feature will carry over into the reading of the next collection of sayings, Proverbs 10:1–22:16, sayings that are not so explicitly associated with Yahweh. Even though wisdom is much more a matter of one's own search in the later collection, the perspective set out in chapters 1–9 becomes the background against which readers understand wisdom's origins and availability. Wisdom calls; individuals must respond.

Wisdom's Themes, 8:4-11

Verses 4 and 5 find Woman Wisdom either narrowing the focus of her audience or making a rather derogatory judgment about the nature of her audience. In v. 4 NRSV translates "O men" as "O people," implying that Woman Wisdom makes no sexual delineation in her understanding of the audience.[2] The only discrimination is between the wise and the foolish. Her call is to all those who are foolish. Wisdom's address to the foolish may also implicate readers. Since in v. 5 the focus is narrowed to all those who are foolish, readers initially respond by placing themselves in the best light ("surely she does not mean me, too"); only after readers' initial denial do they, too, come to recognize the need to attend to her teaching. The discrimination is between those who will learn and those who will not.

Wisdom commends the nature of her message in vv. 6-11. Its value rests upon its moral uprightness and street value. Here Wisdom reiterates the claims put forward in preceding instructions. She offers noble things (*nĕgîdîm*, v. 6) and upright things (*mêšārîm*, v. 6). She contrasts her words of truth (*ʾĕmet*, v. 7) with the abominations of the evil ones (*tôʿăbat śĕpātay rešaʿ*, v. 7). Her claim is that her words are grounded in righteousness and have no part of what is perverse and twisted (*ʿiqqēš*, v. 8). Verse 9 is of special interest in that she finds support for her claims from those who have found wisdom. The question is, can her claims be born out by those who have not found wisdom? Is wisdom's benefit truly publicly and freely available?[3]

The appeal that concludes this section asserts that wisdom's value is far greater than silver or gold. Woman Wisdom simply comes out and admonishes youth to receive her discipline before they receive silver or gold. This assertion is especially appropriate given the context in which she makes the appeal. In the marketplace there is intense competition for value. True value is what catches the shrewd trader's eye. Similarly, the marketplace informs the imagery of the teaching of Qoheleth. His search is for that which is most valuable (What "gain," *yitrôn*, is there under the sun?).

Skills for the Public, 8:12-21

Now Wisdom begins to speak more specifically about her attributes. This section may be divided into two subsections, both identified by the use of the first person pronoun "I" (vv. 12 and 17). The opening subsection, vv. 12-16, lists a series of skills that define Wisdom's work as a counselor for kings. The NRSV translation of "knowledge" and "discretion" in v. 12 might just as easily be translated as "shrewdness" (*ʿormâ*) and "devices" (*mĕzimmôt*). These are skills of mental adroitness and acuity. We might refer to these features as Wisdom's cleverness.[4] [Words for Wisdom in Retrospect] We would be quick to observe that v. 13

Words for Wisdom in Retrospect

AΩ It is informative at this point to look back to the opening verses of this section of instruction (1:1-7) to compare the concepts set out in the opening verses with these in vv. 12 and 13. Notice the same terminology in both: "wisdom" (*ḥokmâ*), "shrewdness" (*ʿormâ*), "knowledge" (*daʿat*), and prudence or "devices" (*mĕzimmôt*). This provides a helpful framework for readers as these same wisdom attributes are now associated with more than just a concept, but with a person who was with Yahweh at creation.

In the introduction, these were concepts perhaps difficult to conceptualize in real life. Associated in this closing poem with Wisdom herself, the terminology takes on a new personality. They become personal, in other words. Making Wisdom personally available to all students is one of the goals of the sages.

For further reading, see Michael V. Fox, "Words for Wisdom," *ZAH* 6/2 (1993): 149-69; and Avi Hurvitz, "Wisdom Vocabulary in the Hebrew Psalter: A Contribution to the Study of Wisdom Psalms," *VT* 38 (January 1988): 41-51.

immediately responds by asserting the moral implications of such skills. It is true, however, that the language of v. 13 abandons the first person style of vv. 12 and 14. Readers therefore wonder whether the skills set out in vv. 12 and 14 are not separated by this assertion of their moral uprightness because such skills of cleverness too easily fall into disrepute. Verse 13c seems to provide a comment on 13b and 13a. These skills are commended by their use in the courts of kings and rulers, vv. 15-16.

The second subsection in vv. 17-21 returns to an idea set out already in v. 11 concerning the value of wisdom in the marketplace. The subsection is framed by references to love: Wisdom's benefits come as reciprocation for those who love her (v. 17). Her love is expressed, however, in materialistic terms, an idea readers have already encountered in 3:14 and 8:10. Verses 18, 19, and 21 speak explicitly about the rewards of riches, wealth, gold, and silver. The function of v. 13 within vv. 12-16 seems analogous to that of v. 20.

Egyptian Ennead

The idea of Wisdom being a procreation of Yahweh rather than a creation carries the implication that she is herself an aspect of the deity. One could say she is Yahweh in another form, Wisdom. While she is indeed distinct from the creator, she is yet a part of the creator. Although such an idea is truly questionable in the Bible, it is not so unusual in the ancient world where we find a similar example in the Egyptian creation myths.

The most common creation myth, or cosmogony, in ancient Egypt is the Heliopolitan cosmogony. It focuses on a group of nine gods (thus, "Ennead" or "nineness"), all of whom come from Atum, "the all." Atum brings forth Shu ("air"—male) and his sister Tefnut ("moisture"—female). From their union come another generation of deities, Geb ("earth"—male) and his sister Nut ("sky"—female). From this union come two sets of twins, Seth and Osiris, brothers, and Isis and Nephthys, sisters. While these nine are individuals, they are all at once Atum in a manner not dissimilar to the Christian trinity of Father, Son, and Holy Spirit.

For further reading, see Leonard H. Lesko, "Egyptian Religion: An Overview," *ER* 5:37-54; Karl Luckert, *Egyptian Light and Hebrew Fire* (Albany NY: SUNY, 1991); and Bryan Schafer, ed., *Egyptian Religion* (Ithaca NY: Cornell University Press, 1991).

Ennead

Illustrations of Heliopolitan Ennead ("Nine Gods"). From right to left the deities are: Re the Creator, Atum, Shu and Tefnut, Geb and Nut, Osiris and Isis, and Horus the king.

Verse 20 seems to intrude between this assertion of materialistic benefits to inform readers that there is nothing morally questionable about obtaining such benefit from wisdom. Wisdom herself travels morally upright paths. Thus, anyone who receives instruction from her must get behind her on the path.

Wisdom's Identity Established at Creation, 8:22-31

Wisdom's self-description reaches new heights in these verses. Her attributes are no longer merely confined to the practical needs of mortals and their mundane confines. Rather, she now discloses her universal and cosmological dimensions, and particularly her relationship to Yahweh. The opening verse asserts that the Lord "created" wisdom. Although the word used is the same as that in Proverbs 1:5, "to acquire" (*qānāʾ*),[5] one should not think that Yahweh acquired wisdom as a mortal does. Verse 23 has wisdom asserting that she was "set up, established" (*nissaktî*), thus reinforcing the notion that wisdom comes from Yahweh in some sense (e.g., Ps 139:13b). Clifford observes the negative expressions that serve as a feature of the description of the process of creation. The process of asserting what was *not* there during creation establishes an affinity between Proverbs 8:22-29 and Genesis 1, reiterating the deity's act of creating wisdom.[6] Verse 24 uses the imagery of birth, however, implying that wisdom was procreated instead of created. The implication is that she is Yahweh's offspring. [Egyptian Ennead]

While readers should be cautious about reading metaphorical language too woodenly, it is clear that the poet attributes to wisdom a primordial character. Verses 24-29 set out wisdom's antiquity by alluding to different stages of creation. Even before there was any watery deep—before mountains, hills, heavens, and earth, before establishing order out of chaos—wisdom was there. Especially significant in this larger context is the possible allusion to humanity in 26b. NRSV's translation, "the world's first bits of soil," renders a Hebrew phrase that could also mean the "beginnings of dust." The term "dust" often functions as a metaphor for humanity (e.g., Job 4:19; 10:9; 21:26; 30:19; 34:15; Eccl 3:20; 12:7) and here would reiterate wisdom's antiquity relative to human temporality.

The final two verses of this section pose an even more difficult crux. NRSV translates the Hebrew word *ʾāmôn* in v. 30 as "master worker." The implication is that Wisdom, begotten by Yahweh, was a kind of craftswoman who assisted Yahweh in creation. Readers not only reflect upon her personhood, but also upon her shared identity with Yahweh as co-creator. The two occurrences in the verse of the Hebrew verb "to be" (*'ehyeh*), though translated here as "I was," are the words of identification used by Yahweh at Sinai: "I am" (Exod 3:14).[7] An alternative translation takes the term *'āmôn* to denote "a little child, or ward," as in Lamentations 4:5, "The tongue of the infant sticks to the roof of its mouth for thirst." In the former translation there is consistency with previous portrayals of Woman Wisdom's cleverness and service as an advisor, in this case to Yahweh at creation. In the latter instance there is support in the imagery of delight and laughter that ensues with v. 31. Wisdom's laughter and delight is that of a child who plays with Yahweh's creation. The play, or delight, of wisdom continues in her call to humankind to seek her out. Readers may imagine Wisdom's "delighting in the human race" being reflected in the human response of delight that comes as God allows humankind to find Wisdom. This joy is also a theme the writer of Ecclesiastes will pursue more programmatically (e.g., 2:24; 3:12, 22; 5:18; 8:15; 9:7; 11:9).

Wisdom Has Yahweh's Favor, 8:32-36

The final section of the poem returns to the familiar language and style of the opening appeal. The call to listen and the assertion of blessedness in v. 32 is expanded in vv. 33 and 34. Verse 34 specifies what the youth is to listen for in order to become wise: discipline. Verse 34 metaphorically implies that blessedness comes from a watchfulness "at wisdom's gates."

The address to "children" in v. 32 echoes previous parental appeals (e.g., 7:24; 4:1). Readers make the adjustment in the denotations of the words, however. This is no longer the parent speaking; rather, it is Woman Wisdom using the familiar maternal (and paternal) language of parental appeal. The concluding motive clause legitimizes her call in two ways. First, in v. 35 there is an appeal to Yahweh's pleasure. Readers recall Proverbs 3:13 where finding happiness (*'ašrê*) is the end result of discipline. Here it is happiness or "favor" (*rāṣôn*) from Yahweh. The implication is that Yahweh's delight is in Wisdom as well. Secondly, the two verses contrast life and death. Readers have seen several times that wisdom brings life (e.g., 4:13, 23; 10:17). Here the dichotomy is reasserted. Readers may make the connection with a similar set of alternatives set out in Deuteronomy 30:19 (cf. Sir 15:17).

CONNECTIONS

The Pragmatism of Thoughtfulness

It seems that pragmatism has become the supreme good in modern culture. Classically defined, pragmatism has to do with "concrete outcomes in one's actual life."[8] As one might apply pragmatism to one's ideas, and especially to one's beliefs, one should expect a connection between "knowing the meaning of a [concept or idea] and what to expect if it is true."[9] The ultimate value of any activity, therefore, is in seeing in advance what kind of real-life outcomes there might be to it.

An article in an educational journal raises the question about the practicality of a liberal arts education. [Liberal Arts] Since education has become a commodity like nearly everything else, consumers (students and parents) are asking about the real value of an education in the marketplace. Probably the most frequent question concerns job preparation. "What will this degree prepare me to do?" students ask. "Will my child be able to get a job paying $35,000.00 out of college?" goes the parental inquisition. Such challenges have sent institutions of higher learning into a deep "navel-gazing" mode trying to answer the question: does a liberal arts education really pay? Is it pragmatic? Can we see in advance the real-life outcomes there might be?

The poem in Proverbs 8:1-36 does not really answer the question raised in such terms. The social environment and educational needs of individuals are quite different today from when this poem was

---

Liberal Arts

While the education offered by Wisdom is probably initially for people who will be serving in some administrative setting—a professional program—the breadth of that education, as implied by Wisdom herself, invites comparison to modern conversation among contemporary educators. Current debates over the meaning of "liberal arts," for instance, are perhaps useful in thinking about the relative narrowness or breadth of one's education.

The term liberal arts has come to be used as more of an idea than as a technical term or a specific curriculum in colleges and universities. Many have used it broadly as a means of differentiating between vocational education and more traditional modes of education in the humanities, the arts, and the sciences. However, where once one could justify such a dichotomy between professional education and

a liberal arts education, there is a trend toward the liberal arts as foundational to professional training. "College and university faculties should require every student, regardless of major subject or career objective, to achieve a baccalaureate education that encompasses a broad study in the natural and social sciences and in the humanities" ("Panel on the General and Professional Education of the Physician").

For further reading, see Bruce A. Kimball, *Orators and Philosophers: A History of the Idea of Liberal Education* (New York: College Board Publications, expanded ed., 1995); and Francis Oakley, *Community of Learning: The American College and the Liberal Arts* (New York: Oxford University Press, 1992).

"Panel on the General and Professional Education of the Physician" in Jerry Gaff, *New Life for the College Curriculum* (San Francisco & Oxford: Jossey-Bass, 1991), 35.

Philosophy

Medieval representation of philosophia. In this illustration, Philosophy (with crown and scepter) consoles the prisoner (reclining) by displacing the four muses with the trivium and the quadrivium.

Boethius, Consolation of Philosophy. France. Ms. 3045, Fol.3. 15th C. Bibliotheque Municipale. Rouen, France.

written, and readers should not expect such a direct relation. But parallels between Wisdom's benefits and contemporary education might get us thinking if we use those benefits as a starting point for our reflections. For instance, it is intriguing that the implied student in this poem is one who finds a role of service offering counsel at the courts of kings. Yes, there is employment. One cannot help feeling, however, that such employment is but the most superficial of outcomes for one who begins to embrace the primordial existence of Wisdom. And Wisdom's own call holds out the possibility of reward (gold and silver), but definitely moves beyond such attractions (v. 19).

We have to acknowledge also that Wisdom promotes her kind of education in the marketplace where the competitive demands on the time and abilities of youth are many. She talks the language of that setting; she competes with those who are only concerned about the best price and whether there is profit or loss. However, Wisdom uses the language of stark pragmatism to move beyond the values of the marketplace; she calls people to a different set of values. For Wisdom, the pragmatic values of educational outcomes are but the beginning point. To be certain, a broad, liberal arts education pays in terms of jobs and skills. But it keeps paying in other ways, too. It influences selfhood and develops character, both of which are vital to a meaningful life and a healthy community. Or as one of this author's colleagues has been known to respond when parents ask why send their children to a liberal arts college: "so they won't be clods."

NOTES

[1] Duane A. Garrett, *Proverbs, Ecclesiastes, Song of Songs* (NAC 14; Nashville: Broadman Press, 1993), 106, quoting D. Kidner, *The Wisdom of Proverbs, Job, and Ecclesiastes* (Downers Grove: InterVarsity, 1985), 77.

[2] Roland E. Murphy, *Proverbs* (WBC 22; Nashville: Thomas Nelson, 1998), 46, translates similarly, "To you, O men, I call out; to all humankind, my cry."

[3] Garrett, 107, cites Luke 7:35 as a restatement of this principle: "Wisdom is vindicated by all her children."

[4] William McKane *Proverbs* (OTL; London: SCM Press, 1970), 346-47, thinks these attributes reflect Wisdom's worldly occupation; she is not unfamiliar with the ways of the world.

[5] Murphy, *Proverbs*, 47, translates the word in v. 21 as "begot."

[6] Richard Clifford, *Proverbs* (OTL; Louisville: Westminster John Knox Press, 1999), 46.

[7] Murphy, 53. The occurrence of the verb is all the more noticeable, according to Murphy, since there is a "general tendency in Proverbs to avoid the verb 'to be' in favor of juxtaposition or simply comparison."

[8] Cheryl Misak, "American Pragmatism: Pierce," *Routledge History of Philosophy* 7, ed. C. L. Ten et al. (London & New York: Routledge, 1994), 357-58.

[9] Ibid., 358.

FEASTING AT WISDOM'S TABLE

Proverbs 9:1-18

Chapter 9 of the book of Proverbs functions as a concluding poem to the entire collection of instructions contained in Proverbs 1–9. The poem makes explicit what has heretofore only been implied: Woman Wisdom has a diabolical opponent in Woman Folly. In the poem dealing with this "other" woman (vv. 13-18) readers encounter Wisdom's competitor, Folly, personified in a fashion similar to Wisdom herself. In fact, we shall see that there are some striking similarities between these two. Through the juxtaposition of these two women readers are afforded the opportunity to look back on the admonitions from Woman Wisdom about the "other" woman who seduces young men. [Structure at a Glance: Proverbs 9]

Structure at a Glance: Proverbs 9

AΩ The structure of the poem consists of three main sections set out as follows:

Vv. 1-6: Wisdom's Feast
Vv. 7-12: Humility and the Fear of Yahweh
Vv. 13-18: Stolen Water, Hidden Bread

The three sections outline the treatment of these two women. Verses 1-6 sound familiar to descriptions of Wisdom already encountered in 1:20-33 and 8:1-36. However, scholars are doubtful about whether this final poem comes from the hand of the same author as the other Wisdom poems (Whybray; McKane). Verses 7-12 seem to be an intrusion; that is, these verses were not originally conceived to be a part of the poem contrasting Woman Wisdom and Woman Folly. Verses 13-18 conclude the juxtaposition of the two women by portraying Folly as the "other" woman whose sexual exploits with unsuspecting, foolish men only lead to death and destruction.

William McKane, *Proverbs* (OTL; London: SCM Press, 1970), 359. McKane sees little influence of the instruction style.
R. N. Whybray, *The Composition of the Book of Proverbs* (JSOTSup 168; Sheffield: JSOT, 1994), 43-48.

COMMENTARY

Wisdom's Feast, 9:1-6

The concluding image of Woman Wisdom is that of her preparing a great feast. Readers have already encountered the imagery of the sacrificial meal in the instruction concerning the adulteress in 7:14. In this concluding poem it is Wisdom who prepares the sacrificial meal. The opening description of Wisdom as a "house-builder" has

Slaughter vs. Sacrifice

AΩ McKane notes the difference between *ṭābaḥ*, "slaughter," and *zābaḥ*, "sacrifice." While they are synonymous in one sense, the latter word, *zābaḥ*, refers to slaughter for cultic purposes, thus religious sacrifice. The former word is used more frequently for the ordinary slaughter of animals for food.

The use of *zābaḥ*, "sacrifice," in 7:14 implies that the woman enticing the young man is a cultic prostitute. There may be some significance that in our passage Woman Wisdom only "slaughters," *ṭābaḥ*, the animals she prepares for the feast. While the terms are similar, the ironic parallels between the two women are provocative. It seems that Wisdom is not offering a cultic sacrifice. Rather, the feast she prepares is certainly not cultic.

One possible reflection invites speculation on the secularity of what Wisdom has to offer. As an alternative to Folly's sexual favors, which are cultic in nature, Wisdom offers knowledge and intelligence, which might well be construed as an alternative to what might be experienced in cultic participation. Readers know already that wisdom begins with the "fear of Yahweh." But this fear may well be conceived in terms not associated with worship.

Ritual Slaughter of Oxen. Colored relief from the tomb of Ni-anch-nesut, Saqqara. 2300 BC. 5th-6th Dynasty. Old Kingdom. Staatliche Sammlung Aegyptischer Kunst. Munich, Germany.

For further reading, see Gary A. Anderson, "Sacrifice and Sacrificial Offerings (OT)," *ABD* 5:870-86; idem, *Sacrifices and Offerings in Ancient Israel*, HSM 41 (Atlanta: Scholars Press, 1987); Tony W. Cartledge, "Sacrifice," *MDB*, 783-84; and Hans-Josef Klauck, "Sacrifice and Sacrificial Offerings (NT)," trans. Reginald H. Fuller, *ABD* 5:886-91.

multiple connotations. On the one hand, the phrase brings to the fore the woman's role as maintainer of the well-being of the home. This both anticipates the concluding poem in Proverbs 31:10-31 and forms an intertextual relationship with biblical traditions of other great women who nurtured and protected their homes.[1] The word "house" also may refer to a temple or a shrine as in 2 Samuel 7:1-14 and 1 Kings 8:18. In this case, the metaphoric possibilities require the reader to reflect upon what a sacrificial feast in Woman Wisdom's temple might possibly refer to. [Slaughter vs. Sacrifice] The image of hewing "seven pillars" parallels house-building in v. 1 and is easily interpreted by readers as the associated task of providing the supports on which the house is to be constructed. Scholars have reflected extensively upon other possible significances for the "seven pillars" of Wisdom, but nothing is certain. [Wisdom's Seven Pillars]

Wisdom's Seven Pillars

This intriguing phrase offers readers little clue as to its referent or origins. Several explanations for the meaning have been sought on the assumption that the reference was to some literal architectural formation of ancient house-building. The noted "four-room house" of antiquity has been converted by the substitution of the number seven to signal "many pillars," and thus a very grand house (thus Bernard Lang). With that in view, others have argued that the image was a cipher for the composition of the Book of Proverbs. The seven pillars are the seven chapters with special headings (Clifford; Murphy).

Jonas Greenfield proposes that there has been a mistranslation of an original phrase that had the "Seven" as the subject of laying pillars. The translation of 9:1 would be "Wisdom has built her house, The Seven have set its foundations." The word seven connects with an ancient Near Eastern tradition of seven sages, the *apkallu,* who existed before the flood and were humans especially endowed with wisdom by Ea, god of wisdom in Babylonian mythology. These specially endowed sages then in turn instructed humankind in wisdom. Gilgamesh himself, who although he ruled Erech after the flood, is considered "master of the *apkallu.*" Later literature associated the *apkallu* with wisdom. The text in Prov 9:1 may be making an allusion to this very ancient connection.

For further reading, see Jonas Greenfield, "The Seven Pillars of Wisdom (Prov. 9:1)—A Mistranslation," *JQR* 76/1 (July 1985): 13-20E; Erica Reiner, "The Etiological Myth of the 'Seven Sages,'" Orientalia, NS 30 (1961): 1-11; and Jeffery H. Tigay, *The Evolution of the Gilgamesh Epic* (Philadelphia: University of Pennsylvania, 1982).

Richard I. Clifford, *Proverbs* (OTL; Louisville: Westminster John Knox Press, 1999), 105.

Bernhard Lang, "Die sieben Säulen der Weisheit (Sprüche IX 1) im Licht israelitischer Architektur," VT 33 (1983): 488-91.

Roland E. Murphy, *Proverbs* (WBC 22; Nashville: Word, 1998), 58.

It is with this background in view that Wisdom makes her familiar call to the naive and those who lack insight. Verses 1-3 portray her preparation and vv. 4-6 her invitation to the banquet. Eating her bread and drinking her wine lead to life and to understanding. Again, readers are called upon to stretch their imaginations. The metaphor is intended to provoke thoughtful reflection. What is Wisdom's bread upon which a diligent learner might feast? What is the bread and wine that leads to life and understanding? Clearly, the feast provokes the thought of some kind of union with this woman. Verse 4 identifies those to whom Wisdom calls: the simple and naive (*petî*); those who lack heart (*lēb*). The tone changes from invitation to command in v. 5. Those who accept *must* eat and drink, for, as v. 6 clarifies, to eat and drink at Wisdom's table is to begin travel on the path that leads to life and understanding. Despite the sexual overtones, however, it is not a sexual liaison to which these people are invited. Rather, Woman Wisdom invites the simple and naive to come and learn from her. The bread and wine Wisdom offers stands in opposition to that which is stolen and comes from the "other" woman (e.g., 9:17; see 4:17).

Humility and the Fear of Yahweh, 9:7-12

Even though these verses seem rather abruptly to intrude upon Woman Wisdom's appeal, readers could easily interpret them as answering the above questions about "food" for reflection. These verses are not haphazardly arranged. Verse 7a opens with the theme of the scoffer and 12b concludes with that same theme, providing an inclusio for the contents. The contents open with reflections upon instructing scoffers. Verse 7 sets out the two topics that will be addressed in vv. 8 and 9: scoffers and the wicked versus the wise and the righteous. One should not waste one's time with scoffers or the wicked. Rather, one should spend one's time with the wise and the righteous. The admonition implicates the reader, however, not as one who teaches wisdom, but as one who could potentially be taught.

Ultimately, intellectual arrogance and unrighteousness prevent one from feasting at Wisdom's table of learning. The concluding verse in this set, v. 10, makes unambiguous the importance of submission to Yahweh as the beginning of wisdom. Further, this verse duplicates the statement that opens the entire collection of instructions in 1:7. As such, these two provide an inclusio marking the beginning and ending of the entire collection of instructions in chapters 1–9.[2]

As abruptly as she was interrupted, Wisdom reappears in v. 11, characterized by the first person mode of address. The sense of v. 11 seems conveniently to follow the admonitions in vv. 4-6 and thus reinforces the scholarly view that vv. 7-10 are intrusions into Wisdom's speech. Her appeal is, again, to long life (e.g., 3:16, 18; 4:13; 8:35). The conclusion in v. 12 is not so clear, however. It seems to be asserting a rather radical independence and self-reliance over the submissive attitude proposed in vv. 7-10. Bearing the responsibility for one's scoffing seems a reasonable outcome for one of such arrogance. [Responsibility for One's Ignorance]

Responsibility for One's Ignorance

Verse 12 appears to be an assertion of one's responsibility for becoming wise or simply spending life as a scoffer. In the context of vv. 7-12, which deal with those who simply cannot learn, this observation is relevant. Requiring the responsibility to be born by another relieves Wisdom, and the sages, of having to take a clear position on whether or not there are certain incorrigible classes of people who simply cannot learn.

For further reading, see Michael V. Fox, "Who Can Learn? A Dispute in Ancient Pedagogy," in *Wisdom, You Are My Sister*, FS R. E. Murphy (CBQMS 29; Washington: Catholic Biblical Association, 1997), 62-77.

Stolen Water, Hidden Bread, 9:13-18

The similarities between Woman Folly and Woman Wisdom are inviting in a double sense. In the poetic sense the author of the poem is creating irony. It is ironic that someone so similar to Woman Wisdom could be so deadly. In a second sense, however, the poet reflects his bias about the power of women to seduce youths into the wrong lifestyle. Verse 13 makes an unambiguous statement about Woman Folly's lack of control. She is loud and ignorant. The lack of bodily control is antithetical to the wisdom ethos. One who cannot control her speech is one who is not knowledgeable. If she lacks control in those vital areas, other parts of her body lack control as well.

Verses 14-16 are surprising in their depiction of Woman Folly's affinities with Woman Wisdom. Like Wisdom, Folly also sits at the "high places" of the town (i.e., Prov 8:2a), beside the way (i.e., 8:2b). She calls to passersby (i.e., 8:4) who are simple and lack insight (i.e., 8:5; 1:22). Woman Folly calls to those who are vulnerable to her own feast. It is a feast of stolen water and hidden bread. And the feast precedes the fool's descent to the place of the dead, v. 18.

The proverb in v. 17 reflects the subversive nature of Folly's feast, provoking for readers a retrospective look at the opening instruction in 1:8-19. We have enough of the pieces of this puzzle to form an idea of what this riddle-like proverb in 9:17 is about. This woman is like the adulteress in Proverbs 7, and adultery is a form of stealing. She, like Wisdom herself, uses sayings to justify her call. Indeed, secret sexual liaisons are momentarily pleasurable and satisfying. Interestingly, the very first instruction in the collection addresses stealing; the highwaymen lay in wait to take what is not theirs. Whether it is jewels or illicit sex, both activities stand in contrast with Woman Wisdom's call. Both activities lead inexorably to destruction.

CONNECTIONS

Learning to Teach from Two Women Who Care

The ancient poet's use of feminine imagery for caring invites modern readers to begin reflection with the recognition of both the power of gender differentiation and the notions of caring in our own society. It may well be that learning to "care" about others is at the heart of being a good teacher. However, caring by itself is not enough.

Both of these women are presented as caring a great deal about youths. One's caring is immoral, however, and the other is held up as authentic. The traditional bias in modern society is that men "care about" and women "care for," according to Joan C. Tronto.[3] However, Tronto suggests, the stereotype is morally insufficient. It is not that caring is feminine that makes it morally legitimate, but rather the nature of the care that is given. Questions of the morality of caregiving are raised by recognizing whose needs are being met. Whether caregiving creates dependencies or autonomy further complicates matters. To whom care is given intensifies the question still further.

To assume the role of a teacher and to call individuals to embrace wisdom is to give expression to the desire for relationship and care. Though both teachers in this poem are women, and thus evoke for modern readers notions of caring, they offer different kinds of care to be sure. Both women direct their attention to the naive and inexperienced. The one woman cares because she wishes them to become more wise. The other woman cares because she wishes to exploit them. The one act of concern is selfless, the other is selfish.

Imparting wisdom is itself an act of providing the opportunity for autonomy and freedom since it is wisdom that gives such autonomy. The call of Woman Wisdom is ultimately one to forge a relationship that will liberate. From her point of view students must become masters. There can be no sense of any kind of codependency. It is interesting that the union formed with one woman might easily be misconstrued as a union with the other woman. The difference is that a relationship with the other woman enslaves and suppresses. Her existence is maintained only through codependencies. She is neither independent herself, nor does she offer such independence for those who eat at her table.

Excellent teaching does not create codependencies, either. Rather, teachers are to care for students in such a manner that they are free to learn on their own. The outcomes of a relationship with a caring teacher is that one become independent intellectually, emotionally, spiritually, and economically.

NOTES

[1] Claudia Camp, *Wisdom and the Feminine in the Book of Proverbs* (Almond: JSOT Press, 1985), 137-38.

[2] It may well be that at one time 9:10 was the original conclusion to the book of instructions, and v. 13ff. were added in a subsequent edition.

[3] Joan C. Tronto, "Women and Caring," *Gender/Body/Knowledge,* ed. Alison M. Jaggar and Susan R. Bordo (New Brunswick and London: Rutgers University Press, 1986), 174.

RIGHTEOUSNESS VS. WICKEDNESS

Proverbs 10:1-32

The Proverbs of Solomon, 10:1–22:16

At the center of the Book of Proverbs is the collection titled "The Proverbs of Solomon." These sayings are thought to be among the oldest collection of the entire book.[1] Readers should not be concerned that the oldest sayings are not at the beginning of the book, however. Rather, such an editorial arrangement suggests that this collection functions as a core around which other collections are appended (e.g., chs. 1–9; 25–29). In fact, these sayings and proverbs pose a greater reading challenge than the materials in Proverbs 1–9, because at first glance they appear to be arranged in little more than

The Judgment of Solomon

The painting depicts the tradition of Solomon's famous judgment between the competing claims of two women that each was the mother of one child, 1 Kg 3:16-28.

Nicolas Poussin. 1594–1665. *Judgment of Solomon*. 1649. Louvre. Paris, France.

Sayings and Proverbs

AΩ We will refer to the materials contained in 10:1–15:33 as sayings rather than proverbs. This will develop the distinction between assertions that merely make observations (thus, sayings) and those that may bear great levels of figurative or metaphorical meaning (thus, proverbs). For instance, most of the statements in 10:1–15:33 make observations that have literal meanings. The saying in 11:15 expresses the danger of people outside of the community. Offering a guarantee for loans to such outsiders is risky. To be sure, readers benefit greatly by understanding the social setting behind such an assertion, but there is not much basis for further significance here.

By contrast, 14:4 may be treated as a proverb, since it has both literal and figurative meaning. It concerns oxen and grain on the literal level, but these images may take on other significances by virtue of what they represent to a farmer and a businessperson. While farmers must incur the cost of providing feed for the oxen, their overall return is less if they have no oxen at all. The same is true for any business. Hence the oxen are related to grain the way any engine is related to fuel, or business to cost. Such relationships invite reflection upon these other levels of application.

For further reading, see G. B. Caird, *The Language and Imagery of the Bible* (London: Duckworth, 1980); James L. Crenshaw, "Wisdom Literature," *MDB*, 962-65; Roland E. Murphy, "Wisdom in the OT," *ABD* 6:920-31; and J. G. Williams, "The Power of Form: A Study of Biblical Proverbs," in *Gnomic Wisdom*, ed. J. D. Crossan (*Semeia* 17; Chico CA: Scholars Press, 1980), 35-58.

---

random lists. [Sayings and Proverbs] There simply are not modern literary analogies that enable us to have a clear idea as to how we should read such lists.

Nevertheless, scholars have come to recognize that the editors of these proverbs and sayings did arrange them in smaller groups. Usually dominant themes, shared terminology, and linguistic patterns are the keys to such groupings.[2] The task for readers is not simply to reflect upon individual sayings, but to attend to such themes, terminology, and patterns in order to recognize larger groupings and relationships within the collections. Scholars have recognized, for instance, that the thirteen chapters of Proverbs 10:1–22:16 may be subdivided into three smaller sections: 10:1–15:33; 16:1-31; and 17:1–22:16. The sections vary in their thematic concerns and in the kinds of parallelism that dominates. The sayings in 10:1–15:33 are characterized by parallelism that is "antithetical," or contrastive, as we shall call it here. This means that opposing or contrasting ideas or characters are paired together for the purpose of comparison and reflection. The sayings in 17:1–22:16, on the other hand, are characterized by parallels that are more "synthetic," or reiterative. This means that complimentary ideas are doubled and therefore develop comparatively similar thoughts and images. The sayings in 16:1-33 are predominantly reiterative, and reflect a rather decisive break with those in 10:1–15:33. But it is the theological motifs and themes of chapter

16 that make it stand out from the larger context of 10:1–22:16. Thus the oldest collection of proverbs, 10:1–22:17 reflects three major units: 10:1–15:33; 16:1-33; and 17:1–22:16. We turn first to consider the sayings in chapters 10:1–15:33.

What Does Wisdom Profit?, 10:1–15:33

In ways similar to the groupings of the three larger sections mentioned above, there are smaller groupings of sayings within this section. [Semantic, Syntactic, and Thematic] Such groupings may consist of as many as nine proverbs (e.g., 16:1-9) and as few as a pair (as in 10:27 and 28). Sometimes pairs of sayings are joined together in larger clusters (e.g., 10:27-28, 29-30, 31-32). Such groupings often function in the sayings to indicate breaks between collections, sometimes also defining special thematic concerns of materials contained within collections. In the case of 10:1–15:33 such a series of sayings both opens and closes the unit. Proverbs 10:1-5 is a grouping of sayings, symmetrically arranged, that invites reflection upon the potential outcomes of wisdom. Similarly, 15:31-33 close the unit with reflections on those behaviors that lead to wisdom. The main purpose of this opening cluster of proverbs and sayings is to define what wisdom is all about. The closing collection reiterates this opening assertion. Thus, as in Proverbs 1:20-33 and 9:1-18, the editors have bound the collection with a thematic framework of definitive ideas and images. Wisdom is concerned in some ways with "profit."

Semantic, Syntactic, and Thematic

AΩ These three terms are useful tools for understanding possible relationships between sayings. The word semantic refers to those aspects of words that convey meaning. In our usage here it will designate relationships between sayings based upon the common use of similar vocabulary. We will frequently see groups of sayings that share the language and imagery of speech in order to assert the various ways proper speech is of benefit to one who wants to be wise (e.g., 16:21-24, 27-30). Syntactic relationships are those based on patterns of word sequences. This is not so easy to see in English translation. It is quite evident, however, in Hebrew. We have already mentioned one kind of syntactical arrangement such as the chiasm, where words are paralleled in an A B B A fashion. Thematic relationships refer to the use of common ideas or topics. The importance of such categories is in recognizing that all of these (and others) are techniques by which the sages arranged their sayings and proverbs.

For further reading, see James Barr, *The Semantics of Biblical Language* (Oxford: Clarendon, 1961); and Johannes P. Louw, "Semantics," *ABD* 5:1077-81.

The opening group of sayings in 10:1-5 asserts a theme that is affirmed throughout the entire collection, and is therefore the title of the treatment of these verses: "What Does Wisdom Profit?" At the heart of the question is the assumption that seems to be present in these sages' views that one "gets ahead in life" by practicing wisdom. To be sure, getting ahead may be defined variously in terms of finance, community reputation, social relationships, business practices, and home life. In 10:2, for instance, the saying moves from the category of business profit to the reality of the fear of dying: "Treasures gained by wickedness do not profit, but righteousness delivers from death." However, in this saying there is an overwhelming confidence in prolonging life and profiting financially. This confident view is of particular interest since it is challenged by the interest of the later sage, Qoheleth (Ecclesiastes). Qoheleth questions even this, however. His opening assertion, in fact, is followed by that very question: "What do people gain from all the toil at which they toil under the sun" (Eccl 1:3; 3:9; 5:18, 15; see 7:12; 10:10, 11)? The Hebrew words here translated as "profit" and "gain" in Proverbs and Ecclesiastes, respectively, are admittedly not the same Hebrew words. Both sentences nevertheless reflect a sage's investigation about the outcomes of wisdom and work: is righteousness indeed more profitable than wickedness? Is appropriate speech better than inappropriate speech? Does it pay to commit oneself to the fear of the Lord? What does it mean to "profit" anyway? In other words, by reading Proverbs and Ecclesiastes together, as this commentary does by treating the two books together, readers experience one of the most interesting phenomena of the Bible: diverging, even competing, understandings of truth. One may infer that truth is reached through the juxtaposition of contrasting ideas.

"Is wisdom profitable?" is a theme that runs throughout 10:1–22:16. It is a question that will continue to perplex the sages of ancient Israel, as we shall see. The question of what advantage there might be for the righteous one who strives to be wise, in fact, reaches even beyond the confines of these two books of Proverbs and Ecclesiastes. It is surely on the mind of that post-exilic poet who sought to address the satan's chilling question in the folktale of the suffering innocent: "Does Job fear God for nothing?" (Job 1:9).

Righteousness vs. Wickedness, 10:1-32

The opening chapter of 10:1–15:33 is dominated by sayings that contrast either the righteous and the wicked or behaviors that are associated with such people (vv. 2, 3, 6, 7, 11, 16, 20, 21, 24, 25, 28, 30, 31, and 32). One of the most recognizable defining characteristics of both the wise and the righteous is proper speech. It is a theme revisited several times throughout the chapter (vv. 6, 11, 13, 14, 18, 19, 20, 21, 31, 32). By these wisdom values—righteousness vs. wickedness and proper vs. improper speech—the ancient sages offered the criteria by which one could reflect on the relative profitability of wisdom. [Structure at a Glance: Proverbs 10]

Structure at a Glance: Proverbs 10

AΩ An overview of the concerns and themes of the chapter is suggested below as a guide for organizing reading. The symmetrical arrangement indicated by the indents suggests that the focus concern on speech (vv. 6-20) is to be understood as framed by moral and ethical principles.

> Vv. 1-5 Yahweh at the Center
>> Vv. 6-12: Recognizing Them by Their Speech
>> Vv. 13-20: The Speech of the Wise
> Vv. 21-32: The Righteous Are the Wise

Four sections or groupings of sayings may be isolated on the basis of sayings that function to mark thematic boundaries: 1 and 5; 6 and 11; 13 and 20; 21 and 32. We should not assume that the present structural portrayal consists of sayings that have tight thematic, linguistic, or syntactic similarities. The sayings in the latter part of the chapter are only loosely connected. Further, one should not surmise that these sayings were necessarily preserved with the idea of being read within collections. Rather, one should reflect on sayings and proverbs individually and only then consider how individual sayings might relate to others.

After reading this chapter, however, readers may recognize a kind of chiastic structure to the various groups. The two outer groups of sayings (vv. 1-5 and 21-32) are similar in that they highlight Yahweh and righteousness; the two inner groups of sayings are similar in that they emphasize speech, both its importance to wisdom and its role in characterizing the wise.

COMMENTARY

Yahweh at the Center, 10:1-5

These opening five sayings are arranged thematically in a chiastic structure: v. 1—the wise child (A); v. 2—the profitability of wickedness vs. righteousness (B); v. 3—assertion of Yahweh's care for the righteous (C); v. 4—the profitability of diligent work (B'); and v. 5—the definition of a wise child (A'). Set out graphically the thematic relationships might look as follows:

> A (v. 1) The wise child
>> B (v. 2) The profitability of wickedness vs. righteousness
>>> C (v. 3) Yahweh's care for the righteous
>> B' (v. 4) The profitability of diligent work
> A' (v. 5) The wise child

The verse in the structurally central position, v. 3, is a Yahweh saying. Readers will encounter Yahweh sayings frequently throughout the collection and will recognize them as making explicit references to the deity name as legitimation for the claim made. Such a structural arrangement of individual sayings may invite reflection on the sages' convictions that at the heart of human wisdom is the assertion of ultimate reliance upon the deity. This conviction we have already encountered in chapters 1–9 in a more elaborate instructional form. In the present collection the view serves as a thematic touchstone between Proverbs 1–9 and

Proverbs 10–22. Likewise, the reference to "the child" continues to emphasize the idea of instruction of youth that begins in chapters 1–9. The theme occurs again in 13:1 and 15:20, key points in the collection.

Nevertheless, diligent work must accompany one's faith to realize the benefits of wisdom. We shall see that the chapter concludes with three pairs of sayings, 27-28, 29-30, and 31-32, that again assert the profitability of wisdom and righteousness. They provide a fitting conclusion to chapter 10. In two cases, vv. 27 and 29, the pairs are introduced with assertions about the fear of Yahweh. Underlying these sayings is the common assumption that Yahweh sustains an ordered universe that rewards righteousness and work. However, it is not clear which one is dominant and to what extent the natural order of the universe works independently of Yahweh's intervention.

Recognizing Them by Their Speech, 10:6-11 (12)

A second group of sayings is implied by the repetition of 6b and 11b. These two half-lines (stichoi) of poetry are identical and read: "And the mouth of the wicked conceals violence." Such repetition may serve as a device to mark the boundaries of this particular group (and other groups) of sayings. The weakness of relying upon such rhetorical markers is that one might also expect the two boundary verses to stand in some thematic relationship with each other. This is not the case here. Verse 6a does not offer a convincing thematic connection to 6b: "Blessings are upon the head of the righteous, but the mouth of the wicked conceals violence." At least the two halves of v. 11 are more directly related to each other since both have to do with speech (imagery of the mouth): "The mouth of the righteous is a fountain of life, but the mouth of the wicked conceals violence." We see similar repetition in vv. 8 and 10 in the phrase "the babbling fool will come to ruin."[3] Verse 10b therefore seems out of place since its opposing stichos concerns the dissimulator "who winks the eye." Verse 8b seems to be in the proper place relative to 8a, contrasting the "wise of heart."

Sayings on speech outline the short cluster in vv. 6-11 and thus anticipate revisitation of the same theme in Ecclesiastes (e.g., 1:8; 4:6; 5:2; 12:10, 11). Within the boundaries of vv. 6-11 there are contrasts between the righteous and the wicked (vv. 6, 7, 9, and 11) and the wise and the foolish (vv. 8 and 10). There may be two sets of sayings in this section that might be read as pairs: 6-7 and 8-9. Such positioning of two pairs invites readers' reflection upon their relationship with each other. How do the ideas of righteousness and wisdom counterpoise the ideas of wickedness and foolishness? With wisdom, readers are confronted with both the received traditions and with something that is self-evident in nature. This implies the possibility that righteousness is simply a matter of what is commonly known and readily available to all who would but examine the world about them.

In the case of vv. 6 and 7, we encounter two sayings that contrast the righteous and the wicked. Both 6a and 7a share similar terms for righteous, *ṣaddîq*, and blessing, *běrākôt*. Both 6b and 7a share similar terms for the wicked, *rěšāʿîm*. Verses 8 and 9 are not so closely connected through language. Still, they would appear to be concerned about related themes. Perhaps v. 9 functions to comment on v. 8a by further defining what it means "to take commandments" (*miṣwôt*). Verse 9 defines the "wise heart" of v. 8 by offering an example: it is someone who "walks in integrity." Wisdom, then, is further defined by the values that result from the contrast of these verses. In 9b the image of the one "who perverts" (*měʿaqqēš*) his way stands in opposition to the one "who walks in integrity." Only the one who walks in integrity can be assured of security as an outcome.

Verse 10 would seem to comment further on the immediately preceding half-line in 9b. In 9b we have just encountered an allusion to one who "perverts" his way. Such a one is further characterized as "winking the eye," also a metaphor for deceit and subterfuge. Such ones—who pervert the way and who wink the eye—cause trouble and pain. Verse 12, although outside of the implied boundary of this grouping, could well be read as a saying that has been added because of the linguistic connection to v. 11. Both share the verb "to conceal or hide" (*yěkasseh* and *těkasseh*). Against the assertion of v. 11b—that the wicked conceals violence—v. 12b asserts that love conceals or covers all transgressions.[4] The juxtaposition of these two verses, however, invites reflection on the relationship between wise speech and the attitudes of love and hate.

The Speech of the Wise, 10:13-21 (22)

Verses 13-21 are a still more loosely defined group of sayings. Both outer sayings concern the topic of speech and contrast proper speech with that of a fool. Six of the nine sayings (vv. 13, 14, 18-21) address the topic of speech, while three concern the rewards of certain lifestyles (vv. 15, 16, and 17). Smaller groupings within this collection provide the challenge of further reflection, however. Verses 13-14 are thematically related, sharing common language, "wisdom" and "the wise" (*ḥokmâ* and *ḥăkāmîm*). Verses 15 and 16 are syntactically similar and have in common the word "ruin" (*mĕḥittat*). Verse 17 would seem to comment on v. 16, especially 16a, in that both trace the path to "life" (*lĕḥayyîm*). Verses 18-21 share the common topic of speech and should be taken as a small group within the larger loose collection. The art of the poet is in utilizing one physiological aspect of the process of speech—lips, tongue, words—to stand for the whole process. This is called synecdoche.

Readers will be hard pressed to recognize any carefully defined or readily evident structure to this section of chapter 10. Still, we may encounter this section of sayings as a chiastic sequence of topics on, first, speech (vv. 13-14), profit (vv. 15-17), and speech (vv. 18-21).

A juxtaposition is again set up between topics that asks readers to consider the profitability of proper and improper speech. Readers are therefore to reflect upon the central sayings in this group (vv. 15-17), which seek out the "way to life" through either righteousness or wisdom. The verses mix the images of the fortress, the right way, righteousness and wisdom. [The Way] Further, in view of the sayings at the outer boundaries of this unit (vv. 13 and 21), proper speech is a vital component of the right way.

The Way

AΩ The Hebrew word "way" (*derek*) is a most common word. It occurs frequently in conjunction with words such as "path" or "step." Perhaps its commonness is what provokes extensive figurative significance in the wisdom literature and throughout the Old Testament. It may refer, for example, to a path on which people pass, as in Gen 35:3 or Eccl 10:3. The word may refer to courses of nature, as in Prov 6:6. It may refer to human ethical behavior, as in Ps 5:8 and many occurrences in the Proverbs. The image may be taken even more abstractly to refer to the will and purposes of God, as in Job 26:14 and 40:19.

In the wisdom literature the sages see the human predicament as one of finding the right way, the appropriate path, behavior, response, indeed, the will and purposes of the Lord. The need to choose the correct way that is in harmony with the order of the universe is certainly a justifying cause for having wisdom.

Engraving illustrating John Bunyan's *Pilgrim's Progress*. Pilgrim's travels lead him to a town called Vanity Fair.

For further reading, see Norman Habel, "The Symbolism of Wisdom in Proverbs 1-9," *Int* 26 (1972): 131-57; and Michael V. Fox, "What the Book of Proverbs Is About," in *Congress Volume Cambridge 1995* (VTSup 66; Leiden: E. J. Brill, 1997), 153-67.

Verse 22 is a Yahweh saying and seems to be unrelated to the preceding group of sayings. On closer examination the saying offers comment on vv. 15 and 16 by asserting the true source of wealth. It further corresponds to vv. 6-7, specifying that Yahweh is the source of blessing. However, it shares the word "makes rich" (*taʿăšîr*) with v. 4. We may therefore be reminded of the sages' overall concern to assert the profitability of wisdom and righteousness (cf. Eccl 1:3; 3:17; 8:10-13). Verse 22b is of special significance in this connection, depending upon how it is read. NRSV's translation, "and he adds no sorrow with it," implies that Yahweh's blessing comes without any sorrow. In this sense it recalls the psalmist's assertion that he had never "seen the righteous forsaken or their children begging bread" (Ps 37:25). Verse 22b may also be translated "and toil (*ʿeseb*) adds nothing to it," calling to mind the assertion in Psalm 127:1: "Unless the LORD builds the house, those who build it labor in vain." This statement, though using a different word root for "labor" (*ʿāmēlû*), is intended in the psalm and perhaps also in the saying to assert the Lord as the ultimate source of all blessing. If there is an echo, it takes on darker implications in Ecclesiastes, which also asserts, "There is nothing better for mortals than to eat and drink, and find enjoyment in their toil" (*baʿămālô*), 2:24. For Qoheleth, toil without the assurance of Yahweh's blessing is all that there is.

The Righteous Are the Wise, 10:23-32

The final group of sayings, with the exception of v. 26, all contrast the righteous with the wicked and explore which behavior, righteous or wise, is more profitable. The words for righteous and wicked, *saddîq* and *rāšāʿ*, occur in seven of the final ten sayings (vv. 24, 25, 27, 28, 30, 31, and 32). There further appear to be at least two main subgroups of sayings, vv. 23-25 and vv. 27-32. Verse 26 serves as an independent saying dividing the two subgroups. The noticeable distinction between these subgroups is the thematic sequencing. In vv. 23-25 the topic introduced in each first line concerns the wicked. The second line follows with an observation about the righteous. The positions of these topics are reversed in vv. 27-32, where each saying opens with an observation about the righteous or its equivalent.

The three sayings in vv. 23-25 are of further significance because they reflect a progression of thought.[5] The opening saying actually contrasts the actions of the wise and the foolish. Not surprisingly, however, the actions of the foolish are "wrong" (*zimmâ*),[6] the same

kind of behavior one would expect of the wicked (*rāšāʿ*). "Dread"
awaits the wicked and represents the state in which they live: the
results of their actions are not fully realized in the present, but are
inevitable, v. 24. Finally, the tempest comes, v. 25, and sweeps the
wicked away. The reader is tempted, then, to read v. 26 in the same
context. Even though v. 26 offers a simile on laziness and recalls a
different theme treated already in v. 4, one cannot help now but
think of laziness in the same category as *zimmâ*, v. 23. Both behaviors are foolish and inevitably face the same fate as that of the
wicked.

The final grouping, vv. 27-32, appears to comprise three pairs of
sayings. Verses 27 and 29 are both Yahweh sayings and are paralleled with sayings on the righteous. Verse 27 reflects on long life for
those who fear Yahweh, the righteous, and the contrasting short
years of the wicked. Verse 28 contemplates the reality of the "hope"
(*tôḥelet*) for the righteous and the disappointing "expectation"
(*tiqwat*) for the wicked. Similarly, v. 30 interprets v. 29. The Lord's
"way" is a stronghold. The result is that the righteous shall never be
moved; by contrast, the wicked shall not remain in the land. The
saying associates retention of land with the blessing and security of
faith in Yahweh. The concluding pair continues the motif of contrasting righteous and wicked, while revisiting the theme of speech
already encountered in the chapter (vv. 6b, 8b, 11, 13, 14, 18, 20,
and 21). These two sayings are a fitting recapitulation of the dominant concerns of the chapter: righteous vs. wicked; the
characterization of the righteous as wise; and wisdom as a phenomenon that comes to expression through proper speech.

CONNECTIONS

What Does Wisdom Profit?

Information is the catchword of the post-modern age. The term
"post-modern" generally designates the era of intellectual rebellion
against the fundamental assumptions, structures, and strategies of
meaning that characterize the modern age. One of the central concerns of the modern age, for instance, has been science and its
assumptions. The key assumption that has now fallen into severe
questioning is that science ever provided any kind of method of
reaching truly value-free, that is, unbiased, knowledge. One of the
fundamental assertions of post-modern intellectualism is that all

knowledge is shaped by limited and therefore contextually bound perspectives and conclusions. The notion of any kind of absolute truth must be abandoned for more pluralistic ideas of truth. Information is available to all; what constitutes knowledge is in the minds of individuals.[7]

Mastering the many accesses to this information, then, is the hallmark of the educated person. However, information on its own is of little help in making the universe a meaningful place. It must be ordered and arranged. A library with no card catalogue, with no index, is a fitting analogy to the information age in which we live. How does one know where to go? What are the relationships between the categories? How does raw information join together to make knowledge? How does a person gain access? Such impulses, though obviously not stated in these terms, were behind the thinking of the ancient sages who began to order these sayings. Something like a conviction that information became knowledge when the learners committed their lives to Yahweh was foundational in this mode of thought. In other words, Yahweh became the center point from which various strands of thought, experience, and observation had their beginnings and endings.

This does not mean that there were no conflicts or that experience was always self-evidently harmonious. Rather, it was for the learner to make the connections. We have in this opening collection a confident assertion that, if one but learns the ways of the wise, one will make the connections that lead to prosperity. The world turns on justice so that the wicked will eventually be punished and the righteous will prosper (vv. 2, 3, 6, 7, 9, 11, 16, 20, 21, 22, 25, 27, 28, 29, 31, 32). Diligent work is rewarded with prosperity (vv. 4, 5, 15, 26). Proper speech is a way of determining who is who (vv. 6, 11, 13, 14, 18, 19, 20, 21, 31, 32). What individuals say and do determines who they are and whether they will receive the blessing the Lord has in store for the righteous. The connection between wisdom and righteousness is no clearer than here: it makes good sense to serve the Lord.

What might it mean to live in a world such as this? Individuals would spend their lives knowing that everything fits into a harmonious whole, in theory. Everything would exist for a purpose and contribute a vital link to some part of the whole. The task for all humanity would be to find its appropriate place in the universe so engineered with such acute attention to every detail. Wickedness, poverty, and suffering could all be explained in terms of ignorance, laziness, or sin. Education would not be so much about learning how to figure things out as about memorizing the patterns of order underlying society and the universe. Society would need only to learn how things worked. Individuals would then locate their place within that society. Religion would be defined in terms of quantifiable behaviors—worship, good deeds, study, service—instead of the day-to-day flux of inscrutable relationships between God,

Waiting for Godot

Waiting for Godot is a modern play written in the absurdist style by Samuel Beckett. Absurdism generally aims to portray the meaninglessness of existence through the mocking of conventional modes of creating meaning. The struggle with meaning is captured in the following exchange between Gogo (Estragon) and Didi (Vladimir), wherein the most natural response—to help someone in need—is made to have cosmic significance.

Set designer Steve Gilliam illustrates perfectly the starkness of the set needed for the play. *Waiting for Godot.*

(In response to Estragon's uncertainty about responding to Pozzo's cry for help:) Vladimir: "Let us not waste our time in idle discourse! (*Pause. Vehemently.*) Let us do something, while we have the chance! It is not every day that we are needed. Not indeed that we personally are needed. Others would meet the case equally well, if not better. To all mankind they were addressed, those cries for help still ringing in our ears! But at this place, at this moment of time, all mankind is us, whether we like it or not. Let us make the most of it, before it is too late! Let us represent worthily for once the foul brood to which a cruel fate consigned us! What do you say? (*Estragon says nothing.*) It is true that when with folded arms we weigh the pros and cons we are no less a credit to our species. The tiger bounds to the help of his congeners without the least reflexion, or else he slinks away into the depths of the thickets. But that is not the question. What are we doing here, *that* is the question. And we are blessed in this, that we happen to know the answer. Yes, in this immense confusion one thing alone is clear. We are waiting for Godot to come.

For further reading, see John Killinger, *World in Collapse: The Vision of Absurd Drama* (New York: Dell, 1971); and Bob Mayberry, *Theatre of Discord: Dissonance in Beckett, Albee, and Pinter* (Madison: Farleigh Dickenson University Press, 1989).

Samuel Beckett, *Waiting for Godot* (New York: Grove Weidenfeld, 1982), 51a and b.

people, and events. In fact, nothing is ultimately inscrutable except the Lord, and the Lordself is revealed through wisdom.

The questioning in Ecclesiastes sounds harsh in comparison to the ideal world described above. This later sage calls our attention to the ways in which society and the universe do not in reality reflect such ordered control. Qoheleth's questioning is not so different in tone from that of Gogo and Didi, Samuel Beckett's two characters who continue to wait for Godot—even though it is clear that Godot is not coming.[8] Life for these two characters is nothing more than passing the time, engaging in meaningless talk so they will not have to think. [Waiting for Godot] To those like Gogo and Didi, thinking has the opposite effect from that in the Proverbs. Instead of providing a basis for confidence, thinking reveals the emptiness and absurdity of all existence. Words, even empty palaver, become a way of creating some kind of order and meaning against a meaningless, empty, absurd backdrop of reality.

NOTES

[1] Richard J. Clifford, *Proverbs* (OTL; Louisville: Westminster John Knox Press, 1999), 3; Leo Perdue, *Proverbs* (IBC; Louisville: Westminster John Knox Press, 2000), 158: "The individual sayings, however, likely covered a wide span of time, encompassing the early monarchy through the initial generations of the postexilic period."

[2] See Ted Hildebrandt, for instance, "Proverbial Pairs: Compositional Units in Proverbs 10-29," *JBL* 107/2 (1988): 207-24; also, Roland E. Murphy, *Proverbs* (WBC 22; Nashville: Thomas Nelson, 1998), 64-69.

[3] This is only so in the Hebrew text, however. The Greek text of v. 10 reads, "but the one who rebukes boldly makes peace."

[4] See the NT reinterpretation in 1 Pet 4:8.

[5] Otto Plöger, *Sprüche Salomos (Proverbia)* (BKAT 17; Neukirchen: Neukirchener Verlag, 1984), 29.

[6] See similar usage of the word in Hos 6:9 and Job 31:11.

[7] For further reading, see Elizabeth Deeds Ermarth, "Postmodernism," RHP 7:587-90; and D. Harvey, *The Condition of Postmodernity* (Oxford: Blackwell, 1992).

[8] Samuel Beckett, *Waiting for Godot* (New York: Grove Weidenfeld, 1982), 51a and b.

JUSTICE FOR THE RIGHTEOUS

Proverbs 11:1-31

By comparison with chapter 10, Proverbs 11 does not consist of such clearly evident groupings of sayings. Clearly, v. 1 shares vocabulary with 10:32 in the Hebrew word *rāṣôn*, translated "acceptable" in v. 32, and "delight" in 11:1. It is of further interest that 11:1 is a Yahweh saying, which speaks of just weights and measures. Verse 11:32 speaks of the rewards of the righteous and the wicked. One could infer that the two sayings on measures and rewards, beginning and ending chapter 11, provide the most fitting framework for reflecting upon the fates of the righteous and the wicked. This thematic echo presses further still the overall concern of the section with the profitability of wisdom. [Structure at a Glance: Proverbs 11]

Structure at a Glance: Proverbs 11

AΩ The following structural scheme might facilitate reading.

Vv. 1-2 Honesty Is Yahweh's Policy
    Vv. 3-15 Deciding One's Destiny
    Vv. 16-22 Fateful Behavior
    Vv. 24-30 A Certain Outcome
    V. 31 The Righteous "Repaid" on Earth

The main groupings of the chapter are vv. 3-15, 16-22, and 24-26. The remaining few sayings in 27-30 are related, and perhaps structurally so, but are best separated from these three groups. Verse 2 is independent. Within vv. 3-15 there are at least two subgroups that reflect upon the fates of the righteous and the wicked: vv. 3-8 and 9-14. Verse 15 appears to continue broadly the themes of vv. 9-14, although it is distinctive enough to stand on its own. Verse 16, a saying on the gracious woman, is balanced by v. 22, which reflects upon the beautiful woman who lacks sense. Verses 17-21 comprise another cluster of sayings that contrasts the fates of the righteous and the wicked.

There is a possible relationship between 11:1 and 11:31 suggesting a thematic echo framing the entire chapter. These two verses share similar vocabulary. The Hebrew text of 11:31 has the word *yĕšullām*, "repaid," and 11:1 speaks of the *'eben šĕlēmâ*, "accurate weight." Both words, "repaid" and "accurate," share the Hebrew root *šālam* on which other Hebrew words meaning wholeness, soundness, and welfare are based.

COMMENTARY

Prophets and Sages

There is certainly a danger in assuming that knowledge, especially of such ethical values common to all members of ancient societies, would have been the exclusive intellectual property of one group within a particular society. One is justified, therefore, in reckoning the ethical and moral convictions of the sages to be also those of prophets, priests, and others. While prophetic oracles come to us in different genres from those of wisdom, there was nevertheless a strong interchange of ideas across the culture—as implied by Prov 11:1.

In the cases of the sayings, readers will frequently encounter strong connections, both in form and substance, with laws found in the Old Testament law codes. The difference between a law code and a saying is their hypothetical accessibility to people. Citizens carry sayings around within them; law codes, by contrast, are externally regulatory (see Westermann). One should compare Deut 19:14, 27:17 and Prov 22:28, 23:10; Deut 23:16 and Prov 20:10; Deut 16:20 and Prov 10:2, 11:19, 12:28, 16:31, 21:21.

For further reading, see Joseph Blenkinsopp, *A History of Prophecy in Israel/Judah* (London: SCM Press, 1983); idem, *Sage, Priest, Prophet* (Louisville: Westminster John Knox Press, 1995); idem, *Wisdom and Law in the Old Testament* (Oxford: Oxford University Press, 1983).

Claus Westermann, *Roots of Wisdom,* trans. J. Daryl Charles (Louisville: Westminster John Knox Press, 1995), 40-41.

Honesty Is Yahweh's Policy, 11:1-2

The opening saying reminds readers of both prophetic and legal texts that express a desire for honest transactions in the marketplace. The eighth-century prophet Micah, as one example, condemned evil balances (e.g., 6:11), and such views were later legislated in the Josianic reforms (e.g., Deut 25:15). The saying is revisited in various forms throughout the entire collection of proverbs (e.g., 16:11; 20:10, 23). [Prophets and Sages] The symbolism of a balance may be expanded for the modern reader. The use of a balance in the afterlife to determine one's final fate was common in Egyptian mythology. That this verse should open several collections of sayings on the fates of the righteous and the wicked is therefore doubly appropriate. [Balances in the Egyptian Book of the Dead] Verse 2, however, stands on its own and does not share any thematic, semantic, or syntactic similarity with the immediate context. Nevertheless, it articulates a familiar adage, colloquially expressed as "pride goes before a fall" (cf. 15:33; 16:18; 18:12).

Deciding One's Destiny, 11:3-15

This larger group of sayings generally addresses the destinies of the righteous and the wicked, although in vv. 9-14 (15) there is a noticeable change from the destinies that accrue to individuals to those that accrue to the community. Verses 3-6 seem to exhibit some commonness of theme but do not necessarily stand as a group. Verses 3 and 6 contrast characteristics of the "upright," *yĕšārîm,* and the "treacherous," *bōgĕdîm.* Verses 3 and 5 share imagery of guidance in the path or way. Verses 5 and 6 would appear to be a pair connected thematically, syntactically, and semantically. Both verses contrast the fates of the righteous and wicked. Verse 4 offers several possibilities for connection by contrasting the efficacy of wealth and righteousness in the face of death or suffering. The saying is formulated, however,

Balances in Egyptian
Book of the Dead

Balances served a very pragmatic purpose of weighing in the metalworking trades of antiquity. The balance had a mythological significance in the judgment scenes from the *Book of the Dead*. This text is a collection of texts originally written in the pyramids of fifth and sixth dynasty Egyptian pharaohs and on the interior of coffins of Middle Kingdom members of noble classes. The texts contained magical incantations that were believed to

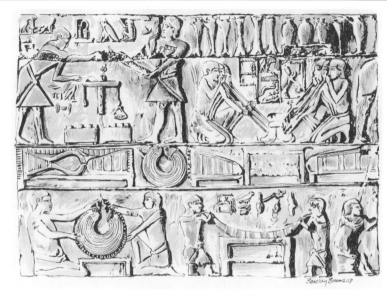

Tomb relief depicting goldworking scenes. Note balance in upper left. *Sakkarah*, tomb of Mereru-ka.

be useful to the dead as they passed through the underworld. In the great hall of judgment stands *Mayet*, spirit of justice. *Anubis*, one of the deities of the underworld, watches the scales to see that the heart, which is being weighed, does not lie (see [The Heart]).

Part of the text that was to be recited by the one being judged included a repudiation of sins. There were forty-two sins specifically that were repudiated before forty-two deities, each of which was responsible for one specific. As Jack Finegan notes, "Although the Book of the Dead in most of its parts and in most of its use was a book of magical charms, it reveals a perception of the truth that happiness after death is dependent upon the ethical quality of earthly life."

For further reading, see "Book of the Dead," MMM 2:257-61; "Egypt," MMM 6:727-36; and M. Lurker, *Gods and Symbols of Ancient Egypt*, rev. Peter Clayton (Great Britain: Thames and Hudson, 1984).

Jack Finegan, *Light from the Ancient Past*, vol. 1 (Princeton NJ: Princeton University Press, 1959), 101.

in terms of "profitability," and thus echoes the same question that is posed in 10:2 and implied throughout chapters 10–15.

Verse 7 stands out as the only saying that is not contrastive; both statements in the verse reinforce each other. The Hebrew text is corrupt, reading something like, "When the wicked die, their hope perishes; and the hope of strength passes away." NRSV translates the word that might be taken as "strength, or vigor," *ʾônîm*, as *ʾawonîm*, "the godless, or unjust."[1] In contrast to the independence of v. 7, vv. 8 and 9 seem to pair together on the basis of a shared verb, the Niphal of *ḥālaṣ*, "to be rescued, delivered," and the opposition between the righteous and the impious. Verse 9 transitions into a string of sayings that reflect upon the wider implications of righteousness and wickedness for the community. Both 9 and 12 share reflections on the implications for the community of foolish speech: "the mouths of the godless" in v. 9a opposes "the man of

Community Ethos in Antiquity

The development of Western Culture is characterized by a growing emphasis upon the individual over the claims of the community. What a contrast this creates with antiquity where, generally speaking, the community was more important than the individual. Aristotle argued that there could be no human life apart from the *polis* (the community); that is, one could not be fully human without living in community.

To a great extent, this perspective is shared by the ancient Hebrew and expressed in these sayings. Many of the sayings in Proverbs argue for what one might call moral individualism. That is, individuals have their own moral consciences and are singularly responsible for moral choices they make. Only such an assumption could explain the many admonitions to individuals to receive wisdom. In that way they would make choices informed by wisdom. Nevertheless, individuals are more or less absorbed politically, socially, and legally by the group of which they are a part. The implications are that the ultimate good is that which accrues to the community, not to the individual.

For further reading, see Paul D. Hanson, "Community," *ABD* 1:1099-1103; and idem, *The People Called: The Growth of Community in the Bible* (San Francisco: Harper/Collins, 1986).

---

understanding who remains silent" in 12b. Both verses consider the destruction that comes to one's neighbor, *rē'ēhû*. These verses surround vv. 10 and 11, both of which depict the city (*qiryâ* and *qāret*) that prospers because of the good that comes to the righteous and the misfortune that comes to the wicked (e.g., 11:28a and 29). The framing verses, vv. 9-12, joined with the two inner verses, vv. 10-11, leave the impression that it is ultimately the propriety of speech that is of such benefit to the community at large. [Community Ethos in Antiquity]

The thematic concerns of vv. 9-12 could easily be extended to the next three verses as well, since vv. 13-15 reflect upon the social implications of "gossip," "guidance," and "strangers." The "gossip" or "slanderer" (*rākîl*) of v. 13 poses an interesting contrast, however, to the behavior of the wicked of 10:6 and 11. The wicked in these two sayings "conceals violence"; the "slanderer" fails to conceal a word or keep a confidence.

Fateful Behavior, 11:16-22

Verses 16 and 22 may function as markers for a group of sayings (vv. 17-21) on the fates of the righteous and the wicked. The two outer sayings, vv. 16 and 22, do not show any apparent connection other than that they are both about women. The NRSV translation of v. 16 is based upon the LXX translation. The Masoretic version lacks lines b and c of the present translation and therefore consists only of "A gracious woman gets honor, but the aggressive (masculine!) gains riches." In this form, 16a seems to foreshadow the statement in Proverbs 31:30, "Charm is deceitful and beauty is vain, but a woman who fears the LORD is to be praised." The Greek translator added lines after stichs "a" and "b," since it was likely unclear how a female could be compared to a male.[2] Adding v. 16 to this group, however, forces readers to reflect at a higher level, recalling that wisdom and its righteousness is a feminine principle (e.g., Prov 1:22-33; 8:1-31; and 9:1-6) and often stands over against the domination of the masculine.

Verses 17-21 revisit the theme of contrasting fates for the righteous and the wicked. The NRSV translation of v. 17 does not do justice to the ambiguities of this opening verse. The subject of the saying could just as easily be "rewarding oneself" as opposed to "those who are kind." In this case the claim would be that those who are not kind to themselves will not be kind to others. Later sages, such as Jesus ben Sirach, also urge the importance of some measure of self-interest: "Do not deprive yourself of a day's enjoyment; do not let your share of desired good pass by you" (Sir 14:14). The following verse, v. 18, might then function to establish a boundary to any self-centeredness that leads to wickedness. Verse 19 provides the climax of the three in its conclusion that those who pursue wickedness shall die, and is finally punctuated by a Yahweh saying in v. 20. The language and passive voice of v. 21—"will not go unpunished—suggests still further reflection on the claim in v. 20, that Yahweh is involved in judging the wicked. Interestingly, the cliché statement "abomination of Yahweh" (*tôʿăbat yhwh*) of v. 20 and the idiom "be assured" (*yād lĕyād*), along with other vocabulary shared by these two, are combined in 16:5.

A Certain Outcome, 11:22-31

The final sayings of the chapter seem to be a loosely connected group, if they are connected at all. Readers will observe that vv. 23, 30, and 31 are sayings about the righteous and thus may function as a general framework for reflecting upon those sayings within. Verse 23 revisits a theme encountered in v. 7 and provides contrast with reflection upon the hope of both the righteous and the wicked. Verse 31 concludes the entire chapter by asserting that the reward for both righteousness and wickedness is "in the land," a phrase that likely has more to do with the certainty of retribution than with the contrast between present life and afterlife. ["Afterlife" in the Old Testament Literature]

Verses 24-26 appear to have a thematic interconnection in reflecting upon the paradox of generosity and prosperity. A similar kind of paradox stands behind related sayings of Jesus (e.g.,

---

"Afterlife" in the Old Testament Literature

The reflections upon God's judgment of the wicked inevitably surface Christian assumptions about death and the afterlife. For many Christians it is difficult to think of death apart from the post-Easter experience of resurrection. In this view, Jesus was awakened from death to new life, and thus precedes all of his followers in that new life (see [The Jaws of Death] and [Theodicy]).

No such concept informs the thinking of the Old Testament writers, however. For them death is the end of life. Life, defined in its fullest expression as praise of Yahweh, ceases when death encroaches (Ps 30:8-10; Isa 38:16-20). Thus, not only did life cease, but praise did as well. The Psalms give expression to the deep disappointment and even anger at death's incursions (Pss 6 and 102), despite the value of long life and old age held by others (Prov 16:31).

One of the most intriguing expressions of the foreboding of death comes in Eccl 12:1-8. Death is the culmination of a process of growing old, a process of losing one's faculties and gradually returning to the dust from whence one comes. Indeed, this later sage wonders who knows what comes after this life (Eccl 6:12b).

For further reading, see L. R. Bailey, *Biblical Perspectives on Death* (OBT; Philadelphia: Westminster, 1979); Norman R. Gulley, "Death," *ABD* 2:108-11; and Bruce Vawter, "Intimations of Immortality and the Old Testament," *JBL* 91 (1972): 158-71.

Mark 4:25; Luke 19:26). Those who give liberally are those who prosper. If we read these three as thematically related, v. 26 would seem to be the climactic verse because it offers the most concrete image of one kind of generosity. The verse imagines the wealthy farmer who plays the market, so to speak, withholding his grain until he pushes the prices up, then selling at an exorbitant profit. Such would appear to be the sort of behavior condemned by the prophet Amos (e.g., 8:4-8).

Verses 27-29 do not share any thematic or semantic connections. However, they are syntactically similar; each of the three verses opens with the Qal masculine participle functioning as a noun. The similarities stop there, however: v. 27 contrasts the one who "seeks" good with the one "seeking" evil; v. 28 abandons the contrastive style in statement "b" by simply commenting on statement "a," which concerns the one who "trusts" in his wealth. Verse 29 parallels v. 28 syntactically because its "b" statement develops the "a" statement with comment and not simply a contrastive statement. What specifically is to be understood by the phrase "the one who troubles his house," beyond the general supposition of bringing some sort of shame to his family through foolish behavior, is uncertain. The word *'ākar*, "to trouble," occurs in the context of Jacob's accusation against his sons Simeon and Levi for their murder of Hamor and Shechem for the rape of Dina (Gen 34:30).[3]

The concluding verses 30 and 31 are both reflections on the righteous one (*ṣaddîq*). The NRSV translation of v. 30b stems from the LXX rendering of *ḥākām*, "wise," as *ḥāmās*, "violence." This creates a statement contrasting the fruit of the righteous with that of violence. One intriguing possibility that retains the Masoretic text is the understanding of *lōqēaḥ*, ordinarily rendered as "to take," as an image of understanding and comprehension, "to understand." This is its general meaning in Proverbs 1:3, for instance. The translation of 30b would then be "'one who understands souls' is wise." As such, this translation would also have the advantage of retaining the text as its stands.[4] Verse 31 concludes the chapter by returning to an image of just retribution for the righteous, echoing the concerns for equity and fairness that began the chapter in the saying on honest balances in v. 1.

CONNECTIONS

On Life's Fairness

"It is simply not fair for me to pay taxes and then have the government give my money to people who don't work," some say. "It's just not fair," one businessman recently exclaimed. "I give my offerings, I pray, I worship, I care for the sick and poor. Why are my children dressed in rags? Why is my house in disrepair? Why is my health failing?" We have all probably thought or even voiced words such as these. More than we know, or are willing to admit, most people are profoundly persuaded by the principle that life should be fair. This chapter begins and ends with concrete images of economic justice. The collection of sayings we have considered here are sandwiched between assertions of the justice of the Lord's scales, with the implication that people get what they deserve in life. We have seen that the chapter is dominated by sayings that contrast the fates of the righteous and the wicked. The righteous prosper, the wicked do not. One should think these to be comforting thoughts. Certainly, such views represent the confident expressions of that ordered and harmonious reality described in the preceding chapter.

Philip K. Howard's book *The Death of Common Sense* explores the way Americans practice justice.[5] The tacit assumption of the book is that Americans do not practice law any longer. Rather, they expect the law to do all of the work for them. Because society now strives for exactitude, the notion of common law has been replaced by ironclad rules. Howard's narrative traces specific examples of people abandoning reasonability and common sense for written law—concerning everything. The idea of reasonable people behaving with accountability is abandoned in favor of a statute concerning even the most minuscule activity. In other words, Howard's thesis is more about how Americans use the law than it is about the law itself. The unhealthy way we believe in law leads to the claim that "law is suffocating America." One can even muse in reflection whether it is law that is ultimately so suffocating, or the presumption that life ought to be fair.

As we read the ancient sages' assertions of a just and moral universe, we also wonder how they might have thought about such issues. Were the views expressed in their sayings and instructions like statutes, providing bases for people to cry out whenever justice was ostensibly violated? Or were they more like common law, assertions of general principles that guided common sense? We are not able to say with any measure of certainty how the sages held their beliefs, but the alternatives posed between common law and statutory law provide us an analogy for thinking about how we might hold to our own views of a just universe. There are broad, general, overarching principles of justice by which the universe is governed. These are not written in stone, however. When injustice occurs, arbitration must take place. Peace must be negotiated anew, adhering as much as is possible to the general principles of justice. A new equilibrium must be established that takes into account both the general principles and the experiences of injustice. But speaking in absolute terms, as though one were quoting from the statute book, violates common sense.

NOTES

[1] Richard Clifford, *Proverbs* (OTL; Louisville: Westminster John Knox Press, 1999), 122, takes the verse as concerning wealth, thus climaxing the first six verses.

[2] William McKane, *Proverbs* (London: SCM Press, 1970), 430-31; Clifford, *Proverbs*, 124.

[3] McKane, *Proverbs*, 429-30, where he comments on the phrase "to trouble his house" (*'okēl bĕtô*); Clifford, *Proverbs*, 126.

[4] See the argument of Daniel Snell, "'Taking Souls' in Prov XI:30," *VT* 33/3 (1983): 362-65.

[5] Philip K. Howard, *The Death of Common Sense* (New York: Random House, 1995).

FOUNDATIONS FOR SUCCESS

Proverbs 12:1-28

Proverbs 12 reiterates the overall exploration of the profitability of wisdom, which concerns the entirety of Proverbs 10–15. Like other opening sayings in the section—10:1, 13:1, 14:1, and 15:2—12:1 asserts the importance of wisdom by reflecting upon the student's receptivity to discipline and reproof. Readers may construe the chapter in two halves. The second half of the chapter is introduced in v. 15, which asserts that the difference between the fool and the wise is that the latter listens to the counsel of the wise. This is related to the concerns of v. 1, and thus may function as an introduction to the second half of the chapter. The concern of the wise and the foolish is developed specifically through an emphasis upon the importance of proper speech. This provides a more focused definition of the difference between wise and foolish. [Structure at a Glance: Proverbs 12]

Structure at a Glance: Proverbs 12

AΩ The outline below provides a guideline for reading.

Vv. 1-7: Security and Stability of the Righteous and Wicked
Vv. 8-14: The Righteous and the Wicked
Vv. 15-23: Fools, Folly, and the Importance of Speech
Vv. 24-28: Retrospect

Thematically arranged clusters of sayings are possible in this chapter (cf. Clifford and Perdue for readings that do not see such structure). After the thematic statement in v. 1, vv. 2-7, with the exception of v. 4, portray the contrast of the righteous and the wicked. Part of that contrast is conceived in terms of the comparison of outcomes from their mutual lifestyles. Verses 8-14 continue the theme of vv. 2-7, but with agricultural imagery. Verse 14 provides a turning point in its anticipation of the theme of speech. Verse 15, by returning to the concerns of v. 1, becomes an opening for the second half of the chapter. Verses 15-21 address various specific aspects of appropriate speech as a means of discriminating between the wise and the foolish.

The final five verses of the chapter would seem not to have any thematic unity at all. Indeed, the case for such thematic affinity is especially difficult to make with the apparent corrupt text of v. 26. However, the closing verse, v. 28, is semantically linked to v. 15 and thus provides a fitting retrospective conclusion to the section. Verses 24-27 offer readers the possibility of connecting the sayings, since v. 27 is thematically related to v. 24 and to the topic of the lazy and the diligent. Of the two inner verses, v. 25 revisits the theme of vv. 15-23, speech. Verse 26, depending upon one's construal of its meaning, could be related in a much more general sense to its preceding verse, v. 15. Verse 6 of the chapter seems to anticipate one possible reading of v. 26.

Richard Clifford, *Proverbs* (OTL; Louisville: Westminster John Knox Press, 1999), 129.
Leo Perdue, *Proverbs* (IBC; Louisville: Westminster John Knox Press, 2000), 168-69.

COMMENTARY

Security and Stability of the Righteous and the Wicked, 12:1-7

The opening statement asserts the connection between knowledge and work: to get the one you must invest discipline, which also involves rebuke from masters. Pedagogical intentions clearly stand behind such a saying: the instructor has the authority to use negative motivation for his student. Verses 2-7 follow, contrasting the righteous and the wicked. Verse 2 implies that the good are those who submit to the discipline of their teachers. The results are the Lord's pleasure. Verse 3 is balanced by the closing verse in the cluster, v. 7. Both sayings reflect upon the relative stability of the righteous and the wicked. Both sayings open with general assertions of security and then reinforce the assertion with a focused, descriptive qualifying statement. In v. 3b the imagery appeals to the everyday reality—in an agricultural land where water is scarce—of the importance of good root systems. [The Land] For plants not to be moved, they must have deep, healthy root systems. Verse 7b presses the theme of stability even further by using the term "house," which can refer both to one's dwelling and to one's heritage. The

The Dead Sea

The Land

The image of "deep roots" reminds readers of the importance the land plays in the thinking of these ancient teachers. In biblical literature the land carries with it important theological connotations. In Deuteronomy the land is the sign of Yahweh's blessing to his people (see [Deuteronomic Land Tradition]). Here, though, one must first attend to simple geographical realities.

Palestine is located in a subtropical region with a generally short rainy season and a longer dry season. Rainfall varies significantly from north to south; desert regions are adjacent on the east and the south, the Mediterranean Sea on the West. In the mountainous areas to the north, rainfall varies from 11.5 to 47.5 inches per year. In the more desert areas rainfall is of 7.5 to 11.5 inches per year, a bare minimum for plant life (Pritchard). In such a land, where water can be scarce, plants survive by developing deep and elaborate root systems. This facilitates water storage and, thus, survival through the dry months.

For further reading, see John W. Rogerson and Philip R. Davies, *The Old Testament World* (Englewood Cliffs NJ: Prentice Hall, 1989).

J. B. Pritchard, *The Harper Concise Atlas of the Bible* (Great Britain: Harper Collins, 1991), 36.

The Good Wife

AΩ The *'ēšet ḥayil*, or "good wife" (or "capable woman" in Prov 31:10, NRSV), in v. 4 requires comment both because readers will encounter the term again in chapter 31, and because it raises the questions of a woman's role in the biblical world. While attitudes toward women are not uniform throughout the Old Testament, it must be conceded that males headed the Israelite family. Male control and leadership translated into socially significant institutions through the transmission of property and ownership, and thus had a negative impact upon the social standing of women. Feminist biblical critics would argue that the relegation of women to socially inferior positions gained further expression and reinforcement in the biblical literature through the subversion and masking of any stance that saw a woman's role as more than devotion to the well-being of her husband. The official position would have been that a woman only prospered as the male head of the family, and the male children, prospered. Wisdom itself, however, provided an avenue to appreciate the unique contributions and independence of women.

Marrying a foreign woman, from the perspective of the status quo, could be even more dangerous (e.g., Prov 5:3-5; 6:24-35; 9:13-19). A woman from outside the community could bring different values and thus assert a negative force upon her husband, his family, and the larger community ethos. The identity of wisdom with the persona of a woman is surely an acknowledgment of such power without abandoning the importance that individuals should marry within the community (Prov 1:20-33; 8:1-21; 9:1-12).

For further reading, see Phyllis A. Bird, "Women (OT)," *ABD* 6:951-57; Athalya Brenner, *The Israelite Woman: Social Role and Literary Type in Biblical Narrative* (Sheffield: JSOT, 1985); and A. Y. Collins, ed., *Feminist Perspectives in Biblical Scholarship* (Chico CA: Scholars Press, 1985).

---

house imagery in the context of a comparison of the righteous and the wicked seems to be asserting that the righteous have a rewarding and meaningful future (cf. 11:29).

Readers may find it provocative to reflect on the interior sayings, vv. 4, 5, and 6, in relationship to the framing statements on discipline and stability. Although v. 4 is neither thematically, semantically, nor syntactically related to vv. 5-6, a rationale for its inclusions in these interior verses might derive from its implied relationship to v. 3. Verse 4 reflects on the good wife, *'ēšet ḥayil,* and implies her role in establishing her husband's reputation. In relationship to v. 3, the reputation certainly contributes to the extension of one's dynasty (cf. 11:16 and 22). [The Good Wife] The vocabulary of vv. 5 and 6, not to mention the themes, suggests that these two sayings are paired with each other. Both contrast the "righteous" (*ṣaddîqîm / yĕšārîm*) and the "wicked" (*rĕšāʿîm*). Verse 5, however, deals with the internal aspects of the righteous and wicked—"thoughts"—while v. 6 deals with the external features—"words." The contrast between the internal and external characteristics of individuals raises the provocative thought that what is hidden becomes visible in one's speech. This point anticipates the general concerns of the section of sayings beginning with v. 15. [House]

House

AΩ The "house" (*bayit*) is a term laden with symbolic significance in the Old Testament. In this chapter we encounter it in v. 7 (e.g., 9:1; 14:1). At its most literal level it denotes a dwelling place for families (e.g., Gen 19:10; Ps 68:6). As a dwelling place it may also denote a dwelling place for many things: for prisoners (Gen 39:20, *bêt hassohar*); for women (as in a harem, Esth 2:9, *bêt hassohar*); for worship (as in a temple, 1 Kgs 7:12), as well as a receptacle for other kinds of activities. The term may also denote a family, or household, the people who live in the house (Deut 6:22, 11:6). In this regard house may also designate a family of descendants (e.g., Gen 18:19). This particular significance provides the decisive play on words in the narrative of Yahweh's promise to David (2 Sam 11:11).

When the sage asserts that the "house" of the righteous stands in contrast to the overthrowing of the wicked, he is clearly inviting the reader to think on more than a single, literal level. The house of the righteous is indeed a dwelling place in the present, but it also connotes a person's descendants.

For further reading, see Serge Frolov and Vladimir Orel, "The House of YHWH," *ZAW* 108/2 (1996): 254-57; and Thomas L. Thompson, "'House of David': An Eponymic Referent to Yahweh as Grandfather," *SJOT* 9/1 (1995): 59-74.

Righteous vs. Wicked, 12:8-14

Verses 8 and 14 suggest a framework on the theme of sensible action. In doing so, they lead to reflection upon speech as a premier expression of such sensibility. Unfortunately this can only be appreciated in Hebrew. The phrase translated "good sense" in v. 8 is literally "the mouth of intelligence," or "prudence" (*lĕpî-śiklô*). In v. 8 the term *pî* is used idiomatically to express "measure," thus "the measure, or extent of" something (e.g., Lev 25:16; Hos 10:12). NRSV translates simply "one is commended for good sense." The evidence of such intelligence results in public commendation. This public-private motif in v. 8 invokes the similar contrast evident in vv. 5-6. Readers looking ahead see that the next occurrence of the word mouth (*pî*) is in v. 14, a saying that both emphasizes the importance of speech, and, like v. 8, explores the consequences of that good speech. Verse 9 artfully confronts readers with the concrete categories of hiddenness vs. evident activities in order to illustrate sensible activity. A "better than saying," verse 9a counterpoises the "light" regard (*niqleh*) for certain people in a community, even though they openly have a servant (implying wealth), with other people who openly have regard for themselves and have no evidence of bread. Verse 9 therefore seems, again, to offer a play on what is seen and what is hidden.[1]

Verses 9, 11, 14, 24, and 27 all convey important images related to the theme of work. Such sayings give expression to the conviction that idleness can lead to failure. Clearly, wisdom cannot be profitable if individuals are unwilling to be diligent in their work.

The later sage, Qoheleth, finds that even diligent work is not in itself absolute (e.g., Eccl 2:20-23; 4:4; 6:7). A still later sage, Jesus ben Sirach, presents a picture that appears somewhat elitist. He distinguishes between those that "work the land" and those who study the law. In other words, the one "devoted to the study of the law of the most high . . ." (Sir 39:1) is uniquely different from the one who "handles the plow" (Sir 38:25). Still later sages, including Sirach, encourage those who study the law with such devotion also to be occupied with labor of the hands, implying work's virtue (Sir 7:15 and 22).

The imagery of vv. 10-12 seems to reflect the influence of an agricultural situation. Verse 10 contrasts the care the righteous and wicked give to their animals. Verse 11 contrasts the one who works his land with the one who does not. Verse 12 (even though there are textual ambiguities in 12a) concludes with an image encountered in v. 3 regarding the roots of the righteous. Verse 11 echoes v. 9 in its use of the vocabulary of work, '*ōbēd*, and the results of that work, either the lack of food (v. 9) or having plenty of food (v. 11). Verses 10 and 12 are similar in their contrast of the internal dispositions of the righteous and wicked. In v. 10b there is the "mercy" (*raḥămê*) of the wicked. In v. 12a the wicked "covet" (*ḥāmad*). Verses 13 and 14 are thematically paired with the imagery of the mouth or lips. Both sayings reflect upon the importance of good speech. As the text stands in MT, there is a further semantic connection between vv. 12-14 and the words translated (in NRSV) as "the proceeds" in v. 12a (*mĕṣôd*), and "ensnared" in v. 13 (*môqēš*), both synonyms for netting or trapping.[2] With explicit anatomical language concerning speech (i.e., mouth), v. 14 invites readers to look back to v. 8 and consider how these examples of internal dispositions and sensibilities climax in public speech.

Fools, Folly, and the Importance of Speech, 12:15-23

The second half of the chapter is introduced with a saying that echoes the concerns of v. 1. It portrays the ones who fail to submit to proper discipline and thus believe "their own way is right." These people are fools (*ĕwîl*), and the saying sharpens the thought of v. 1 by offering an example of what it might mean to "hate to be rebuked." Verse 16, which is paired with v. 15, further reflects upon the way of the fool and returns to an idea implied by the examples of sensible action in vv. 8-14: the contrast between one's internal disposition and external action. "Fools show their anger," but the clever conceal (*kōseh*) provocations. How such vexation is displayed or contained is the broader subject of the following verses. Speech plays an important role. In v. 23, the concluding verse in the group, the same or similar vocabulary of v. 16 recurs: "the clever" (*ʿārûm*), "the fool" (*ʾĕwîl*), "folly" (*ʾiwwelet*), and the verb "to cover or conceal" (*kōseh*).

Perhaps vv. 17-20 could be read as a group of sayings.[3] Verse 17b concludes with the characterization of "deceit" (*mirmâ*), and v. 20a opens with the same language (*mirmâ*), "deceit." Verse 17, however, seems to be more concerned with one's testimony in the law court, the city gate. Verse 20 appears to revisit the familiar contrast between internal disposition and external results: deceit in the heart versus the counsel of speech. The two internal sayings, vv. 18 and 19, are paired thematically and semantically. The language depicting speech is readily evident: the use of the term "tongue" (*lĕšôn*) is a convention called synecdoche (cf. Prov 10:18-21) whereby an aspect or part of a phenomenon symbolizes or represents the whole. The word is shared by both sayings. Verse 18, however, appears to be more concerned with the contrast between constructive versus destructive speech. Verse 19 revisits the concerns of v. 17, honest speech, though not necessarily in the setting of the law court.[4]

Verse 21 seems to intrude because it does not concern the themes of either speech or the discipline of wisdom. It contrasts the fates of the righteous and the wicked and apparently has no connection either with what precedes in v. 20 or with what follows in v. 22. The LXX translation perhaps offers the only possible connection between vv. 21 and 20 in its rendering of *yĕʿunneh*, "encounter or meet," as *aresei*, "to be pleasing or gratify." Verse 22 is a Yahweh saying that returns to the overall interest in honest speech. This verse offers theological reinforcement to the other sayings whose authority rests only on observation. We have already seen above that v. 23 echoes the statement in v. 16 and thus recalls the important pair of statements in vv. 15 and 16. Verse 23 is different from 16, however. In the one, the clever person conceals knowledge; in the other, he conceals vexation. Both reflect the importance of self-control, and in the context of the reflection on speech, claim that words provide the media of disclosure.

Retrospect, 12:24-28

These concluding verses appear to be only a loosely connected group of sayings. Verses 24 and 27 return to related themes stated in 9-10 and 14. Verses 25 and 26 return to the theme of proper speech. As a concluding statement, v. 28 asserts with confidence that the fate of the righteous leads only to life, and in doing so, echoes the imagery of v. 15 by recalling the motif of "the way." Once we see that vv. 24-27 revisit themes already treated in the chapter, the symmetrical arrangement becomes even more apparent. The outer sayings on diligence provide a framework for reflecting upon the urgency of proper speech. Textual difficulties abound in both vv. 26 and 27, thus making questionable the rather convenient distribution of themes suggested here.[5]

CONNECTIONS

On the Educated Person

One of the most common questions parents ask when searching for a town in which to settle is "What about the schools here?" The question reflects their concern that their children get the best possible education through the particular public school system. While many parents are indeed convinced that private schools are the answer, many public schools offer opportunities for students to excel and achieve. But one must ask whether the program alone is enough to provide the necessary education. Too often these same parents think that education is merely about filling a child's head with knowledge when there is so much more.

Among his various correspondences, Mark Twain wrote a stern letter to his brother Orion in 1878. It seems that Orion, having seen his brother, Samuel Clemens, make it big in writing, set out to do some of his own publication. He sent a manuscript to Clemens (Twain) titled *Journey in Heaven*. Having read the manuscript, Twain began his reply to Orion with the following: "Every man must *learn* his trade—not pick it up. God requires that he learn it by slow and painful processes. The apprentice hand in blacksmithing, in medicine, in literature, in everything, is a thing that can't be hidden. It always shows."[6] In offering this response Twain was reminding his brother that there was a great deal of work yet to be done on the new novel before publication. With such an observation he also was acknowledging that learning is a long, slow, toilsome process no matter what the particular task is. Part of that process consists mainly of long hours of disciplined work.

The mixing of sayings in this chapter assert the importance of diligent work, the love of discipline as the basis of knowledge, and the ethical virtues of such work. Such assertions invite us to ask what it meant to the sages to be an educated person. The question is not out of date, to be certain. One has but to read the current literature on education to see how many and how varied are the views on what it means to be an educated person today. While we shall have opportunity to reflect on this point frequently throughout this commentary, the connection between work and education implied in this chapter suggests that there is more to knowledge than academics. The outcomes of education are many and multifaceted. Common sense tells us that no institution can adequately prepare students for everything. Being thoughtful and reflective, having some understanding of and appreciation for beauty and art, having the heart and sense of responsibility to make one's contribution to community, being a diligent worker—all go together to create a composite picture of the educated person. Educators as well as parents should give to students as many opportunities as is possible to do the things that society will demand of them. However, none of these is realized without careful, thoughtful, diligent work.

NOTES

[1] Raymond Van Leeuwen, *Proverbs* (NIB 5; Nashville: Abingdon, 1997), 125.

[2] Roland E. Murphy, *Proverbs* (WBC 22; Nashville: Word, 1998), 88. Note Murphy's judgment regarding the corruption of v. 12a.

[3] Murphy, *Proverbs*, 70, acknowledges the possibility and refers to R. Scoralick, *Einzelspruch und Sammlung* (BZAW 232; Berlin: de Gruyter, 1995).

[4] The LXX translates the Hebrew adverb 'ēd as *marturion*, "witness," suggesting that the term was understood by that ancient reader in a forensic sense.

[5] See Murphy, *Proverbs*, 88; William McKane, *Proverbs* (OTL; London: SCM Press, 1970), 447; and O. Plöger, *Sprüche Salomos (Proverbia)* (BKAT 17; Neukirchen: Neukirchener Verlag, 1984), 153, for discussions of the difficulties of *yātēr mērē'ēhû* in v. 26 and the difficulties of understanding *yaḥărok* in 27a along with the grammar of 27b.

[6] "To Orion Clemens, Keokuk," in *The Selected Letters of Mark Twain*, ed. Charles Neider (New York: Harper & Row, 1982), 101.

THE ESSENTIALS
OF EDUCATION

Proverbs 13:1-25

The collections of sayings in this chapter continue to reflect the sages' concern with the value of wisdom. Here they address the topic through the more focused problem of pedagogy. How does one obtain wisdom? What assumptions must be shared between instructor and pupil? Verse 1 reiterates the importance of discipline; v. 13 asserts the essentiality of listening to the word; and v. 24, one of the closing verses, asserts the importance of corporal punishment as motivation to the student. Readers have already encountered this conviction in 10:13b in reference to fools. As in the preceding chapters, this chapter also has sayings that contrast the righteous with the wicked (vv. 5, 6, 9, 21, 22, and 25). However, the absence of any Yahweh sayings makes the chapter unique in the entire collection of 10:1–22:16.[1] [Structure at a Glance: Proverbs 13]

Structure at a Glance: Proverbs 13

ΑΩ Readers might find the following organization helpful in their interpretation of the chapter:

Vv. 1-6 Wisdom and Speech
Vv. 7-11 Wealth, Poverty, and Righteousness
Vv. 12-19 Instruction and Discipline
Vv. 20-25 Wisdom and Prosperity

With close attention to the sayings and their contexts, readers may see that the sayings in this chapter are not clustered haphazardly. (Roland E. Murphy disagrees with the overarching thematic connections observed by R. N. Whybray and with this present treatment.) The interrelationships along thematic and semantic lines allow readers to infer possible intentional arrangements and to explore their implications within the chapter. The main lines of division suggest the (above) groupings, which outline the treatment here. There are thematic correspondences between 12 and 19; 13 and 18; 14 and 17; 15 and 16—all of which might be organized around the general theme of education's value in vv. 12-19.

Verses 7-11 seem also to function as a group. Most recognizable are the thematic and semantic connections between vv. 7 and 11. Both verses share the word for riches (*hôn*) and concern reversals of either presumptions on appearances or of fortunes. This leaves two loosely related series of sayings on either side of the two central units, vv. 1-6 and vv. 21-25. (Raymond VanLeeuwen believes vv. 1-4 are bound together as a unit.)

Roland E. Murphy, *Proverbs* (WBC 22; Nashville: Word, 1998), 99.

Raymond Van Leeuwen, *Proverbs* (NIB 5; Nashville: Abingdon, 1997), 131.

R. N. Whybray, *The Composition of the Book of Proverbs* (JSOTSup 168; Sheffield: JSOT, 1994), 99-100

COMMENTARY

Wisdom and Speech, 13:1-6

This opening unit of sayings stands apart from vv. 7-11 since its sayings seem to function independently as a sequence of connected observations. Verses 2 and 3, concerning the importance of guarding one's speech, are paired as sequential reflections upon the scoffer (*lēṣ*), v. 1. Verses 5 and 6 are paired similarly. Both vv. 3 and 6 offer generalizations commenting upon the particular observations of vv. 2 and 5. There are close semantic connections between vv. 2 and 3: the vocabulary "mouth," synecdoche for speech, and "life," or "desire," the Hebrew for which is *nepeš*. In v. 2b the term *nepeš* denotes the "desire" of the wicked; in 3a the same term denotes the "life" or "soul" of the one who guards his mouth. The play between the imagery of vv. 2 and 3 succeeds because the mouth is used both for speaking and eating. Eating is an image of appetite and consumption. In general, proper speech directs one's appetites. The one who guards his words, v. 3, guards his appetites for things that can eventually lead to destruction.

The unit offers several reflections upon the learner's discipline of "listening" to the rebukes of his teacher. From the "fruit" of his teacher's words a student will eat good things. In other words, education leads to prosperity. But a student, like his instructor, must guard his mouth. Those who do more speaking than listening will not know prosperity, since they will not learn. Verse 5 comes back to the topic of honest speech, allowing a broader significance of speech than instruction alone. Verse 6 generalizes that righteousness "guards" the way of the upright, thus returning to imagery used in v. 3, where "guarding" one's mouth keeps one's life. The central saying, v. 4, shares vocabulary with vv. 2 and 3 in its reflection upon the "desires" or "appetite," *nepeš*, of the lazy and the diligent. Verse 3 reflects upon the importance of diligent work in order to realize the objects of one's desire. Asserting the efficacy of diligence in this context makes even more important the need for some kind of restraint (see 4b and 2b), thus calling for the moral restraints set out in vv. 5 and 6.

Wealth, Poverty, and Righteousness, 13:7-11

This group of sayings shares similar kinds of interconnections as those seen in the preceding group. Verses 7, 8, and 11 are explicitly concerned with either wealth or wealthy people. Verse 10 makes an

Wealth and Poverty

AΩ Within the framework established by the concept of retribution, wealth and poverty stand as two opposing outcomes for one's activity in life. Wealth is one of the rewards of righteousness and therefore provides some measure of security (13:6). Poverty is the result of laziness, generally speaking. Readers have encountered these ideas already in 10:4-5; 11:16; 12:11-12; and 13:4, and will encounter them in nearly every remaining chapter of this collection.

It is nevertheless the responsibility of the rich to care for the poor and avoid oppression (e.g., 11:24-26; 14:31). This social obligation is consonant with the Deuteronomic legislation that also reinforces care for the poor, Deut 15:1-11. The sages recognized the possibility that poverty results not from laziness but from social injustice. The saying in 13:23 provides a stark reminder of the sages' awareness of this reality.

For further reading, see Trevor Donald, "The Semantic Field of Rich and Poor in Wisdom Literature of Hebrew and Akkadian," *Oriens Antiquus* 2 (1964): 27-41; Sue Gillingham, "The Poor in the Psalms," *ExpTim* 100 (1988–1989): 15-19; J. David Pleins, "Poor, Poverty," *ABD* 5:402-14; and R. N. Whybray, *Wealth and Poverty in the Book of Proverbs* (JSOTSup 99; Sheffield: JSOT, 1990).

---

observation that could be of great relevance to the wealthy. Verse 9 contrasts the righteous with the wicked, which, in the context of these observations about wealth, heightens the possibility for the association of wealth with either wickedness or righteousness.

Verse 7 revisits a motif readers have encountered already in chapter 12 (and 11:24), the contrast between appearances and reality. Some people try to look wealthy and are not, while others appear poor and have great wealth. Such a statement invites further reflection upon the possible connotations of wealth: is the saying simply referring to material wealth, or might one who is wise be considered wealthy in another manner of speaking? Verse 8 is thought to be corrupt by some, since its final two words match those of 13:1b.[2] In this context, the present state of the saying seems to extend the reflection of v. 7 by focusing upon the usefulness of wealth in times of danger. The saying turns on the irony that the poor person need not be concerned with the possibility of being robbed. This irony might be of special relevance to the people in v. 7 who pretend to be rich. [Wealth and Poverty]

The concluding three sayings round out the group by revisiting two of the overall themes of the chapter, indeed of the entire collection. Verse 9 contrasts the life of the righteous and the wicked. The imagery of light in v. 9 is interesting because of its metaphoric value as life. In Ecclesiastes the same image is used as a metaphor for life (e.g., Eccl 12:2). [The Rejoicing Light] Verse 10 revisits the urgency of taking counsel to obtain wisdom. Verse 11 concludes the group with another reflection on wealth. Wealth that comes from nothing (*mēhebel*), it is concluded, becomes small, or

---

The Rejoicing Light

AΩ Readers may pause to appreciate the language and imagery of this ancient poetry. The NRSV translates v. 9a as "The light of the righteous rejoices . . . ." Clearly the image of light is used to describe some feature shared both by the righteous and the wicked. In 9b the parallel term, "lamp" (*nēr*), in reference to "the wicked" is extinguished, so the action relative to the light and the lamp is at least consistent there. The term for rejoice is *yiśmāḥ*, a common word denoting the expression of happiness or joy. Standing in relationship to the word "light," readers are confronted with an interesting mix of metaphors—"rejoicing light."

The rich background of sacred traditions and literature is probably assumed by the writer. In Hebrew literature, light is an expression of life. The very first words out of the creator's mouth assert its preeminence. All of life comes after light (e.g., Gen 1:1ff). Darkness symbolizes that uncreated, lifeless, and formless void out of which the creator fashions all creation. When light is extinguished, as in the case of this saying, the image of death is irresistible. Life characterized by rejoicing implies the profitability of righteousness. Readers will also find that the connections between life and rejoicing serve as a dominant thematic statement in the work of the later sage, Qoheleth (e.g., Eccl 2:24-26; 3:12-13; 3:21; 5:18-20; 8:15; 9:7; 11:7–12:8).

For further reading, see William McKane, *Proverbs* (OTL; London: SCM, 1970), 461; Michael V. Fox, *Qohelet and His Contradictions* (JSOTSup 71; Sheffield: JSOT, 1989), 63-64; and Norbert Lohfink, "Qoheleth 5:17-19—Revelation by Joy," *CBQ* 52 (1990): 625-35.

---

diminishes. In contrast to 11b, where the assumption that wealth may also come from careful, systematic building of wealth, 11a seems to imply that the best wealth is that for which one has had to work and save. This concluding saying foils the opening observations, v. 7, by juxtaposing "nothing" with "pretense" in the two opening stichs. In this way readers may conclude that it is better to have the appearance of poverty while taking the pains to build a wealth that lasts.

Instruction and Discipline, 13:12-19

The next group of sayings is evidently clustered both thematically and chiastically. The technique of arranging the pairs of sayings to form an envelope, so to speak, functions both to unify the collection and to focus attention on those sayings at the center of the structure. While readers ordinarily read lists from top to bottom in sequence, having recognized such a structure requires readers to abandon sequential reading and to be willing to make some hops and skips as they go. Readers should keep in mind a structure as proposed in [Chiastic Arrangement of vv. 12-19].

This is not to suggest that within this group there are no linear connections to which to attend. We encounter within vv. 12 and 14 the imagery of the "tree of life/fountain of life" (see [Tree of Life]). The two images provide a framework within which the three sayings function. Verse 12 makes a general assertion on the

Chiastic Arrangement of vv. 12-19

AΩ The structural arrangement in this unit of the chapter employs the stylistic technique called "chiasm." We have already encountered this in Proverbs 1 (see
[Women and Wisdom]).

V. 12: Delaying gratification and realizing longing
  V. 13: Failure to heed instruction
    V. 14: Good teacher and faithful messenger
      V. 15: Good sense and cleverness
      V. 16: Good sense and cleverness
    V. 17: Good teacher and faithful messenger
  V. 18: Failure to heed instruction
V. 19: Delaying gratification and realizing longing

We might consider reading vv. 12 and 19 as a pair of sayings on delaying gratification
and the fulfillment of longing. Verse 19b abandons this theme by returning to the overall
concerns of instruction and discipline. Verses 13 and 18 raise the theme of the failure to
heed instruction and discipline. Verses 14 and 17 compare the faithful messenger and the
good teacher; both have the purpose of steering one in the direction of life and prosperity.
At the center are vv. 15 and 16, which reflect upon good sense and cleverness, and which
return readers to the overall concern of the entire chapter, especially evident in vv. 1-6.

---

fulfillment of one's longings. Verse 13, while castigating the one
who despises teaching, also affirms the final reward, *yĕšullām*, for
those who keep the teacher's commandment. Verse 14 extends this
idea by asserting that wise instruction turns one from the snares of
death, and it functions as a climactic statement in the progression
of the three verses by returning to the fountain of life image.

Verses 15 and 16 invite reflection as a pair through their obvious
thematic connections. Both sayings assert the value of wisdom. In
v. 15 prudence, or "good sense," is contrasted with the "way" of the
faithless. "Way" is used to denote the ethical and moral choices one
must make: one set of choices leads to favor; another leads to ruin.
A second contrast follows between the "clever," *ʿārûm*, and the fool,
kĕsîl. The clever one acts with knowledge; the fool displays folly.

Wisdom and Prosperity, 13:20-25

The concluding six verses provide helpful retrospective on the
sayings and the main themes that have been included in the
chapter. But the arrangement of the themes in these closing verses
do not lend themselves to linear reading. There seems to be, rather,
a double framework that invites reading with skips as above. Verse
20 reiterates the chapter's concern with obtaining wisdom, and as
such takes readers back to vv. 18, 13, and the opening verse in the
chapter. The penultimate saying, v. 24, balances the concern for

Corporal Punishment in the Bible

The saying in 13:24 asserts the importance of corporal punishment in the rearing of children. The opening saying, 13:1, has a legitimizing effect by its claim that such punishment produces the more important outcome of education. The importance of the parents' roles in maintaining parental authority, even if through physical means, is reasserted in yet another collection, 23:13-14, 22-25. In fact, the collection of Solomonic sayings opens with an image that juxtaposes proud and ashamed parents, 10:1. Nevertheless, corporal punishment is a most vivid expression of the need for control, not surprising in a context that frequently urges various kinds of constraint over the activity of one's body (e.g., 13:2-3; 14:30; 15:18, 31; 16:32; 19:15).

Anthropologists tell us that the body is one avenue for understanding society. It functions as a symbolic form upon which culture inscribes its rules, beliefs, and practices evident for all to see. Through the daily habits of bodily care—from table manners, acts of deference and courtesy, to toilet habits and routines—the body gives unwitting expression to a society's highest values and norms. A body that violates these habituated controls, whether consciously or unconsciously, undermines social control and the facade of cosmically grounded social order (see, for instance, Mary Douglas).

Patriarchalism as a "systematic dominance of men" in society achieves its aims through an ideology that identifies women with nature and therefore as objects to be dominated and controlled (King). In the same way that nature is to be dominated and controlled, in other words, so are women. Further, since women are sources of reproduction, they naturally have an affinity with children, and children are therefore also objects to be dominated and controlled. One can see the emphasis of this bias in Prov 5:15-23, for instance, where a man's wife is depicted with imagery that speaks of nature and maternity. The question readers must ask is whether there are other models of education that do not necessarily rest upon such male dominance models, and thus do not require such potential for human oppression.

For further reading, see Raymond Westbrook, "Punishments and Crimes," *ABD* 5:546-56; Susan Griffin, *Woman and Nature: The Roaring Inside Her* (New York: Harper & Row, 1978); and Sherry Ortner, "Is Female to Male as Nature is to Culture?" in *Woman, Culture and Society*, ed. Michele Rosaldo and Louise Lamphere (Palo Alto CA: Stanford University Press, 1974).

Mary Douglas, *Natural Symbols* (New York: Pantheon, 1982).

Ynestra King, "Healing the Wounds," in *Gender/Body/Knowledge,* ed. Alison M. Jaggar and Susan R. Bordo (New Brunswick and London: Rutgers University Press, 1986), 121.

wisdom with its own concern for wisdom and a more focused reflection upon corporal punishment. In a context so heavily devoted to education (of "children," see vv. 1 and 22), one possible conclusion must be that corporal punishment is an acceptable means of motivating learning.[3] [Corporal Punishment in the Bible]

A second theme is recalled in vv. 21 and 25, that of the contrast between the fates of the wicked and the righteous. These two sayings recall other such assertions in the chapter such as vv. 5, 6, and 9. There is possibly another implied connection between vv. 20 and 21 deriving from the semantic play on the verb *yērôaʿ*, "to suffer harm," in v. 20b,[4] and the noun *rāʿâ*, translated in v. 21a as "misfortune." Of further significance is the use of the same three consonants in v. 20b, *rōʿeh*, as in the following v. 21a. The two words have different meanings: the former, "companion," the latter, "misfortune." With such semantic and orthographic connections, readers may be inclined to search for and imagine behavioral parallels between those who are companions of fools (20b) and those who pursue sinners (21a). In this way readers might conclude that to fail to acquire wisdom not only leaves one a companion of fools, but also a wicked person.

Verses 22 and 23 bring the preceding themes together by reflecting on the inheritance of youth—potentially wisdom and prosperity, according to the tenor of these collections of sayings— as well as the fate of the unrighteous. The link between vv. 22 and 21 is apparent in the reflection upon "sinners." In 21a misfortune pursues sinners; in 22b the treasure of the righteous is the wealth of sinners. Similarly, v. 23 reflects upon the newly plowed field of the poor and the fact that it produces plenty of food, even though it is swept away through injustice. Verse 25 picks up the motif of food (*ʾōkēl*), sharing the same word with v. 23, and concludes that the righteous, not the wicked, have enough to satisfy their appetites.

CONNECTIONS

Education, Maturity, and Liberation

The talk of America continues to be on education. On can scarcely read a newspaper without seeing the politicizing of education in nearly every article, accompanied by a debate from every possible viewpoint. For example, one commentator observes the paranoid behavior of parents in seeking the best, most expensive education they can find for their eighteen- to nineteen-year-old children. The trend is feeding (or being fed by) the growth in popularity of educational consultants: people who advise students on preparing a "winning application" for college or on preparation for the ACT and SAT exams. The commentator argues that at the root of all the activity is prestige—especially for the parents—not the education itself. The tragedy is that not only are there so many parents who are willing to risk bankruptcy to obtain such an education, but youths very early in their lives begin to become virtual middle-aged adults, "compiling records of achievement in arts, sports and community service in the hope that admissions officers will cry 'Amazing!' and put the financial screws to their parents."[5]

Without condemning all current and future activities of preparation for post-secondary education, it might be nevertheless worthwhile for us to ask ourselves both what is driving such fierce competition and what it takes to obtain a good education for our children? Could there be a misunderstanding of what education is all about? In view of the legitimizing function of 13:1 and 24, for instance, readers might consider how parents, as agents for cultural ideology, dominate their children and use education as a way to perpetuate dominance in society. Such behavior bespeaks parents' own lack of awareness of how culture has shaped and controlled their own thinking. Children become pawns of a much larger interest in superimposing social control worldwide. Parents are unwitting participants in teaching their children to wield an ideology of control. In this scenario, education is not for liberation from the narrow ideologies that confine and imprison humanity, but a tool for perpetuating the narrowness of selfishness, self-exclusiveness, and fear.

If we can grant the assumptions of Proverbs 13:15-16 on good sense and cleverness, and if we affirm that good teachers are indeed faithful messengers in vv. 14 and 17, then the outer sayings of vv. 12 and 19 are of some potential import. What does delayed gratification have to do with education? Is it possible that the sage is here providing the insight into breaking free from oppressive ideologies?

What college instructor has not recognized the dramatic difference between the study habits of traditional students (normal college age) and those of nontraditional students, who after a few years away from formal education come back to complete a degree or realize a goal that was put off until some indefinite point in the future? It is not only study habits that differ. There is a kind of maturity and worldly knowledge that intensifies the flames of interest and curiosity. The older student's perspective is shaped by a world that understands the relevance of a mature grasp of all kinds of knowledge and skill. The simple truth is that the kinds of synthetic and reflective activities and attitudes modeled in the Proverbs originate in the life practice of mature learners and teachers who seem only too aware of the realities of culture's influence.

Unfortunately the assertions regarding delayed gratification in vv. 12 and 19 probably have the effect of encouraging students *not* to wait on their commitment to knowledge and wisdom. Delaying such involvement only further postpones the positive outcomes of learning and thus makes the heart sick. However, delaying the gratification of education ought to be weighed against present-day understanding of the importance of developmental aspects of the educational process. Only adults who understand the nature of social control and oppression have a ready insight into the liberating effects of education.

NOTES

[1] R. N. Whybray, *The Composition of the Book of Proverbs* (JSOTSup 168; Sheffield: JSOT, 1994), 99-100.

[2] Richard J. Clifford, *Proverbs* (OTL; Louisville: Westminster John Knox Press, 1999), 136.

[3] Ibid., 99-100; Whybray argues that at one time v. 24 closed the collection, since it offered such a pointed response to v. 1. Compare Roland E. Murphy, *Proverbs* (WBC 22; Nashville: Word, 1998), 98-99.

[4] A Niphal imperfect of root *r ʿ ʿ*.

[5] Russell Baker, "It costs plenty to be able to boast about a college kid," in *The Kansas City Star* (30 May 1996): metro section, 5.

WISDOM IN PUBLIC

Proverbs 14:1-35

The chapter opens with a reflection on the efficacy of wisdom (cf. 9:1, 10:1, and 13:1), that echoes the larger concern of the Proverbs of Solomon in chapters 10–15. While this collection mostly calls for readers' attention to catchword relationships between individual sayings, there appear to be some larger thematic groupings of sayings. One of the most persistently recurring themes contrasts the wise with the foolish (e.g., vv. 1, 3, 6, 7, 8, 9, 16, 17, 18, and 24).
[Structure at a Glance: Proverbs 14]

Structure at a Glance: Proverbs 14

AΩ Even though the overarching structure is not drawn from tightly connected clusters of sayings, readers might still find the following arrangement of sayings helpful in reflection.

Vv. 1-9 The Wise and the Foolish
Vv. 8-15 The Wisdom of Righteousness
Vv. 15-18 Portraits of Fools
Vv. 18-24 The Wise and the Foolish
Vv. 25-26 Wise Speech
Vv. 27-34 Wisdom for a King

The play of the interrelationships between these sayings is never more evident than in the several small units of sayings. Verses 1-9 seem to be delineated as a group by the overall theme contrasting the wise with the foolish (vv. 1, 3, 6, 7, 8, 9). Further, vv. 2 and 9, both of which contain references to deity, allude to matters of religious discipline, possibly serving as boundaries for a group of sayings within (Whybray). The references to deity in both provide cosmic legitimation for the claims of the sayings within. Vv. 8-15 appear to be arranged in a chiastic structure, with thematic oppositions between vv. 8 and 15, 9 and 14, 10 and 13, 11 and 12. (This accords with the observation of Duane Garrett.) While closing this previous grouping, v. 15 then opens yet another grouping contained in vv. 15-18. Verses 15-18 and 19-24 comprise the final two groupings in the first major section in the chapter (vv. 1-24). This section is concluded with two Yahweh sayings in vv. 26 and 27, recalling the opening Yahweh sayings in v. 2. Verses 28-35 consist of a group of sayings within a framework of sayings on the king and kingship (vv. 28 and 35).

Duane Garrett, *Proverbs, Ecclesiastes, Song of Solomon* (Nashville: Broadman Press, 1993), 142-43.
R. N. Whybray, *The Composition of the Book of Proverbs* (JSOTSup 168; Sheffield: JSOT, 1994), 100-102.

COMMENTARY

The Wise and the Foolish, 14:1-7

The opening three sayings state the dominant theme of vv. 1-9 as well as of 1-24, which is the contrast of the wise and the foolish.[1] NRSV translates v. 1 as "The wise woman," emending the Hebrew text from a plural "wise women" to the singular. It is not uncommon to emend the text further to read the subject of 1a as (Woman) Wisdom by deleting the Hebrew word for "women."[2] This has the advantage of making 14:1 an echo of 9:1, which also talks about Woman Wisdom. That she "builds her house" contributes to the foreshadowing of the poem on the capable wife (NRSV) of Proverbs 31:10-31. Verse 2 is a Yahweh saying, which associates wisdom with the "fear of the LORD." This saying contrasts the images of "walking uprightly" and "departing from" or "turning aside from" the way. The familiar image of "the way" has moralistic significance. Verse 2 contrasts wisdom with folly. The saying asserts speech as a criterion for distinguishing the wise from fools, echoing concerns already encountered in 12:13-16, especially v. 15. The idea is that through speech, fools bring punishment upon themselves. Wise speech, by contrast, preserves the wise.

Verses 4-7 continue the motif of speech initiated in v. 3. This is most evident in v. 5, which most likely concerns testimony in a judicial setting (cf. v. 25). The saying is not only about falsehood, but falsehood in a context where absolute truth is essential. Giving accurate testimony is a fundamental obligation in a court of law. Readers may recall a connection with similar concerns in Exodus 20:16 and 23:2b-3. Verse 6 reflects on the "scoffer," the *lēṣ*, who seeks wisdom and cannot obtain it. [The Scoffer] Given the motif

---

The Scoffer

AΩ The scoffer, or *lēṣ* in Hebrew, is one who should be classed among the larger category of fools. He is foolish because he "values his opinions overmuch" (Crenshaw). This definition is helpful, but there is an aspect of the *les* that the characteristic of overconfidence does not quite capture. Proverbs 22:10 associates "strife" (*mādôn*) with his behavior. When he is driven away, quarreling and conflict cease. Such language implies, therefore, that there is a kind of aggressiveness about his attitude as well. So much so that, according to Prov 9:7, whoever tries to discipline the *lēṣ* receives abuse for his trouble.

As the term occurs in the Proverbs, the *lēṣ* is one who is incapable of possessing real wisdom because he cannot

learn (e.g., Prov 1:22; 9:8; 13:1; 14:6; 15:12; 21:24; 24:9). Interestingly, the Hiphil stem of the word occurs in Job 16:20 and 33:23. In the former passage it carries a related meaning of scorner, or one who derides. It seems an apt description of Job's friends. Ironically, its occurrence in Job 33:23 depicts merely an intermediary, or one who intervenes. The psalmist concludes that the *lēṣ* should be avoided altogether, Ps 1:1.

For further reading, see C. Barth, *"lys,"* in *TDOT* 7:547-52; H. N. Richardson, "Some Notes on *lys* and its Derivatives," *VT* 5 (1955): 163-79; and idem, "Two Addenda, . . ." *VT* 5 (1955): 434-36.

James L. Crenshaw, *Old Testament Wisdom* (Atlanta: John Knox Press, 1981), 81; also cited there is W. O. E. Oesterly, *The Book of Proverbs* (London: Methuen and Company, 1929), LXXXIV-LXXXVII.

contrasting the wise with fools, the *lēṣ* stands as but one example of the fool. Verse 7 also notes the absence of knowledgeable words in the fool.

Verse 4 is of special interest to readers reflecting upon the inner connections of vv. 1-7. How does the saying in v. 4 relate to this larger context? It does not appear to have anything to do with either the topic of speech or with the contrast between wisdom and foolishness. The verse stands out from its context, however, because of the stark agricultural imagery that does not explicitly address the thematic concerns of the larger context of vv. 1-7. It may be, however, that the saying is included as an example of foolishness from a farming perspective.[3] Indeed, v. 4 is much more a proverb than a mere saying, apparently having multiple levels of significance. Readers are not unfamiliar with its content. It is not uncommon to hear someone today describe a foolish person in analogous kinds of imagery: "he is one bale short of a load"; "she is not the sharpest knife in the drawer"; "the wheel is turning but the gerbil is dead"; etc. On the most immediate level the proverb in v. 4 concerns the results of a lack of oxen: no produce. On another level, oxen signify the engines that produce the farmer's profit. They are to the farmer's crops as wisdom is to his proper speech. Inserted here, we have a metaphorical way of reiterating the relationship between wisdom and speech, or folly and the lack thereof. In the Hebrew text the implied relationship between v. 3, contrasting the speech of fools and the wise, and v. 4 seems to be reinforced orthographically in that both sentences open with the Hebrew preposition *bĕ*, which may be translated as "in, with, or by." The opening of v. 3 might literally be translated "with the mouth of a fool"; v. 4 might literally be translated "with no oxen."

The implied connection between vv. 3 and 4 further allows one to read vv. 4-7 as a cluster of sayings that reflect upon the stated theme of vv. 1-3, the contrast between the wise and the foolish as evidenced in speech. Verse 5 does not mention either wisdom or foolishness, and readers must infer that "the faithful witness" corresponds with wise behavior. Verse 6 revisits the *lēṣ*, whose skepticism is promoted through his speech (see [The Scoffer]). We have already encountered the assertion of this character's unteachability in 13:1. Verse 7b makes the concluding observation that in the presence of the fool there are no knowledgeable words.

The Wisdom of Righteousness, 14:8-15

These verses may be read as a group on the basis of their apparent chiastic arrangement. As in 13:12-19 (see [Chiastic Arrangement of vv. 12-19]), the apparent symmetrical arrangement of sayings assist readers' reflections on the possible main point of such an arrangement. Consider the following structural arrangement:

V. 8 "The clever and the fool"
  V. 9 "Moral behaviors, sacrifice, and the fool and the upright"
    V. 10 "The heart and its bitterness"
      V. 11 "The destruction of the house of the wicked"
      V. 12 "The destruction of one who follows his own way"
    V. 13 "The sadness of the heart"
  V. 14 "The results of moral and immoral behaviors"
V. 15 "The simple and the clever"

The outer sayings, vv. 8 and 15, contrast the presumptuousness of the fool with the discernment of the wise. These two verses have both language and imagery in common. Both speak of "the clever" (*ʿārûm*), in 8a and 15b; the image of "this way" in 8a parallels "his steps" in 15b; both sayings attribute presumption, or naivete, to the fool.

Verses 9 and 14 take the thinking further by pairing sayings about fools and the perverse: the fool scoffs at the guilt offering, the *ʾāšām*. [The ʾāšām] The perverse get what they deserve; presumably they, like their foolish counterparts, have not taken seriously the guilt offering either. While there are no shared vocabulary words between vv. 9 and 14, v. 9b describes the "upright," and v. 14b describes the synonymous "good one," *ʾîš tôb*.[4] Verses 10 and 13 appear to be paired more closely to each other, since both reflect upon a person's internal disposition. The verses share the word for "heart" (*lēb*) in 10a and 13a. They share the word for "joy" (*śimḥâ*) in 10b and 13b. Verse 10 asserts that the pain born on the inside cannot be fully shared or understood by any other. Verse 13 actually reinforces the claim of v. 10 by observing that, even though laughter appears on the outside, the inside is in pain. What is more, laughter always turns to pain.

Readers will look back to this saying when they read through Ecclesiastes (e.g., Eccl 7:2-7). The problem in Ecclesiastes is not that joy always turns to pain but rather how to turn pain into joy. Readers of both books therefore experience a reflective conversation between a sage and his tradition. Ecclesiastes tries to articulate what cannot easily be articulated, as Proverbs 14:10 states; in doing so,

The 'āšām

AΩ The extent of the scoffer's behavior is seen in his scoffing at the 'āšām (Prov 14:9), one of the important sacrifices for sin in ancient Israel's expiatory system. (Readers should note the difficulties of the text in v. 9: subject-verb agreement in stich a; meaning of *rāṣôn* in opposition to the cultic image of the 'āšām; and the allusion to cultic matters in the Proverbs, generally. LXX radically reinterprets the verse to address the houses of the impious and just. See Roland E. Murphy.)The term means "offense" and denotes the particular sacrificial offering on behalf of that offense, which reestablishes covenant between God and people, whether individuals, priests, or the community at large. This sacrifice is similar to a second kind of expiatory sacrifice, the sin offering, or *ḥaṭṭāʾt* (cf. Lev 5:14-26; 7:1-6). The thought of anyone scoffing at the means of removing alienation between God and humankind is absurd and only functions to intensify the extreme foolishness of such fools.

Burnt Offering
Illustration of a relief from Sainte Chapelle, Paris, of a lamb being offered (incorrectly) in a fire.

Rarely do readers encounter references to the system of temple worship and sacrifice in wisdom literature *per se*, although the sages certainly understood this important institution in the life of the people of ancient Israel. Ecclesiastes, for instance, speaks directly about the appropriate attitude with which one should venture to the temple to make vows (Eccl 5:1-7). The language of "abomination," a priestly concept, readers have already encountered several times in the Proverbs (e.g., 6:16; 8:7; 13:19; 15:8; 16:12). The term is used with a sense of both purity and ethical behavior. In Prov 14:9 the word 'āšām may only be used metaphorically as "offense" to stand in opposition to *rāṣôn*, "delight."

For further reading, see Gary A. Anderson, "Sacrifice and Sacrificial Offerings (OT)," *ABD* 5:870-86; Roland DeVaux, *Ancient Israel*, trans. John McHugh (London: Darton, Longman & Todd, 1961), 424-30; and T. H. Gaster, "Sacrifice in the OT," *IDB* 4:147-59.

Roland E. Murphy, *Proverbs* (WBC 22; Nashville: Thomas Nelson, 1998), 101.

however, he is himself driven to the conclusion that happiness and joy is only seldom available for humanity (e.g., Eccl 2:24-26; 3:12-13; 3:2; 5:18-20; 8:15; 9:7; 11:7–12:8). Whether this happiness Ecclesiastes advocates is only superficial, as is indicated in Proverbs 14:13, will be for readers of the later work to decide.

The central pair of sayings, vv. 11 and 12, offers an observation about the fates of the righteous and the wicked and then a generalization about how such fates apparently come upon people. Verse 11 states an interesting contrast between the apparent permanence of the wicked and the actual permanence of the upright. The use of "house" in reference to wicked and "tent" in reference to the upright adds sarcasm to intensify the point (cf. [House]). Houses are permanent; tents are not. But in this case, the more permanent house of the wicked is destroyed while the transitory tent of the upright flourishes. Such a fate reinforces the axiom that appearances are unreliable. This idea is then asserted in v. 12 that what appears to be the right way may, in fact, be the way that leads to death.

Once arriving at the central pair of sayings, readers may reflect on how the problem of appearances relates to all of the pairs in the group. Verses 8 and 15 have to do with presumptuousness and thus with the inability to see beneath the superficiality of appearances. Verses 10 and 13 concern the contrast between the joy that is externally visible and the internal experience of great pain. Scoffing at the guilt offering in v. 9 is an example of the failure to discern the importance of such ritual activity. One can only compare such activity with that of the fool who reaps what he sows in v. 14.

Portraits of Fools, 14:15-18

Verse 15 acts as a turning point for the next four sayings, each of which contrasts wisdom with folly. Notice the similarities in vv. 15 and 18. Both reflect on the behavior of "the simple" (*petî* and *pĕtaʾîm*) and the "clever" (*ʿārûm* and *ʿărûmîm*). Verse 16 is paired with v. 15 by restating the contrast between naivete and acute awareness. Verses 15b and 16a virtually restate each other: "the clever consider their steps; the wise are cautious and turn away from evil." Verse 16b stands in close thematic relationship with 15a, comparing the behaviors of the "simple" who believe everything and the fool who "throws off restraint, and is trusting."

Verse 17 (cf. v. 29) also has the vocabulary contrasting foolish with wise behavior. Quick temper is not only declared to be characteristic of foolishness, but it also follows the description in 16b as an example of another kind of lack of restraint. Verse 17b is translated in NRSV as "and the schemer is hated," a topic readers have already encountered in 12:12. The "schemer" (*ʾîš mĕzimmôt*) is deliberate in his thinking, whether or not normative value is attached to the outcomes of his thoughts. Such deliberation is a good contrast to the short-tempered fool in 17a. The problem is why such deliberate thought should attract ill will from others. Obviously, such deliberation can indeed have negative outcomes and thus be construed as scheming. If the final word of 17b is translated from *yissâ'* rather than from *yissāne'*, thus emending the text, as the LXX translation implies it might be, then we have a sense that fits with the contrast set up in the saying. The deliberate or patient person "bears a lot" rather than "is hated." This translation therefore implies the virtue of such discipline of mind.[5]

The Wise and the Foolish, 14:18-24

Just as in the preceding group of sayings, vv. 15-18, the closing statement opens the following group. That is, v. 18 also acts as a turning point. Readers have seen that the language on the simple and the clever in v. 18 parallels the same language in v. 15. Again, the language of "inheritance" (*nāḥălû*) and "crowning" (*yaktirû*) in v. 18 parallels the similar language of "crown" and "garland" in v. 24. These two outer verses form an inclusio containing materials readers may relate together. Verse 19 describes the final fate of evil people as one of service to good people. The sayings that follow provide criteria for defining "good" behavior according to their relative treatment of the poor.

Verses 20 and 21 form a pair with each other through common vocabulary and a shift in point of view on the same topic. The common vocabulary is "the neighbor." In v. 20 the neighbor is the one who hates the poor. In v. 21 the neighbor is the poor person who is hated by the rich. The shift in point of view implicates readers. If readers affirm the truth of v. 20, then they are easily included within the group that is condemned for such behavior in v. 21. Thus the progression of thought develops with a further reflection in v. 22 on the judgment of the machinations of planning evil. In the context of vv. 20 and 21 readers relate such machinations of evil and good with the problem of the treatment of the poor. Verse 23 offers a general statement that potentially challenges the moral validity of poverty in general. If readers accept the premise of v. 23, that all work is profitable, then the poor exist because they do not work enough.

Readers may anticipate the words of a later sage, Qoheleth, who is rethinking some of these assumptions. His observations and instructions question the efficacy of work in his opening statement: "What do people gain from all the toil at which they toil under the sun?" (e.g., 1:3). Such questioning seems to be seeking an alternative explanation for poverty. Indeed, the much deeper assumption, that somehow ordered reality is understandable and provides a basis for confidence that one may prosper and enjoy one's prosperity, is also seriously questioned by that later sage (e.g.,

Eccl 3:1-8, 9-15). In fact, Qoheleth probably more than any other sage recognizes the disparities between appearances and reality (cf. Prov 14:12-13), especially those between joy and sadness, meaning and absurdity, even righteousness and wickedness.

Verse 24 closes the group of sayings with language that parallels the language in v. 18. NRSV emends the text of v. 24 in two places: first, by changing "riches" in 24a to "wisdom"; second, by changing "folly" in 24b to "the garland." The change in 24b makes good sense. The change in 24a too facilely follows the implications of the LXX. However, the MT in 24a, if retained ("riches") provides yet a further assertion about poverty. Not only does work prevent poverty, but wisdom does as well by making one wealthy.

Wise Speech, 14:25-27

These three sayings revisit themes stated earlier in the collection. Verse 25 reiterates and completes the thought of v. 5. Initially the truthful witness is simply one who does not lie. Here such a one actually saves lives. While the language seems to betray an original concern with legal testimony, in this context readers may also associate that testimony with instructions from the sage. The climactic admonitions of the collection are in vv. 26 and 27. Both are Yahweh sayings, both completing the thought first articulated in 14:2. In the earlier saying the concern is to identify behavior that is fitting for one who fears Yahweh. In these two verses the concern is to state that "the fear of Yahweh" results in long life and an inheritance.

Wisdom for a King, 14:28-35

The concluding eight sayings are provocative in that, while they revisit themes already encountered, they are placed within a framework of two sayings on kingship. Verses 28 and 35 set out the stresses of kingship: on the one hand, without people, the king is ruined; on the other hand, foolish servants will incur the king's wrath. [Wisdom and Kingship] The sayings between these two invite a point of view that acknowledges their possible application to the king's responsibilities and to the institution of kingship. Thus, slowness to anger (readers have encountered similar language in 14:17) and the tranquility of mind (vv. 29 and 30) are essential to maintaining an administrative balance of judgment. The sayings on oppression of the poor and the fate of the wicked (vv. 31 and 32) have a new relevance beyond the concerns of the ordinary citizen.

Wisdom and Kingship

There is a general consensus that ancient Israel's wisdom tradition has as one of its sources of origin the international political environment. Sayings within the collection of Proverbs often portray the importance of the king's counselors and servants (e.g., Prov 15:35). Additionally, the sayings affirm the role of the kings as God's regent with the purpose of maintaining justice and the social order (e.g., Prov 16:10-15; 25:1-7). The narrative traditions of the Bible reinforce this notion in the stories about Solomon's supplication for wisdom (1 Kgs 3:9), about his discernment (1 Kgs 3:16-28), and about his compositions and renown (1 Kgs 4:29-34).

Of course, this does not mean that all kings successfully maintained justice, nor that all people felt kingship was to be so highly regarded. The most influential history within the Bible, the Deuteronomistic History (Joshua, Judges, Samuel, and Kings), portrays kings as leading Israel astray from commitment to Yahweh (e.g., 2 Kgs 17:1-23, esp. v. 21; Jer 23:1-4; 25:33-38; 22:1-17). Several of the wisdom sayings criticize kings for cruelty and oppression (e.g., Prov 28:15; 29:2, 4). The later sage, Ecclesiastes, simply resigns himself to the arbitrariness of royal power (e.g., Eccl 8:2-4), though such references may be to foreign kings and not to Israel's kings.

For further reading, see Joseph Blenkinsopp, *Sage, Priest, Prophet* (Louisville: Westminster John Knox Press, 1995), 9-64; and James Miller, *The Origins of the Bible* (New York: Paulist, 1996).

It is the king who must ensure justice and equity. Referring again to Ecclesiastes, readers will see that the royal persona—the character through whose eyes and voice the observations of the book are ostensibly offered, especially in 1:12-2:26—doubts that such justice and equity exist (cf. Eccl 4:1-3). One of the initial ironies established in the book of Ecclesiastes is that the opening observations of life's inequities come from a king, whose responsibility it is to maintain such equity and justice.

Reading the final section in Proverbs 14:28-35 offers some special interest in that the themes seem to follow sequentially in pairs. Verses 29 and 30 assert the internal disposition of the king; vv. 31 and 32 concern the social circumstances in the kingdom; and vv. 33 and 34 address the ideals of wisdom and righteousness, perhaps as guides for the head of state. However, these sayings also seem to be arranged chiastically if we observe common catchwords and aural cues. Consider the following graphic representation of the arrangement of sayings and themes. The italicized words at the end of each line represent the link to other lines of poetry, as is explained in the following paragraph.

V. 28 Kingship topics (*melek, rāzôn*)
  V. 29 Internal disposition of the king: understanding (*těbûnâ*)
  V. 30 Internal disposition of the king (*lēb*)
    V. 31 Social circumstances of kingdom (the poor)
    V. 32 Social circumstances of kingdom (the wicked)

V. 33 Internal disposition of the king: the mind (*lēb*)
V. 34 Internal disposition-external reality: righteousness
V. 35 Kingship topics (*melek, rĕṣôn*)

For instance, vv. 28 and 35 share the word "king" (*melek*) and topics concerned with kingship. Verse 28 concludes with the word "prince" (*rāzôn*), which in Hebrew sounds similar to the word opening v. 35, "delight" (*rĕṣôn*). Verses 29 and 34 share words for "exalt," coming from the same Hebrew root, *rûm*. Verses 20 and 33 both reflect on the "mind" (*lēb*). At the center of the chiasm are two sayings that comment upon each other: v. 31 concerns those who oppress the poor; v. 32 concerns the wicked. In such close proximity to each other the verses imply that those who oppress the poor are themselves wicked.

CONNECTIONS

Wisdom and Public Discourse

What has public policy to do with religion? The question is prompted by this chapter's collection of sayings that blend several perspectives on the wise and the foolish with a concluding reflection upon the importance of kingship. Government, public policy, and wise decision-making somehow must go together even though their interests at times seem to stand in opposition. In a constitutional democracy, such as that privileged in the United States, it is the public, not just the king's advisors, that must be wise decision-makers.

"Trash talk" has become the popular approach to public political discourse. Generally what is meant by this term is a brand of communication that feeds on the emotions rather than appealing to a higher sense of reason and logic. And while everyone is guilty of using such approaches to persuasion, it is the media who probably should be held as accountable as any for promoting this in the United States. Well-known radio and television people, with high-energy personalities and overzealous ideological commitments, dispense their brand of political commentary daily to a public that grows increasingly cynical with each passing election year. Indeed, gross inequities, government wastefulness, attitudes of entitlement and privilege, just as heartless prosperity and the breaking of public trust, warrant extreme measures. But people who must make decisions in the public square would be wise to listen to the sages of ancient Israel: "The simple believe everything, but the clever consider their steps" (Prov 14:15). The rush to invest oneself heavily in the witty and glitzy contemporary wisdom of those who crank it out like so much sound-byte sausage is not wise, and ultimately in no one's best interest. Only informed, patient, and responsible conversation will suffice as a basis for effective decision-making.

Wise decision-making on matters of public concern—with the emphasis upon "wise"—is of concern to the Christian community. Foy Valentine, former director of the Southern Baptist Convention Christian Life Commission, provides the following four guidelines for public debate and decision-making:[6]

- We all must understand that robust public debate is indispensable to a healthy democracy.
- This debate is not a spectator sport. Responsible citizens can and should participate in reasoned dialogue on important public issues.
- Consumers of media as well as media owners, managers, and personalities need to devote their considerable talents to developing a responsible and civilized dialogue.
- Parents, teachers, clergy, and others who do the hard work of equipping people to be good citizens should be commended and supported in their work.

An assault mentality informs our current approach to public debate. Perhaps the word "debate" itself conjures up images of contestants opposing each other in tense matches of question and answer, driven by the pressure of time and the scrutiny of a camera. With so much at stake, people with differing points of view are driven to questionable rhetorical strategies. Where does reasoned thought take place? When does honest exchange of doubt and ambiguity happen? Who is able to help a nation move beyond the superficialities of personality and outcome to an ongoing process of genuine engagement of the social problems that profoundly affect the nation?

Wise rulers are those who realize that their glory resides in the greatness of their people (Prov 14:28). Their delight is in the prudence of their advisors (and also their people). Perhaps the criteria for electing officials to lead government ought to include something more than whether they take the population by the storm of their rhetoric. Perhaps the criteria ought to include the way they help us, indeed inspire us, to listen to each other in addressing a government's challenges.

NOTES

[1] Leo Perdue, *Proverbs* (IBC; Louisville: Westminster John Knox Press, 2000), 171, states the contrast to be between the "righteous wise and the wicked fool."

[2] Roland E. Murphy, *Proverbs* (WBC 22; Nashville: Word, 1998), 101-03; William McKane, *Proverbs* (OTL; London: SCM Press, 1970), 472.

[3] R. N. Whybray, *The Composition of the Book of Proverbs* (JSOTSup 168; Sheffield: JSOT Press, 1994), 101.

[4] Verse 9 is plagued with serious textual difficulties. See Murphy, *Proverbs,* 101 and McKane, *Proverbs,* 476.

[5] See McKane, *Proverbs,* 468. Murphy, *Proverbs,* 102, sees such an emendation as unnecessary, however.

[6] Printed in the *Kansas City Star* (8 June 1996), E-12. These four were developed by participants in colloquia on public discourse sponsored by the Center for Christian Ethics, Dallas TX. Foy Valentine was Director of the Christian Life Commission of the Southern Baptist Convention for twenty-eight years.

THE DISCIPLINE OF REASON
AND RELIGION

Proverbs 15:1-33

With Proverbs 15 readers come to the conclusion of the initial collection of sayings in the "Proverbs of Solomon," which began in 10:1. This chapter reiterates the important themes encountered up to this point and anticipates the central concerns of chapter 16. The important themes are those that have underscored the many assertions throughout of the profitability of wisdom. For instance, there have been repeated reflections upon children who listen to their parents' instruction or students who attend to the teachings of the wise. Proper speech is the evidence of knowledge. Proper decision-making is the difference between the fates of the wise and the foolish. The fates of the wicked and the righteous are also connected to wisdom and foolishness, thus joining wisdom with a moral and ethical motivation. The fear of Yahweh is the beginning and ending of wisdom, and in chapter 15 it becomes a dominant theme. [Structure at a Glance: Proverbs 15]

Structure at a Glance: Proverbs 15

AΩ The occurrence of nine Yahweh sayings, about one-third of the total number of sayings in this chapter (vv. 3, 8, 9, 11, 16, 25, 26, 29, and 33), anticipates the central theological concerns of ch. 16. In terms of a meaningful structural arrangement of sayings, readers may find the following outline helpful.

Vv. 1-4 Advice for a King
Vv. 5-12 The Fool before the Lord
Vv. 13-19 The Inside Matters
Vv. 20-33 Retrospect on Solomon's Sayings

Readers who pause to search for structure and interconnection will recognize familiar catchword techniques and inclusion devices linking together sayings and groups of sayings. Verses 1-4 are dominated by a speech motif (v. 3 is the exception) and may actually be an extension of the royal theme in 14:28-35. Verses 5 and 12, through catchwords and theme, create an inclusio for a group of sayings on wisdom and instruction. Verses 13-17 are dominated by the imagery of "rejoicing" and by the catchwords of "heart" (*lēb*, "mind") and "good" (*tôb*, "better"). Verses 18 and 19 stand each on its own, although both return to themes readers have encountered already in 15:1. The final cluster of sayings are continued in 20-33. This final collection may be broken into three separate subgroups. Verses 20-24 return to the theme of the wise versus the foolish and the accompanying evidence for such behaviors. Verses 25-27, positioned at the center of the three subgroups, reassert the moral-theological underpinnings of wisdom. Verses 28-33 return to observations about the importance of learning wisdom, the theme that opens the entire collection.

COMMENTARY

Advice for a King, 15:1-4

These opening four sayings assert the importance of soothing language. Verse 1 contrasts language that brings people together with words that drive them farther apart. If we read these verses in the context of 14:28-35, then a chief administrator such as a king must be attentive to such matters of conciliation. Indeed, both the king and the teacher must be aware of the power of language. The book of Ecclesiastes will remind readers that "the words of the wise are like nails" (12:11) and that the teacher, Qoheleth, sought to find "pleasing words" (12:10). The NRSV translates Proverbs 15:2 as "dispenses knowledge," while MT has "makes knowledge good." This latter idea might well be consonant with Ecclesiastes 12:10, if it may be allowed that speech may be polished, "adorned or embellished."[1] Verse 4 concludes with the image of the gentle tongue, or "healing tongue" in MT. The saying appeals to an image readers have already encountered, the "tree of life" (e.g., 3:18; 11:30; cf. 10:11; 14:27; 13:14), implying that proper speech is a source of life and vitality.

Embedded within this discourse on proper speech, v. 3 asserts that the "eyes" of Yahweh are in every place. Given the context, readers may wonder why not the "ears" of Yahweh also. Nevertheless, the image provides a clear statement about Yahweh's presence. Yahweh's activity is "looking out" (*ṣōpôt*) for "the evil and the good." In the present group one understands the reference to be to the evil and good that might come from one's speech.

The Fool Before the Lord, 15:5-12

Verses 5 and 12 appear to function as an inclusio (see [Inclusio with Two Women]) for these sayings. Both contrast the wise and the foolish. They use common language in describing the fool as one who does not "heed admonition" or "rebuke" (*tôkaḥat*, or *hôkēaḥ*), both terms that come from the same Hebrew root. Overall, the sayings deal with the importance of wisdom and instruction by contrasting the wise and the foolish. Verses 5-7 may, however, be read as a subgroup on instruction; in that case, the remaining verses, vv. 8-11, might be read as a response that moralizes the instructions in vv. 5-7.

Verses 5 and 7 both comment on the discipline that is necessary to obtain wisdom. Verse 7 appropriately follows v. 5 by observing that the wise ones spread wisdom. It is incumbent upon one who would learn, therefore, to be receptive. Verse 6 offers a motivation, first by implying that wisdom is a characteristic of those who practice righteousness (thus, one should be receptive to wise instruction), and second by urging that such wisdom and righteousness is rewarded. NRSV's translation of v. 6 corrects the MT by removing the preposition *bĕ*—"in, with, or by"—from the opening of 6b and placing the same preposition at the beginning of 6a, according to the LXX translation. Still, what might be meant by "trouble befalls the income of the wicked" in 6b most likely means that the wicked can derive no benefit from it.[2]

Verses 8-11 consist mainly of Yahweh sayings with only one saying in the group (v. 10) returning to the overall concern of 5-12, the importance of discipline. Verse 10 uses the same vocabulary as vv. 5 and 12: "discipline" (*mûsār*) and "rebuke" (*tôkaḥat*). Verses 8 and 9 are paired in their use of common language and in their thematic concerns. The language of sacrifice, with its attending notions of purity and abomination, makes these verses somewhat unique in the collections of sayings (cf. 14:9). Both verses contrast the righteous with the wicked. They further provide an interesting contrast with Ecclesiastes' remarks on the relative importance of sacrifice (cf. Eccl 5:1-6). Verse 8 offers an intriguing parallel between sacrifice, *zebaḥ*, and prayer, *tĕpillat*. Such an equation raises questions about the changing views within the Hebrew community of such religious activities. [Prayer] Verse 11 returns to the observation in v. 3 concerning the presence of Yahweh. Not only is Yahweh present in every place (through his eyes), but Yahweh knows the internal workings, "the hearts," of humans as well. The parallel between Sheol and Abaddon, mythic imagery for death, and the human heart functions to emphasize the inscrutability of both. Only Yahweh understands both. What is more, from a human perspective, understanding the human heart is like trying to understand death. "Who knows?" as Ecclesiastes says (Eccl 3:20-22). [Sheol and Abaddon]

Sheol and Abaddon

AΩ The saying in 15:11 is an assertion of Yahweh's power as creator over against the relative inferiority of humanity. The two terms Sheol and Abaddon, both names for the underworld (see [The Jaws of Death]), occur only three times together in the Old Testament (Job 26:6; Prov 15:11; 27:20). The word Abaddon comes from the Hebrew root *ʾābad*, which in its Qal stem means "to perish." The etymology of Sheol is more complex and is not much help in appreciating the usage of the word. The most simple connection is with the Hebrew root *šāʾal*, "to ask." A euphemism is implied here, though. The term would refer to "that place asked about." Another possible explanation of the derivation from "to ask" assumes necromancy as a background, and the one who inquires of the dead about the future (see 1 Sam 28:1-19).

In any event the terms refer to the place or abode of the dead (e.g., Gen 37:35; 1 Kgs 2:6; Job 17:16). It is interesting that one "goes down" to Sheol (Job 17:16; Ps 88:3-4; Deut 32:22); often those depths are contrasted with the height of heaven (Amos 9:2; Job 11:8). The underworld is a place of darkness (Job 17:13; 18:18) and quiet.

For further reading, see W. F. Albright, "The Etymology of *Seʾol*," *AJSL* 34 (1918): 109-10; Theodore J. Lewis, "Dead, Abode of the," *ABD* 2:101-105; and N. Tromp, *Primitive Conceptions of Death and the Nether World in the Old Testament* (Chicago: Loyola Press, 1969).

Prayer

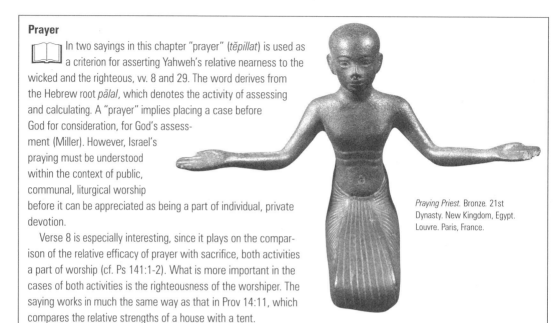

In two sayings in this chapter "prayer" (*tĕpillat*) is used as a criterion for asserting Yahweh's relative nearness to the wicked and the righteous, vv. 8 and 29. The word derives from the Hebrew root *pālal*, which denotes the activity of assessing and calculating. A "prayer" implies placing a case before God for consideration, for God's assess-ment (Miller). However, Israel's praying must be understood within the context of public, communal, liturgical worship before it can be appreciated as being a part of individual, private devotion.

Praying Priest. Bronze. 21st Dynasty. New Kingdom, Egypt. Louvre. Paris, France.

Verse 8 is especially interesting, since it plays on the compar-ison of the relative efficacy of prayer with sacrifice, both activities a part of worship (cf. Ps 141:1-2). What is more important in the cases of both activities is the righteousness of the worshiper. The saying works in much the same way as that in Prov 14:11, which compares the relative strengths of a house with a tent.

Readers are reminded here of the frequent prophetic condemnations of sac-rificial ceremony in the absence of justice and purity of heart (Mic 6:6-8; Amos 5:21-24). Even prayer offered in the context of temple worship was to be offered in purity (Isa 1:10-17). Perhaps these sayings in Prov 15:8 and 29 come from an era when, because of the destruction of the temple, prayer became a rival ritual act, perhaps over the objections of purists who felt that only proper sacrifice at the altar of the temple could suffice to maintain relationship to God. [See Samuel E. Balentine for a discussion of the emergence of prayer to a status equivalent with sacrifice.]

For further reading, see James H. Charlesworth, "Prayer in Early Judaism," *ABD* 5:449-50; Jacob Neusner, *From Politics to Piety* (New York: Ktav, 1979); and S. Talmon, "The Emergence of Institutionalized Prayer in Israel in Light of the Qumran Literature," in *Qumran: Sa piété, sa theologie et son milieu*, ed. M. Delcor (BETL 46; Paris and Louvain, 1978).

Samuel E. Balentine, Prayer in the Hebrew Bible (Minneapolis: Fortress, 1993), 273-75.

Patrick D. Miller, They Cried to the Lord (Minneapolis: Fortress Press, 1994), 38-39; paraphrasing Sheldon H. Blank, "The Confessions of Jeremiah and the Meaning of Prayer," HUCA 21 (1948): 337-38, n. 2.

The Inside Matters, 15:13-17 (18 and 19)

Verses 13-17 form a group of sayings connected through catch-words and a chain of related thoughts. Verses 13 and 14 form a pair joined by the opening words, "heart" and "mind" (*lēb*). Verses 16 and 17 form a pair of "better than" (*tôb*) statements, both of which concern with the theme of poverty. The saying in the middle of the group, v. 15, combines both catchwords, *tôb* and *lēb* in the second stichos, thus linking vv. 13 and 14 with 16 and 17.

An interesting progression of thought is at work within these sayings. Verse 13 and 14 concern a person's internal dispositions. They both contrast the internal emotions with the external effect: cheer within yields cheer without. This idea parallels the ensuing claim in v. 14 that speech is the result of knowledge. We have encountered such contrasts between internal and external dispositions already in 14:30 and 12:20. Even Ecclesiastes recognizes that the internal disposition affects one's external actions (Eccl 8:1). But v. 15 offers an application to a real problem: can one who is poor ameliorate his suffering by facing poverty with the appropriate disposition? This would be the implication of the two statements in v. 15. Are readers to understand that the way to address the suffering poverty brings is by maintaining a cheerful heart, a positive attitude, or a balanced emotional state? Or is this a form of denial that too easily glosses over real social problems?

Verses 16-17 take the question further. Verse 16, a Yahweh saying, states that religion joined with poverty is better than wealth conjoined with trouble. Verse 17 is not a Yahweh saying but expresses a similar idea: poverty, represented by a table of vegetables, with love is better than wealth, represented by the "fatted ox," conjoined with hatred. Both sayings rest on the assumptions set out in vv. 13 and 14. One may wonder, however, whether the author of this saying was himself wealthy or poor. On the other hand, readers again anticipate the words of Ecclesiastes, who may himself have been wealthy and concluded that all is absurdity (Eccl 2:1-11). [Theodicy]

Verses 18 and 19 apparently stand on their own. There may be some thematic connection between vv. 17 and 18 in the conclusion of 17b with the word "hate" (*śin'â-bô*) and the opening of 18a with "hot-tempered" (*'îš ḥēmâ*). Verse 18 recalls the concerns of the opening four sayings (vv. 1-4) with its interest in anger (*ḥēmâ*). Verse 19 contrasts two different kinds of categories, laziness and

Theodicy

The term *theodicy* denotes the phenomenon of maintaining belief in the justice and righteousness of God in the face of disconfirming experiences. Although the term is not in the Old Testament, it provides the conceptual umbrella for readers' understanding of the many questions about innocent suffering and righteous retribution within (e.g., Jer 12:1; Job 21:1-16; Gen 18:22-33). James L. Crenshaw notes that the concept was never merely theoretical in the Old Testament. The issue of God's just governance of the universe involved society itself, from economics, to social disparity, and including individuals' rights. Little wonder that the wisdom literature took the question so seriously. The sages' conviction of the order and harmony of creation had to withstand an awesome challenge from all disconfirming realities, including the Babylonian captivity.

The Old Testament literature documents Israel's commitment to hold on to belief in God's justice, even when he decreed the sacrifice of Abraham's firstborn (Gen 22), or his own firstborn, Israel (Hos 11:1-11). If theodicy is indeed the beginning point for theological reflection, theology takes on a defensive posture, bearing the weight of justifying evil before praise can take place.

The confession of Yahweh's presence may be taken as an assertion of theodicy. Nothing happens without the Lord's knowing it; no event falls outside the order of the Lord's universe. The wisdom tradition gives fullest expression to the struggle to maintain a good faith commitment to God's righteousness. While asserting God's presence, as in Prov 15:3, the tale of Job makes clear that the maintenance of such views exacts high prices in the realm of human surrender and submission.

For further reading, see James L. Crenshaw, "Theodicy," *IDBSup*, 895-96; Leo G. Perdue, *Wisdom in Revolt* (JSOTSup 112; Sheffield: JSOT Press, 1991); and R. J. Williams, "Theodicy in the Ancient Near East," *CJT* 2 (1956): 14-26.

James L. Crenshaw, "Theodicy," ABD 6: 444-47.

moral uprightness. The implication is that industriousness is given moral value. On the other hand, there may be humor in the images. The lazy person always has an excuse for not working—in this case that excuse consists of the "thorns" along his way.

Retrospect on Solomon's Sayings, 15:20-33

The concluding section of sayings recapitulates several themes readers have encountered throughout the opening five chapters of the "Proverbs of Solomon." The sayings are gathered rhetorically in three subgroups, the two outer groups paralleling each other. The inner group functions as a kind of central focus. Verses 20-24 concern wisdom and folly, education and instruction. Verses 25-27 contrast righteousness with wickedness and Yahweh's judgment. Verses 28-33 return to the themes of the initial subgroup, only here the appeal to Yahweh reinforces and legitimizes the claim that one's desire for discipline is wisdom. Moreover, these closing verses complete an inclusio for the entire section, Proverbs 10:1–15:33, by returning to the themes encountered in 10:1-4, which initially assert the idea of wisdom's profitability.

Verses 20-24 concern the themes of wisdom and folly and foreshadow Ecclesiastes' "test" of wisdom and folly (e.g., Eccl 2:1). Verse 20 returns to the images of 15:5, 13:1, and 10:1 concerning the pleasure wise children give to their parents. Verse 24, perhaps the climax of this initial group, offers the broadest statement justifying both the success of wise children and the joy it brings to parents: "the path of life leads upward for the wise," avoiding the downward slope toward Sheol for fools. Within these two sayings there are examples of folly and wisdom. Verse 21 begins with a general statement that folly causes rejoicing only to those who lack sense. By contrast, 21b moralizes the understanding person's behavior. That person "walks straight ahead." The verbal root for "to walk straight" is the same root encountered in the noun "the upright" (*yāšār*). Thus, as in v. 19, where industriousness is moralized—using the same root, *yāšār*—v. 21 has a similar moralizing strategy. Verse 22 offers another example of folly by asserting that there are no plans where there is no council. Verses 21 and 23 balance each other in their use of the image of "joy" (*śimḥâ*) to characterize their examples of wisdom or folly. In v. 23 joy is the result of a timely answer, something only a wise person could possibly appreciate. The combination of terminology provides a background for the theological implications of "joy." Ecclesiastes interprets joy as the "answer" of God to the plight of humanity (e.g., Eccl 5:18-20; 9:7-10) in what is perhaps one of the climactic statements of the book of Ecclesiastes. Joy may be all that is left when everything else is absurd. In v. 23 something as simple as the right word at the right time provides joy.

Verses 25-27 provide a moral center for these closing sayings (vv. 20-33), both metaphorically and literally. Metaphorically, they appeal to Yahweh as the source of wisdom's order. Literally, these three moralizing verses stand in the center of two outlying groups of sayings on wisdom and folly (vv. 20-24 and 28-33). All three of these assert explicitly or implicitly Yahweh's judgment upon wickedness. Verse 25 observes that Yahweh will protect the widow by tearing down the house of the proud. Verse 26 returns to the abomination formula readers have encountered in vv. 8 and 9 to assert the contrast between evil plans and pleasant words. The imagery of v. 27 is not new; Proverbs 11:29 also speaks of the one who "troubles his house" (cf. 15:6). Readers have also encountered the sages' disapproval of "ill-gotten gain" in 1:19. The attitude toward bribery will occur again in 17:8, 19:6, and 21:14. In v. 27, the implication is that Yahweh guarantees life to those who hate bribes since it is through bribery that one's profit is inappropriately obtained.

Verses 28-33 each contain either explicit or implicit references to hearing, heeding, or reflecting upon instruction, good news, or prayer. With such language and imagery, this opening section (Prov 10–15) on the profitability of wisdom comes to a close. The implication is that apart from one's attentive listening, people may not receive wisdom or any of its attending advantages. The opening image of the righteous person's activity is one of "pondering," or "musing." Psalm 1:2 translates the same Hebrew word, *yehgeh*, as "meditates" (NRSV). The emphasis is more upon how one receives words than it is on the immediate answer one might offer. The wicked, by contrast (v. 28b), have answers bubbling out of their mouths. It would be easy to take v. 29 in two ways. The most obvious sense is that Yahweh does not listen to the words (the prayers?) of the wicked in the way that he does the righteous. But also, Yahweh's self is one who ponders the right answer to the prayers of the righteous (Eccl 5:5-6).

Verses 30 and 31 continue the motif of hearing and listening. In 30b the benefits of "good news" are stated plainly as "refreshing the body." Verse 30a, however, is more challenging. To what does the metaphor "light of the eyes" refer? Ecclesiastes contrasts the "sight of the eyes" with the "wandering of desire" (Eccl 6:9). Desire is unrealized, but seeing implies a more concrete experience. In v. 30, both the pleasing sight and the good word have positive internal consequences. Verse 31 is paired with v. 30 through the theme of hearing and the specific catchwords on hearing: the words translated "news" (*šĕmûʿâ,* v. 30) and "heeds" (*šōmaʿat,* v. 31). Verse 31a qualifies 30b by reflecting upon "wholesome admonition" (*tôkaḥat ḥayyîm*). The implication is that the good word is one that provides the admonition of life. People who receive this will dwell with the wise.

   The final two sayings are paired by their mutual catchwords for "instruction" or discipline (*mûsār*). Verse 32b links with v. 31 by continuing the motif of "heeding of admonition" (*šōmēaʿ tôkaḥat*). The assertion in v. 32 parallels previous statements in 15:20, 13:1, 12:1, and 10:1, which is ultimately a concern of the entire opening collection. It is self-destructive to reject instruction. The closing verse reiterates this now common theme by equating religious piety with this instruction. By doing so, piety, with its attending humility, properly precedes wisdom. Ultimately the profitability of wisdom derives from Yahweh's hand.

CONNECTIONS

Religion and Human Knowledge

The first half of the closing saying of the chapter, v. 33a, equates fearing Yahweh and the discipline of wisdom. The second part of the saying, v. 33b, asserts that humility must precede glory. In relationship to the opening statement of v. 33, humility implies religious surrender. In other words, seeking Yahweh means first humbling oneself. Only then may one obtain the glory that comes from wisdom. This is most certainly an assertion that intellectual activity cannot be embraced without also embracing religious faith.

   Biblical scholars like to debate whether such an assertion of religious priority reflects a conviction that emerged during the post-exilic period, or whether the sages would have held such views in the pre-exilic period.[3] In the former case, heavy editing of collections of wisdom sayings would have overlaid older, more secular collections of sayings with later assertions of the theological character of wisdom. In addition, there would have been a desire to intimate through the rhetoric of the sequence of collections this same theological priority. This might help to explain why the beginning, middle, and end of the Proverbs are strong statements of the preeminence of Yahweh. The purpose of such theological editing would have been to respond to a view of reality that rested upon human reason and cognition rather than Yahwistic revelation.

One reason that this approach is so attractive to biblical scholars is that it parallels the contemporary struggle to understand the relationship between a modern, non-supernatural worldview with that of an ancient, supernatural worldview. Christians find themselves torn in just such a way. There are claims that grow from their faith as well as their society. The former are founded upon assertions that are pre-scientific; the latter are scientific throughout. How should one understand the relationship between science and religion without becoming an intellectual schizophrenic?

Ian Barbour's *Religion in an Age of Science*[4] opens with a discussion of four different ways of relating science and religion. First is open conflict, where either science "swallows" religion or religion "swallows" science. The weakness here is that both reduce the other to something less than what it is. A second kind of relationship seeks to keep the two absolutely independent. Each stays in its own realm, using different methods of thought, beginning from unrelated starting points. Unfortunately, life itself, Barbour concludes, is not nearly so neat and tidy. A third relationship attempts to develop dialogue between science and religion, seeking to find some common methodological approaches and aiming to understand the boundaries between the two. A great deal of mutual understanding is afforded through such approaches. However, the risks include glossing over the absolute differences that do exist. Barbour's final category is called integration. Utilizing categories from nature, both science and religion seek to find a new reality that forges a new synthesis for the content and methods of investigation of each discipline.

If it is true that the explicit theological elements of the wisdom tradition did not emerge until after the exile, it is also clear that Barbour's first three categories are not quite sufficient to appreciate what those sages were doing. Something along the lines of the complete integration is represented in sayings such as that in 15:33. The groundwork for understanding the verse in this way—and all of the Yahwistic verses in Proverbs 10–15—has already been laid in chapters 1, 8, and 9 where wisdom becomes a person. Wisdom is no longer a mere object but is now a subject itself. Yahweh is portrayed as the creator of wisdom, apart from whom creation did not come into existence. Wisdom was at Yahweh's side while he created (Prov 8:30). Wisdom became something new; Yahweh as her creator has a new relationship with wisdom, a personal relationship.

So must it be for Christians and the way they hold knowledge vis-à-vis faith. Knowledge is not merely objective reality, but takes on its own subjectivity in relationship to the creator of all the universe. Coming to know and understand the universe means coming to know the creator of the universe.

NOTES

[1] William McKane, *Proverbs* (OTL; London: SCM Press, 1970), 478.

[2] Ibid., 486. See also R. E. Murphy, *Proverbs* (WBC 22; Nashville: Thomas Nelson, 1998), 110.

[3] Compare the introductions of McKane, *Proverbs*, and R. N Whybray, *The Composition of the Book of Proverb* (JSOTSup 168; Sheffield: JSOT Press, 1994). For a readable explanation of these different views see R. E. Clements, *Wisdom in Theology* (Grand Rapids: Eerdmans, 1992),151-79.

[4] Ian Barbour, *Religion in an Age of Science*, Gifford Lectures, vol. 1 (San Francisco: Harper Collins, 1990).

THE CENTER
OF THE UNIVERSE

Proverbs 16:1-33

Proverbs 16 is of special importance, since it introduces the second subcollection of Solomonic sayings and also stands at the very center of the collection titled "Proverbs of Solomon." The Masora notes that 16:17 is also the central verse of the entire collection of the book of Proverbs. [The Masoretes] Such a strategic position in the center of the book might explain why the number of Yahweh sayings increases so dramatically in this chapter. Eleven of the total thirty-three sayings are Yahweh sayings in the chapter (vv. 1-7, 9, 11, 20, 33). The first nine, with the exception of v. 8, are a set collection of Yahweh sayings. Clearly, this chapter asserts the fear of Yahweh as the fundamental principal of wisdom. The variation in the style of these sayings further reinforces the chapter's distinctiveness. Readers immediately recognize the absence of antithetical, or contrastive, sayings. The sayings are predominantly synonymous, or reiterative (see ch. 17). [Structure at a Glance: Proverbs 16]

Structure at a Glance: Proverbs 16

AΩ Even though ch. 16 begins the second half of the Sayings of Solomon, it stands out from the other chapters because of the predominance of Yahweh sayings. For this reason, we have postponed the introductory discussion of the second half of this section until ch. 17. The purpose is to concede the possible function of ch. 16 as a kind of theological center point around which both units in chs. 10–15 and 17–22:16 are structurally related. As far as the structure of the chapter itself is concerned, readers might consider two broad sections as follows:

I. Vv. 1-15 *Yahweh and the King*
  Vv. 1-9 Yahweh and Human Limitation
  Vv. 10-15 On Kings and Kingship
II. Vv. 16-30 *The Wise and Wicked Ways*
  Vv. (16) 17-20 Watching One's Way
  Vv. 21-25 Speech that Is Pleasing
  Vv. 26-30 The Way of Wickedness

The groupings of the sayings structure the chapter broadly into two halves, vv. 1-15 and vv. 16-33, with smaller subgroups evident within each half of the chapter. Most obvious to readers is the opening section on Yahweh, vv. 1-9, followed by a collection on the king and kingship, vv. 10-15. The juxtaposition of these two groups provides ample opportunity for thinking about the relationships between king as deity and deity as king. Verse 16 may stand on its own as a gloss on the two preceding groups and function as a connection between the two halves.

Verses 17-20 seem to be connected by catchwords on the theme of "watching one's way"; vv. 21-25 are organized by catchwords and themes regarding "speech." The proverbial significance of v. 26 introduces the themes of a closely connected group in vv. 27-30. This group concerns the wicked and antisocial use of speech. Verses 31 and 32 depict types of people that counter such wicked ones. The concluding sayings return to the motif of Yahweh's absolute rule as stated in 16:1ff.

COMMENTARY

Yahweh and Human Limitation, 16:1-9

Both vv. 1 and 9 make a similar observation: there is a limit to human understanding. Both contrast a person's planning and arranging with Yahweh's implementation. In addition to being Yahweh sayings, the two share the vocabulary of "heart" (*lēb*) and "humankind" (*'ādām*). These semantic connections suggest that the two verses function to mark the boundaries of the cluster of sayings within, and possibly to declare the central thematic idea.[1] [Human Limitation] Verse 2 elaborates on v.1 by offering an example of the differences between the human and the divine point of view. Humans see externalities; Yahweh tests the spirit. The ensuing v. 3 has a similar contrast between externals and internals—human works versus human plans. Opening with an imperative implies that the saying functions as an instruction based upon the conclusions of the preceding two sayings. Since the mortal perspective cannot appreciate the outcome of an action, it is best to trust that outcome to Yahweh. Yahweh establishes the planning. Verse 3 is also of interest because of the idiomatic Hebrew expression for "commit" (*gōl*). The word *gōl* literally means to "roll." Thus one who is

Human Limitation

In seeking to lay out for youth the order of the universe, the sages were not remiss in asserting the place that humans occupied. They frequently asserted that there is a boundary to human potential. As G. von Rad puts it, "Its aim is, rather, to put a stop to the erroneous concept that a guarantee of success was to be found simply in practicing human wisdom and in making preparations."[11]

For further reading. Peter Berger and Thomas Luckmann. *The Social Construction of Reality*. New York: Basic Books, 1970. John Rogerson. *Anthropology and the Old Testament*. Sheffield: JSOT, 1984.

Gerhard von Rad, *Wisdom in Israel*, trans. James D. Martin (London: SCM Press, 1972), 101.

"committing" oneself to the Lord is to "'roll' unto the LORD your works. . . ." This figure of speech also occurs in Psalms 37:5 and 22:8.[2] The idea is perhaps to turn one's way over to Yahweh.[3]

The next three sayings, vv. 4, 5, and 6, focus on the motif of Yahweh's judgment. Verse 4 justifies the admonition of v. 3: all phenomena within the Lord's creation have a purpose; the existence of wicked people is justifiable as the cause of the day of trouble. Verse 5 opens with an abomination formula (cf. 11:20; 12:22; 15:9, 26) and asserts that the "arrogant" will not go unpunished. The term "wicked" is left open-ended in v. 4, until v. 5 focuses upon the problem of the wicked person's arrogance. Verse 6 seems to respond to the preceding claims about judgment by offering an observation on atoning for sins. The language of atonement, *yĕkūppar,* is priestly language, recalling images of sacrifice and sacred ritual.[4] However, the language of 6a derives from the moral ethical sphere. "Loyalty" (*ḥesed*) and "faithfulness" (*ʾĕmet*) are here offered as the means of atonement. By paralleling these two moral behaviors with the "fear of the LORD" in 6b, the implication is that these human activities take the place of the ritual sacrifices in the temple (cf. 20:28). Of even greater significance is the role such assertions play in maintaining theodicy, the very question that falls under the scrutiny of Ecclesiastes (e.g., 3:16-17; 8:17). By shifting the contingency of atonement to human faithfulness, the creator of the universe is less likely to be challenged for suffering and evil. In this saying the Lord's word makes sense: all phenomena fit into an appropriate place, even the wicked. Their appropriate place is the day of judgment.

Verse 7 might well be paired thematically with v. 6. Both open with the Hebrew preposition *bĕ,* "in, with, or by"; both speak of human moral behavior. In v. 6 such behavior yields atonement for sin; in v. 7 such behavior, expressed by the phrase "ways of people" (*darkê ʾîš*), yields the Lord's delight and eventually peace with one's enemies. As such, v. 7 continues the response to the assertion on atonement. Verse 8 comments further with a better-than-statement, here defined with the word "righteousness," *ṣĕdāqâ.* The thrust of the statement is that poverty with righteousness is better (more profitable, beneficial) than "large income" without justice, *mišpāṭ.* Readers may take pause to consider from whose point of view such a saying might be valid. People who have ample income would hear this quite differently than people who are impoverished. Verse 9 closes the group by reminding readers of the starting point, v. 1: ultimately, Yahweh determines all things. Humans make plans; Yahweh establishes actions.

On Kings and Kingship, 16:10-15

This group of sayings concerns the king and kingship in general, and in several sayings draws explicit parallels with the actions of Yahweh in the preceding section. [Kingship and Yahweh] The six sayings are in pairs: vv. 10 and 11 concern the king and justice; vv. 12 and 13 concern the king and righteousness; vv. 14 and 15 concern the king's wrath and pleasure. Verse 10 is of interest, since the same word for pagan divination, *qesem*, is here attributed to the king as a means of his obtaining inerrant decisions in judgment (e.g., Deut 18:10; 2 Kgs 17:17; 2 Sam 14:17-20). The saying attributes authority to the king (in judgment) that is analogous to the way 16:1 attributes inerrant decisions to Yahweh. Verse 11 returns to the familiar image of balances and scales (see 11:1 and 20:23), sharing the word for "judgment" (*mišpāṭ*) with v. 10. The verse contains a Yahweh saying asserting that Yahweh's judgment, represented by the imagery of "honest balances and scales," is just. The saying underscores the preceding claim that the king's judgment comes by oracle. Readers may revise their reading of v. 10—where

Kingship and Yahweh

The strong affinity between the king and Yahweh, the national deity, is explainable in part by the broader Near Eastern context in which Israel came to flourish. Simply put, in the nations surrounding Israel, kings were considered to be divine in varying degrees. In Egypt, for instance, one stele dedicated to king Ni-maat-Re ascribes deity to the king by identifying him with Re, the sun god. One line reads, "He is Re, by whose beams one sees, He is one who illumines the Two Lands more than the sun disc." In Mesopotamian notions of kingship the king was more likely simply to be thought of as "the son of god" as in the following "Petition to a King": "Thou [*in*] thy judgment thou art the son of Anu, Thy commands, like the word of a god, cannot be *turned back*" (Pritchard).

In Israel the king was not divine, but by virtue of his appointment he was certainly considered to be sacrosanct. The language of "sonship" (e.g., Pss 2:7; 89:26-27) reflects a process of elevating a mortal to the status of divinity. Ancients likely understood this elevation to have taken place through a ceremonial adoption by the deity upon an individual's ascension to the royal throne. Nevertheless, the poetic language elevates the king's status to a near mythological level (Ps 110:1, 3). Because of such an identity with Yahweh, poets referred to the king as the one who sustained the people's lives (Lam 4:20) and protected them by establishing and maintaining justice (Pss 45:4; 72:1-4).

For further reading, see F. Frick, *The Formation of the State in Ancient Israel* (Sheffield: JSOT, 1985); Keith Whitelam, "King and Kingship," *ABD* 4:40-48; and idem, "The Symbols of Power: Aspects of Royal Propaganda in the United Monarchy," *BA* 49 (1986): 166-73.

James B. Pritchard, *ANET* (Princeton: Princeton University Press, 1958).

Illustration from a Hittite relief depicting a god (the larger figure) with his arm surrounding the king (the smaller figure) as they walk side-by-side.

the implication is that the king uses divination to gain discernment—to understand that Yahweh is nevertheless the source of the king's decisions.

Verse 12 opens with the "abomination" formula, characterized by the use of the Hebrew word *tô'ăbat*, which readers are accustomed to seeing in reference to sayings about Yahweh. The saying about kingship echoes the most recent abomination saying regarding Yahweh (v. 5). In this saying it is an abomination for kings to do evil; their thrones are only established by righteousness. In other words, the office of king is to ensure that justice prevails across the kingdom. While there might indeed be evil people in the kingdom, the ultimate reversal of social order is here represented by the idea that the king himself might do evil. Verse 13 follows with an assertion that reinforces the claims of v. 12. The king's delight rests upon "righteous lips." Readers who recall the importance of the spoken word to the sages, and indeed to the good life (e.g., 12:18, 22; 14:23; 14:25; 15:4), may recognize that "righteous lips" is not merely a reference to speech. It is not enough, in other words, merely to speak of righteousness without doing it. Rather, righteous speech is the outpouring of the righteous heart.

Verse 14 opens a third pair in this group with a contrasting reflection upon the king's wrath. The saying makes an interesting connection with "righteous lips" in v. 13 through the image of the "messenger of death," both images of communication of some sort. Yet another interesting connection is implied between vv. 14 and 6 in the words "appease" (v. 14) and "atone" (v. 6). Although the English words are different, they are actually the same Hebrew word (*kāpar*) and imply similarities between atonement for sinners before Yahweh and appeasement of the king's anger. Verse 15 offers a contrasting image of the king's pleasure, connoted by the phrase "In the light of a king's face." From the point of view of the servant, perhaps the court counselor, appeasing the king means remaining alive. Is this image a basis for thinking about the analogous aims of religion?

The Way of Pleasant Speech, 16:16-24

The next group of sayings is perhaps more clearly read as two smaller groups, vv. 17-20 and 21-24, with one independent saying in v. 16. Verse 16 may remind readers of the more general assertions of the benefits of wisdom encountered in Proverbs 3:13-14 and 4:5. The sayings in this section continue to reflect upon the juxtaposition of Yahweh as the source of all wisdom and kingship as an office of wealth and power. Verse 16 provides an evaluative reflection upon kingship and wisdom. The implication is that it is better to have the latter.

Verse 17 is the middle verse in the entire book of Proverbs. At this juncture it is an apt reiteration of the sages' understanding of life as a path upon which one travels and has the ultimate decision regarding the direction of travel. Together, vv. 17 and 20 would seem to offer parallel images of people who are careful to "watch" their ways. In this case there are two sayings that function as an inclusio marking the outer boundaries of the sayings within. Verse 17b has the image of "guarding one's way" in parallel with the highway of the upright. The implication is that to turn from evil requires attention to one's actions. Likewise, v. 20a opens with the image of one who is "attentive to a matter." The translation "matter" renders a term that could just as easily be translated "word" (*dābār*). This offers a possible connection with the ensuing subgroup, vv. 21-24. Such people find happiness in their trust in Yahweh. The inner sayings in this group may be taken as examples of "watching" one's way. Verse 18 is paired thematically with v. 17 and urges that pride and arrogance precede a fall. Readers will encounter a variant in 18:12.[5] Verse 19, a better-than saying, observes that it is better to be lowly and poor than "dividing the spoil with the proud."

Verses 20-24 are dominated by speech motifs; v. 20 could well offer a play on the term "word" as a means of introducing these verses. Verse 21 functions with 24, again, as an inclusio. Not only do both verses contain speech imagery ("lips" and "words"), but both exploit the imagery of "sweetness" to describe those words. In v. 21 the translation "pleasant" renders the Hebrew word for "sweet" (*meteq*).[6] Verse 24 uses the image of the "honeycomb" (*ṣûp-dĕbaš*) as a metaphor for pleasant words (see 15:26b). Within this framework on speech, v. 22 asserts the importance of wisdom, using the Hebrew word *śēkel*, by contrasting it with the discipline, or "punishment," of fools, which is folly. The use of the term *śēkel* connects with v. 20 and the occurrence of the word *maśkîl*. Vocabulary with the same root also occurs in v. 23, *yaśkîl*, "causes to be prudent." Verses 21b and 23b bear great resemblance in that both have the phrase "increases persuasiveness," *śĕpātayim yōsîp leqaḥ*. Verse 23 returns to the important connection between wisdom and proper speech begun in v. 20.

The Way of Wickedness, 16:25-33

Verse 25 introduces the closing section of sayings by returning to an idea stated at the beginning of the chapter: appearances deceive humans (cf. 14:12). Two subgroups conclude the chapter's collection: vv. 27-30 address examples of negative speech in order to provide a contrast with the group in vv. 20-24; vv. 31-33 address the themes of righteousness in order to reiterate the emphases of vv. 1-9 and thus round out the sayings in the chapter. Verse 26 introduces vv. 27-30, which consist of sayings on ways that lead to death. All of the sayings refer to or imply negative modes of speech. Verse 26 concerns the appetite of workers and appears to be totally unrelated in this context.[7] However, in a context that is concerned about speech, the appetite is a bodily function that includes the mouth: the mouth consumes. The clever play on soul=life and soul=hunger, and then mouth=means of speech and mouth=means of satisfying hunger, however, creates more than a patronizing nod to day laborers. As the mouth gives strength to the laborer through consumption of food, it also gives life to the soul, and thus to the community, through proper speech. The deeper, proverbial significance of the mouth therefore provides the possibility that toil is not only a matter of "what goes into the mouth" but "what comes out of the mouth that defiles" (cf. Matt 15:11). Of course, the later sage, Ecclesiastes, will subvert this possible deeper interpretation by asserting that toil is indeed only for the appetite (Eccl 6:7).[8]

The ensuing vv. 27-30 all concern behaviors of wicked people. All of the behaviors are characterized by inappropriate speech. In Hebrew vv. 27-29 are very distinctive, all opening with the word for "man," *'îš*, followed by a modifier. Verse 27 concerns the "scoundrel," *'îš bĕlîyaʿal*, who concocts evil; the perverse person, *'îš tahpukôt*, who spreads strife, follows in v. 28; the violent person, *'îš ḥāmās*, who entices his neighbors, is the third in the series in v. 29. Verse 30 does not open with the same formula but is nevertheless thematically related, since it describes one who plans perverse things. His winking of the eye, *'ōṣeh ʿênāyw*, signals his deceitfulness (cf. 10:10).

The final three verses return to more normative examples for the community. In v. 31 the elderly are valued members of the community. They exist because they have lived lives of righteousness. Clearly, death is not feared in this image of old age (cf. Eccl 12:1-8). Verse 32 revisits the theme of self-control (cf. 14:17; 15:18). Possibly readers may see this as a comment on v. 31. The only way to achieve righteousness is through self-control. Finally, v. 33 revisits the concerns of 16:1-9 by asserting the Lord's ultimate

Urim and Thummim

AΩ These terms denote media by which the will of God was determined, usually in response to a specific question voiced by a cultic functionary. We do not know exactly what the media looked like or were made of, but likely they were objects that could indicate yes or no responses.

In Exod 28:30 and Lev 8:8 the chief priest carries the *'ûrîm* and *tūmmîm* on his body. In Exod 29:5 and 29:30 readers may draw the inference that the objects were small enough to be carried on the breast pieces of the priest. There are some traditions that suggest that the devices were not only for the priest. Num 27:21 explains that Joshua had access to the *'ûrîm* and *tūmmîm* for purposes of discerning the outcomes of battles.

For further reading, see Bill Bellinger, Jr., "Urim and Thummim," *MDB*, 945; and Merlin Rehm, "Levites and Priests," *ABD* 4:297-310.

control over all activity. The secrecy of "casting the lot" does not prevent Yahweh's rendering the decision. [Urim and Thummim]

CONNECTIONS

Knowing Human Limitations

The sages asserted Yahweh's incomparability by declaring human inferiority and limitation. Such denigration of humanity facilitates the defense of the creator and the justification of his rule (see [Theodicy]) The disparity between humans and the deity raises a number of provocative questions about the nature of human limitation. We tend to conceptualize human limitation in some spatial sense where the deity is large and humans are small. In the biblical story the episode of the human quest to build a tower to reach the heavens is a good illustration (Gen 11:1-9). What presumption and hubris we see in such frail, human endeavors. In fact, the spatial conception of God's relationship to the universe—somehow out beyond the heavens—curtails readers' imagination and ability to reflect upon human limitations. Another and perhaps better example helps us think a bit differently.

John Allen Paulos, the mathematician, has made a name for himself among a popular audience by making advanced concepts in mathematics available to an "innumerate" society. In one book, *Beyond Numeracy,* he discusses the concept of limits as the central assumption of calculus.[9] Paulos offers an example of the concept by posing the following challenge:

> Take a circle that is one foot in diameter and inscribe in it an equilateral triangle. Now inside this triangle inscribe a circle and then inside the smaller circle, inside of which you next inscribe a regular pentagon. Continue with these nested inscribings, alternating between a circle and a regular polygon whose sides increase by one with each iteration.[10]

While one imagines that the outcome will be virtually infinite until a single point is reached, what happens is quite surprising. As each polygon increases in sides, it becomes more like a circle until what is left is exactly that, a circle about 1/12 the size of the original circle. The limit is a circle. Each successive attempt to inscribe only produces another circle the same size.

Here we have an intriguing analogy to human limitation. While readers tend to think of human limitations as relative to those things that are external to us, the most important limitations are those that are within. What is more, the figure of human limitation in this analogy is itself a symbol of perfection, a circle. As in the mathematical calculation of limits, so it is with humanity: once we reach the perfect, the infinite, we cannot go beyond it. All of our activities and imaginations of good and evil, like polygons inscribed with a perfect circle, never move beyond the limit. The point at which such an analogy is helpful is in the reflections upon human limitation as a basis for human self-abnegation. Limitation so conceived is a basis for celebration, since it is a basis for knowing what is perfect. Human limitation does not therefore become a basis for disaffirming human dignity and worth.

NOTES

[1] See R. N. Whybray, *The Composition of the Book of Proverbs* (JSOTSup 168; Sheffield: JSOT, 1994), 88-89; Raymond C. Van Leeuwen, *Proverbs* (*NIB* 5; Nashville: Abingdon, 1997), 158.

[2] On the view that *gôl* derives from the root *galâ*, "to reveal," instead of the root *gālal*, "to roll," see William McKane, *Proverbs* (OTL; London: SCM Press, 1970), 497; and O. Plöger, *Sprüche Salomos (Proverbia)* (BKAT 17; Neukirchen: Neukirchener Verlag, 1984), 190.

[3] Van Leeuwen, 158.

[4] McKane, *Proverbs,* 498.

[5] Van Leeuwen, *Proverbs,* 161, notes 25:6-7 to be a concrete example of this saying.

[6] *BHS* proposes *meteg,* or "bridle," here since the sages are often concerned about restraining the speech (e.g., 27:1).

[7] Thus Plöger, *Sprüche Salomos,* 195.

[8] Roland Murphy, *Proverb* (WBC 22; Nashville: Word, 1998), 123.

[9] John Allen Paulos, *Beyond Numeracy* (New York: Vintage Books, Inc., 1992), 127-32.

[10] Ibid., 127.

LESS IS MORE

Proverbs 17:1-28

Wisdom and the Good Life, 17:1–22:16

The general theme of the profitability of wisdom continues in this second collection of sayings under the heading of "The Proverbs of Solomon." Taking this section as a whole, readers revisit many of the themes they have already encountered throughout the collection in 10:1–15:13 and 16:1-33. For a brief explanation of why we single out chapter 16 for individual treatment and begin with chapter 17 as the opening to the second subsection, see the introductory remarks to chapter 16.[1]

Chapter 17 opens with a stark image of the virtue of wisdom in v. 2. Together with v. 1, the opening two verses are sandwiched between two Yahweh sayings: Proverbs 16:33, which closes chapter 16 and 17:3. These foreshadow the concerns of the central chapters of the collection, chapters 19 and 20, which are dominated by sayings about the role of knowledge within relationships between humans and Yahweh. Chapter 22 concludes the collection with several sayings on the theme of wealth and poverty, both topics related to wisdom and the individual's relationship to Yahweh. These two themes further define the meaning of the good life and the profitability of wisdom.

As mentioned above (see Introduction) however, readers encounter a drastic stylistic change with this collection of sayings. Instead of the contrastive, or antithetical, style of sayings, we now read a reiterative, or so-called "synonymous" style.[2] Instead of various degrees of opposition, each half-line, or stich, restates its alternate stich as a variation, complement, or extension of the original statement. This change also contributes to a greater variability in the forms of sayings contained within the section.[3] In chapter 17, only vv. 9, 22, and 24 continue in the so-called "antithetical" style.

Less Is More, 17:1-28

Most immediately difficult about reading chapter 17 is its apparent lack of any overall structure. In the first half of the Proverbs of

Structure at a Glance: Proverbs 17

AΩ Readers would find it helpful in reading this chapter to compare the readings of a few different scholars. Interestingly, R. N. Whybray, who has championed the notion of interconnectedness in the deliberate arranging of these sayings, finds "no sign of a comprehensive structure" in this chapter. By contrast, Duane Garrett isolates four "inclusio or chiasmus collections," which he indicates to be collection 1, vv. 9-13; collection 2, vv. 14-19; collection 3, vv. 20-22; and collection 4, vv. 23-26. In his scheme, vv. 2-9 are simply random proverbs. We suggest the following structure to facilitate reading.

Vv. 1-3 The Prudence of Wisdom
Vv. 4-8 The Test of Speech
Vv. 9-15 Intense Relationships
Vv. 16-20 The Love of a Friend
Vv. 21-28 Coping with Foolish Children

The opening two groups of sayings are suggested by the sayings that function as possible boundaries: in 16:33–17:3 one may read the two Yahweh sayings as an inclusio (vv. 33 and 3). In the case of vv. 4-7 the imagery of speech within vv. 4 and 7 also potentially indicates boundary or inclusio sayings. In vv. 9-15 only vv. 9 and 13 counterpoise each other thematically. There is some question about the relationship of vv. 14 and 15. Although there is no tight semantic sequencing in vv. 16-20, recurring terms such as "mind" (*lēb*) and "love" (*'ohēb*) suggest some coherence. A chiastic structure appears to govern vv. 21-28; this structure would therefore imply some overarching coherence to the sayings contained within.

Again, readers must look carefully to find thematic, linguistic, and syntactic coherence in this collection of sayings. Thematic coherence is not as clear as in chs. 15 and 16, the concluding and introductory chapters to the first and second subsections of the overall collection "The Sayings of Solomon." Readers should also be reminded that the conventions of symmetry and coherence may be more in the minds of readers than in the minds of the editors of these sayings. (Roland Murphy's skepticism is wisely noted.)

Duane Garrett, *Proverbs, Ecclesiastes, Song of Songs* (NAC 14; Nashville: Broadman Press), 158-63.

Roland E. Murphy, *Proverbs* (WBC 22; Nashville: Word, 1998), 128.

R. N. Whybray, *The Composition of the Book of Proverbs* (JSOTSup 168; Sheffield: JSOT Press, 1994), 110.

Solomon (Prov 10–15 [16]) thematic, syntactic, or linguistic interconnectedness provide a means for structuring the collections of individual sayings. The frequent charge that the sayings are haphazardly arranged is probably justified here when we compare this chapter with the preceding chapters. And yet, there does seem to be some possible interconnection among the sayings. [Structure at a Glance: Proverbs 17]

COMMENTARY

The Prudence of Wisdom, 17:1-3 (16:33–17:3)

The two Yahweh sayings in 16:33 and 17:3 provide background for reflection upon the topics of the household contained in 17:1 and 2. The Yahweh sayings affirm the deity's silent sovereignty over human public behavior. Decisions rendered by lot are themselves from the Lord. Just as the smelting furnaces are for silver and gold (v. 3), so Yahweh tests the heart. Smelting is a process of removing the outer material so that the purer, inner material will remain. The image of silver and gold is one of assaying whether they are the genuine elements, something that can only be determined by looking through the shiny exterior. Similarly, only by knowing an individual's heart, which is hidden from one's public persona, may one determine whether an individual is also genuine.

Verses 1 and 2 share interest in matters stemming from the household, a setting encountered already in 11:29 and 15:27. Verse 1 asserts that the bounty and richness of the feast is not the determinant of good table fellowship. Verse 2 addresses the topic of the prudent slave who takes over his master's inheritance. [Slaves and Inheritance] The aim of both sayings is to reinforce the importance of the prudence that stems from wisdom. The son who lacks wisdom will be disinherited, and the slave who has wisdom will become a member of the house. These two sayings are related, then, by something more than household concerns. Both sayings portray an absence of wisdom where it should be present. The meal of wealth with strife is a table that lacks wisdom. The household where the slave usurps the place of the heir is a household lacking wisdom. The outer Yahweh sayings are especially relevant at this point. They also are concerned about what is not visible or is absent from the viewer's gaze. The onlooker may indeed see the lot cast, but does not see that its decision is Yahweh's. Likewise, people may see the color of silver and gold, but without knowing what is inside—

Slaves and Inheritance

Slaves in the ancient Near East were the property of their masters, yet the practice of keeping slaves took forms quite unlike those familiar to the New World of the 17th and 18th centuries AD. The language for slavery does not eliminate ambiguity. The term *'ebed*, "servant," is typically translated slave (e.g., Prov 17:2; Exod 21:2), but it comes from a root that simply means "to work." Other narrative contexts imply some kind of "servant" within the household, but may not use the term *'ebed*. For instance, Num 22:22b depicts Balaam riding with his "two servants," *nĕ'ārāyw*, "youths." The same word in a feminine form functions similarly in Gen 24:61 with reference to Rebekah's "maids."

The Deuteronomic law makes a distinction between Hebrew slaves and foreign slaves. Non-Israelite slaves were moveable property whereas Hebrew slaves could not be sold but had to be freed after six years of indenture (Deut 15:12-18). The main source of non-Israelite slaves was probably warfare. Those captured in warfare became slaves of the state. They found employment at court and even within the temple precincts. Ezek 44:7-9 condemns the introduction of such foreigners to serve in the temple service.

Nevertheless, the law codes do not make the distinction between foreign and Hebrew slaves as regards their membership in the family. They were to share in the family's worship (Exod 20:10; 23:12), share in the sacrificial meals (Deut 12:12, 18), and take part in the Passover festival (Exod 12:44). In one narrative tradition Abraham would have considered his slave as his heir (Gen 15:3), and in 1 Chr 2:34-35 a slave marries his master's daughter. Job 3:19 implies that when the master died, the slave obtained freedom automatically.

Job's protests of innocence provide some further insight. He argues that he has not denied his slaves justice, which confirms his piety. Moreover, he assumes that the God who created him is the creator of the slaves as well (Job 31:13-15). Clearly, the literature implies that slaves were welcomed into the family, were protected in varying degrees in Hebrew society, and could therefore become quite at home within a family. So much so, according to Prov 17:2, that they could become heirs in the master's house.

For further reading, see Muhammed A. Dandamayer, "Slavery (ANE)," *ABD* 4:58-62; S. Scott Barctchy, "Slavery (Greco-Roman)," *ABD* 4:65-73; and Raymond Westbrook, "Biblical and Cuneiform Law Codes," *RB* 92/9 (1985): 247-64.

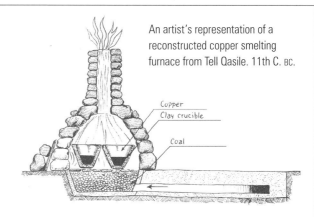

Mining Silver and Gold

The language and imagery of mining and smelting precious metals is well-known in the Bible (e.g., Job 28:1-11). The term for mining is the Hebrew word *zāqaq*. The actual process of smelting is thought to be of Hittite origin around 1400 BC. Most likely the technique traveled down the coast to the Sea Peoples and thereby was introduced to the Semitic peoples living in the Canaan land.

The mining of silver and gold was not as common or plentiful as copper or bronze, an alloy of copper and tin. One might infer that the making of weapons was far more important than that of jewelry. Silver and gold were used for different purposes and were not mined in Palestine.

For further reading, see R. J. Forbes, *Metallurgy in Antiquity* (Leiden: E. J. Brill, 1950); and Charles F. Pfeiffer, ed., "Metallurgy," in *The Biblical World: A Dictionary of Biblical Archaeology* (Grand Rapids: Baker Book House, 1966), 382-88.

An artist's representation of a reconstructed copper smelting furnace from Tell Qasile. 11th C. BC.

revealed only through smelting—they do not know whether they are real. [Mining Silver and Gold]

The Test of Speech, 17:4-8

Three of the five sayings in this group concern evil speech, vv. 4, 5, and 7. Verse 4 associates the evildoer (*mēra‘*) with those whose speech is wicked, thus, the "liar" (*šeqer*). As with the first sayings in this group, there is an abrupt contrast between the assertion in v. 3, which alludes to the Lord's testing of one's heart, and the depiction of the evildoer, whose speech makes immediately clear the nature of this ways. In verse 5 the saying continues the topic of evil speech by focusing upon the particular sin of mocking the poor. The same phrase translated here as "insult their Maker" occurs in 14:31, where the behavior is not one of speech but of oppression. Job 31:16 refers to withholding from the poor, which teaches that oppressing the poor may be a passive act. The reference to God as maker (creator) also has a parallel in Job. In defending himself against the possible accusation that he has treated his slaves unjustly, Job appeals to the belief that he would be liable before God, since God created both Job and his slaves: "Did not my maker make him?"(Job 31:15). The final saying concerning speech is v. 7, which expresses a familiar theme on the inappropriateness of certain kinds of speech to certain kinds of people. If it is inappropriate for a fool to have fine speech, how much more inappropriate is false speech to a ruler.

Two sayings in this group, vv. 6 and 8, are not related to false speech at all. Verse 6 affirms both youth and age. Children and grandparents receive glory from each other. The statement is much more in line with the themes of the household encountered in 17:1 and 2. By juxtaposing children with grandparents, the sage asserts an aspect of household that concerns the importance of its "linear descent."[4] A household may have longevity, especially for the wise. Verse 8, concerning the prosperity that results from a bribe or a gift, provides an interesting conclusion to the group of sayings. NRSV's translation assumes that the saying concerns the one who gives the bribe. It is difficult, however, to know whether the Hebrew term *bĕʿālāyw*, which means "its lord," refers to the one who gives the bribe or the one who receives the bribe.[5] Thus it is difficult to determine whether the bribe is an act of deceit and dishonesty, as in the examples of false speech, or if this is an example of the clever behavior of one who is wise (cf. 18:16). As in other instances of wise sayings, the ambiguity between a gift given to ensure favor or the gift given gratuitously is probably left up to the reader.

Intense Relationships, 17:9-13, 14, and 15

Verses 9 and 13 counter each other on the topic of friendship and reciprocal ill-treatment of one's house. Verse 9 alludes to the act of returning good for evil treatment by invoking the role of forgiveness in friendship. Verse 13 envisions the outcomes of returning evil for good treatment. In v. 9, one "forgives transgressions" and thus builds friendship. By contrasting the two behaviors of forgiving transgression and "dwelling on disputes," the saying asserts that the ultimate aim is cultivating love and friendship. In v. 13, if one "returns evil for good," one puts one's house at risk. The outcomes of such behavior are clearly connected to those of vv. 1, 2, and 6.

The three sayings within the outer framework (created by vv. 9 and 13) treat topics that may be juxtaposed with the outer sayings themselves. Verse 10 follows the assertion of forgiveness in v. 9 by reflecting upon the appropriate rebuke. What makes a rebuke appropriate or inappropriate is not the act, but the person toward whom such a rebuke is directed. One rebuke toward the discerning makes more difference than a hundred beatings on a fool. In contrast to v. 9, though, it is not clear that v. 10 is encouraging such rebukes as a means of instruction. Because of a person's ability or inability to understand, forgiveness may be the only appropriate response. Verse 11 contemplates the punishment directed against one whose evil leads him to rebellion. Perhaps this saying envisions the kind of social rebellion described in the biblical narrative of Absalom's revolt, 2 Samuel 15–17.[6] The "cruel messenger" (*mal'āk 'akzārî*), perhaps a messenger from the king announcing the inevitable fate of such rebelliousness (cf. 16:14), is envisioned as the source of the inevitable rebuke. Verse 12 implies that the inevitable punishment that results from encountering a bear robbed of her cubs is better than that which follows a fool's folly. In the larger context of vv. 9-13, one is more likely to find forgiveness in the former instance than in the latter. An affinity with v. 10 is evident in the use of the fool as a point of comparison. Both sayings portray the utter futility of finding any hope for a fool and his folly.

It is difficult to determine whether vv. 14 and 15 belong to the cluster in vv. 9-13, although both sayings deal with related images or topics. The saying in v. 14 compares the beginnings of an argument, with its disagreement and strife, to a small opening in a dam. The inevitable result is increasing quantities of water seeping through. Reading this saying against a context concerned with forgiveness and retribution (vv. 9-13), advice not to let strife get out of control seems appropriate. Verse 15 is a Yahweh saying and contemplates a finer application of the preceding assertions about forgiveness and retribution. The imagery is both legal and cultic. A judge who justifies the wicked and condemns the righteous is impure before the Lord. This is a common theme among the sages (e.g., 11:20; 12:2; 15:8; 24:24-25) as well as the prophets (see Isa 5:23; Amos 5:7). It seems that this saying provides a qualification to the important assertion in v. 9 concerning forgiveness. One must wonder about the relationship between "covering" a sin as an act of forgiveness (v. 9) and "covering a sin" in the sense of declaring someone just and innocent when they are actually guilty (v. 15). The question is whether forgiveness on an individual level necessarily applies on a social level. The advice that applies to the household may not apply for society at large. The logic of the saying further complements v. 13, which concerns the appropriateness of one's response to good treatment.

The Love of a Friend, 17:16-20

These sayings show few signs of tight semantic and syntactic sequencing. In any event readers encounter common and related themes within. For instance, the words translated "mind," vv. 16

and 20, and "love," vv. 17 and 19, render the Hebrew words *lēb* and *'ohēb*, which suggest a possible semantic connection within these sayings. The occurrences of "love" remind readers of the preceding sayings on forgiveness, friendship, and the household (vv. 9, 13, and 14). Verse 16 opens with a saying that reflects upon the foolishness of fools. The clear implication is that the price of an education is wasted on a fool (see also 26:7). We may infer from the reference to "price" (*mĕḥîr*) that wisdom teachers were paid for their instruction. Readers further wonder about the existence of schools in ancient Israel. The allusion to foolishness and the accompanying identification with the fool motivate readers to attend carefully to what follows.

Verse 17 compares friendship with kinship. The problem in understanding the saying is whether friendship compares favorably or negatively with kinship relationships. Proverbs 18:24 might offer some commentary by admitting both possibilities. Some people only pretend friendship, and some friends are closer than brothers. Friendship is as friendship does, in other words.[7] Verse 18 returns to the image of one who lacks sense. The symbol of his senselessness is making a pledge, providing collateral, for a friend. The love of a friend apparently should not extend to the provision of financial backing. The term translated "neighbor" in v. 18 is the same word rendered "friend" in v. 17. The problem of providing financial backing or security may be read in light of the treatment in 6:1-5: sometimes it is necessary, but it is risky. The later sage Jesus ben Sirach is not so adamant in his advice on this point. Sirach 29:14-17 makes it clear that only shameless people are unwilling to provide security on a loan for their neighbors. He acknowledges the risks involved (e.g., "Being surety has ruined many who were prosperous . . ."), but concludes that one should "Assist your neighbor to the best of your ability, but be careful not to fall yourself." In Proverbs 17:18, the broader context on neighbors and "the one who loves" (Prov 17:19) makes difficult the advice not to provide security for a neighbor. Verse 19 and its language therefore invites readers to reconsider v. 17 and the previous saying in v. 9 on seeking love by forgiving transgressions. The problem is how to connect the first part of the saying in v. 19 to the latter. The one who "loves transgression" is one who "loves strife." In 19b, however, one who "builds a high threshold" seeks "broken bones." The two parts of the saying seem thematically unrelated, but metaphorically both make passage, whether into a room or into a relationship, difficult. Verse 20 concludes with an image of the twisted heart or mind. The two parts of the sayings compare the outcomes of inappropriate thoughts and words. Both lead to failure.

Coping with Foolish Children, 17:21-28

Some readers may recognize the possibility of a small collection in 21-25,[8] but it is unclear how these sayings were assembled together. There appears to be a chiastic arrangement of these eight verses around the topic of the fool and the shame of his parents as they cope with their foolish offspring. One might consider reading together vv. 21 and 28; vv. 22 and 27; vv. 23 and 26; and vv. 24 and 25.

> V. 21 The parent of a fool has no joy
>   V. 22 The cheerful heart vs. downcast spirit
>   V. 23 Secret perversion of justice
>   V. 24 The wise vs. the fool
>   V. 25 Foolish children grieve parents
>   V. 26 Injustice toward the innocent
>   V. 27 Few words, cool in spirit
> V. 28 Fools who keep quiet appear wise

The pair of sayings forming the center of the chiasm, vv. 24 and 25, both reflect upon the nature of the fool and the displeasure he brings to his parents.

Verse 21 recalls the familiar topic of educating children, already encountered in 10:1 and 13:1, and fits in with the frequent concern in this chapter with the household. The point of view is that of the parent. Verse 28 expresses the point of view that may also be that of the parent and offers some potentially ameliorating advice in response to v. 21: fools that keep quiet are considered wise. There may still be hope for joy if one's foolish children can simply refrain from speaking. The observation in v. 22 also provides comfort. Allowing misfortune, especially the misfortune of foolish children, to make the spirit downcast, "dries up the bones." Reading v. 27 in comparison to v. 22 evokes reflection upon the internal disposition of an individual. In the context concerning a parent's foolish children, again, there is hope if the fool does not open his mouth. Similarly, parents who are "cool in spirit" may be able to retain a "cheerful heart" about their children. Verse 27 also pairs well with v. 28. Both sayings concern the importance of silence.

Verse 23 describes the wicked as aiming to pervert the ways of justice. They accept secret bribes. In the context on the fool and his parents, a parent must weigh the consequences. Is it better to have a fool or to have a child who is wicked? On the other hand, if a fool can remain silent enough to be thought intelligent (v. 28), then such deception is at least potentially as injurious to society as the wicked person who takes secret bribes. Verse 26, the counterpart of v. 23, recognizes the danger of reversing the proper order of things: imposing a fine on the innocent is like the flogging of the noble for his integrity. Both actions are reversals of the desired order of society. Further, such behaviors may be the kinds of actions that result from secret bribes. The question is whether concealing that one has a foolish child, v. 28, is the kind of behavior that might result in analogous reversal of social order. Is it right that a fool might be considered intelligent due to strategic silence? Is it right that slaves should obtain an inheritance because they are merely wise (v. 2)?

The central verses of the group, vv. 24 and 25, return to the theme articulated in v. 21. Verse 24 contrasts discerning people and fools. The fool, though he searches the earth, can never seem to find wisdom. Or, possibly, precisely because he is always looking to everything but wisdom, he remains a fool. Thus, as v. 25 reasserts, fools bring grief and bitterness to their parents.

CONNECTIONS

When Is Less Really More?

How do we define the good life? Most people don't really spend much time defining it. Such an exercise is usually reserved for academic conversations in college or graduate school. Nearly everyone's stereotype of a philosopher is one who strokes his chin and gazes into thin air with a blank expression upon his face, while reflecting upon what is good. To be sure, it is an image that persuades most folk to steer clear of the question altogether. Still, most of us have some assumptions about the good life, and those assumptions are born out in the ways we live our lives. We have reasons for getting more education, for instance, or for building bigger houses, for taking on new and more challenging occupations, for moving to newer neighborhoods, and so on. From the places we eat our meals to the places we worship on Friday,

Saturday, or Sunday, to the ways we cast our votes, we are giving expression to what we truly believe about the good life.

The opening and closing sayings in chapter 17 seem to give expression to the ethos that less is actually more. It is better to have the barest sustenance with peace than to have the greatest feast with strife, v. 1 tells us. Even a fool is not recognized as long as he keeps his mouth shut, the concluding saying claims. Both sayings remind readers about the sages' view of the good life: one does not find it in many words or great worth. It may rather be measured by what one does *not* have or do.

In a more modern setting the idea that "less is more" is not foreign to us. We do not accord it much value, however. In developing some of the wilderness philosophies of Henry David Thoreau, Ralph Waldo Emerson observed that "Things are in the saddle and ride mankind."[9] Like Thoreau, Emerson recognized the pace that business and industry had set for defining the notion of the good life late in the nineteenth century. There was no time for reflection, little or no appreciation of nature, or the environment and the human place in it. Life was pervaded and defined by the goals of consumption and the accumulation of more things. Quality was defined by quantity: who could achieve the most or the biggest. One should probably not judge that generation too harshly. Things have not actually changed much since their day. The claim that "less is more" speaks to the present day.

But what could such a phrase mean in real terms? Here again the ancient sages have given a few ideas. Saying less rather than saying more is a good starting place. The emphasis is on quality not quantity. Wisdom advocates saying the right word at the right time (e.g., 15:1, 23; 16:24; 17:28) rather than saying things all the time without taking into account their appropriateness (e.g., 14:3; 12:13; 13:3). Taking care with the quality of what one says requires taking care with the quality of what one thinks, believes, and does. Wisdom turns the tables on our assumptions about what is good and what is not good. The quality and value of life is redefined in less quantitative terms. The processes of human life instead of the outcomes of human life take the central position. The profit that wisdom brings is thus potentially a notion that is determined by human relationship and community good.

NOTES

[1] See Leo Perdue, *Proverbs* (IBC; Louisville: Westminster John Knox Press, 2000), 180. Perdue, as most commentators, treats Prov 16 as the opening chapter to the second subsection of 10:1–22:16.

[2] See the list of scholars who have moved away from this terminology in Roland Murphy, *Proverbs* (WBC 22; Nashville: Word, 1998), xxiii.

[3] William McKane, *Proverbs* (OTL; London: SCM Press, 1970), 501.

[4] Perdue, *Proverbs,* 182.

[5] McKane, *Proverbs,* 502, takes the saying to concern "the judicious use of a bribe." See Murphy, *Proverbs,* 129, for a fuller discussion of this ambiguity.

[6] McKane, *Proverbs,* 510.

[7] See Raymond Van Leeuwen, *Proverbs* (*NIB* 5; Nashville: Abingdon, 1997), 168, who notes 1 Sam 18:1-24 and 2 Sam 1:26 regarding a friendship like brothers.

[8] R. N. Whybray, *The Composition of the Book of Proverbs* (JSOTSup 168; Sheffield: JSOT Press, 1994), 111; Murphy, *Proverbs,* 131 only cautiously.

[9] Ralph Waldo Emerson, from his "Ode, Inscribed to W. H. Channing," *Poems*, quoted in Roderick Nash, *Wilderness and the American Mind*, rev. ed. (New Haven and London: Yale University Press, 1973), 87.

THE GOOD LIFE
AND ITS SOCIAL CONTEXT

Proverbs 18:1-24

The strategy of arranging sayings in this chapter most closely resembles that in chapter 17. Therefore readers must exercise the same kinds of imaginative ways of connecting the various sayings. The grouping of the sayings is not clearly evident. There are, however, smaller units within the chapter that combine two to four sayings. Most of these units may be discerned in Hebrew on the basis of euphony and semantic connections. [Structure at a Glance: Proverbs 18]

COMMENTARY

The Fool as Antisocial, 18:1-3

The opening three sayings show an interesting possible progression of thought from the antisocial person, v. 1, to the fool, v. 2, to the wicked one, v. 3.[1] However, each saying has its own concern. Verse 1 poses difficulties because the translation, "the one who lives alone," is only a good guess as to the meaning of the Hebrew word *niprād*, the Niphal of *pārad*, which means to "divide" or "separate."[2] The implication is that those who separate or isolate themselves from others do so against the best advice of the sages. With this reading the emphasis of the saying is upon the importance of one's community. The second part of the verse suggests the error of implied individualism: living alone is like disregarding "sound judgment." Verse 2 follows easily upon the opening saying both semantically and in terms of its thematic concern. Verse 2a asserts that the fool does not delight in under-standing, which one immediately equates with the absence of sound judgment and the individualistic desires of the person who lives apart from community. The implication is that antisocial people are themselves foolish. Another possible connection between vv. 1 and 2 is in the use of the two Hithpaʿel forms, *yit-gallâ* (1b) and *běhitgallôt* (2b), both sharing the broad lexical meaning of "uncover, lay bare, reveal." In v. 1 this is translated as "showing," and in v. 2 it is translated as "expressing." In both cases, the true character of the individuals is revealed by their actions: one is antisocial, the other is known by the expression of his own ideas.

Verse 3 does not demonstrate the same kind of semantic connec-tion as vv. 1 and 2. However, that a saying on wickedness should follow two sayings on foolish behavior invites readers to make con-nections between the ideas of wickedness and foolishness. We may read the implication that such resistance to sound judgment as encountered in the opening two sayings inevitably leads to wicked-ness. In addition to wickedness comes dishonor and disgrace. If we read the sayings with the MT, *rāšāʿ*, "the wicked," then v. 3 seems only remotely connected to the people described in vv. 1 and 2. If we read the passage with the LXX, *asebeis*, which translates the Hebrew *rešāʿ*, "wickedness," then v. 3 is a gloss on the activities of the people of vv. 1 and 2 rather than on the people themselves.

The Power of Words, 18:4-8

These verses are dominated by the imagery associated with the activity of speech; especially significant are words like "lips," "mouth," and "words." The motif of depth is present in both v. 4 and v. 8, functioning as an inclusio. In v. 4 the image of "deep waters" provides metaphorical background for reflection upon the impact of an individual's words. In v. 8 words "descend" into the belly and are like "hidden treasure." The question is whether to take these two ideas of descent and hiddenness positively or nega-tively, especially in view of the implications of vv. 5, 6, and 7 on subverting justice and the speech of fools. In v. 4 the question is whether deep waters is an image of profundity and fullness, or of hideousness and danger. [Water and Chaos] If one reads the two halves of the verse as being related in a reiterative sense, then 4a is a posi-tive assertion of profundity and fullness of meaning, since the images used in 4b are of fountains and streams. The image of a fountain is frequently used in reference to the "fountain of life" and is therefore a positive image (e.g., 10:11; 13:14; 14:27; 16:22).[3] In

Water and Chaos

Because rainfall was scarce in Palestine, water was a highly valued commodity. The presence or absence of water could mean the difference between harvest and famine for the agricultural society that populated the region. Like the metaphorical use of bread, water conveyed ideas of both life and death. The ancient Hebrews' land-locked civilization further contributed, possibly, to a psychological predisposition to the sea. The sea was a source of mystery and terror, to be sure. Ancient cosmology conceived of the earth as floating upon the waters of chaos. These waters of chaos reflected the uncreated aspect of the universe against which God's ordering principles stood.

"The deep" as an image of water came to give expression to those primordial, uncreated, chaotic waters that preceded all things (Gen 1:1). The great flood (Gen 6–9) came to pass through a reversal of the creation order that initially held them in check. In the Babylonian creation epic *'enuma 'elish,* the waters of the chaotic deep were personified in the goddess Tiamat. Tiamat, the goddess of salt water, along with her husband, Apsu, the god of sweet water, were those evil characters whom Marduk defeated and shaped into the world, with Babylon as its principle city. In the biblical story not only did God divide the waters initially in order to create the heavens and earth (Gen 1:6), but after the flood itself, there was a new creation as well.

For further reading, see A. H. W. Curtis, "The 'Subjugation of the Waters' Motif in the Psalms: Imagery or Polemic," *JSS* 23 (1978): 244-56; John Day, *God's Conflict with the Dragon and the Sea,* UCOP 35 (Cambridge: Cambridge University Press, 1985); David H. Hart, "Tiamat," *MDB*, 917; and Choon Leong Seow, "Deep, The," *ABD* 2:125-26.

The destructive and salvific forces of water are captured in this Raphael painting, c. 1518.

Raphael (School of). 1483–1520. *The Crossing of the Red Sea* from *The Story of Moses*. Fresco. Logge, Vatican Palace. Vatican State.

this case readers would understand that the topic concerns the words of the sage or the wise person. If one reads the verse in a contrastive sense, however, then v. 4a is about deception and ineffectiveness and 4b is about the power of the sage's speech to overcome such deception. The ambiguity itself provokes further thought since speech may both conceal and deceive as well as reveal and inform. Clifford states the meaning of the saying in terms of Proverbs 20:15: "The purposes of the human mind are like deep water, but the intelligent will draw them out."[4]

Verse 8 puts together two images: one concerns the whisperer or slanderer, *nirgān*, and another evokes thoughts of one's appetite. The slanderer has an appetite for slanderous behavior; it is a "taste" that resembles one's attraction to "delicious morsels." The negative image of slander in v. 8, standing in opposition to v. 4, suggests that one might indeed take the initial saying (v. 4) as an image of deception, since slander is itself a deceptive behavior. Deep waters create the potential for hiddenness. On the other hand, the negative image in v. 8 could just as easily stand as a foil for the positive assertion of the depth and profundity that is associated with wise speech, and thus provide a fitting climax to vv. 5-7 on foolish speech. Slander is a good example of such foolish speech. One could go further still and recognize that wise words both conceal and reveal simultaneously. Wisdom comes from recognizing when words are one or the other. Moreover, wisdom consists of using words at the right time either to conceal or reveal.

Verses 5-7 offer three examples of foolish speech. Verse 5a concludes with the words "not good" (*lō' tôb*; cf. 16:29; 17:5; 26). Readers may recall that with such language the sages set out the order of their social worlds. The overall concern of the saying is for the subversion of justice. The idiomatic expression for such subversive activities, here translated as being "partial to the guilty," is to "lift the face of the wicked." [The Face] The concern with perverting justice in the law court is addressed in the Covenant Code (e.g., Exod 23:1-3). There one reads of a concern with taking the side of the wicked, as well as with being partial to the poor, presumably over against the wicked. It is interesting that the law court represents not only the possibility of the perversion of justice, but a key testing ground for the sages by which one recognizes appropriateness or inappropriateness of speech. Readers will recall also that sometimes such perversion of justice is not a matter of speech at all, but of a bribe (e.g., 17:23).

Verses 6 and 7 are paired on the topic of the speech of the fool. The semantic connections are obtained through their sharing

The Face

AΩ In Hebrew the word for face, *pāneh, pānîm* (pl.), has several significances, the most obvious of which is its literal reference to the human face. Other terms that might also indicate the human face through synecdoche are "nose," *'ap,* and "eye," *'ayin.* Interestingly, the term "face," *pāneh,* functions as an anthropomorphism when used in reference to the deity. In such cases it may designate the deity's presence (e.g., Exod 33:14-15; Deut 4:37). Thus the term comes to be equated with the deity's person (e.g., Gen 33:10; Job 33:26). The language is analogous in reference to kings. Thus, to see the face of a king is to go into his presence. Seeking an audience with a king is analogous to the activity of divination. The word's metaphorical meaning is of interest here, since the notion of innocence is indicated in this saying with the phrase "lifting the face" with reference to a person.

Since it is with the face that people give expression to their emotions, the face came to stand for one's entire countenance and emotional state. When the face is bowed (looking to the ground), it may indicate awe or reverence (e.g., Num 22:31) or anger or sadness (e.g., Gen 4:5). In this latter case, to cause a person's face to raise is to give cause for celebration and cheer. The saying in Prov 18:5 seems to envision the wicked one's ironic cause for cheer through a subversion of justice.

For further reading, see Samuel E. Balentine, *The Hiding of the Face of God* (Oxford: Oxford University Press, 1983); Joel Drinkard, Jr., "Face," *ABD* 2: 743-44; and Carol Start Grizzard and Marvin E. Tate, "Presence," *MDB,* 709.

---

of the words for "fool" (*kěsîl*), "lips" (*śiptê*), and "mouth" (*pî*). Verses 5 and 6 are connected through the term translated "strife" (*rîb*), a term that typically designates a courtroom controversy. That a lawsuit seems to be envisioned is suggested by v. 5. The only judgment that should be rendered in a law court goes against the fool, whose words subvert justice. Ultimately such foolish speech is in the fool's own worst interest. It is of further interest to speculate that the foolish one might not be either of the litigants, but the judge himself.[5]

Social Security, 18:(9)-14

These sayings function well as a group in that all of them reflect upon behavior that poses some kind of a threat. Verses 10-12 actually represent a core of verses establishing the motif of safety and security. Verse 9 may serve as a transition between the previous group on speech and the following group on security. It actually equates laziness to destructiveness, thus the threat is posed both to the community and to one's self-interests. The community is threatened, since one cannot provide for oneself and thus must rely upon the community to provide one's needs. Such behavior is a threat to oneself, since it leads to one's own want.

Verses 10-12 seem to be related by various images. The tower of strength (*migdal 'ōz*) of v. 10 is something one finds in a strong

City Architecture

The image of the strong city requires some basic differentiation between cities with walls and those without. The most important architectural feature of the ancient city was its fortification. The city wall with its accompanying gate complex and lookout towers provided the measure of protection envisioned in this saying. Villages, however, smaller settlements outside of the great city wall, were not usually so fortified.

The defensive towers that stood on either side of the gate complex provided a vantage point for viewing those who approached the gates. Usually at the center of the city was the acropolis, which formed an inner citadel. The acropolis was the highest point in the city. It might function as an internal stronghold and also might serve as the residence of the governor of the city. Security would be most heavy in this part of the city, both due to its height and due to the importance of the residents of the citadel.

This illustration of the main gate of Megiddo shows the strategic importance of city gates during Solomonic times.

More modern Hellenistic and Roman cities were characterized by a grid of streets running perpendicular to each other. Through this arrangement the city was divided into square blocks. In the Greek city an open square, the *agora*, served as a common meeting place and market. This central square took over the function of the more ancient city gate complex.

For further reading, see John Baines et al., "Art and Architecture," *ABD* 1:401-61; C. de Geus, "The Profile of an Israelite City," *BA* 49 (1986): 224-27; F. Frick, *The City in Ancient Israel* (Missoula MT: Scholars Press, 1977); David C. Hopkins, "City/Cities," *MDB*, 157-58; and Y. Shiloh, "Elements in the Development of Town Planning in the Israelite City," *IEJ* 28 (1978): 36-51.

city, *qiryat 'uzzô*. [City Architecture] Note the same vocabulary for "strong" shared in these two sayings, *'az*. Verse 12 inserts the image of destruction or brokenness, the appropriate foil to the images of towers, cities, and walls. But the trio of sayings does not concern a city's defenses only. Rather, v. 10 is speaking of faith in Yahweh as the strong defensive tower of the righteous. Readers have encountered Yahweh sayings and other sayings asserting the security of the righteous many times already (e.g., 10:2, 9, 25, 29; 11:4, 6, 8, 21). The implication is that something as ethereal and immaterial as faith could have the substance of a high city tower. The ensuing saying in v. 11 comments on the immateriality of faith by alluding to the wealthy person who believes wealth to be equivalent to a fortified city wall. The saying ridicules this notion by asserting that such a view exists only in the imaginations of the wealthy.[6] The implication is that wealth does not come close to faith in Yahweh. The concluding verse of the three, v. 12, contemplates the contrast between trust in Yahweh and trust in one's wealth. The saying recognizes that often what determines whether one places faith in one or the other is pride and haughtiness of spirit. It takes humility to trust Yahweh. Destruction comes when pride prevents people from committing their faith to Yahweh.

Verses 13 and 14 reflect upon actions—or better, states of mind—that pose threats to security. The saying in v. 13 takes readers back to aspects of foolish speech in vv. 4-8. Readers should probably not confine the saying's significance to legal contests alone, as in vv. 4-8. General discourse may be envisioned here. Offering an answer before really hearing leads to folly and public shame. In the present context, which concerns one's trust in Yahweh, the same prideful attitude that rejects faith in Yahweh is tantamount to answering before hearing. Rejecting trust in Yahweh therefore leads to public shame. Verse 14 also alludes to previous sayings that are concerned with the importance of the spirit in fending off disease (e.g., 14:13; 15:13; 17:22). Without such strength of spirit, one is vulnerable. However, what is it that mends the sick spirit? This verse invites readers to remember the reference to the haughty spirit in v. 12 and the inevitable fall that follows. What, after all, causes the spirit to become humble, receptive, and trusting?

Words at Work, 18:15-19 (20-21)

It is back to school in this group of sayings. Verse 15 really seems to stand on its own as an admonition to learn wisdom. It functions as a marker for the approximate midpoint of the chapter, or perhaps as simply a call to learn the material that follows. The sayings that follow warrant such a call, however, because they pose views that would seem to reverse some generally held assertions about the "real world" of conflict, especially in the law courts. In the context of legal struggle v. 16 is an important point of departure. On the one hand, the saying's subject matter could concern bribes, as 15:27, 17:8 and 23. In this case, it reflects upon a means to assume victory in court. On the other hand, the word "gift" (*mattān*) may be totally neutral, not necessarily implying any attempt to pervert justice at all. Readers must decide as they process the ensuing sayings. Verse 17 presents the legal process: the plaintiff presents a case, then cross-examination follows. It is noteworthy that of this group of sayings, v. 17 is the only one that reflects the critical process of searching for the truth. Verse 16 is possibly about bribery, v. 18 about casting lots, and v. 19 about securing victory through power.

Verse 18 reflects upon legal decisions reached on the basis of the lot (*haggôrāl*). The verse attests to the difficulty and perhaps the cost of extensive cross-examination, which v. 17 describes. The critical process of determining the truth is drawn out, expensive, and inevitably yields ambiguity. Proverbs 16:33 offers a legitimating comment on the use of the lot, since the decision is actually from Yahweh. Unfortunately, there is little evidence that the lot was really used in a legal context or in society at large. As Murphy points out, the references in the Bible are mostly religious contexts.[7] The text of v. 19a is obscure, but the *qĕrē* reading of the Hebrew *midwānîm* as *midyānîm*, "quarreling," "disputing," links vv. 18 and 19. Both are about such disputes among powerful enemies. Verse 19a seems to project the possibility of being in conflict with one who was once an ally or brother who is now at odds. This is surely a comment on the need for decision by lot, since the case could go on indefinitely due both to the resolve of the offended and the apparent resources available to see such a case through to resolution.[8]

Verses 20 and 21 return to the topic of speech already encountered in vv. 4-8. The two sayings stand as a pair and share the challenging imagery of "eating one's words," or at least the "fruit" of one's words. In both cases, the market value of proper speech is being called to mind. [The Hand of the Tongue] The "fruit" of such speech is the payment one receives, presumably for such public work. These sayings suggest that one might make quite a successful living out of knowing what to say at the right time. While the

---

The Hand of the Tongue

AΩ The phrase in 18:21 translated "power of the tongue" derives from a starker image in Hebrew: "the hand of the tongue." With the mixing of these two aspects of the human body we have a provocative image requiring some explication of the possible metaphorical significances of hand and their derivations.

While the term hand, *yād* in Hebrew and *cheir* in Greek, literally refer to "the hand" (e.g., Gen 48:17; Ps 73:23), they occur more frequently in various metaphorical functions to denote power or ability (e.g., Deut 16:17, "as they are able"; Josh 8:20, "they had no power"). This may be so because of the hand's typical activity of holding. It is not a vast leap from the activity of holding something to controlling it, thus to exercising authority over it. The hands were also used in symbolic gestures of authority such as bestowing blessings.

The activity of laying on hands for the purpose of passing on a blessing plays a central role in Jacob's blessing of Ephraim and Manasseh, where the right and left hands convey different levels of authority (Gen 48:14-20). Likewise, it is through hands that healing power is conveyed.

Thus, the term "hand" is frequently used to express power and authority and agency. Abraham gives Hagar into the "hand" of Sarah, his wife (Gen 16:6, 9), and Potiphar gives all of his property into Joseph's "hand" (Gen 39:8). When speaking of the "hand" of the tongue with such usage in mind, there is attached the understanding of the great authority as well as responsibility that goes along with speech.

For further reading, see Scott Nash, "Hand," *MDB*, 456; and J. Bergman, W. von Soden, and P. Ackroyd, " *yād*," *TDOT* 5:385-426.

verses clearly stand on their own as a pair, that they follow the section on legal disputation is of further possible significance. This is especially true in light of v. 6, which asserts that foolish speech creates disputes. With at least four means of winning a court case—the bribe, cross-examination, the lot, and pure power—these verses in vv. 20 and 21 offer the intriguing possibility that proper speech is as important as any in either avoiding court, or if necessary, winning at court. In fact, the references in v. 21 to life and death elevate yet more the importance of one's words (cf. Prov 13:2).

Everyday Concerns, 18:22-24

The final three sayings may be read as a cluster, since they all deal with everyday, family, or community relationships. Situated at the close of this chapter's collections, they function as an effective counterbalance to the opening sayings on those people who are antisocial and keep to themselves. Verse 22 presents as a Yahweh saying an image of finding a wife. She is called a "good thing" and is the measure of Yahweh's goodness. Readers may think of this verse as foreshadowing the discussion in Proverbs 31:10-31, since there we will read an extended poetic reflection upon the "good wife."

It is interesting that the search for a wife is followed in v. 23 by a reflection on the poor and the contrast between the power of rich and poor. The saying reflects the vulnerability of the poor vis-à-vis the rich: the rich can speak their minds. The poor spend their time speaking graciously, while the rich speak harshly. The saying invites readers to remember the preceding sayings on the importance of the tongue, especially the market value of an individual's speech. It seems logical, then, along with considering the power disparity between rich and poor, also to consider the possibility that speech is important in breaking out of poverty.

Verses 22 and 23 present images of power disparity: husband and wife, rich and poor. The concluding saying, v. 24, offers an image of friendship that compares real friendship, one that has depth, with one that is superficial. In view of the preceding two sayings, where power disparities are real, readers may be provoked to wonder whether there can be friendships of depth where there are such power inequities. Friendships seem more likely to be superficial—only for show—in cases where such power disparities exist. The cluster of sayings evokes readers' reflections upon the different kinds and levels of friendships available within society, and guides them to probe beneath the surface to discover the complexities of social existence. While the sages value social existence over individualism (cf. 18:1), they do not seem to promise that social existence is easy.

CONNECTIONS

Individual and Society

The opening saying regarding the self-indulgence of a loner and the concluding sayings on friendship give us our points of departure for reflection upon the importance of an individual's social context. For all of the emphasis the sages placed upon the success of individuals, they never forgot that what is in the best interest of individuals is their building a strong society. For that reason, all of these activities—speech, the lawsuits, responsibility to others, etc.—must be stressed for their implicit assumption that they contribute to the good of the larger community.

Many of us began reading Daniel Defoe's *Robinson Crusoe* while in grade school. Viewed from the perspective of a child or adolescent, it is one episode of adventure and challenge after another. Crusoe, shipwrecked on what appears to be a desert island with nothing but wild animals, builds himself a secure fortress, outfits himself with supplies from the wrecked ship and whatever else he can gather. He then survives alone, learning and living the life of an adventurer. Adult readers might recognize, however, another challenge within Crusoe's adventures. Only an adult who appreciates the importance of community, friends, and family recognizes the loneliness of an individual to be the ultimate challenge.

In assessing his situation, Crusoe lays out the Evil and the Good that arise from his situation as though he were keeping a ledger. Of the six evils he enters in the ledger, three have to do with aloneness. In addition to having little hope of recovery, having no clothes, and being defenseless, Crusoe also adds: "I am singled out and separated, as it were, from all the world to be miserable." "I am divided from mankind, a solitaire, one banished from human society." "I have no soul to speak to, or relieve me."[9] From an adult's perspective, Crusoe's facing the challenge of survival alone would seem to be the greatest challenge of all. The mark of maturity and indeed wisdom is the recognition of the importance of community. Part of

Defoe's purpose in writing *Robinson Crusoe*, no doubt, was the exploration of the importance of society.

Of course, anyone who has read the book knows that Crusoe was not alone. His man Friday becomes a source for rediscovering the meaning of community. The irony of reading Defoe's classic novel is that in a world increasingly populated and continually pressing in on us, we still feel lonely, and indeed have come to think that life must be accomplished through individual action alone.

The ancient sages knew the importance of community and went to pains to arrange sayings so their readers had to understand that all of the activities of the individual were contextualized by the strong affirmation of community. The sages' concern that speech be appropriate stems from their larger concern about life within a community of relationships. One is accountable to one's community for what and how one speaks. Similarly, foolishness is a relative term. The key criterion for determining foolish behavior is its impact upon one's social setting. Does it cause good or evil for those around? In fact, the very image of Yahweh's strength, the city, presupposes the centrality of the community.

NOTES

[1] Otto Plöger, *Sprüche Salomos* (BKAT 17; Neukirchen: Neukirchener Verlag, 1984), 210.

[2] See William McKane, *Proverbs* (London: SCM Press, 1970), 519, for a discussion of *niprād*; Roland Murphy, *Proverbs* (WBC 22; Nashville: Word, 1998), 134.

[3] Murphy, *Proverbs,* 135.

[4] Richard Clifford, *Proverbs* (OTL; Louisville: Westminster John Knox Press, 2000), 170.

[5] Note also the chiastic structure in the syntactical arrangement of these two sayings. Verse 6a opens with "the lips of the fool," 6b with "his mouth"; v. 7a opens with the "mouth of a fool," 7b with "his lips."

[6] Compare R. B. Y. Scott, *Proverbs, Ecclesiastes* (AB 18; New York: Doubleday, 1965), 112, who takes the LXX alternative reading for v. 11b: "It covers him like a high wall."

[7] Murphy, *Proverbs,* 137.

[8] See McKane, *Proverbs,* 520, for a discussion of the textual difficulties. Murphy, *Proverbs,* 137, notes the concern in Deut 1:16-17 for law cases between fellow Israelites as background for Prov 18:19.

[9] Daniel Defoe, *Robinson Crusoe* (New York and Scarborough, Ontario: The New American Library, 1961), 69.

ON GETTING AN EDUCATION

Proverbs 19:1-29

The chapter is dominated by sayings on the importance of knowledge and instruction. It is reasonable to suppose that these sayings were assembled to have the overall effect of an instruction.[1] However, clusters of sayings that form rhetorical units are even rarer here than in chapter 18. The challenge to readers is to isolate links and connections between individual and pairs of sayings so that they might reflect on possible thematic connections between the still larger units of material. [Structure at a Glance: Proverbs 19]

COMMENTARY

Consider Poverty, 19:1-4

These opening four verses might imaginatively be read as a unit, since both vv. 1 and 4 utilize references to the poor. As we have encountered previously, v. 1 makes a strong implication that righteousness is connected to poverty (see 28:6). The verse is not saying, however, that poverty equals righteousness, thus idealizing impoverishment in some sense. Rather, v. 1 asserts that it is not worth giving up poverty for wealth if it also means sacrificing integrity. While the situation envisioned in the saying seems to be one of gaining wealth through lying, the character of Job, who would not sacrifice his integrity even though he had lost all, provides an interesting twist on the saying (cf. Job 2:9; 27:5). It is Yahweh at the end of the narrative who distinguishes between Job and his pious friends on the basis of who spoke the truth (Job 42:8). In doing so, Yahweh affirms Job's, and thus this saying's, insistence upon integrity over wealth. Proverbs 19:4 provides an antithetical thought to the celebration of poverty in v. 1. The saying observes that poverty is nevertheless a lonely condition; "the poor are left friendless." Readers must reflect upon the costs of poverty, and indeed the costs of righteousness. In v. 1 the term *raš* is used of "poor," whereas in v. 4 readers encounter the term *dal.* These two terms are virtually synonymous and are used most frequently in the Proverbs to designate poverty.[2]

The inner two sayings, vv. 2 and 3, allow readers some alternatives in reflection upon poverty and righteousness. Verse 2 connects with v. 1 through the shared word for "good" (*tôb*). What is not good in v. 2 is having the desire to act without the necessary knowledge to direct that action. Verse 2 contrasts v. 1 by counterpoising images of travel. Verse 1 offers an implicit comparison through a "better than" statement. The opening statement (1a) extends the image of "walking" (*hōlēk*). In this image integrity is a "walk": one "walks in integrity." Verse 2b counters with the image of "moving hurriedly" (*ʾāṣ bĕraglayim*). In this image, by contrast, one moves too hurriedly and "misses the way." By countering these two images, plodding integrity of 1a—even if accompanied by poverty—is privileged over aimless and directionless activity of 2b. Verse 3 provides a further point of reflection on the preceding sayings with its notion that it is folly that leads to one's ruin. The irony within this saying is that, even though it is folly that causes one's ruin, the fool blames Yahweh. Readers have one example of such folly in v. 2, undirected action, and therefore a reason to agree with vs. 3 that it is truly a fool who would blame the Lord for one's own foolish actions. In a context opened with celebration of poverty that may be the result of righteousness, one may give pause to consider the implication that the real threat is not wealth but foolishness.

What Is False and What Is True, 19:5-9

This complex of sayings is arguably a unit, since both 5a and 9a, functioning to form an inclusio, begin with the same phrase: "A false witness will not go unpunished." We have already seen how similar repetitions of terminology and phrases function to isolate groups of sayings that might be read as thematically related (e.g., 10:6-11; 14:28-35; 15:5-12; 16:1-9). To be sure, the language alludes to the law court where reliable testimony is to be given for the purpose of discovering the truth. In the framework of a collection of sayings that function as a basis for instruction, the idea of reliable testimony is not unrelated to the interests of education or, for that matter, to the interests in the functioning of everyday society. The emphasis upon perjury as a serious crime (cf. 12:17; 14:5, 25; and 21:28) implies that any teacher who fails to teach the truth is like someone who commits perjury. The extended implications are significant: the truths that society relies upon may be founded upon lies themselves.

Verses 6 and 7 stand as a pair of sayings that address the opposite sides of an argument: wealth and poverty (cf. 14:20). Verse 6 observes the popularity of one who is noble in spirit or generous. The phrase translated as "seek the favor" is in Hebrew *yĕḥallû pĕnê-nādîb*, "stroke the face." This image suggests that there is an active process of currying the favor of great people. We encounter it in examples in the biblical narrative illuminating of the meaning of *yĕḥal*. While Moses was on Mt. Sinai in God's presence and delayed to return to the people, the people began to commit sin in Moses' absence. When the Lord saw the people's wickedness and was about to destroy them, Moses "implores the LORD" (*yĕḥal mōšeh 'et-pĕnê*), using similar language to that in this saying. Moses "strokes the face of the Lord," in other words, mollifying God's anger (Exod 32:11). In v. 6 the rich are loved because of their generous gift-giving. Verse 7 makes an observation that contrasts this in reference to the poor: the noble are loved because of their generosity, but the poor are hated even by their families. In light of v. 6 readers naturally conclude that the poor are hated because they have nothing to give. The two verses work together to create a contrast similar to that encountered in vv. 1 and 4: choose poverty with integrity and loneliness, or wealth with popularity. Verse 7 contains a third stich translated by NRSV as "When they call after them, they are not there." A more literal translation of the Hebrew text is "One who pursues words, they are not." Some commentators say it is a "corrupt remnant of a lost couplet."[3] Others argue that it is a variant of 7b, the immediately preceding stich.[4] [LXX on Proverbs 19:7]

In the opening unit (vv. 1-4), however, readers are invited by v. 3 to revise the implications of vv. 1 and 2 so that folly, not wealth or poverty, is the problem. Something similar happens in v. 8. Here wisdom is put forward as the appropriate choice between wealth or poverty: it is neither wealth, which preserves one's life, nor poverty,

LXX on Proverbs 19:7

The comparison between the Hebrew MT and the LXX is of little help in sorting out the textual problem in 19:7. NRSV has three lines of poetry instead of two. The translation is based upon the assumption that 7c, the third line of poetry in v. 7, is a response to 7a and b. On its own 7c might simply read, "the one pursuing words, they are not." Not only does the sentence not make any sense on its own, but it is unclear how this half-line might follow thematically the preceding lines of poetry.

One may compare v. 7 with the LXX to get an idea how the Greek translators read the verse. In theory it is possible to reconstruct the Hebrew text based upon the translation given in the LXX. This assumes, of course, that the MT reflects an earlier stage of the tradition than the LXX. Upon comparison of the two versions, however, readers find that v. 7 in the Greek text is still much longer than the Hebrew text, and says something quite different. One is justified in concluding therefore that not only is the present Masoretic form of 7c corrupt, but it may well have been corrupt for the Greek translator, who then reconstructed it along with 7a and b to say something entirely different (McKane).

For further reading, see Emmanuel Tov, *Text Criticism of the Hebrew Bible* (Minneapolis: Fortress; Asen/Maastricht: Van Gorcum, 1992).

William McKane, *Proverbs* (OTL; London: SCM Press, 1970), 527. See also Franz Delitzsch, Proverbs, vol. 2 (COT; Grand Rapids: Eerdmans, 1950), 24-25.

which takes one's life. Only wisdom allows one "to prosper." In v. 8 such prosperity is indicated by the Hebrew phrase *limṣōʾ-tôb*, "to find good."

The Great and the Small, 19:10-12 (13-14)

This initial group of three sayings in vv. 10-12 concerns the attributes of administrators. The pair of sayings in vv. 13-14 return to the common themes of foolishness and the inevitability of Yahweh's control, and thus appear not to be related to the preceding three sayings. These final two sayings, however, offer interesting points of reflection as they require that readers consider the fact that people with administrative responsibility also have foolish children and quarreling wives. As such, the day-to-day features of life make even powerful people rather common.

Verse 10 asserts the inappropriateness of a fool's living in luxury. The overall effect of the saying is comparative and argues "from the lesser to the greater," *a minore ad majus* (e.g., Prov 11:31; 15:11; 17:7; 19:10; Job 4:19; 15:16). [A Minore Ad Majus] Luxury is to fools as power is to slaves; if the one is inappropriate, how much more the other. Verse 11 asserts the importance of an even temper, as readers have already seen in 14:29, 15:18, and 17:14. Nothing in particular requires that this saying be about kings or princes, but its proximity to v. 12 invites reflection upon its applicability to royalty as well. The final line of v. 11 also frames the concern with an even

A Minore Ad Majus

AΩ This Latin phrase translates the Hebrew phrase *"Mi-qal va-homer,"* meaning "from the lesser to the greater." It is significant as a rule of midrashic interpretation. Midrash is a mode of interpretation that attempts to investigate the meaning of a text beneath the superficial, literal level of a text. The ancient view of the inspiration of texts concluded that, if truly inspired, a text ought to have multiple significances and applications. The principle of *"mi-qal va homer"* is simply a rule of deriving meaning at a deeper level than the literal level of a text by arguing that if a circumstance applies to a lesser situation, then it surely applies to a greater situation.

Philip Alexander explains with the following citation from the Baraita of Rabbi Ishmael:

On one occasion the fourteenth of Nisan [Passover] fell on a Sabbath. The Benei Bathyra forgot and did not know whether or not the Passover overrides the Sabbath. They said: 'Is there anyone who knows whether or not the Passover overrides the Sabbath?' They were told: 'There is a certain man who has come up from Babylonia, Hillel the Babylonian by name, who has studied with the two greatest men of the age, and he knows whether or not the Passover overrides the Sabbath.' So they summoned Hillel and said to him: 'Do you know whether or not the Passover overrides the Sabbath?' He said to them: . . . 'It is a case of *qal va-homer.* If the daily offering, neglect of which is not punished by "cutting off" (*kāret*) overrides the Sabbath, then is it not logical that the Passover offering, neglect of which *is* punished by "cutting off," will override the Sabbath?' (Babylonian Talmud, Pesaḥim 66a).

For further reading, see David Daube, "Rabbinic Methods of Interpretation and Hellenistic Rhetoric," *HUCA* 22 (1949): 239-64; and James Kugel, "The 'Bible as Literature' in Late Antiquity and the Middle Ages," *Hebrew University Studies in Literature and the Arts* 11 (1983): 20-70.

Philip S. Alexander, ed. and trans., *Textual Sources for the Study of Judaism* (Chicago: University of Chicago Press, 1990), 59.

---

temper. Verse 12 is explicitly about the rule of the king. Ancient images of lions depict the animals as both grand and ferocious. [Lions] Such ferocity invites readers to consider the power of the restraint involved in holding back such emotion. If there is something beastly about the royal temper (or the common administrator!), imagine the struggle to maintain a controlled emotional demeanor.

The sayings in vv. 13 and 14 return to family matters, foolish children and their father, the quarreling between the prudent wife and her husband. The image of the foolish child in v. 13 returns to the theme of foolishness set out in v. 1 and also revisited in v. 10. Readers will also recall the frequent references to parental disappointment with children and the implications that are associated (e.g., 10:1; 17:21, 25). Likewise, the image of the "nagging wife" will be revisited periodically throughout the collection (e.g., 21:9, 19; 25:24). In association with sayings about the temper of administrators and the assumption that fathers play some role of

Lions

The imagery of the lion is frequently used in reference to kings (e.g., 30:29-31). There is archaeological evidence that lions once roamed Palestine during the Iron Age. Unfortunately lions have not survived until the modern era. Bears and leopards are now more common in the region.

The Talmud calls the lion "the king of beasts" (Hag 13b). The occurrences in the Hebrew Bible are more metaphorical than literal, however. Jacob's blessing to his sons and Moses' blessing to Israel compare both Judah and Dan to lions (Gen 49:9 and Deut 33:22). Israel as a whole is called a lioness in Num 23:24. The mothers of the kings of Judah are also referred to as lionesses who bring forth young lions (Ezek 19:2-9). David himself is remembered as having the heart of a lion (2 Sam 17:10). In Solomon's temple carvings of lions were incorporated into the decorative architecture (1 Kgs 7:29).

For further reading, see Louis Isaac Rabinowitz, "Lion," in EJ 5:262-76; and Edwin Firmage, "Zoology," *ABD* 6:1109-67.

Stone relief of a lion attacking a bull. Located on the east stairway of the Apanada.

Lion and Bull. Relief. Achaemenid art. 6th–5th C. BC. Persepolis, Iran.

administration in the home, this saying may imply an interesting analogy between family and kingdom. If administrators are like both fathers and husbands in temper, the saying illustrates the nature of irritations that require restraint and the difficulty of exercising restraint given the prerogatives of the two characters. Verse 14, then, functions in two ways: to contrast the good wife with the nagging wife and to contrast control with lack of control. If one may grant a measure of certitude about one's inheritance, then there could be even less certitude about finding a good wife. Of course, Yahweh retains his own sovereignty and as such reveals the relative impotence of human wisdom, especially in matters of the choice of one's spouse. While the good wife is a blessing indeed in this saying, she is just as much a surprise (e.g., 31:10-31). The saying provides further comment on the similar notion expressed in 18:22.

Motivation, 19:15-19

These verses follow a progression of ideas that are only remotely related in theme. Readers may see connections if they view them from the perspective of the problem of an individual's motivation to action. There is a progression from a saying on the fate of the lazy, which leads to sleep, v. 15, to a saying on the excesses of a violent temper, v. 19. In the cluster of five sayings (e.g., vv. 15-19), v. 17 stands as the central saying: two sets of sayings are symmetrically balanced on either side. Verse 17 offers a specific observation on the motivation toward kindness to the poor. This verse represents the most explicit reference to any particular activity in the group. Verses 18 and 19 may be suggesting possible modes of motivation for instruction.

Verse 15 is about laziness, returning to the theme of an instruction already encountered in 6:6-11. The results of laziness are inactivity, hunger, and, as readers will encounter in 21:25, death. Such implications provide a provocative contrast with v. 14, suggesting that even though one has inherited house and wealth, and enjoyed Yahweh's blessing through one's wife, one must still account for the daily provision. Verse 16 observes that keeping the commandment, *miṣwa,* leads to life. The question is whether this is Yahweh's commandment or the commandment of the wisdom teacher. In the shadow of v. 15, readers logically wonder whether lazy people will either follow the Lord's commands or that of a teacher. One would think that the outcomes of laziness would be acknowledged as having self-evident validity that requires no religious legitimization. This is especially intriguing in relation to v. 17. This verse contains a Yahweh saying requiring readers to reconsider whose commandment is at stake in v. 16. Caring for the poor is indeed Yahweh's commandment in Deuteronomy 15:1-11. Further, the sages themselves urge proper care for the poor (e.g., 14:21, 31). The motivation is that caring for the poor is like borrowing from the Lord. There is no risk because the Lord always repays debts in full. Sirach 29:8-13 envisions that what money one gives away in alms is actually a source of profit from God. In retrospect, the lazy person will never be able to meet the commandment to care for the poor, thereby obeying either Yahweh's commands or the teacher's. Since readers already know that laziness leads to poverty (e.g., 6:10-11; 10:4; 13:4; 15:19), they may explore an interesting contradiction. Since the lazy cannot keep the command to care for the impoverished, they must further rely upon others within their community to keep the command so the lazy will not be so impoverished.

The final two sayings offer a conclusion with a warning. Verse 18 is a saying admonishing parents (or teachers) to discipline their children. The saying assumes that motivating one's children is only possible while they are young and therefore there is some urgency

kĕtîb-qĕrē' in Proverbs 19:19

AΩ The two terms *kĕtîb* and *qĕrē'* designate early distinctions between various readings within the ancient Hebrew text. The term *kĕtîb* may be translated "what is written," and the word *qĕrē'* may be translated "what is read." When there was some doubt about the vocalization of a particular Hebrew word in the written text, scribes would write into the margins of the text an alternate set of vowels to be substituted for the consonants in the written text. By making such a substitution of vowel pointing, a new meaning for the word in the text was derived. If modern translators choose the *kĕtîb* tradition, that is the written tradition, they translate with the vowels as written in the text. If they choose the *qĕrē'* tradition, they translate with the vowels substituted in the margins of the text.

At v. 19 there is in the MT the designation that the word written (thus *kĕtîb*) as *gĕrāl* should be pronounced (thus *qĕrē'*) as though it were *gĕdāl*. The difference in meaning is significant in 19:19. The former, the *kĕtîb* reading, would not make sense at all, since it would be taken as an adjectival form of *gorāl*, "lot." The latter reading, which uses an adjective meaning great or large, produces the better reading "great anger" (see Roland Murphy). Richard Clifford also notes the *qĕrē'* reading as the basis for his treatment of the saying.

Richard J. Clifford, *Proverbs* (Louisville: Westminster John Knox Press, 2000), 178,

Roland Murphy, *Proverbs* (WBC 22; Nashville: Word, 1998), 141.

---

about it. With the preceding references to laziness and the command to care for the poor fresh in mind, the object of the discipline seems clear. It is so one's children will not be lazy themselves and thereby become poor; so they will not fail to keep the commandments, which leads to death. Verse 18b is provocative. It is not clear whether this half of the saying envisions death resulting from the harsh discipline, or whether death is the result from failing to discipline.[5] It seems clear that corporal punishment was indeed practiced in antiquity as a part of child rearing. Murphy observes that Deuteronomy 21:18-21 "sets definite limits to any lethal treatment of rebellious sons."[6] Verse 19 seems to make the thought unambiguous by reflecting upon the man of extreme temper. [*kĕtîb-qĕrē'* in Proverbs 19:19] We have encountered this person before in 14:17, 29, and 15:18. Further, there are accompanying public consequences through the paying of a fine. One can therefore easily project the relevance of this saying in a courtroom setting. However, in the present context of sayings, especially following a saying on the disciplining of children, violent temper is inappropriate.

Ground Rules for Education, 19:20-27

Even though the sayings in this group are not particularly thematically related, we delineate this group at vv. 20 and 27 because of the similarity of these two outer sayings. Both are imperatives, directed at the learner, to receive instruction. The two sayings recall similar imperatives for children to listen to the instructions of parents in the collection in Proverbs 1–9 (e.g., 3:1; 4:1). In these two sayings, then, we have the boundaries of the collection as well as a possible thematic touchstone to which readers may return to reflect on the inner sayings. The admonition to receive "advice" (*ʿēṣâ*) and "instruction" (*mûsār*) is placed into a larger perspective in v. 21. That perspective is grounded by the appeal to Yahweh as legitimation and asserts the priority of religious illumination over the rigors of disciplined learning. The two sayings, vv. 20 and 21, are connected semantically by their use of the words *ʿēṣâ* and *ʿăṣat*, the former translated "advice," the latter, "purpose."

Verses 22 and 23 might be read as the object of the instruction that comes both from the Lord and from one's teacher. Verse 22 urges that what is desirable in a person, presumably from both instruction and religious experience, is loyalty, *ḥesed*. Returning to the thought of 19:1, the full sense of v. 22 implies that it is better to be poor and have integrity than to be wealthy and be a liar. The Yahweh saying that follows in v. 23 reiterates that one finds life and security in one's religious practice. Readers might well conclude that to choose the poverty stemming from one's religious faith is nevertheless to be secure and suffer no harm.

The three sayings that follow, vv. 24, 25, and 26, reflect on people who are most at risk of failing to receive instruction, especially that instruction that is promoted in vv. 22 and 23. The first person at risk is the lazy, *ʿāṣēl*, v. 24. The sarcasm is clear: lazy people cannot even feed themselves. It further stands as a decisive contrast to the kind of rest of which v. 23 speaks. The lazy person rests, even sleeps, with his hand in the serving dish. How could this one ever be able to receive instruction? The scoffer in v. 25, *lēṣ*, is also at risk of failing to receive instruction. The saying asserts that the only positive effect of punishing a scoffer is that good might come to the simple, *petî*. Presumably this benefit accrues to the simple through observation of the beating (cf. 21:11). A further implication is that scoffing is as much defined by attitude as it is by speech. In such a case it is obvious that a scoffer could not receive instruction. Finally, those who do violence to parents, the fountainhead of wisdom, also are at risk of failing to receive instruction. The question is whether the violent treatment of parents follows because the children are shameless, or children are shameless because they do not honor their parents.[7]

Verse. 27 deserves further comment as an example of the difficulties in translating the idioms of another language. The NRSV translates "Cease straying, my child, from the words of knowledge, in order that you may hear instruction." Although this translation captures the intent of the sayings, it misses the irony. A literal translation of the Hebrew text is "Cease, my son, to listen to instruction, in order that you may stray from words of knowledge." This admonition says, at face value, just the opposite of the previous translation. The irony of the Hebrew version is that readers must interpret an imperative that counters everything that has been said by the sages up to this point. It follows that failing to listen causes one to stray from knowledge, the very thing the sages sought to prevent.[8]

For Whom There Is No Hope, 19:28-29

The two closing sayings provide a fitting conclusion to this chapter. Verse 28 returns to the image of the lying witness (v. 5). The images of speaking lies and swallowing iniquity, however, appear to be contradictory. The Hebrew word for "swallow," *yēballaʿ*, may be emended to read "gush forth," *yabbîaʿ*, as in 15:28: "the mouth of the wicked pours out evil."[9] The final saying in v. 29 also returns to the image of punishment for scoffers and fools. These two, the unreliable witness and the liar, stand as emblems of those who refuse to heed instruction and thus are uneducable.

CONNECTIONS

Education and Society's Ideals

We have seen several times already that the ancient sages were concerned about the importance of education. Wisdom was at the core of meaningful and successful living. It should be understood that behind such an assertion are fundamental assumptions of the very nature of society. Why, one might ask, does a society idealize an educated public? The liberal tradition in which the nineteenth century philosopher John Stuart Mill stood imagined an educated public that was bettering itself through free thought and experiments in living.[10] While it is not clear that the ancient sages had in mind such an education for every person in their society, modern democratic society certainly does.

The seventeenth century English Puritan poet and scholar John Milton wrote his *Of Education* in hopes that the Puritan revolution in England would restore society to a more pristine Christian state. This Christian society required a certain kind of leader emboldened by intellectual, spiritual, and emotional abilities and commitments. Thus Milton wrote, the end of education is "to know God aright, and out of that knowledge to love Him, to imitate Him, to be like Him," and "to perform justly, skillfully, and magnanimously" all the duties of public and private life.[11] Milton envisioned a kind of national regeneration as the basis for his society. And for that society Milton laid out a broad curriculum that addressed the physical, intellectual, aesthetic, and religious aspects of the inhabitants of this society. It was based upon the classics: the ancient languages, the great Greek and Latin playwrights, law, politics, literature, theology, and the Bible. The breadth of this education probably says more about his ideals of society than it does about either the curriculum or what pupils were actually able to learn.

The same is surely true of the sages of ancient Israel. Their convictions about education probably say more about their visions of society than anything else. Certainly the literacy rate of the ancient Israelite world limited to a very narrow upper class the realized benefits of education.[12] For a fool to be in a position of luxury or power was not fitting (19:10). It was a society where the wicked were overpowered by the wise and righteous, where the lazy got exactly what they earned, where it was truly better to be poor than to be a liar. This is an ideal world to be sure, but it became the basis for an extraordinary commitment to education. Is it possible that a society can only have an excellent system of education if there is some high vision for what that society should be? Perhaps it is not possible for teachers to teach unless they possess within their souls the conviction that there is a purpose for all of their labors. In other words, one cannot simply embrace the sages' advice on education without also giving some consideration to the much larger question of their, and our, vision for society.

NOTES

[1] R. N. Whybray, *The Composition of the Book of Proverbs* (JSOTSup 168; Sheffield: JSOT Press, 1994), 113; cf. Roland Murphy, *Proverbs* (WBC 22; Nashville: Thomas Nelson, 1998), 142, who doubts one can speak of intentionality of arrangement here.

[2] R. N. Whybray, *Wealth and Poverty in the Book of Proverbs* (Sheffield: JSOT Press, 1990), 14-23.

[3] William McKane, *Proverbs* (OTL; London: SCM Press, 1970), 526.

[4] R. B. Y. Scott, *Proverbs, Ecclesiastes* (AB 18; Garden City NY: Doubleday, 1965), 117, states, "The second and third lines are probably alternatives, representing with line 1 different forms of the same saying."

[5] McKane, *Proverbs,* 524, similarly notes this ambiguity. O. Plöger, *Sprüche Salomos* (BKAT 17; Neukirchen: Neukirchener, 1984), 224, notes that the verse is along the same lines as 23:13, which urges that harsh discipline will not kill a child.

[6] Murphy, *Proverbs,* 145.

[7] McKane, *Proverbs,* 531-32. Plöger, *Sprüche Salomos,* 227, implies that shamefulness derives from the treatment of parents.

[8] Note Murphy, *Proverbs,* 146, who adds that there is no "certain translation" of this verse. Richard Clifford, *Proverbs* (Louisville: Westminster John Knox Press, 2000), 179, interprets the verse as ironic advice.

[9] Thus, *BHS*.

[10] See John Stuart Mills's *On Liberty*, ed. Elizabeth Rapaport (Indianapolis, Cambridge: Hackett Publishing, 1978), 55-56.

[11] John Milton, *Areopagitica and Of Education*, ed. George H. Sabine (Arlington Heights IL: Harland Davidson, Inc. 1951).

[12] James L. Crenshaw, *Education in Ancient Israel* (ABRL; New York: Doubleday, 1998), 32-40, 280-81

THREATS TO THE GOOD LIFE

Proverbs 20:1-30

As in chapter 19, no single or recurring theme dominates the entirety of this chapter. Readers find instead small clusters of sayings linked together by language and theme. Verses 1-4 appear to be disparate and unrelated.[1] Nevertheless, each of the topics—wine, the king's anger, strife, and laziness—poses a threat to an individual's happiness and society's success. The images indeed appear unrelated, but each one leads to its own kind of destruction. Verses 5-12 are set apart by their concern with penetrating that which is hidden in the human heart. Verses 13-19 are concerned with the ancient world of commerce and the challenge of making a profit. Verses 20-25 concern different dimensions of Yahweh's relationship to humankind. More importantly, according to R. N. Whybray, these final verses are part of a much larger collection that extends from 20:20 to 21:4.[2] [Structure at a Glance: Proverbs 20]

AΩ **Structure at a Glance: Proverbs 20**
Consider the following arrangement of sayings.

Vv. 1-4 Things that Destroy Life
Vv. 5-12 Penetrating the Human Heart
Vv. 13-19 Making a Profit
Vv. 20-25 Relationship to Yahweh
Vv. 26-30 Yahweh, the King, and His People

Readers must continue in this chapter to watch for the thematic, semantic, and syntactic cues that suggest clusters of sayings. However, this chapter seriously tests the hypothesis that ancient editors systematically arranged sayings into clusters according to catchwords, repetitions, and general themes. Readers may find related themes and boundary markers function to distinguish at least five groups of sayings. On the other hand, readers may also find that the above five groups are only a strained interpretation and that many other possibilities are just as likely.

Murphy does not dismiss the existence of smaller possible units. He acknowledges catchwords in vv. 1-2 ("good"), vv. 4-7 ("friend," "poor"), Yahweh sayings in vv. 3, 14, 17, and 21. However, he sees no "obvious structure" to this chapter (Murphy).

Roland Murphy, *Proverbs* (WBC 22; Nashville: Word, 1998), 142.

COMMENTARY

Things that Destroy Success, 20:1-4

Even though these opening four sayings do not appear to be related, all four of them deal with subjects that pose a threat to a person's happiness and prosperity. The opening verse asserts that intoxication prevents one from being wise. Wine is called a "mocker" (*lēṣ*), the same Hebrew epithet that occurs in 19:29 (cf. 23:29-35) in parallel with the foolish. In the latter case, however, it is translated as "scoffer." Such behavior, and those who practice it, await judgment. Readers will also remember that Woman Wisdom is portrayed as serving wine at her banquet (9:5) whereas her counterpart, Woman Folly, serves only water with bread. The assumption in that passage (9:5) seems to be that there is a difference between consumption of wine for purposes of drunkenness and more legitimate usage of the substance. (see [Drunkenness in the Bible])

A second example of a destructive threat is in the king's anger.[3] Readers have already encountered the theme of the king's anger in 19:12. The saying in 20:2 anticipates similar sayings about kingship later in the chapter and in the collection (e.g., 20:26, 28; 21:1). The audience for this saying is certainly not ordinary people. Rather, the audience consists of those who have such access to the king that would allow potential provocation.

Verses 2 and 3 deal with the results of some kind of provocation. In v. 2 the king's anger is provoked; in v. 3 readers encounter one who potentially does the provoking. It is not wise to provoke the king; it is not wise to become embroiled in conflict. With v. 4, a reflection upon the dangers of laziness, readers look back upon four verses that address four threats to happiness and prosperity. Verses 2 and 3 deal with conflict and strife; only a fool would welcome such behaviors. Verses 1 and 2 evoke the reader's consideration of what phenomena bring on such conflict. Intoxication curtails an individual's wisdom and ability to make judgments; such an incapacitated state leads to foolish action. Laziness leads to no action at all.

Penetrating the Human Heart, 20:5-12

This group of sayings is collected with a thematic point in mind. Verses 5 and 12 provide the thematic boundaries by supplying reflections upon the problem of discerning what is hidden. Verse 5 uses the image of deep water to assert the impenetrability of an individual's inner thoughts (cf. 18:4). It is the intelligent person who can draw from such depths the meaning of either his own or another's thoughts. Verse 12 is one of several Yahweh sayings in this chapter. It asserts that the creator of the most important means of discernment—eyes and ears, watching and listening—is Yahweh. Yahweh, who watches and listens to all things, is the source of understanding that which is hidden within the hearts of people.

The sayings between these two boundary sayings call for such discernment in the wise. Verse 6 reflects upon the problem of loyalty. Many people proclaim themselves loyal, but actually identifying a loyal person requires the discernment of the intelligent person. Verses 5b and 6b are related in the juxtaposition of the "intelligent," *'îš tĕbûnâ,* and the one "worthy of trust," *'îš 'ĕmûnîm.* The concluding rhetorical question of 6b, "who can find," *mî yimṣā,* seems to lead appropriately into the following saying in v. 7, which answers an implicit question of how to recognize the righteous. One recognizes righteous ones by their integrity (e.g., 13:22 and 14:26). Verse 8 identifies discernment as one of the most crucial roles of the king. Readers have already encountered the theme of the king as an insightful judge (e.g., 16:10, 12, 13; also 2 Sam 14:17; 1 Kgs 3:16-28 for narrative examples). Verse 9 comments further on v. 8. It casts implicit doubt on whether any person can claim to be pure, especially in the face of the king's scrutiny. One may recall the previous sayings where people frequently think their ways to be pure in their own eyes (16:2).[4]

The Yahweh saying in v. 10 takes up the familiar theme of false weights and measures (cf. 11:1, 16:11; 20:23). These are abominable to the deity because of their use in the attempt to deceive. It takes individual discernment to recognize the people who use them. Verse 11 offers one final example of what is hidden to all but the discerning. Children's behavior betrays whether they are pure and right (cf. v. 7, where the children of the righteous are the best evidence of their integrity). The reason discernment is necessary is because the behavior of a child may only be "playacting" in his or her deeds, making it difficult to determine the purity of the act.[5] The saying in v. 11 offers the person of discernment the criteria for such a reflection as that in v. 7.

Making a Profit, 20:13-19

The sayings in vv. 13-19 are not so neatly connected as those in vv. 5-12 appear to be. On close reading, however, it is not difficult to associate these sayings with the problems of commercial activities. Verse 13 asserts that sleep leads to poverty, an implicit connection between laziness and sleep (e.g., 19:15). In both vv. 12 and 13 the eyes play a vital role. In v. 12 they are crucial for discernment; in v. 13 they must remain open so as to permit work that leads to prosperity. The image in v. 14 is that of the marketplace and the practice of haggling over the price of an item. The way of the businessperson is one of concealing from the opponent (the buyer or seller) one's true feelings. It is a humorous saying in its contrast between the public and private feelings of the buyer. Following a saying on the value of a commodity, the saying in v. 15 reflects on the relative value of knowledge. As rare as gold is, precious jewels are more rare, and such is speech informed by knowledge. Knowledge is especially appropriate in the marketplace.

Yet another rule of thumb for the businessperson concerns the familiar theme of giving credit to strangers, v. 16 (cf. 6:1-5; 11:15; 17:18; 22:26; 27:13). The idea is that when dealing with a person who gives credit for strangers, one should also require collateral immediately. The occurrence of the words *zār* and *nokrîyā*,[6] which are used elsewhere to designate foreign women, suggests to some that the problem is not loans to strangers, but to prostitutes. Readers have here then a criterion for questioning sound judgment.[7] Both vv. 16 and 17 share the Hebrew word *'ārab* (*'ārēb* in v. 17). In v. 16 it means to "make surety"; in v. 17 it is an adjective meaning "sweet." The two are related to the theme of dishonest gain. Verse 17 moderates somewhat the distrust that inheres in the statement in v. 16. Dishonesty is not good in any who practice it, to be sure. However, a strict business practice such as is put forward in v. 16 leaves little room for "heart."

The concluding two sayings in this group provide reflections on the commonsense business practice of taking advice. While v. 18 seems to reflect a provenance of warfare, the general admonition that success comes only from following sound advice is universally true. As a measure of caution, however, the following saying, v. 19, considers that in confiding in counselors one risks gossip. A wartime strategy as well as a plan for the marketplace is put at risk if it is shared with a gossip. Discretion is therefore as vital to success as obtaining counsel. Verse 19 shares the Hebrew root *'ārāb* with vv. 16 (translated "surety") and 17 (translated "sweet"), implying a possible linking of thought. In v. 19 the word is a reflexive form of the verb and contemplates a different kind of relationship than that proposed in vv. 16 or 17.

Relationship to Yahweh, 20:20-25

These six sayings may easily be read as part of a much larger context framed by 20:20–21:4.[8] The outer boundaries of the unit consist of two clusters of sayings, each with three Yahweh sayings in them (20:22-24; 21:1-3). In addition to the Yahweh sayings, the thematic concern with kingship also provides a unifying aspect. The sayings in 20:20-25 reflect on Yahweh's relationship with human beings, especially in providing the certainty that evil will be repaid.

The opening saying asserts the inevitability of failure for those who "curse" their parents (see also Exod 21:17; Lev 20:9; Deut 27:16). The word curse, *měqallēl*, finds some balance in the concluding saying of the group, v. 25, which reflects upon "wild talk," or "rash speaking," *yāla'*. In v. 20 the concern is a curse of one's parents; the saying in v. 25 concerns the making of a vow without reflecting on whether one can really pay the vow (a topic considered in Eccl 5:1-6). Both examples of unreflective speech suggest that the results are grim. Verse 21 provides a scenario in which an individual might find himself cursing parents. It implies that the unscrupulous gain of an estate might come from mistreating one's parents. NRSV translates with the *qěrē'* tradition, meaning "hastily." The *kětîb* reading would be "greedily." [*kětîb* and *qěrē'* in 20:21] Readers have already encountered sayings that reflect upon the idea of "quick wealth" and the trouble such behavior brings to the household

kětîb and qěrē' in 20:21

AΩ The designations *kětîb* (what is written) and *qěrē'* (what is read) are placed in the margins of the Hebrew text and indicate the scribal activity that preceded and continued through the work of the Masoretes (see [**The Masoretes**] and [*kětîb-qěrē'* in 19:19] for fuller explanations).

In the case of the term in v. 21, for instance, the difference between the written tradition and the read tradition is the substitution of the vowel letter *hē* for the consonant *ḥet*. The two letters look very similar and are easily mistaken. The difference in the spelling of the words in question appears in transliteration as (k) *měbōḥelet* (q) *měbōhelet*. The tradition that was pronounced, thus *qěrē'*, takes the word from a different root altogether. The meaning of the phrase concerns an inheritance gotten by haste rather than greed.

Care of Parents

📖 On several grounds readers may deduce the importance of caring for parents in antiquity. The saying in v. 20 has affinities with both the Decalogue and the covenant code. In Exod 20:12 we hear the admonition to "honor your father and your mother"; in Exod 21:15 and 17 we hear injunctions against either striking or cursing parents. The laws are sanctioned by death. It is obvious therefore that a saying on parents in such a context is not likely to have been addressed to children for the purpose of proper behavior. Rather, the sayings surely envision a period when older adults lose their ability to contribute to society. They are not simply to be cast aside by their adult children. Abusing parents is the indication of such disregard.

Some question arises, however, as to the enforceability of such an admonition. Clearly the saying in v. 20 uses language quite different from the legal formulations mentioned above. One's "lamp" being extinguished is quite different from one being executed by the state. Perhaps by the time of the proverbial saying there was no possible appeal to the state for enforcement. Thus the only sanction is that of Yahweh. The religious sanction fills the gap created by a diminished or absent legal authority (see McKane).

For further reading, see Cyril S. Rodd, "The Family in the Old Testament," *BT* 18 (1967): 19-26; Hans Walter Wolf, *Anthropology of the Old Testament*, trans. Margaret Wohl (Philadelphia: Fortress, 1974); and C. J. H. Wright, "Family," *ABD* 2:761-69.

William McKane, *Proverbs* (OTL; London: SCM Press, 1970), 541.

Ethic of Nonresistance

R. B. Y. Scott sets this saying (20:22) within the framework of his own notion of a progression of ethical development evident within the literature of the Bible. Gen 4:24,
Lamech's song intoning the glory of multiple vengeance, reflects a primitive "desert vengeance."
The legal admonitions of *quid pro quo* (Exod 21:23-25) may reflect a later stage of thinking where
equity becomes a constraining factor in retaliation. And, still later, Deut 32:35, Moses' "Song,"
reflects thinking that substitutes divine revenge for personal revenge and eventually leads to the
idea of nonresistance (Lev 19:18; Prov 25:22) (Scott).

Such a neat development of ethical thought is probably more difficult to demonstrate than
Scott's position assumes. For one thing, the biblical tradition speaks far more frequently about
retaliation than it does non-retaliation. One would also question the principle of *quid pro quo*
thinking in the cases of capital punishment (e.g., "life for life," Deut 19:21). In Matthew's thought
(Matt 5:43-48) the principle is not ethical but religious. God's mercy is to be imitated.

For further reading, see H. H. Cohen, "Talion," *EncJud* 15:741-42; Bruce T. Dahlberg,
"Retaliation," *MDB*, 757; and John H. Tullock, "Retribution," *MDB*, 757.

R. B. Y. Scott, *Proverbs, Ecclesiastes* (AB 18; New York: Doubleday, 1965), 122.

(e.g., 13:11; 15:27a). The concluding word in v. 21, *tebōrāk*, "to be blessed," takes readers back to the opening words of v. 20 concerning parents. Indeed, a blessing should come from parents. But parental blessing will not happen if their children mistreat them. [Care of Parents]

The three sayings that follow are all Yahweh sayings, the first cluster of three in the overall unit contained by 20:20–21:4. The saying in v. 22 comes at a strategic moment in this context to imply that Yahweh is the one who ensures the appropriate punishment of all evil, even those who curse their parents in order to obtain the inheritance prematurely. On the face of it, however, it is a saying that teaches nonresistance. [Ethic of Nonresistance] Readers have encountered sayings on false measures several times already (e.g., 20:10). Besides reminding readers of the cluster of sayings on commercial practices in vv. 13-19, this saying implies that Yahweh both sees and repays even the most secret of evil practices. The concluding saying gives approval to the assumption that humans are limited in their capacity to control their destiny. Yahweh alone understands the ways of humankind (cf. 16:9; 19:21). Verse 25 is a good example of the extent of human foresight: people speak rashly in making a vow, and then discover they lack the wherewithal to meet the obligation.

Yahweh, the King, and His People, 20:26-30

These final five sayings may stand in a larger group that extends to 21:4. The general theme is kingship. Verse 27 is a Yahweh saying.

The final two sayings of the chapter are provocative observations in relationship to the thematic context.

Verse 26 addresses the king's ability to maintain justice. The assertion is very similar to that in v. 8. The image is not one of warfare, however, but one of threshing wheat by driving a cart over the grain. The act of crushing separates the kernel of wheat from the surrounding husks. The ensuing verse, v. 27, asserts that it is through the human spirit that Yahweh scrutinizes the inner thoughts of a person. Following v. 26, which celebrates the king's powers of discernment, readers may connect the two thoughts. The king's innermost thoughts are the discerning powers by which he separates the wicked from the righteous. Verse 28 concludes the explicit reflection upon kingship by maintaining the importance of his throne. The opening stich, 28a, urges that loyalty, *ḥesed,* and faithfulness or truth, *'ĕmet,* preserve the king's throne. This reiterates the assumption that the king's job is to maintain justice. NRSV translates 28b with the LXX, which substitutes righteousness, *dikaiosune* or *ṣedeq,* for a second *ḥesed,* which exists in the MT. [*ḥesed* and *'ĕmet* and the King]

The concluding two sayings invite readers to reflect upon possible connections with those preceding. Neither explicitly concern kingship. However, in the context of kingship and discernment, v. 29 offers a pragmatic point of view. The king's discernment, however much sentimentalized, is as much a function of years of practice as it is anything else. Gray hair is not only a metaphor for long life, but for wisdom as well. The final verse of the chapter also requires some reflection. As it stands, it concerns the value of corporal punishment. NRSV translates the *kĕtîb* reading, giving the verbal idea of cleansing or polishing. The *qĕrē'* tradition changes to

ḥesed and 'ĕmet and the King

AΩ In its present form the MT implies that the subject of v. 28 is the dual idea of "steadfast love" and "faithfulness." The king is the object of their watching and protection. The critical text suggests making the king the subject of the sentence, as would be implied in 28b, which reads "he establishes his throne by 'steadfast love' (*ḥesed*)." In this case 28a simply asserts that the king, being the subject of the sentence, is the one who ensures that "faithfulness" and "loyalty" flourish in his kingdom and thus promotes unity across the kingdom.

William McKane proposes that retaining the present MT, with the king as object of the protection of "steadfast love" and "faithfulness," possibly bears greater and more heightened significance. Following Gemser, who suggests the possibility that these two figures are "guardian angels" of the king, McKane cites several other biblical connections that might reinforce, if not the elevation of the two to quasi-divine status, then at least their function in an active sense of watching over the king. For instance, Ps 61:7 reads (NRSV) "appoint steadfast love and faithfulness to watch over the king." McKane cites two passages that allude to Yahweh's covenant with the house of David, in which the terms *ḥesed* and *'ĕmûnâ* occur as means of ensuring the Lord's covenant (2 Sam 7:15-16 and Ps 89:33 ET). It seems more likely that these two concepts are aspects of Yahweh's relationship to the king. The information is too incomplete to hypothesize the possibility of their being angelic beings.

For further reading, see Donald W. Misser, "Truth," *MDB,* 936; Wayne E. Ward, "Grace," *MDB,* 347; and H. J. Zobel, "ḥesed," *TDOT,* 44-64.

William McKane, *Proverbs* (OTL; London: SCM Press, 1970), 546.

a nominal idea, something along the notion of a massage. Either way there is a harsh conflict created between beatings and the idea that they are medicinal and therapeutic. The use of the phrase "innermost parts," *ḥadrê-bāṭen,* is shared with v. 27 inviting readers to recall the role of the king to maintain justice. Only a king has both the power to detect and to eliminate evil from the realm. Corporal punishment is one way he might accomplish his multiple tasks.

CONNECTIONS

The End Is Always the Beginning

Seldom do we think about the collapse of a society. When we do it is in some imagined cataclysmic, apocalyptic form, coming as the final pronouncement of some deity's intervention in the world. Hebrew literature envisions the finality of a society's collapse and disappearance dramatically by describing a time when Israel would be nothing but a proverb (*māšāl*) and a "by-word" (*lišnînâ*) among the nations. That is, their disappearance from the face of the earth should be so total they are only remembered in sayings of derision (e.g., Deut 28:37; Jer 24:9; Ps 44:14). But we might pause to reflect on the societies that have come and gone on the face of the earth, including ancient Israel, and keep in mind the sages' frequent warnings about those things that stand as threats to a society's good life. Too frequently we reflect only on the threat that brings an end to that which is established without also contemplating the new possibilities that accompany the completion of one form of human civilization.

A very complex society thrived for over a millennium in the lowlands of Central America (300 BC to AD 800). The ancient Mayas developed a sophisticated calendar system so accurate as to make intercalation (our "leap years") unnecessary. Their technology was highly developed as was their worldview advanced. Art and architecture flourished and economies brought prosperity. Archaeologists have been mystified at the relative speed of Mayan demise at what appears to be the height of its social and cultural flourish. There have been many attempts to explain the collapse of this great society in terms of natural disaster, warfare, internal peasant revolt, and so on. But none of these explanations has been widely accepted, because no single explanation fits with the evidence.

More recent research has argued that as city-states were collapsing in the southern regions of Central America, related cultures were rising in the north. These new cultures were not identical with the old, but related. This suggests that the model of a monolithic collapse is not as accurate as a model that acknowledges change, relocation, and new expansion. So while the old civilizations did indeed come to an end, there were many new beginnings that had their origins in the so-called collapsed societies.

The sages of ancient Israel were always offering warnings about activities, practices, beliefs, and peoples that put at risk an individual's (and a community's) enjoyment of the good life. Failing to honor parents, being led astray by poor judgment, failing to work, etc. all subverted the best interests of both the individuals and their society. Such negative activities bring an end to a certain kind of lifestyle, but they do not end life altogether. They perhaps redefine life from a certain, and perhaps a limited, point of view. Therefore, in contemplating one's actions, one's beliefs, it is important to hold in balance the fear of losing that which is established with the hope of new possibilities that only emerge once the established modes of existence have run their course.

NOTES

[1] R. N. Whybray, *The Composition of the Book of Proverbs* (JSOTSup 168; Sheffield: JSOT Press, 1994), 115-17; Otto Plöger, *Sprüche Salomos* (BKAT 17; Neukirchen: Neukirchener Verlag, 1984), 231-32.

[2] Whybray, *Composition,* 116-17.

[3] The word translated "provokes him" is a Hithpa el participle plus suffix and bears some consideration as to whether it is reflexive, denoting the king's anger, or an active verb, denoting the provocation of the king. See R. B. Y. Scott, *Proverbs, Ecclesiastes* (AB 18; New York: Doubleday, 1965), 119. Verse 3 also has a Hithpa el of the verb *gālâ.*

[4] Plöger, *Sprüche Salomos*, 234.

[5] Richard Clifford, *Proverbs* (Louisville: Westminster John Knox Press, 2000), 182, explains the multiple meanings that inhere to the Hebrew word *yitnākkēr.*

[6] *Nokrîya* is the *qĕrē'* reading implying an understanding that foreign women were here designated. *Kĕtîb* has *nokrîm.* NRSV translates the *kĕtîb* tradition.

[7] Duane A. Garrett, *Proverbs, Ecclesiastes, Song of Songs* (NAC 14; Nashville: Broadman, 1993), 177.

[8] R. N. Whybray, *Composition,* 115-16. Roland Murphy, *Proverbs* (WBC 22; Nashville: Word, 1998), 149-50, does not adopt this hypothesis.

WISDOM AND WICKEDNESS

Proverbs 21:1-31

As indicated in the discussion of Proverbs 20, the opening four verses of chapter 21 may easily be read as the conclusion to the cluster of sayings beginning in 20:20.[1] Alternatively, one may read this chapter of sayings roughly as a unit of its own. The opening two and closing three sayings are Yahweh sayings, asserting the deity's autonomy over against human ingenuity. Taken as such, the strategy for reflection would be to hold in tension the many and varying assertions of wisdom's benefits with the fundamental assumption that Yahweh always has the final word in human affairs. Further, the occurrence of the "contrastive" style of sayings, so common in Proverbs 10–16, resumes in this chapter. [Structure at a Glance: Proverbs 21]

Structure at a Glance: Proverbs 21

AΩ Readers may find the following organizational suggestions helpful as they read.

Vv. 1-4 Royal Surrender
Vv. 5-8 Haste Makes Waste
Vv. 9-19 Miscellaneous Sayings
Vv. 20-24 The Treasures of Wisdom
Vv. 25-31 A Concluding Miscellany

The dominant themes concern human wisdom (vv. 1, 16, 20, and 22) and human wickedness (vv. 4, 6-8, 10, 12-15, 18, 21, 24, 26-29). Two sayings concern the diligent and the lazy (5 and 25), two concern wives (9 and 19), and one concerns a threat to a person's obtaining wealth (v. 17). Firm thematic or semantic connections among larger clusters of sayings are not apparent beyond two or three sayings.

The opening four verses, vv. 1-4, serve both to conclude the thematic concern with kingship begun in 20:26 and to urge Yahweh's absolute autonomy from human wisdom. Verses 5-8 associate obtaining treasure with acts of wickedness. Verses 9-10, set off by an inclusion created by two sayings on wives (vv. 9-19), contain a broad miscellany of sayings mostly concerning the wicked. Verses 20-24 return to statements that promote the characteristics and prosperity of wise behavior. Verses 25-31 conclude by returning to the theme of the fate of the wicked, punctuated with two Yahweh sayings, vv. 30 and 31.

COMMENTARY

Royal Surrender, 21:1-4

Against the assertions of the king's autonomy, which we have already encountered (e.g., 16:10, 14, 15; 20:2, 26, 28), this opening saying is provocative. Ultimately, whatever glory may accrue to the king because of this opening saying, it is Yahweh who stands behind the king. It is clear in this case that the king does not rely on human counselors, his courtiers, or ministers of state. He relies upon Yahweh only.[2] Such a statement provides appropriate balance to the saying in

Public vs. Private Religion

📖 Verse 3 counterpoises public (sacrificial) religion with private morality by asserting that Yahweh prefers the latter over the former. In the larger context of biblical literature, there is indeed a repeated emphasis upon individual moral character. In fact, readers have already encountered similar teaching in Prov 15:8: "The sacrifice of the wicked is an abomination to the LORD, but he loves the one who pursues righteousness." The apparent prejudice toward personal moral behavior over public sacrificial religion is regarded as a prophetic bias (e.g., Jer 6:20; 17:9-10). Not only did prophets accuse the community of moral lapses, but individuals as well. Prophetic denouncement of individual behavior had its ultimate outcome in the well-being of society as a whole.

It is unlikely that the saying in Prov 21:3 is attempting to undermine the importance of the sacrificial system, however. More likely, the saying recognizes that it is possible to pollute and weaken the significance of the sacrificial system by failing to maintain personal righteousness and justice in conjunction with it. The prophets condemned temple worship if it was not accompanied by appropriate moral behavior (e.g., Isa 1:12-17). But the temple was also a part of the prophetic vision of restoration and Yahweh's presence with his people (Ezek 44–48). The thrust of this thinking is that personal integrity and morality validate the officially sanctioned practice of public sacrifice.

For further reading, see Aubrey R. Johnson, *The One and the Many in the Israelite Conception of God* (Cardiff: University of Wales Press, 1961); Douglas A. Knight, "Ethics in the Old Testament," *MDB,* 267-70; Temba L. J. Mafico, "Ethics (OT)," *ABD* 2:645-52; J. R. Porter, "The Legal Aspects of Corporate Personality in the Old Testament," *VT* 15 (1965): 361-68; and John W. Rogerson, "Corporate Personality," *ABD* 1:1156-57.

---

v. 4. Both verses share the image of the heart." While v. 4 obviously concerns wicked people and not the king, it is still the person with such intellectual pride who, unlike the king, cannot be directed by Yahweh. The phrase translated "proud heart" (*rĕhab lēb*) stands in contrast to the often encountered phrase "to lack sense" (*ḥăsar lēb*, e.g., 6:32; 7:7; 9:4, 16; 10:13; 11:12; 12:11; 15:21; 17:18),[3] implying that pride derives from the possession of intellect.

Within the boundary of these two sayings—one concerning the submissive king, the other concerning the resistant intellectual—are two more Yahweh sayings. Readers have encountered both of these in previous contexts (15:8 and 16:2). By reading these sayings against the context of kingship, one may encounter some provocative implications. The king, whose responsibility is to maintain justice across his land, must recognize that justice and righteousness are more important than sacrifice. The sequence is provocative. Righteousness and justice must be initiated from within the heart; sacrifice follows as a public response. [Public vs. Private Religion]

Haste Makes Waste, 21:5-8

While the sayings in the chapter appear to have more of a miscellaneous character to them, readers may recognize a progression of thought in vv. 5-8. Verse 5 reminds readers of the importance of diligent planning. The contrast to such diligence is not laziness, as would make more sense, but haste. Verses 6-7 offer two examples of the kind of haste that may be envisioned in v. 8.

Verse 6 envisions the person who speeds up the process of obtaining wealth by lying. If such activities are the result of one's "plans" (*maḥšĕbôt*, v. 5), then, indeed, one will come to want. The inevitable result is death. Interestingly, the occurrence in v. 6b of the word "vapor," *hebel*, informs the usage of the term in the book of Ecclesiastes, wherein the sage finds many other activities that do not, in the long run, provide any gain. Violence logically follows such unprofitable and dishonest behavior. Verse 7 observes that violent acts eventually take their toll on the wicked who perpetrate them. The idea is not new here. Readers have seen that the sages often gave expression to the belief that the wicked would be ensnared in their own deeds (e.g., 12:13; 13:14; 14:27). Verse 8 offers a more general observation on the comparative ways of the pure (*zak*) and the guilty person (*wāzār*).[4] By association, one may also infer that the person who lies is one who plans (v. 5) an inappropriate pursuit of wealth.

Miscellaneous Sayings, 21:9-19

Verses 9-19 read more like a miscellaneous collection than anything else.[5] It is nevertheless interesting to consider vv. 9-19 as a group, since the opening and closing sayings share identical topics concerning the "contentious wife." Further, both sayings in vv. 9 and 19 are "better than" sayings. Readers might be tempted to surmise that the sayings contained within the two boundary statements would concern domestic matters. They do not, however. The themes of the sayings from vv. 10-18 mostly concern wickedness and the wicked.

The domestic conflict pictured in vv. 9 and 19 remind readers of a topic already encountered in the collections. Proverbs 19:13 has already addressed the nagging and contentious wife. Readers are further reminded that the male perspective here fails to reflect upon what possible social and environmental conditions contribute to the wife's contentiousness. Both sayings picture lonely spots as better alternatives to domestic conflict, here portrayed as originating solely with the wife. [Corner of a House]

Corner of a House

ΑΩ While sayings in vv. 9 and 19 are related in their concern with a "contentious wife," visual-izing the significance of the hyperbole in v. 9 requires some elaborating on the architectural background. Unfortunately, archaeologists have not found any houses with preserved roofs, so precise knowledge is unavailable. NRSV's translation "the corner of a housetop" envisions something akin to the arrangement depicted in 2 Kgs 4:10. In that narrative a chamber with walls is built atop the roof. Because access to the roof was likely from the outside, such a room was more likely to have been built on the corner, where two walls conjoined.

This is certainly not the only possible reconstruction of the text. The LXX translates the Hebrew *pinnat gāg,* "corner of the roof," with the word *hupaithrou,* "in the open air." This would imply living exposed on the corner of the roof. It does not apparently have any notion of the room on top of the roof and it certainly renders the image more extreme: it is better to be exposed to the elements on top of the roof than to live with a contentious wife (McKane).

For further reading, see John S. Holladay, Jr., "House, Israelite," *ABD* 2:308-18; Yigael Shiloh, "The Four-Room House—Its Situation and Function in the Israelite City. *IEJ* 20 (1970): 180-90; and idem, "The Casemate Wall, the Four-Room House and Early Planning in the Ancient Israelite City," *BASOR* 268 (1987): 3-15.

William McKane, *Proverbs* (OTL; London: SCM Press, 1970), 553-54.

Garrett groups vv. 10-13 as sayings on merciless behavior. Both vv. 10 and 13 are examples of merciless behavior; vv. 11 and 12 are sayings on the benefits of watching such merciless ones be punished.[6] Verse 10 observes that the wicked are incapable of offering mercy to their neighbors. If one reads v. 13 against v. 10, poverty is an example of the result of such refusal to be merciful. If the wicked are incapable of mercy, then the scoffer is incapable of learning, as readers have already seen (e.g., 19:25). Verse 11 asserts, however, that there is pedagogical value for the simple in observing the punishment of the scoffer. The wise, by contrast, always take learning to heart, suggesting an implicit similarity between the wise and the simple. Verse 12 is linked to v. 11 through the use of Hiphil forms of the Hebrew word *śākal,* meaning "to look at" or "have insight." In v. 11 *běhaśkîl* is translated as "instructed." In v. 12 *maśkîl* is translated as "have insight." Verse 12 returns to the contrast between righteous and wicked behavior as in v. 10. Here, in a sense parallel with v. 11, the righteous person watches as the house of the wicked is destroyed. Another meaning arises as NRSV takes *ṣaddîq,* in v. 12, as "the Righteous One," meaning God. The implication is that God is doing the watching, not some righteous person. Despite the parallelism with v. 11 through the shared ideas of watching and observing, a human person, especially one who is righteous, could not be the subject of the participle *měsallēp,* "to overturn," translated in NRSV as "casts down," in the second half of v. 12. Such intervention must be reserved for the deity alone.

Again, readers cannot avoid the conclusion of the miscellaneous nature of vv. 14-18. Three of the sayings are possibly related to the theme of justice (vv. 14, 15, and 18), while the other two concern common themes of wisdom (v. 16) and pleasures (v. 17). The saying on the benefits of the bribe as a tool to avoid anger returns to an idea already encountered in 17:8 and 18:16. On the possibility of the bribe as subverting justice, see 15:27b and 17:23. Perhaps both dimensions are envisioned by placing v. 14 in proximity to v. 15. Together, both assert the benefits of secret agreements as long as there is no subversion of justice. In this context of the discussion of justice, v. 18 poses a challenge. While the literal sense of "ransom" (*kōpēr*) cannot be satisfied by the sense of this saying,[7] an exchange or substitution seems to be the main idea. Clearly, there is a contrast implied in the fates of the righteous and wicked. The idea is that the evil fate that might befall the righteous is directed toward the wicked. The classic example is Haman swinging from the gallows built for Mordecai (Esth 7:10).[8] The story captures the irony created by the secret machinations of the powerful, represented by Haman, and the grinding of the slow wheel of justice for the righteous, represented by Mordecai, and reflects the very contrast created by the present vv. 14 and 15. Verse 16 recalls the image of the "way" as both a metaphor for life and as a symbol for ethical purity. The implication is that wickedness is an imprudent choice, and imprudence necessarily leads to its own kind of punishment. Similarly, it is imprudent to prefer pleasures that take one away from work. The inevitable fate is poverty.

The Treasures of Wisdom, 21:20-24

This group of sayings stands out both because of its concern with beneficial features of wisdom and its structural arrangement. Of the five sayings, v. 22 stands in the central position as a short narrative illustrating the power of wisdom. The sayings that precede and follow v. 22 list the benefits; v. 22 offers an example. The NRSV translation of v. 20 allows the contrast between the sage and the fool. The wise is much more cautious than the sage about preserving his treasure. There is a possibility that "treasure" has a double meaning in this saying. On the one hand, treasure may be devoured by the fool. This implies a temporal significance, and one could infer that the referents are silver, gold, and jewels. However, the sages are interested in those benefits that are often counterpoised with earthly riches, thus allowing the possibility of reflecting upon another kind of treasure. The ensuing sayings explore what some of those precious treasures are.

The wise celebrate the prudence of righteous behavior in v. 21. The rewards for such pursuit are life and honor. Life and honor stand in contrast to monetary treasure and give clear indication of the sorts of things that the wise hold to be most dear. Verse 22, positioned at the center of the short collection of sayings, has more of a narrative character about it. We will encounter its subject matter again in Ecclesiastes 9:13-16. The saying celebrates both the cleverness of one sage who outsmarted a city of warriors as well as the power of wisdom, which, properly wielded, is a vital weapon of war. The concluding sayings in vv. 23 and 24 reflect the values of cautious speech and humility. Readers have encountered the value of using speech reservedly (e.g., 13:3; 15:23; 18:13). One wonders, however, how the sages could maintain such caution in speech and simultaneously assert the importance of instruction. Verse 24 puts forward presumptuousness and haughtiness as criteria for defining the scoffer. Readers recall the impossibility of the scoffer ever learning (e.g., 19:25, 29; 21:11); here it is made clear why that is so.

A Concluding Miscellany, 21:25-31

Three of the concluding six sayings concern the wicked or wicked behavior: vv. 26, 27, and 29. As readers have already seen, the final verses are Yahweh sayings that balance the opening four sayings in the chapter. Verse 25 is a saying describing the behavior of the lazy. Readers recall 19:24 and the sarcastic attitude toward laziness there. Here the statement is almost contradictory. Desire or craving is motivation for most people; for the lazy it is detrimental. The idea suggests that laziness precludes any real desire, or that there is only desire and that without effort. There is therefore no real fulfillment of desires. Verses 25 and 26 share a semantic connection in the use of the Hebrew word for "desire" (*ta'āwâ*). The linguistic affinity may provoke readers' interest in the details of the relationship between the two sayings. The Hebrew text of 26a implies the anteceding subject, the lazy, as its own subject. In this case, the lazy stands in contrast with the righteous, not the wicked. The NRSV translation of "the wicked" stems from the LXX's expansion of 26a to include *asebes*, "the wicked," based upon the inclusion of *ṣaddîq* in the Hebrew text of 26b.

As in 21:3, v. 27 reminds readers that sacrifice is subordinated to ethical behavior. Here is the first time the word for wicked, *rěša'îm,* is used in the group. Logically, it follows the reference to the right-eous in v. 26b. Verse 29 takes the behavior further by asserting that the wicked lie. The "hardening of the face" is an idiom to express deceit. The saying parallels v. 27 through its motif of outward appearances; the outward appearances are contrasted with an indi-vidual's ways (v. 29) in a sense similar to the contrast between public sacrifice and ethical purity (v. 27). Verse 28a is appropriate in the midst of 27 and 29, though it is not clear what it means in its entirety. Readers have encountered the subject of the "false witness" already (e.g., 14:5, 25; see also 29:5, 9), but the implica-tions of joining the idea with the statement in 28b about a "good listener" are not clear at all. Murphy suggests that the nuance is one of counterpoising false testimony with the testimony of one who listens. "This would be a careful observer whose words in reply will stand permanently and convincingly because they have been well thought out, and they are honest."[9] Alternatively, the sayings may contrast the fate of the liar with the fate of the witness who imme-diately follows and has had the benefit of previous testimony.[10]

The final two sayings form a pair to provide a Yahwistic frame-work for the entire collection of sayings in chapter 21. Verse 30 fundamentally reasserts the claims of vv. 1-3. Three key wisdom terms—"Wisdom" (*ḥokmâ*), "understanding" (*tebûnâ*), and "counsel" (*ʿēṣâ*)—are used to illustrate the scope of the claim. An example follows in v. 31. With all of the preparations one might make for the day of battle, the victory belongs to Yahweh.

CONNECTIONS

"The Turning of the Times"

Having now gotten a grasp of how the sages thought about their world, one likely finds it difficult to visualize the wickedness to which the sages often referred. Was it real, or was it merely a concept? Had evil become a saying or a proverb so concretized in its symbolic framework that it did not have any place in the real world? Such is the danger of working with proverbs and sayings. They lose their life, so to speak, and readers must constantly find ways to revisualize, or rematerialize, what the sages were talking about.

The *Letters and Papers from Prison* of Dietrich Bonhoeffer, the Lutheran pastor and theologian of the early twentieth century,

Dietrich Bonhoeffer (1906–1945)

Bonhoeffer was a German pastor and theologian whose life culminated in martyrdom for his belief that Christians could not remain silent while the Third Reich carried out its campaign of terror, racism, and world war. As a result of his outspoken opposition, his participation in underground anti-Reich subversion, and his support of a plot on Hitler's life, Bonhoeffer was imprisoned by the Gestapo in 1943 and executed in April 1945.

He is best known for his Christian classic *The Cost of Discipleship,* first published in 1937. Through the remarkable efforts of his family and his friend, Eberhard Bethge, Bonhoeffer's *Letters and Papers from Prison* have allowed modern readers to experience the faith he wrought while facing his final days of this life.

For further reading, see Eberhard Bethge, Renate Bethge, and Christian Gemmels, *Dietrich Bonhoeffer: A Life in Pictures* (Philadelphia: Fortress Press, 1986); and Eberhard Bethge, *Bonhoeffer: Exile and Martyr* (New York: Seabury Press, 1975).

[Dietrich Bonhoeffer (1906–1945)] contain several poems that Bonhoeffer wrote from Tegel prison during the years 1943–1944.[11] One poem in particular captures the despair of the imprisonment and the darkness of evil. In it readers hear the stark descriptions of hopelessness along with Bonhoeffer's yearning for liberation and justice that stem from his vision of judgment that will one day come. One passage from his "Night Voices in Tegel" is particularly illuminating of what true evil and wickedness has been about in the context of modern-day readers.

> Twelve cold, thin strokes of the tower clock
> Awaken me.
> No sound, no warmth in them
> To hide and cover me.
> Howling, evil dogs at midnight
> Frighten me.
> The wretched noise
> Divides a poor yesterday
> From a poor today.
> What can it matter to me
> Whether one day turns into another,
> One that could have nothing new, nothing better
> Than to end quickly like this one?
> I want to see the turning of the times.

Violence (v. 7), arrogance (v.4), the absence of mercy (v.10), and injustice (v. 15) all lead to the cry of pain that is unheard (v. 13). Life then becomes a meaningless tedium that merely passes an evil time. That is the thrust of Bonhoeffer's poem as well as some of the images of this chapter of the Proverbs. Against the backdrop of what would eventually happen to Bonhoeffer, the only turning of the times he saw was on the day of his own execution, 9 April 1945, in Flossenburg prison. To the Christian world, Bonhoeffer's death was a martyrdom that stood at the end of a trajectory of evil that grew from an extraordinary series of wicked acts perpetrated against all of humanity. Such palpable evil causes even the strongest of the faithful to despair in the darkness. Bonhoeffer saw it, heard it, and resisted it, and death was the only redemption he had from it.

The particular acts of wickedness mentioned in this collection of sayings are themselves testimony to the sages' understanding of an extraordinary darkness. In the Proverbs they stand at the head of a trajectory of thought that would be visited fully in later wisdom works. The story of Job testifies to one righteous person's encounter with meaningless despair. In Job readers are reminded again of contemporary sufferers, struggling to "see the turning of the times." Qoheleth, the sage behind the book of Ecclesiastes, also testifies to an incomprehensible darkness. His is a level of despair and darkness unparalleled elsewhere in the Bible. Readers are reminded that meaning derived from observations of order in nature cannot be validated simply by excluding the disorder also evident in nature.

NOTES

[1] R. N. Whybray, *The Composition of the Book of Proverbs* (JSOTSup 168; Sheffield: JSOT Press, 1994), 115-16.

[2] R. B. Y. Scott, *Proverbs, Ecclesiastes* (AB 18; New York: Doubleday, 1965), 125, speculates that within 1a are two statements that have been editorially combined. One concerns the king's sovereignty, the other Yahweh's control.

[3] William McKane, *Proverbs* (OTL; London: SCM Press, 1970), 558.

[4] Reading with NRSV, which translates *wāzār* as cognate with an Arabic root meaning "guilty." The MT could also be taken as *waw + zar* = "and strange."

[5] Whybray, *Composition*, 117-18.

[6] Duane A. Garrett, *Proverbs, Ecclesiastes, Song of Songs* (NAC 14; Nashville: Broadman Press, 1993), 181.

[7] McKane, *Proverbs,* 561, explains that the *kōpēr* was a monetary payment; further, the righteous person needs no ransom. See R. E. Murphy, *Proverbs* (WBC 22; Nashville: Thomas Nelson, 1998), 160.

[8] Scott, *Proverbs, Ecclesiastes,* 126, quoting Rashi.

[9] Murphy, *Proverbs,* 161.

[10] Scott, *Proverbs, Ecclesiastes,* 126; cf. Richard Clifford, *Proverbs* (Louisville: Westminster John Knox Press, 2000), 193-94.

[11] Dietrich Bonhoeffer, *Letters and Papers from Prison,* ed. Eberhard Bethge (New York: Macmillan, 1971), 351.

THE PROFITABILITY
OF WISDOM

Proverbs 22:1-16

With these sixteen verses we conclude the collection titled "The Proverbs of Solomon," 10:1–22:16, and the smaller subsection that begins in 17:1–22:16, by returning to the general themes of the profitability of wisdom. The majority of sayings in this chapter concern wealth and poverty (vv. 1, 2, 4, 7, 9, and 16), providing perhaps the starkest examples for readers of wisdom's claims to its profitability. We are further reminded of the interrelationship between the sayings in Proverbs and the book of Ecclesiastes by the assertion of 22:1 on the "good name" (Eccl 7:1). Clearly the sages who stood within Israel's wisdom tradition continued to reflect upon the meaning of these sayings, providing each generation of subsequent readers opportunity to hear an implicit and ongoing dialogue about such matters. [Structure at a Glance: Proverbs 22:1-16]

Structure at a Glance: Proverbs 22:1-16

AΩ The following broad subdivisions may help readers distinguish the broad topics contained within this final section.

Vv. 1-5 A Good Name with Wealth
Vv. 6-16 Instructing Children for Prosperity

The sayings in this chapter are organized thematically with more readily recognizable markers. Verses 1-5 are linked through their juxtaposition of topics on wealth, wisdom, and Yahweh. Verses 1 and 2 concern wealth and poverty, vv. 3 and 5 concern wisdom, and vv. 2 and 4 are Yahweh sayings.

The second section is framed by vv. 6 and 16. A parallelism exists between vv. 6-7 and vv. 15-16 that suggests the thematic context of the sayings within (Duane A. Garrett makes this structural observation). Verses 6 and 15 concern the disciplining of children, the aim of wisdom, while vv. 7 and 16 concern wealth and poverty, one of the hoped-for outcomes of such discipline. Two smaller, thematically determined clusters may be found in this concluding section in vv. 7-9 and vv. 10-14.

Duane A. Garrett, *Proverbs, Ecclesiastes, Song of Songs* (NAC 14; Nashville: Broadman Press, 1993), 186-87.

COMMENTARY

A Good Name with Wealth, 22:1-5

This set opens by asserting the priority of a good reputation over wealth. Readers remember one of the opening sayings of the entire collection, 10:7, that contrasts the reputations of the wicked with the righteous. Sirach much later elaborates that a name, or reputation, outlives a person as well as wealth (Sir 41:12). Ecclesiastes, on the other hand, parallels a good name with death and precious ointment with the day of birth (Eccl 7:1). The question of an individual's reputation in the Proverbs saying (22:1), however, is whether one can have wealth as well as a good name. The ensuing context, vv. 1-5, suggests that it is possible if one is both compassionate and wise.

Such compassion might begin with the recognition that both rich and poor have in common their stance before the Lord, as v. 2 asserts. The concern for one's reputation takes priority over wealth, but not in the same way as the remembrance of one's ultimate origins. Job's assertion of innocence has a foundation in this very affirmation: God gives light to each person's eyes (Job 31:15; cf. Prov 29:13). A good example of how one's reputation works is implicit in the saying in v. 3, which readers encounter elsewhere (14:16; 27:12). The saying contrasts the "clever" (*ʿārûm*) with the "simple" (*pětāyîm*) and compares the two in terms of their caution and carelessness. Both of these are behaviors that help to determine how they got their names. As a general rule, though, readers now must reflect upon the danger of forgetting their own origins (v. 2) and the potential threat such omission has upon one's reputation (v. 1). Perhaps the most explicit affirmation thus far of the connection between one's faith and wealth comes in v. 4. It baldly asserts that the reward for humility and faith includes riches, honor, and life.[1] Readers have encountered a related idea in 21:21. Verse 5 concludes by returning to a contrast similar to that in v. 3, only here between "the perverse" (*ʿiqqēš*) and the one who "is cautious" (*šômēr napšô*). Not only are two kinds of people contrasted, as in v. 3, but two "ways" of life are also. One way is full of thorns and snares, the other is not (cf. 15:19). The clever see the danger (cf. v. 3), the simple do not. Seeking wealth without taking care for the poor, and one's own reputation, is costly and even dangerous.

Instructing Children for Prosperity, 22:6-16

As mentioned above, vv. 6-7 parallel vv. 15-16 thematically, providing a pair of framing doublets for these concluding sayings. [Semantics of vv. 6-7, 15-16] The sayings in the section offer examples that provide a rationale for the proper inculcation of basic wisdom values. The parallels with 10:1-5 suggest a further thematic frame—"the profitability of wisdom"—for the entire collection

Semantics of Vv. 6-7, 15-16

AΩ The semantic parallels in the outer verses of this group of sayings are worth pausing over. Through such parallels the sages created groups and clusters of sayings, which taken together suggest the possibility of considering the internal sayings as having thematic interconnectedness.

Both vv. 6 and 15 are about teaching children. The NRSV has "children" as the subject of v. 6 and "a boy" as subject of v. 15. In Hebrew the two sayings look even more similar. Both sentences have the word "youth," *na'ar,* as the subject. Both end with the same preposition with varying suffixes—"from it," *mimmennâ* and *mimmennû.* Further, both vv. 7 and 15 concern the relationship of rich to poor. V. 7 asserts the financial rule of rich over poor. Verse 16 observes that oppression of the poor, presumably by the rich, leads to ruin. As a response to v. 7 readers conclude that this is a balancing warning. Both sentences use the same word for "rich," *'āšîr.* There is a clear contrast between "rule" in v. 7 (*yimsôl*) and "oppress" in v. 16 (*'ōšēk*).

(10:1–22:16). Readers recall that 10:1 opens with a reflection on a "wise son," followed in 10:2 with a saying on the "treasures" of the wicked.

The NRSV translation of v. 6 has a familiar sound to it, even though the Hebrew text requires some interpretation. The saying is an imperative and therefore seems somewhat out of place among the collections of observations (cf. 14:7; 16:3; 19:18, 20).[2] The Hebrew literally reads "according to the mouth of his way," which is conventionally rendered "according to his way" or "the way he should go." The LXX leaves the verse out entirely. One could just as easily render the phrase that is translated "in the right way" as "according to his own way," implying possibly that education might be tailor-made in some fashion to an individual child's stage of development. [A Child's Way] Read against v. 15, however, it is not likely that the sages had any such notion of "individualized education" in mind, although they certainly understood teaching children to be different from teaching adults.[3] The goal of a proper education is to drive "folly" out of the hearts of young people. The association of vv. 7 and 16 also provides a provocative interrelationship through their reflections upon the rich and poor. Verse 7 reminds readers of the reality of both wealth and the vast disparities it may create within society (cf. v. 2). Readers are reminded of the prophetic message decrying oppression of the poor by the wealthy (Mic 2:2; Isa 5:8-10; Amos 8:4-6). Verse 16 ultimately provides a rejoinder in asserting that such behavior is self-defeating in the end. If the appeal to the commonalties between rich and poor (v. 2) is not enough reason, then the very pragmatic appeal in v. 16 should be: "Oppressing the poor in order to enrich oneself, and giving to the rich, will lead only to loss."

A Child's Way

AΩ The Hebrew phrase in 22:6, translated by NRSV as "in the right way," invites consideration, since it is taken by some to mean "according to the child's ability." (William McKane ascribes this view to Helmer Ringgren, *Sprüche/Prediger,* ATD 16/1 [1962].) The difficulty is in the phrase "his way" (*darkô*), which implies a certain individuality to the quite common concept of "the way." The term "way" is most frequently understood as objectively determined over against the particular contexts from which individuals might experience that way. It seems unlikely, then, that the phrase is to be understood in any sense that abandons the notion of "way" as ethical guidelines or traditional views, which children must measure themselves against.

Nevertheless, it may be that what the saying means is something like "after the fashion of a child" or "in a child's way." That is, it recognizes that adolescents in general have certain characteristics as opposed to adults. Verse 15 seems to reinforce this by focusing on a child's foolishness. Later Jewish literature, such as the *Pirkei 'Abot*, seems to

recognize some correspondence between a child's development and level of difficulty of pedagogical content. One passage reads:

> At five years one is fit for the Scripture,
> At ten years for the Mishneh,
> At thirteen for the Commandments,
> At fifteen for the Talmud,
> At eighteen for the bride-chamber,
> At twenty for the pursuing (a calling),
> At thirty for authority. [Quoted in Lemaire]

For further reading, see R. E. Clements, "The Relation of Children to the People of God in the Old Testament," CBQ 21 (1965–1966): 195-205; James L. Crenshaw, *Education in Ancient Israel* (ABRL; New York: Doubleday, 1998); André Lemaire, "Education (Israel)," *ABD* 2: 305-12; Hans Walter Wolff, *Anthropology of the Old Testament,* trans. M. Kohl (Minneapolis: Fortress Press, 1981); and C. J. H. Wright, "Family," *ABD* 2:761-69.

André Lemaire, "Education (Israel)," ABD 2:307.
William McKane, *Proverbs* (OTL; London: SCM Press, 1970), 564.

Verses 7-9 could be read as a cluster, because vv. 8 and 9 also comment on the claim put forward by v. 7. Verse 7 asserts the social reality of rich and poor. Verse 8 reflects an agricultural setting and appeals to the authority of nature's cycles: sowing and reaping. It quickly moves from the concrete observations of nature to a more abstract inevitability. Punishment for the wicked—those who commit injustice against the poor—is as inevitable as sowing and reaping. The NRSV translation of 8b, "the rod of anger will fail," requires readers infer from 8a that sowing injustice is "the rod of anger" in 8b. The image of reaping what one sows is certainly not new. Readers have encountered the idea in 11:18 and possibly in 12:14. Still more familiar is the application of the idea by the prophet in Hosea 8:7, and by New Testament writers (e.g., Matt 3:10; Gal 6:7-8). Verse 9 offers a vision of one who is generous and shares with the poor as stark contrast to the one showing injustice. Blessings are in store for those who are generous to the poor. The one who does so is referred to in Hebrew as having a "good eye" (cf. 28:22; 23:6 for *raʿ ʿayin*, "evil eye"). [The Good Eye]

The sayings in 10-14 invite readers' special reflection because of their concern with the familiar wisdom theme of proper speech. Only v. 13 departs from this theme with its concern for laziness. Verse 10 opens with the familiar warning about the scoffer (*lēṣ*), whose attitude is reflected in his speech. The scoffer only creates

The Good Eye

AΩ The phrase translated by NRSV as "those who are generous" renders a very old phrase that has its origins in the belief in the power of a look or a glance. The concept of the "evil eye" was common in ancient folklore and was known among the ancient Greeks and Romans as well. Readers encounter it elsewhere in the Proverbs several times (e.g., 23:6; 28:22; note also Deut 28:54 for opposing language). In the Proverbs the "good eye" is translated as generosity; the "evil eye" is translated as stinginess.

There is a related idea in the broader ancient Near Eastern context that makes the phrase appear somewhat tame by comparison. In ancient Mesopotamia the eye might be used to symbolize the presence of an all-seeing deity. Likewise, in ancient Egypt, coffins might be decorated with eyes on the side to signify the invocation of a divine curse upon any who would disturb the tomb. It was common for individuals to wear amulets and participate in magic to counter the effects of an eye that was thought to convey a curse.

Eye Idols

Scholars do not understand the significance of "eye idols" like these illustrations from Tell Brak, Jemdet Nasr, c. 3000 BC. One view is that they symbolize divinity.

For further reading, see Alan Dundes, ed., *The Evil Eye: A Folklore Casebook* (New York and London: Garland Publishing, Inc. 1981); Richard Cavendish, ed., *Man, Myth and Magic: The Illustrated Encyclopedia of Mythology, Religion and the Unknown.* New York, London, Toronto, Sydney: Marshall Cavendish, 1995), s.v. "Eye."

division and quarreling (cf. 21:24). By contrast, v. 11 speaks of those who love purity of heart and speech. Such people are sought out, in contrast with the scoffer. Verse 12 climaxes the sequence of three sayings by comparing Yahweh's responses. He watches over knowledge, but he overthrows words that are false. In retrospect, these three sayings, all on proper speech, reflect a progression of responses to ensure proper speech. In v. 10 there is a human response—"drive out a scoffer"; v. 11 speaks of the royal response to "gracious speech"—the kings' friendship; and v. 12 speaks of Yahweh's response—"overthrows the words of the faithless."

Two examples of improper speech come from the mouth of the fool and the foreign or "strange" woman (vv. 13-14). Of course, v. 13 portrays the lazy person as one who speaks in hyperbole in order to avoid work. It would take a fool to believe the words of such a one. Employers need to know in advance who is lazy, but they need not test by hiring; they need only listen to the individual's speech. Similarly, the foreign woman, who poses a threat toward cultic purity, is also identified by her words.

CONNECTIONS

The Journey's End

The Sayings of Solomon come to an end with this final collection of sayings on success and wisdom. Readers may readily affirm the passion with which the ancient sages pursued the importance of education. But where does it lead, and where does it end? Young Gershon Loran, in Chaim Potok's *The Book of Lights* (1981), provides a point of view from which modern readers of the Proverbs might continue their reflection.

Loran is a rabbinical student whose world has been shattered by the deaths of his parents, friends, and relatives. He struggles with the reality of evil and suffering, and carries his own fear and indecision around with him. His study of Talmud leads him to the study of Jewish mysticism in the Kaballah, "The Book of Lights," and it is here that he comes closest to understanding the darkness that surrounds him in his world. Ironically, it is when Gershon is literally in darkness that he hears the taunting voice reminding him that he prefers illusions to reality. In the darkness there are no illusions, just cold hard reality. Only in the light may illusions survive.

Gershon's fears come in the form of darkness and quiet voices. For it is in the dark that Gershon perceives the unanswerable questions that torment him. In one compelling scene darkness, after having deeply perturbed Gershon by raising questions, says,

> I leave now, it is almost light. Your illusions will soon return. Ponder my questions. I do not make the journey from the other side merely to torment you. We can make a cautious alliance, you and I. You have a mystic sense, and an eagerness to break old barriers and confront the new.[4]

It is this "cautious alliance" with darkness that is so central to education and its ultimate outcomes. Without it, there is only illusion.

The scene reminds readers that education is about the bewilderment and perplexity of the darkness. Instead of spending time denying perplexity, those who truly wish to learn must embrace their perplexity. Only in embracing the reality of darkness can true light come. Further, much of what passes for knowledge is only illusion. As we conclude the sayings of Solomon, with their strong emphasis upon education and the affirmation of the wisdom of Yahweh, we may begin to search for that cautious alliance with the darkness that helps us to understand the illusions created by the light. On the one hand the human ability to obtain wisdom, to work, to choose wisely, to speak properly, and to walk a path that is morally pure is at the heart of wisdom's aims. On the other hand, it is all for naught apart from one's total and ultimate submission to Yahweh and the exercise of his total control. Ultimately, one must embrace one's own darkness and ignorance of the ways of the Lord in order to obtain the light of wisdom. It is at the threshold of the abandonment of knowledge that true knowledge is found.

NOTES

[1] See Roland Murphy, *Proverbs* (WBC 22; Nashville: Word, 1998), 164, who explains that the absence of the "and" in Hebrew after *'ănāwâ*, "humility," is a result of the grammatical convention called "asyndesis." This justifies the reading of line b as a result of line a.

[2] Richard Clifford, *Proverbs* (Louisville: Westminster John Knox Press, 2000), 196.

[3] William McKane, *Proverbs* (OTL; London: SCM Press, 1970), 564, disagrees with those who translate in this fashion. See also Murphy, *Proverbs*, 164-65.

[4] Chaim Potok, *The Book of Lights* (New York: Fawcett Crest, 1981), 325.

BETWEEN RICH AND POOR

Proverbs 22:17–23:11

Instructions for Success, 22:17–24:22; 24:23-34

Having completed the Sayings of Solomon (Prov 10:1–22:16), readers are immediately struck by the change in style of the sayings in 22:17–24:22. The sayings that follow this initial unit, regarded by scholars to be an appendix of sayings, 24:23-34, differ somewhat in style and are therefore thought to stand independently from 22:17–24:22. The first instruction, 22:17–23:11, is actually one of three large collections within the overall collection. Readers encounter a second, more loosely connected collection of instructions in 23:12–24:22 ("Between Envy and the Fear of the Lord"). The final section, 24:23-34, has been added as an appendix to these "Words of the Wise."

With the opening admonition of 22:17 readers may be reminded of the opening admonitions of parental addresses in chapters 1–9. The sayings in 22:17–24:22 are characterized by imperatives and motive clauses, which define the instruction form. This collection of instructions, however, contains much smaller units than those in chapters 1–9. Readers should bear in mind that the style is not consistent throughout the entire collection.

The NRSV separates the section from the preceding section (10:1–22:16) with a heading, "The Words of the Wise," that is extrapolated from the occurrence of a similar heading in 24:23; it does not occur as a heading in MT. In actuality, both the MT and the LXX open the collection with the phrase "Incline your ear and listen to the words of the wise." The extrapolation takes place, rather, in the LXX.[1] The main reason for reconstructing the phrase as a heading is that the heading of 24:23, "These also are of the wise," clearly indicates the assumption of a collection called "Words of the Wise." What is more, it is clear that a new section does begin at 22:17. On these bases, scholars extricate the phrase from the middle of v. 17 and treat it as the superscription to the entire unit.[2]

For most of the twentieth century scholars have regarded this section of instructions to be an adaptation of the Egyptian "Instructions of Amenemopet."[3] [Amenemopet] Similarity in thought,

Amenemopet

AΩ This is the name of an Egyptian scribe who wrote a collection of instructions that many believe to be closely related to the collection in Prov 22:17–24:34. Some date the work of this lower administrator as early as the twelfth dynasty (1186-1070 bc), while others say it is as late as 6th-7th centuries BC. (Compare Pritchard with Beyerlin.) The nature of its influence upon the biblical text is debated on several grounds. Most significant is the relative degree of direct or indirect influence the collection might have asserted on the biblical writer. Scholarly consensus seems to be that there was some influence. However, the Hebrew wisdom tradition retains its own distinctiveness.

One scholar observes that Amenemopet was not a high official in the Egyptian administration. Further, unlike his predecessors, Merikare and Ani, he reflects much more the mixture of traditional Egyptian wisdom with the popular traditions and beliefs of the land (McKane).

For further reading, see James L. Crenshaw, "The Contemplative Life in the Ancient Near East," in *CANE* 4:2445-69; P. Overland, "The Wisdom of Amenemopet and Proverbs," in *Go to the Land I Will Show You,* ed. Joseph E. Coleson and Victor H. Matthews (Winona Lake: Eisenbrauns, 1996); Donald B. Redford, "Ancient Egyptian Literature: An Overview," in *CANE* 4:2223-41; and Edward F. Wente, "The Scribes of Ancient Egypt," in *CANE* 4:2211-21.

Walter Beyerlin, *Near Eastern Religious Texts Relating to the Old Testament* (London: SCM, 1978), 49.

William McKane, *Proverbs: A New Approach* (OTL; London: SCM Press, 1970), 105-106.

James Pritchard, *Ancient Near Eastern Texts,* 3rd ed. (Princeton NJ: Princeton University Press, 1969), 421.

instruction form, and specific phrases has convinced many readers of a direct literary influence of the Egyptian instructions bearing upon the Hebrew. While there can be no doubt that ancient Israel's sages shared with their milieu the thoughts and speech forms of wisdom, one must be cautious in the absence of more definitive evidence about arguing for such direct literary dependence. One of the most frequent appeals for evidence is in reference to Proverbs 22:20: "Have I not written for you thirty sayings of admonition and knowledge. . . ." This statement parallels Amenemopet 30: "See thou these thirty chapters: They entertain; they instruct."[4] The meaning of the Hebrew word *šilšôm* in 22:20 is a key component in the argument for literary dependence on the Egyptian text.

At the heart of the argument is the *kĕtîb-qĕrē'* that is associated with the word *šilšôm* (see [*Kĕtîb-Qĕrē'* in 19:19] and [*Kĕtîb and Qĕrē'* in 20:21]). The *kĕtîb* (written) tradition is *šilšôm*, allowing a translation of "the day before yesterday." The *qĕrē'* (spoken) tradition is *šālîšîm,* and could be read either "thirty" or "adjutant," as in some kind of officer. The LXX reads the term as a number, *trissos,* thus reinforcing an interpretation as a number not an office. The parallels between *Amenemopet* offer further confirmation in that a similar phrase occurs within its contents, plus other parallels of form and content.

The Hebrew text, thought to parallel the Egyptian, might be translated in another way, however. One alternate reading of the

MT might be, "Have I not written for you formerly. . . ,"[5] referring
to some previous setting of instruction. Taken in this way, the language is less similar to the phrase in the Egyptian instructions and
thus provides even less of a basis on which to argue that the
Hebrew sage was relying directly upon the thirty chapter divisions
of the Egyptian instruction.

   The structure and contents of the Hebrew collection further
weaken the argument of direct dependence upon the Egyptian
instructions. It is conventional to divide the Hebrew text into
thirty instructions on the strength of the *qĕrē*ʾ reading of 22:20.
However, the entire collection does not seem to be a unity, as
would be implied in such a heading. The verses contained in
22:17–23:11 appear to be common;[6] the materials in 23:12–24:22
and 24:23-34 show much more variation. In 22:17–23:11 there is
an introduction (vv. 17-21) followed by ten negative admonitions,
nine of which use the negative particle, *ʾal.* The opening (vv. 22-23)
and closing instructions (23:10-11) both address the oppression of
the weak and appeal to the one who will take up their cause
(Yahweh and a redeemer). These two instructions could be construed as forming a rhetorical device, an inclusio, to mark off a unit
of instruction that is to be read as one.[7] The second half of the collection, 23:12–24:22, contains many instructions that are
thematically repetitive (e.g., envying the wicked, 23:17-18; 24:1-2;
24:19-20; drunkenness, 23:20-21; 23:29-35) and that insert the
rhetorical appeal of the parent or instructor as introduction (23:12-
16; 23:19; 23:22-26; 24:3-4; and 24:13-14).[8] While the Egyptian
Instructions of Amenemopet may indeed stand in the background
of these sayings to some extent, a direct dependence upon them
cannot be demonstrated.

Between Rich and Poor, 22:17–23:11

The first unit of instructions may be subdivided into two smaller
sections: an introductory appeal, 22:17-21, and the instructions
proper, 22:22–23:11. The instructions in 22:22–23:11 consist
largely of negative admonitions of the sort we have already encountered in Proverbs 3:21-35. In this collection such negative
admonitions are joined together to create a rhetorical effect that
identifies and positions readers as people who are mediators
between the socially powerful and socially weak.

COMMENTARY

An Introductory Appeal, 22:17-21

The opening five verses form an introductory appeal that is similar to the parental appeals found in Proverbs 1–9. The thrust of the appeal from the parent is to listen so that, when the time comes, one will be able to produce accurate speech. Verse 17 opens with the imperative to listen; v. 21 concludes with a purpose clause that sets out the purpose or aim of the listening. As mentioned above, v. 17 contains language that scholars believe to have been the original heading for the collection in 22:17–24:22.

Verses 18-20 have various rhetorical effects. Verse 18 is the motive clause for the admonition to listen. The image of retaining the instruction within one's stomach conveys the idea of preparedness. We have encountered such imagery in the admonition to "write upon the heart" (4:21) and "bind around the neck" (6:21 and 7:3). The image of retaining in the stomach, though similar, is different.[9] Verse 20 is a rhetorical question referring to previous instructions, though it could also refer to the significance of the instructions that follow. The NRSV translation, while interesting, seems to assume direct literary dependence upon Amenemopet. Verse 19 is a purpose clause and the central sentence of the introduction.[10] We treat it last because it asserts that trust in Yahweh is the ultimate point of listening to instruction. Readers may find the relationship between vv. 17 and 19 provocative. Verses 17 and 18 seem to point to a purpose for instruction that is not necessarily tied to piety. Verse 19 requires readers to recontextualize somewhat the admonition in v. 17. The outcome of "hearing" and "applying the mind" is broader than one's own well-being. Now the proper response of speech is subsumed under the heading of Yahwhistic piety.

The concluding verse, a purpose clause summing up the entire introductory appeal, presses upon the audience the importance of truth and accuracy. Such is the outcome of careful listening and remembering. The final phrase, "to those who sent you," is intriguing because of the assumptions it makes regarding its audience. The audience seems to be some kind of mediator or emissary, thrust into a professional role analogous to middle management. Readers may find it helpful therefore to imagine themselves between the demands of conflicting perspectives: the demands of an employer and the demands of one's own employees. It further foreshadows similar assumptions in the remaining instructions about

Structure at a Glance: Proverbs 22:22–23:11

AΩ The unit comprising 22:22–23:11 consists of ten sections, each with its own motive clause. Nine of the sections consist of negative admonitions, opening with the negative particle, *'al*. One section (v. 29) consists of a rhetorical question. Only v. 28 lacks a motive clause. The themes of the prohibitions situate the audience at court. The repetition of the admonition concerning the removing of the "ancient landmark" (vv. 28 and 23:10-11) may function both structurally as an inclusio and metaphorically to call the young courtiers to attend to tradition. Readers may find the following outline helpful in organizing their reading.

I. 22:22-23 "Do not rob the poor"
II. Vv. 24-25 "Do not associate with hotheads"
III. Vv. 26-27 "Do not give pledges for financial security"
IV. V. 28 "Do not remove the ancient landmark"
V. V. 29 "Only the skilled will serve kings"
VI. 23:1-3 "Do not desire the king's delicacies"
VII. Vv. 4-5 " Do not wear yourself out to get rich"
VIII. Vv. 6-8 "Do not eat the bread of the stingy"
IX V. 9 "Do not waste words on fools"
X. Vv. 10-11 "Do not remove the ancient landmark"

readers who, though highly educated and in a responsible professional position, nevertheless serve others who are more powerful.

Ten Admonitions, 22:22–23:11

The second subsection in this unit of instructions consists of ten
admonitions, most of them stated in the negative. [Structure at a
Glance: Proverbs 22:22–23:11] The title "Between Rich and Poor" at the
head of this section not only reflects some of the dominant topics
of instructions within, but the assumption that the audience is in a
middle management position. The extremes of the instruction
swing between the oppression of the weak/poor (vv. 22:22-23 and
23:10-11) and the avoidance of the lifestyle of the rich (23:1-8).
The people to whom these instructions are addressed have some
power (enough to oppress the weaker, to desire the wealth of their
betters) but must watch themselves in the presence of superiors. We
see this clearly in the fifth instruction, 22:29, where one who is
skillful serves kings not commoners. That this individual holds
some middle management position seems clear.

Three times throughout this unit there is reference to oppression
of ones with more vulnerable social statuses. These include the first
instruction (22:22-23), the fourth instruction (22:28), and the
tenth instruction (23:10-11). The first deals with the poor; the
fourth and the tenth deal with moving boundaries. The final
instruction (vv. 10-11) includes an additional concern for

encroachment upon the land of "orphans." In these latter two, the fourth and the tenth instructions, the young manager is admonished not to subvert the order of justice by secretly seizing land from those who cannot defend themselves in a court of law. This echoes the admonition in 22:22-23, which also assumes that the person of weaker status cannot obtain justice in the courts. In both cases, another, more powerful individual makes the legal appeal. Such an ethos is also reflected in the Covenant Code (Exod 23:1-2, 6).

Instructions six (23:1-3), seven (23:4-5), and eight (23:6-8) reverse the concern from deception to being deceived oneself. All three instructions, which form the central panel of the collection, offer warnings about the deceptions of the wealthy, wealth itself, or people who are themselves deceptive. The imagery of a meal functions in the two outer instructions as a basis for warning about the need to exercise control over the appetite. Readers have already seen how meals set by Woman Wisdom and by Woman Folly function as metaphors for engaging in certain kinds of proper or illicit behaviors (see Prov 9:1-6; 9:13-18). These three instructions warn of the deceptiveness of wealth and power. The ruler's delicacies are "deceptive food"; wealth takes wings and flies away as soon as one

Classical Tragedy and Comedy

The situations of an individual's life imagined by the ancient sages evoke speculation about the sages' critical assumptions regarding the dramatic possibilities for some of their characters. For instance, how might the court servant who was caught between the demands of his service to both superiors and inferiors be dramatized? Lacking any knowledge of the sage's dramatic assumptions, readers are left to rely upon more familiar western critical assumptions.

Dramatic tragedy traces a series of events in the life of an important character that culminate in some kind of catastrophe. Aristotle's *Poetics* explained the purpose of such tragedy was to evoke pity and fear and thus produce in the audience a catharsis of these emotions. Tragic characters, however, tend to change with the times, thus reflecting the values of the context in which dramatic tragedies are performed. In Elizabethan England, for instance, Shakespeare's *King Lear* reflects upon both the good king and fundamental understandings of love and loyalty. In Arthur Miller's *Death of a Salesman*, the tragic figure, Willy Loman, while of middle-class background, reflects the ultimate twentieth-century fall due to a false consciousness of reality.

Comedy, by contrast, is much lighter in tone than tragedy, tends to be amusing, and usually ends happily. Generally wit and humor dominate the portrayal of humanity and its incongruities. While tragedy might be thought of as exploring humanity in its ideal state, comedy explores humanity the way it is: made ridiculous by its faults and limitations. The human body is the constant threat to a higher and nobler human behavior. In *Sir Gawain and the Green Knight*, for instance, it is the control of one's sexual behavior that tests the true knight's loyalty. At the same time the minutest failure subverts the seriousness of social control over natural bodily functions. Such subversion exposes the high calling of courtly codes of conduct as ironic.

Taken comedically, the admonitions in Prov 22:17–23:11 to the middle managing court servant may actually subvert the importance of the position altogether (e.g., who could really maintain such poise and balance?). Taken tragically, the admonitions to maintain balance are the means to true heroism.

For further reading, see Leo Aylen, *Greek Tragedy and the Modern World* (London: Methuen, 1964); Oscar G. Brakett, *Perspectives on Contemporary Theatre* (Baton Rouge: Louisiana State University Press, 1985), 80-103; and Hugh Holman, Jr., *A Handbook to Literature*, 3rd ed. (Indianapolis and New York: The Odyssey Press, 1972).

possesses it; and currying favor with something or someone who is ultimately deceptive has the reverse effect.

People who are neither rich nor poor, who have power and authority enough to deceive and yet are themselves ambitious enough to be deceived, are also vulnerable to other kinds of threats. Prohibition two (22:24-25) concerns making friends with a person who cannot control his temper—a hothead. The danger is taking on such behavior and falling into the traps that come from the loss of control of one's temper. In instruction three, friendships that come at the cost of providing collateral on debts are too costly, especially if one does not have the collateral (22:26-27). The cost is more than the gain. Being overly ambitious leads to other bad decisions. Instruction nine (23:9) depicts the desperation that follows when one wastes words by addressing a fool. Since fools only despise words of wisdom, nothing is more ineffective and therefore costly.

CONNECTIONS

Formula for a Tragedy

The classical understanding of tragedy features heroic characteristics or activities that ultimately contribute to a hero's downfall. [Classical Tragedy and Comedy] The advice to the implied middle manager in this section takes for granted a recipe for his downfall and thus evokes readers' recollections of similar tragedies where highly skilled and noble people fail to succeed through some failure to choose proper behavior. Through the abuse of his own power and authority, or through his ambition to rise to greater power, the middle manager runs the risk of toppling his own position. An art film titled *Big Night* portrays the conflict between ambition and excellence, reflecting similar tragic consequences.

It is a story of two immigrant brothers, Primo and Secundo, and their attempt to start a restaurant in America that serves authentic Italian food. Primo is the ambitious brother who sees America as an opportunity to become rich and famous. Authentic Italian food is simply a means to that end. If the customer wants pasta with every meal—whether it is authentic or not—the paying customer is always right. Secundo is the purist who sees the restaurant as a means of serving only the finest and most authentic Italian food. He is far more interested in maintaining some integrity with the cultural background. Therein lies the conflict of the story: finding the middle way. What is the middle way between such extreme views without sacrificing parts of each of those views?

Most people live their lives in the tension between competing values. By competing values I mean equally valid yet opposing perspectives and worldviews. Unfortunately, they do not spend much time reflecting upon it. Individuals are challenged to be effective in the positions they are in, and yet they are considered unambitious if advancement is not a goal. On the other hand, constantly looking for the next higher position or a better paying job may so consume individuals that they are not effective in their present positions. Being satisfied, accepting oneself, can be good if it functions as a strategy for making one better. However, pressing forward out of a sense of dissatisfaction can also be regarded as a symptom of a kind of pathology. One could be equally construed as not having good self-esteem or as one who can never be happy. The middle position is always fraught with such difficulties.

To find the middle position, must one sacrifice one's commitment to excellence? No, but one must think about excellence beyond the boundaries of one's own self. One's striving for excellence must remain in contact with the real world of one's existence. Does embracing the real world of one's existence require the surrendering of one's ambitions? Again, no, but one's ambitions must be tempered by the circumstances of one's relationships, one's abilities, and the opportunities that present themselves.

NOTES

[1] Roland E. Murphy, *Proverbs* (WBC 22; Nashville: Word, 1998), 169.

[2] See Murphy, *Proverbs,* 169; Richard J. Clifford, *Proverbs* (OTL; Louisville: Westminster John Knox Press, 1999), 204.

[3] Leo Perdue, *Proverbs* (IBC; Louisville: Westminster John Knox Press, 2000), 200; see also James Pritchard, *Ancient Near Eastern Texts,* 3rd ed. (Princeton NJ: Princeton University Press, 1969), 421-25.

[4] Pritchard, 424.

[5] R. N. Whybray, *The Composition of the Book of Proverbs* (JSOTSup 168; Sheffield: JSOT, 1994), 133, relying upon the *kĕtîb* tradition of the text.

[6] Perdue, *Proverbs,* 200, states: "The first instruction is the lengthiest in this collection as is the part most dependent on Amen-em-Opet."

[7] R. N. Whybray, *Composition,* 134, quoting A. Niccacci, "Proverbi 22:17–23:11," *Studii Biblici Franciscani Liber Annuus* (Jerusalem) 29 (1979): 42-72.

[8] Whybray,132-147.

[9] William McKane, *Proverbs: A New Approach* (OTL; London: SCM Press, 1970), 374, sees such imagery as evidence of strong awareness of Amenemopet. He cites the instructions within that collection: "Better is a man whose talk (remains) in his belly than he who speaks out injuriously."

[10] Richard J. Clifford, *Proverbs*, 206, notes that the word "Yahweh" is the "eighteenth of thirty-six words."

BETWEEN ENVY AND THE FEAR OF THE LORD

Proverbs 23:12–24:22

The second unit of instructions under the heading "Words of the Wise" begins with 23:12. The most pronounced similarity between the Proverbs and *Amenemopet* ends with 23:11.[1] The admonitions contained within presuppose an educational setting rather than a court setting and may remind readers of the parental instructions of Proverbs 1–9. Common topics as well as an admonitory style reinforce the apparent similarities. For instance, both collections warn about prostitutes (vv. 26-27), reinforce obedience of parents (vv. 12-28), and exhort against envying wrongdoers (vv. 17-18). The admonition to learn wisdom, v. 12, further establishes a connection with Proverbs 1–9 by reiterating one of the dominating themes of that collection as well as the entire book of Proverbs. The two references to Yahweh in 23:17 and 24:21 provide the theological foundation for the rest of the sayings and may function as a theological inclusio. [Structure at a Glance: Proverbs 23:12–24:22]

Structure at a Glance: Proverbs 23:12–24:22

AΩ The section may be further subdivided into four sections based upon introductory appeals similar to those in chs. 1–9. Within these four major sections there is a collection of miscellaneous instructions. Readers will observe clearly defined topics as in chs. 1–9, as well as the rhetorical form reminiscent of parental instruction. Readers may find the following organization of the chapter helpful in reading:

Vv. 23:12-18 Wisdom, Instruction, and the Fear of the Lord
Vv. 19-21 On Drunkenness and Gluttony
Vv. 23:22-24:12 A Miscellany of Instructions
Vv. 24:13-22 Attitudes Toward the Righteous and the Wicked

Readers should not think that these instructions are randomly arranged. There seems rather to be a thematic inclusio created by the first and final instructions, 23:17-18 and 24:19-22. Both admonish the child to fear Yahweh (23:17b and 24:21), the only places in this subcollection that Yahweh's name is mentioned. Both admonish against envy of the wicked (23:17a and 24:19). Both use similar language to appeal to the future hope of those who place piety before material desires (23:18 and 24:20, 22).

COMMENTARY

Wisdom, Instruction, and the Fear of the Lord, 23:12-18

The imperatives and negative admonitions in these verses remind readers of the opening admonitions in Proverbs 1–9 (e.g., 3:1-2; 4:1-4; 5:1-2). In vv. 13-14 there is a sudden shift in the addressee. Instead of addressing the child, these verses address the parent concerning the matter of corporal punishment as a means of discipline. Commentators who divide the whole of these chapters into "thirty sayings" on the basis of similarity with *Amenemopet* [2] simply isolate vv. 13-14 from the others as a separate instruction. Other approaches include citing the precedent for such abrupt changes in address in non-biblical wisdom literatures. [3] Another possibility is that the poet is quoting another saying in vv. 13-14 as legitimization for his own admonition to his son.

Readers have already encountered such sayings on punishment in the Solomonic collection, chapters 10:1–22:16 (e.g., Prov 19:18; 22:6) and will encounter them again in 29:17. Readers have also encountered in 4:1-9 a very deliberate quote of a parent that functions to legitimize the speaker's own admonitions to his son. That vv. 13 and 14 are a quote seems a strong possibility. [On Quotations] In this case, the verses in question are actually in agreement with the overall tenor of the context. Thus, one may suppose that the poet quoted a saying in order to reinforce his instruction. In any event, vv. 15-16 seem to counter a reading of the preceding verses that is too harsh. These verses portray great parental pride in children (or students) who excel in wisdom.

On Quotations

AΩ Apparent textual incongruencies where there are changes in grammatical person or even lapses in logic may be accounted for by hypothesizing the ancient convention of quoting. In modern practice quotes are introduced with language that indicates to the reader that a quote follows. The quote in 4:1-9 is much more clearly marked with introductory language than in 23:13-14. But in Hebrew convention it is possible for writers to offer a quote without such clear markings. Although we see such language evident in passages such as Prov 4:1-9, it need not be there at all in order to have a quotation.

Michael V. Fox offers this advice for identifying a quotation within Hebrew literature. He says most importantly readers must distinguish between potential quotes the speaker agrees with and those the speaker disagrees with. In the latter case, a disagreement could be alternatively construed as a contradiction unless it can be identified unambiguously as a quotation of another source.

For further reading, see James Barr, "Paul and the LXX: A Note on Some Recent Work," *JTS* 45 (October 1994): 593-601; Robert Gordis, "Virtual Quotations in Job, Sumer and Qumran," *VT* 31 (October 1981): 410-27; idem, "Quotations as a Literary Usage in Biblical, Oriental and Rabbinic Literature," *HUCA* 22 (1949): 157-219; Steve Miyise, "Does the NT Quote the OT Out of Context?" Anvil 11/2 (1994): 133-43; and Pancratius C. Beentjes, "Invented Quotations in the Bible: A Neglected Stylistic Pattern," *Bib* 63/4 (1982): 506-23.

Michael V. Fox, *Qohelet and His Contradictions* (JSOTSup 41; Sheffield: The Almond Press, 1989), 25-28.

We encounter the instruction proper in vv. 17-18. Here the assurance of a future hope is offered in place of harboring envy for sinners. An alternate translation suggests that individuals *are* to envy those who fear Yahweh.[4] The appeal against envy of the wicked is a common theme. We encounter it again in 24:1 and 19 for instance, and have already encountered it in 3:31. The idea of desiring what the pious have is reinforced in v. 18 with the argument that it is those people who have a future and a hope that will not be cut off.

On Drunkenness and Gluttony, 23:19-21

The second instruction in this section opens in v. 19 with a second parental appeal. The use of the term "way" invokes previous appeals to pathway imagery in other collections (e.g., 3:17; 4:11, 26; 5:21; 14:12; 16:2, 25). The implication is toward moral instruction; parents are concerned about proper behavior.

Drunkenness in the Bible

Wine was one of the important commodities of ancient Palestine because the climate was especially suited for growing vineyards. In the biblical story the grapevine, with its accompanying wine production, symbolizes both the fertility of the land and God's blessing of the people (e.g., Deut 6:10-11; Hos 2:12; Jer 5:17).

With wine being such a major commodity, however, the danger of over-consumption was real, and wine was intoxicating (Hos 4:11). Generally speaking, Israel's story is not sympathetic with drunkenness. Such a state became a basis for public shame (Gen 9:21) and an image for failed leadership (Isa 28:7-9). Wine even functioned as a figure for the disaster that Yahweh would bring upon the nation (Isa 49:26; Jer 25:27-29). The early Christian writers recalled Jesus' opponents accusing him of drunkenness (Matt 11:19), thus indicating the pejorative implications of such behavior. Paul himself warned of the threat of drunkenness in the early church (Rom 13:13; 1 Cor 5:11).

For further reading, see Nigel Graham, "Vinedressers and Plowmen: 2 Kings 25:12 and Jeremiah 52:16," *BA* 47 (March 1984): 55-58; Alan W. Jenks, "Eating and Drinking in the Old Testament," *ABD* 2: 250-54; Lucio Milano, ed., *Drinking in Ancient Societies*, HANE 6 (Padua: Sargon, 1994); and Jo Ann H. Seely, "The Fruit of the Vine: Wine at Masada and in the New Testament," Brigham Young University Studies 36/3 (1996–1997): 207-27.

Andrea Pisano. 1295–1348/9. *The Drunkenness of Noah.* Marble relief. c. 1344. Museo dell'Opera del Duomo. Florence, Italy.

The instruction itself addresses the problems of drunkenness and gluttony. It is not only the sages who have made the connection between these two excessive behaviors, but the Deuteronomist as well. In Deuteronomy 21:20 drinking wine and gluttony are connected with stubbornness and rebellion. One wonders whether drinking wine and gluttony cause the youth's stubbornness and rebellion, or whether the rebellion causes the drinking and gluttony. [Drunkenness in the Bible] The instruction here makes clear that one of the outcomes of too much eating and drinking of wine is poverty. The effects of overeating and consumption of alcohol make it impossible for one to work. Without work there is poverty.

A Miscellany of Instructions, 23:22–24:22

We continue the approach of isolating and organizing the instructions according to the parental appeals. Verse 23:22 opens another section with a general admonition to make parents happy, here by obtaining wisdom. Accompanying this parental appeal are several instructions: vv. 27-28, against the foreign woman, or prostitute; vv. 29-35, on addiction to strong drink; 24:1, on envying the wicked; 24:3-9, on the benefits of wisdom; vv. 10-12, on rescuing those condemned to death. The unit might appear to conclude in 23:8 with an instruction on the threat posed by the prostitute. By the criteria of the preceding instructions, however, readers will recognize yet another parental appeal in v. 26, suggesting that vv. 26-28 is an instruction separate from the accompanying units. The problem of reading vv. 26-28 as separate from vv. 22-25 is that these latter verses seem only to have parental address and lack the instruction itself. For that reason readers should read vv. 26-28 as the instruction belonging to the introductory admonition in vv. 22-25. Verses 22-25 therefore provide an opening appeal for several instructions.

Proverbs 23:22-25. Murphy interprets these opening verses as a unity arguing that the appeals to parents in vv. 22 and 25 form an inclusio.[5] Clifford, on the other hand, argues that there are two separate introductory units: one in vv. 22-23 and the other in vv. 24-25. He observes a parallelism between 22 and 24 consisting of positive and negative imperatives: "listen to // do not despise, acquire // do not barter away."[6] The theme of v. 23—"buy truth"—is not in the LXX and seems to move beyond the parent teacher theme. For this reason some scholars believe v. 23 to be an intrusion into this unit.

Proverbs 23:26-28 offers warning against the "prostitute." While the cultic prostitute may indeed be envisioned here (see comments on 7:10-20), there is good reason to understand the larger category of "strange" or "foreign woman" instead. The LXX translation suggests that the Hebrew text originally said *zārâ,* "foreign woman," rather than *zônâ,* "prostitute." Usually LXX translates *zônâ* as *gunē pornē,* as in 5:10 and 7:5. But, in 23:27, LXX renders the word as *allotrias oikos,* "another house," which could easily function as a paraphrase of the Hebrew *zārâ,* "foreign," especially given its association with "foreign house" in 5:10. By adopting an emendation here one would not be eliminating the admonition against enjoining a prostitute.[7] Rather, taking the language metaphorically allows one to retain the text as its stands, with *zônâ,* and to envision the foreign woman as well as the prostitute. Both are condemned.[8] The imagery applies to both: the "deep pit" is used for the capture of unsuspecting animals. The "narrow well," while employing an image of fertility and sustenance, as in 5:15-23, adds a negative value. This is one well that provides only limited sustenance. The social importance of a woman's ability to bear offspring is challenged. Rather than giving, this woman takes like a robber and actually increases the number of unfaithful people.

Proverbs 23:29-35 offers a second instruction on the threat of addiction to wine. There is no parental appeal opening this poem, but rather a series of riddle-like leading questions. Verse 30 answers the questions raised in v. 29. The instruction proper comes in vv. 31-35. The list of questions in v. 29 attempts to capture the life of one who is frequently drunk: woe, sorrow, strife, complaining, unexplainable wounds, and redness of eyes. Since modern readers do not understand every nuance of the language used in the description, it would be unwise to equate these descriptions with behaviors of modern-day alcoholics. Nevertheless, readers' imaginations are provoked by the extensiveness of the portrayal.

The poet has elevated the topic of alcoholic addiction to a level of metaphoric consideration by using similes of the serpent's bite and adder's sting (v. 32). In biblical lore, the serpent is a creature who is most alluring yet who wreaks havoc for humankind. However, one should not take the poetic metaphors so woodenly. For example, the admonition in v. 31 not to look at wine does not mean that it is the *look* of wine that addicts. Rather, the appearance of the wine only entices and allures. It is the human response to its metaphorical sting—the loss of sensibility and memory, the loss of balance and physical control—that so seriously concerns the sage.

Proverbs 24:1 makes a rather significant change of direction from the chronic drunk to the behavior of the wicked. Again, there is no parental admonition introducing this warning, only an opening negative admonition. The verse recalls 23:17 and anticipates a related admonition in 23:19 (cf. Pss 37:1 and 73:3). Like a refrain, the admonition not to envy the wicked keeps coming back interspersed with other instructions.

While the wicked are described as devising violence and talking of mischief, the juxtaposition of this instruction with the preceding one on the chronic drunk is provocative. With the placement of this admonition so close to the warning about strong drink, readers wonder whether sages are suggesting that chronic drunkenness is a kind of wickedness. In both cases their "minds" (*lēb*, v. 33 and v. 2) produce perversities or trouble. The implied difference is that the wicked is in full control of his sense; the chronic drunk produces similar outcomes while being out of control. Ultimately, the ends of both are related.

Proverbs 24:3-9. It is not difficult to read these verses as five independent sayings.[9] However, readers may also find that the sayings are loosely connected with the other. None of these verses is an instruction—characterized by imperatives, negatives, admonitions, or motive clauses. Rather, each resembles the sentence sayings readers have encountered in 10:1–22:16. Readers recall the metaphoric use of wisdom as a house-builder from 9:1 and 14:1 and thus readily understand v. 3 as a symbolic statement of wisdom's benefits. Verse 3 therefore introduces a series of reflections upon the nature of wisdom's benefits. Verses 5 and 6 illustrate the power of wisdom by invoking the contrast between military strength and military strategy. Verse 7 is both a reflection on wisdom's benefits and an anticipation of the contrast between wisdom and folly, which follows in vv. 8-9.

Verses 8-9 echo the previous negative admonition in vv. 1-2 against the devices of the wicked. In v. 2 the concern is the devising of wickedness; in v. 9 it is devising folly, the opposite of wisdom. Verse 9 parallels v. 8 by equating the planning of wickedness and the devising of folly. Folly is not depicted here as a mere lapse in wisdom. Rather, like wickedness, folly is deliberately planned. A fool is therefore no different in one sense from one who deliberately commits wicked acts or from a scoffer.

In v. 9 readers encounter the phrase "the devising of folly," which translates the term *zimmat* as "devising." In this context "devising" has negative value. The term is cognate with the term *mĕzimmâ*, translated in 1:4 as prudence and there understood as a desirable trait. In fact, clustered in that introductory context "prudence" is offered as one of the ultimate outcomes of the collection of instruction (cf. 3:21; 5:2 and 8:12).

However, *mĕzimmâ* is not a term that always carries a positive value. In other contexts it has a negative significance (e.g., Pss 10:2; 10:4; 21:11). Psalm 139:20 describes a person who opposes God as one who speaks of God "maliciously," *limzimmâ*. Proverbs 12:2 observes that a person of *mĕzimmôt* is to be condemned. Thus when readers encounter the cognate *zimmâ* in Proverbs 21:27 and 24:8, with negative connotations, it should not be too much of a surprise. Here, obviously, the term is not concerned with prudence as much as it is with scheming. It designates the endeavor of secretly planning to subvert some decent activity or to commit some questionable act.[10]

Proverbs 24:10-12, the concluding three verses in this collection of instruction, may also be read as a unit. To do so, readers must equate the "day of adversity" of v. 10 with the challenge of "rescuing those taken away to death" of v. 11. NRSV translators have further taken v. 11 as a conditional sentence, an unlikely translation given the fact that v. 11 opens with an imperative, "save." Clearly, v. 12 pictures some kind of accountability for not responding appropriately to those people who are so distressed, as v. 11 describes. One is to intervene and "save" those being taken away. Yahweh is the one who "weighs the heart" (see also 16:2) and therefore sees whether one's failure to deliver is sincere or not. The problem is, of what does v. 11 speak?

There is no question that people are being led to death, perhaps execution. One can imagine a scenario where those accused unjustly, thus who are innocent, are executed. One may bring to this text the present-day concern over the effectiveness of capital punishment, for instance. If the execution of criminals is shown not to be an effective means of criminal deterrence, of protecting society, or of administering justice for crimes, might this admonition become a basis for engaging our involvement in rescuing those who are bound for execution?

Attitudes toward the Righteous and the Wicked, 24:13-22

In 24:13 we arrive at the fifth and final parental admonition in this section. It distinguishes the final cluster of instructions from the preceding ones. Readers encounter another parental appeal in v. 21, but this is likely a resumption of the original address in v. 13 rather than the beginning of a new one.

An opening admonition on the benefits of wisdom is followed by three instructions: vv. 15-16 concern criminal activity; vv. 17-18 address proper attitudes toward the punishment of the wicked; vv. 19-20 present the familiar warning against envying the wicked. The closing instruction, which appeals to Yahweh, asserts the value of a kind of benign resignation toward both Yahweh and the king. One should know one's place both in the universe and in the kingdom.

Verses 13-14 portray the parent comparing the consumption of honey with the reception of wisdom. Like honey wisdom has its own kind of sweetness. With wisdom one gets a future and the assurance that future hope will not be cut off. This general statement offers a fitting introduction to the specific concerns of wisdom that follow in the remaining instructions.

Verses 15-16 admonish against criminal activity. Readers have seen the image of one who "lies in wait" in 1:8-19 and recall the teaching on the fate of such ones. If we adopt NRSV's translation, we may take this as an instruction directed to those who are already sympathetic with such instruction. However, MT addresses this to the wicked: "Do not lie in wait, wicked one, against the abode of the righteous." Most regard the "wicked one" as a gloss, since it would be the only occurrence in the book where the wicked was addressed by the teacher.[11]

The instruction is important because it provides insight on the nature of the "future hope" that the preceding instruction mentions (v. 14). It does not mean that the righteous will not fall, but that they will recover. Or to put it another way, the future hope for the righteous does not preclude suffering; it simply assures success and fulfillment in the long run. By comparison, the wicked is swept away.

Verses 17-18 pair conveniently with vv. 15-16. The word that NRSV translates as "overthrown" in v. 16 is used again in an infinitival form in v. 17, "when your enemies fall." This parallel implies some equation between "your enemies" and "the wicked." The instruction admonishes the righteous *not* to rejoice over the destruction of the wicked. The threat in v. 18 is that the Lord will see this rejoicing in another's defeat, consider it evil, and relent from his anger against the wicked. While the idea is surely that punishment belongs to the Lord alone, this must raise further questions about that future hope for the righteous. Could it really be that the justice due the wicked is somehow made contingent upon the proper attitude of the righteous toward the wicked? We will encounter the converse of the argument again in the next section of sayings, 25:21-22.

Verses 19-20 reiterate one of the broad thematic concerns of the entire section by returning to the question of the future of the wicked. Verse 19 opens with the admonition that one should neither become angered at the way of the evildoer, nor envy him (cf. 24:1 and 23:17).

Verses 21-22 conclude the unit by reminding youths that Yahweh, not unlike the king, is above all and is therefore guarantor of the order of justice. We have seen little expression of any appeal to Yahweh or God in these verses. His name occurs in 24:21 and 23:17. An implicit appeal to God is present in 24:12 in the words "he who keeps watch over your soul."

CONNECTIONS

Future Hope

The framework of this collection of instructions admonishes not to envy the wicked, because they have no future. But there is a difference between one's future destiny and one's future fate. We use such terms differently in modern parlance. Fate implies a future over which one has no control or choice. Some outside force acts and human society and individual members of society follow its inevitable course. Destiny, by contrast, connotes a concern with the future, but it does not so convey the idea of inevitability. One's destiny comes as a result of one's choices. Such a view acknowledges that outside forces alone do not determine the future.

Scientists are always speculating on the future, it seems. They are continually trying to quantify the impact of some new scientific discovery or technological application. The human genome project, for instance—the task of mapping all of the approximately 100,000 genes in human DNA and sequencing the approximately three billion chemical bases that make up human DNA—was begun in 1990.[12] As the twentieth century—indeed the millennium—came to a close, researchers had completed the project. The impact of the project is massive in theory: humans will have the information about what genes contribute to the development of, if they do not completely determine, human characteristics and behaviors.

The ethical implications alone are enormous. Such knowledge will increasingly lead to the technology to manipulate the human gene, which in limited ways it is already doing. What behaviors should be manipulated? What human characteristics should be factored in or out? Who are the ones who decide such matters? Is the decision simply one of properly handling the technology, or one of determining whether it should be handled at all? What if such notions as wickedness, which presuppose human decision-making and choice, are shown to have genetic determinants? Where once humanity thought itself liberated by knowledge from the tyranny of ignorance, is this new knowledge simply raising the level of human fate to a higher level? Perhaps, but the element of human choice is still operative.

Another area of fascinating recent research concerns the age of the cosmos and its inevitable demise. Only ten to twenty billion years old right now, our cosmos is apparently still in the first phase of a four-stage process of dying. It will die when the energy dwindles and galaxies shrink.[13] One could indeed speak of our universe as having a fate rather than a destiny. And yet, within a frame of reference that has a finite existence with inevitable and inexorable results, humankind still exercise choices about what knowledge will be authoritative, what the implications of that knowledge will be, how to improve life, and whether to replicate or even to clone life. Such choices within the larger framework are not necessarily fated to happen. Rather, as a species that creates meaning, we cherish life's possible meanings. In other words, even in the most modern scientific terms, humans choose their destinies in full view of their inevitable fates.

The sages of Israel were concerned about human destiny. The instructions they offered concern those areas where human society has a choice about its future. The admonition not to envy the wicked, based upon the observations of the past, is also a statement about an individual's destiny. There is a choice, and it has an effect upon one's future.

NOTES

[1] This reflects R. N. Whybray, *The Composition of the Book of Proverbs* (JSOTSup 168; Sheffield: JSOT Press, 1994), 141. Roland E. Murphy, *Proverbs* (WBC 22; Nashville: Word, 1998), 174, notes that the break is justified on the basis of the similarity between *Amenemopet* and vv. 1-11. Alternatively, Richard J. Clifford, *Proverbs* (OTL; Louisville: Westminster John Knox Press, 1999), 199, has expanded the "Words of the Wise" to three major sections: introduction, 22:22–23:11; concerns of youth, 23:12-35; and the destinies of the good and the wicked, 24:1-22.

[2] Thus, William McKane, *Proverbs* (OTL; London: SCM Press, 1970), 385-86; also Duane A. Garrett, *Proverbs, Ecclesiastes, Song of Songs* (NAC 14; Nashville: Broadman Press, 1993), 196-200.

[3] Whybray, *Composition,* 142, cites parallels with "Words of Ahiqar ll. 81-82," where similar abrupt shifts in topic occur. Clifford, *Proverbs,* 212, seems to imply the verses function ironically.

[4] McKane, *Proverbs,* 387.

[5] Murphy, *Proverbs,* 176.

[6] Clifford, *Proverbs,* 213.

[7] Ibid., 389.

[8] Murphy, *Proverbs,* 177.

[9] McKane, *Proverbs,* 396; Garrett, *Proverbs, Ecclesiastes, Song of Songs,* 198.

[10] See S. Steingrimsson, "ZMM," *TDOT* 4:87-90.

[11] Murphy, *Proverbs,* 181; Clifford, *Proverbs,* 206; McKane, *Proverbs,* 403.

[12] See one of many websites, titled "About the Human Genome Project," <http://www.ornl.gov/TechResources/Human_Genome/about.html>.

[13] I rely here on Ron Cowen, "From Here to Eternity," *Science News* 151 (5 April 1997): 208-209.

MORE WISE WORDS: THE COURT AND WORK

Proverbs 24:23-34

The heading over these verses in 23a clearly indicates the presumption of the collection titled "Words of the Wise." On this basis scholars believe them to be another appendix added after the materials in 23:12–24:22 and 22:17–23:11. It is difficult to say that there is any particular focus in these passages similar to the rhetorical emphasis upon "the middle way" in 22:17–23:11 or to the connecting theme "the future hope" in 23:12–24:22. There are, however, two topics within these verses: honesty at court and work. Since readers assume this collection to have been added as an appendix, it is the readers' task to incorporate the significance of these topics into the relevant preceding frameworks.

Readers will notice that these materials seem to be rather miscellaneous. We have grown accustomed to seeing parental admonitions, imperatives, and motive clauses. There are none here. There is also no reference to Yahweh or to wisdom, further suggesting that these verses are appended and not intended to stand on their own as a distinct collection.

Still, the two topics seem to be interlocked by the placement of the sayings. Verses 24-26 generally deal with the court; vv. 28-29 return with a focus upon being a proper witness. Verse 27 interrupts the topic on the court with an assertion about proper preparations for work, and the topic resumes with the poem in vv. 30-34 on the farmer's field.[1] [Structure at a Glance: Proverbs 24:23-34]

> **Structure at a Glance: Proverbs 24:23-34**
>
> AΩ At least two commentators, Roland Murphy and Richard Clifford, mention the possibility that there is a parallel structure in these verses around the themes of court conduct, speaking and thinking, and one's attitude to work. Such arrangement would challenge the above claim that this addendum is merely a collection of miscellaneous verses.
>
> Murphy sets out the following suggestion based upon Meinhold's study:
>
> Conduct in court: (Judges: vv. 24-25)
> (Witnesses: v. 28)
> Speaking, thinking: (Honest speech: v. 26)
> (Harmful speech: v. 29)
> Attitude to work: (Positive: v. 27)
> (Negative: vv. 30-34)
>
> Richard J. Clifford, *Proverbs* (OTL; Louisville: Westminster John Knox Press, 1999), 216.
> Roland Murphy, *Proverbs* (WBC 22; Nashville: Word, 1998), 185, quoting A. Meinhold, Die Sprüche (ZB; Zürich: Theologischer Verlag, 1991), 410.

COMMENTARY

The Court, 24:23-26, 28-29

NRSV translates the Hebrew phrase "to regard the face," *hakkēr pānîm*, as "partiality in judging." We have encountered this expression throughout the sayings section (e.g., 18:5) and will see it again in 28:21. The point of view is clearly that of those who administer justice in the courts, and it is a warning against their subverting of justice. Verses 24 and 25 specify the nature of the subversion: in this case it is declaring the wicked to be innocent rather than *vice versa*. Exodus 23:1-2, a small segment of the Covenant Code, seems to recognize both sides of such subversion by asserting the possibility of privileging those people who would appear to be righteous. The concluding reflection in Proverbs 24:26 seems to recognize the one-sided interpretation of vv. 24-25. It makes the general statement that one is to strive for honesty at all times. [The Kiss in the Bible]

Verses 28-29 shift the point of view from the administrator of justice to those who contribute to the process by serving as witnesses. Verse 28b asserts that bearing witness "without cause," *ḥinnām*, is a matter of bearing false witness (see the treatment of 1:17 and 3:30). In other words, bearing witness "without cause" is apparently irrational because there is no justification for the testimony. It is a matter of perjury. On the other hand, v. 29 seems to go one step beyond the admonition against perjury to an admonition against revenge. Thus, revenge is not a basis for offering testimony against someone.

The Kiss in the Bible

The act of giving a kiss is given metaphorical significance in Proverbs 24:26 by paralleling it with the act of giving an honest answer. Both are therefore mutually reinforcing images of goodness and community.

The act of kissing, or of touching the lips to another person's lips, cheek, hand, etc., was a custom of greeting and acceptance, perhaps even friendship and respect in the ancient world. While the act could have erotic significance (e.g., Prov 7:13; Cant 1:2; 8:1), more often it was used in greeting or departing (Gen 27:26-27; 29:11; 50:1; 1 Sam 10:1; Ruth 1:9). It also occurs in contexts where the symbolism is negative, for example, as an act of idolatry (1 Kgs 19:18; Hos 13:2) or an act of betrayal (2 Sam 20:9).

Perhaps the most famous kiss in the Bible for Christians is that of Judas's betrayal of Jesus (Mark 14:44-45; Matt 26:47-56; Luke 22:47-53; compare John 18:2-11). Ironically, this kiss has multiple significances. Readers know that it is not a kiss that results in goodness and community. For the disciples, the kiss of Judas is the ordinary greeting of a disciple to his rabbi. For those seeking to take Jesus' life, it is the kiss of death.

For further reading, see Jeffery Cohen, "An Unrecognized Connotation of *nsq peh* with Special Reference to Three Biblical Occurrences (Gen 42:40; Prov 24:26; Job 31:27)," *VT* 32 (October 1982): 416-24; William Klaasen, "Kiss (NT)," *ABD* 4:89-92; and idem, "The Sacred Kiss in the New Testament: An Example of Social Boundaries," *NTS* 39 (January 1993): 122-35.

Work, 24:27, 30-34

Verse 27, which interrupts the sayings on the workings of the court, returns to the image of house-building (cf. 9:1; 14:1; 24:3-9). The thrust of the sayings concerns making proper preparations before one begins to build a house. The sayings obviously have some concrete reality in mind, but the metaphorical possibilities abound. With the emphasis upon work and preparation, the sayings foreshadow the poem that follows in vv. 30-34, which uses the sorry state of the lazy person as an object lesson.

We have seen this autobiographical style of instruction in 7:6-20. The poem opens with the first person point of view, describing the scene of an unkempt vineyard. The observer knows, presumably, that this is the field of one who is lazy (e.g., 6:9-11; 19:24; 22:13; 26:13). If he did not know it, he could deduce it from the state of the field's being overgrown. One of the differences between this occurrence of the instruction and that in 6:9-11 is the further assertion of the man's "stupidity." The observer makes the equation between laziness and stupidity. The vineyard in such a state will not produce; poverty is inevitable. Thus, in the concluding saying, vv. 33-34, the observer reflects on the connection between laziness and poverty. [Care of a Vineyard]

CONNECTIONS

Passing Judgment

Would you hire that person to come work in your vineyard? This appendix, whether intentionally or not, creates for readers an interesting dilemma: we sit in the seat of judgment upon the one whose field is overgrown. If the observer, our teacher, who bears witness against him, is correct, then the farmer is lazy and stupid. But, as judges, we have to ask ourselves whether that may be known from the state of the field alone. Surely, one would have to know the man also. Our pious imaginations begin to spin out the most obvious conclusion when we see the overgrown state of things, and especially the wall that has fallen down. Anyone who would not repair the wall must be both lazy and foolish, right? Can we be satisfied with the facile circumstantial evidence of the rundown field? What is more, can we sit in judgment without reflecting upon our own abilities to maintain the appearance of order?

One of John Cheever's delightful short stories, "The Enormous Radio," explores the theme of uncovering one's true identity, or self-realization. Through the mysterious mechanical difficulties of a brand-new radio, Jim and Irene Westcott hear the conversations of their neighbors through the radio. They soon discover that they have access to the most intimate conversations—the arguments,

The Wine Harvest. Tapestry. 16th C. Loire Region. Musée du Moyen Age (Cluny), Paris, France.

Care of a Vineyard

There are hundreds of references to the tending and cultivation of the vine, in Hebrew, *gepen*. The implication is that such agriculture was widespread in ancient Palestine; so much so that the vine became a symbol of Israel. The climate of ancient Palestine was well-suited for growing vineyards. But the care of a vineyard, including preparation of the ground, planting, pruning, and harvesting, was time-consuming and intensive work.

References in the Bible suggest a vineyard could grow either on hillsides (Ps 80:8-10; Jer 31:5; Amos 9:13) or in valleys (Num 13:22-24). Protection of the vineyard through the building of protective hedges or walls is also attested (Jer 49:9; Isa 5:1-6). Pruning took place when the grapes appeared on the branches (Lev 25:4; Isa 18:5). Harvest of the grapes for wine production required the building of a wine vat or press in which to crush the grapes to obtain the juice from the fruit (Isa 5:2). The wine producing process then followed.

For further reading, see Irene Jacob and Walter Jacob, "Flora," *ABD* 2:803-17; Jane M. Renfreuer, "Vegetables in the Ancient Near Eastern Diet," in *CANE* 1:199-202; J. F. Ross, "Vine, Vineyard," *IDB* 4:784-86; and idem, "Wine," *IDB* 4:849-52.

the financial difficulties, and marital problems—of all the people who live in the
apartment building with them. Irene, who
stays at home, cannot keep herself from listening in, and then grows suspicious that the
troubles her neighbors have might be hers,
too. The radio and its focus upon everyone
else's problems force Jim and Irene to confront their own problems. Self-realization,
then, is a matter of cutting through the veil
of denial that allows people to maintain some
semblance of order.

Wine Press
An ancient wine press from Capernaum in Israel.

As we look at the lazy person whose field is
grown over, we might take a lesson from Jim and Irene. Just as
readers have a special affinity with the couple, so do the people
gazing at the overgrown field. As we read the short story, we listen
to everyone else's problems through the eyes of Jim and Irene. We
also experience the revelation that apparently happy couples have
domestic problems of which we were not aware. And finally, we
readers are motivated to examine our lives and confront our own
hidden problems. What does our judgment of the overgrown field
reveal about those of us who pause to gaze upon it? It may well be
that it reveals more about us than it does the owner of the field.

NOTE

[1] Leo Perdue, *Proverbs* (IBC; Louisville: Westminster John Knox Press, 2000), 217,
suggests a structural arrangement of superscription, v. 23a; discourse on judgment
(24:23b-26, 28-29); and an autobiographical discourse on household labor (2:27, 30-
34).

DISCRIMINATING KINGS, COURTS, AND CHOICES

Proverbs 25:1-28

Proverbs of Solomon Copied by Hezekiah's Officials, 25–29

Having completed our reading of a third major collection of instructions (22:17–24:33), we return to more sayings. The collection is clearly demarcated with a heading in 25:1, "These are the proverbs of Solomon that the officials of King Hezekiah of Judah copied." The heading in Proverbs 30:1, "The words of Agur son of Jakeh," provides the concluding boundary mark for the materials contained in chapters 25–29. The collection of sayings contained within these chapters resembles in style the materials readers have read in 10:1–22:16. There are mainly sayings within these chapters. However, unlike the earlier collection, readers will recognize the admixture of instructions along with the sayings. Further, there are longer sayings in this collection. We did not encounter, for instance, any four-line sayings in 10:1–22:16 as we will in this collection (e.g., 25:4-5).

We mention in the introduction to this commentary that it is likely that a literary tradition flourished by the time of King Hezekiah (715 to 687 BC), to whose reign this collection of sayings is attributed in 25:1. The collection was likely assembled for the purpose of educating young people who would live their lives in service to the court.

These chapters divide into two major subsections: chapters 25–27 and 28–29. Just as the Sayings of Solomon (10:1–22:16) consist of two discernible subsections, there are also easily observable distinctions between the collections in these two parts. Chapters 25–27 comprise instructions and sayings, while chapters 28–29 consist exclusively of sayings. Further, the first subsection uses similes and nature imagery; the second section uses almost exclusively contrastive, or antithetical, parallelism.

Strategies for reading both sections greatly resemble those readers have used in 10:1–22:16. The use of verbal, thematic, and syntactic linking devices, especially in 25–27, facilitate the clustering together of independent sayings and admonitions. Theological themes are not

Structure at a Glance: Proverbs 25

AΩ In addition to the possible inclusio that obtains in vv. 16 and 27, readers might further organize the chapter's groupings as follows:

Vv. 2-7 On Royal Discernment
Vv. 8-10 In the Court of Law
Vv. 11-15 Speech: The Means of Judgment
Vv. 16-28 On Things in Excess

Strategic rhetorical devices within this chapter organize the collection into the following groupings: vv. 2-7a; vv. 8-10; vv. 11-15; vv. 16-20, 24-25, 27-28. The first half of the chapter provides an interesting thematic movement in three discernible sections. The opening section contains observations about kings and kingship (vv. 2-7), the next section reflects upon the court (vv. 8-10), and the final section considers speech. These three contain sayings with interrelated themes. If readers use the inclusio in vv. 16-28 as a thematic touchstone for reading the groupings in the second half of the chapter, many if not most of the sayings or instructions are related to excessive behaviors. [It should be noted that at least two scholars regard 25:2-28 as a separate "wisdom book" divided into two parts: vv. 6-16 and 17-28. See G. E. Bryce, "Another Wisdom-'Book' in Proverbs," *JBL* 91 (1972): 145-57; and Raymond C. Van Leeuwen, *Context and Meaning in Proverbs 25–27* (SBLDS 96; Atlanta: Scholars Press, 1988).]

as common, however, in these chapters in contrast to 10:1–22:16. There are only six Yahweh sayings in the entire collection: three in chapter 29 (vv. 13, 25, and 26); two in chapter 28 (vv. 5 and 25); and one in chapter 25 (v. 22).

Discriminating Kings, Courts, and Choices, 25:1-28

No single theme dominates chapter 25 as a touchstone for arranging all of the sayings. However, certain sayings and instructions may be grouped together based upon form, verbal links, and thematic content. For instance, the sayings in 2-7a share the word "king" (*melek*). This is obviously a verbal link that contributes to the thematic unity of the opening grouping of sayings. The chapter breaks into vv. 1-15 and vv. 16-28, with both halves consisting of yet smaller groupings of sayings and instructions. Although there is little thematic unity in either half, there may be the indication of some intended structural unity. Verses 16 and 27 might function as an inclusio for the latter half of the collection; both verses share verbal and thematic links with each other (honey [*děbaš*] and the idea of excess). [Structure at a Glance: Proverbs 25]

COMMENTARY

On Royal Discernment, 25:1, 2-7

At the head of the chapter the superscription attributes the sayings to Solomon and their "copying" to Hezekiah. Clifford offers a plausible rationale for regarding the superscription's historicity. Hezekiah's reign is known in Hebrew literature as a time of reform after the destruction of the northern kingdom in 722 BC (2 Kgs 18–20; 2 Chr 29–30). Copying and editing traditional materials and sacred literature, especially in the wake of the influx of refugees

Meaning of 'āṭaq

AΩ NRSV translates v. 1 to say that the officials of King Hezekiah "copied" the sayings of Solomon that are included in the present chapter. The translation "copy" comes from the LXX translation of the Hebrew heʿtîqû, the Hiphil of 'āṭaq, as *exegrapsanto*, "to copy out or write out." The Latin Vulgate translates the word as *transtulerunt*, meaning "transfer." In both of these cases there seems to be an ancient understanding of a process of transmission. R. B. Y. Scott's translation of the verse, in fact, uses the word "transmit."

This is convenient for those who search for some explicit reference to the process of transmission behind the Scriptures. It is unwise, however, simply to rely upon the LXX and the Latin translations when other occurrences of the word *āṭaq* in the Hebrew Scriptures suggest possible alternative meanings. While the word occurs in contexts where the base meaning of "movement" is clear, there is not any other occurrence that appears to convey the idea of transmission. Thus, in Gen 12:8 Abraham "moves on"; similarly, in Gen 26:22 Isaac "moves from there." In Job 14:18 God moves or removes mountains.

In other words, as Stuart Weeks concludes, "It is hard to see how 'abandon' or 'remove' could become 'copy' or 'pass on.'" Even those scholars who admit the possibility of its meaning "collect" do so only cautiously (e.g., Murphy; Clifford). For readers of the NRSV, the implications of Prov 25:1 for a general theory of Scripture transmission must be held with the same caution that applies to any hypothesis.

For further reading, see M. Carasik, "Who Were the 'Men of Hezekiah' (Proverbs XXV,1)?" *VT* 44 (1994): 289-300.

Richard J. Clifford, *Proverbs* (OTL; Louisville: Westminster John Knox Press, 1999), 219.

Roland E. Murphy, *Proverbs* (WBC 22; Nashville: Word, 1998), 190.

R. B. Y. Scott, *Proverbs, Ecclesiastes* (AB; New York: Doubleday, 1965), 153.

Stuart Weeks, *Early Israelite Wisdom* (Oxford: Clarendon Press, 1994), 44.

---

to Judah from the North, would have been a part of those reforms. A collection of sayings that would be useful at court could well have been a part of such reform activity.[1] Readers may accept as a general guideline the patronage of kings in the production and preservation of wisdom sayings. [Meaning of 'āṭaq]

Verses 2-7 are linked by the shared theme of kingship and kings. The quality of the king's discernment provides a basis for the development within the sayings. Verse 2 opens with a comparison between God's glory and the king's glory. God hides things; kings search hidden things out. Note the verbal link between vv. 2 and 3 on the term "search." Verse 2 contains the infinitive form of the word *ḥāqar*, "to search"; v. 3 contains a nominal form, *ḥēqer*, "searching, inquiry." [Riddling God's Mystery] It follows in v. 3, then, that if kings search out the deep things of God, then kings like deities must be inscrutable.

The next verses invite readers to see the discernment of the king as a process of separation. The saying in v. 4 alludes to the process of smelting silver, one of separating the dross from the pure substance. Verse 5 parallels the structure of v. 4 and draws an explicit comparison to the king's judgment in removing the wicked from

Riddling God's Mystery

Prov 25:2 is probably more concerned with the assertion of royal discernment than with exploring God's mystery. Even so, the statement in v. 2a is an extraordinary confession of the sages' theology.

The saying gives readers pause to think about how Yahweh reveals. In the biblical narratives God's self-disclosure to humans, while awful and inspiring, is always partial and incomplete. God's self-disclosure is not so complete that a mediator is unnecessary. This idea is recalled in the portrayal of the people at Sinai requesting Moses to intercede on their behalf with Yahweh (Exod 20:19). Moreover, God's self-revelation is not without ambiguity. The Lord promises Moses that he will see all of the deity's goodness and will hear the name while also urging that Moses cannot see the face of God (Exod 33:19-23). The prophets are remembered as ones who struggled to understand the announcement of God's purposes (e.g., Isa 6:11-13; Jer 12:1-6). If there was hope that God's ways could be discerned, as Prov 25:2b implies, then God's mystery was a basis for confidence. If, alternatively, mystery was a confusing and impenetrable shroud, then Qoheleth's cry "who knows? (Eccl 2:19; 3:21; 8:1) becomes a confession of intellectual darkness and spiritual despair.

For further reading, see Walter Brueggemann, *Theology of the Old Testament* (Minneapolis: Fortress, 1997), 333-72; and Raymond C. Van Leeuwen, *Context and Meaning in Proverbs 25–27* (SBLDS 96; Atlanta: Scholars Press, 1988).

his kingdom. It is the king's responsibility to see that justice and righteousness are maintained, (cf. Prov 16:12).

The final two verses in this sequence comprise an instruction: a negative admonition (v. 6) accompanied by a motive clause (v. 7). The implication of the admonition has to do with an individual putting on false airs: standing with the great is a kind of presumptuousness that invites scrutiny. In the king's court where critical discrimination is important, presumptuousness can work against one's own self-image. The motive clause, here in the form of a better-than saying, implies that one should use the king's discriminating tastes to one's own advantage.

"What Your Eyes Have Seen"

NRSV along with NIV renders the latter part of v. 7 (7c) as the opening statement of vv. 8-10 rather than the concluding statement of vv. 6-7. Later versions of the LXX (for instance, Symmachus) read 7c as though it is connected with v. 8, "What your eyes have seen, do not bring out to the multitude quickly." This is, in fact, the way that most commentators read the passage (e.g., McKane; Murphy; Clifford).

Duane A. Garrett, however, retains the MT over against the LXX translation and explains that the sentences make sense following v. 7, the topic of which concerns public humiliation. He argues that "no one wants to have to look his peers in the face while being publicly humiliated by a superior." This is an interesting proposal, but it seems to assume that the emphasis in 7c is upon being seen rather than, as the text itself says, what one sees. Realigning the sentence with v. 8, with NRSV and NIV, seems more likely.

Richard J. Clifford, *Proverbs* (OTL; Louisville: Westminster John Knox Press, 1999), 223.

Duane A. Garrett, *Proverbs, Ecclesiastes, Song of Songs* (NAC 14; Nashville: Broadman, 1993), 205.

William McKane, *Proverbs* (OTL; London: SCM, 1970), 580.

Roland E. Murphy, *Proverbs* (WBC 22; Nashville: Word, 1998), 191.

In the Court of Law, 25:8-10

NRSV translates v. 7c as the beginning of the instruction in vv. 8-10. The MT takes vv. 8-10 as a simple instruction about the dangers of bringing every matter to court.[2] NRSV's translation is difficult, however. Rushing to court on the basis of what one has seen implies that individuals who behave in this way are professional witnesses of some sort (cf. 24:28). The admonition in vv. 9-10 does not seem to fit this scenario, however. ["What Your Eyes Have Seen"] Verses 8-10 are connected through the common use of the word "case" (*rîb*), and therefore make unlikely a separation between v. 8 and vv. 9-10.

If with MT we read the text as beginning with v. 8 proper, we have a simple admonition not to be too hasty to take conflict into the public courtroom. The motive clause that accompanies in v. 8 suggests that the outcome will be public shame and humiliation.[3] On this basis, vv. 9-10 urge one to take one's case directly to one's opponent (one's neighbor), not relying upon the council of another (such as a judge).

Speech: The Means of Judgment, 25:11-15

The next grouping of sayings all have in common a connection with proper speech, a well-established wisdom theme. The previous cluster of sayings have both addressed the king's judgments and offered advice about the place of judgment, the court. It is appropriate next to address one significant vehicle of such discernment, speech. Verses 11-14 are comparative statements introduced with the particle "like." The word itself is not in the text, but it is clearly implied in the arrangement of the poetry. Verses 11-12 are connected with the word "gold"; vv. 13-14 both use weather imagery.

Verses 11 and 12 combine to illustrate a word that has a "right fit." Such a word—the "right" word—is like finely tooled gold in a silver setting. For the teacher, this may be the metaphorical "teachable moment." The right time is when the right word from the teacher and the student come together. Such a meaning might be inferred from Proverbs 15:23. The phrase in 11b translated by NRSV as "fitly spoken" is the Hebrew '*al 'opnāyw*, however, and it is uncertain in its meaning. Taken from the noun *open*, the word carries the idea of "manner" or "mode." From this meaning comes the basis for the derivation that has to do with circumstances. McKane suggests taking the word from the noun

Mount Hermon

Mount Hermon, one of the three highest peaks in the Hermon range at the southern end of the Anti-Lebanon range, is snow-capped year round.

'opān, "wheel," in which case the dual form of the word, *'opnāyw*, implies that sayings were like two wheels turning. A good word, with its two parallel parts, would be a "well-turned" word.[4] The

next two verses, 13-14, combine weather imagery to characterize other instances of proper or improper speech. Honest messengers are compared to soothing cool on a blistering hot day. The image of "snow" does not mean one may necessarily infer that it snows during the month of June in Palestine.[5] More likely the image suggests the use of snow cooled into spring water that is offered as refreshment during the harvest. By contrast, the refreshment that never comes in the form of rain is like the one who boasts in public of his gifts and then never delivers. The concluding saying juxtaposes two powerful realities: the king and speech (the tongue). Proper speech can persuade kings. The saying is careful to qualify a kind of "softness" that must accompany such persuasion. With "patience" readers are reminded of other guidelines of self-control already encountered in the collections of sayings (e.g., 14:29; 15:18; 16:32). When these conditions are met, the tongue is arguably more powerful than the king.

On Things in Excess, 25:16-28

The materials in the second half of the chapter do not follow a thematic arrangement as clearly as the materials in the first half. Readers must attend to syntactical and/or formal matters more carefully. Verses 16 and 27-28 are about excess. Verse 28 follows with a saying about self-control, an appropriate response to the threat of overindulging. Verse 21 with its motive clause in v. 22 serves as a dividing point for the collection and utilizes imagery of eating. Verses 18-20 are all similes, that is, explicit comparisons. In translation the comparative particle "like" introduces each sentence. Verses 23-26 are not so evidently similar. Three of these four could be construed as thematically linked to the subject of speech (vv. 23, 24, and 25). Verses 25 and 26 are similes. Verse 24 is a "better than" statement.

Verse 16 provides the opening of this second half of the chapter with an image of a good thing that is overused. Honey is the symbol of what is good, but too much of it makes one vomit. The implication is that restraint heightens the pleasure. Verse 17 is paired explicitly in that its second stich opens with the identical particle "otherwise" (*pen*) and uses the same verb as in the second stich of v. 16 (*śaba*). Verse 17 observes that neighbors are a good thing, but too much of them creates animosity. Verse 18 is linked with v. 17 by its use of the word "neighbor" (*rēa*). The saying imagines giving false testimony against one's neighbor (although neighbor may also imply opponent at court—see v. 9). Such behavior at court surely does not create the environment for successful social relations. Verse 19 might well be linked to v. 18 by the similarities between the Hebrew word for "tooth" (*šēn* v. 19) and for "sharp" (*šānûn,* v. 18). Verse 19 connects thematically with the falsehood depicted in v. 18. One who bears "false witness" against a neighbor has become one who is a "faithless person in time of trouble." If the MT is retained, v. 20 seems to be connected with v. 19 by the words "faithless person" (*bôgēd,* v. 19) and "clothing" (*beged,* v. 20). NRSV relies upon LXX in this translation, which both removes the phrase in 20a, "like one who takes off a garment on a cold day," and adds 20c, "Like a moth in clothing or a worm in wood." The versions, in other words, indicate severe textual variation. The idea is that a saddened heart cannot voice songs of mirth.[6] Verse 20 creates an interesting counterpoint with v. 16. Verse 16 has the image of an excess of honey; v. 20 has the image of vinegar, the opposite of honey.

Verses 21 and 22 invoke the eating imagery begun in v. 16, only here in reference to one's enemies. These four lines of poetry are difficult to read, however, without thinking of their treatment in Romans 12:17-21. In fact, the command to feed one's enemies seems remarkably similar to Jesus' command to love one's enemies and pray for them (Matt 5:44). The claim in Proverbs 25:21 that treating enemies with kindness is the best way to inflict punishment upon them is reminiscent of 24:17-18. Readers may recall in that instance that the admonition is to withhold any rejoicing at the failure of one's enemies. Only in such a case would Yahweh intervene on behalf of the innocent.

Verses 23-26 form an interesting foursome. Verses 23 and 25 use the imagery of water—one rain, the other cool water—to describe the efficacy of different kinds of speech (cf. v. 14). Verse 23 is concerned with secret words; v. 25 is concerned with good news proclaimed openly and loudly. Both 24 and 26 are concerned with different kinds of individuals. Verse 24 pictures the nagging wife; v. 26 pictures the righteous person whose resolve to do only righteousness wavers before the wicked. Both are therefore negative images. Verse 27 and 28 reiterate the importance of self-control by invoking the image of excess, which began the second half of the chapter (v. 16).

CONNECTIONS

The Doctrine of Enough

The sayings in this chapter illustrate well one of the fundamental assumptions of the wisdom literature: to be wise is to be discriminating. The chapter begins by implying that as kings discern between good and bad, right and wrong, so must individuals be discerning about everyday life. Metaphorically speaking, daily life is like a courtroom wherein one must be constantly handing down verdicts on what is and is not proper speech in this or that relational situation. What makes for proper speech is not merely the assertion of many words; speech is proper when there is a coming together of the right time with the right person. Recognizing the right time requires that individuals be as discerning as kings. The closing half of the chapter takes the idea of discrimination to a logical conclusion by urging that there can be too much of a good thing. Discernment is all about knowing when and where enough is enough. In everyday parlance there is such a thing as a law of diminishing returns, where the extra effort (or investment) for an additional experience of pleasure or an extra rewarding experience is more than the reward itself. Put another way, the extra cost is not worth the minimal gain. Discernment permeates everyday life.

The 1996 report titled *The State of the World* seems to recognize this fundamental principle when it states, "One of the most fundamental flaws of market-based economies is that the prices they use to guide buying decisions and allocate resources rarely reflect the full costs of environmental damage."[7] Determining whether the costs of any kind of activity are really worth the gain is a fundamental economic necessity of a global community with burgeoning population and shrinking natural resources. A careful analysis recognizes the inherent necessity of denial that must accompany the coalition of industrialized nations as they continue to promote unbridled consumption. Consumption is the watchword for the modern state that desires to be prosperous.

As countries continue in the cycle of elections of leaders, ministers, and presidents and continue to raise questions of policy regarding issues beyond the environment, the central issue is the relative cost versus the gain. How does a democratic nation define freedom to allow the maximum opportunities for individual prosperity, growth, and dignity and also to inculcate a philosophy of the common good? Or to put it another way, is it possible for freedom to take on such radical extremes that individuals do not see the importance of their contribution to the nation-state? When is freedom for the individual enough? [An Ecological Market]

The common sense promoted in the teaching of the ancient sages acknowledges a kind of law of diminishing returns. Sometimes the cost of certain actions, even good ones, is not worth the gain. Self-control therefore becomes a definitive attribute for individuals. As individuals embrace such a principle for their personal lives, they project the principle onto the interests and concerns of the larger society and eventually the global community. There is also a personal sense in which the doctrine of "enough" has relevance. Individuals in the West at the onset of the twenty-first century are so driven by the desire to consume that there is little time for qualitative reflection. The needs of the world aside, the quality of individual life often takes second place to the importance of the quantity of possessions.

An Ecological Market

"To make the market system reflect rather than obscure ecological realities, societies need to enforce a principle that is at once radical and obvious: that people and businesses should pay the full costs of the harm they do to others."

David Malin Roodman, "Harnessing the Market for the Environment," in *State of the World,* ed. Linda Starke (New York & London: W. W. Norton & Co., 1996), 169.

NOTES

[1] Richard J. Clifford, *Proverb* (OTL; Louisville: Westminster John Knox Press, 1999), 219.

[2] Roland E. Murphy, *Proverbs* (WBC 22; Nashville: Word, 1998), 188; Clifford, *Proverbs,* 223.

[3] NRSV reads v. 8 as a motive clause opening with the particle *kî,* "for," rather than *pen,* "lest."

[4] William McKane, *Proverbs* (OTL; London: SCM, 1970), 584; see also Murphy, *Proverbs,* 192.

[5] R. B. Y. Scott, *Proverbs, Ecclesiastes* (AB; New York: Doubleday, 1965), 155, writes that he has seen such unseasonably cool weather at that time of the year, however.

[6] See Murphy, *Proverbs,* 189 and 193; Clifford, *Proverbs,* 225; McKane, *Proverbs,* 589.

[7] David Malin Roodman, "Harnessing the Market for the Environment," in *State of the World*, ed. Linda Starke (New York & London: W. W. Norton & Co., 1996), 169.

WHAT IS A FOOL?

Proverbs 26:1-28

In addition to a broad three-part structure, this collection features characteristics that readers have encountered in chapter 25, especially the frequent use of simile. Most of the sayings in this chapter are therefore comparisons, although there are also other forms. The three-part structure of the chapter does not diminish the necessity of attending to smaller sub-groupings within the overall collection. For instance, vv. 4-5, 6-7, and 20-22 form independent thematic units of thought within the larger grouping. Catchwords form semantic connections—for example, "quarrel" and "fire" in vv. 20-21; "gossip" in vv. 20 and 22; "lips" in vv. 23-24; and "hate" in vv. 26 and 28.[1] [Structure at a Glance: Proverbs 26]

Structure at a Glance: Proverbs 26

AΩ The three-part structure of the chapter makes it convenient to read the overarching themes. The opening section, vv. 1-12, deals with the fool (*kĕsîl*), which establishes an important touchstone for reading the following two sections. The ensuing sections, vv. 13-16 and vv. 17-28, though thematically different, are more focused treatments of kinds of foolish behavior. The final series in vv. 17-28 may be broken into four smaller units: vv. 17-19, 20-22, 23-25, and 26-28. Readers may recall the images of the fool while reading about the lazy person in vv. 13-16. Likewise, lying, vv. 17-28, is a further kind of foolishness. Hence, the following outline may guide one's reading.

> Vv. 1-12 The Glory of a Fool
> Vv. 13-16 Lampooning the Lazy
> Vv. 17-28 The Deceived Are the Deceivers
> Vv. 17-19
> Vv. 20-22
> Vv. 23-25
> Vv. 26-28

COMMENTARY

The Glory of a Fool, 26:1-12

These opening twelve sayings are clearly connected semantically. The word for fool, *kĕsîl*, recurs within each saying, excepting v. 2, in both singular and plural forms. [Previous Encounters with the Fool] Verses 4-5 and vv. 6-7 are paired thematically with each other within the larger context. Verse 1 is a programmatic statement that glory for a fool is misplaced. Readers recall 25:13, where snow in harvest time is used as an example of rarity and something out of place. Given the

---

Previous Encounters with the Fool

AΩ The prevalence of sayings on the fool in this chapter reminds readers of similar references throughout the sayings of Solomon. Perhaps the most frequent term in Proverbs for the incorrigibly foolish is *kĕsîl*. The term occurs some seventy times in the Hebrew Bible. In Proverbs this person stands in contrast with the wise (e.g., Prov 10:1; 15:2, 20) and with the clever (e.g., 12:23; 13:16) and parallels the scoffer (e.g., 19:29). Apparently there is hope for neither. Sometimes people may be called foolish because they are naive and inexperienced. In such cases, the sages use the word *pĕtî*, "simple" or "naive" person. This term occurs some fifteen times in Proverbs. These are not hopelessly foolish people, however (e.g., Prov 7:7; 8:5). Individuals who are referred to as *'ĕwîl*, "foolish," are not inherently foolish. They are, however, resistant to instruction (e.g., Prov 10:8; 15:5), mocking (e.g., 14:9), and quarrelsome (e.g., 20:3) This term occurs some twenty-seven in the Hebrew Bible. These individuals can learn, but will not until they have the will to learn (e.g., Prov 16:22; 27:22).

Other kinds of behaviors the sage refers to as foolish are more serious and sinister than those set out above. The one who does not love discipline and is mentally subhuman in a sense is called a *ba 'ar* or a brute. The term occurs five times in the Bible (e.g., Prov 12:1; 30:2). A still more sinister kind of foolishness is embodied by the person the sages call a *nābāl*, a "fool," whose behavior is close to sinful. This person lacks moral and social refinement (e.g., Prov 17:7; 30:22). This person always scoffs at instruction and is therefore uneducable.

For further reading, see Sheldon Blank, "Folly," *IDB* 2:303-304; Kenneth Hoglund, "The Fool and the Wise in Dialogue," in *The Listening Heart,* ed. Kenneth Hoglund et al., FS Roland Murphy (Sheffield: JSOT Press, 1987); and Jack Weir, "Fool/Foolishness/Folly," *MDB,* 305-306.

---

assumption of the regularity of the seasons, honoring a fool is a serious subversion of order. However, given the possibility of such reversal, the implication might be that fools obtain glory more frequently in society than one would think possible. Verse 2 also utilizes the motif of things misplaced in urging that an "undeserved" curse is ineffectual. The term translated "undeserved" is the adverb *ḥinnām* (cf. 1:17 and 3:30).[2] Verse 3 responds to these two opening statements by asserting that the only thing appropriate for a fool is a whip for his back. The fool is neither teachable nor potentially of any use to society.

This incorrigibility of the fool raises ethical problems for one who is wise. To what extent should one try to teach a person who is so uneducable and of such limited potential? Verse 4 asserts that to try to do such an impossible task makes oneself look like a fool. Verse 5 asserts that failing to teach a fool allows the fool to believe that, in fact, he really knows what he is talking about. Readers may consider v. 5 against the danger implied in v. 1: honor for a fool is like a subversion of the order of creation. It may be that the only proper response to the fool is the severe one pictured in v. 3. On the one hand, that response is a corrective response; on the other hand, the whipping does not make any pretensions about the potential of the fool. Mercifully (although some might say unfortunately!), whippings no longer play a vital role in pedagogy.

An interesting chiasm structures vv. 6-10 on the themes of ineffectualness and social danger created by both the fool and the ones who hire fools:

V. 6 Physical danger: "cutting off one's foot"
  V. 7 Ineffectualness: "proverb in the mouth of a fool"
    V. 8b Reiteration of v. 1: threat of "giving honor to a fool"
  V. 8a Ineffectualness: "proverb in the mouth of a fool"
V. 9 Physical danger: "archer who wounds everyone"[3]

The outer sayings, vv. 6 and 10, utilize metaphors of physical danger to convey the problems of engaging the service of a fool. In both cases, not only does the task fail, but one is potentially in danger of being injured. Verses 7 and 9 offer illustrations of the ineffectualness of a proverb in the mouth of a fool. Not only are fools irresponsible, they are also uneducated. Verse 8, the central saying in the chiasm, reasserts the programmatic claim of v. 1: one should not give honor to a fool. The image depicts yet another failure of the order of the cosmos. The stone that sticks in the sling is not only ineffectual; it is also dangerous to the one who is using the sling. [The Sling]

The concluding sayings, vv. 11 and 12, provide closure on the section by reasserting the fool's incorrigibility. The image of the dog returning to its vomit appeals to a very base nature of things. Clearly this sage had the lowest regard for fools and their foolishness. But the image also compares the fool's ability with that of instinctual behavior. A fool's ignorance is

---

The Sling

Within the catalog of ancient weaponry, the sling seems a rather benign weapon and most likely evokes sentimental responses due to its association with the biblical story of the shepherd, David (1 Sam 17:40-50). In fact, the sling was quite a deadly weapon due to its accuracy and range. For military purposes, slingers would more likely be catalogued with archers rather than with close range infantry.

The sling consisted of two leather cords joined together by a patch of cloth or leather. The projectile fit into the patch. The two cords were grasped and swung to gain velocity. One of the cords was released, thus freeing the projectile to travel its course (e.g., Judg 20:16; 1 Chr 12:2).

For further reading, see Joel F. Drinkard, "Weapons/Warfare," *MDB*, 955-57; and Mark J. Fretz, "Weapons and Implements of Warfare," *ABD* 6:893-95.

Gian Lorenzo Bernini. 1598–1680. *David*. 1623–1624. Marble. Galleria Borghese. Rome, Italy.

merely instinctual and therefore inescapable. This is why the final saying is such an exclamation point. Readers may well have thought at this point that there could be nothing lower than a fool—whose best instincts are merely to be a fool—but, apparently, there is something still more self-deluded than a fool. Those are people who think themselves above the plight of the fool, imagining that they have obtained wisdom. Murphy refers to this as an "astounding proverb," since it raises questions about both stages of folly and the truly wise person who must nevertheless acknowledge his limitations. The saying expresses a view that wisdom has its dangers. The most significant danger is the blindness to one's own limitations.[4]

Lampooning the Lazy, 26:13-16 (17-19)

Laziness is another kind of foolishness (cf. 24:30-34; 6:6-11). However, the tone of these sayings is different from that in v. 12. We get the impression of the sage's sense of humor through the use of exaggeration and irony. True, laziness represents for the sage a threat to success, but the way of identifying this threat seems to be much more lighthearted in these verses.

Verses 17-19 are not formally a part of this subgroup. They neither show explicit verbal links with the section on foolishness nor with the immediately preceding section on the lazy person. However, they are about foolish behavior. Further, they anticipate the sayings in vv. 20-28 in their portrayal of negative social behavior. Hence, readers may read them as transitional sayings inserted here to provide movement from one kind of social threat to another.

Readers should also imagine the ones making such observations. We have already encountered the topics of vv. 13 and 15 in Proverbs 22:13 and 19:24. It appears the present collection is simply reusing these sayings. The ridiculous excuse in v. 13 is intended to make hearers chuckle at the energy devoted to the avoidance of work. Similarly, the depiction of the lazy in v. 14 is matchless in depicting the energy spent on the avoidance of work. The image of one being so lazy that he falls asleep before being able to feed himself is likewise hyperbolic. The lazy people's expenditure of energy to avoid work is intensified in v. 16 by mentioning their own self-deception. Readers recognize in vv. 13-15 the motif of comparison: in v. 13 the extreme exaggeration; in v. 14 the activity to avoid activity; in v. 15, the most unlikely of events—inability to feed oneself. These are concluded by the exaggerated observation of lazy people's self-deception. They think they are wiser than others who, by their cautious answers, show themselves to be wise. The number seven in the verse may be an allusion to the mythical seven anti-diluvian sages of Mesopotamian lore.[5] Taken in this way, the exaggeration is complete: the lazy are not just wise in their own eyes, they are wise in comparison to the most wise.

The Deceived Are the Deceivers, 26:17-28

Verses 17-28 comprise the third subsection of sayings in this chapter. The opening verses, 17-19, differ from the preceding sayings in that they return to the use of simile. Although they are different in form, they introduce four sets of sayings that may be loosely related as examples of foolishness. Though they all address quite different thematic materials, they offer a series of evocative reflections to the chapter.

Verse 17, translated by NRSV as taking a "passing dog by the ears," evokes reflection upon certain kinds of foolish behaviors (perhaps one's own fits of anger? e.g., 15:18; 17:14; 20:3[6]). Meddling in another's affairs is simply going out of the way to invite trouble into one's life. One might get involved in another's affairs through deception and offering false reports, v. 18 observes. Covering one's actions by claiming to have been joking does not diminish the severity of the action. This image of deception offers a useful transition to the several sayings that concern deception and lying in the remaining three units of thought.

Readers become even more aware in vv. 20-22 that the concern is with the problem of public appearances and private behavior. Verses 20-22 assert the destructiveness of the "whisperer" (*nirgān*), the one who keeps quarreling stirred up by passing on information secretly. Readers have already encountered the problems associated with gossip (e.g., 16:27-28). In vv. 20 and 21 the observation addresses the social effect. Verse 22 shifts to the subjective experiences of the one who keeps things so stirred up.

Verses 23-25 are also connected to the theme of deceitful speech. Verse 23 makes a general statement about "smooth lips," an image of deceit. NRSV follows the LXX in this translation. The MT literally reads "burning lips." It is "burning lips" that are equated with the "evil heart." The image of a "glaze" covering a clay pot alludes to the process of providing a burnished, or highly polished, finish. The idea is that of deception and the requisite skill to detect what is both pure silver on the outside as well as within. [Pottery Making] The verse anticipates what is to follow in vv. 24-25, where readers

---

Pottery Making

The image of "smooth lips" and an "evil heart" is illustrated with an appeal to ancient pottery making. If the NRSV translation is correct, the image is one of a clay pot with a glazing, or a burnished finish that conceals the dull-looking clay interior.

Pottery making was an important industry in the biblical world. Frequently poets and prophets appeal to the pot-making industry as an analogy to God's relationship to humankind (e.g., Job 10:8, 9; Isa 45:9). Several kinds of vessels mentioned in the Bible indicate the extent and variety of pottery making (e.g., Jer 19:11; Lam 4:2), although there is not much detail in the Bible about the process itself.

Two Potters at the Kiln. Painted wood and stucco. Middle Kingdom. Egyptian Museum. Cairo, Egypt.

The key factors in pottery production were the quality of clay and the technology for throwing and firing the clay. The potter's task was in both preparing the clay and then shaping and finishing the clay product. Clay had to be worked (treaded in Isa 41:25) to remove foreign debris. This ensured a uniform texture. The potter then shaped it in various ways, depending upon the technology available.

Before the availability of a turning wheel (Neolithic period, 10,000–4,000 BC), the potter shaped the clay from a ball, gradually pressing it into shape, or rolled it into lengths and coiled it. Turning boards were used in the Chalcolithic period (4000–2000 BC), with refinements in the technology progressively added through the Bronze (2000–1200 BC) and Iron (1200–550 BC) ages. Technological advances allowed greater stylistic variations to be applied deliberately, with greater uniformity

For further reading, see J. L. Kelso, "Pottery," *IDB* 3:846-53; Nancy L. Lapp, "Pottery," *ABD* 5:428-44; and Carla M. Sinopoli, *Approaches to Archaeological Ceramics* (New York & London: Plenum Press, 1991).

---

encounter further sayings on "the one who hates" (*śônē'*), translated in NRSV as "the enemy."

Verses 26-28 also seem to function as a unit. Verse 26 offers an intriguing image of the undoing of the enemy in the context of "the assembly" (*qāhāl*), a technical term for the body of worshipers in Israel or for a judicial gathering. On the other hand, it could be a judicial assembly that is visualized. While either of these possible connotations of *qāhāl* pose some interesting possibilities, it may well be that the *qāhāl* only denotes the society at large. This general sense seems to be the implication in Proverbs 5:14. Verse 28 concludes with another image of deception, reminding readers of the image in v. 19.

CONNECTIONS

The Self-deception of the Fool

The self-deception of fools seems to be their greatest downfall, perhaps the very reason they can never be wise. Fools always think that they are already in possession of wisdom when they are not. One of the axioms of wisdom is therefore that one must always be open to self-criticism and reflection. Many changes of fortune have taken as their point of departure this singular reality.

One of Shakespeare's greatest tragedies, *King Lear*, portrays the unraveling of a kingdom due to the failure of its king to acknowledge his own insolence and limitation. The plot turns on the king's decision to divide his kingdom among his three daughters and their husbands, setting aside his regal authority while still retaining the title of king. In his aim to assure that there would be no future strife by making all inheriting parties happy, he instead ensures that there will most certainly be civil war. He apparently has no sense of the realities of power. The tragedy, of course, is that Lear is so unaware of himself and his blindness that he cannot see clearly until his sons-in-law, the husbands of his daughters Regan and Goneril, have overthrown him as king. The king's blindness and inability to rule with a critical acumen is established early in the play when he fails to recognize which of his three daughters actually loves him the most. Goneril and Regan flatter their father with empty words of love. Cordelia tells him the truth, that her love is defined by her duty and nothing more, but her duty proves truer and more reliable than her sisters' boasts of loving devotion. Regan sums it up at the end of Act I, scene I when she says of her father, "'Tis the infirmity of his age: yet he hath ever but slenderly known himself."

Such a pronouncement is judgment upon all who think they have finally arrived at wisdom. The difference between living well and merely living is in this self-reflectiveness that allows one to see how dangerously close to being a fool one actually is. Such ability to be self-critical allows the possibility of other points of view, other cultural perspectives and practices, values that compete for central authority. Such self-criticism allows one to love others as one loves oneself.

The ability to embrace such a principle as a discipline for one's life is one of the hallmarks of education. Educated people learn to be self-aware and thus self-critical. One of the educational outcomes of the modern academy is student "self-awareness." The absence of this faculty leads to all sorts of excesses in modern society.

NOTES

[1] Roland E. Murphy, *Proverbs* (WBC 22; Nashville: Word, 1998), 198; Richard J. Clifford, *Proverbs* (OTL; Louisville: Westminster John Knox Press, 2000), 228.

[2] On the *kĕtîb-qĕrē'* in v. 2b, see Murphy, *Proverbs,* 197; William McKane, *Proverbs* (OTL; London: SCM, 1970), 600. F. Delitzsch, *The Book of Proverbs,* vol. 2, reprint (COT 6; Grand Rapids: Eerdmans, 1952), points out that Ibn Ezra retained both as a means of maintaining a double meaning.

[3] Duane Garrett, *Proverbs, Ecclesiastes, Song of Solomon* (NAC 14; Nashville: Broadman, 1993), 212.

[4] See Murphy, *Proverbs,* 201 for other references; Clifford, *Proverbs,* 232, treats the problem of the sayings as "self-satisfaction" rather than blindness to one's deficiencies.

[5] Clifford, *Proverbs,* 233.

[6] Ibid., 233.

FOCUS ON THIS DAY'S WORK

Proverbs 27:1-27

With Proverbs 27 we arrive at the conclusion to the first sub-collection in chapters 25–29. Unlike chapters 25–26, this chapter is not so clearly or conveniently organized. It makes much greater demands upon readers' ability to detect the internal connections.

The opening sayings admonish caution about one's confidence in the future. One cannot "know" about tomorrow. The concluding instruction in vv. 23-27, which also serves as a conclusion to the collection in chapters 25–27, begins with the same word in an infinitival form, "to know" (v. 23). Its instruction focuses upon what an individual *can* know. The contrast between what may and may not be known anticipates Qoheleth's despair over what he feels is unknowable. One can know, however, one's work in the present. [Structure at a Glance: Proverbs 27]

Readers encounter a greater variety of rhetorical forms in this chapter. While the explicit comparison is a frequent occurrence here, there are also "better-than" statements (e.g., vv. 5 and 10), as well as a

---

Structure at a Glance: Proverbs 27

AΩ Some scholars believe that the overall structure of the unit reflects a tendency to pair the sayings together (see Murphy; Van Leeuwen). Verses 2 and 10 bound the initial grouping of sayings concerning the importance of friendship. While v. 2 does not specifically share language with v. 10, the idea of a contrast between an outsider (*zār*) over against a friend (*rē'ăkā*) provides an interesting connection. At least three sets of paired sayings offer connections within this thematic frame. Note especially vv. 5 and 6 and their sharing of the term "love" (*'āhāb*) and vv. 9 and 10 and their sharing of the term "neighbor" or "friend" (*rē'ēhû*). The second grouping joins various sayings concerning different kinds of people and behaviors. These sayings are more loosely organized, but vv. 23-27 is a distinct unit of instruction on the theme of diligence and hard work. It may function as a kind of parabolic coda on both the chapter and the sub-collection (Whybray). Readers will find provocative linguistic connections between vv. 11 (*hăkam*) and 12 (*'ārûm*), and thematic connections between vv. 15 and 16 and vv. 18-22. The discussion below will therefore be arranged along the following general lines:

Vv. 1-10 The Need for a Friend
Vv. 11-22 Parental Advice on People
Vv. 23-27 Tend Your Flocks

Raymond Van Leeuwen, *Context and Meaning in Proverbs 25–27* (SBLDS 96; Atlanta: Scholars Press, 1988), 142.
Roland E. Murphy, *Proverbs* (WBC 22; Nashville: Word, 1998), 206.
R. N. Whybray, *The Composition of the Book of Proverbs* (JSOTSup 168; Sheffield: JSOT Press, 1994), 126.

number of instructional elements, especially vv. 23-27. One scholar suggests that there may be a deliberate attempt to juxtapose different forms.[1] For instance, v. 1 opens with a negative admonition and v. 10 closes the opening section with a negative admonition. Then follow instruction, v. 2; observations, vv. 3-4; a "better-than" saying, v. 5; observation, v.v. 6-7; comparison, v. 8; and an observation, v. 9.

COMMENTARY

The Need for a Friend, 27:1-10

Verses 2 and 10 provide an inclusio concerning friends or neighbors. Admittedly, the language in v. 2 concerns an outsider or foreigner and thus not explicitly a friend. However, one outside the community who offers such evaluation is not bound by the same constraints of one's own self-evaluation. It is therefore hard to imagine any outsider to one's community who offers any kind of praise (*hallēl*) not being considered a true friend. Verse 1 leads into v. 2 through a verbal connection between the word translated "boast" in v. 1 and "praise" in v. 2 (*hallēl*). While there is no thematic connection, both words come from the same Hebrew root. Nevertheless, whether it is confidence in the future or confidence in oneself, both these sayings admonish that such praise should come from someone else. This provides an interesting echo to the sages' earlier concerns about foreigners (see chs. 1–9).

Verses 3 and 4 offer comparisons and have parallel structures. [The Syntax of 27:3, 4] For all of the syntactical parallelism, though, thematically the two sayings have little to do with each other. There is perhaps a kind of relationship in that both seem to concern the

---

The Syntax of 27:3, 4

AΩ Syntax concerns the way linguistic elements are positioned within a sentence. For instance, in the sentence "The dog bit the boy," we see a syntactical sequence of subject (S: "dog"), verb (V: "bit"), and object (O: "boy"). A second comparatively similar sentence, "The car hit the wall," differs completely in theme and sense, but it has the same syntactical sequence as the first sentence: (S: "car"), (V: "hit"), and (O: "wall").

Proverbs 27:3 and 4 have similar syntax and thus function as a pair, even though thematically they are unrelated. Both

stichs of both sayings establish comparisons, the second stich of each offering the most extreme example. In v. 3a, for instance, we see the following pattern: noun (N: "stone") + modifier (M: "heavy"), noun (N: "sand") = modifier (M: "weighty") and 3b noun clause (NC: "fool's provocation") + modifier (M: "heavier") + comparative particle plus pronoun (CPN: "than both of them"). A similar scheme might be set out for v. 4. Readers will notice that v. 4 abandons the pattern in the second stich by substituting a rhetorical question.

Jealous and Zealous

AΩ The Hebrew word translated as "jealous" in v. 4, *qin'â*, is of special interest, since it is the same word that is often translated "zealous" in the Hebrew Bible. Jealousy is a pejorative term for envy. The term also implies an extreme intolerance of a rival or a rivalry, as in the case of Gen 30:1, the episode of Rachel's "envy" of Leah. The use of the word in Prov 6:34, for instance, is illuminated by the husband's anger over an adulterous rival (cf. 6:32-35).

By contrast, "zeal" typically has a more positive value. It often connotes the passionate pursuit of some goal. Taken to its extreme, zeal becomes fury, as in Zech 8:2. We see zeal in the biblical narratives when people are passionate in their service of Yahweh (e.g., 2 Kgs 10:16) and for the service of the temple (e.g., Ps 69:9). Readers naturally tend to privilege zeal for Yahweh over jealousy about a rival.

It is interesting, however, that the outcomes of the two emotions often lead in the same directions. Through Jehu's zeal for Yahweh, all of the remaining people loyal to the house of Ahab are slaughtered (2 Kgs 10:1-11). A husband's jealous anger over a rival suitor to his wife could conceivably have the same outcome.

For further reading, see John McOlley, "YHWH and His Zealous Prophet: The Presentation of Elijah in 1 and 2 Kings," JSOT 80 (Spring 1998): 25-51; and Patrick D. Miller, Jr., "The Most Important Word: The Yoke of the Kingdom (Deut 6:4)," Iliff Review 41/3 (Fall 1984): 17-29.

---

limits of an individual's toleration. Verse 3 asserts that the fool's provocation is intolerably heavy. Verse 4 asserts that while one might be able to withstand someone's anger, one cannot withstand a person's jealousy. [Jealous and Zealous]

A third pair of sayings comprising vv. 5 and 6 are joined both thematically and linguistically. These two share the word for love, *ʾāhāb*, and both address the importance of friendship. Verse 5 is a "better than" saying and makes a more general statement about honesty in relationships: a rebuke that is out in the open is better than love that is concealed. True love, in other words, is not something that can be concealed. Verse 6 explores this motif of openness vs. hiddenness. Kisses can conceal an enemy's true feelings.

Having thus far encountered sayings that worked as pairs (vv. 1-2, 3-4, 5-6), vv. 7 and 8 appear to be unrelated both syntactically and thematically. Verse 7 concerns the experience of being sated with food; v. 8 concerns the question of wandering from home. Verse 7 may be taken symbolically; satiation with food is perhaps an analogy for satiation with many aspects of life. Likewise, the wandering of a bird from home may provide a beginning point for reflecting upon why humans wander from home. Is the latter related to satiation of some sort?

One scholar urges the possibility of reading four verses, vv. 7-10, as a unit in an "ABAB" alternating structure.[2] If we examine this proposal we see that vv. 7 and 9 share the vocabulary of *nepeš*, translated "appetite" and "soul," respectively. The same verses also

Perfume and Incense

The translation in v. 9b, "but the soul is torn by trouble," derives from the LXX. The MT is difficult and appears corrupt. (See many proposed solutions in McKane.) Whatever the second half of the line says, it clearly stands in parallel with terms translated as "perfume" and "incense" in 9a. The overall meaning of the verse must recognize the comparison or contrast with these two terms and the reality they connote.

Perfume and incense are used for social occasions. In Prov 7:16, the adulteress perfumes her bed to make it alluring to the youth she aims to seduce. Likewise, Prov 21:17 observes that wine and perfume ("oil"), the elements of festivity and social gathering, are costly and will leave one penniless. Perfume and incense are metonyms, therefore. They function as figures of speech that utilize the attributes of something—in these cases, of social occasions—to represent or stand for that thing. It may well be that perfume and incense here, as aspects of great social gatherings, are used to establish a contrast with images that connote more intimate and private relationships.

For further reading, see Athalya Brenner, "Aromatics and Perfumes in the Song of Songs," JSOT 25 (Fall 1983): 75-81; Bruce Cresson, "Incense," *MDB*, 405-406; Victor H. Matthews, "Perfumes and Spices," *ABD* 5:226-28; and G. W. VanBeek, "Frankincense and Myrrh," *BAR* 2 (1960): 99-126.

William McKane, *Proverbs* (OTL; London: SCM, 1970), 612-13.

Perfume flasks or alabastrons, also called "Tear Bottles," found in Jerusalem. Terracotta. Height 10cm. Private Collection. Vienna, Austria.

share the words for "sweet," *mātôq* and *meteq*. The contrast between spurning what is sweet and desiring what is bitter in v. 7 anticipates the contrast between gladness and sadness in v. 9. [Perfume and Incense] Verses 8 and 10 are also suggestively related. The bird that wanders from its nest and the need to return to one's home in times of trouble are images that evoke emotions related to homelessness and need. They call for the response in v. 10 not to forsake a friend since one will not be welcomed at home in times of trouble.

Parental Advice on People, 27:11-22

Nothing is more pragmatic in the present than recognizing different kinds of people and their behavior. This second section of chapter 27 addresses some of the most practical problems youths might face. There seems to be a clear break with the preceding verses, however, in that there is less tendency to pair sayings together. Readers will not see in these next verses the close verbal and thematic connections encountered in vv. 1-10. Still, readers may find it useful to subdivide this unit into two sections: vv. 11-17 concern certain kinds of activities, and vv. 18-22 seem to focus more particularly on kinds of people.

Verses 11-17 are collected under the rubric of the parents' advice in v. 11. Here there seems to be a kind of justification of the parents' teaching in the outcome of the youth's life (cf. 23:15). The motive for the child's obedience is the parents' shame, not the child's. This reminds readers why parents get so involved in their children's lives. To outward observers it is because of the parent's desire for the child's success. However, honesty demands that parents (and children!) recognize how parent's reputations and instructions are validated or negated by the child's performance.

Readers have encountered already the topics of vv. 12 and 13 in 22:3 and 20:16. Verse 12 follows well on v. 11 by its opening with a key synonym for wise, "the clever" (*'ārûm*). Those who are clever hide from trouble; the naive walk right into it. Some sound advice follows in vv. 13 and 14. Readers may read these as examples of the kinds of behavior the clever seek either to practice or to avoid. Making loans to those outside the community is to be avoided. However, if one must do so, one should get collateral. Verse 14, taken as a depiction of one who is naive, is another saying that both recognizes a law of diminishing returns and the significance of timeliness. There are times when even offering a blessing upon one's neighbors will get one into trouble. If a blessing is too loud and untimely so that it wakes one's neighbors from their sleep, they will regard the blessing as a curse. A blessing that is offered as flattery and thus insincerely is a still more serious form of deception.[3]

Verses 15 and 16 concern the "contentious wife," a topic readers have already seen in 19:13. The translation of v. 16 is challenging. NRSV's translation of "restrain her" (*ṣōpnêhā*, "hide her") in 16a takes the feminine singular suffix "her" as referring to v. 15's reference to the contentious wife. Verse 16 does not necessarily follow v. 15, however. For that reason the connection established by the translation is guesswork.[4] The second half of v. 16 is even more difficult to translate. Literally it could say, "the oil of his right hand calls." The juxtaposition of oil with wind seems to convey the idea that restraining one's contentious wife is impossible. Verse 17 concludes this small subsection with a parallel between the proverbial images of iron sharpening iron and people learning from other people. The language is interesting in that the word "face," *pānîm*, means both the edge of a blade (cf. Eccl 10:10) and verbal expression or wit (cf. Prov 15:13).[5] Thus iron sharpens the "face" of iron like a person sharpens the "face" of a person. The figure is therefore a fitting conclusion to the parent's appeal to "be wise" and a relevant introduction to the following section in which the sayings address different kinds of people.

Verses 18-22 may be read as a series of character observations. There is reflection upon the human heart (v. 19), human greed (v. 20), knowing people by their reputations (v. 21), and the fool v. 22). The opening saying in v. 18 compares the tending of a fig tree to tending to the concerns of one's master, perhaps keeping the master's instructions. Both bear fruit. It is good advice for people who are in the employment of another, but it is also good advice for students who should heed their master's teaching. Readers are reminded of the opening admonition in v. 11. The use of agricultural imagery invites analogies with learning. This anticipates the metaphorical possibilities of the concluding instruction in vv. 23-27.

Verse 19 reiterates the concern of v. 17 both linguistically and thematically. The recurrence of the word "face" (*pānîm*) conveys various implications. Water reflects the face of the one who looks into it. Thus, looking into the "face" (perhaps wit or intellect?) of another person's heart (*lēb ha'ādām*) reflects one's own learning. The saying stresses that the best learning is done in relationship to other people. Verse 20 connects semantically with v. 19 and thus invites reflection upon possible parallels. As humans face each other in learning, so death (Sheol and Abaddon) and human desire, "the human eyes," stand juxtaposed as counterparts: neither can be satiated. The image of the insatiability of human desire is revisited in the opening observations of Qoheleth (Eccl 1:8b).

The final two sayings in this subsection are related by the idea of testing and refinement. In v. 21 the praise of others tests individual character the way a refining fire tests the purity of gold or silver. Readers will recall the opening of the chapter and the concern that one should not praise oneself but allow others only to do so. Here the praise of others is the ultimate test of one's value. Submit a fool for the same kind of testing, and he is proved only to be a fool.

Tend Your Flocks, 27:23-27

The concluding five lines of poetry form a coda-like recapitulation of the opening sayings in 27:1, which admonish one not to boast about tomorrow. This conclusion urges the kind of work that must be done today. The agricultural imagery functions metaphorically in the same way that v. 18 functions. One's flocks and herds provide livelihood in the same way that a teacher's instructions provide guidance and wisdom. The produce of one's flocks and herds allows one to make provision for what is truly important: one's household. If we occupy ourselves with the concerns of the present, the future will take care of itself.

The concluding assurance regarding the provisions for one's "household" (*bêtekā*) invokes the image of wisdom's house in 9:1 and 14:1. Wisdom is about learning to build a household, whether it is woman wisdom or the student. Moreover, building a household is a task of providing the proper nourishment, material and intellectual, for all who live within.

CONNECTIONS

The Future in the Present

This conclusion in vv. 23-27 is sound advice, especially as reflection upon the riddles and hidden mysteries that occupy God and kings (e.g., 25:1-3). The admonition for one to take care with present responsibilities is a bit of pragmatism that undoubtedly grows from a benign skepticism that one may know much about the future. It further reflects a studied confidence in the present. The only thing one can know about the future lies in the present.

Such a focus upon the present, however, is not akin to the way many of us practice our faith. Rather than focusing upon the present, we tend to let our attention drift to the future. Such a strategy for living comes to us honestly as communities of faith have for millennia concerned themselves more with eschatological matters than with matters of more immediate import. Eschatology is a vital component of living faith. As the New Testament proclaims, there is an eschatological element of faith that has already been realized; for some, the resurrected Christ is but a beginning of a soon-to-be-completed establishment of God's final reign.

Even so, extending one's success off into the future in the face of failure is a strategy for making life meaningful when the structures of social reality change or when opposition prevents one from carrying out one's purposes. The problem with living for the future is that it relegates the present to a demonstrably inferior status. Values of human relationships, personal responsibilities, and obligations, as well as the basic worth of individuals all change if the present loses its significance. Suffering in the present can lose its social impact if one's immediate circumstances are inferior to some hoped for happiness that is projected onto the future.

Even having flocks and herds to tend in the present suggests something about the perspective of this sage. For those who have nothing to tend in the present, there can be no firm grasp upon the future. Thus, the abdication of the present for the future is perfectly understandable. The future is all there is to live for. For those who have responsibilities to tend in the present, careful attention to those responsibilities will lead such people to the future. To return to the practice of faith, it is easy to have faith in the future when we have possessions that will lead us to the future. It is much more difficult to have faith in the future when we have nothing in the present.

NOTES

[1] S. Weeks, *Early Israelite Wisdom* (Oxford: Clarendon, 1994), 30-31.

[2] Duane A. Garrett, *Proverbs, Ecclesiastes, Song of Songs* (NAC 14; Nashville: Broadman, 1993), 217.

[3] Richard J. Clifford, *Proverbs* (OTL; Louisville: Westminster John Knox Press, 1999), 239.

[4] Ibid., 238; Roland E. Murphy, *Proverbs* (WBC 22; Nashville: Word, 1998), 208.

[5] Clifford, *Proverbs,* 239.

A JUST ECONOMY

Proverbs 28:1-28

The final two chapters of sayings in this collection (chs. 28–29) appear to have no clear organization or thematic unity. Their similarities appear only in comparison to the preceding chapters 25–27. Most evident is the change in the rhetorical form of the sayings. The predominance of the comparison sayings, which readers encounter in chapters 25–27, gives way to the contrastive sayings such as those we encountered in 10:1–22:16, the Sayings of Solomon. There is also a drastic change in content, a decided absence of nature imagery, and a resurgence of moral and ethical topics. In particular, there is a return to the contrast between the righteous and the wicked in both chapters. [Structure at a Glance: Proverbs 28]

COMMENTARY

The Ruler and His Poor, 28:1-13

The opening three verses provide a possible thematic touchstone for our reading of both chapters 28 and 29. These three verses not only contrast the righteous and the wicked, they also reflect upon righteous rulers versus wicked rulers. They then define a ruler's righteousness in terms of the care that is given to the poor within his kingdom. Admittedly, there are difficulties in squeezing the theme of v. 2 into this scheme. Clearly the theme of v. 2 is concerned with "rulers" (*śārêhā*) and thus fits broadly into the thematic scheme. However, the criteria for good rulers are not specifically concerning the justice they provide for the poor. Rather it is the "lasting order" that they bring to the land. "Lasting order" only comes, however, because the ruler is a knowledgeable person. One could assume that proper care for all constituents in a society falls under the broad topic of "lasting order." Some scholars believe the saying to have arisen in reflection upon the phenomenon of many leaders who took the throne in the final days of the northern kingdom (cf. 2 Kgs 15:17-

---

Structure at a Glance: Proverbs 28

AΩ There may be more clues to structural organization than readers might initially imagine. A possible thematic super-structure organizes the sayings under the rubric of righteous rulers. (The structure of these two chapters adopted here rests mainly upon the ideas of Malchow.) Prov 28:2-3, 15-16; 29:2, 16; and a concluding Yahweh saying in 29:26 are general sayings on righteous vs. wicked rulers. Further, the sayings roughly divide each chapter in half, making four major subsections between the two chapters. The contents of each chapter deal predominantly with questions of social concern. Throughout the materials of ch. 28, there is an alternation between the law vs. the rich and the poor. Chapter 29 continues the concern with the poor but substitutes sayings on the fool in place of the law.

There are hints that the arrangement of sayings in the two halves of ch. 28 parallel each other. The first three verses of each half begin with the same sequence of topics. Prov 28:1-3 opens with a general saying contrasting the wicked and the righteous followed by two sayings on rulers. Likewise, vv. 14-16 open by contrasting the righteous and the wicked and also have two sayings on the ruler following them. In the case of vv. 3 and 15, the criterion for determining a just ruler is how he provides for the poor. The ensuing sequence of sayings in both halves continues to focus on the rich and the poor. Verses 4-13 are further distinctive through their reflection upon *tôrâ* along with concern for the poor.

There is then a thematic touchstone for interpretation of the sayings that readers encounter in these closing chapters of the collection in Prov 25–29. The following chart suggests the way the two halves of ch. 28 both parallel each other and organize their reflections.

28:1	Wicked vs. righteous	V. 14	Humble vs. hardhearted
Vv. 2-3	Rulers and the poor	Vv. 15-16	Rulers and the poor
Vv. 4-5	Keeping the law	Vv. 17-18	Examples of judgment
V. 6	The poor	V. 19	Work and poverty
V. 7	The law vs. greed	V. 20	The greedy punished
V. 8	Kindness to the poor	V. 21	Poverty subverts justice
V. 9	Failure to keep law	V. 22	The miser (greedy)
V. 10	Judgment on evil	V. 23	Health of rebuke
V. 11	Wisdom rich vs. poor	V. 24	Robbing parents to get rich
V. 12	Righteous vs. wicked	V. 25	The greedy
V. 13	Public vs. private sin	V. 26	Trust in one's own wits
		V. 27	Giving to the poor
		V. 28	Righteous vs. wicked

B. Malchow, "A Manual for Future Monarchs," CBQ 47 (1985): 238-45, as quoted in Roland E. Murphy, *Proverbs* (WBC 22; Nashville: Word, 1998), 213-14.

29; 17:1-18).[1] Modern readers, however, may look for many other possible historical contexts to fit the saying.

The translation of v. 3a, "A ruler who oppresses the poor," is an emendation of the MT, which literally reads, "A poor person who oppresses the poor." The adjustment to the text, substituting "ruler" (*ʿāšîr* or *rōʾš*) for "poor" (*rāš*), seems logical given the larger context of the chapter. However, in a literary world where there are frequent reversals of a reader's expectations, the text as it stands could envision a person who once was poor, who comes to power through the unlikely reversal of fortune, and then continues to engage in economic practices that are oppressive to poor folk.[2] Such reversals that allow slaves to become kings are loathed in Proverbs 30:21-23. Both the reversal and the lack of popularity of the one who obtains the throne are envisioned in Ecclesiastes

4:13-16. Qoheleth seems to accept the possibility as a part of the natural order of things.

Verses 4 and 5 assert the alternate theme for the remainder of the sub-collection (vv. 1-13). Verse 4 asserts the importance of *tôrâ* against our thematic touchstone in vv. 2 and 3. Exactly what is meant by *tôrâ* is not certain, even though NRSV translates the term "law." Readers will recall from earlier treatments (see [Torah Psalm]) that the term *tôrâ* broadly denotes instruction of a teacher, a priest, or a parent. However, it came to have a more focused signif-icance in the second temple period in denoting the Mosaic instruction, or law. *Tôrâ* was a specific reference to what has now become the Pentateuch, or first five books of the Bible. In the absence of compelling evidence that the term here means Mosaic law, it is probably better to take the more general significance. In any event, the meaning of the saying seems certain: forsaking authoritative instruction (*tôrâ*) assists the works of the wicked. Verse 5 sharpens the focus of v. 4 by asserting that wickedness is defined as a lack of justice (*mišpāṭ*).

Verses 6-11 (with the exception of vv. 9-10) are sayings that alter-nate thematically on *tôrâ* and proper treatment of the poor.[3] Verse 6 is a "better than" saying contrasting the integrity of the poor with the dishonesty of the rich. Verse 7 returns to *tôrâ* but contrasts those who keep to it with gluttons. The context allows readers to think of a glutton as more than one who merely drinks or eats too much (e.g., Prov 23:20; Deut 21:20). In Deut 21:20 the rebellious child is termed a *zôlēl*, or glutton, and may be disowned by parents. The saying in Proverbs 28:7 imagines gluttonous people as those who have enough to waste. Verse 8 returns explicitly to the rich and poor and assumes a kind of implicit order in the universe that protects the poor. Those who take "com-missions" (*nešek*) or charge "interest" (*tarbît*) will lose their money to those who show mercy on the poor. [Interest and Commission]

Verse 9 alternates back to the theme of *tôrâ* and claims that even the most pious activities are abominable to the Lord if they are not in accordance with the instructions of *tôrâ*. The language of 9b implies that Yahweh is only responding in kind to those who reject *tôrâ*: if

Interest and Commission

AΩ The difference between "commission" (*nešek*) and "interest" (*tarbît*) is that one is taken off the amount of the loan, and the other is added onto the repayment of the loan (McKane). The charging of interest on loans is known as early as Hammurabi's Babylon. With the minting of coins under the influence of the Persian empire (e.g., Ezra 2:69; 8:27), the practice of charging interest was made somewhat easier among the Judean refugees. It is interesting that the Hebrew word translated as "commission" stems from a word meaning "to bite" (*nāšak*). The term "interest" simply means "increase."

Both the charging of a commission and interest are outlawed for fellow Israelites in Lev 25:36-37, although it was permissible to charge interest to foreigners (Exod 22:25 and Deut 23:20). The prophet Ezekiel regards the charging of interest as a practice that separated the righteous from the abominable (e.g., 18:8, 13, 17; 22:12).

For further reading, see G. A. Barrois, "Debt, Debtor," *IDB* 1:809-10; Bruce Frier, "Interest and Usury in the Greco-Roman Period," *ABD* 3:423-24; and Harold S. Songer, "Coins and Money," *MDB*, 162.

William McKane, *Proverbs* (OTL; London: SCM Press, 1970), 627.

one does not "listen" to instruction, Yahweh will not listen to that person's prayer. A more explicit retributive image follows in v. 10. People who mislead the upright into evil will fall into disasters of their own making. The saying is interesting because it abandons the bipartite form characteristic of most of the sayings. Here, the third stich assures that, even though the upright have been led into paths of evil, if they are truly blameless (*tāmîm*), they will still inherit good.[4] The topic of stich C alludes to "inheriting" as one way of becoming rich. This easily fits in with the larger themes of the overall passage. Verse 11 contrasts the rich, who think they are wise, with the truly wise who see through the facade of the rich. In a word, rich people are not necessarily wise.

Verses 12 and 13 conclude the opening sub-collection with general sayings on the contrast between righteous and wicked. Verse 12 is a thematic duplication and also functions, with v. 13, to conclude the section. The similarities between vv. 12 and 28 are obvious. NRSV's translation of v. 12 emends the Hebrew text from "to rejoice" to "to triumph," however.[5] The emendation facilitates the parallelism between vv. 12 and 28, but is not necessary for it. An emendation would not be necessary if "to rejoice" were taken metonymically to signify triumph. Further, rejoicing of the righteous, given the larger context of the chapter, results when there is a righteous ruler. Verse 13 comments that true prosperity comes when there is absolute honesty and public acknowledgment of transgressions. In juxtaposition with v. 12, v. 13 may be putting forward yet another criterion defining the righteousness of the king.

NRSV's translation of v. 13 using the words "confesses" and "mercy" risks being overlooked because of readers' familiarity with those terms. One scholar observes that "v. 13 is the only sentence in Proverbs which contains a reference to the confession of sin, and that *môdeh* [to give thanks or praise] has the sense of confessing sin only here and in Ps. 32:5."[6] The Hebrew term *môdeh*, translated in NRSV as "confesses," is a Hiphil form of *yādâ*, "to throw or cast," which in this form means to "give thanks and praise" (e.g., Pss 44:8; 54:6; 99:3; 138:1). "I" language, that is, language that seems to stress individuality, usually occurs in psalms that function liturgically in the context of public worship. One possible implication of its occurrence here is suggesting that confession of sin is inextricably bound to the confession of faith through public worship. In Proverbs 17:9 one effectively conceals offenses from others by forgiving them. This is a virtue. Concealing one's own offenses, however, is not as virtuous.[7]

The Ruler and His Riches, 28:14-28

As we have already seen above, the opening three verses, vv. 14-16, provide a kind of thematic touchstone that connects the sayings that ensue. While vv. 15-16 clearly parallel vv. 2-3 in their treatment of rulers, v. 14 is slightly different from v. 1. If one takes "fear" to mean "piety," then one can make a reasonable case for v. 14 contrasting the pious with those who are impious. This parallels the contrast between righteous and wicked in v. 1. However, the word for fear (*mĕpaḥēd*) is not necessarily a term for piety. Rather, it stands in parallel with a word for "hardened heart" (*maqšeh libbô*) and therefore implies a virtue more like submissiveness and tenderness rather than righteousness.[8] Tenderness and submissiveness are necessary for a ruler who would be aware of the needs of the poor in his kingdom.

Verses 15 and 16 reflect upon unjust rulers. The ruler's power is imagined as that of roaring lions or charging bears; just as there is no way to stop such beasts, there is no stopping such power. One must simply get out of their way. Verse 16 contrasts the ruler who lacks understanding with one who hates unjust gain. It may well be that the lack of understanding, perhaps in the sense of having a hardened heart, leads to "cruel oppressions." Could it be that such oppressions come because rulers are not clever and are thus out of touch with the suffering they inadvertently cause? However, if rulers lack understanding but hate unjust gain, one could suppose there would not be cruel oppression and that they would have long lives. Could such a reading of the saying suggest that moral virtue is of more import in a ruler's work than intellectual virtue? Readers may recall that v. 2 also speculates upon the performance of an "intelligent ruler." There, however, intelligence prevents rulers from "unjust gain."

The strategy of thematic alternation applies much more randomly in this half of the chapter. Verses 17 and 18 contain two sayings that reflect upon the fates of the unrighteous. The theme follows well from the concern for "unjust gain" of the king in v. 16. NRSV's translation of v. 17 envisions a murderer "burdened" with the blood of another; most scholars take this to refer to a murderer who is on the run. The Hebrew word translated "burdened," *ʿāšuq*, is literally "oppressed" and is an unlikely context for its occurrence. Even so, the verse envisions the practice of allowing certain people to find asylum in designated cities (e.g., Deut 19:1-10; Josh 20.) Verse 18 is a more general statement about the "crooked" falling into their own snares. The two sayings, vv. 17 and 18, are linked by

Tilling the Land
An Egyptian model from the sixth–eleventh dynasties depicts the work of tilling the ground using a single plow and two oxen yoked together.

Team of Plowing Oxen. Painted wood. Egyptian. Middle Kingdom, 1st Intermediate Period. 16 cm x 23 cm. Louvre. Paris, France.

their punning on the words "burdened," *ʿāšuq*, and "crooked," *neʿqaš*, and by the use of synonyms for death, *bôr* and *šāhat*.[9]

Verses 19-22 treat various aspects of wealth versus poverty. Verse 19 offers a different perspective from that which we saw in the first half of the book. It asserts the importance of work over against "worthless pursuits" in the avoidance of poverty. This same view is expressed in 12:11. Verses 20 and 22 reflect upon those who are "in a hurry" to get rich. The ethos of the sages caused them to be suspicious of getting in a hurry and tended to associate premature wealth with evil intentions (cf. 19:2; 20:21). Waiting on God to provide timely reward is the supreme value. Verse 21 is of interest because of its indirect interest in matters concerning the rich versus the poor. In the first place, its distinction is in asserting what is "not good." We see far more often sayings that assert what is either "good" or "better." A court of law would be the more appropriate background for this sentence. In the second place, the circumstances that make this a true saying have to include impoverished people since impoverished people may be so because someone did not show them partiality. Readers may ask what it would take to subvert justice, especially if it were for a just cause, such as rectifying and eliminating poverty.

Verses 23-28 open with a saying on honest rebuke. True friends are those who may be brutally honest (cf. 19:25; 25:12; 27:5). In the present context one might construe the saying to assert flattery as another possible way of obtaining wealth. Verse 24 concerns seizing property from parents. The prophet Micah is remembered as having condemned such activity (cf. Mic 2:2). But readers are called upon to imagine not only in what way parents would be robbed, but also that the robber might argue that it was not a crime. Clifford imagines a scenario in which children who remain at home even after marriage gradually take over the household and the wealth before it is legally theirs.[10] Verse 25 is about a person who seeks to be wealthy. Here is a Yahweh saying where greed is contrasted with trust in Yahweh. Only through such trust can one find riches. Verse 26 abandons the general theme of wealth versus poverty to elaborate the notion of trust (*bôṭēaḥ*) that is introduced in v. 25. Both sayings share this vocabulary. Trusting one's own wits stands in sharp contrast to trusting in the Lord. Presumably, walking in wisdom means also trusting in Yahweh.

Verses 27 and 28 conclude the chapter by reasserting themes that govern most of the sayings in the chapter: concern for the poor and the comparison between righteous and wicked. Verse 27 contrasts v. 25 by reflecting upon the riches that come to those who give to the poor. Ignoring the cries of the poor is the surest way to poverty. Verse 28 explores the result of unrighteous rulers: righteous people go into hiding in order to avoid the injustice that permeates society.

CONNECTIONS

Rich and Poor Are Inextricably Bound

This chapter of sayings reminds the reader of the importance of care for the poor. The reality of poverty is made even more poignant in contrast to the competing reality of those who are wealthy. The problems an impoverished community raises for a just ruler are enormous. The sayings seem to be aware that as important as work, diligence, persistence, and piety is the economic system that makes all of it work. How does a ruler ensure an economy that both privileges the creation of wealth, thus favoring the wealthy, and creates opportunities and protections for the poor? The dilemma confronts every society, and it is seldom addressed effec-

Martin Luther King Jr. and the Letter from Birmingham

Martin Luther King Jr. (1929–1968), African-American preacher and theologian, provided arguably the most influential voice of leadership advocating black civil rights through the early sixties in the United States until his assassination in 1968. In 1963, while serving as president of the Southern Christian Leadership Conference, King came under attack from clergy because of his public statements and his imprisonment. His letter from a prison in Birmingham, Alabama, seeks to answer those criticisms. In so doing, he maintains the tradition of providing a timely word for Christians even though imprisoned (as, say, Dietrich Bonhoeffer or Paul the Apostle).

For further reading, see Richard Lischer, *The Preacher King* (New York: Oxford University Press, 1995); Lewis V. Baldwin, *There Is a Balm in Gilead: The Cultural Roots of Martin Luther King, Jr.* (Minneapolis: Fortress, 1991); and Martin Luther King, 1929–1968, *The Speeches of Martin Luther King,* (United States: MPI Home Video, 1988).

---

tively. Perhaps one of the guiding principles is understanding the relationship between the rich and the poor.

In his "Letter from Birmingham City Jail," Martin Luther King, Jr., reminded his audience of the principle of connectedness. [Martin Luther King Jr. and the Letter from Birmingham] While the letter offers explanation for his nonviolent approach and the urgency of moving immediately, one of his opening observations is of singular importance.

> Moreover, I am cognizant of the interrelatedness of all communities and states. I cannot sit idly by in Atlanta and not be concerned about what happens in Birmingham. Injustice anywhere is a threat to justice everywhere. We are caught in an inescapable network of mutuality, tied in a single garment of destiny. Whatever affects one directly affects all indirectly. Never again can we afford to live with the narrow, provincial "outside agitator" idea. Anyone who lives in the United States can never be considered an outsider anywhere in this country.[11]

It seems that the idea of interconnectedness was for King as important to an economy as it was to a rationale for civil rights. Leaders and members of society must understand that what happens to the rich and the poor affects everyone. Members of a community are just that: members of something that is much larger than their individual needs and concerns. Our modern day celebrates the elevation of the individual to such an extent that it has overshadowed the reality of this community principle. Society's task is to identify the inequities that exist and eliminate them. Allowing inequities to stand only hurts the well-being of the whole. The question is whether modern, wealthy, privileged American society is spiritually and intellectually able to wrestle with such problems.

NOTES

[1] According to William McKane, *Proverbs* (OTL; London: SCM Press, 1970), 630, the Deuteronomistic History suggests that many rulers in the North brought on political instability that led to its downfall.

[2] Both Roland E. Murphy, *Proverbs* (WBC 22; Nashville: Word, 1998), 211, and Richard Clifford, *Proverbs* (OTL; Louisville: Westminster John Knox Press, 1999), 243, retain the MT without emendation.

[3] Duane A. Garrett, *Proverbs, Ecclesiastes, Song of Songs* (NAC 14; Nashville: Broadman, 1993), 222, believes that vv. 3-11 establish a two-part parallel arrangement through these alternations of thematic concern.

[4] Murphy, *Proverbs,* 213, notes the verse is overloaded and suspects that 10b has been added. *BHS* would delete stich C instead of B.

[5] See Murphy, *Proverbs,* 216.

[6] McKane, *Proverbs,* 627; Murphy, *Proverbs,* 216

[7] Clifford, *Proverbs,* 245.

[8] NIV translates "Blessed is the man who always fears the LORD."

[9] This reading emends MT from *bĕ'eḥāt* to *bĕšāḥat.*

[10] Clifford, *Proverbs,* 247.

[11] Quoted from Martin Luther King, Jr., "Letter from Birmingham City Jail" (Philadelphia: American Friends Service Committee, 1963).

SOCIETY AND GOOD GOVERNMENT

Proverbs 29:1-27

This concluding chapter in the final Solomonic/Hezekian collection is very similar to chapter 28. Again, the dominant form of saying is the antithetic or contrastive type, and the opposition between the righteous and the wicked is the most common thematic characteristic throughout. The same subtexts as in chapter 28 continue here. Verses 4, 12, 14, and 26 continue the reflection upon the righteous "king" or "ruler." Further, there continue to be periodic references to the teaching of children (vv. 3, 15, and 17). These various social concerns positioned under the rubrics of the righteous versus the wicked, and the model righteous king, imply an overall thematic concern with good government.[1] [Structure at a Glance: Proverbs 29]

Structure at a Glance: Proverbs 29

AΩ Readers may subdivide this chapter broadly into two halves: vv. 1-14 and vv. 15-27. Verse 1 deals with discipline and a person who refuses to learn. Verse 15 opens with the topic of discipline, sharing with v. 1 the word for "reproof," *tôkāḥôt*. Following vv. 2 and 16, in parallel sequence, are sayings on the results of authority of the righteous vs. that of the wicked. Verses 2 and 17 offer sayings on the discipline for children. Verses 4 and 18 concern the stability of the land.

There seems also to be a linear arrangement of the sayings in this chapter. Verses 2 and 12-14 frame the first half of the collection with sayings on the righteous ruler. Since v. 7 first raises the topic of the poor, which is revisited in vv. 13 and 14, then the natural subdivision in this opening half is vv. 1-6 and 7-14. The second half of the chapter has a framework on kingship, vv. 15 and 26. The first half of that subunit is more concerned with teaching children, especially slaves (vv. 20 and 21). The latter half consists of more general reflections on anger, crime, and trust in Yahweh. The parallels and framing devices are suggestive for reading and interpreting the overall aims of the collection:

V.1 One who is reproved (*tôkāḥôt*)	V. 15 The rod and reproof (*tôkaḥat*)
V. 2. Righteous vs. wicked	V. 16 The rule of the wicked
Vv. 12-13 The righteous ruler	Vv. 17-21 Rule of children and servant
V. 14 Kingship and the poor	Vv. 26-27 The just ruler

The structure of the chapter is suggested as follows:

Vv. 1-6 Righteous kingship and education
Vv. 7-14 Provision for the poor
Vv. 15-21 Teaching wisdom
Vv. 22-17 General social concerns

COMMENTARY

The Righteous King, 29:1-6

The various sub-themes set out in these verses cohere around the social implications of the rule of the righteous king. Verses 1-4 alternate on various aspects of learning and kingship, while vv. 5-6 are a pair of reflections upon the righteous and the wicked.

The opening verse offers a candid reflection on a familiar topic: some people just cannot learn or change. We have already encountered reflections on the eventual fate of such people in 12:1 and 15:10 (cf. Exod 32:9; Deut 31:27). Such people are incapable of learning, and the constant rebukes from instructors eventually shatter them into a state from which there is no recovery. Verse 3 offers a more concrete example of the concerns in v.1. Some children please their parents; some squander their inheritance on prostitutes. Verse 2 returns to the overall thematic assertion of chapters 28 and 29 on kingship and righteousness (e.g., 28:2-3, 12, 15-16, 28; 29:16, 27). Readers may wonder about the rule of a king and the problem of people who cannot or will not learn. But v. 4 provides a more concrete problem. Stability comes to a land because of justice. Certainly part of that justice has to do with fair maintenance of the economy of the land, as might be implied in NRSV's rendering of stich B as "one who makes heavy exactions ruins it." [Economic Justice]

While the sayings that conclude this opening section, vv. 5 and 6, are about a flatterer and a transgressor, in the larger context they provide lenses through which to view the king. Those who obtain

---

Economic Justice

AΩ The theme of economic justice is suggested throughout the chapter in sayings that explicitly concern rights of the poor (e.g., 29:7, 13, 14). Matters of just taxation, which is the conventional way of reading v. 4, would also seem to speak to the responsibility of the king to avoid "heavy exactions." However, the word NRSV translates as "heavy exactions," and which readers construe as having to do with taxation in some way, is the Hebrew *tĕrûmôt*. The word means literally "things lifted up," stemming from the root *rûm*, to be high, exalted, or lifted up. The term is not one that on its own denotes taxation, even though it commonly denotes contribution or offerings for cultic purposes (Exod 25:2; 30:14; Deut 12:6, 11; Ezek 45:13, 16). (Duane A. Garret takes the term as "bribes.")

More typical language for taxation would include *mekes* from the root *kāsas*, "to compute" (Num 31:28), or the Aramaic term *mindâ* (e.g., Ezra 4:13; 6:8; 7:24), cognate with the Hebrew feminine noun *middâ*, from the root *mādad*, meaning "to measure." What is interesting, however, is that the Hiphil verbal form of *rûm* occurs in Num 31:28 as the subject of the noun *mekes*. The command in that context is to "lift" or "cause to be lifted" a tax or exaction. So it may well be that the noun that comes to function as contribution is related to the idea of taking a tax.

For further reading, see Gösta W. Ahlström, "Administration of the State in Canaan and Ancient Israel," *CANE* 1:587-603; J. A. Sanders, "Tax, Taxes," *IDB* 4:520-22; and Daniel Snell, "Taxes and Taxation," *ABD* 6:338-41.

Duane A. Garrett, *Proverbs, Ecclesiastes, Song of Songs* (NAC 14; Nashville: Broadman, 1993), 228.

their ends through flattery are not to be trusted. This goes for a
king as well. In the end, both the flatterer and the transgressor are
snares and traps. The connection between these two sayings stems
form the verbal correspondence between the synonyms for trap and
snare, *rešet* and *môqēš.*

Care for the Poor in the "Thoughtful" Society, 29:7-14

Verses 7-14 function as a second sub-collection, opening with a
saying on the poor and closing with two sayings that address the
topic, vv. 13-14. The series in vv. 8-11 reflects upon scoffers and
fools and provides relevant counterparts to the topic of the education of children.

The saying in v. 7 compares the knowledge that righteous and
wicked people have concerning the rights of the poor. The specific
language translated "rights" (*dîn*) may imply some kind of judicial
setting.[2] The saying is relevant thematically in its contrast of the
righteous and wicked, in its concern for the poor (*dallîm*), and in
its recognition of the importance of knowledge, an aspect of
wisdom. The reference to knowledge provides a basis for readers to
connect the following four sayings, which seem to be laid out in
alternating fashion, just as in vv. 1-4 above.[3]

Verse 8 parallels v. 10 semantically. Verse 8 contrasts the scoffers,
'anšê lāṣôn, with the wise; v. 10 contrasts the "bloodthirsty," *'anšê
dāmîm,* with the upright. It may well be that by paralleling v. 8 on
scoffers with v. 10 on criminals, the overall sense of the danger of
scoffers intensifies. One thinks of a scoffer as a criminal, in other
words. Verses 9 and 11 contrast the wise and the foolish. Verse 11
might be a lens through which to understand v. 9. The behavior of
the fool is such that it makes a mockery of any proceeding of a
court. The two outer sayings in this unit, vv. 8 and 11, both have
phrases that contrast the foolish and the wise person's ability to
hold back their anger.

The final verses in the first half of the chapter, vv. 12-14, work
together to reiterate the concern for the righteous ruler and the criterion of a society's provision for the poor. Verse 12 asserts an
important means of recognizing rulers: their court. If a ruler's officials are wicked, then so are they. Verse 13, the only Yahweh saying
in the first half, emphasizes a basis on which one might argue to
care for the poor—Yahweh created both rich and poor (cf. 22:2).
On the other hand, since Yahweh is to blame for the existence of
the oppressor—the rich person—is the oppression that follows
legitimate? Verse 14 helps readers to understand the importance of

v. 12 and the righteousness of the king. The Lord may well have made both the oppressor and the oppressed, but it is the judgments of the king that maintain justice in the social realm.

The Society of Yahweh, 29:15-27

These verses comprise a parallel response to the first half of the chapter. The final conclusion is that righteousness ultimately comes from Yahweh. Verses 15-17 are sequentially parallel to vv. 1-3. Verses 26-27 offer observations on the righteous ruler, reminding readers of one of the recurring themes of chapters 28–29.

Verses 15-18 alternate between concern with education and concern with the role of the righteous king. One could easily see these verses as a further contrast on public authority versus private education (in the home).[4] Verses 15 and 17 reflect upon the discipline and education of children, seeing corporal punishment as a kind of "tough love" (cf. 13:24; 19:18; 22:15; 23:13-14). Neglecting to give a child this kind of attention is shameful. In v. 15 the mother is shamed with no mention of the father. Verse 3, however, refers to the father's shame and neglects the mother (NRSV translates *'abîw* as "his parent" instead of "his father" in v. 3). Verse 18 considers society's need for prophecy. The word "prophecy" translates the Hebrew word *ḥāzôn,* which in prophetic literature denotes the vision or revelation that prophets receive. It occurs in Proverbs only here. The word is paralleled by the word *tôrâ,* translated in the Proverbs as instruction. As noted earlier, the term came eventually to designate what we now refer to as the Pentateuch. There is no way to be certain of its meaning here. Further, although it is provocative, it is ultimately unanswerable whether the wisdom saying advocates appeal to a prophet over one's appeal to intellect.[5]

Righteous Rule

Pharaoh Seti I nurses at the breast of a goddess. Such affinities with deity ensured the king's righteous rule on earth.

Prophecy and Law

AΩ The saying in v. 18 makes an interesting juxtaposition between "vision" (*ḥāzôn*) and "instruction" (*tôrâ*). The two terms are interesting in their own rights. Vision is a term that occurs typically in prophetic contexts, denoting the prophetic task of envisioning the will of God (e.g., Hos 12:11; Ezek 7:13; 1 Sam 3:1) and receiving through that vision some divine communication. The term functions in titles of prophetic books (e.g., Nah 1:1) and defines the nature of oracles that are included in books (2 Chr 32:32).

Torah (*tôrâ*) designates in Proverbs the instruction of the sages. However, it came to be a technical term for Mosaic Law in the second temple period, and eventually the first five books of the Hebrew Bible. The question raised in this verse is whether prophetic activity is being equated with wisdom instruction or Mosaic Law? In the former case, the implication might be that wisdom is moving beyond human observation to more ecstatic modes of authority, which would seem to be a departure from the worldview of wisdom. The latter implication is that wisdom may now be identified with Mosaic Law.

William McKane suggests the saying reflects the second temple period when the authority of the old prophetic office was dying out and the Mosaic Law was taking its place. The implications for kingship are also significant. Readers may wish to examine the biblical narrative of Josiah's seeking a prophetic word form Hulda the prophetess (2 Kgs 22:14-20). In that episode the newly discovered law code (22:8-10) is not so authoritative that the king neglects to seek a prophetic word.

For further reading, see John Barton, "Prophecy (Postexilic Hebrew)," *ABD* 5:489-95; Joseph Blenkinsopp, *A History of Prophecy in Israel* (Philadelphia: Fortress, 1983); and John J. Schmitt, "Prophecy (Preexilic Hebrew)," *ABD* 5:482-89.

William McKane, *Proverbs* (OTL; London: SCM Press, 1970), 638.

However, NRSV makes explicit here that when prophecy or vision generally is lacking, there is no guidance for the people or the king. [Prophecy and Law]

Verses 19-21 form a cluster of sayings on the theme of educating servants. Verses 19 and 21 share terms for "slave" (*ʿebed*); vv. 19 and 20 share terms for "words" or "things" (*dĕbārîm*). While the emphasis upon "words" is relevant to education, that the servant is the one to be educated creates a special situation. Verse 19 makes clear that words alone are insufficient apart from corporal punishment. However, the covenant code provides a boundary for such punishment (cf. Exod 21:20-21, 26-27). Likewise, Proverbs 29:21 asserts that pampering a slave will only lead to a negative end. Readers might wonder how this view is any different from the attitude toward the education of one's own children in v. 15. Verse 20 considers the one who is too quick to speak, perhaps to form a judgment. In between the two sayings on educating a servant, the saying in v. 20 serves to direct the reader's attention away from pedagogies other than those through speech. Although, if "words" are analogous to "deeds,"[6] then haste in deeds, perhaps in the punishment of a servant, is also to be viewed cautiously.

Verses 22-23 are paired with the synonyms "anger" (*'ap*) and "spirit" (*rûaḥ*). We have seen sayings on anger already (e.g., 14:17, 29; 15:18) and sayings where both these words are paired (e.g., 14:29; 16:32). Verse 22 simply observes that uncontrolled anger leads to conflict. The inability to control such anger may have to do with pride, as v. 23 implies. Lowliness of spirit (humility) is the first step in finding such control.

Verse 24 is important since a society depends upon the effective workings of the courts. The saying is related to Leviticus 5:1 on giving witness. One who knows of a crime and fails to testify should be punished. If because of a friendship one refuses to bear witness against a criminal, then the oath that is invoked to determine the truth (enforced by Yahweh, see [Job's Oath]) falls upon the witness as well as the criminal.

The conclusion to the chapter follows with vv. 25-27. Both vv. 25 and 26 are Yahweh sayings. Verse 25 urges trust in Yahweh rather than fear of people. Verse 26 stresses that social justice ultimately comes from Yahweh. It is therefore more important to seek Yahweh than to curry favor with a king. As a reflection upon the preceding saying, v. 26 provides a boundary for regarding even a king: the king never receives the reverence due Yahweh alone. Verse 27, the final saying in the collection of chapters 25–27, contrasts the righteous with the wicked by invoking the criterion of justice and abomination. The former is the central governing social principle; the latter assumes that Yahweh is ultimately the judge. The verse begins with the Hebrew letter "*taw*," the final letter in the Hebrew alphabet, implying conclusion and completion.

CONNECTIONS

The Government and the King

The chapter arranges sayings so that readers face the reality that good government, effective education, and the righteous king are all greater than the sums of their parts. Even the sayings give expression to a multifaceted reality that informs each subject's thinking about the nature of good government. But, as intriguing as the problems of education are, that there is a collection of sayings setting out these competing social realities and their competing values implies something about the sages' expectations of the level of education of the person of faith.

John Stuart Mill, a nineteenth century British economist and philosopher (1806–1873), is known for his systematic rethinking and application of the utilitarian philosophy of Jeremy Bentham to the moral and political issues of his time and society. In exploring the constituent elements of good government, Mill shows the then current notion of "Order and Progress" to be of little use in defining good government. The components of order are at odds with the components of progress. Rather, Mill understands good government to be government that makes the individual community members good.

> It [the foundation of good government] consists partly of the degree in which they promote the general mental advancement of the community, including under that phrase advancement in intellect, in virtue, and in practical activity and efficiency; and partly of the degree of perfection with which they organize the moral, intellectual, and active worth already existing, so as to operate with the greatest effect on public affairs.[7]

Such is the function of this collection of sayings. Indeed, they are concerned with the opposition between those whom one must educate and the uneducable. The implication is that the criterion for the effective government of a king is his provision and maintenance of justice for all members of the society, especially the disenfranchised and the powerless that live within his society. These problems are the fabric of these very instructions. Instruction in the Proverbs consists of the struggle with the intellectual challenges that stand behind the social dilemmas confronting a society. It is the well-educated, the thinking community, that will have the intellectual and spiritual abilities to wrestle with the problems of society.

NOTES

[1] Roland E. Murphy, *Proverbs* (WBC 22; Nashville: Word, 1998), 220, doubts that the governing theme of the collection concerns kings.

[2] Murphy, *Proverbs,* 221.

[3] Duane A. Garrett, *Proverbs, Ecclesiastes, Song of Songs* (NAC 14; Nashville: Broadman, 1993), 229, also sees such a connection. He calls it an ABAB pattern with catchwords on "wise" and "fool."

[4] Ibid., 231.

[5] KJV translates as "vision"; NAS translates as "vision." See Murphy, *Proverbs,* 222-23; Richard Clifford, *Proverbs* (OTL; Louisville: Westminster John Knox Press, 1999), 253-54; William McKane, *Proverbs* (OTL; London: SCM Press, 1970), 638.

[6] Murphy, *Proverbs,* 223.

[7] John Stuart Mill, "Representative Government," in *On Liberty and Other Essays*, ed. John Gray (Oxford and New York: Oxford University Press, 1991), 229.

RIDDLED WITH QUESTIONS

Proverbs 30:1-33

Looking at Wisdom Backward and Forward, 30–31

The final two chapters of Proverbs are appendices that have been attached to help sum up and close out the ideas in the various preceding collections. We may consider the two chapters in roughly four parts. Both chapters 30 and 31 have opening instructions set under the headings of unknown people. We know nothing of Agur, 30:1. It is also of great interest that within this Israelite collection there is a non-Israelite author, "Lemuel, king of Massa," 31:1. We will read the materials in 30:1-9 as a unit and the materials in vv. 10-33 as a collection of different instructions only loosely connected with each other. Proverbs 31:1-9 stands under the heading of the instructions from king Lemuel, and 31:10-31 closes the book of Proverbs with a retrospective on the *ʾēšet ḥayil*, "the capable wife/the valorous woman."

These final four sections both provide retrospect and give the reader a prospect of Ecclesiastes, which in most ancient and modern canonical lists immediately follows Proverbs. The retrospect allows readers to revisit themes of kingship, righteousness versus wickedness, and the general ethos of wisdom's efficacy. These familiar themes and values are put forward here in mostly new forms, especially the numerical sayings of 30:21-33 (only otherwise encountered in Prov 6). The numerical format of these sayings, tied closely through their emphasis upon nature, is familiar to readers thematically. The new format, however, allows readers to experience the topics anew.

The chapters also provide a prospect to Ecclesiastes, because there is both theological questioning and instruction that comes from a king. Readers of Ecclesiastes will see that Qoheleth (the Hebrew name of the book; see Introduction to Ecclesiastes) offers his wisdom, initially, through the voice of a king. We will discuss 30:1-9 as a montage of perspectives that both challenge and defend wisdom's assumptions about Yahweh and its own authority. We shall see a similar juxtaposition of perspectives repeatedly throughout the book of Ecclesiastes. Further, the concluding chapter of Proverbs opens with an admonition from a king. The poem on the "capable wife"

(*ʾeset ḥayil*), while not likely authored by this king, or his mother, nevertheless stands within the perspective of this opening royal framework. Even this concluding poem, then, anticipates well the opening of Ecclesiastes, which puts forward its instructions as echoing a king's point of view.

Riddled with Questions, 30:1-33

The penultimate chapter of the book of Proverbs combines a cacophony of voices that raise questions as well as offer answers. The answers, however, are cast in what sound more like riddles. No single theme dominates the collection. In fact, just the opposite is true. A wondrous variation of ideas and forms seems to be the rule. Nevertheless, the heading, "The Words of Agur son of Jakeh. An oracle," invites readers to consider the possibility that the entire unit derives both its authority and its origins from this source (cf. Eccl 1:12–2:26). Taken in this way, Agur's oracle includes serious questioning, vv. 1-9, and clever numerical sayings interspersed with instruction, vv. 10-33. [Structure at a Glance: Proverbs 30]

Structure at a Glance: Proverbs 30

AΩ The chapter may be divided into more than two major sections. While we are reading vv. 1-9 together in this treatment (following R. N. Whybray's suggestion that "curse" in v. 10 seems to connect more with vv. 11-14 than with what precedes in vv. 1-9.), this is not the only possible way to coordinate the chapter's arrangement. Richard J. Clifford, for instance, arranges vv. 1-10 into a section because he sees vv. 1-5 and 7-9 as two coherent units separated by v. 6 and concluded by v. 10. Verse 10 has the same syntax as v. 6, and for that reason is included in the opening verses. Leo Perdue, on the other hand, is less sure about placing v. 10 with vv. 1-9. He simply refers to it as a "redactional insertion." The LXX treats vv. 1-14 as a unity, although, as mentioned above, not under the heading of "The words of Agur." In the LXX these verses follow 24:1-22 and are themselves followed by what is now 24:23-34. It is interesting that an ancient reader did not see 30:1-14 as being joined with 30:15-33. A natural break may indeed occur, since the sayings in vv. 11-14 are not themselves numerical sayings as are most of those in 15-33. Although vv. 11-13 list phenomena, they do not enumerate them.

There are at least two different voices within the opening unit (vv. 1-9): one raising questions, vv. 1-4; and one offering the perspective of pious submission with a prayer, vv. 5-9. A miscellaneous collection of numerical

sayings follows (cf. Prov 6:16-19). These concluding riddle-like sayings do not appear to be connected by any dominant theme, although there may be connections through catchwords (Murphy; Clifford).

Readers may find the following organization helpful as they work through the chapter.

    Vv. 1-9 Who Knows?
      Vv. 1-4b Questioning
      Vv. 5-9 The Response of Prayer
    Vv. 10-33 Enumerating Instruction
      V. 10 Don't meddle in others' matters
      Vv. 11-14 On parents and the poor
      Vv. 15-16 Things that cannot be satisfied
      V. 17 Scorn for parents
      Vv. 18-19 Ways that are hidden
      V. 20 The way of an adulteress
      Vv. 21-23 Reversals of order
      Vv. 24-28 The small are great
      Vv. 29-31 The nature of kings
      Vv. 32-33 Instruction on restraint

Richard J. Clifford, *Proverbs* (OTL; Louisville: Westminster John Knox Press, 1999), 257.

Roland E. Murphy, *Proverbs* (WBC 22; Nashville: Word, 1998), 226-27.

Leo Perdue, *Proverbs* (IBC; Louisville: Westminster John Knox Press, 2000), 253.

R. N. Whybray, *The Composition of the Book of Proverbs* (JSOTSup 168; Sheffield: JSOT Press, 1994), 149-50.

COMMENTARY

Who Knows? 30:1-9

The opening section is provocative and difficult to read for several reasons. First, the superscription uses prophetic language, "an oracle" (*hammaśśāʾ*), yet what follows does not appear to be like any prophetic oracle with which biblical readers might be familiar. The attribution to Agur does not help, since he is not known in biblical literature. Second, v. 4 suddenly abandons the grammatical first person for a series of rhetorical questions. Are we to understand the speaker of vv. 1b-3 to be asking these questions? Do they have as their rhetorical subject God (that is, the answer to each question points toward God) or humankind (their answer points to a person)? If the former, then they are offered as a pious response to the preceding assertions of the doubter. If the latter, then they are offered by the initial speaker to elaborate his doubt that humans, who are finite, may know the things of God. Finally, vv. 5-6 offer a pious assertion that God's word cannot fail. First person language returns in vv. 7-9, but now readers must determine whether the speaker is the initial voice or another.

Verses 1-4 are translated by NRSV as a unit, which implies that we are to hear the same speaker throughout. In this case v. 4 is a part of the original speaker's questioning. The Hebrew word *hammaśśāʾ* in v. 1a may mean "oracle," as in NRSV, or "burden," as in Jeremiah 17:21. It can also denote a "Massaite," that is, a member of Arabian tribe, as in Genesis 25:14 and 1 Chronicles 1:30. Scholars believe that it should be taken as a reference to the Arabian tribe. In this case, Agur is a Massaite. More significantly, these words are attributed to a non-Israelite chief.[1] Verses 2 and 3 introduce the rhetorical questions of v. 4 by calling attention to the irony that, since wisdom comes from God (one of wisdom's central theological tenets), one cannot be wise if one has not ascended to God. In these questions, this speaker is being radically literal in his interpretation of human inferiority to God. The questions in v. 4 make this clear: what human being and his son have achieved any of these things necessary to find wisdom? The obvious answer is no one. This idea occurs also in Deuteronomy 30:12-14, although that text makes the opposite point: "No, the word is very near to you; it is in your mouth and in your heart for you to observe" (v. 14). The end result in Proverbs 30:4 is an intellectual weariness with reflecting upon the origins of wisdom, v. 1. Such assertions of frustration and weariness accompany other literary reflections upon

"I Am Weary"

AΩ NRSV's translation of v. 1 is highly reliable but gives readers no idea of the state of the MT, the process of reaching such a translation, or any inkling of other possible translations. As the MT stands it is possible to read v. 1 as an address: "An oracle of the man: to Ithiel, to Ithiel and to Ucal." The LXX translation reads, "my words are to be feared, my son, keep them," suggesting that the present text of the MT may be corrupt. Scholars usually seek to redistribute the consonants in this line of poetry in search of other possible meanings. However, two important criteria govern such redistribution: first, the consonants given in the Hebrew text must be retained, and second, meanings must be sought that are consistent with the larger context of despair and doubt.

Several other meanings are possible. One proposal is, "O that God were with me, O that God were with me." A second is, "Who has exerted himself much with God, who has exerted himself much with God and triumphed?" A third is, "I am not God, I am not God that I should have power." Finally, a fourth is, "There is no God, there is no God and I cannot know anything" (McKane; Garrett). The NRSV translation provides a particular understanding of the text in its present form, but readers must be cautious not to think that this is absolutely certain. Some things we simply cannot know.

For further reading, see Richard Clifford, "Observations on the Text and Versions of Proverbs," in *Wisdom, You Are My Sister* (CBQMS 29; Washington, DC: Catholic Biblical Association, 1997); and Haber Heriberito, "The LXX and the Bible: Matter for Thought," *JBQ* 24 (1996): 260-61.

Duane A. Garrett, *Proverbs, Ecclesiastes, Song of Songs* (NAC 14; Nashville: Broadman, 1993), 236.

William McKane, *Proverbs* (OTL; London: SCM Press, 1970), 644.

---

knowledge, too (e.g., Pss 73:22; 92:6). Readers who have made their way through Proverbs to this point are themselves perhaps willing to identify with this speaker's frustrations. ["I Am Weary"]

Verses 5-9 consist of a pious response to the questions in vv. 1-4 and a prayer that asserts a kind of middle ground for those who recognize the reasonable doubts of the speaker of vv. 1-4. This does not mean, however, that the speaker does not wish to continue his search for wisdom. In vv. 5-6 we hear the voice of pious confidence asserting the reliability of the word of God. The assertion of v. 5 that the "word of God is pure" is nearly identical to such assertions in Psalm 18:30. Proverbs 30:6 bears strong resemblance to Deuteronomy 4:2 in its admonition not to add anything to the word of God (see Sir 18:5-6).

Verses 7-9 offer a first person prayer addressing the deity (vv. 7 and 9). This is unique in the book of Proverbs. The prayer returns to a theme readers have frequently seen—wealth and poverty (e.g., Prov 10:4, 15; 13:7, 8; 14:20; 18:23; 22:2, 7; chs. 28–29). What is striking is the suppliant's apparent recognition of the impact of sociological circumstances on one's faith. Neither riches nor poverty are desirable. The fullness that results from wealth leads to the denial of the Lord. The want that results from poverty leads to crime and profaning God's name.

From the reader's perspective, our supplicant offers a kind of middle ground as a basis for relationship to God. This middle ground begins with reality as one sees it: one may not deny the existence of either poverty or wealth. One must acknowledge that one's understanding of God may be shaped by one's social situation. Searching for wisdom is seeking for a middle ground between serious questioning (e.g., vv. 1-4) and pious prayer. The sage there is neither stupid, as he states ironically, nor has he ascended to heaven. Rather, he has absolute proof of wisdom's central theological claims.

Enumerating Instruction, 30:10-33

The second half of the chapter consists of a few instructions and several numerical sayings. There does not seem to be any structured sequence of thematic clustering. Verses 10 and 32 seem to be instructions. Verse 10 is unambiguous in its use of a prohibition. The action of "putting the hand to the mouth" in the context of the foolish behavior implies an admonition in v. 32. Verses 15a and 17 are sayings of the sort we read in chapters 25–29. The balance of the material in this section is formulated in the more stylized form of numerical sayings.

Verse 10 is not connected thematically to any others, unless perhaps one considers that both vv. 10 and 11 use the word for curse (*qālal*).[2] The cursing of a servant (v. 10) and the cursing of a parent (v. 11) are thematically much different. Readers might wonder, however, how a curse may be efficacious, unless it is one where the object of the curse is guilty in advance (cf. Prov 26:2). In the case of the servant, such guilt would make speaking to his master at least legitimate. Nevertheless, one should not get involved in the affairs of others.

Verses 11-14 do not contain numerical sayings of the type that we see in the remainder 30:15-33 (see above). Readers easily recognize the absence of the typical sequencing of phenomena according to numerical increments. But the verses are related formally to those that follow in that they list several phenomena. These verses present four people who are repugnant to the sages. Their behavior is antisocial and therefore unwholesome for the community. In the Hebrew text each line opens with the word "generation" (*dôr*), establishing a rhetorical pattern that holds together the four different kinds of people mentioned. The two outer people, mentioned in vv. 11 and 14, are guilty of very specific crimes: cursing parents and devouring the poor. Readers familiar with the

Covenant Code (Exod 21–23) will remember that cursing parents is condemned (Exod 21:15, 17). The two central descriptions, in vv. 12 and 13, characterize generally the people who would perpetrate such acts. Such people fail to recognize their ways; they have problems with self-awareness. In addition to their being unaware of their sinfulness, the sages conclude that they are so because they are arrogant (cf. Prov 6:17; 21:4). Verse 14 reflects upon the poor and thus implies some connection between one's personal treatment of parents and one's public attitude toward and treatment of the poor.

Verses 15-16 have to do with certain kinds of insatiable appetites. Verse 15a seems to stand on its own, however, putting forward an example from nature of a creature with an insatiable appetite, the leech. The leech's "two daughters" are its suckers at either end. The image is an introduction to more metaphorical concerns that follow in 15b and 16. There we encounter other phenomena that are insatiable.

Beginning with 15b, readers encounter the first numerical saying of the section, this one arranged in threes and fours (cf. vv. 18-19, 21-23, 29-31). Three of the four are feminine nouns—Sheol, earth, and fire. Even though the word for womb is a masculine noun, it too is a feminine image. Of the four, only Sheol is not described. McKane would say that all four are metaphors for a woman's sexual appetite.[3] More likely the images have much broader metaphorical possibilities, most obviously their connection with death and the underworld.[4]

Verse 17 abandons the numerical style to return to the topic of v. 11 regarding parents. It stresses the importance of proper respect and obedience for parents. The saying turns on the *lex taliones,* the "law of retaliation." In the absence of any procedural adjudicating body, the law of retaliation often governs the community's law. Readers encounter the principle in Genesis 9:6 and in Exodus 21:12.

The implication is that guilty people must be punished in such a way that they suffer the same injury and pain as that of the person they injured. As a principle of law the *talion* is thought to provide a more consistent form of justice, since it does not rest upon class differences or economic status. If it is the eye that offends through its scorn for a parent, then it is the eye that will be eaten out by ravens and vultures.[5]

Although verses 18-19 do not reflect the classical riddle form, they seem to function as riddles. The verses return to the form of the numerical saying. Built upon the numbers three and four, it is the fourth in the list—the man with a "girl"—that stands out from the other phenomena in the sequence. While the key to understanding the phenomena is the sage's lack of understanding, it seems that the nature of the phenomena contributes to the concealment of that understanding. All four are connected by the word "way." As the ways of the eagle, the snake, and the ship are only momentarily evident to the onlooker, so are the ways of a man and a young woman. The furtiveness of relationships between a man and women leads onlookers to form only superficial judgments. However, the verse reads more like an expression of the onlooker's wonder and sheer delight than his insight into the psychology of relationships between men and women.

Verse 20 offers an observation about the way of the adulteress. The observation does make an explicit statement that it is concerned with three or four phenomena as do the verses immediately preceding it. However, the saying clearly has affinities with what precedes, since it has four stichs, the final three of which are governed by three verbs: "eats (ʾoklâ), wipes her mouth (ûmāḥătâ pîhā), and says (weʾomrâ). . . ." It is possible to read the adulteress's actions as an attempt to conceal her behavior, that is, to make her way as mysterious as that of the three preceding phenomena. Onlookers would not necessarily recognize her for what she is; "she eats, wipes her mouth," thus hiding all of the evidence of her behavior.

Verses 21-23 are another set of sayings built upon the pattern of threes and fours in sequence. The word that occurs in each line of poetry, thus forming a linguistic connection, may be translated both "under" and "instead," *taḥat.* The particular series of topics is especially distinctive, since we have seen the sages consider analogous reversals.[6] What makes these phenomena "reversals" is the assumption that the world rests upon a system of created order. [Wisdom and Order]

There is the recognition that slaves can supplant heirs in 17:2; 19:10 asserts the impropriety of such an occasion. Qoheleth reflects upon a similar reversal in Ecclesiastes 4:13-16, where a young man in prison becomes the king. We have already seen the unlikelihood that fools will eat. In 12:11 and 28:19 fools do not eat because they do not work. The Bible's narrative tradition preserves accounts of the "unloved woman" getting a husband (e.g., Gen 29:30-31). Under the law she has the right to retain her status as wife, and her children's inheritance is protected (Deut 21:15-17). Readers may recall the important biblical narrative of the maid who supplants the mistress (Gen 15:1-6). The idea of reversal even becomes an important allegory in Paul's understanding of the logic of law versus grace and religious status (cf. Gal 4:21-31).

Wisdom and Order

In the introduction to Proverbs we referred to the theology of wisdom as an ordering of the universe. Scholars frequently refer to the way sages understood their world as an ordered world in which the highest good was to understand and live in accordance with that order. Roland Murphy has defined the work of Israel's sages as one of "seeking order." The view of an ordered universe in antiquity probably derives from an Egyptian milieu and the idea of *maat*. The term means many things, but chief among them are the ideas of truth and justice, both fundamental principles for the workings of Egyptian society.

In ancient Israel, the order of the universe was most apparent in nature (Prov 3:19-20). The belief in a creator made nature the supreme validation of a deity who maintains a just and meaningful universe (cf. Prov 8:22-36; Eccl 1:5-11). That the sages frequently appealed to nature as warranting the validity of their instructions also provides evidence of the importance of order. Evident in nature were the principles for survival and prosperity (e.g., 6:6-11); for justice and the principle of righteousness (Job 12:7-9); for the assumption that all things have a proper place and time (Eccl 3:1-8).

The notion of order did not mean that there could not be variation and change. There was no strict determinism in the Israelite world. For one thing, there was mystery: appearances did not always align with reality (e.g., Prov 18:17; 20:6); plans did not always succeed (e.g., Prov 16:1, 33; 20:24); wisdom was not always evident (e.g., Job 28:12-28). Sometimes, the best predictions based upon the ordered universe were subverted (e.g., Prov 17:2; 28).

For further reading, see Leo G. Perdue, *Wisdom in Revolt* (JSOTSup 112; Sheffield: JSOT Press, 1991), 12-31; and Gerhard von Rad, *Wisdom in Israel*, trans. James D. Martin (Britain: SCM Press, 1972), 144-76, 263-83.

Roland Murphy, "Wisdom in the Old Testament," ABD 6: 920-31.

Verses 24-28 contain a list of creatures that perform amazing feats even though they are considered small and defenseless. The numerical sequence is abandoned in this saying, although the wisdom of these creatures is upheld. Size matters little in view of the extraordinary accomplishments of these tireless, boundless creatures.

Verses 29-31 are another saying in a sequence of three and four. The fourth is the dissimilar phenomenon featuring the king and perhaps the main point of the entire saying. There is textual difficulty in v. 31; the translation "rooster" derives from the LXX rendering, *alektor*. One implication of these analogies is that kingship is merely an imitation of nature, thus providing legitimization for its place in society.

Verses 32-33 are read by NRSV as an instruction. The final series of similes holds together around the common language translated "pressing" (*mîṣ*). The idea is that too much pressure causes situations and circumstances that lead to drastic, sometimes irreversible changes.

CONNECTIONS

"It is better for them to believe . . ."

Miguel de Unamuno's character, Don Emmanuel, provides an interesting background for reflecting upon the questions of the doubting sage that open this chapter (vv. 1-4). Don Emmanuel, as presented through the knowing eyes of Angela Carballino, is a simple parish priest who has doubts about his faith. However, his care for his people, his consistency in bearing their burdens, and his affirmations of the doctrines of the church make it impossible for the townspeople to see him as he really is. Only Angela and her older brother Lazarus come to see the priest for what he is and what he really believes. Angela's suspicions are aroused occasionally when she notices that the priest's voice grows silent when he comes to the Credo's words, "I believe in the resurrection of the flesh and life everlasting." [Credo] She wonders why he will never answer her personal and probing questions about his own faith. Yet, the people of the village love him, especially his demeanor at mass and his authority in upholding the doctrines of the church.

It is Angela's brother, Lazarus, who finally tells her that Don Emmanuel, the priest, in seeking to convert him had urged him to "feign belief even if he did not feel any." The simple faith of the village people, and the order created by that belief, was far more important than one's own disbelief. Lazarus says, "For a saint he is, Sister, a true saint. In trying to convert me to his holy cause—for it is a holy cause, a most holy cause—he was not attempting to score

---

Credo

Credo is a Latin word that means "I believe." In the course of the Latin mass, the Nicene Creed follows the Gloria and asserts a confession of faith in Christ, setting out the major articles of the church's doctrine. Unamuno's narrative assumes readers know that Don Emmanuel would have been reciting the credo, along with his communicants, in the context of worship. The confession of faith in the resurrection of the dead and eternal life is the closing confession of the creed. The Nicene Creed is as follows:

I believe in one God, the father almighty, maker of heaven and earth and of all things visible and invisible; and in one Lord Jesus Christ, the only-begotten son of God, begotten of his father before all worlds. God of God, light of light, very God of very God, begotten, not made, being of one substance with the Father, by whom all things were made. Who for us men and for our salvation came down from heaven. And was incarnate by the Holy Ghost of the virgin Mary and was made man; and was crucified also for us under Pontius Pilate. He suffered and was buried. And the third day he rose again according to the scriptures. And ascended into heaven. And sitteth on the right hand of the Father. And he shall come again with glory, to judge both the quick and the dead; whose kingdom shall have no end. And I believe in the Holy Ghost, the Lord and Giver of Life, who proceedeth from the Father and the Son, who with the Father and the Son together is worshipped and glorified, who spake by the Prophets. And I believe in one Catholic and Apostolic Church. I acknowledge one Baptism for the remission of sins. And I look for the Resurrection of the dead, and the Life of the world to come.

a triumph, but rather was doing it to protect the peace, the happiness, the illusions, perhaps, of his charges." And thus Lazarus himself becomes a willing participant in the priest's ministry. At one point, the priest disciplines Lazarus from inveighing against local superstition, because, he argues, "It's better for them to believe everything, even things that contradict one another, than to believe nothing."[7]

As we reflect upon Don Emmanuel's words, we might ask ourselves whether we believe it better to believe even contradictory things than to believe nothing at all. The frustration in the sage's words in vv. 1-9 make our reflection even more intense. Reading the final form of the text, on the one hand, we have a serious epistemological challenge: how can one know? On the other hand (vv. 7-9), the prayer recognizes that one cannot simply let faith go. And like Unamuno's priest and Lazarus, we suspect that there must be a certain intellectual willingness, perhaps a participation in the suspension of disbelief, that individuals are required to offer in order to maintain that faith. But, upon doing this, faith in God makes a difference that is real and tangible. Faith is so real that even the true nonbeliever may conclude that belief in everything is better than none at all.

NOTES

[1] Roland E. Murphy, *Proverbs* (WBC 22; Nashville: Word, 1998), 226; Richard J. Clifford, *Proverbs* (OTL; Louisville: Westminster John Knox Press, 1999), 260.

[2] Clifford, *Proverbs,* 263, observes that syntactically vv. 10 and 11 are similar in their use of "not" (*'al*) + imperfect second person verb + "lest" (*pen*).

[3] William McKane, *Proverbs* (OTL; London: SCM Press, 1970), 656.

[4] Clifford, *Proverbs,* 265.

[5] For further reading, see Calum Carmichael, "Biblical Laws of Talion," *HAR* 9 (1985): 107-26; H. B. Huffmon, "Lex Taliones," *ABD* 4:321-22; William A. Mueller, "Self-Defense and Retaliation in the Sermon on the Mount," *RevExp* 53 (January 1956): 46-54.

[6] See Raymond Van Leeuwen, "Proverbs 30:21-23 and the Biblical World Upside Down," *JBL* 105 (1986): 599-610.

[7] Miguel de Unamuno, "Saint Emmanuel the Good, Martyr," in *Abel Sanchez and Other Short Stories*, trans. Anthony Kerrigan (Chicago: Regnery Gateway, 1956), 207-67.

A WOMAN'S WISDOM

Proverbs 31:1-31

The final chapter of the book contains two independent sections. Verses 1-9 contain an instruction from a non-Israelite source; vv. 10-31 contain a poem on the "capable wife/valorous woman." These two provide readers an opportunity to reflect upon the opening instructions in Proverbs 1. Since Proverbs 1 also consists of an opening instruction followed by a poem on wisdom, readers must now reconsider their presumption that the teacher was a male parent. We must now consider the instructions as coming from the mother, since in this closing chapter that is certainly the case. Further, as readers attend to those instructions, they may find them to anticipate the book of Ecclesiastes. The guidelines this royal mother lays down for her son will echo as readers encounter Qoheleth's reflections.

The link between Proverbs 1 and 31 continues in the poem on the *ʾēšet ḥayil*, the "capable wife." It is widely accepted that this closing poem provides, along with chapters 1–9, a framework into which other sayings and instructions have been collected.[1] Readers are challenged to associate the wife with Woman Wisdom herself. The affinities become clearer once readers begin thinking along these lines. Both wife and Wisdom are incomparable (e.g., 2:4; 3:14-15; 8:10-11; 31:29); both build a house or household (e.g., 9:1; 14:1; 31:27); both begin with the fear of Yahweh (e.g., 8:22-23; 31:30). In a word, this woman in Proverbs 31 is no ordinary wife. The implications of these similarities reinforce the admonition to say to wisdom, "you are my sister," recalling that "sister" functions as an allusion to wife (e.g., 7:8).[2]

COMMENTARY

The Words of a King's Mother, 31:1-9

As noted above, the chapter is divided clearly into two poems, each with its own unique structure. In the opening poem (vv. 1-9), there is

Aramisms

AΩ In 31:2 the word for "son" is not the Hebrew *ben* but the Aramaic word, *bar*. Aramaic was a language similar to Hebrew that dates to around 2000 BC. Aramaic comes to have an influence upon biblical writers especially after the fall of Jerusalem and after a generation of Israelites had lived in Babylon. However, the language was known in the pre-exilic period. The narrative in 2 Kgs 18:26, the taunt of Hezekiah by the Assyrian Rabshakeh, depicts the servants of the king requesting that the Assyrian speak to them in Aramaic so the people of the city would not understand the threats posed by the Assyrian armies. One implication of the narrative is that Aramaic was used at court, as a language of diplomacy, even before the fall of Jerusalem.

The flourish of Aramaic as the official language of the Persian court explains its influence upon writers of that still later era. Several sections of late biblical books are written in Aramaic (Ezra 4:8–6:18; 7:12-26; Dan 2:4b–7:28; Jer 10:11). The narrative in Nehemiah depicting Ezra's reading from the Scripture during the new year celebration also includes "interpretation" (Neh 8:8). While it is not certain what this word denotes, it may well be that interpretation was in actuality translation. Translation could conceivably have been necessary after reading from a Hebrew text due to the Aramaic speaking populace and their inability to understand Hebrew. This occurrence of an Aramaic word in Prov 31:2 may argue for the lateness of this particular instruction.

For further reading, see Frank Moore Cross, "The Development of the Jewish Scripts," in *The Bible in the Ancient Near East*, ed. G. E. Wright (Winona Lake IN: Eisenbrauns, 1979), 170-264; Stephan A. Kaufman, "Languages (Aramaic)," *ABD* 4:173-78; and Joseph Naveh, "Aramaic Script," *ABD* 1:342-44.

---

a symmetry that subdivides the poem into two halves, excluding the superscription (vv. 1-2). Verses 3-5 open with a negative admonition, "Do not give" (*'al tittēn*); vv. 6-9 open with the imperative, "Give" (*tĕnû*). The opening admonition is concerned thematically with alcohol and women; the latter admonition suggests a use of alcohol for other than royal consumption: so those in misery might forget their suffering. By caring in this way for those who are suffering, the king can maintain justice (vv. 8-9). The imperatives that open vv. 3, 4, 6, 8, and 9 are characteristic of instruction (e.g., chs. 1–9).

Verses 1-2 form a superscription identifying the source of the instruction that follows. As in 30:1 readers encounter the name of a character otherwise unknown in the Hebrew Scriptures, Lemuel. As the line is divided in Hebrew, the NRSV correctly translates *maśśā'* literally as "burden" or "oracle." Most scholars read this word as in 30:1 to be a place in Northern Arabia, based on the identification in Genesis 25:14.[3]

Verse 2 begins with strong negative assertions in NRSV: "No, my son! No, son of my womb! No, son of my vows!" A literal translation of the MT would be something like, "What, my son? What, son of my womb? What, son of my vows?" There is obviously strong rhetorical intention in the repetition and the use of interrogatives. The strong and unambiguous negative imperatives following in vv. 3 and 4 perhaps allow readers to infer the negative rhetorical tenor of v. 2 and thus derive the rather dynamic translation of NRSV.[4] [Aramisms]

The negative admonitions in vv. 3 and 4, followed by a motive clause in v. 5, concern women and wine. It is interesting that this mother warns her son against women. Verse 3b parallels "women" with "those who destroy kings." However, it may be that she has in mind a certain kind of woman, perhaps those members of the king's harem. The maternal warning sets up a possibly helpful contrast for readers with the poem on the capable wife in vv. 10-31. Wine, v. 4, causes leaders to forget and therefore to sacrifice their judgment. This is a logical follow-up to the mother's admonition against women who would destroy the kings.

Verses 6-7 urge the use of wine for people who are perishing. Whether this is advocated as public policy cannot be ascertained. It is interesting, nevertheless, that the properties of wine are recognized, so that it might be used as a painkiller—the opium of its day! Wine causes the poor to forget their poverty and remember no more their misery. The concluding two verses parallel each other in their syntax and in content. They both urge the king to maintain justice. This is the real purpose of the king rather than using power and wealth for women and drink.

The Right Woman, 31:10-31

This poem on the "capable wife," or "woman of great value," follows a mother's admonitions to her son, the king. Although the poem is clearly independent from the instructions in vv. 1-9,[5] it provides provocative comment on the mother's instructions there. Under the heading attributing the materials to Lemuel, readers continue to read the poem as a part of the preceding instruction. Further, readers not looking for possible significances beneath the surface of the poem may initially read the poem as describing the features of the perfect wife. But a closer examination suggests the possibility of interpreting the poem as describing the one woman who is much more than the right wife for a king. She looks a lot like Woman Wisdom herself. [Woman's Affinity with Wisdom]

An intriguing balance forms between this poem in vv. 10-31 and Proverbs 1:20-33. That opening poem concerns wisdom and her call to all to come listen to her. This poem may also be interpreted as portraying Woman Wisdom. The opening poem is structurally set out in a chiastic formation; this poem is also in a chiastic

---

Woman's Affinity with Wisdom

Claudia Camp has argued that the image of Woman Wisdom forms an "inclusio" or framework around the instructions in the book of Proverbs. Not only does the framework serve the purposes of forming literary boundaries, but makes a "theological statement" as well. By introducing and concluding the collection of Proverbs in this book with the image of Woman Wisdom, the editors responsible for inserting the image invite a certain kind of interpretation.

It is not entirely clear what theological implications such a framework might have on the collected materials contained within it. Even so, the following diagram seeks to illustrate Camp's point by identifying those affinities between the woman in Prov 31:10-31 and Woman Wisdom in ch. 1 and other parts of Proverbs (see Camp, 188-89).

1. Mother's teaching (*tôrat 'ēm*):	31:1-9	and vv. 1:8
2. "More precious than jewels":	31:26	and 3:15 (8:11)
3. "Finding" (*māṣā'* woman of worth:	31:10	and 3:13, 18
4. No lack of "gain":	31:11 *šll*; 3:14 *sḥr*; 8:21 *yēš*	
5. Incomparable:	31:29	and 3:15
6. Depth of feeling for:	31:11	and 3:18; 4:8; 8:17, 21
7. Provides security:	31:21	and 8:34
8. Worth evident in city gates:	31:31	and 1:21; 8:3

Claudia V. Camp, *Wisdom and the Feminine in the Book of Proverbs* (Sheffield: Almond, JSOT Press, 1985), 179-91.

---

arrangement. In addition, this concluding poem is an acrostic; that is, each line of the poem begins with a letter of the Hebrew alphabet in sequence. The technique conveys completion and fullness. [Structure at a Glance: 31:10-31]

Verses 10-12 open with the epithet "a capable wife" (*'ešet ḥayil*). The translation "capable" does not capture the wide range of meanings that can be conveyed by the word *ḥayil*, however. The word also carries with it images of power and strength, as of valorous warriors. The subject of *ḥayil* is certainly not ordinary. The question concerning the possibility of finding such a woman implies both the necessity of a search and the difficulty of success. The question "who can find . . ." echoes Job's query about wisdom (Job 28:12). Regarding one's finding a wife, readers may recall Proverbs 18:22: "He who finds a wife finds a good thing, and obtains favor from the LORD." Finding wisdom, like finding a wife, is a gift from God. The challenge and the hope for finding a wife and wisdom rests in one's trust in God. The image of the woman's value exceeding jewels reinforces our suspicions. Readers have encountered this image in 20:15, which asserts that knowledge is worth more than jewels. In 3:15, Woman Wisdom is herself more dear than jewels.

Verses 11 and 12 offer the point of view of her husband. By viewing the wife, Wisdom, from the husband's point of view, readers have the rhetorical perspective to understand the pragmatic aspects of Wisdom. "Trust" is the exact outcome of observing

Structure at a Glance: 31:10-31

AΩ Unfortunately, in English readers cannot see clearly the craft of the poet. This poem is an acrostic poem, meaning that each line of poetry begins with a successive letter of the Hebrew alphabet. There are 22 letters in the Hebrew alphabet and 22 lines of poetry here.

But the artistry does not stop there. Duane Garrett believes that there is an elaborate chiastic pattern that also governs the composition and reading of the poem. Readers might make sense of the poem in two mirroring halves as follows:

A. High value of good wife (v. 10)
  B. Husband benefits (vv. 11-12)
    C. Wife works hard (vv. 13-19)
      D. Wife gives to poor (v. 20)
        E. No fear of snow (v. 21a)
          F. Children clothed in scarlet (v. 21b)
            G. Coverings for bed, wife wears linen (v. 22)
              H. Public respect for husband (v. 23)
            G'. Sells garments and sashes (v. 24)
          F'. Wife clothed in dignity (v. 25a)
        E'. No fear of future (v. 25b)
      D'. Wife speaks of wisdom (v. 26)
    C'. Wife words hard (v. 27)
  B'. Husband and children praise wife (vv. 28-29)
A'. High value of good wife (vv. 20-31)

This structure is quite clever and as in other such structures we have encountered requires that readers be able to move forward and backward to compare line with line. But its demand upon readers probably only occurs retrospectively. A far more readily evident structure observes two halves of the poem, with an introduction and a conclusion. Vv. 10-12 begin with the husband's trust. The next eight verses (vv. 13-20) provide descriptions governed by the recurring motif "the work of her hands." The second main section consists of the next seven verses (vv. 21-27) and is governed by the motif of "the care of her household." The conclusion consists of the final four verses (vv. 28-31) and shifts the point of view from that of the woman to those whom she helps: her family and, of course, the sage.

Vv. 1-3: Woman's Husband's Trust
Vv. 13-20 The Work of Her Hands
Vv. 21-27 The Care of Her Household
Vv. 28-31 Praise from Beneficiaries of Her Work and Care

For further reading, see D. N. Freedman, "Acrostics and Metrics in Hebrew Poetry," *HTR* 65 (1972): 367-92; Will Soll, "Acrostic," *ABD* 1:58-60; and L. Alonso-Schöckel, *A Manual of Hebrew Poetics* (Roma: Editrice Pontificio Istituto Biblico, 1988), 190-91.

Duane Garrett, *Proverbs, Ecclesiastes, Song of Songs* (NAC 14; Nashville: Broadman, 1993), 248.

Wisdom's instructions in 3:23: "Then you will walk on your way securely and your foot will not stumble." The word translated "gain" in NRSV renders the Hebrew word *šālāl,* which is ordinarily translated "booty or plunder." It frequently accompanies pronouncements of doom and destruction brought by foreign nations (e.g., Isa 10:6; Ezek 29:19). When readers see that this woman provides plenty of "plunder" for her husband, they may recall that the word *ḥayil* also connotes might and valor and wonder exactly what this is to imply.

It is further interesting that the word "plunder" is used in the opening instruction, Proverbs 1:13. There it is clear that plunder is gained through crime and the slaughter of innocent victims. Readers are set up, in other words, in 31:11. They must wait in suspense to find out what kind of "plunder" the woman brings to her family.

Verses 13-20 continue enticing readers to compare the work of this wife to the work of Woman Wisdom. One of the most

Ancient Persian Textile Making
This figure from ancient Susa portrays a woman holding a spindle in one hand and material the other.

apparent connections is the recurring motif concerning "the work of her hands." This hand imagery recurs in vv. 13b, 16b, 19, and 20, signifying its importance in the poem. By this point in the poem, readers are indeed suspicious of the poet's aims, however. We recall now that there is a very explicit image for the power and efficacy of Woman Wisdom's hands in 3:16: "Long life is in her right hand; in her left hand are riches and honor." What we are going to see in 31:13-20 reads like an expansion on that statement in 3:16. This woman in the guise of an ordinary wife is most extraordinary in her power to make the good life happen.

In vv. 13 and 19 her hands are involved in making fabric from wool and flax with distaff and spindle. These are peculiar images to the eyes of modern readers; this woman is a creator in nearly every sense. She not only fashions the articles of clothing, she makes the fabric from the raw materials. In v. 14 she is portrayed as a woman of commerce, involved in large market enterprises. The word "merchant" in 14a translates the Hebrew word *sôḥēr*, a participial form of a root that means "to go around," "to traffic." The same root is used in Proverbs 3:14 where we read of Woman Wisdom's "income," *saḥrâ*. Both women are employed in making a profit. Verse 18 revisits this same theme with similar language. Again we see the word "profitable" (*saḥrâ*) and thus are curious to see how vv. 15-17 illustrate the nature of her "income," her profitability. Verse 18 is an exact quote of 3:14: *kî ṭôb saḥrâ*. In 3:14 it comes as a better than statement: "for her income is better than silver"; in 31:18 it is translated, "She perceives that her merchandise is profitable."

Verses 15-16 portray different features of her ambition. In v. 15 she rises early to take care of the needs of her household. If readers are troubled by the poet's use of *šālal* in v. 11, they may be even more troubled by the use of *ṭerep*, "prey," as an image of her provision for her household in v. 15. If she were a lioness, there would be no problem since the word is most typically used to denote the kill of animals (e.g., Job 24:5). However, despite the suggestion that 31:15c is a gloss to explain the use of the term,[6] forms of the word are used in other late segments of Scripture to indicate food for humans. The Hiphil form of the same root is used, for instance, in Proverbs 30:8. Malachi 3:10 clearly uses the same noun, *ṭerep*, to denote food in the temple storeroom.

This characteristic of diligent work will recur in v. 27. In v. 16 she is not only a hard worker, but a clever one as well. She "considers" a field. Here is wisdom in action. The word translated "consider" is the Hebrew *zommâ*, a verbal form of an important wisdom word we have already encountered several times. We have observed in Proverbs 24:9 that fools can devise or consider sin, and in Zechariah 8:14-15 that God can devise either good or evil. The power to devise a plan, however, is one of the characteristics of the wise (e.g., Prov 1:4b). Woman Wisdom herself possesses the power to create such devices (e.g., Prov 8:12). Finally, v. 17 is a summary statement that attributes strength to this woman. Her work is profitable because she is strong, she is clever, and she is a hard worker.

Verses 19 and 20 close this initial half of the poem concerning "the work of her hands" by pairing together two lines of poetry. Each stich illustrates some defining feature of this woman's impact upon society. The two words for hand used in these two verses alternate in usage at the beginnings of each stich, forming a chiasm. The image of the distaff and spindle is one of creativity and industry. The assertion in v. 20 supplements the idea of industry with a balancing image of care and concern for the poor and helpless.

Verses 21-27 are held together by a slightly different motif than the first half of the poem. Here we see how this remarkable woman cares for her household: her husband and children. Both vv. 21 and 27 have the word "house" (*bayit*), which provides the thematic boundaries of the unit. The point of view changes in v. 28 from that of the woman and her works to that of her children and husband, and finally, of the sage. Readers see in this part of the poem an imaginative exposition of the statement in Proverbs 14:1, that "The wise woman builds her house. . . ."

Verse 21 continues the description of the way this woman provides for her household. Exactly what the phrase "her household is clothed in crimson" means is not clear. Why the color of a garment would provide extra protection from the cold is not known. One strategy for interpretation is to follow the LXX translation, which reads the Hebrew word as though it were "double" instead of "crimson."[7] Double clothing would indeed protect from the cold. By retaining crimson, however, readers of NRSV must assume that the color connoted quality clothing, which might also be construed as reliable protection in the cold.[8] The following verse, v. 22, might reinforce this interpretation since it also speaks of her own quality of dress. Verse 23 is the first explicit reference to the way that a particular family member benefits from her work (compare v. 12). Her husband is known in the city gate. Because of his domestic security, he can devote himself to matters of public concern.

We now may recognize an interesting pattern that is developing in the arrangement of these verses. Verse 21 speaks of how her household is clothed; the key word for clothing is the Hebrew *lābûš*. Verse 22 then speaks of what she "makes" for herself to wear using the Hebrew word *ʿāśĕtâ* (again, the word *lĕbûšâ*, "clothing," recurs here). Then v. 23 is specifically about the benefits to her husband. In v. 24 we see again an assertion of what she "makes," using the same word as in v. 22, *ʿāśĕtâ*. In v. 25, which deals generally with the way she herself is dressed (compare this with v. 17), we encounter the word for clothing again, *lĕbûšâ*. In v. 26 we have a reference to her teaching, undoubtedly a reference to the way she teaches her children. This provides a reference to the other members of the household to balance the reference to her husband in v. 23. In other words, we have a progression of similar language in two sets of three poetic lines, vv. 21-23 and vv. 24-26. Verse 27 closes the segment on her household with the assertion that she looks after her family, and there is not a lazy bone in her body. The interconnectedness of vv. 21-26 are illustrated as follows:

V. 21 *lābûš*   clothed
   V. 22 *ʿāśĕtâ . . . lĕbûšâ*   makes clothing
     V. 23 benefits to husband
   V. 24 *sādîn ʿāśĕtâ*   makes linen
     V. 25 *ʿōz-wĕhādār lĕbûšâ*   strength and dignity her clothing
     V. 26 teaches children

Verses 28-31 close the poem by emphasizing the praise that comes from both family members and the sages themselves. In v. 28 the voices of both her children and her husband rise up in response. This response balances the opening statement about her husband's trust (v. 11). He trusts in her, and her family praises her. Their devotion and commitment surpass any such commitment to any other. They acknowledge that there are many such women who have excelled. Verse 30 would be inappropriate in the mouth of either husband or children, however. Readers hear the voice of an onlooker, perhaps a sage partial to wisdom teaching. His remark should not be construed as a denigration of beauty, however. Readers may recall that in Proverbs 5:15-19 beauty contributes to marital fidelity. The MT reads "a woman who fears Yahweh . . . ," but the LXX has "a woman of knowledge." It may well be that originally the poem and thus the valuable woman was not necessarily associated with Yahwistic piety. Readers may refer to Proverbs 1:1-6 to recall the introduction's perspective on knowledge. In Proverbs 1:7 there is clearly a strong equation between knowledge and Yahwistic piety. In the final form, the wise woman, Woman Wisdom herself, is a servant of Yahweh. As such she experiences the benefit from the work of her hands, and her fame goes before her into the city gate.

CONNECTIONS

The Tenderness of Power

This closing description of the valorous woman leaves no doubt in readers' minds why the ancient sages believed a society succeeds. Her strength, determination, skill, diligence, devotion, and cleverness provide the foundation for the success of her family and the success of her community. One must search for a person such as this woman, and there is no guarantee that one will find her. This is no ordinary woman or wife who scrapes and toils at the bidding of an overbearing husband. This is a woman who is independent in every sense and only chooses to share her good with her husband and her family. This is Woman Wisdom for whom we seek. One of the most striking contrasts between this poem and a more modern portrait of a woman is in her combination of industry and mercy (vv. 19-20).

Dagney Taggert is the extraordinary woman character in Ayn Rand's classic novel, *Atlas Shrugged* (1957). The author creates a world in which there are people who get things done and people who make no contribution, either because of laziness or incompetence, and only sponge off of the produce of the others. The ratio of the one to the other is quite unbalanced, so that the producers finally get fed up with the majority of those people who spend their lives living off of the work and creativity of others.

Maat

This is an image of the Egyptian goddess, Maat, thought by some scholars to be the origins of Israel's Woman Wisdom. She wears the feather, the symbol of truth, as her headdress.

Goddess Maat. Bas-relief. Painted stone. Egypt. 19th Dynasty. Museo Archeologico. Florence, Italy

When the producers quit, society begins to crumble. Dagney Taggert, daughter of a railroad tycoon and sister to an incompetent brother who nevertheless inherited the railroad presidency—because he was male—is a provocative counterpart with our Woman Wisdom. She is every bit as tenacious a competitor and a worker; she is a hard-line pragmatist who lives to make things happen. She has no tolerance for laziness or incompetence and no patience with people who seek to blame others or for the easy answers to explain their misfortunes. Her motto would surely be, "if it is to be, it is up to me."

The world that Ayn Rand creates in this novel, the boundaries of which are defined by her radical Objectivist philosophy, has no room, however, for compassion. [Objectivist Philosophy] There is no place for explanations of poverty; there is no assumption that society owes anybody anything. It is a world of extreme social Darwinism, where belief in God is only for the weak or the lazy. And it is here that we see in such relief our biblical picture of the mighty Woman Wisdom. She *is* compassionate, although she will

Objectivist Philosophy

The basic principles of Rand's Objectivist philosophy are usually portrayed through the lives of the main characters in her novels *The Fountainhead* (1943) and *Atlas Shrugged* (1957). At the heart of her views are assumptions about human nature: humans are rational beings who operate on the basis of choice. There is no such thing as determinism; humans are not victims of forces or realities beyond their control.

Objectivism rejects any notion of the supernatural. Thus, its metaphysics emphasizes that "what you see is what you get." Humankind and their survival is an end in itself, and all humans must work toward their own best self-interest. Thus Objectivism rejects altruism in that it is not ultimately in the best interest of an individual's survival. Such views are strikingly different from the assumptions of the ancient sages.

For further reading, see Leonard Peikoff, *Objectivism: The Philosophy of Ayn Rand* (New York: Penguin, 1991); Ayn Rand, *Introduction to Objectivist Epistemology*, 2d ed. (New York: Meridian, 1990); and idem, *The Virtue of Selfishness* (New York: Signet Books, 1964).

---

not tolerate foolishness. She *does* extend a helping hand to people who cannot help themselves, although she would teach that they should find ways of being productive. She *does* fear Yahweh, but would admonish her children to work as though their lives depended upon themselves alone. In other words, this pragmatic woman of the Bible is both tough and tenderhearted. It is the *mix* of this tough pragmatism and tenderness that makes her so extraordinary, and perhaps so difficult to find.

NOTES

[1] R. N. Whybray, *The Composition of the Book of Proverbs* (JSOTSup 168; Sheffield: JSOT Press, 1994), 162-63; Claudia V. Camp, *Wisdom and the Feminine in the Book of Proverbs* (Sheffield: Almond, 1985), 179-208; Carol A. Newsom and Sharon H. Ringe, eds., *Women's Bible Commentary: Expanded Edition* (Louisville:Westminster John Knox Press, 1998), 159.

[2] Roland E. Murphy, *Proverbs* (WBC 22; Nashville: Word, 1998), 43, comment on vv. 4-5.

[3] Murphy, *Proverbs,* 226; Richard J. Clifford, *Proverbs* (OTL; Louisville: Westminster John Knox Press, 1999), 269.

[4] William McKane, *Proverbs* (OTL; London: SCM Press, 1970), 260, translates, "Listen, my son. . . ," based upon proposed affinities with the Arabic *ma,* "listen." Duane Garrett, *Proverbs, Ecclesiastes, Song of Songs*, (NAC 14; Nashville: Broadman, 1993), 246, prefers the NIV translation as, "O, my son, O son of my womb. . . ."

[5] LXX has the poem last in the book, but following 25:1-7 instead of what is now 30:1-9.

[6] See McKane's discussion, *Proverbs,* 667-68.

[7] Clifford, *Proverbs,* 276.

[8] McKane, *Proverbs,* 669.

ECCLESIASTES

INTRODUCTION TO ECCLESIASTES: THE LEGACY OF SKEPTICISM

Turning from Proverbs 31:31, readers encounter a second wisdom book, named in the Greek tradition Ecclesiastes. The Hebrew name of the book is Qoheleth,[1] a name worthy of further comment below. In beginning to read the book of Ecclesiastes after completing the Proverbs, readers move from the instruction of a king's mother recounted by her son the king (Prov 31) to the words of another king. These have been passed on in tradition as the words of "the son of David, king in Jerusalem" (v.1). Readers may make a connection between these two royal perspectives. That connection between the two books gives us pause at the outset of this commentary to reflect upon the possible purposes of the canonical sequence of the two books.

Ecclesiastes in the Canon

In the present Jewish canon the book is included among the Writings, the third section of books that follows in date and authority the Law and the Prophets. Within the present Jewish sequence of holy books, Ecclesiastes does *not* actually follow Proverbs. Rather, it has been grouped with four other books known as the "Scrolls," or *mĕgillôt*, which are to be used as a liturgical reading within the context of the Feast of Booths (*sūkkôt*). Thus the book follows Song of Songs within the larger arrangement of Ruth, Song of Songs, Ecclesiastes, Lamentations, and Esther. Readers in that canonical tradition therefore do not simply "turn a page" in their Bibles, as suggested above, from Proverbs 31 and begin reading the words of yet another king.

Only in the most ancient canonical lists did the book of Ecclesiastes follow Proverbs, having attained canonical status as one of the books of Solomon—along with Proverbs and Songs. The Greek canonical tradition has preserved that sequence.[2] Since Christian Bibles are more or less based upon the Greek tradition of the church, modern Christian readers encounter Ecclesiastes as immediately following the book of Proverbs. Thus, the traditionally held Solomonic authorship of both books functions as an additional stance from which readers might reflect upon the way both books are in conversation with each other.

Authorship

From another point of view, the book of Ecclesiastes questions the tradition of Solomonic authorship. For one thing, the book itself does not consistently maintain its implication that Solomon was the author. For instance, the reader's deductions of Solomonic authorship from 1:1 and 1:12 are overturned in 12:9-11, which describe Qoheleth as a teacher and professional sage, not a king. What is more, after the introduction to the book, 1:12–2:26, the persona of a royal teacher altogether disappears and does not occur again. Rather than autobiographical testimony, readers easily recognize that the opening royal imagery is artificial. While it is not impossible for people of power, with extensive administrative responsibilities, to have a moral sense, it strains readers' credulity to think that a king as powerful as Solomon really wrestled with the moral and religious dilemmas described in various places of the book.

Once readers can begin to consider the difficulty of holding to the notion of a literal Solomonic authorship, the differing voices within the book leads them to hypothesize alternative ways of thinking about authorship. The book consists of a central core of first person accounts (1:3–12:8) surrounded by third person reflection upon the content and/or the person offering those accounts (1:1, 2; 12:8; 12:9-14). In addition to these changes in perspective, the internal inconsistencies seem to imply more than one point of view, thus possibly more than one author. For instance, in some places wisdom is denigrated (e.g., 1:18-19), in others it is affirmed (e.g., 2:13; 7:11); in 2:17 the speaker says he hates life, but elsewhere he affirms life (e.g., 9:4-6; 11:7).

The hypothesis of multiple sources or multiple editors, however, has not been persuasive.[3] It is far more likely that a sage, someone steeped in ancient Israel's intellectual tradition, wrote the book. This would be someone who utilized the ancient conventions of pseudonymity in order to construct an authoritative reflection upon the very claims of the traditional wisdom school. It is possible that this person constructed a narrator (1:1) and a character named Qoheleth (1:3) whose reflections and observations are the basis of dialogue between narrator and reader.[4] The contradictions are reflections of the real world the sage is seeking to explain, and the truth sought out stands only as such contradictory claims about reality are considered at face value and not merely glossed over.[5] In this commentary we will assume that there was a real sage who taught about life's contradictions. An anonymous writer passed on his teachings in the form of this book, in which he has collected and framed those teachings. This person is sympathetic with Israel's wisdom tradition, both its interest in order and its openness to reflect upon disorder.[6]

Ancient Near Eastern Context

Readers will recognize the Jewish influences upon the book within the first few lines. The appeal to the Solomonic tradition (1:1,12), for instance, assumes readers to have a basic grasp of that Davidic/Solomonic history. Further, the book's themes also make contact with biblical traditions. The themes of wisdom vs. folly (e.g., 2:12-13), of creation (3:11), of unjust suffering (e.g., 4:1), of faithfulness in one's religious obligations (e.g., 5:4) are all common within the Bible, not to mention the wisdom tradition contained in the Proverbs, Job, and some Psalms.

Like many other biblical works, however, Ecclesiastes bears remarkable evidence of influence from outside those traditions that make up the Bible. Thus readers find warrant to seek further information on this background as a means of understanding the arguments and artistic forms the sage is using within this book. It is unclear whether the Hebrew writer actually depended upon these other documents as he wrote. Suffice it to say that there are parallels, both in genre and in content, with a breadth of materials that stem from non-Jewish traditions.

In terms of content, readers find striking similarities between Ecclesiastes and Mesopotamian texts. The so-called "Dialogue of Pessimism," which recognizes the fundamental problem of retribution, says: "Go up to the ancient ruin heaps and walk around; look at the skulls of the lowly and the great. Which of the skulls belongs to someone who did evil and which to people who did good?" (see Eccl 2:14).[7] Likewise, the Gilgamesh Epic, an ancient Akkadian myth, offers advice very similar to Qoheleth's advice. Siduri, the "ale-wife," says to Gilgamesh as he is about to undertake his adventure to seek his deceased partner, Enkidu: "Let thy garments be sparkling fresh, Thy head be washed; bathe thou in water. Pay heed to the little one that holds on to thy hand, Let thy spouse delight in thy bosom! For this is the task of [mankind]" (see Eccl 9:7-9).[8]

Similarly, Egyptian texts offer helpful comparisons, especially in terms of genre. The instructional features of Ecclesiastes parallel the instructional genre of ancient Egypt, especially that of royal instructions. "The Instruction of Hor-dedef" and "The Instruction for King Merika-re" are two examples that are similar in form to the opening of the book (Eccl 1:11–2:26), where readers hear a royal voice.[9] Of course, the royal voice does not offer instruction in these opening verses of Ecclesiastes, neither does it continue throughout the entire book. One of the "Harper Songs" of the first "Intermediate Period" is similar in its skepticism as well as its advice:

> I have heard the words of Ii-em-hotep and Hor-dedef,
> With whose discourses men speak so much.
> What are their places (now)?
> Their walls are broken apart, and their places are not—
> As though they had never been!

The advice (see Eccl 2:24; 3:13, 22; 5:18)that grows from such skepticism is:

> Make holiday, and weary not therein!
> Behold, it is not given to a man to take his property with him.
> Behold, there is not one who departs who comes back again![10]

Date of Origin

Scholars conclude that linguistically, socioculturally, and theologically the book reflects a much later time period than the age of the Solomonic empire. Such conclusions are based upon comparisons with other extra-biblical documents, but also upon a growing awareness of the cultural and historical characteristics of the late post-exilic period. The linguistic characteristics of the book point to a time when Aramaic was a dominant language. This would be a time after the Persian empire came to dominate the Palestinian world, sometime after the sixth century BC, establishing the earliest possible date for the book's origin.[11] Greater accuracy in dating is sought by many scholars by hypothesizing a Ptolemaic setting for the origins of the book (301–200 BC). The book was apparently known by the writer of Jesus ben Sirach, written around 185 BC, thus providing a point no later than which it could have been written. To most scholars the book betrays the economic and social circumstances of a period within that framework as early as 300 BC, as late as 150 BC.[12] A less widely held view, though recently well argued, is that the imaginative thought of Qoheleth reflects the earlier Persian period.[13]

Although questions remain about the date of origin, it is clear that the writer is deeply engaged in the world of Jewish ideas that flourished in the post-exilic period. His use of proverbs and sayings, rhetorical questions, and other didactic forms of speech focus for readers the wisdom background from which he originates. While most readers find Qoheleth to be offering a mighty challenge to his wisdom traditions, his theological assumptions clearly locate him within the mainstream of post-exilic Judaism. He assumes a single God who is creator of the world, who has the power to correct the injustices of the world. He assumes humankind to be weak, having come from dust and returning to dust. He knows the traditional contrast between the fates of the righteous and the wicked, only he takes this as a starting point for raising questions about his tradition rather than offering the usual affirmations. He is in the midst of a crisis of meaning; things in his world do not measure up to his traditional beliefs. He therefore comes across as one who, like Job, subverts the views of his community of faith. For this reason, Qoheleth's theological assumptions are of central interest to anyone who reads the book of Ecclesiastes.

Theology

In no way can readers think of Qoheleth, the sage behind the book of Ecclesiastes, as a systematic theologian. He is not systematic nor is his concern only theological. Nevertheless, he makes certain theological assumptions that help readers identify him with a tradition of thought given expression within the Bible. Readers have already seen in Proverbs that the sages' worldview placed great emphasis upon the matrix of human contingency and created order. The essence of the good life lay embedded within the ability of a wise man to deduce the good from the harmonious workings of the creation order. The collected sayings and instructions within Proverbs provide an image of a meaningful and discernible universe (see Prov 3:19-20; 8:22-31).[14]

The importance of creation as a theological foundation for the book of Ecclesiastes is expressed in the form of a framework for the instructions within the book. Readers might equate the role of creation in Ecclesiastes with what is today called "natural theology." It assumes that the natural world is a component in understanding God's nature, first and foremost as the end result of God's act of creating and ordering it. The order of human relationship as well as God's purpose of human society may be derived through careful analysis of the natural order.[15] As this view is worked out in other places in the Bible, nature is an avenue for knowing God. As natural theology comes to an expression in more contemporary contexts, nature stands over against God, making the idea of God's direct revelation less necessary and less discernible. The opening and concluding poems of Ecclesiastes offer reflections upon creation (1:4-11) as well as the human dilemma and its implications within that creation (11:9–12:7). This kind of framing technique recalls the similar convention in Proverbs 1–9, which personifies wisdom as a woman in both the beginning of the collection, 1:20-33, and at the conclusion, 9:1-12. However, there is no persona of wisdom in Ecclesiastes that stands next to the deity.

In Ecclesiastes the sage finds that the once reliable order of the universe, which guaranteed goodness and assured justice, is not in fact reliable in an unqualified sense. The sage's purpose is to turn up the power of magnification, so to speak, and have a closer look to see how traditional views may be held and where they need to be qualified. The moral fabric of his world is rather in shreds (4:1-2), from the height of political power (5:8-9) to the ordinary citizen (8:10-11). While the sage holds out the hope that God will indeed judge the deeds of all people (3:17; 5:6-7), the cosmic basis upon which to admonish moral behavior seems remote (3:16; 7:15-17; 9:2). The confidence that creation reveals some predictable and reliable moral order has vanished for this teacher. God cannot be known (3:14; 7:14). Moreover, what the creator of the universe has done cannot be undone (7:13); indeed, God is responsible, as creator, for that which is twisted and perverted in human existence. There is an order to creation, but it is an endless and impenetrable cycle beyond the ken of humankind (1:4-11; 3:1-9). The endless cycles of seasons, circuits of the wind, and well-timed activities of human society only serve to remind the sage that order has itself become burdensome and meaningless. It is against such theological and cosmic assumptions that the sage fashions his instruction, through a message that nevertheless argues the possibility of some happiness in a terribly meaningless world.

The Message of the Book

The crisis of traditional theological and cosmological assumptions is troublesome indeed. This alone would be an important touchstone in accounting for the frequent judgment throughout the book that all is "vanity" (*hebel*). However, the sage seems to be offering a confession that moves beyond the mere recognition of ambiguity and inconsistency in the universe. The thrust of the message concerns *how* the search for meaning continues rather than *what* that meaning is to be. The book portrays a teacher whose aim is to model for his students the importance of making relative judgments. He calls attention to the dangers of absolutes and the vulnerability of unquestioned assumptions. The benefits of his instruction are not in their seminal grasp of new sweeping reforms. Rather, they provide ways of coping with meaningless circumstances that never seem to change. Readers may think of this teacher's insights as minor adjustments, nuances of color and sound, perceptible only to those who are asking the questions the way Qoheleth is asking them. Or, they may agree with his premise that in the face of unyielding madness and folly, it is still possible to find enjoyment. It is a gift of God, to be sure, and is as unpredictable and undeserved as any other reality. Nevertheless, enjoyment is still commended. In contrast to the sage advice of Proverbs 10:1, the wise are counseled to abandon the search for profit (Eccl 2:10-21) for it never satisfies (5:13-17; 6:7-9). Death is inevitable (3:19-22), life is full of pain and suffering (2:23), God is unknowable, and yet it is entirely possible to enjoy one's lot in life (5:18-20).

So, without any delusion of getting ahead, of pleasing God, or of actually changing the inexorable facts of existence, it is still better to be wise than a fool (7:11-12), better to draw near to worship in an attitude of respect than in one of disrespect (5:1-5), better to live in the moment than in the past (7:10). One should make the most of one's time—whatever it is (9:10)—should seek God while youth allows (12:1-2), and should take advantage of every opportunity to enjoy what has been made available for one's enjoyment (9:7; 11:7-8). In other words, the meaning of life is not found in the macro-assumptions one holds, but in the way one manages life's micro-significances. The little things count the most to make life full and meaningful.

Literary Genre and Structure

The subtlety of this message is conveyed through the genre of the book as well as the structure. There are a number of ancient forms that resemble Ecclesiastes' dialogical format, its call for enjoyment, and its instructional rhetoric.[16] The fiction of Solomonic instruction invites readers to hear these words as the teachings of a king whose voice calls authoritatively from beyond the grave. The irony of an authoritative call from the grave, however, serves to reinforce the subversion of traditional assumptions and approaches.

The structure of the book, while disputed among scholars, further illuminates the subtleties of the instruction. Most scholars recognize two main sections: 1:1–6:9 and 6:10–12:14. The challenge for readers is in understanding the relationship between the two sections. Guidance for reading might be sought in Qoheleth's own dialectical mode of reasoning, which is represented in the following phrase: "on the one hand, . . . but on the other." It is better to live than die, he says (9:4-6), but those who have died are better off (4:2). Another example is his view that wisdom does not profit (1:17-18; 2:13-16), but it does give one an advantage when there is also an inheritance (7:11). It has been noted above that the opening poem, 1:4-11, reflects a concern with creation, and the closing poem, 11:9–12:7, reflects the anthropological response to the inevitable implications of God's creation.

The strategy for readers is therefore not so much one of finding a logical argument as much as listening to a sage debate with himself. The point-counterpoint movement reinforces the sage's attention to subtleties. For everything that moves forward, there is a force tugging in the opposite direction. He raises questions based upon his experiences and readers must listen to the different perspectives; some traditional, others quite untraditional. As we understand Qoheleth's point of view, we also enter into his arguments, rejecting some and retaining others. But even more than detecting some resolution in Qoheleth's thinking, readers themselves learn by experience a process of deliberating on life's and faith's riddles.

The internal structure reflects further subdivision. The two halves may be divided into two further halves. For one recent scholar each half of the book contains a series of reflections (1:2–4:16; 6:10–8:17) followed by ethical implications (5:1–6:9; 9:1–12:8).[17] While 5:1–6:9 does not follow 1:2–4:16 in any direct sense by addressing similar topics, it is clear that there is some rhetorical change that warrants subdivision. For that purpose, these categories of subdivision are followed in this commentary. However, for others, no such symmetrical overall structure is available. The book consists mainly of a string of reflections punctuated by affirmations to "enjoy life" while one is able. Four such affirmations appear in the first half of the book (2:24-26; 3:12-13; 3:22; 5:17-19), while three follow in the second half (8:14-15; 9:7-10; 11:9-10), subdividing the book into its various instructions.[18] Readers are cautioned not to make too much of modern literary conventions that risk imposing upon the ancient text an appearance that could never have been intended.

NOTES

[1] Throughout this commentary I shall refer to the book as "Ecclesiastes," utilizing the name most readers are familiar with. I will use the name "Qoheleth" to refer to the implied author and sage whose wisdom the book contains.

[2] See Roger Beckwith, *The Old Testament Canon of the New Testament Church* (Grand Rapids: Eerdmans, 1985).

[3] See James L. Crenshaw, *Ecclesiastes* (OTL; Philadelphia: Westminster, 1987) for a discussion of these options.

[4] See Michael V. Fox, "Frame narrative and composition in the Book of Qohelet," *HUCA* 48 (1977): 83-106. More recently, *A Time to Tear Down & A Time to Build Up* (Grand Rapids: Eerdmans, 1999), 363-77.

[5] Choon-Leong Seow, *Ecclesiastes* (AB 18C; New York: Doubleday, 1997), 38-39.

[6] Regarding pseudonymity, readers should note that the Apocryphal book "Wisdom of Solomon," while attributed to Solomon, makes no pretense that it was not written in the late 1st century BC. Likewise, readers of the Proverbs cannot forget that this book is a collection of several collections. The final form of the book bears the mark of the collector or editor.

[7] *ANET*, 601 (IX).

[8] Ibid., 90 (iii).

[9] Ibid., 414, 419.

[10] Ibid., 467 (both quotations).

[11] R. N. Whybray, *Ecclesiastes* (NCB; Grand Rapids: Eerdmans, 1989), 14-15.

[12] Roland E. Murphy, *Ecclesiastes* (WBC 23A; Waco: Word, 1992), xxii-xxiii; Whybray, *Ecclesiastes,* 4-5; Crenshaw, *Ecclesiastes,* 49-50.

[13] Seow, *Ecclesiastes,* 21: "the second half of the fifth and the first half of the fourth centuries BC."

[14] For the terminology of a theological framework consisting of anthropology, cosmology, and theodicy, see Leo G. Perdue, *Wisdom and Creation* (Nashville: Abingdon, 1994), 34-48.

[15] See James Barr, *Biblical Faith and Natural Theology* (Oxford: Clarendon Press, 1993).

[16] Perdue, *Wisdom and Creation*, 194-202, notes the "Righteous Sufferer poems," the "Dialogue of Pessimism," "The Songs of the Harper," the "Grave Biographies," and the "Royal Instruction."

[17] Seow, *Ecclesiastes,* 46-7.

[18] Perdue, *Wisdom and Creation,* 204-205, quoting François Rousseau, "Structure de Qohelet I 4-11 et plan du livre," *VT* 31 (1981): 200-17; see James L. Crenshaw's extensive summary of several approaches to the structure of the book, *Ecclesiastes*, 34-50.

REFLECTIONS ON A ROYAL POINT OF VIEW

Ecclesiastes 1:1-3

The Meaning of Life: Requiem for a Skeptic, 1:1–2:26

The book opens with four rather distinctive introductory features: a superscription (v. 1), a thematic statement (vv. 2-3), a poem asserting that the created order is itself wearisome and predictable (vv. 4-11), and finally, an autobiographical statement of a king who poses as Solomon (1:12-2:26). This latter subsection of the opening unit implies a perspective from which the reader is to understand the origins of the observations.

The superscription (v. 1) attributes authorship to the observations that follow. Readers will ponder how Qoheleth (v. 1) can be a king (v. 12), and further what it might mean that such dismal prospects as Qoheleth holds come from the observations of a king. The thematic statement (vv. 2-3) foreshadows the thematic concerns that are to follow. In these verses one of the definitive themes of the book is first stated: "vanity of vanities, all is vanity." The question about what people "gain from all the toil," takes up the validity of conclusions that more traditional readers might have drawn

Structure at a Glance: Ecclesiastes 1:1–2:26

AΩ The structural arrangement of this opening unit, 1:1–2:26, allows us to make an important point about the relationship between the chapters in the book and the sense of the discussion within the book. The following overview of the opening unit of the book indicates the major units of thought.

1:1   Superscription
1:2-3 The Theme of Vanity
1:4-11   Conclusions Drawn from Creation
1:12–2:26 Conclusions Drawn from a King's Testimony

Scholarly debates over the structure of the book tend to originate more in assumptions readers bring to the text rather than in what is in the text itself. Of one thing we can be certain, however—that the chapter divisions only approximate the actual rhetorical arrangements of the arguments. Chapters 1 and 2 are a good example, since they stand as a unit mainly because of the dominant rhetorical strategy of the first person report that begins in 1:12. Chapter 2 begins right in the middle of that argument. Readers should not let the chapter headings prevent them from reading 1:12–2:26 as a unity. Likewise, 1:4-11 is a distinct unit, elaborating upon the question raised in vv. 2-3. Readers should not be surprised throughout the commentary to see that units of thought move beyond the units prescribed by the chapter and verses of the book.

from such statements as those in Proverbs 10:1-5, that are certain that at least wisdom pays off in the end. Not only are these conclusions available on the basis of inferences drawn from creation, but a king, King Solomon himself, has reached them as a result of his own careful investigations. [Structure at a Glance: Ecclesiastes 1:1–2:26]

COMMENTARY

Superscription on Lineage of David, 1:1

The superscription in v. 1 invites readers to reflect upon the much larger story into which this book is placed. Those who are familiar with Proverbs will recall the collection in 22:17 that begins with an attribution of words (*dibrê*) to the wise (cf. Prov 24:23). We must be aware that passing on these traditions was the work of many, not just one. Yet the attribution of origins to royalty, such as here—"the son of David"—is also common in Proverbs (e.g., Prov 1:1; 10:1; 25:1; 30:1) The phrase is obviously used to allude to Solomon and most likely derives from the author's reflection upon what is now located at Ecclesiastes 1:12, where a particular son is apparently imagined: he reigns in Jerusalem, over Israel. The referent of such a statement could only be Solomon since it was only after this king's death that there were two nations, Israel and Judah, with two capitals, Samaria and Jerusalem.

The author's appeal to Solomon is entirely appropriate to his purposes, however. There was a strong tradition associating wisdom's flourish with this important king's reign (e.g., 1 Kgs 5:12). For the reader who has read both Proverbs and the larger biblical story, the words of Qoheleth are a part of a now familiar context. Because of such connections, we will use the larger wisdom tradition attributed to Solomon as an intellectual touchstone for these words. By invoking Solomonic lore, the character of Solomon himself now speaks from his "rest" (thus "requiem") in the grave. It is ironic for later readers that the fate of one as great as Solomon is the same grave that awaits all. Yet another irony is that one so apparently troubled in life at last finds his "requiem."

The Hebrew name "Qoheleth," which is translated into Greek and transliterated as "Ecclesiastes," raises its own set of problems. The name occurs seven times in the book (1:1, 2, 12; 7:27; 12:8, 9, 10). In v. 1 the NRSV translation is "the Teacher," and it leaves readers seeking to abandon the Solomonic connection as quickly as they took it up in v. 1. At what time was this king ever a teacher, readers rightfully wonder. Other English translations render the word "the Preacher," implying that the ancient social context

Qoheleth

AΩ The term translated "Teacher" in NRSV is *qōhelet* in Hebrew. The term derives from the Hebrew root that means "to assemble," *qāhal*. The Greek translation of the term as *ekklesiastes* is not unrelated in that it denotes an individual "who sits or speaks in the *ekklesia*, that is, an assembly of local citizens" (Whybray).

The word *qōhelet* in Hebrew is a feminine participle most likely denoting one who assembles or gathers. That such a person could be envisioned as having some kind of official status is implied by other uses of feminine participles in the Bible to designate such officials. (e.g., Ezra 2:55-57, though all the following are treated as proper names instead of titles in NRSV: *hassōperet, pōkeret-haṣṣĕbāyîm*).

Alternatively, one might infer that this assembler had the task of "assembling" instructions and sayings rather than assembling people. This would be more closely tied to the idea implied in Eccl 12:9. However, the word *qāhāl*, which is the root of *qōhelet*, occurs most frequently with reference to people rather than inanimate objects. Thus the implication that Qoheleth was an assembler of people, not sayings, seems more in keeping with the majority of the evidence.

For further reading, see Choon-Leong Seow, *Ecclesiastes* (New York: Doubleday, 1997), 95-97; and O. Kaiser, "Qoheleth," in *Wisdom in Ancient Israel* (Cambridge: Cambridge University Press, 1995), 83-93; see especially n. 2, p. 83.

R. N. Whybray, *Ecclesiastes* (NCB; Grand Rapids: Eerdmans, 1989), 2.

---

behind these instructions is quite different from the more generic translation, "Teacher" (e.g., the RSV, the KJV, and the NAS). Unfortunately, neither translation adequately solves the ambiguities created by the attribution to a son of David who was king in Jerusalem. Both translations derive from contexts much later than the one in which the book of Ecclesiastes was itself produced. [Qoheleth]

The Theme of Vanity, 1:2-3

These two verses set forth the theme of the book. Verse 2 states a nearly unbelievable proposition: vanity of vanities, all is vanity. The phrase "vanity of vanities" utilizes a conventional Hebrew superlative: a singular noun in construct relationship with the plural of the same noun (*hăbēl hăbālîm*). If we grant that all is really in vain, then the logical question is whether anything—work, pleasure, wisdom, and reflection, even religion—is profitable. Indeed v. 3, a rhetorical question, functions as a response to the assertion of v. 2. [Vanity] What a contrast this offers to the traditional proverbial view on life's outcomes. Traditionally, diligent work, thoughtful speech, and deliberate action lead to the good life. The assertion the sage is offering here questions what profit there can be in view of life's absurdities.

Vanity

AΩ The word translated "vanity" in the NRSV is the Hebrew word *hebel*. It occurs thirty times in the short book of Ecclesiastes and is one of the key thematic terms of Qoheleth's argument. The meaning one might find in a lexicon is "vapor" or "breath." That meaning fits, for instance, with its use within the context of Isa 57:13, where the prophet imagines the idols of his audience being susceptible to a puff of wind.

In Prov 21:6 *hebel* has the metaphorical sense of ephemerality, which illuminates the saying's negative judgment on the act of lying in order to obtain treasure. In a similar way, Job gives voice to the insignificance of his life by calling it *hebel*, a breath (Job 7:16). In Isa 49:4 the idea of vanity is indicated in the parallel phrase that pictures the expenditure of strength for nothing (*ḥinnām*). We may also note its occurrence in Prov 31:30 to indicate the deceitfulness of youth and beauty. The

This illustration updates the Sisyphus myth by substituting a character in contemporary western attire for the ancient Greek figure.

word indicates the total untrustworthiness of that to which it is an attribute. One cannot place much stock in youth or beauty; they vanish like the wind.

Fox believes that the best English equivalent to Qoheleth's use of *hebel* is "absurdity." He especially focuses upon the significance it derives from Camus's *Myth of Sisyphus* (see **[Albert Camus and the Modern Word]**).

Sisyphus was one of the Homeric characters and was known as the craftiest of men. He tricked Hades (death) into allowing him to return to the upper world on the ruse that his wife was not performing her sacred duties to his dead corpse. He is most known for the special punishment he incurs in the underworld. He is compelled to roll a big stone up a steep hill. Before it reaches the top of the hill, the stone always rolls down and Sisyphus has to begin all over again. It is absurd because the activity is never completely accomplished.

With Sisyphus's eternal punishment in view, absurdity is defined as "a disparity between two phenomena that are supposed to be joined by a link of harmony or causality but are actually disjunct or even conflicting" (Fox, 31). By using the word *hebel* to describe all of existence, Qoheleth is asserting his assumptions of a prevailing order as well as his observation that that order is only imagined.

It is of further interest to observe the kinds of things that the sage calls *hebel* and chasing after wind: work (2:11, 19, 21, 23; 4:4, 7, 8); pleasure (2:1; 6:9); wisdom (2:16; 4:13-16); speech (6:11; 5:7); life (3:19; 6:12; 7:15; 9:9; 11:10); death (11:8); God's justice (8:10, 14) (Fox, 39-45).

For further reading, see Michael V. Fox, "The Meaning of *Hebel* for Qohelet," *JBL* 105 (1986): 409-27; and J. Priest, "Humanism, Skepticism and Pessimism in Israel," *JAAR* 36 (1968): 311-26.

Michael V. Fox, *A Time to Tear Down & A Time to Build Up* (Grand Rapids: Eerdmans, 1999).

Verse 3 contains the word translated "gain" or "profit" (*yitrôn*) and is distinctive to Qoheleth. It comes from the Hebrew root *yātar* meaning "to surpass or exceed" and functions within the book to maintain the commercial metaphor by which Qoheleth seeks to understand the meaning of life's complexities. However, the word does function in other ways. It may denote the idea of benefit rather than profit. This particular meaning of the word seems to apply in 2:11, 13; 10:10, 11.[1]

The implications of Qoheleth's question in v. 3 are perhaps more evident in the sage's use of the phrase "under the sun" (*taḥat haššāmeš*), another phrase that occurs frequently and distinctively in Ecclesiastes. By that phrase Qoheleth denotes the experience common to all humankind, something appropriating an anthropological universal. Experiences "under the sun," however, are distinct from those that have "perished" (9:6). Thus, the realm of human experience does not include that of the dead. Likewise, Qoheleth draws a clear distinction between God's domain and that of humans in 5:1-6. Fox notes the term to be functioning inclusively even though it does not include all aspects of human experience.[2]

One of the equally perplexing problems for readers is deciding whether these words in vv. 2-3 are Qoheleth's words or whether this is the judgment of his editor after reading his teachings. Readers who pause over v. 2 will see that the verse speaks of Qoheleth in the third person. We will encounter this again in 7:27 and 12:8. The challenge will be for readers to decide whether they come to a similar conclusion as that of either Qoheleth or his editor who makes the attribution in v. 1.

CONNECTIONS

What Does It Profit?

Ecclesiastes opens in vv. 2-3 with a theme addressed in Proverbs 10:1-5. The claim before us attempts to position the ensuing observations by suggesting that the main criterion by which one determines the worth of anything, and perhaps people as well, is its utility. In modern Western society we have seen this debate carried to the realm of education. Parents wish to know the value of an education. Educators, even more, are driven to quantify the outcomes of an education.

John Henry Newman, nineteenth-century British cleric and scholar, who converted to the Roman Catholic church after years of arguing for the catholicity of the Church of England, offered an important essay titled *The Idea of a University* (1852). He outlined, among other things, the uses of knowledge, and saw himself standing in opposition to those who believe that knowledge is always necessarily pragmatic, utilitarian, or even quantifiable. For instance, Newman disputed John Locke (1632–1704), the British philosopher of the Enlightenment, as one who urged such pragmatism in education. Newman quotes Locke as saying, "Can there be any thing more ridiculous that a father should waste his own money, and his son's time, in setting him to learn the Roman language, when at the same time he designs him for a trade, wherein he, having no use of Latin, fails not to forget that little which he brought from school, and which 'tis ten to one he abhors for the ill-usage it procured for him?"[3] In contrast, Newman is equally convinced that it is absurd to think that knowledge must be so confined to one's profession. Education is something that is quite separate from such quantifiable modes of assessment. By this he challenges the idea that the value of education is its utility. The debate continues today, in terms of the whether students need a broad-based education or a much more focused education.

Clearly Qoheleth operates within a framework, a wisdom tradition, which believes that education, experience, speech, work, etc., have their outcome in some very pragmatic application. It is from within this frame of reference that this ancient sage begins his questioning. Perhaps the degree to which we agree or disagree with his conclusions is related to the degree to which we grant his beginning assumptions: that life can itself be quantified in such pragmatic ways. In spite of his tradition, the world that Qoheleth sees is one where things are much more uncertain. His experiences lead him to the conclusion that even the best things don't "add up" in ways one might expect them to in order to assure pragmatic outcomes. And while such statements could be frustrating, even disconcerting for modern readers, they could also be a new beginning. Too frequently readers understand Qoheleth's questioning as reflecting a kind of agnosticism of desperation. However, it may well be that his observations precipitate an intellectual liberation that leads to unquenchable joy. That liberation consists of ridding oneself from the assumption that everything has to add up, that everything has to be pragmatic.

NOTES

[1] See Choon-Leong Seow, *Ecclesiastes* (AB 18C; New York: Doubleday, 1997), 103-104.

[2] Michael V. Fox, *A Time to Tear Down & A Time to Build Up* (Grand Rapids: Eerdmans, 1999), 165. This is a revision of his *Qohelet and His Contradictions* (JSOTSup 71; Sheffield: JSOT, 1989) and will be used throughout this commentary on Ecclesiastes.

[3] Quoted from J. Henry Newman, *The Uses of Knowledge*, ed. Leo L. Ward (New York: Appleton–Century–Crofts, 1948), 59-63.

CONCLUSIONS DRAWN FROM CREATION

Ecclesiastes 1:4-11

The argument that nothing is profitable and that all things are pointless and therefore absurd continues in vv. 4-11 by appealing to creation for evidence. In Proverbs nature is a common source of authority for the ancient sages (e.g., Prov 6:6-8; 25:13, 14, 23; 26:1). Here, Ecclesiastes appeals to nature's cycles as evidence that nothing ever really changes. Everything simply goes in a big circle. The final conclusion toward which the argument presses is that human activity makes absolutely no impact on the course of events. In other words, there is "nothing new under the sun" (v. 9).
[Structure at a Glance: Ecclesiastes 1:4-11]

COMMENTARY

The Unchangeable Elements of Life, 1:4-7

The sage opens in v. 4 by contrasting images of motion and motionlessness; he describes great activity and yet insists that all activity is ultimately stagnant. Things go round and round and yet things go nowhere. Time passes and nothing changes. Generations succeeding generations go through the same processes with nothing to show for all of the expended energy. This fundamental contradiction is the basis of the sage's interpretation of

Structure at a Glance: Ecclesiastes 1:4-11

AΩ The passage may be considered in the following arrangement. Verse 4 opens a poem that is responding to the rhetorical question put forward initially in v. 3: "What do people gain from the toil at which they toil under the sun?" Michael V. Fox treats v. 3 as belonging to the poem in vv. 4-11. By contrast, R. N. Whybray argues that v. 3 is separate.

Vv. 4-7 Sun, wind, water
Vv. 8-9 Eye, ear, word
Vv. 10-11 Still nothing new

The poem in vv. 4-11 conveniently divides into three parts: vv. 4-7; 8-9; and 10-11. Verses 4-7 concern three aspects of nature: sun, wind, and water. Verses 8-9 shift the topic to human phenomena perceived by eye and ear, concluding with the assertion that "there is nothing new under the sun." Finally, vv. 10-11 extend the argument by anticipating the possibility that there might actually be something new. The pronouncement is that, since there is a lack of human remembrance, human perceptions are therefore unreliable as a basis for claims of newness. Readers should consider what parallels may be observed in the symmetrical relationship between the natural phenomena of sun, wind, and water (vv. 4-7) and the human phenomena of eye, ear, and word (vv. 8-9).

Michael V. Fox, *A Time to Tear Down & A Time to Build Up* (Grand Rapids: Eerdmans, 1999), 164.

R. N. Whybray, *Ecclesiastes* (NCB; Grand Rapids: Eerdmans, 1989), 38-39.

nature's cycles, and further his use of them to defend his thesis that all is vanity and nothing is profitable.

The term in v. 4 translated "generation" (*dôr*) by NRSV gives readers pause for reflection since its meaning may be broader than mere human cycles of life. In Isaiah 51:9 the term is a generic term for time itself. By invoking it in Ecclesiastes, the sage is not necessarily staking his argument on mere human life spans.

Rather, the notion of time itself fits in with the much grander cosmic imagery invoked through the circularity of sun, wind, and water. There may furthermore be an allusion to Psalm 72:5 where the length of the king's reign is to be lengthened in measure against the generations of sun and moon.[1]

Verse 4 also uses the explicit language of "coming" (*bā'*) and "going" (*hōlēk*). These terms establish a motif that unifies vv. 4-7. In each of the descriptions of sun, wind, and water, the words for coming and going recur. Even though more conventional language describes the motion of these natural phenomena, they also, just like the generations, are always coming and going.

The images of sun, wind, and rivers in vv. 4-7 convey well this theme of busyness that accomplishes little. Verse 5 begins by stating that "the sun rises." But after it rises it "comes" (*bā'*) and hurries to its place. The affinity with a similar image in Psalm 19:6 evokes recognition. The language of hurrying in the Psalm emphasizes the irony of the sage's observation. The sun's only activity is to hurry to get back to its beginning point in order to repeat the cycle again

Sun Mythology

It may well be that Ecclesiastes has in mind the common mythologies of the sun. In Greek mythology the sun was a deity, though a minor one. He drove his chariot every day from east to west. At nights he returned to the east by sailing around the northerly oceans in a huge cup.

In Egyptian mythology the sun god, Re, traveled in a boat across the sky to make his east-west journey. At night he traveled in another boat through the underworld. There, in order to be reborn for the new day, he had to defeat the evil god Apophis. Readers should compare these with Ps 19:5-6 where the sun is a man running a race across the sky.

For further reading, see Veronica Ions, *Egyptian Mythology* (New York: Peter Bedrick Books), 82; and Byron E. Shafer, ed., *Religion in Ancient Egypt* (Ithaca: Cornell University Press, 1991), 7-87.

This illustration of an ancient Egyptian painting depicts the sun god Re in the Barque of Millions of Years, in which he crossed the heavens each day.

and again. [Sun Mythology] Verse 6 likewise opens with the wind literally "going" (*hôlēk*). The NRSV translates with a more idiomatically correct term, "blowing." Yet, the term "going" preserves the image that is begun in v. 4. The wind goes, and it circles, and circles, and circles. Verse 7 likewise invokes the image of rivers "going" (*hōlĕkîm*) to the sea, yet the sea never fills up, an image not uncommon in Greek drama. [Aristophanes' "Clouds"] For the image of the rivers and sea to be effective, however, readers will probably infer the poet's assumption of a process of evaporation. It is not necessary to take these images as woodenly literalistic, however. Exactly *how* this circular process happens is not here the concern. The sage's observation is that there is great activity, but that nothing really progresses.

The Subjectivity of Human Experience, 1:8-11

The sage now changes his approach and considers the human point of view in contrast to the natural. There follows another trio of phenomena to balance those in vv. 4-7, only these are peculiarly human activities. NRSV translates v. 8a as "All things are wearisome." Weariness is a fair description given the preceding observations. However, the Hebrew word "things" (*haddĕbārîm*) may also be translated "words," which would not be an inappropriate translation. Ecclesiastes uses the same term to mean "words" in 5:2; 6:11; 7:21; and 9:17. The double significance of

---

Aristophanes' "Clouds"

Scholars typically point out that in v. 7 Ecclesiastes' observation about the rivers flowing into the sea is similar to that of Aristophanes in his play *The Clouds*: "The sea, though all the rivers flow to it, Increaseth not in volume" (Whybray). Aristophanes was one of the most well-known comedy writers of ancient Athens. He lived during the Athenian golden age (c. 450–388 BC). His play *The Clouds* is in many respects an attack on the "modern" education of the time.

The satire is achieved by portraying the educated as seeking merely the power to subvert truth by asserting weaker arguments over stronger arguments. In the "thinkery," or school (*phronisterion*), Socrates is portrayed as allowing two allegorical characters—"Just Discourse" and "Unjust Discourse"—to teach Phidippides. They teach by engaging in a debate with each other over their relative merits. The dialogue quoted here emphasizes the importance of tradition by associating "new maxims" with Unjust Discourse's methods.

Just Discourse: Come here! Shameless as you may be, will you dare to show your face to the spectators?
Unjust Discourse: Take me where you will. I seek a throng so that I might better annihilate you.
Just Discourse: Annihilate me! Do you forget who you are?
Unjust Discourse: I am reasoning.
Just Discourse: Yes, the weaker reasoning.
Unjust Discourse: But I triumph over you, who claim to be the stronger.
Just Discourse: By what cunning shifts, pray?
Unjust Discourse: By the invention of new maxims.
Just Discourse: . . . which are received with favour by these fools. (*He points to the audience.*) [Cited online at http://classics.mit.edu/Aristophanes/clouds.html.]

At the play's conclusion the Phronisterion, or "Thinking shop," is burned by the father of Phidippides.

R. N. Whybray, *Ecclesiastes* (NCB; Grand Rapids: Eerdmans, 1989), 42-43.

haddĕbārîm connects the natural phenomena of vv. 4-7 (thus "things") to the human "words" mentioned in the context of vv. 8-11.

The remaining two phenomena in v. 8 are seeing and hearing. These are means of human perception, the very ways humans recognize the circularity of which Ecclesiastes, as representative of humankind, speaks. Interestingly, seeing, hearing, and then speaking form yet another cycle of phenomena that repeat without end. As though it were not enough that nature has nothing new to offer, humans observe nature and simply say the same things again and again, much like the sage's own words that will follow.[2] In other words, life offers an endless variety of activity that goes nowhere. Every generation compounds words of reflection upon them and there is nothing new.

The conclusion in v. 9, "what has been done is what will be," is fully warranted from Qoheleth's perspective. Existence and all of its varying types of events is utterly predictable. The observations of nature's cycles in vv. 5-7 serve as proof. Life's phenomena are tediously repeated. In Proverbs predictability is a positive judgment. It assures that the world is ordered, that God is trustworthy, and that wisdom is and will be profitable. It is difficult, however, to read this sage's conclusions as affirming that principle of predictability. He acknowledges in v. 10 that people will claim there are truly unprecedented phenomena. He dismisses such claims in v. 11, however, as a failure of human memory. Thus Ecclesiastes asserts the limitations both of human perceptions (v. 8) and of human memory (v. 11).

CONNECTIONS

The Transformative Power of a "New" Vision

The great prophet of the Babylonian exile, Deutero-Isaiah, envisioned the days of absence from Jerusalem culminating in Yahweh's new day. The things of old would pass away because the Lord would do something new with his people (Isa 42:9). The new song God's people would sing is certainly reminiscent of the words of yet an earlier prophet, Ezekiel, who saw God's people coming through the Babylonian exile with a new heart and a new spirit (Ezek 11:19). In fact, the culminating vision of the Christian canon is of a new heaven and a new earth, projecting upon the direst of

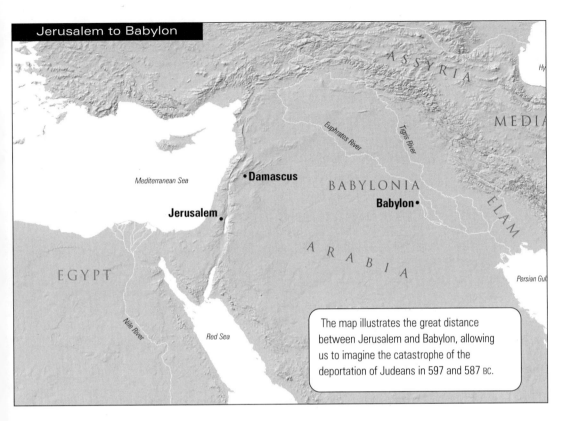

Jerusalem to Babylon

The map illustrates the great distance between Jerusalem and Babylon, allowing us to imagine the catastrophe of the deportation of Judeans in 597 and 587 BC.

situations a meaningful future for those who endure to the end. And yet, the power of Ecclesiastes' observations, which take readers ever nearer to their own personal, secret darkness, invites them to reflect upon the daily struggle for a meaningful existence.

Viktor Frankl, holocaust survivor and well-known psychotherapist, died in September 1997. What he called "therapy through meaning" explicates the term "logo-therapy," which was used by his peers to describe his psychotherapeutic techniques. He explained, in terms of Maslow's hierarchy of human needs, that the apex of "self-actualization" is a function of the human "will to meaning." In his book, *The Unheard Cry for Meaning*, Frankl explained how this will to meaning is realized. His explanation provides readers a basis for reflecting upon Ecclesiastes' despair. He says:

> Specifically, this is a possibility to do something about a situation confronting us, to change a reality, if need be. Since each situation is unique, with a meaning that is also necessarily unique, it now follows that the "possibility to do something about a situation" is unique also, insofar as it is transitory.[3]

Ecclesiastes' despair stems from the apparent inability for change because the cycles of nature are so repetitive. The sage has lost the hope of anything new, and thus anything really meaningful within the realm of these major cycles of life. Life's repetitive tedium, reinforced by the inexorable cycles in nature, simply confirms the utter meaninglessness of existence. However, the sage does acknowledge much energy, activity, and motion. This "transitoriness," as Frankl calls it, is a part of human existence; it is the basis for change even within the larger and unchanging cycles of the natural world. Human perceptions and words do not simply have to repeat the cycles of nature. They can envision and evoke something new within these macro-cycles of history.

At the same time, the human will for meaning allows humankind to take risks on relationships, on commitments, on God, and on God's future. It was just such a call to take risk and to envision something new that served as the prophetic basis for hope.[4] Only death can extinguish the spirit that yearns for meaning. It is the Christian message that, through Christ, even in death there is resurrection and new hope. Thus, with Ecclesiastes and his dark despair, we refuse to believe that the search for meaning must be so unsuccessful. We continue to search, to trust, to commit, to believe in hopes of finding that transforming meaning that comes from our ability to create something new out of the larger and endless cycles of existence in which we live.

NOTES

[1] See Michael V. Fox, "A Study of Antef," *Or* 46 (1979): 393-423.

[2] Michael V. Fox, *A Time to Tear Down & A Time to Build Up* (Grand Rapids: Eerdmans, 1999), 167-68.

[3] Viktor Frankl, *The Unheard Cry for Meaning* (New York: Basic Books, 1978), 38.

[4] Walter Brueggemann, "The Prophetic Word of God and History," *Int* 78 (1994): 239-52.

WHAT IS CROOKED CANNOT BE MADE STRAIGHT

Ecclesiastes 1:12-18

Conclusions Drawn from a King's Testimony, 1:12–2:26

Having experienced the extraordinary claims of the sage (1:2-3), and supporting evidence from nature (1:4-11), readers now encounter the king himself, who also puts forward similar conclusions. The persona of kingship is advanced, however, only as a rhetorical device. The persuasiveness of the conclusions intensifies if the speaker possesses the status of a king. Who more than a king would have the power and responsibility to maintain justice, to change society? Who more than a king could see how truly difficult such a responsibility is? However, readers soon discover that the king's point of view ceases to exist after 2:26. The autobiographical voice ends; the perspective of wealth and power halts; in fact, the epilogue to the whole book identifies the speaker, Qoheleth, as a teacher and arranger or collector of sayings and instructions rather than as a diplomat, legislator, and judge (Eccl 12:9-11).

The function of this testimony from an imaginary king in 1:12–2:26 must be understood against the background of kingship roles in the larger ancient wisdom tradition. Some idea may be gained by recalling proverbial sayings that deal with kingship. Proverbs 25:1, for instance, says that kings "search things out." Raising riddling questions about ultimate meaning is therefore justified. The king in Ecclesiastes more closely resembles the king encountered in Proverbs 30:1-4, Agur, whose experiences force him to the precipice of despair. He, too, recognizes the limitations of wisdom. The king in the book of Ecclesiastes, however, takes the questioning a step further.

As mentioned in the introduction, readers are further led to infer that the royal figure is Solomon. This is significant in that Solomon traditionally represents the height of royal wisdom (1 Kgs 3:16-28; 4:29-34; 10:1-10). He is held in high esteem as a patron of those who collected and passed on sayings and instructions (Prov 1:1; 10:1; 25:1). He is remembered also as possessing those things that come as

---

Structure at a Glance: Ecclesiastes 1:12–2:26

AΩ Readers may find helpful the following outline of the unit's organization and structure.

Vv. 1:12-18 What Is Crooked Cannot Be Straightened
Vv. 2:1-11 The Challenge of Understanding Pleasure
Vv. 2:12-17 Is Wisdom Worth It?
Vv. 2:18-26 Pleasure and Toil, Wisdom and Folly

One strategy for recognizing structure in this entire section (1:12–2:26) is to search for some formal criteria such as the repetitive phrases. The occurrences of sayings, for instance (e.g., 1:15, 18; 2:13, 14), might function as generalizing conclusions to arguments and observations. Likewise, phrases such as "I said to myself" (1:16; 2:1) or "I turned" (2:12, 20) might also help to differentiate units of thought.

More likely the structure of the unit derives from its broad thematic concerns. Readers encounter four major segments of thought: 1:12-18 describes the investigation and introduces the investigator and his preliminary conclusions. 2:1-11 describes the investigation of wisdom and folly. 2:12-17 asks whether wisdom is worth the effort. 2:18-26 reflects on pleasure and toil, wisdom and folly.

---

a result of wisdom: wealth, power, and faith. Yet even readers who are sympathetic with Solomonic lore could not be expected to have forgotten Solomon's failures. According to tradition, his wives turned his heart away "after other gods" (1 Kgs 11:4). Adversity struck his kingdom after his death through the shortsighted policies of his son, Rehoboam (1 Kgs 12:1-11). A person who brought the experiences of such manifest successes and devastating failures would quite naturally raise dynamic questions about wisdom and the mystery of God. [Structure at a Glance: 1:12–2:26]

What Is Crooked Cannot Be Straightened, 1:12-18

These opening verses set out the nature of the inquiry that follows. Not only will it be systematic, but it will revisit those themes that help readers to reflect upon the profitability of wisdom generally. Verse 12 elaborates the identity of the investigator. Such an investigation as will be described in succeeding verses befits the grandeur of a king such as Solomon. Verse 13 defines the nature of the investigation. The objects of the investigation include everything, *kol.* The method of investigation is wisdom. One of the results will show whether wisdom is an adequate means of exploring all things under the sun. Verses 14-15 set out in advance the findings; vv. 16-17 offer a reassessment of the king's means of inquiry; and v. 18 offers a final reflection on the nature of the task.

COMMENTARY

The Investigation, 1:12-13

We have already noted the use of the term Qoheleth, translated "The Teacher" in 1:12. In the present context perhaps the phrase should be rendered "I am Qoheleth." The phrase "king of Israel" identifies this speaker as Solomon since traditionally there were no other kings, besides David, who reigned over "Israel" in "Jerusalem." The NRSV translation renders the verb "to be" in v. 12 to denote that the speaker is no longer king—"I was king"— although it might also imply continued action that began in the past—"I have been king," and still am.[1] Either way, the narrative voice is looking reflectively upon an investigation that certainly took place in the past. The results of that investigation are reported in this book.

Verse 13 is translated "I applied my mind," which means something like "I resolved." The Hebrew phrase is important, and taken literally is "I set my heart." It is a phrase that makes contact with sayings in Proverbs. Those who have read Proverbs will recall the frequent references to "the heart" in the sayings (e.g., Prov 4:21; 15:32; 19:18; see [The Heart] and [Jesus and the Heart]). The investigation is to proceed "by wisdom," that is by employing wisdom as a tool. The use of the Hebrew preposition *be* indicates instrumentality here as in other places in the book (e.g., 2:3; 7:23; 9:15). The object of Qoheleth's investigation is "all that is done under heaven," and we pause to wonder what the author means. If we take the introductory poem in 1:4-11 as any indicator, then the investigation focuses upon humans and nature as each illuminates the other. So the sage is interested in not just what humans do, but what happens to them as well. The sage's conclusion is set out in advance: "it is an unhappy business that God has given to human beings to be busy with." The term translated "business" (*ʿinyan*) is distinctive to Qoheleth (e.g., 2:23, 26; 3:10; 4:8; 5:3; 8:16) and stems from the verb *ʿānâ*. The verb has four distinct meanings: (a) to answer; (b) to be occupied with (e.g., 1:13; 3:10); (c) to be oppressed; and (d) to sing or chant.[2] Readers naturally wonder what relationship there is between the "business" God has given to all humans and the task Qoheleth has given to himself. Is the task of investigation all that has been done under the sun also the task of humankind?

The Findings, 1:14-15

Qoheleth asserts here the results of the investigation, and he begins by making the extraordinary claim that he saw "all" the deeds done under the sun. What does he mean by "all"? What is the extent of Ecclesiastes' world that might fall within the boundaries of this "all"? Of course, readers may restrict this "all" by the statement in v. 13, where we read "all that is done." But the sage is interested in what happens to humans (e.g., old age—12:1-8) as well. Apparently, the investigation may be confined to whatever is relevant to human experience. Readers should nevertheless attend to the way that the investigation proceeds in order to define exactly what the speaker means by this frequently recurring term "all." What is more, the sage's conclusion is that "all" is "vanity and chasing after wind." This negative judgment makes identification of the extent of the inclusiveness of "all" even more urgent. ["Striving After Wind"]

Verse 15 is a saying much like those we encounter in the Proverbs. As in the instructions in the Proverbs, sayings in the context of an argument or instruction often function to sum up, illustrate, and authenticate the argument they accompany (e.g., Prov 1:17; 24:33-34). This is no different in the case of the saying in v. 15, "What is crooked cannot be made straight, and what is lacking cannot be counted." Following the conclusions in vv. 13 and 14, which assert the burden and the futility of human existence, this saying in v. 15 emphasizes the impossibility of changing one's fate. The saying may have been composed by the author, perhaps to reinforce his claim of the futility of finding order and meaning in his world. The twistedness of which he speaks, however, is not a result of human activities, but God's. What God has twisted cannot be straightened by human effort.[3]

"Striving After Wind"

AΩ The phrase translated by NRSV as "chasing after wind," *rĕʿût rûaḥ*, is one of Ecclesiastes' hallmark statements of futility. He uses it here and in five other places in conjunction with another characteristic term, "vanity," *hebel*. In 4:6 the phrase "striving after wind" occurs by itself (see 2:11, 17, 26; 4:4; 6:9). The translation "chasing" strikes a balance between two possible meanings of the term *rĕʿût*, depending upon its derivation. If the infinitive derives from the root *rāʿâ*, "to tend or graze sheep," the image is one of pasturing. If it derives from the Aramaic root *rĕʿay*, "to desire," the image is one of pursuing vigorously. Either way, the idea has to do with great exertion for little more than a breath of wind in return.

For further reading, see Choon-Leong Seow, "Qohelet's Autobiography," in *Fortunate the Eyes that See*, ed. A. Beck et al., FS D. N. Freedman (Grand Rapids: Eerdmans, 1995), 257-82; and H. C. Shank, "Qohelet's World and Lifeview as Seen in His Recurring Phrases," *WTJ* 37 (1974): 57-73.

Reassessment of Method and Conclusion, 1:16-18

The reassessment of the investigation provides fitting closure on this introductory section. Here we witness again the introspection of the speaker. He wrestles with his own identity as one who "acquired great wisdom, surpassing all who were before" him and the incumbent responsibility as king to "search out" wisdom "to know madness and folly." His dilemma between responsibility as king and awareness of the futility of such a search as a wise man confronts readers again and again throughout the book. The conclusion, according to NRSV, is not that wisdom itself is folly, but that *knowing* wisdom is folly. [Composition of Sayings]

The internal dialogue is indicated in v. 16 with the expression provided by NRSV, "I said to myself." Clearly a quote is implied in the translation. In Hebrew the construction introducing such a quote is even more clear, since it creates a redundancy between the words *dibbartî*, "I said," and then *lēʾmōr*, "saying," which is not translated in NRSV (see [On Quotations]). The effect is to portray the inner debate that continues within the mind of the king.

Verse 17 is perplexing because it adds to the objects of investigation "madness and folly." Both vv. 16 and 18, by contrast, continue only to assert "wisdom" (*ḥokmâ*) and "knowledge" (*wadaʿat*) as the objects of investigation. According to Seow, there is good reason to suspect that the original Hebrew text had "wisdom and knowledge of prudence."[4] As the text stands now, readers must infer that to understand wisdom and knowledge means also to understand their opposites, madness and folly. Verse 18 is yet another saying, perhaps modified by the sage to reinforce his claims. Readers may recall that the sayings in the Proverbs also understand the learning of wisdom to come with pain. In fact, pain is the only way it may be learned well. Proverbs 22:15 says, "Folly is bound up in the heart of a boy, but the rod of discipline drives it far away." Qoheleth modifies this somewhat so that even the end result, the attainment of wisdom, is itself painful. Looking back upon the introductory section, having wisdom and knowledge in a world that is crooked and unchangeable is ultimately futile and abysmally frustrating. What greater pain is there than to have the ability and insight to change things, but to live without the possibility of doing so?

Composition of Sayings

In addition to many other traditional wisdom genres embedded within the book (e.g., "better than" sayings, instruction, malediction and benediction, autobiographical narrative, example story, anecdote, parable, antithesis, rhetorical questions; see Crenshaw), this sage frequently uses the traditional saying, such as these in 1:15 and 18, to reinforce his arguments. In fact, two major collections of sayings are roughly fitted into the overall structure of the argument at 7:1-12 and 10:1-20.

It is interesting, however, that these sayings assume a traditional form and function, but in content are not so traditional. It may well be that Qoheleth himself composed them for his own purposes. Alternatively, he may well have taken more traditional sayings over and modified them to function ironically within his argument (Murphy).

For further reading, see R. N. Whybray, "The Identification and Use of Quotations in Ecclesiastes," VTSup 32 (1981): 435-51.

James L. Crenshaw, *Ecclesiastes* (OTL; Philadelphia: Westminster, 1984), 29.

Roland Murphy, *Ecclesiastes* (WBC 23A; Dallas: Word, 1992), 13.

CONNECTIONS

What Is Crooked . . .

What a hopeless conclusion: what God makes crooked cannot be straightened. Though humans try, ultimately they cannot make a difference in such matters. Such a sentiment intensifies when we hear it in the voice of one of such great power and wealth, whose reputation preceded him as a leader who made a difference.

But Qoheleth himself might have benefited had he compared his hopelessness with the circumstances of other leaders who faced similar unjust decrees from God. Consider the image of Nehemiah reconnoitering the broken-down walls of Jerusalem in the late hours of the night, alone but for a few trusted officials, calculating the costliness of his vision of rebuilding, and no doubt reckoning with the real possibility of dismal failure. We can imagine another fitful internal conversation about his resources, the surrounding opposition, and most importantly, whether rebuilding the wall of Jerusalem really constituted God's will as once Nehemiah had thought. After all, it was God who allowed the calamity of Jerusalem's destruction to happen (Neh 1:4-11).

It is the metaphorical power of Jerusalem's wall that is so significant. It is no less significant than the hedge around God's servant Job (Job 1:10). Indeed, it is only when the hedge or the wall of faith and religion is down that one is able to see reality in all of its starkness. Annie Dillard's extraordinary essay on awareness of the worlds that surround us, *Pilgrim at Tinker Creek*, offers several metaphors for seeing at new depths and levels of magnification. There is the "artificial obvious" over against the "natural obvious," terms by which Dillard distinguishes between the limited bits one is *taught* to see and the infinite depth that is available to be seen.[5] But having seen it as Job and Nehemiah did, and perhaps as Qoheleth did as well, finding meaning is like rebuilding a new wall, or replanting a new hedge.

Mother Theresa died in fall 1997. [Mother Theresa] Her passing invites us to reflect upon Ecclesiastes' words in 1:15 with perhaps a greater vantage point of insight. Who was less powerful than she? Who recognized more than she did the crookedness of the world with its teeming masses of impoverished, homeless, suffering, nameless people in the streets of Calcutta, India? She did not waste her time arguing before governments about the injustices of society, nor did she reason with scholars about new political theories. She simply cared for people, helping them until she died. She did not

Mother Theresa

Mother Theresa was born Agnes Gouxha Bojaxhin in 1910, the youngest daughter of an Albanian builder. She joined the Order of Our Lady of Loreto in Ireland in 1928 and took the name of Theresa after Saint Therese of Lisieux (1873–1897).

Saint Therese's life's mission in her own words was to "make God loved as I love Him, to teach souls my little way." She was canonized in 1925 as Saint Therese and proclaimed by Pope John Paul II to be a "Doctor of the Church" 19 October 1997.

Mother Theresa traveled to Calcutta, India, to begin teaching in 1929. In 1946 she had a life-changing experience, which she recounts as follows: "I realized that I had the call to take care of the sick and the dying, the hungry, the naked, the homeless—to be God's love in action to the poorest of the poor. That was the beginning of the Missionaries of Charity" (see http://ascension-research.org/teresa.html).

straighten any of the crookedness of the world, but she made an unforgettable impact—built a hedge— not only for the people for whom she cared directly, but for the entire world watching. Meanwhile, we debated and reasoned, in all of our wisdom.

NOTES

[1] R. N. Whybray, *Ecclesiastes* (NCB; Grand Rapids: Eerdmans), 48.

[2] Choon-Leong Seow, *Ecclesiastes* (AB 18C; New York: Doubleday, 1997), 121.

[3] Michael V. Fox, *A Time to Tear Down & A Time to Build Up* (Grand Rapids: Eerdmans, 1999), 172. Also see Robert Gordis, *Koheleth: The Man and His World* (New York: Schocken, 1968), 211, for discussion of vocalizations for *litqōn*, "to straighten," and *lĕhimmānôt*, "to count."

[4] Seow, *Ecclesiastes,* 125.

[5] Annie Dillard, *Pilgrim at Tinker Creek* (San Francisco: Harper-Collins, 1974, 1999), 16-32.

THE CHALLENGE OF UNDERSTANDING PLEASURE

Ecclesiastes 2:1-11

The report of the inner conversation and brooding of the king continue in this initial stage of the royal investigation. Using the figure of Solomon, Qoheleth continues to explain his search for a way to understand pleasure as an aspect of wisdom, madness, and folly. Readers may remember that the preliminary results of the investigation have been reported in a general fashion in 1:14, 17: "all is vanity and a chasing after wind." We anticipate with great interest, however, the way a king might have conducted an investigation of pleasure. There certainly would be no stinting upon the extent to which he participated in every possible pleasure. [Structure at a Glance: Ecclesiastes 2:1-11]

COMMENTARY

A Pointless Test, 2:1-3

The report begins with the king's description of his own inner debate: "I said to myself. . . , but this also was vanity." We have already encountered this type of language in 1:16, and it contributes to the narrative strategy that governs the overall section contained by 1:12–2:26. The test consists of this king's self-awareness of his own happiness as he conducts the everyday work of ancient kings. Verse 1 sets out the idea of "testing" or "trying" (*'ănassekâ*) and thus emphasizes the experimental nature of the king's activities. It is difficult to envision a laboratory, though, since v. 1 also makes clear that "pleasure" (*śimḥâ*) is the object of the investigation. The phrase that parallels "pleasure" is "to see good" (*rĕ'ēh bĕṭôb*), or "enjoy oneself." Seeing good means experiencing good.[1] Readers find such an idea enticing, but quickly hear the king say, looking back upon his investigation, that pleasure is "vanity" (*hebel*) just as all other aspects of human existence. [Pleasure]

Verse 2 echoes the saying in Proverbs 14:13, which asserts that one may simultaneously laugh and be sad, may have joy along with grief. In that saying as in Ecclesiastes 2:2, laughter is paralleled with pleasure, and both behaviors appear to conceal a deeper reality invisible to onlookers. Readers may question the sage's conclusion: that pleasure and laughter are "madness" and "uselessness." Readers may also question whether this conclusion stems from the fact that madness and uselessness contribute to a kind of self-indulgence or because through them individuals may subvert reality. In the case of the story of David (1 Sam 21:13-14), the subversion of reality through his feigning madness (*wayithōlēl*) saves his life. The narrative context illuminates a possible connection between laughter and madness: both are incoherent and thus subvert any control that is exerted upon the body.

There would seem to be another contradiction in v. 3 besides that of using both wine and wisdom in a legitimate investigation of pleasure. Some readers feel that the phrase NRSV translates "how to lay hold of folly" (*le'ĕḥōz*) contradicts the overall sense of v. 3. Why, they reason, would one who is being guided by wisdom in his search seek to "lay hold of folly"? Is the discovery of folly in some sense a strategy (rather than a conclusion) for discovering what is good?[2]

An emendation of the text at this point seems possible. The prepositional *lāmed* is detached and, through the addition of the letter *'āleph*, the two form the negation "not." The phrase then becomes "and not to lay hold of folly." This reading is advantageous in that the sense of the phrase is now consistent with what readers have learned in Proverbs: folly stands in opposition to

Pleasure

AΩ The Hebrew word translated as "pleasure" (*śimḥâ*) covers a broad range of experiences (Fox). The term, which occurs eight times in the book, may designate "deep joy" or "happiness" (e.g., Isa 30:29; Pss 21:6; 122:1; 126:3). More frequently the word refers to activities of "merrymaking" (Esth 9:17; 1 Sam 18:6). The term may refer to superficial emotional responses when there is very little deep-seated joy (e.g., Ps 137:3). It even occurs in Proverbs as a pejorative term (e.g., 21:17). Some of the things that contribute to *śimḥâ* in Qoheleth's reflections in the present passage include food, wine, gardens, singers, and perhaps concubines. None of these, for all of the "pleasure" they give to the king, escape his judgment of being vanity and absurdity, *hebel*.

Michael V. Fox, *A Time to Tear Down & A Time to Build Up* (Grand Rapids: Eerdmans, 1999), 113-15.

wisdom, and therefore folly would not be a strategy of an investigation guided by wisdom.[3] Alternatively, to grasp folly is to mark out the boundaries of wisdom.

The ultimate purpose of the investigation either way is to determine whether pleasure can be thought of as "good" for mortals. It is difficult to overcome the suspicion, however, that the sage is simply rationalizing the pleasures that accompany his life. Perhaps it is for that reason that Qoheleth later reminds us that he is guided by his mind and by wisdom. As readers see, these provide the controls for his experiment. Whether wisdom is sufficient to control experiments that require one to "cheer his body with wine" is suspicious, especially as we recall the sayings and admonitions on use of wine in the Proverbs (e.g., 23:29-35).

All that Gives Pleasure, 2:4-8

The activities summarized in vv. 4-8 indicate the areas to which the king directed his investigation and experience of the good. In v. 5 the king says he planted gardens and forests; in v. 6 he says he constructed great pools of water from which to water the gardens and forests; in v. 7 he reports his acquisition of servants through whom he obtained their children, his purchase of great flocks and herds; in v. 8 he reports that he also gathered great treasure, whatever was the delight of kings, and in addition, accumulated many concubines. Readers familiar with Proverbs 31:1-9 may be immediately caught in the awkward suspense between sound instruction in the Proverbs and the present king's activities. The king's openness about his extensive acquisitions, construction projects, and especially his investigation of pleasure contradict the advice on wine and women given by King Lemuel's mother.

And yet, who could argue that such constructive activities as planting gardens, parks, and fruit trees were not worthwhile? The word for "parks" in v. 5 (*pardēsîm*) is a Persian loan word; it comes into Greek as *pardeisos*, from which we get our word paradise. Verse 6 reads as though it were an ancient inscription describing the architectural accomplishments other ancient Near Eastern kings.[4] [Hanging Gardens of Babylon] Biblical references to the existence of pools are moreover frequent in the Bible (e.g., 2 Sam 2:13; 4:12; 1 Kgs 22:38; 2 Kgs 18:17; Isa 7:3; 22:9) References to gardens in Song of Songs 4:12 also imply the commonness of such construction activities for kings. Further, the reference to "fruit trees" allows readers to connect with another significant biblical paradise story in

Hanging Gardens of Babylon

D. J. Wiseman's 1983 Schweich Lectures on *Nebuchadrezzar and Babylon* provide a relevant backdrop for readers' reflections on the architectural feats of ancient kings. Nebuchadnezzar, known in the biblical story as the king who destroyed Jerusalem and deported Judeans to Babylon, is attested in inscriptions as a great builder, not only in Babylon, but in at least twelve cities across his vast empire.

Part of his building activities included his Palace Gardens, for which, according to one inscription, he "formed bricks into the likeness of a mountain and built a large step-terraced *kumma* . . . structure as a royal abode for [himself] high up between the double walls of Babylon" (Wiseman). Underneath the extension of this structure

Maarten van Heemskerck. 1498–1574. *The Hanging Gardens of Babylon.* Pen and brown ink. 20.3 cm. x 26.7 cm. Louvre. Paris, France.

was a series of underground canals to provide water and drainage. The height of the structure, extending at times into the clouds, could well give the impression of being a "hanging" garden.

D. J. Wiseman, *Nebuchadrezzar and Babylon* (The British Academy: Oxford University Press, 1983), 56-57.

Genesis 1. This king sought pleasure to the extent of attempting to recreate a primordial paradise.

While it is clear that the recipient of all of this activity was primarily the king himself ("I made myself gardens . . ."), some of the activities seem more constructive and others more self-indulgent. For instance, readers might justifiably see the building of pools, gardens, and forests as worthwhile construction. The acquisition of slaves as the labor forced to accomplish such work seems distasteful to modern readings, of course. But readers should observe that v. 7 makes the distinction between slaves that were purchased (*qānîtî*) and those that were born in the house as children of other slaves. They would have different status. The accumulation of flocks and herds might be explained as necessary to provide for the numerous members of the king's household. Perhaps the accumulation of silver and gold is a means of making such acquisitions and providing such support.

However, readers wonder about "the treasure of kings and of the provinces" and about the following acquisitions in v. 8. The word "treasure" within the phrase "treasure of kings" (*sĕgullat mĕlākîm*) occurs elsewhere in the Bible to describe Israel as Yahweh's "private possession" (e.g., Exod 19:5; Deut 7:6; 26:18). In NRSV's translation the treasures are not only fit for kings. They are also "of the provinces" (*hammĕdînôt*), implying that the definition of treasures is broader than only what might be fit for a king. Alternatively, it may rather be that that the provinces are themselves the possession of the king.[5] Within wisdom's world, concubines would seem excessive; at least, they would pose a threat from a mother's point of view (Prov 30:1-9). Readers may wonder about the credibility of the king, recalling the simple youth of Proverbs 7:6-8 who was caught up in the adulterous affair. We cannot avoid the suspicion that this king, too, is "carrying fire in his bosom" (Prov 6:27-28).

Yet, readers' concerns may be unnecessary since the phrase translated "concubines" (*śiddâ wĕśiddôt*) is uncertain and derives more from its position in parallel with the phrase "the delights of the flesh" (*wĕtaʿănûgōt*). In the context of Song of Songs 7:7 the word "delights of the flesh" has connotations of eroticism, but in Proverbs 19:10 it simply refers to "luxury." The specific delights of the flesh might just as easily refer to some other aspect of the king's wealth.[6]

Indeed, Striving after Wind, 2:9-11

The conclusion to this opening test of pleasure and work begins with another declaration of the king's status relative to predecessors. The pedigree he reasserts in v. 9 consists of his greatness, his consumption, his wisdom. These aspects of his royalty contribute to an implicit challenge of wisdom's claims. We have heard this already in 1:16, but here it achieves a more pointed significance. In the context of the investigation of pleasure we recognize this king as one who has received all that wisdom itself has to offer: "the reward for humility and fear of the LORD is riches and honor and life" (Prov 22:4). He has also proven that wisdom's negative appraisal on pleasure is not quite correct: "Whoever loves pleasure will suffer want; whoever loves wine and oil will not be rich" (Prov 21:17). The king has used his wisdom to gain these things, and pleasure has not robbed him of anything. Or has it?

The use of the term "desired" in v. 10 (*šāʾălû*) is reminiscent of Solomon's dream traditions wherein the king is instructed to "ask" his wishes of God (1 Kgs 3:5, 10, 11, 13; 2 Chr 1:7, 11). There, of course, he does not ask for material possessions, but for wisdom. The "reward" for his toil was all of these luxurious pleasures. The word rendered "reward" in NRSV is an interesting word: *ḥeleq*, "lot," "portion," or "reward." Here his "lot" is the result of his toil. This word is one of Qoheleth's favorite words. It occurs several times throughout the book (e.g., 2:10, 21; 3:22; 5:18; 9:6, 9;

11:2), and we must be careful to understand some boundaries on the translation "reward."

In 2:21 the term is translated not as "portion" or "lot," but as "all," implying all that a man has from his toil. In 3:22 the term is translated "lot," as it is in 5:18. The translation in 9:6 is "share" and in 9:9, "portion." In 11:2 the word is translated "your means," again implying all that has resulted from one's toil. Clearly, all these translations carry with them the idea of something one receives or inherits (as in Deut 10:9; 12:12; 14:27, 29), but not apart from one's own work or activity. So, one's lot or share is partly what one brings upon oneself.[7]

The distinction between wisdom and all the things that give pleasure is not so clear, however. There is a disparity between the "eyes" and the "heart" in the wisdom teachings in Proverbs. Appearances can deceive if one is not discerning (e.g., Prov 16:2; 17:24). Thus, the language of the king in summary sounds reckless. His unrestrained experience of pleasure leads him to the conclusion that there is nothing to be gained from any of it.

CONNECTIONS

Pleasure in Perspective

Karen Farmer cites Rabbi Kushner's book title *When All You've Ever Wanted Isn't Enough* (1986) as an apt description of the meaning of this king's investigation of pleasure.[8] True, there is an attempt on the part of the speaker to couch his description in the form of a lab report—this is a serious investigation guided by wisdom (vv. 3, 9). However, his words read more like a reflection upon his own life's work than they do an investigation. For one thing, it takes time to accumulate the wealth he speaks of; it takes time to do the building he describes. And while he intended for all his pleasure-seeking to be guided by wisdom, what we are reading here is a sober confession that his entire life has been motivated by one goal: the desire of his eyes (2:10) for wealth and luxury. It is indeed the retrospection of one who has learned something about himself and about pleasure: pleasure is not enough to make life meaningful.

Luke's Gospel echoes this finding in its parable of the man who built larger barns (Luke 12:13-21). The story comes in the context of Jesus' instruction about greed. The parable portrays the unfortunate results of being so focused upon material possessions that one fails to find the more substantive concern of life—one's soul! The man who saw God's provision of abundant wealth (the bumper crop) simply as an opportunity to make more wealth (by building barns to store the grain to sell it for a profit later) missed the point of both the blessing and the purpose of his life. God calls the man a fool and demands the man's soul on the very night of his success. He is a fool because he fails to see that such abundance only achieves significant meaning as it is put in its right place: it is God's.

Kushner concludes his little book on Ecclesiastes by observing that this short book is read in the autumn during the Jewish festival of Sukkot. [Sukkot] Sukkot comes just after Rosh Hashanah, "New Year," and Yom Kippur, "Day of Atonement," times of deep introspection and self-examination. Legend has it that on Rosh

Sukkot

AΩ The term *sukkot* means "booths" or "tabernacles" and denotes one of three major Hebrew festivals in the Bible (cf. Deut 16:1-17; Lev 23:4-38). In Exod 23:16; 34:22 it was a time of ingathering from the threshing floor and winepress, and was thus the last of the three festivals connected with the agricultural season.

Biblical critics early in the 20th century sought to identify *sukkot* with a hypothetical new year festival of enthronement. Sigmund Mowinckel in particular interpreted the Enthronement Psalms as liturgical pieces for the new year's celebration of Yahweh's enthronement. The new year's festivals of ancient Babylon functioned in some sense as a pattern against which one might hypothesize the

Leopold Pilichowski. 1869–1933. *Sukkot*. 1894–1895. Oil on canvas. 42.5" x 53". Gift of Mr. and Mrs. Oscar Gruss. The Jewish Museum. New York.

existence of similar celebrations in ancient Israel. Gerhard Von Rad located a ceremony of covenant renewal within this hypothetical new-year festival. His evidence consisted largely of the portrayals of reading the law during the Feast of Booths in Neh 8 (see Deut 31:10-11). Unfortunately, there is no reference to such activities during the festival, nor any rabbinic tradition that suggests them. In modern practice *sukkot* is part of a complex of festivals in the autumn that mark both the end of the agricultural season (ingathering) as well as the beginning of the new agricultural year (Rosh Hashanah).

For further reading, see Louis Jacobs, "The Religious Year," in *Judaism: A People and Its History*, ed. Robert M. Seltzer (London & New York: Collier MacMillan Publishers/MacMillan Publishing Co., 1989), 235-41; and Jacob Neusner, "Judaism," in *World Religions in America*, ed. Jacob Neusner (Louisville: Westminster John Knox Press, 1994), 151-76.

Sigmund Mowinckel, *Psalmenstudien II* (1922).

Gerhard Von Rad, *The Problem of the Hexateuch and other Essays*, trans. E. W. Trueman Dicken (London: SCM Press, 1984).

Hashanah God determines who will live and who will die over the next year. In this season of self-examination, of transition from the old year to a new one, the building of the "booth," the flimsy little makeshift hut to commemorate the travel through the wilderness to the land of promise, we find a stark reminder of the significance of human pleasure. It is not a substantive goal for finding life's meaning. It is rather a makeshift booth, temporarily erected as we are passing through, much like human life itself.

NOTES

[1] Choon-Leong Seow, *Ecclesiastes* (AB 18C; New York: Doubleday, 1997), 126.

[2] Thus James L. Crenshaw, *Ecclesiastes* (OTL; Philadelphia: Westminster, 1987), 78.

[3] Seow, *Ecclesiastes,* 127; Michael V. Fox, *A Time to Tear Down & A Time to Build Up* (Grand Rapids: Eerdmans, 1999), 179.

[4] Crenshaw, *Ecclesiastes,* 79, refers to the Mesha inscription in which the king mentions his construction of water reservoirs.

[5] Seow, *Ecclesiastes,* 130.

[6] Ibid., 131-32.

[7] Fox, *A Time to Tear Down,* 109-11.

[8] Karen Farmer, *Who Knows What Is Good?* (Grand Rapids: Eerdmans, 1991), 157.

IS WISDOM WORTH IT?

Ecclesiastes 2:12-17

The investigation continues with the king's interest now turning to wisdom and folly. The brooding investigator has already introduced readers to the conclusion that all is futility, especially work and pleasure. Here he returns to the question of whether wisdom is really better than folly (see 1:17). While wisdom is indeed an advantage, its benefits are marginal and should cause one to be cautious in giving too much time to its pursuit. Ultimately, both fools and the wise suffer the same fate: death.[Structure at a Glance: 2:12-27]

COMMENTARY

Wisdom's Answer to Real Life, 2:12-14a

The king states his investigation rather directly in v. 12a. NRSV translates the final phrase of the verse as though "madness and folly" form two separate topics in addition to wisdom. It may rather be that here we have a hendiadys—one thought through two words (the Greek *hēn dia dyoin*, "one through two")—so that readers could imagine the object of investigation to be something like "inane folly."[1] A more interesting problem is how 12b makes sense in relationship to 12a and introducing the appeal to tradition (vv. 13-14) and the conclusion (vv. 15-17). In NRSV's translation the king asks in 12b, "For what can the one do who comes after the king?" and concludes, "Only what has already been done." Readers rightly wonder how this question regarding the king's successor relates to the

Textual Emendation in 2:12b

AΩ Verse 12b is further problematic in that it does not readily reveal a connection with the opening question in 12a regarding wisdom and folly. In Hebrew it reads, "what of the man who comes after the king." One proposal is to read v. 12b in relationship to v. 11, assuming that the two verses are arranged in an alternating thematic structure—A, B, A, B, etc. In this case 12b, assuming we understand what it is saying, becomes a reason for the king's despair over "all the works of his hand" (v. 11). Likewise, v. 13 responds to v. 12a. But the text itself is further troubled and requires consideration at the sentence level.

One further proposal is that the verb meaning "to do" (*ya'aseh*) has dropped out of the MT and must be added. Adding this to the text explains the NRSV translation, "What can the one *do* who comes after the king?" Alternatively, the Hebrew word translated "what" (*meh*) may be translated as "who," which would be consistent with its occurrence in Pss 8:5; 144:3; Job 21:15; 7:17; and 15:14. This translation of *meh* is further consistent with the LXX translation, "who is the man?" (*tis anthrōpos*). The phrase would read "who is

the one who comes after the king?" While this solves the difficulties in the first part of the phrase, it still does not clarify what is being asked about the person who follows the king.

As the text stands the final phrase begins with the direct object indicator, *'et*, implying that a finite verb precedes. The only verb present is there because of an emendation in the text ("to do"). One recent proposal is to read "the king" (*hammelek*) as an interrogative *he* plus participle (*molek*), "does he rule," or "will he rule" (*hammōlēk*). This requires a revocalization of the construct form of "after" (*'ăhărê*) to "after me," (*'ăhăray*). Thus the sentence would read, "Who is the one who comes after me? Will he reign over that which has already been done?" The idea is that for all of the creativity of one king's work, another comes along and inherits it. In relationship to the interest in madness and folly, the temporary nature of even the greatest works of a king provides a fair example (Fox; Murphy; Seow).

Michael V. Fox, *A Time to Tear Down & A Time to Build Up* (Grand Rapids: Eerdmans, 1999), 182-83.

Roland E. Murphy, *Ecclesiastes* (WBC 23A; Dallas: Word, 1992), 21.

Choon-Leong Seow, *Ecclesiastes* (AB 18C; New York: Doubleday, 1997), 133-34.

king's opening resolution to investigate wisdom and inane folly. The observation in the form of a rhetorical question apparently illustrates the inefficacy of wisdom. Even a king, with all of his power and wisdom, leaves his work and wealth to a successor who takes credit for it. That king then does whatever he pleases. [Textual Emendation in 2:12b]

Verses 13 and 14 are crucial to the argument being made here and further indicate to readers one of the stylistic characteristics of the book's author. The king asserts baldly that there is an advantage in having wisdom. Compared to folly, it is like light to darkness. In v. 14a the speaker cites a traditional saying: "The wise have eyes in their head, but fools walk in darkness." This serves to reinforce his observation of wisdom's relative benefits and to assert a more traditional view. Little do readers suspect that what follows is going to subvert the authority of the traditional view. ["Excess" and the Persian World]

Readers have already seen in 1:15 and 19 that the sage uses sayings to reinforce his arguments. Sometimes he uses traditional sayings in order to refute them by adding comments and observations about them. One scholar refers to this convention as the "broken aphorism."[2]

In the case of 2:12-17 this use of the traditional saying plays a key role in shaping the structure of this overall unit. There is an

"Excess" and the Persian World

Twice in v. 13 Qoheleth refers to one idea "excelling" another so as to indicate that it is comparatively an advantage. He returns to this question in one of his concluding observations in v. 15. The words in vv. 13 (*yitrôn*) and v. 15 (*yōtēr*) are related in their basic meaning of "advantage or surplus." These are important words because of their frequent occurrences (1:3; 2:11, 13, 15; 3:9; 5:9; 6:8, 11; 10:10, 11) as well as their implication that the author is using language from the world of commerce to shape his metaphors for understanding what is "good" in life.

One recent scholar argues that this language betrays the Persian time period as the historical background for the writing of the book. The introduction of coinage, the establishment of an elaborate system of taxation, and the granting of what should be considered economic incentives on the western fringe of the Persian Empire (thus, Palestine or Yehud) help to explain the apparent concern of our writer to couch his discussion in such economic terms (Seow).

For further reading, see Samuel E. Balentine, "The Politics of Religion in the Persian Period," *After the Exile*, ed. J. Barton and D. Reimer (Macon GA: Mercer University Press, 1996), 129-46; and J. L. Berquist, *Judaism in Persia's Shadow* (Minneapolis: Fortress, 1995.)

Choon-Leong Seow, *Ecclesiastes* (AB 18C; New York: Doubleday, 1997), 21-33.

---

observation based upon Qoheleth's experience (v. 13), which is supported by a traditional saying (14a). As we follow the argument, further information infuses a new perspective on the saying (14b). This new perspective does not negate the saying's validity, but throws a new light upon its authoritative claim. The new observations are then incorporated into Qoheleth's argument (v. 15) that leads to a conclusion (vv. 16-17).

Real Life's Answer to Wisdom, 2:14b-17

Readers of Proverbs may remember the assertions in the Proverbs that compare the wise with the fool (e.g., Prov 10:1, 8; 12:15, 23; 14:1, 7). With such claims in mind, we are not surprised to hear that indeed the wise have an advantage over fools. We are not prepared, however, to consider that in view of death the advantage is not as great as we might have supposed. Qoheleth recognizes that "the same fate befalls all of them." That same fate, of course, is death. Death happens to all living things, and this recalls for readers the story of Adam and Eve in the garden of paradise (Gen 2:4–3:24). In the face of death, knowledge (the tree of the knowledge of good and evil) and wisdom seem to have only relative value.

Verse 15 continues; the very next question that comes from the king's mouth is, logically, "why have I been so wise?" The term in Hebrew translated "so very" (*yôtēr*) occurs several times in the book and denotes an excess. The sage's question implies that it is possible to be too wise, presumably to devote too much time to obtaining wisdom. Given the king's conclusion that the same fate comes to the fool as to the wise, one should not spend too much time on wisdom at all. This conclusion allows one perhaps to maintain wisdom's importance, but requires that one begin to think about a kind of balance between wisdom and other aspects of life. The additional observation in v. 16 compounds the king's conclusion. It is possible that the pursuit of wisdom is itself "vanity," since there is no enduring remembrance of either wise people or fools. The implication is that memory plays a vital role in establishing the true worth and value of all things (cf. 1:11). The ease with which something or someone is forgotten is the measure of lasting value.

Qoheleth sees these things—the advantage of wisdom, the inevitability of death, the forgetfulness of people—and concludes that he really hates life (v. 17). The fleeting nature of all such phenomena reminds Qoheleth of striving after wind. Such an activity to the sage is the height and depth of absurdity. We sense here the same kind of weariness we have already encountered in Proverbs with another king who was searching for wisdom (see Prov 30:1-4). His search led to a kind of personal self-deprecation. In Ecclesiastes, the king has moved beyond blaming himself; he holds someone—anyone—other than himself entirely responsible.

CONNECTIONS

On Getting Ahead

The influential world of commerce and its effects upon Qoheleth's thought becomes unambiguously clear in this passage. The writer takes the implication of profitability in life (Prov 10:2) and makes it an economic question: is wisdom profitable? Will it help one "get ahead" in life? This creates a remarkable interface with questions that seem to be on the mind of nearly everyone these days who is concerned with getting ahead. In this passage Qoheleth's assumptions of the profitability is thwarted as he seems to recognize a law of diminishing returns. It is this immutable law that leads to his conclusion that more is not necessarily better.

One of the more entertaining texts from antiquity comes from ancient Egypt and is titled "The Satire on the Trades." It was written for schoolboys in the scribal school and dates originally from the Middle Kingdom or earlier (2150–1750 BC).

Middle Kingdom (2150–1750 BC)

The term "Middle Kingdom" designates a period in ancient Egypt and illustrates one of the conventional methods of reconstructing Egyptian history. The period is connected to the present text in that Qoheleth's ideas, dating as early as the 5th century BC to as late as the 2d century BC, share some of the same ideas as those set in the Middle Kingdom of ancient Egypt. While Egypt is mentioned in Herodotus's histories (5th century BC), it is the 3rd century BC priest, Manetho, to whom modern scholars turn for this historical taxonomy of Egyptian dynasties. Manetho divided Egypt's history into the reigns of thirty pharaonic dynasties. Various clusters of dynasties, depending upon their relative political strength, accomplishments, and origins, provide a firm basis upon which to differentiate them and the major political eras.

The Middle Kingdom consists of dynasties 11 and 12 and reflects a more well-established and politically settled time. This contrasts with the preceding Intermediate Period of dynasties 7-10 that was a time of political turmoil and national disunity marked by the intrusion of Asian nomads into their land.

For further reading, see Peter A. Clayton, *Chronicle of the Pharaohs* (London: Thames and Hudson, 1994); and Donald B. Redford, *Egypt, Canaan and Israel in Ancient Times* (Princeton NJ: Princeton University Press, 1992), 71-97.

[Middle Kingdom (2150–1750 BC)] The schoolboys copied the text in order to learn how to write. The text sets out the various aspects of several different professions in order to urge the benefits of learning to be a scribe. "The small building contractor carries mud, . . . He is dirtier than vines or pigs from treading under his mud." Another line reads, "The embalmer, his fingers are foul, for the odor thereof is (that of) corpses." Another reads, "The laundry man launders on the river, a neighbor of the crocodile." The poem concludes that only the life of the scribe, the one who knows how to write, has any kind of advantage. "But if thou knowest writing, then it will go better than (in) these professions which I have set before thee."[3]

Clearly ancient Egyptian sages anticipated some of the very same kinds of questions people are still asking today. Such questioning applied to ancient Israel, too. Fathers wished for their children every advantage and took pains to provide the appropriate instruction for them. For biblical sages there was the comparable certainty that wisdom's precepts offered the "way" to "get ahead." For Qoheleth, however, there was a ceiling on all of the benefits of wisdom: death. He recognized that in the face of death's inevitability, one simply cannot get far enough ahead by wisdom to warrant the extension of so much value to it. One must therefore learn to seek wisdom with one eye on the other realities of this existence. Allowing oneself to admit that the beginning and end of all things may not be contained in the world of wisdom provides liberation to formulate a doctrine of "enough." One should indeed take what is available from wisdom, but should recognize that there are other ways of looking at things, other worthwhile activities, other perspectives that make wisdom relative.

NOTES

[1] Michael V. Fox, *A Time to Tear Down & A Time to Build Up* (Grand Rapids: Eerdmans, 1999), 182; Choon-Leong Seow, *Ecclesiastes* (AB 18C; New York: Doubleday, 1997), 133, takes the *waw* as "explicative," yielding the sense "irrationality, that is, folly."

[2] R. N.Whybray, *Ecclesiastes* (NCB; Grand Rapids: Eerdmans, 1989), 21.

[3] See *ANET*, 432-34. Compare this with Sir 38:24–39:11.

A REVIEW OF TOIL, PROFIT, WISDOM, AND FOLLY

Ecclesiastes 2:18-26

Verses 18-26 comprise the closing unit of thought in this introductory section on the king's personal investigation of the good, 1:11–2:26. The final reflection reviews earlier conclusions regarding toil and its profitability, wisdom and its negligible advantages over folly. The king's conclusions reach a climax in their negative appraisal of God. Ultimately, God has made things the way they are (v. 24), so that humans can do nothing but accept them. We have encountered this resignation already in 1:13, the very beginning of the king's reflections. At the end of the king's reflections, such radical honesty provides structural closure as well as a reminder of the theological implications of the royal investigation. [Structure at a Glance: Ecclesiastes 2:18-26]

These deliberations leave no other option than to place responsibility for the situation squarely upon God's shoulders. This conclusion leads to Qoheleth's assertion that humans simply must learn to find happiness in their pointless, futile toil.

Structure at a Glance: 2:18-26

AΩ Structurally, there are two larger subunits of thought (vv. 18-23 and vv. 24-26) that can be subdivided into four smaller units of thought. Verses 18-23 portray the king offering a reprise of his earlier conclusions; vv. 24-26 stress the theological implications of his conclusions. Qoheleth's favorite phrases, "vanity," or "striving after wind," punctuate these assertions. Consider the following outline of the four subunits of thought.

Vv. 18-19 Toil and Wisdom Are Pointless
Vv. 20-21 Despair Over the Wise Leaving Prosperity to Fools
Vv. 22-23 Conclusion that All the Days of Humanity Are Pain
Vv. 24-26 Find Happiness in Toil, Since It Is God's Gift

Readers should attend to the relationships between two subunits that make up these closing nine verses of ch. 2. The claims in vv. 18-23 comprise three of the four smaller subdivisions of thought and remind readers in three forceful assertions that there is no getting ahead from one's toil, nor is wisdom a factor in long-term outcomes. Verses 18-19 revisit earlier themes beginning again with Qoheleth's stress on his hatred of his toil and his uncertainty of outcomes. Verses 20-21 intensify those emotions by asserting the king's despair over his toil since his wisdom has come to naught. Verses 22-23 open with a question that grows from the king's despair over futility and concludes that humanity's plight is pointless and frustrating. All three pairs conclude with "vanity," *hebel*.

COMMENTARY

All the Days of Humanity Are Pain, 2:18-23

Readers immediately recognize the resumptive use of "I hate," the same opening phrase as in v. 17. Here it signals connections with v. 17, the concluding verse in the preceding section, even as the body of these ensuing verses clearly indicates a new topic. There is a similar occurrence of this resumptive repetition in 2:11-12. The term "toil" in v. 18 means more than mere work, since the speaker indicates that he must "leave it to those who come after me." The term is metonymic for the products of the speaker's toil.[1] The word "toil" (*ʿāmal*) occurs nine times in vv. 18-26 (vv. 18—twice; 19—twice; 20—twice; 21—twice; 24—once), signaling its thematic centrality to this concluding passage. The reasons for Qoheleth's dismay become clear in v. 19, where he makes a comparative statement about the wise and fools. Whereas readers have come to expect that the wise have an advantage in everything (e.g., Prov 18:4-8; Eccl 2:14), here wisdom has made no such impression on the king. The fool is as likely as the wise to inherit the product of the king's toil. The use of the opening phrase "who knows" indicates the king's skepticism that there might be any principle of justice by which the transaction will take place. ["Who Knows?"] Qoheleth's favorite phrase, "indeed, this was *hebel*" concludes v. 20.

The opening of v. 20 sounds familiar; the speaker "turns" to consider the implications of his conclusions as in vv. 11-12. Here the verb is not *pānîtî* ("I turned") but *sabbôtî* ("I returned" or "I turned back"), though the two seem to function in the same way. The king returns to despair, the complete abandonment of hope, regarding

---

"Who Knows?"

AΩ The phrase "who knows" (*mî yôdēaʿ*) stands out at the opening of v. 19. It occurs a total of ten times in the Hebrew Bible (2 Sam 12:22; Joel 2:14; Jonah 3:9; Ps 90:11; Esth 4:14; Prov 24:22; Eccl 2:19; 3:21; 6:12; 8:1). Its occurrence in the wisdom literature marks a distinctive usage within the Hebrew Bible. This usage is especially important for understanding the special concerns of the book of Ecclesiastes.

In the occurrences in non-wisdom books in the Bible, the phrase gives expression to the phenomenon of absolute freedom. Nothing illustrates the function of freedom as a hopeful idea as clearly as the episode in 2 Sam 12. David is explaining to his servants why in the death of his child he has ceased to grieve, and while the child was alive he

mourned. The explanation for his grieving begins with the phrase "Who knows?" and asserts that while the child was alive, there was hope; the outcome was not predictable. There was the possibility that Yahweh would be gracious and restore the child's health. By contrast, in its wisdom occurrences the phrase *mî yôdēaʿ* becomes a term of skepticism. The unpredictability of outcomes, the idea behind the notion of freedom, becomes a basis for despair or at least the expression of doubt. This is clearly the case in the occurrences in Ecclesiastes.

For further reading, see James L. Crenshaw, "The Expression *mî yôdēaʿ* in the Hebrew Bible," *VT* 36 (1986): 273-88; and idem, "Qoheleth in Current Research," *HAR* 7 (1983): 41-56.

Job's Anger

The language of v. 23 has certain affinities with Job's own accusations of God, especially in Job 30:17-18. The setting of the poem (chs. 29–31) is Job's final defense. He describes former days in ch. 29, the present, including the intensity of his suffering, in ch. 30, and then takes an oath of innocence in ch. 31. The climactic oath in ch. 31 has the rhetorical effect of forcing the deity's hand, if this is conceivable. The long-silent creator must now either condemn Job, since he enforces the oath, or acquit him as innocent. After a pause for another friend to speak, Yahweh does in fact speak.

Job's description of his suffering in 30:17-18, like Eccl 2:23, uses the alternating night and day motif to structure the statement. In Job 30:16 we read, "days of affliction take hold of me" (*yo'ḥăzûnî yĕmê-'onî*). In Eccl 2:23 we read, "For all their days are full of pain, and their work is a vexation" (*kî kol-yāmāyw mak'obîm wāka'as 'inyānô*). In Job 30:17 we read that Job's pain does not rest (*wĕ'ōrqay lo' yiškābûn*). In Eccl 2:23 we read that the human heart does not rest (*lō' šākab libbô*). Both verses use the same verb for rest or lie down (*šākab*), and both use a cognate of the Hebrew word for toil and suffering.

For further reading, see Michael B. Dick, "The Legal Metaphor in Job 31," *CBQ* 41 (1979): 37-50; Georg Fohrer, "The Righteous Man in Job 31," in *Essays in Old Testament Ethics*, ed. J. L. Crenshaw and J. T. Willis (New York: KTAV Publishing House, 1974), 3-22.

---

all of the things he has produced. He helps his readers realize that the fool is as likely as the wise to receive benefit from his own toil. His despair is made even clearer in v. 21 as he moves from the particularity of his own observations to their general applicability for all society. The sage speaks of the experiences of "a man" (*'ādām*) or "one" (NRSV) rather than of what he himself has experienced. But he clarifies further that it is he himself who has the problem. One who has not toiled receives the good while one who has toiled receives nothing. He concludes this section with his favorite phrase, everything is *hebel*, but adds to it that such circumstances create a "great evil," by which he means, most likely, a great injustice.[2]

Qoheleth's thought therefore returns to the question raised at the beginning of the book, "what is there for humans in all their toil?" (1:3; NRSV: "What do people gain from all the toil at which they toil under the sun?"). The question evokes the frequently offered answer, which is the theme of the discussion up to this point: everything is *hebel.* Verse 23 explains why: days and nights of pain and vexation are the lot of humankind. The statement echoes some of the same language readers hear spewing from the mouth of Job in anger. [Job's Anger] In Ecclesiastes, there is a quiet and superficial resignation that covers the deeply entrenched bitterness and disappointment. The speaker resigns himself, because there is apparently nothing he can do to change his situation. God alone is the one who can change things, and God will not. Qoheleth's resignation is superficial, however, because he is still quite passionate about identifying the injustices that exist at the core of human existence.

Enjoyment of Toil Is God's Gift, 2:24-26

The royal prologue concludes by returning to the theological implications of the king's observations. Verse 24 serves as an answer, at least a partial answer, to the question raised in v. 22. What is there for humankind? The answer is to "find enjoyment in their toil," because toil is all that is left. In the knowledge that one has no control over the future, the only thing left is the present. The ability to enjoy the present in which one toils is indeed the gift of God.

Verse 24 is the first occurrence of a refrain-like response that occurs frequently throughout the entirety of the book (e.g., 3:12, 22; 5:18; 8:15; 9:7-9; 11:7-12). The words counsel individuals to enjoy their toil but acknowledge that this enjoyment only comes from God. What is more, conclusions about enjoying one's toil also reflect that God gives it arbitrarily. A rhetorical question in v. 25 would seem to reinforce the claim in v. 24 that all comes from God's hand. [Examining the Text of 2:25]

The concluding statement in v. 26 reminds readers that hard work does not ultimately yield profit. God is pleased with one and not with another. Exactly why this is so is never clear. One might read v. 26 as though there were some moral criterion implied, since the term "sinner" (*hôteʾ*) is contrasted with the "good." However, the term *hôteʾ* functions in some places to mean "one who offends" without any moral implications (e.g., 1 Kgs 1:21; 8:31; Exod 5:16; Prov 20:2). Taking the term *hôteʾ* in this way, lacking any moral sense, provides a more consistent reading with Qoheleth's arguments in the preceding verses. Ultimately, any attempt to get ahead is *hebel* and striving after wind. Even conventional moral categories do not adequately explain why one person excels and another does not.

Examining the Text of 2:25

AΩ The text of v. 25 is difficult and NRSV translators have made a decision, first, on the meaning of the Hebrew word here translated as "to enjoy" (*yāḥûs*) and, second, on the first person suffix attached to the concluding preposition making the phrase "from me" rather than "from him" (*mimmennî* or *mimmennô*) (Brueggemann). In the former case, the meaning of *yāḥûš* is uncertain. In the latter case, the implication would be that happiness only comes from the speaker, a royal figure, perhaps Solomon. While this might be a possibility given the speaker's complaint about passing his life's production on to another (see v. 21), given the context's concern with God, the emendation to the third person pronominal suffix, "from him," that is, from God, seems more appropriate. The king thus recognizes that, whether for good or ill, all things come from God.

CONNECTIONS

Living for the Moment

Jesus' teaching to "take no thought for tomorrow" echoes the sage's conclusion of the arbitrariness of the deity (cf. v. 26). The question is age-old and predicated on the assumption that God is absolutely free from humans' understanding of the order of the universe. One has but to reexamine the narratives that comprise the primordial history. The story of Cain and Abel prosaically illuminates a double irony of God's control and sovereignty.

Why does Yahweh choose to "gaze upon" Abel's offering and not Cain's? One commentator explains that it is a mistake to moralize the story. It is not a conflict between Cain and Abel that causes the problem. Rather it is Yahweh who causes the problem. "Yahweh chooses—accepts and rejects. . . . Life is unfair. God is free."[3] There is nothing on the face of the story to indicate a clear reason. Scholars have speculated that since one offering was livestock and the other agricultural, the story privileges one sociological point of view behind the text. While this may be so, the narrative certainly does not develop along these lines. In fact, the second irony is that Abel's name is *hebel*, referring clearly to the brevity and insignificance of his truncated life. Cain, the one who complained about the injustice of things and was even punished for his murderous act, is nevertheless allowed to live and raise offspring. God's justice does not demand Cain's life for his brother's!

What is interesting is Yahweh's response to Cain's anger about the apparent injustice of the deity's receiving one gift and not the other. He gives Cain a choice: "If you do well, will you not be accepted? And if you do not do well, sin is lurking at the door; its desire is for you, but you must master it" (Gen 4:7). The truth is that the universe is not just. But it is equally true that one is held responsible for one's choices and must therefore master the choice to commit evil.

Living for the moment is somewhere in between zeal and resignation. It was not Abel's zealous preparation that caused God to accept his offering; neither was it Cain's insistence on justice that caused God to spare his life. It was, however, Cain's choice to commit murder that forever changed his life. Readers are reminded that the fabric of God's grace is not cut from the bolt of justice. Rather, it defies justice, even transcends it. Living for the moment is living within the grace of the creator. That grace is not something that removes real choices to commit evil. Rather, that grace intensifies the importance of one's choices, since one must bear the responsibility for those choices.

NOTES

[1] See Michael V. Fox, *A Time to Tear Down & A Time to Build Up* (Grand Rapids: Eerdmans, 1999), 186-87.

[2] James L. Crenshaw, *Ecclesiastes* (OTL; Philadelphia: Westminster, 1987), 88.

[3] Walter Brueggemann, *Genesis* (Atlanta: John Knox Press, 1982), 56-57.

EVERYTHING IN ITS PLACE

Ecclesiastes 3:1-15

Turns on the Goodness of Order, 3:1–4:16

The royal testimony now completed, the sage turns to considerations and instructions that continue to develop his opening observations given voice through the person of a king. It is not that there is no order to reality, but that the order seems senseless in light of endless repetition (1:4-11) and unprofitable toil (see 2:18-23). The section beginning in 3:1 opens with another phenomenon rendering the observed order meaningless and impenetrable: death (3:2, 8; 19-21). Ultimately death makes all experiences relative, including those recognized by the sage as central to individual and social existence. These include justice (3:16-22), relationships (4:7-12), religious commitments (5:1-6), and wealth and its benefits (5:9-10; 6:1-9). With these topics the first half of the book of Ecclesiastes comes to a close.[1]

The pervasiveness of allusions to death and the structural significance of its treatment in these next passages give readers pause for reflection upon the overall structure of the book (see introduction). Arguments for a unifying structure of the remaining materials in the first half of the book (3:1–6:9) do not convince readers fully, however. Choon-Leong Seow divides the first half of the book into "reflection" (1:2–4:16) and "ethics" (5:1–6:9), providing convenient categories for further subdivision of the individual ideas.[2] On the whole, however, scholars tend to be cautious when it comes to the reading of large sections such as 3:1–4:16 as though they were thematically connected to one idea. This is especially so when such interpretation appears to impose modern reading and writing conventions upon ancient literary forms. It is better to pay attention to the interconnectedness of individual themes and ideas as one reads than to hold hard and fast to a supposed structural unity.

Everything in Its Place, 3:1-15

This section of the sage's reflection opens with poetry. Thematically and structurally there are parallels between this opening poem in

vv. 1-8 and the poem in 1:4-11. In 1:4-11 nature provides a glimpse into the unending repetition of life's cycles that could function as order. In 3:1-8 it is not nature so much that structures reality, but the cycles of human social behavior. Readers nevertheless get the distinct impression that, though this order is about human society, humans are not themselves in control. Rather, they are subject to the very reality to which they contribute and in which they participate.[3] Again, there is the potential to understand the poem as an assertion of an ordered and meaningful reality. There is equal potential to read this poem as an assertion of the oppressiveness of human existence, precisely because it is so inescapably ordered. These verses may be divided into the poem proper (vv. 1-8) and the sage's reflections upon the poem (vv. 9-15). It seems clear that the two are connected through the recurrence of thematic language: Verse 11 contains the same reference to time we see in vv. 1-8 ("a time to be . . ."). Fourteen pairs of opposites structure each line, with the opening line in v. 2 (on birth and death) paralleling thematically the final pair in v. 8 (on war and peace).

The reflections on the poem in vv. 9-15 consist of an opening question, v. 9, and three responses. The three individual responses each open with the narrator's assertion of personal experience: "I have seen" (v. 10), "I know" (v. 12), and "I know" (v. 14). Thus the unit both asserts a summary of social order and then in retrospect reflects upon the threat this order may pose to meaning.

COMMENTARY

Time Is Order, 3:1-8

The theme of the poem is stated in v. 1: all things have a place or specific time. The NRSV translates 3:1 so that every "matter" has a time and season under heaven. Obviously, nature could be included within the term "everything" here, but the poem only sets out things that concern human society. The word translated "matter," the Hebrew word *ḥēpeṣ* (cf. 3:1, 17; 5:8; 8:6), is in other places throughout the book translated as "desire" or "pleasure" (e.g., 5:4; 12:1b, 10). Here is an example of a word that has multiple meanings within the book. Clearly the context of the poem renders the meaning of desire or pleasure unlikely in that it refers

Structure at a Glance: Ecclesiastes 3:2-8

AΩ One scholar argues that there is a further level of arrangement that would see at least seven pairs of pairs in a chiastic arrangement (for chiasm, see discussion of structure in Prov 1:20-33). This is achieved by assigning to each element of a pair the value of "desirable" or "undesirable." In this case readers could see that the two pairs in v. 2 might be considered either desirable or undesirable: birth = desirable (D), death = undesirable (U); to plant = desirable (D), to pluck up what is planted = undesirable (U). The following diagram aims to capture graphically the emerging structure.

D–U (2x in v. 2)
U–D (2x in v. 3)
U–D (2x in v. 4)
D–U (2x in v. 5)
D–U (2x in v. 6)
U–D (2x in v. 7)
D–U (v. 8a)
U–D (v. 8b)

While such structures may provide opportunities for imaginative reading, readers should be cautious about assigning such values to the phenomena named in the poem. Even within the sage's own argument these phenomenon have different values (see Loader; Murphy).

J. Loader, *Polar Structures in the Book of Qohelet* (BZAW 152; Berlin: De Gruyter, 1969), 240-42.

Roland Murphy, *Ecclesiastes* (WBC 23A; Dallas: Word, 1992), 32.

---

to activities that are not pleasurable or desirable (e.g., death, war, weeping, etc.).[4]

By beginning in v. 2 with birth and death, readers understand that the subject is comprehensive in nature. The poet's approach mixes literal human phenomena with metaphorical equivalents. Thus, in v. 2 birth and death are paralleled with planting and plucking up what is planted. The agricultural image provides a richer metaphorical context against which to interpret otherwise mundane human events. Life and death are like the cycles of planting and harvesting. Life and death give way to activities of killing and healing in v. 3, another pair that has metaphorical qualifiers of breaking down and building up. The word for "breaking down" occurs frequently in reference to stone walls, which were used by farmers to protect crops (e.g., Isa 5:5; 49:17; Ps 80:12). The metaphorical implications suggest that killing is like tearing down a stone wall; sometimes it is necessary. [Structure at a Glance: Ecclesiastes 3:2-8]

The next pair in v. 4 pursues human emotions of weeping and laughing, which are further characterized by the activities of mourning and dancing. The art of the Hebrew poet is further illustrated in the paronomasia created by the word choice. This simply means that the words not only parallel each other in sense but in

Greek Art

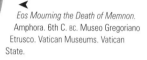 Greek art thought to be contemporaneous with Qoheleth depicts both weeping and dancing. The figures on the Attic vase depict a slain man and women mourning; the statue portrays a woman dancing.

◄ *Eos Mourning the Death of Memnon.* Amphora. 6th C. BC. Museo Gregoriano Etrusco. Vatican Museums. Vatican State.

Kallimachos. *Dancing Maenad.* Roman copy of Greek original. c. 410–400 BC. 143 cm. Museo dei Conservatori. Rome, Italy. ►

sound as well: *libkôt* and *liśḥôq*, for "to weep" and "to laugh"; *sĕpôd* and *rĕqôd* for "to mourn" and "to dance." [Greek Art] The pairs in v. 5 form a provocative puzzle depending upon whether readers understand "casting" and "gathering" of stones metaphorically or literally. The inclination to read gathering stones against an agricultural background, as in 3b, is reinforced by the broad social context. An agricultural worldview shapes the perspectives of biblical writers, and both gathering and throwing stones is a matter of preparing a field for agricultural purposes (e.g., Isa 5:2; 2 Kgs 3:19, 25). Alternatively, throwing stones could be construed as an act of hostility and violence. The Midrash Rabbah on Qoheleth reads sexual imagery into the image of throwing stones. [Midrash Rabbah on Qoheleth] Throwing stones might therefore be a cipher for sexual incontinence; gathering stones stands for sexual continence. The ensuing images of embracing and refraining from embrace in 5b form a possible parallel with the sexual reading of 5a and are only remotely connected with anything agricultural.

Both 5a and 6b utilize the phrase "throwing away," implying the possibility of both thematic and structural connections between the two. But this seems not to be the case. The agricultural imagery of 5a does not quite match up with the allusion in v. 6 to a futile search. The word translated in NRSV "to lose," *lĕ ʾabbēd,* means "to perish, or die" in other parts of the Hebrew Bible. In late biblical

Midrash Rabbah on Qoheleth

The "great midrash" on the book of Qoheleth, or Ecclesiastes in its Greek name, is one of many ancient rabbinic works of biblical exposition. Within the framework of rabbinic literature, roughly consisting of *halakah*, or the rules by which one keeps Torah; *haggadah*, material that illustrates the meaning of the Scripture; *midrash*, a way of interpreting Scripture; *and mishnah*, a way of learning and passing on the *halakah* of Torah, the *midrash* could be best thought of as a vehicle for exegeting Scripture. The Midrashim are the literary works that resulted from the process of interpreting Scripture.

Qohelet Rabbah is therefore a rabbinic commentary on the book of Scripture with the same name. Within the commentary there is a quotation of the book of Qoheleth itself (unlike *mishnah*, which simply quotes the interpretation or the traditional instruction on *halakah*). This *Midrash Rabbah* on Qoheleth is late and probably originated in the 7th century AD.

For further reading, see J. Bowker, *The Targums and Rabbinic Literature* (Cambridge: Cambridge Univ. Press, 1969), 79.

Hebrew the meaning of "to lose" is well attested.[5] The tearing of garments is a common act of mourning in the biblical story (e.g., Job 1:20; 2 Kgs 22:11; Ezra 9:3), and the sewing of garments, although the image is rare, seems logically to be a reversal of such mourning behavior. The next pair concerns a "time for silence" and a "time to speak" and could easily correspond to the implied mourning behavior in 7a. However, readers might also simply recall the frequent references to silence throughout the Proverbs (e.g., 10:19; 13:3; 17:27; 21:23) as a means of maintaining control over one's speech. Thus, 7b need not be taken to reinforce the allusion to mourning in the language of 7a.

The concluding pairs of contrasting statements in v. 8 are connected through the two abstract nouns, "love" and "hate," which are exemplified by "war" and "peace." Together they create a chiasm. Recalling v. 2, readers connect "birth" and "death" as two concrete human experiences that often are associated with love and hate. War and peace are as timely, or appropriate, as birth and death; both pairs of activities take their rightful place within human social existence.

God as the Source of this Order, 3:9-15

The section begins in v. 9 with the same language set out previously, "what gain" (cf. 1:3; 2:22; 5:16; 6:11), as if to invite readers to question whether knowing the source of this order makes any difference for the meaningfulness of human life. Returning to personal observations, the sage argues that, if anything, the order imposed upon human social existence is itself a mystery and adds nothing to the purpose of human toil.

These observations of the sage provide the structure of the response in vv. 9-15. Verses 10-11 open with "I have seen," vv. 12-13 with "I know," and vv. 14-15 with "I know." It is significant that the assertion of "I know" follows the assertion that "I have seen," indicating that the conclusions rest upon reasoning drawn from personal observation. The thematic connection between these verses of reflection and the preceding poem is implied by the repetition in v. 11 of language familiar from vv. 1-8: "He has made everything suitable in its time." Verse 9 opens the section with a rhetorical question. Readers experience again the preceding conclusion that all human activity is pointless since it is not profitable. Verse 10 asserts again the "business" (*'inyān*) God has given to humanity; only here it refers to the predetermined times. The outcomes do not differ, it now seems, from the activities humanity strives for in this existence (1:12–2:26).

Verse 11 stands out as one of the first reflections in response to the rhetorical question of v. 9 and the assertion of God's imposition of order. "He has made everything suitable for its time" evokes reflection upon the Genesis creation account. In that story, the use of the same verb, "to do, or make" (*'āśâ*), dominates the action of the story (see Gen 1:7, 16, 25). By alluding to the creation story, Ecclesiastes may be implying ironically the goodness of all that happens. The term translated in NRSV as "suitable" is in other places translated "beautiful" (*yāpeh*; see also 2 Sam 13:1; Amos 8:13; Prov 11:22). The context of Ecclesiastes 5:17 indicates the term may also have the meaning of "right." The statement further indicates that God is the source of this order. Part of God's activity, v. 11 continues, is to "put a sense of past and future into their minds," despite which humankind "cannot find out what God has done from the beginning to the end." The term translated "past and future" (*'ōlām*) might also be taken as "hiddenness, or darkness" since the root of the word might have that meaning. However, it seems clear that the occurrence of the same word in v. 14 is unambiguously concerned with "futurity," "endurance," and "that which is beyond time." It seems reasonable to infer from the larger context the same significance for the word in v. 11. In contrast to God's making all things in their time, humans have a sense of timelessness and eternity. For this reason humans cannot find out God's work.[6]

In view of such a statement of general human ignorance of God's works, it is doubly ironic that the sage puts forward his own knowledge in vv. 12 and 14 of what is good for humankind and of the implications of God's works. He concludes that what God has made cannot be changed (v. 14); humankind's response is one of simply finding enjoyment in its own work. Indeed that enjoyment is God's gift (v. 13); God has made things this way so that humans will stand in awe (will fear) of God (v. 14). The idea of fear is not that of terror as much as it is one of distance and separation. God has made humankind for a place, too.

The closing statement in v. 15 could serve as an epigram for this passage on the significance of timely order: "That which is, already has been, and that which is to be, already is." Readers have encountered a variation of this thought in 1:9, the introductory poem on nature and its circularity (cf. 1:4-11). In the present passage this final statement is difficult to understand. The general meaning of the phrase "God seeks out what has gone by" seems to be that God seeks to do things God has already done.[7] [The Crux of 3:15] As we probe for some theological significance, we must also bear in mind the larger context. Order establishes both predictability and repetition. In the present context, repetition conceals more about God than it reveals.

The Crux of 3:15

AΩ The final phrase in v. 15, though occurring in a context that concerns life's circularity, nevertheless raises questions. Only with great difficulty are readers able to infer what claim is being made about God's activity.

NRSV translates, "and God seeks out what has gone by." The questions concern the meaning of the object of God's seeking "what has gone by." The Hebrew word *nirdāp*, translated as "seeks out," comes from the root *rādap*, which means to pursue or to persecute. In the Niphal stem (a participle in v. 15), its meaning is passive, thus "what is pursued" or "persecuted." The latter meaning seems to be eliminated by the larger context. This leaves an abstract concept to interpret. One solution stems from the observation that *rādap*, "to pursue," and *biqqēš*, "to seek," are used as synonyms in other contexts (see Ps 34:15; Zeph 2:3 with Deut 16:20), making more certain the narrow idea of seeking (Gordis). Thus God seeks what has been sought or seeks what God has sought before. This translation reiterates the notion of the inescapable circularity of existence.

R. Gordis, *Koheleth: The Man and His World* (New York: Schocken, 1968), 233-34.

CONNECTIONS

"The Plain Sense of Things"

Wallace Stevens (1879–1955) was born in Reading, Pennsylvania (he studied at Harvard, though never graduated). As a poet he is known supremely for his use of unexpected diction and imagery. His poetry often features a concern with points of view and the "interaction of the observed and the observer."[8] His poem "The Plain Sense of Things" opens with the stark assertion that meaning derives from the imagination of the poet. The idea of imagining order, or imagining nature's repetitions to bear the significance of order, provides some contemporary touchstone for our own reflections upon what may be happening in Ecclesiastes 3:1-15.

> After the leaves have fallen, we return
> To a plain sense of things. It is as if
> We had come to an end of the imagination,
> Inanimate in an inert savoir.

As the poem continues, it is not just meaning that results from the imagination, but the absence of meaning, too. Poets have to imagine what a meaningless world would be like:

> Yet the absence of the imagination had
> Itself to be imagined. The great pond,
> The plain sense of it, without reflections, leaves,
> Mud, water like dirty glass, expressing silence
> Of a sort, silence of a rat come out to see,
> The great pond and its waste of the lilies, all this
> Had to be imagined as an inevitable knowledge,
> Required, as a necessity requires.[9]

Not unlike Stevens, Qoheleth imagines a world in which everything has a place and a time, a world that is actively overseen by a creator. But imagination also allows the poet to see that such predictability in and of itself does not guarantee meaningful existence. The cycles that serve to regulate and offer predictability may also create a kind of moribund existence, where there is no variety or diversity, and where predictability becomes an oppressive and inescapable prison. Dullness becomes the plain sense, and the human search for order is a kind of mendacious excuse for the abandonment of a spirit that is open for new and unpredictable experiences.

The plain sense of things is that God's gift is the ability to enjoy one's work and to be able to eat and drink in addition. This perspective is itself a cooperative act between one's own imaginative will and the everyday circumstances of one's life. Individuals choose to participate in a reality where God both conceals and reveals. Or, to put it as the sage has, God seeks after that which is already sought. Individuals who can accept life this way are not therefore on a search for order or meaning. Rather, they are cooperating with the order God has already established, remaining attentive to what there is that is new, original, different.

The new, the original, and different are those truly remarkable events that are not of the usual order. They move beyond the plain sense of things. Jesus of Nazareth was in Wallace Stevens's sense no plain sense sort of person. How electrifyingly imaginative the resurrection is. It is through this decisive act that God declares something absolutely new breaking into this plain sense world. The resurrected Christ calls humankind to move beyond a plain sense kind of life; to be free from endless seeking and speculation, free to play with the imagination, and absolutely assured that the one new thing inserted into this ordered reality calls all people to new life with Christ our brother.

NOTES

[1] Choon-Leong Seow, *Ecclesiastes* (AB 18C; New York: Doubleday), 43-46.

[2] Ibid., 43-46.

[3] See Peter L. Berger, *The Sacred Canopy* (Garden City NY: Anchor Books, 1969), 29-51.

[4] For further reading, see W. E. Staples, "The Meaning of ḥēpeṣ in Ecclesiastes," *JNES* 24 (1965): 110-12.

[5] Seow, *Ecclesiastes,* 162.

[6] Ibid., 163; but compare Michael V. Fox's disagreement in *A Time to Tear Down & A Time to Build Up* (Grand Rapids: Eerdmans, 1999), 212.

[7] Fox, 214.

[8] See Nina Baym, ed., *The Norton Anthology of American Literature,* vol. 2, 5th ed. (New York and London: W. W. Norton & Company, 1998), 1164-66.

[9] Ibid., 1184.

IMAGINING A WORLD OF JUSTICE

Ecclesiastes 3:16-22

Chapter 3 concludes with the sage's assertions of some far-reaching implications of a world that does not turn on human justice.[1] In despairing the pervasiveness of injustice in society, the sage finds that what is even more pervasive is death. In a world where people imagine that justice is the numerator, death is the common denominator.

The relationship of this passage to what precedes is especially challenging for readers. The phrase translated in v. 16 as "Moreover I saw" (*ʿôd rāʾîtî*) implies a disjunction with what precedes. The same phrase has been used in earlier parts of the argument to open a new section or block of thought (e.g., 1:14; 2:13; 3:10). Reading through the claims in vv. 16-22 reveals other phrases, however, that seem to draw from the poetry in vv. 1-8. This is especially so in 17b, "for he has appointed a time for every matter" (*kî-ʿēt lĕkol-ḥēpeṣ*). This phrase is virtually identical to 3:1, which sets out the theme of the poetic unit in 3:1-8. The overall effect upon the reader is to connect the new section (vv. 16-22) with the poetic unit in vv. 1-8 and the comments in 9-15.

The exposition of Qoheleth's thought in these verses is set out symmetrically in four statements. Two are encountered in vv. 16-17 and two in vv. 18-22. Verses 16-17 state that there is injustice and that God nevertheless judges. Verses 18-21 state that life yields death and v. 22 states that life yields pleasure. These two pairs of oppositions and their echoing of the pairs of oppositions in vv. 1-8 function to reiterate the events of human social order as it is regulated by the reality of human nature.

COMMENTARY

The Pervasiveness of Injustice, 3:16-17

The experience of the sage is again captured in the verb "I have seen," and reiterates an emphasis upon this sage's attempts to be as empirical as possible (e.g., 2:13, 24b; 3:10, 22; 4:1, 15; 5:13, 18; 6:1; 7:15; 8:9, 10, 17; 9:13; 10:5, 7). The place of justice in antiquity was the city gate where Qoheleth believes justice may or may not take place. The irony is that vv. 1-8 have just asserted that for everything there is a time, implying the reality of order. However, in the place where justice and righteousness are to prevail, their opposite, wickedness, is also there. [Injustice in the Bible]

Readers are set up, therefore, for the counter assertion in v. 17 that God judges the righteous and the wicked. Scholars have thought this to be contradictory to the claims of v. 16 and have hypothesized that it comes from a secondary hand.[2] Nevertheless, such contradictory claims pervade the entire book and readers may just as easily attribute them to the aims of the sage to illustrate the deity's inscrutability (cf. 3:10-11). What is more, the sage makes a direct appeal to the assumptions set out in vv. 1-8: there is a time for everything. Within the framework of these assumptions, God ensures justice, even though it cannot be observed in human courts.

Injustice in the Bible

The sage joins an august body of biblical witnesses who have dared to raise their voices in disagreement with the received tradition of a universe that turns on justice. Within the sage's own tradition there is, of course, Job, whose arguments lead to an unfortunate impasse: Yahweh challenges back, "Will you condemn me that you may be justified?" (40:8b). The category of justice, as conceived by Job and his friends, is shown to be inadequate for accommodating all of life's exigencies.

The extent to which other of the deity's servants grasp the conundrum of a just deity who allows injustice in his creation is seen in narrative, prophetic, and liturgical literature alike. The psalmist nearly loses faith when he sees "the prosperity of the wicked" (Ps 73:3). Jeremiah reels when he grasps the fundamental inconsistency between his own message and God's enforcement of principles: "Why does the way of the guilty prosper?" (Jer 12:1). Likewise, the patriarch Abraham states the problem most eloquently when

he asks whether the judge of all the earth does not do justice (Gen 18:25).

Even beneath the eschatological reassurances of the earliest Christian missionary is the stark assumption that things must nevertheless be set aright (Rom 8:18). The delays, furthermore, continue into the second and third generations of Christians, who continue to struggle to formulate a response to those who are relentless in their reminder that justice has not yet come (2 Pet 3:1-7).

For further reading, see James L. Crenshaw, "The Birth of Skepticism in Ancient Israel," in *The Divine Helmsman*, ed. James L. Crenshaw and Samuel Sandmel (New York: Ktav, 1980), 1-19; idem, *Theodicy in the Old Testament* (Philadelphia: Fortress, 1983); idem, *Whirlpool of Torment* (Philadelphia: Fortress, 1984); Stephen T. Davis, ed., *Encountering Evil* (Edinburgh: T&T Clark, 1981); and Elie Wiesel, *A Consuming Fire: Encounters with Elie Wiesel and the Holocaust* (Atlanta: John Knox Press, 1979).

The Relative Importance of Justice, 3:18-21

The sage's inner thoughts about the injustices he observes turn to the fate of humankind, which is no different than that of animals. The Hebrew text of v. 18 is difficult grammatically and syntactically. [The Text of 3:18] The sage's comparison is obviously pejorative. The presumption of humankind is that they are above the animals. Death makes it clear that humans are not so different. When it comes to justice, righteousness, and wickedness (cf. vv. 16-17), humankind may also be no different. [God "Testing" Humans] Furthermore, juxtaposing the failure of justice with the fate of humans, namely their deaths, creates an interesting problem: might the sage be laying the groundwork for a reflection upon the possibility of an afterlife?

The sage's line of thought develops in vv. 19 and 20. His assertions move from the comparison of humans to animals in death to speculating on human life after death, a life that is qualitatively different from that of the animals mentioned in v. 21. The idea of identifying humans with animals is not itself new in the Bible. Readers have seen this in the creation story of Genesis 1:24-27. On the sixth day of creation God makes both humankind and the animals. In Genesis 2:7 and 19 Yahweh makes the man and the animals from the dust of the ground. The only difference is he breathes into the man, but not the animals (see Gen 2:7). In Ecclesiastes 3:20 the sage uses the distinctive language of Genesis 2: humans, like animals, come from dust and return to dust (Gen 3:19). Likewise, the wisdom tradition associates humans with

The Text of 3:18

AΩ There are three main textual difficulties in this verse, the first two being the presence of two infinitival forms without a finite verb in the sentence. First, the phrase rendered in NRSV as "God is testing them" translates an infinitival form, *lĕbārām*, from the verb *bārar*, "to choose" or "test"; second, the phrase translated in NRSV as "to show *that*" is also awkward in that it, too, is an infinitival form, *welir 'ôt*. It is taken as a syncopated Hiphil of *rā'â*, to "cause to see," thus "to show." Thirdly, the phrase translated "that they are but animals" seems to suffer from duplicated words (dittography—*šĕhem bĕhēmâ hēmmâ*). Still, translators and commentators are generally agreed that the verse claims God to be setting humans apart from Godself in some fashion by comparing them with animals.

God "Testing" Humans

AΩ The word translated in NRSV as "testing" is *lĕbārām*, from the root *bārar*, to "purify" or "select." The term seems more appropriately translated as "set apart," thus more related to the idea of "select" than "test." The term occurs in contexts where the idea is to "purge" (Ezek 20:38) and "purify" (Zeph 3:9) or "cleanse," "polish" (Isa 49:2). As such, the purpose of testing is to determine whether a thing or a person is pure, or cleansed. The root idea of "select" or "set apart" seems more at home here, however, by virtue of the larger context. Humans are "set apart" from God that they may see they have more in common with beasts, particularly in the face of death.

The idea of God's testing various individuals in the biblical story is not uncommon, however. The more common vocabulary for "test," when the deity intends to determine an individual's or a community's loyalty or trust (see Gen 22:1; Exod 15:25; Deut 33:8; 2 Chr 32:31) is from the root *nāśā'*, to "test" or "try." Interestingly, Qoheleth uses the same word, *nāśā'*, to describe the process behind his instruction in 2:1 and 7:23. While the sage's purpose seems not to be that of "testing God" (as in Exod 17:2, 7; Num 14:22; Ps 78:18, 41; Isa 7:12), the effects of his scrutiny are similar.

beasts (*běhēmôt*). Yahweh's response to Job indeed elevates Job's status by claiming that he is "like" the mighty mythological creature of creation, *běhēmôt* (Job 40:15). Nevertheless, the traditions of Genesis and Job only allow Qoheleth to conclude that both humans and animals must die.

What is perhaps more interesting is the sage's play on the word "place" (*māqôm*) in vv. 16 and 20. In verse 16 the sage begins his observations about the place for justice. Instead of justice, however, he sees injustice. In v. 20 he reflects upon the significance of another place, that place where the body goes when it turns to dust. Of course, in this verse the sage is referring to the dust. Readers may muse, however, about the possible connections between the two places. The sage's certainty that justice is out of its place may only intensify readers' certainty that it, like human life, is swallowed up by the dust of death.

Verse 21 raises the question whether there might be any qualitative difference between humans and animals in relationship to their deaths. The image of the spirit of one going up and the spirit of another going down may well be the sage's recognition of Hellenistic anthropology.[3] The sage rejects this in v. 21 in his use of the skeptical phrase, "who knows?" But he seems to be raising the possibility of death leading to a place and time where the judgment missed in the physical life could take place. The concluding verse of the unit evokes the sage's experiential authority. Here again (cf. 2:24 and 3:12) the sage urges human enjoyment (*yiśmaḥ*) in whatever way there is available. Given the unknowable future and its eventual outcomes (dust), finding enjoyment in the work of one's hands is a gift from God (cf. 2:24-26; 3:12; 5:17-18; 8:15; 9:7-9; 11:9-10).

CONNECTIONS

Justice and the Beasts

In his extraordinary tale, *Ishmael*, Daniel Quinn cultivates a remarkable parable wherein a lowland gorilla, Ishmael, harried by the loss of home and habitat at the hands of ever encroaching human culture, tells his story to a young person who searches for meaning. Ishmael casts his story of human culture as a clash between the values of the "Leavers," hunter/gatherer types who are kind to the environment, and "Takers," human agriculturists who

Life After Death

The assertion of God's certain judgment in v. 17, the query of the joint fates of humans and beasts after death in v. 19, and the expression of doubt that anyone really knows about the direction of both human and animal spirits after death in v. 21 all testify to the interest of the sage in life beyond death. The writers of these biblical texts did not express much confidence that the grave held any hope beyond a gloomy underworld.

Scholars generally agree that a belief in a blessed afterlife emerges in the post-exilic period under various influences. First, the biblical tradition itself contains several ancient narratives that speculate on human immortality. The story of the Paradise garden in Gen 3 presupposes the possibility of immortality for the man and the woman. Similarly, the translation of Enoch in Gen 5:24 as well as the ascension of Elijah in 2 Kgs 2:1-12 both imagine the possibility of transcending death. Second, the failure of the belief that God really rewards the righteous and punishes the wicked, especially in the post-exilic period, creates the intellectual despair that propels the imaginations of still later writers to move justice beyond the grave. One of the expressions of this earliest confidence in a blessed afterlife is in Wisdom of Solomon. This book responds to the call for justice and expresses a Hellenistic anthropology that facilitates immortality.

For further reading, see T. J. Lewis, "Dead, Abode of the," *ABD* 2:102; J. Day, "Belief in Life after Death in Ancient Israel," in *After the Exile*, ed. John Barton, David J. Reimer (Macon: Mercer University Press, 1996), 231-58.

---

use up all natural resources and perpetuate a cultural myth that legitimizes their activities and arrogant attitudes. The Takers, of course, have dominated the scene since the founding of civilization. The only trace that the Leavers were ever present is through their story, preserved and passed on through characters such as Ishmael.

The Taker story, or myth, is one that explains why humans are not like all the other creatures on the planet. [Life After Death] It legitimizes the human claim that their destiny is "to conquer and rule." The Leaver story, by contrast, makes no such differentiation between humans and all other life forms on the planet. The wisdom of the Leavers celebrates "knowledge about what works well for people." "Takers accumulate knowledge about what works well for things."[4] Ultimately, they all share a common resource— the earth—and a common desire for survival.

The sage in Ecclesiastes 3:16-22 is remarkably at one with Ishmael, both in his stark assertion of human affinity with the beasts and in his observation of the failure of one of the most important notions of Taker culture: justice. Without drawing too great a parallel, it is interesting that Qoheleth subverts the dominant paradigm that unrelentingly maintains a universe that turns on the principles of justice. He asserts that where justice should occur there is frequently injustice. Then he appeals to his cultural story, that of God's creation and establishment of justice, and says to himself—as many people do who struggle with the injustices rampant in modern society—someday, somewhere, God will judge.

The appeal to human identification with the beasts offered by the sage in vv. 18-21 is an alternative way of seeking meaning. Humans are not gods, nor even godlike (contrary to what they may believe, based upon the most frequent interpretations of Gen 1:1–2:1). Their place, and thus their perspective, is with the beasts of the field. The adoption of such a story is not denigrating since the beasts, too, are wonders of creation. The creator makes that absolutely clear to Job (chs. 38–42). However, this view of humans as having great affinity with the beasts does offer quite a new outlook on life's purpose and on the categories by which human culture determines its meaning. Furthermore, such a view makes readers of this sage's wisdom now recall the singular importance of natural cycles that shape the search for meaning (cf. 1:2-7; 3:1-8) and the failure of human society to produce anything other than vanity (cf. 1:11–2:26).

NOTES

[1] Not all commentators agree that the canonical ending of the chapter concludes the thought begun in 3:16. James L. Crenshaw, *Ecclesiastes* (Philadelphia: Westminster, 1987), 101-107 and R. Gordis, *Koheleth — The Man and His World*, 234-39 both extend the section to 4:3. Choon-Leong Seow, *Ecclesiastes* (AB 18C; New York: Doubleday, 1997), 169-76; R. N. Whybray, *Ecclesiastes* (Grand Rapids: Eerdmans, 1989), 76-81; and Michael V. Fox, *A Time to Tear Down & A Time to Build Up* (Grand Rapids: Eerdmans, 1999), 217, maintain the canonical boundaries at 3:22.

[2] See Crenshaw, *Ecclesiastes,* 102, for instance, who allows that since such optimism does not pervade other parts of the sage's thought, this verse may well be a gloss.

[3] For Fox, *A Time to Tear Down,* 216, it would be Hellenistic; for Seow, *Ecclesiastes,* 176, who dates the book to the Persian period, the possible external influence, though speculative, is not Hellenistic.

[4] Daniel Quinn, *Ishmael* (New York, Toronto et al.: Bantam/Turner, 1992), 206.

THE RELATIVE GOOD VS. THE ABSOLUTE GOOD

Ecclesiastes 4:1-16

Chapter 4 consists of a series of five "better than" sayings of the kind readers encounter in the book of Proverbs (e.g., 12:9; 15:16-17; 16:19; 21:9, 19; 25:7, 24). Clearly, Ecclesiastes stands in the same tradition as the various authors and collectors of the Proverbs. The thrust of such sayings is to assess the quality of life by positing only a relative good (things could be a lot worse, in other words). Following the assertions of Ecclesiastes 3:16-22, which note the prevalence of injustice, the assurance of mortality, and the absolute certainty that humans are no different from the beasts regarding the afterlife, the rhetorical effect of "better than" sayings is provocative. They provide a reflective response in light of ultimate reality: justice is unreliable, death is inevitable, and life after death is uncertain. Therefore, it is better not to be born than to live, but if one must live, it is better to be alive than to be dead (4:1-3).

Generally, scholars recognize the form critical connections between these sayings ("better than" sayings) if not the thematic connections.[1] Fox

Structure at a Glance: Ecclesiastes 4:1-16

AΩ The chapter is easily subdivided according to its five observations, four of which have "better than" statements (4:1-3; 4:4-6; 4:9-12; 4:13-16). Readers recognize that vv. 7-8 stand out from the five sayings both because it is the central passage, and because it alone lacks a statement of a phenomenon that is relatively good. This unit simply summarizes the difficulties that come to people who are alone.

Fox assigns the loose thematic interconnectedness of these observations according to a chain of shared themes.

A. 4:1-3 The lack of sympathetic fellowship for the oppressed
B. 4:4-6 Jealousy as the fuel for toil
C. 4:7-8 The lone man's pointless labor
D. 4:9-12 The value of companionship
E. 4:13-16 The conflict among successive rulers, showing an injustice suffered by wisdom

The links between units A and B (vv. 1-3 and 4-6) are on the theme of fellowship; units B and C (vv. 4-6 and 7-8) are connected through their allusions to toil; and units C and D (vv. 7-8 and 9-12) are similar in their treatment of aloneness, which introduces the topic of the companion (šēnî) of saying E. The final sayings seem most difficult to fit into this scheme dominated by fellowship, toil, companionship, and competition. Still, readers get the idea for one possible strategy of reading these individuals as a unity.

believes that there is a loose thematic relationship among the sayings; however, he notes that all five sayings, which he lists in alphabetic sequence (e.g., A-E), may be linked around a chain of themes concerning fellowship, toil, loneliness, and companionship.[2] Such an approach is reminiscent of the clustering techniques used in the collections of sayings in the book of Proverbs. The challenge for the reader is to read beyond the singular saying to discover how it might be related to its surrounding context. [Structure at a Glance: Ecclesiastes 4:1-16]

COMMENTARY

Death Better than Oppression, 4:1-3

Following the gloomy reality of death set out in 3:16-22, readers are immediately confronted with the possibility that there could in fact be some experience worse than death. Verse 1 opens with the characteristic affirmation of the horror of endless suffering. This suffering is the sort that comes from the hand of an oppressor, and the sage says nothing to indicate that such oppression is only an occasional phenomenon. The recurrence throughout these verses of the word "oppress" (*ʿāšaq*) conveys the prevalence of the oppression, even though the oppressor is not named. Clearly, oppression and being oppressed is a way of life for some. This sage is not the first to point out such oppression within the Bible, however. The prophetic tradition is full of instances where God's spokesperson called rulers to task for their abusive use of power (e.g., Amos 7:1-3; Isa 1:21-23; Jer 5:1-5). The tragedy of oppression as a given is that the presence of a comforter is not an equally given reality. What in Lamentations is a phenomenon tied to the historical moment of Jerusalem's destruction (Lam 1:2, 9, 16, 17, 21) has now become a characterization for a way of life: suffering may be irremediable.

It is this way of life, a life where there are none to comfort the oppressed, that leads the present sage to conclude initially that death is indeed better than life (v. 2). This cry is not new with Qoheleth. Job, too, has called out in his despair that death would be better than life (Job 3:11-19, 21-23). He even accuses the deity of being his oppressor in life: "Does it seem good to you to oppress, to despise the work of your hands, and favor the schemes of the wicked?" (10:3). Interestingly, Job the sufferer continues the conversation with the deity, perhaps because he is so personally involved and his comforters, who are not suffering, are so detached.

There is however something much more cold and calculating about it in the book of Ecclesiastes. It is not the sage, so far as one

---

Relativity of Death in Sirach

The Wisdom of Jesus ben Sirach is written much later than Ecclesiastes, perhaps between 200 and 180 BC, and under different circumstances. But the sage's attitude toward death is similar. In Sir 41:1-4 the sage notes death's inevitability (v. 4) but urges that its bitterness is related to an individual's particular circumstances at the time of death: it is "bitter" if one has no worries, numerous possessions, and is healthy (v.1). Death is welcome if one is poor, unhealthy, and generally miserable in life (v. 2). Either way, death should not be feared since all die, both those who precede one on the earth and those who follow. Moreover, death is God's decree and humans should simply be resigned to it (v. 4).

Sirach's attitude regarding death's inevitability would seem to parallel an inscription found on Hellenistic tomb markers that trivialized death: *non fui, fui, non sum, non curo* which translated says, "I was not, I was, I am not, I care not." The inscription was so common at one time it was abbreviated NFFNSNC (Ferguson).

For further reading, see Luther H. Martin, *Hellenistic Religions* (New York and Oxford: Oxford University Press, 1987).

Everett Ferguson, *Backgrounds of Early Christianity* (Grand Rapids: Eerdmans, 1987),195.

This marble Hellenistic grave stele from the 4th century BC shows loved ones bidding farewell to each other.

---

may discern, who is suffering. He is only observing, thus passing a detached judgment upon the meaning of another's suffering, something comforters do all too frequently. His words about the lack of a comforter create irony, therefore, when readers recall that Job wants release as much from his comforters as from his own physical suffering (Job 19:2-5). Observers of suffering, no matter how caring, simply cannot share the perspective until they suffer, too (although, they might ease the sufferer's pain!).

The actual better-than saying in v. 3 considers what really cannot be an option—"never to have been born." It is hyperbolic, of course, but indicates something of the extreme to which an observer of suffering may be driven. It would not be accurate to suggest that people who suffer themselves never wish for death. Job is a good example of one who wonders why he did not die (e.g., 3:20-23). The point is that suffering affects even those who are not suffering; those people think death better than life, too. [Relativity of Death in Sirach]

Better to Be Poor and Peaceful, 4:4-6

The prospect of finding comfort in the face of endless suffering and oppression would seem to grow yet dimmer in view of the motivation for all human toil. Verse 4 states that the lot of all humankind, which is meaningless toil, is the result of envy. The statement is closely tied to the theme of work's futility encountered throughout the discussion thus far. In Ecclesiastes the futility of work is fed by its motive: to get ahead or make a profit (e.g., 1:12–2:26). We can only infer the connection that there may be no one to comfort those who are suffering, because everyone sees other people as objects of competition. The price to be paid for having a community to offer comfort in times of suffering is that all toil is performed out of a sense of envy toward another community member. Is the price too high to be paid?

The implied conflict between getting ahead through competitive toil and the lack of a comforter for the oppressed comes into focus in the next two sayings. Verses 5 and 6 are proverbial; v. 6 is the concluding "better-than saying." The author basically agrees with the traditional view on work and laziness (e.g., Prov 6:10; 24:33). In the present context the lazy person is put forward as an example of the extreme approach to avoiding competition. The saying concludes that people who are lazy are fools, and their behavior is self-destructive. The phrase "consume their own flesh" refers to a kind of metaphorical self-cannibalism (Ps 27:2).

As an alternative to laziness, v. 6 counters with an image of moderation: the filling of "one hand" rather than the filling of "two." The image is not new. The wisdom of previous sages has asserted the idea of maximizing one's wealth along with one's quality of life (Prov 15:16; 16:8; 17:1). For the sage who is reflecting upon the futility of work due to human envy (cf. v. 4), the traditional view makes the point. If the ideal result can only be obtained at the cost of surrendering one's peaceful existence—which might be required to have the help of community during times of suffering—then the price is too high. It may be that Qoheleth appeals to a balance between wealth and happiness because his is a social world that fails to value the quality of life alongside the quantity of material possessions.

The Question, 4:7-8

The now familiar formula, "Again, I saw," introduces the third section of the chapter and alerts readers (as in 4:1) that something new may be occurring. It is especially noteworthy that the themes of the three remaining sections have to do with various kinds of paired relationships. In vv. 7-8 there is the relationship that motivates one's foil. This forms a connection with the motive of envy in

vv. 4-6. In vv. 9-12 there is a relationship of mutual care and in vv. 13-16 there is a relationship between a ruler and his successor.[3]

Readers recognize that in this central section there is no "better-than saying." There is only an observation. In the context, however, this observation will be the touchstone for further evaluation of what is relatively good. In contrast to laziness there is toil, but toiling for less and striving for quality of life is better than simply amassing quantity. In v. 7 the sage recognizes the ultimate futility of toiling for no one but oneself.

The use of *hebel*, translated "vanity" here, means more than mere futility and purposelessness. Rather, it carries with it the idea of "enigma."[4] In other words, there is something internally contradictory about depriving oneself of pleasure and then having no other person with whom to share the benefits. The question of v. 8, "For whom am I toiling," is ultimately the question that leads to the kind of soul-searching evaluation that is basic to the discovery of true meaning. The sage has laid the groundwork leading to his assertion that ultimately, meaning is in relationships.

Two Are Better than One, 4:9-12

In the fourth section of the chapter Qoheleth gives clear indication of what is relatively good in light of the enigma of aloneness. Here readers encounter his claim that, when there are two people toiling together, there is a relative good because their joint toil is rewarded. Three illustrations follow in vv. 10-12. Readers should note, however, that the rewards are only pragmatic and not emotional. In contrast to the interests of most modern readers, the ancient sage does not seem to be too concerned about the emotional dimension of companionship. The challenge for modern readers is to move beyond the sage's pragmatism by envisioning the depth of emotional and psychological well-being that may result in companionship.

The first illustration of the pragmatic benefits of companionship is when one falls into a pit. It is doubtful that the sage is only being metaphorical. More likely he has in mind the real world in which pits were used to capture animals (e.g., Prov 26:27; 28:10, 14; 28:18). If one does not travel alone, then one may always be able to escape from such life-threatening situations. The second illustration concerns the reality of sleeping in an environment where there is no heat. One possible setting in which this might be a physical possibility is travel. In a day of travel by foot and with scarcity of roadside inns, pilgrims slept beside the road. The Palestinian nights got cold. With a companion, there could be the possibility of generating warmth. The third example imagines some kind of conflict, either from attack (while traveling?) or simply general conflict. The thrust of the claim is that there is strength in numbers. If two people can withstand a threat better than one, just think what three might be able to withstand.[5]

Better to Be Poor and Wise in Politics, 4:13-16

The final section concerns the relative value of wisdom as illustrated in the problems and realities of political successions. The conclusion to which the sage presses is that, while wisdom can indeed accomplish great things, even wisdom succumbs to the faithlessness of a crowd to its king. The opening verse (v. 13) couches the initial comparison within the "better-than saying." A youth with wisdom is juxtaposed with an aged yet foolish king. Readers may recall that the teachers of wisdom usually gave deference to the wisdom of kings, because they are wise and aged (e.g., Job 32:4-7; Prov 16:10, 13; 25:2). One strategy for reading these verses (vv. 13-16) is suggested by the motif of succession and usurpation of the king. Several biblical stories in fact bear resemblance to the plot of the youthful successor who takes the place of the king. [Narratives Behind the Parable in 4:13-16] Verse 14 continues by affirming the possibility of emerging from prison to become king. The implication is that criminals might become kings. However, since prisons in antiquity were not places for reform but places to pay off debt, it is more likely that the emphasis is upon a rich-poor rather than a righteous-unrighteous dichotomy.[6]

The NRSV translation of v. 15 avoids one of the cruxes of the text and thereby conceals the more likely implication of the entire

---

Narratives Behind the Parable in 4:13-16

The Hebrew Scriptures are rich with narratives about the conflict between an older ruler and a younger successor. Joseph and Pharaoh immediately come to mind (Genesis 37–48), since young Joseph emerges from prison to be the second in command. David and Saul might also roughly fit the scheme. Young David comes from humble circumstances to usurp the popularity of the old King Saul, although he does not come from being imprisoned (1 Sam 18:1-9). Perhaps Jeroboam and Solomon reflect a similar scenario in that the rebellious labor leader was banished by Solomon to Egypt. Later he returned to Israel as the one who would reign in opposition to the Davidic-Solomonic heir, Rehoboam (1 Kgs 11:26-43).

In none of these instances does the narrative match exactly the sage's parable in 4:13. Readers only find slight common points of correspondence. Readers are encouraged to explore other biblical narratives as well as non-biblical narratives for similar parallels. For instance, according to Seow, some of the non-biblical characters who might qualify include Cyrus and Astyges, Antiochus III and Ptolemy Philopater, Ptolemy Philopater and Antiochus Epiphanes, and depending upon the dating of Ecclesiastes, other post-exilic and Hellenistic royal figures.

Choon-Leong Seow, *Ecclesiastes* (AB 18C; New York: Doubleday, 1997), 190.

The Crux of *hayyeled haššēnî*

AΩ The translation "that youth" of v. 15b in NRSV conceals the fact that the phrase in Hebrew means "the second" or "the next youth." There is no reason to emend the phrase itself. There is good textual verification for its presence in MT. Thus the question is simply one of its meaning. Does it refer to the initial youthful usurper of v. 14, or is it introducing a third character, one who usurps the youthful usurper?

The use of the word *šēnî* in other contexts to mean "next" (e.g., Exod 2:13; but see Judg 20:24) indicates that the term may mean something other than "second." In Exod 2, for instance, the word functions in a context where it must designate simply a day later than the earlier day, on which Moses killed the Egyptian, rather than the second day in a sequence of days. (NRSV there translates "the next day.") In Judg 20:24 by contrast, the larger context seems to call for the translation of the word as "second" since the preceding verses designate the preceding day with the adjective "first." A more idiomatic translation would seem to be "the next day." Thus the word may be taken more broadly than the narrow referent in Eccl 4:14. The larger context that indicates a concern with endless change may indeed justify a corresponding introduction of yet a third character. (The discussions of Michael V. Fox and R. N. Whybray are especially helpful.]

Michael V. Fox, *A Time to Tear Down & A Time to Build Up* (Grand Rapids: Eerdmans, 1999), 208.

R. N. Whybray, *Ecclesiastes* (NCB; Grand Rapids: Eerdmans, 1989), 89-90.

---

passage. The references to "that youth who replaced the king" in 15b lead readers to believe that the object of the crowd's devotion is the same individual who emerged from prison to usurp the king in the previous verse (v. 14). It is more likely that the phrase in Hebrew (*hayyeled haššēnî*) refers rather to yet a third individual, a second youth who succeeds the preceding youthful usurper. [The Crux of *hayyeled haššēnî*] In this latter reading the sage is more concerned with the inevitability of ongoing succession than he is with the fact of the possibility of usurpation by youthful kings.

The reference in v. 15 to those "moving about under the sun" translates the Hebrew *haměhallěkîm*, a word used in 1:6 to describe the circularity of the wind's movement. Readers therefore are to associate the crowd with this constant sea of change against which political leaders rise and fall (v. 16). The overall point seems to be that this constant shift of power and succession, although related to the wisdom of youth and frailty of age, is more a function of the vicissitudes of the crowds who follow and forget. One king is great in his day and then, with the coming of a new crowd, that king is forgotten and another king becomes great. It is the perfect illustration that greatness is in the minds of the ruled, not in the (wise) actions of the ruler.

CONNECTIONS

The Fellowship of Suffering

Robert Frost's poem "The Question" captures powerfully the self-conscious loss of confidence in a purposeful, meaningful existence in view of the overpowering reality of aloneness, suffering, and death.

> A voice said, Look me in the stars
> And tell me truly, men of earth,
> If all the soul-and-body scars
> Were not too much to pay for birth.[7]

Readers may hear the voices of Ecclesiastes, Job, Jeremiah, and other suffering servants of the biblical tradition within this poem. Against those voices, we hear a tinkling of hope, like faint wind chimes, in the sage's consideration of the importance of relationships. The Greek world of classical antiquity provides some background against which readers might hear this ancient Jewish sage.

For Aristotle, fourth-century BC Athenian philosopher and student of Plato, friendship was a virtue. Youths in modern society tend to think of friendship as little more than liking someone or enjoying a common interest or pursuit. For Aristotle, however, friendship was sharing with someone that commitment toward the common good. That "good" was carried out in the social context of the city-state (polis) and thus was at the same time an expression of patriotism.[8] Friendship on such terms obviously played a far more serious and central role in the effective and meaningful existence of human society.

The early Christian community likewise developed its notion of fellowship as central to the survival of the community and its members. Christian fellowship (koinonia) is sometimes equated with little more than cookies in the social hall before worship. The New Testament envisions fellowship as a phenomenon that runs much deeper. Fellowship is a community between individuals that grows from communion with the risen Christ.

For the apostle Paul, the basis for fellowship with other Christians was a mystical union with Christ whereby individuals became Christlike to each other (1 Cor 1:9). Being "in Christ" meant, further, sharing also in his suffering and "becoming like him in death" (Phil 3:10). Thus, Christ's suffering is extended to bearing the burdens of other people (Gal 6:2) and seeking the good of others over one's own needs (1 Cor 10:24). In contrast to our sage's emphasis upon pragmatic relationships, there is a far deeper emotional attachment that results for the church. Without denying pragmatism that accrues to any relationship, those relationships in Christ take on a new dimensions when individuals bear others' burdens.

One could not say that the ancient Jewish sage actually is calling for such self-sacrificing relationships among individuals. Nevertheless, he is recognizing in a pragmatic way the difficulties that arise for people who face their existence alone and for whom a partner could help to bear the burdens. The Christian community responds with an invitation to share in Christ's community of suffering. Indeed, that is the only kind of fellowship that the true church is called to offer.

For further reading, see Stanley Hauerwas and Charles Pinches, *Christians Among the Virtues* (Notre Dame IN: University of Notre Dame Press, 1997) and R. Spencer, "Fellowship," *MDB*, 298-99.

NOTES

[1] R. N. Whybray, *Ecclesiastes* (NCB; Grand Rapids: Eerdmans, 1989), 81ff., structures each saying as an independent pericope in his commentary; likewise James L. Crenshaw, *Ecclesiastes* (Philadelphia: Westminster, 1987), 105ff.

[2] Michael V. Fox, *A Time to Tear Down & A Time to Build Up* (Grand Rapids: Eerdmans, 1999), 217.

[3] Roland E. Murphy, *Ecclesiastes* (WBC 23A; Dallas: Word, 1993), 41.

[4] Choon-Leong Seow, *Ecclesiastes* (AB 18C; New York: Doubleday, 1997), 180.

[5] See Seow's fuller discussion, *Ecclesiastes,* 188-89.

[6] Ibid, 191.

[7] Robert Frost, "A Question," *Complete Poems of Robert Frost* (New York: Holt, Rinehart and Winston, 1967), 493.

[8] R. B. Kruschwitz and R. C. Roberts, *The Virtues* (Belmont CA: Wadsworth Publishing Co., 1987), 10.

HONESTY

Ecclesiastes 5:1-7

All Things Considered, Some Sage Advice, 5:1–6:9

The tone of the discourse shifts in 5:1 from objective observation to admonition. The passages in the remainder of the first half of the book no longer allow readers to imagine a dispassionate and somewhat cynical observer offering truculent comments from the side. Rather, the voice comes from one who seems to think that, all other things being equally bad, there are some experiences in life that are better than others. The discussion is couched in the language of direct address. An implied audience, perhaps a student, now comes to the forefront as the object of the admonition: "Guard *your* steps . . ."(5:1), "When *you* make a vow . . ."(5:4), etc. The instructor shifts to imperatives and injunctions rather than simply assuming his audience will understand the implications of his observations.

This final section of the first half of the book consists of two subsections. As noted in the introduction, there is no consensus about the structure of the overall book of Qoheleth. Many scholars choose to avoid tortured attempts to find unity within structural symmetry and design.[1] Still, other scholars see patterns of thought, connecting ideas, and linking vocabulary that at least are suggestive of a broad and deliberate architecture to the book.[2] [The Problem of Structure] Two ideas dominate the conclusion of this opening half of the book: admonitions about honesty in religious practice (5:1-7) and certain inexorable realities about human happiness (5:8–6:9). That these matters should be reserved for the book's direct address section implies that they have surfaced from the preceding observations as being of paramount importance to the sage.

The Problem of Structure

Two excellent summaries of the difficulties of the structure of the book of Ecclesiastes are set out in two commentaries by James L. Crenshaw and Roland Murphy. Both Crenshaw and Murphy set out the extensiveness of the problem and many provocative scholarly treatments. The difficulty of organizing the book rests mostly in defining the genre of the book and thence the purpose of the book. It is one thing if the book is, like Proverbs, more a collection of sayings and observations; quite another if it is more a discourse on some specific topic (Zimmerli). Attempts to read it as more than a collection eventually risk molding the text to fit the theory. Nevertheless, readers soon recognize there to be more cohesion throughout than in a mere collection. Besides, readers of Proverbs have seen how collections may receive larger structuring and shaping into larger units through semantic, syntactic, and thematic connectivity between sayings (see the introduction to Proverbs 10 above, n. 1, and [Semantic, Syntactic, and Thematic] Perhaps it is better to say that the book is at least a "carefully planned composition" (Kaiser).

The most important structural cues are the repetitive language that recurs throughout the work. These may function to mark the beginnings and endings of certain units of thought. For instance, 1:1 and 12:9 both speak of *Qoheleth* in the third person and introduce or mark passages that function as prologue (1:1-11) and epilogue (12:9-14). Other important repetitive language that may well function structurally includes the repetition of the phrase "vanity" (*hebel*) and/or "chasing after wind" (*re'ût rûaḥ*). In 2:1-11, 2:12-17, and 2:18-26, this phrase seems to set off units of thought. Similarly, the phrases "not find" (*lō' māṣā'*) in 7:14, 24, 29, and 8:17 and "not know" (*lō' yāda'*) in 10:15, 11:2, and 11:6 may further subdivide the units of the text. The Masoretic midpoint of the book in 6:9 provides a basis upon which readers might consider how the structure of the first half of the book (Eccl 1:1–6:10) is governed by the phrase "vanity and/or striving after wind" and the structure of the second half (Eccl 6:11–12:8) is governed by the phrases "not find out/not know."

The difficulty of strictly following such repetitive language is illustrated in the preceding passage, 4:1-16. Even though the phrase "vanity/ chase after wind" implies that 3:1–4:6 should be treated as a unit, the phrase "and I turned" in 4:1 signals a new unit of thought within that overall unit. So, which is the basic unit, 3:1–4:6 or 4:1-6?

For further reading, see Addison Wright, "The Riddle of the Sphinx: The Structure of the Book of Qoheleth," *CBQ* 30 (1968): 313-34; idem, "The Riddle of the Sphinx Revisited: Numerical Patterns in the Book of Qoheleth," *CBQ* 41 (1980): 38-51; and Michael V. Fox, "Frame Narrative and Composition in the Book of Qoheleth," *HUCA* 48 (1977): 83-106.

James L. Crenshaw, *Ecclesiastes* (OTL; Philadelphia: Westminster, 1987), 34-49.

Otto Kaiser, "Qoheleth," in *Wisdom in Ancient Israel*, FS J. A. Emerton, ed. John Day, Robert P. Gordon, and H. G. M. Williamson (Cambridge University Press, 1995), 83-93.

Roland Murphy, *Ecclesiastes* (WBC 23A; Dallas, TX: Word, 1992), xxxii-xli.

Walter Zimmerli, "Das Buch Kohelet—Traktat oder Sentenzsammlung?" *VT* 24 (1974): 221-30, quoted in Murphy, xxxvi.

COMMENTARY

Honesty with God

An interesting rhetorical sequence may be noticeable to readers as they make their way through these verses. The argument is structured with two outer imperatives and three inner negative admonitions. The two outer imperatives are distinguished from what follows both by their lack of a negative and their reference to one's general attitude before the deity: "guard your steps" and "fear God." The inner negative admonitions offer specific examples of what such reverence might entail and all concern what one says in the presence of God. [Rhetorical Development in 5:1-7] In this passage an individual's caution before God in the holy place is tantamount to

Rhetorical Development in 5:1-7

AΩ The diagram below sets out each phrase of the poetry in vv. 1-7 with a corresponding description of the rhetorical function (e.g., imperative, explanation, rhetorical questions, etc.).

5:1 (imperative)—"Guard your steps when you go to the house of God;"
   1a (explanation, "for")—"for they do not know . . ."
      5:2 (negative admonition)—"Never be rash with your mouth . . ."
        2a (explanation, "for")—"for God is in heaven . . ."
        3 (explanation, "for")—"For dreams come with many cares."
      5:4 (negative admonition)—"When you make a vow, do not delay . . ."
        4b (explanation, "for")—"for he [God] has no pleasure in fools."
          4c (imperative)—"repay . . ."
          5 ("better-than saying")—"It is better not to vow . . ."
      5:6 (negative admonition)—"Do not let your mouth lead you to sin . . ."
        6b (rhetorical question)—"Why should God be angry . . ."
   5:7 (imperative)—". . .But, fear God."

Choon-Leong Seow, *Ecclesiastes* (AB 18C; New York: Doubleday, 1997), 193.

---

fearing God. But the content of the instruction makes clear that what one *says* to God is the matter for reflection.

Readers may remember that the sage has not been one to stress traditional Yahwistic religion. The confident assertions in the Proverbs that a deity presides over an intelligible universe are conspicuously absent in this book (cf. Prov 16:1, 4, 7, 11; 19:17, 21; 25:21-22; 31:30). We have read that God simply cannot be known by humankind (Eccl 3:11), that, even though there will be justice, it does not exist uniformly in the present (3:15), and that God's gift to humankind is only the potential to enjoy the toil that pervades their existence (2:24). Readers cannot mistake the advice in 5:1-7 as any kind of sentimental appeal to piety. Rather, it is a call for brutal honesty with God and with oneself about the practice of religion, since God has left humankind in an equally no-nonsense circumstance of existence.

The tone of direct address provides a means of following the movement of the instruction in these verses. There is an inclusion made up of two imperatives in vv. 1 and 7: "Guard your steps" and "Fear God." Within these two outer boundaries readers find three negative admonitions that center the sage's concerns about inappropriate speech: "Never be rash with your mouth" (v. 2); "Do not delay in fulfilling it [your vow]" (v. 4); and "Do not let your mouth lead you into sin" (v. 6). These three, all of which concern appropriate speech before God, imply that one of the greatest threats to the practice of honesty with God is one's mouth.

Jerusalem Temple
This photo shows a model of the second temple after it was renovated by Herod the Great in the 1st century BC.
Herodian Temple. Model. c. AD 50. Holy Land Hotel. Jerusalem, Israel.

Honesty Requires Caution

By the inclusion of this admonition toward proper behavior in making vows before the deity, Qoheleth indicates his assumption that his audience participated in temple worship. As a matter of pragmatics Qoheleth recognizes the role temple worship plays in establishing a meaningful existence. The opening verses clearly presuppose the existence of the temple, especially in view of the reference to sacrifice. The term "house of God" is common in the literature of the second-temple era (e.g., Ezra 3:8; 6:22; 8:36; 10:1). The admonition to "Guard your steps" echoes the frequent appeal to the imagery of life as a path or way in other wisdom contexts (e.g., Prov 4:27; Pss 26:11; 119:101). Clearly v. 1 consists of an admonition toward behavior that is ethical and upright and thus defines one of the outcomes of worship. [Translation Difficulty in 5:1]

The appeal to a fool's behavior as a negative example seems appropriate since in v. 2 the sage warns against improper speech in the deity's presence. The argument is that humans are so relatively insignificant, it would be the height of foolishness to tempt one so powerful. Verse 3 makes an even more explicit comparison between a fool's speech and the activities associated with dreams. [Dreams in the Ancient Near East] As NRSV reads the implication, a fool's voice is only heard with many superfluous words, so dreams come with much anxiety. The problem with this interpretation is how such an idea forms a basis for urging proper religious and ethical behavior. Seow argues that dreams are also metaphors for the ephemeral. Thus, the point here is not that dreams are meaningful, but just the opposite, that as dreams are passing and ephemeral, so are a fool's words, especially before God.[3]

With that perspective on the foolishness of words before God, the sage offers one of the clearest examples of such foolishness in failing to keep vows made to the deity. Readers should recall the tradition's concern for the importance of repaying vows (Prov 20:25; Sir 18:22-23). [Vows] In the present context of concern about behaviors that are more or less meaningful, the sage concludes that simply avoiding vows altogether is better than making vows with no commitment to keep them (v. 5). The judgment is harsh: failure to keep a vow constitutes sin (Deut 23:22).

Translation Difficulty in 5:1

AΩ The second part of v. 1 poses both textual and interpretive problems for readers. NRSV rightly translates the segment as a "better than saying": "to draw near to listen is better than the sacrifice of fools." (The *tob* is elliptical [GKC § 133c].) The Hebrew word *yišma'* is translated as "to listen" rather than as its equally viable meaning, "to obey." However, in Deut 5:27 "listen" means to hear *and* obey, and this seems to complete the thought implied by the use of the word *yišma'*. The textual problem is solved in NRSV's translation of the final phrase as meaning that fools "do not know how *to keep from* doing evil" instead of "do not know how *to do* evil," as written in MT. This latter statement makes no sense in the context unless one takes the sage ironically, in which case the ultimate point of the irony would be captured in the NRSV translation. Most translations agree with NRSV (see Crenshaw; Whybray; Seow).

James L. Crenshaw, *Ecclesiastes* (OTL; Philadelphia: Westminster, 1987), 114.

Choon-Leong Seow, *Ecclesiastes* (AB 18C; New York: Doubleday, 1997), 193.

R. Whybray, *Ecclesiastes* (NCB; Grand Rapids: Eerdmans, 1989), 93.

Dreams in the Ancient Near East

Although the interpretation given here to the sage's allusions to dreams is metaphorical, dreams played a key role in religion across the ancient Near East. Dreams were thought to communicate messages from the divine realm to humans about one's physical state of being, about the immediate will of the deity, or about the future. One old message dream has the god Ningirsu, a Sumerian deity, instructing the Sumerian king Gudea of Lagash (c. 2000 BC) to build a temple for the deity. In the ancient Greek Homeric epics, Apollo is the god of prophecy and communicates the future by sending dreams. It is interesting that the Old Testament story of Joseph hinges upon the dream that is sent to an Egyptian king and only interpreted by one of Abraham's grandsons (Gen 41).

Throughout the Old Testament, dreams play a vital role in communicating Yahweh's purposes. People who believed their deity spoke through dreams sought divine guidance at local holy places. The story of Samuel's call is thought by some to be such an example (1 Sam 3:1-18). Since dreams came while asleep, such seekers would sleep on the premises of the sacred site in hopes of receiving some message. This practice is known as incubation.

For further reading, see Abraham Arzi, "Dreams," *EncJud* 6:207; J. M. Everts, "Dreams in the New Testament and Greco-Roman Literature," *ABD* 2:231-32; and B. Kilbourne, "Dreams," *ER* 4:482-92.

> **Vows**
>
> AΩ A vow is a conditional promise to give or to consecrate to God a person or a thing. Such is common practice throughout the ancient Near East and witnessed frequently throughout the biblical story. Individuals promise a tithe (Gen 28:20-22), a sacrifice (2 Sam 15:8), plunder taken in war (Num 21:2), or a person (Judg 11:30-31; 1 Sam 1:11). The vow is one of three different kinds of offerings that falls into the category of "communion sacrifices," or *šĕlāmîm*. There is the sacrifice of praise (*tôdâ*) as in Lev 7:12-15; 22:29-30; then the voluntary sacrifice (*nĕdābâ*) as in Lev 7:16-17; 22:18-23; and finally the votive sacrifice to which suppliants bound themselves by a vow. [Roland DeVaux, *Ancient Israel*, trans. J. McHugh (London: Darton, Longman, and Todd, 1961), 465-66.]
>
> The biblical materials provide evidence of an eventual blurring of lines between these three. The vow came to be a simple promise not dependent on God's granting any favor (Pss 50:14; 61:9; 65:2). The evidence in Lev 27:1-25 implies that later legal thinkers commuted vows down to the payment of money.
>
> For further reading, see K. Joines, "Vow in the Old Testament," *MDB*, 950.

Exactly to whom "the messenger" refers in v. 6 is a matter of debate. Several possibilities present themselves, depending upon whether one understands the term to refer to a divine or a human individual. The LXX reads the Hebrew term *mal'āk* as "angel," implying a lower divinity. It is just as likely that the messenger is a priest or temple official who comes to receive the vow.

The concluding sentence in v. 7 contrasts the admonition to "fear God" with a summary of those things that are ephemeral. If we remember from v. 3 that dreams are ephemeral, then words, like dreams, are also ephemeral. Words behind which there is no commitment should be avoided in the presence of God. The admonition therefore makes all the more stark the importance of taking quite seriously one's relative inferiority to the deity.

CONNECTIONS

The God Who Is Real in Commitment

One scholar argues for a "neuropsychological explanation for the continuance of the 'reality of God.'" His argument responds to a society in which God's existence may only be grasped by reducing God to a concept apprehensible in terms of sciences such as sociology, anthropology, or phenomenology.[4] One wonders just how real such a God so conceived may in fact be to individuals who gather to worship. Nevertheless, one also must grant the

Deism

Deism is a term given to describe a movement in England in the 17th and 18th centuries that sought to scrutinize the supernatural claims of Christianity from a naturalistic point of view. This point of view rested firmly upon the huge strides made by scientific observation and experimentation in understanding the universe and human origins. Its relevance to the 18th century and to Jennens, one of Handel's librettists, is that it provoked strong Anglican polemical response, of which Handel's *Messiah* is part.

By resting upon naturalistic understandings of the universe, the Deists no longer accepted supernatural explanations of biblical miracles. Therefore, fundamental doctrines of the church, such as the incarnation and the divine nature of Jesus, as well as subsequent trinitarian formula, and the miraculous revelation of the Bible, could be explained either in terms of the workings of nature or dismissed altogether. One of the most important anti-deistic polemicists, Richard Kidder, late 17th century bishop of Bath and Wells, wrote a document titled *A Demonstration of the Messias. In which the Truth of the Christian Religion is Proved*, which served as one of the backbones for Jennens's textual structure of the libretto of the *Messiah*.

For further reading, see Ruth Smith, "Intellectual Contexts of Handel's English Oratorios," in *Music in Eighteenth-Century England: Essays in memory of Charles Cudworth,* ed. Christopher Hogwood and Richard Luckett (Cambridge: Cambridge Univ. Press, 1983), 115-33.

---

importance of an attempt to retain, in some fashion, the reality of God in a hostile society.

The question is an old one. Ruth Smith's penetrating and thorough analysis of the eighteenth-century British context that produced Handel's *Messiah* makes clear that there was more going on in that oratorio than merely a musician's miraculous gift from God.[5] The librettist Charles Jennens was himself a highly educated person and deeply engaged in an anti-deistic polemic. [Deism] Whether Handel himself understood or even cared about the implications of such a debate cannot be known. Jennens, a regular librettist collaborating with Handel, was not willing to surrender his faith to a deistic understanding of God. Deism's perspective was one that was profoundly influenced by the scientific breakthroughs of the day, especially some of the possible implications of Newtonian physics. Deists denied a personal deity, thus undermining the doctrines of the incarnation, the trinity, and any miracle. Jennens's strategy in the libretto of *Messiah*, therefore, was to illustrate the miraculous and personal self-revelation of deity by showing how the New Testament story was anticipated ("foretold") in the Old Testament. This prophecy-fulfillment scheme, which structures the movement of the *Messiah's* text (and therefore, Handel's music!), functions to counter the deist's rejection of a deity who is known in no other way than through nature's unyielding cycles.

Up to this point in the book of Ecclesiastes the sage has described a deity who is hidden, and who, for all practical purposes, is unavailable to humanity. Creation was impersonal as its cycles passed without any regard for human society. Humankind, according to the teacher, may indeed have within them the inklings of eternity, a sense of the beauty and timeliness of God's work, but the meaning of it all is impenetrable. The deity, Exilic Isaiah confesses, is one who hides himself (Isa 45:15).

But readers should not attribute to this sage an attitude that resembles closely the deistic perspective on reality and God. In the context of religious devotion and participation in the community's sacred rituals, God becomes very real to Qoheleth. He is so real that even the most jaded, those who feel most frustrated by his absence, dare not violate a sacred vow. God suddenly becomes very real and present at this thought.

Without trivializing the complexity of the sage's commitment to the temple and its cults, there is perhaps a parabolic significance for modern readers buried beneath the sage's instruction. It is only in acts of commitment and devotion, where there is the real investment of life and the possibility of failure, that God becomes real and even personal. Too routinely God's hiddenness becomes the excuse for reluctance and even apathetic participation in the disciplines of celebrating the sacred. It may indeed be better not to tempt the deity by offering slight regard for one's promises. The cost, however, is missing out on the presence of God.[6]

NOTES

[1] Thus R. Gordis, *Koheleth: the Man and His World* (New York: Schocken, 1968); James L. Crenshaw, *Ecclesiastes* (OTL; Philadelphia: Westminster, 1987); and R. Whybray, *Ecclesiastes*, NCB (Grand Rapids: Eerdmans, 1989).

[2] Michael V. Fox, *A Time to Tear Down & A Time to Build Up* (Grand Rapids: Eerdmans, 1999); and Choon-Leong Seow, *Ecclesiastes* (AB 18C; New York: Doubleday, 1997).

[3] Seow, *Ecclesiastes,* 199.

[4] Eugene G. d'Aquili and Andrew B. Newberg, "The Neuropsychological Basis of Religions, or Why God Won't Go Away," *Zygon* 33/2 (1998): 187-201.

[5] Ruth Smith, *Handel's Oratorios and Eighteenth Century Thought* (Cambridge University Press, 1995), especially 141-56.

[6] See S. Terrien, *The Elusive Presence* (San Francisco et al.: Harper & Row, 1978).

ENJOYMENT IS GOD'S GIFT

Ecclesiastes 5:8–6:9

The series of reflections that conclude the first half of the book appear to be somewhat loosely arranged. The challenge for the reader is to determine how the discrete units connect with each other. Scholars are not in agreement. Some see thematic continuity in 5:10-20 quite separate from 5:8-9 and little thematic connection to 6:1-6, 7-9.[1] Other scholars see a great deal of continuity in 5:8–6:9, though they do not agree on what those themes are.[2] [Structure at a Glance: Ecclesiastes 5:8–6:9]

Beyond the search for thematic connections, some of the assertions of the sage in these verses stand all alone in their relevance to the search for the good life and one's ability to enjoy all that one has. The NRSV seems to separate the units of thought based upon the

---

Structure at a Glance: Ecclesiastes 5:8–6:9

AΩ It is useful to have some idea of the variation in scholarly treatment of the structure of these passages. Fox treats 5:10–6:11 separately from 5:8-9, but implies that the individual units within 5:8–6:11 fit together chiastically. As with the units in 5:10–6:11, Fox allows that vv. 8-9 may be loosely connected by theme to the ensuing verses. It is further interesting that in Fox's arrangement, the chiastic arrangement of verses extends beyond the Masoretic center of the book in 6:9. His chiastic structure is as follows:

A. 5:10-12, Introductory observations on satisfaction and dissatisfaction
   B. 5:13-17, The bad case: a man hoards wealth and loses
      C. 5:18-20, The good case: a man is allowed to enjoy wealth
   B'. 6:1-6, The bad case made worse: a man is not allowed to enjoy wealth
A'. 6:7-9, Dissatisfaction
D. 6:10-12, Human ignorance

By contrast, Seow includes the two verses (5:8-9), which Fox excludes, in the overall structure of his arrangement of the section contained in 5:8–6:9. Interestingly, Seow confines the unit to the boundaries implied by the Masoretic center (6:9; 10ET). He notes the lack of scholarly agreement regarding the inclusion of vv. 8-9 either with what precedes (5:1-7) or with what follows (5:10–6:9). Seow includes vv. 8-9 with what follows because of the parallel thematic movement he sees with a preceding passage in Ecclesiastes, 3:16-22 and 4:1-7. He then puts forward his own chiastic arrangement as follows:

  A. 5:8-12, People Who Cannot Be Satisfied
    B. 5:13-17, People Who Cannot Enjoy
      C. 5:18-19, What Is Good
        D. 5:20, Enjoy the Moment
      C'. 6:1-2, What Is Bad
    B'. 6:3-6, People Who Cannot Enjoy
  A'. 6:7-9, People Who Cannot Be Satisfied

Michael V. Fox, *A Time to Tear Down & A Time to Build Up* (Grand Rapids: Eerdmans, 1999), 213.

Choon-Leong Seow, *Ecclesiastes* (AB 18C; New York: Doubleday, 1997), 215-18.

recurrence of the word "to see." Thus, v. 8 opens with "you see," v. 13 identifies a grievous ill "I have seen," v. 18 opens with a subject that "I have seen" to be good, 6:1 begins with an evil "I have seen," and then the conclusion to the entire unit follows in 6:7-8.

It is entirely appropriate that the sage should couch his words here within a framework of observations asserting the immutability of certain phenomena. The book of Ecclesiastes begins in 1:3-11 with assertions of the unchanging cyclical nature of all reality, subverting the compelling optimism of the Proverbs (cf. 10:1–22:16) that one can get ahead, can make a profit, can contribute to real change. It is provocative that the first half of the book now concludes with an assertion of God's unpredictability and inscrutability (5:1-7). An unpredictable and inscrutable deity stands over against predictable and intelligible nature. In the latter case, the sage removes traditional hope for confidence. Yet, ironically, the sage seems to have more confidence in the deity, even though God is above such predictability.

COMMENTARY

People Whose Circumstances Yield No Enjoyment, 5:8-12

Readers will be receptive to the idea that some people cannot find enjoyment because some situations cannot be changed. This frustrating circumstance pervades the entire book and is the determining factor behind so much of the oppression the sage observes. Verse 8 opens the section with a reflection on the impenetrable bureaucracy that exists because all of the officials "watch" out for each other. In 4:1 the sage's concern was for the oppression of the poor; here that same poor person has no hope of appeal because the system is bewilderingly unyielding. Upon reflection, readers may wonder whether the appeal to bureaucratic government offers a way of removing responsibility for oppression from the deity. ["The Protests of the Eloquent Peasant"]

Verse 9 is problematic because it is not clear how this proverb relates to the description of the bureaucratic nightmare for those seeking justice. The NRSV translation implies that the king is to be read as a metaphor for the bureaucracy and urges that the land is still better off despite the breakdown in justice. Exactly how the

"The Protests of the Eloquent Peasant"

The sages acknowledged the existence of both poverty and of horrible oppression of the poor. How different is Qoheleth's apparent indifference to oppression given Israelite Wisdom's participation in the strong protest against such (e.g., Job). This sympathy with protest was not new with the sages of ancient Israel, and resembles the circumstances depicted in an Egyptian tale titled "The Protests of the Eloquent Peasant." Note the challenges offered to the steward in the following challenge of the peasant:

Now then this peasant came to appeal to him an eighth time, and he said: 'O Chief Steward, my lord! One may fall a long way because of greed. The covetous man is void of success; any success of his belongs to failure. Though thy heart is covetous, it is not (of avail) for thee. Though thou robbest, it does not profit thee, who should still permit a man to attend to his (own) business. Thy (own) needs are in thy house; thy belly is full; the grain-measure over-flows—(but) when it is jostled its surplus is lost on the ground. Takers, robbers, appropriators, magistrates—(and yet) made to punish evil. Magistrates are a refuge for the violent—(and yet) made to punish deceit! . . .' (*ANET*, 409)

The tale dates from the Middle Kingdom (2040–1782 BC) and relates the events of a peasant's eventually successful attempt to obtain justice. He had been deceived and robbed by the son of a government official while on his way to the city to purchase food for his family. In the course of the peasant's nine appeals, either to lesser officials, to the chief steward, or to the pharaoh himself, the peasant sets out clearly his view that government officials had an obligation to do justice.

For further reading, see Peter A. Clayton, *Chronicle of the Pharaohs* (London: Thames & Hudson, 1994); John Gray, "The Book of Job in the Context of Near Eastern Literature," *ZAW* 82 (1970): esp. 17-18; and James L. Crenshaw, "Popular Questioning of the Justice of God in Ancient Israel," *ZAW* 82 (1970): esp. 393-94.

land is better off is not specified, unfortunately. It is further puzzling what a proverb about a king could possibly signify in the historical context of Persian or Hellenistic political domination. Textual emendations such as Seow's redistribute the Hebrew letters so that the text refers to an agricultural productivity that is of benefit rather than a king. The phrase might therefore be rendered, "But the advantage of the land is in its provision."[3]

Following vv. 8-9, which create for the reader the anticipation and perhaps the overconfidence that money is the solution to diffi-cult bureaucratic problems, vv. 10-12 challenge the view by exploring some of the unanticipated realities of wealth. The sage says that those who love money will not be satisfied. We have encountered related ideas in 1:8 and 4:8. As money multiplies, so do those who help one consume it. The statement calls to mind those flattering, self-seeking, individuals who attach themselves to wealthy people in order to benefit from the extravagant lifestyle. From the perspective of those who have money, the rationale for the saying "it takes money to get money" is not difficult to understand. The more one has, the more one must spend to have it. The wealthy rely on the poor workers in order to obtain more wealth.

The concluding thought in v. 12 compares the sleep of the servant with that of the rich. The implication that the servant is also poor is clear through the comparison with a rich person. Readers may recall that the poor are subjected to the oppression described in vv. 8-9. The implied conclusion is that it is better to be poor and have to do physical labor than to be wealthy and worry about how quickly one's wealth is being consumed by others (cf. Sir 31:1-2).

People Who Cause Their Own Lack of Enjoyment, 5:13-17

In contrast to people who find themselves in situations that, through no fault of their own, cannot be changed, some people bring their lack of enjoyment upon themselves. Such people cannot enjoy what they have. What is imagined in v. 13 is the hoarding of wealth to one's own hurt. Admittedly, the "grievous ill" or some kind of misfortune, of which v. 14 speaks, is not avoidable and is itself not a result of wealth. However, through unpredictable eventualities hoarded wealth is subject to changes of fate and may be lost, along with all that it affords.

With the birth of an heir, an interesting contrast is established with 4:8. In the earlier reflection, the tragedy was excessive toil and no person such as an heir with whom to share it. In 5:14 there is an heir and nothing to pass on. Again, the implication is that over-confidence in one's wealth simply leads to disappointment, since wealth is subject to what is unpredictable. The overconfidence, however, is something an individual can change. Verse 15 offers a concluding appeal to traditional wisdom. Like Job, who comes from his mother's womb naked and returns there (Job 1:21; see also Sir 40:1), so is this one, who once had it all and succumbs penniless to his inexorable fate, death. The tragedy is not that he dies poor, but that he invests his entire life in something that is so vulnerable to the cyclical yet ever-unpredictable universe.

The final verses in this section (vv. 16-17) offer a general conclusion that reminds readers once again of the overall refrain of the entire book. The explicit language of coming (*šebbāʾ*) and going (*yēlēk*) is reminiscent of the opening poem of the book (1:4, 5, 6) and its motif of inescapable circularity and repetition. There is no gain for any who toil after wind. For those who invest their time and energy in things that cannot endure the test of that yawning chasm of unpredictability, there remains the indignity of possessing only darkness, bewildering pain, and bitterness.

Enjoyment Is a Gift of Good from God, 5:18-20

The sage has seen good, too. However, readers are unable to forget the pathetic vision of the preceding observation of meaninglessness. The good the sage has seen is only relatively good, but against the background of endless, meaningless repetition, relative good must be embraced. Verse 18 asserts that goodness is in the appropriateness or suitability of all those things that contribute to enjoyment: eating, drinking, and seeing good in one's work. Readers should recall the sage's observations in 3:11, where he asserts that God has made all things "suitable" (*yāpeh*) in their time. The same Hebrew word used there, *yāpeh*, is translated in v. 18 (NRSV) as "fitting" and denotes the idea of appropriateness. The appropriateness to which the sage refers in v. 18, however, is not something that comes from human designation. Rather, it is God who determines what is appropriate or fitting. Humanity has nothing to do with it.

Verse 19 clarifies the point. It is not enough merely to have been given riches and treasure, unless one has been "made master" over all of it. The observations in vv. 13-17 offer readers a stark reminder of the unreliability of riches alone in securing enjoyment. God causes people to be able to enjoy wealth and prosperity by making them masters of it. It is a gift from God to be able to take up one's lot or inheritance. That "lot" is indeed from God. It represents potential good, but it also has limitations. Enjoying it means one must stay within the boundaries of that lot.

The summary statement in v. 20 is provocative. Readers find it challenging to determine the specific referent of being "occupied" as well as understanding the overall implication of the verse. As NRSV translates the phrase, it explains how God gives to some the ability to enjoy their wealth: he simply keeps them occupied (*ma'ăneh*) with the "joy of their hearts." That occupation prevents a consciousness of the surrounding evil so that people may enjoy the gifts from God. Does this refer to both people who can and cannot enjoy their lots from God?[4] If so, then God's gift is more like a painkiller, an anesthetic, that prevents the kind of honest look at reality the sage has been describing throughout his own book. The theological implications are even more serious: God is therefore one who is dishonest; religious faith is little more than a drug.

An alternative meaning of *ma'ăneh* is "answer," implying that God's answer to human toil is through the joy that does come to some. Reading *ma'ăneh* as "answer" has good precedent in the Proverbs (e.g., Prov 15:1, 23; 16:1; 29:19; Job 23:5). What is more, the sentence might not be taken as a description of life, but as an injunction toward a certain response to life: "he should not brood over the days of his life, for God answers through the joy of his heart." As a climax to the sage's assertion of good, this verse then functions as an admonition to enjoy life without any hesitation, if indeed the deity has put it in one's power to do so.[5]

When God Does Not Cause One to Enjoy, 6:1-6

The opening two verses are thematically set apart from vv. 3-6. Verses 1-2 return to the theme of wealth and prosperity while vv. 3-6 reflect on an individual example of one who has not been given the ability to enjoy his wealth and prosperity. All six verses are treated together here since both themes are introduced with the formulaic reference to what the sage has "seen" in v. 1. These opening verses almost mirror preceding examples. Verse 1 echoes the statement in 5:13, where the sage asserts his awareness of "a grievous ill." In 6:1 he states his awareness of an "evil." Obviously, the two examples of bad fortune are not exact parallels. In 5:13-17 the loss of wealth is through a bad venture; in 6:1-2 it is because someone else receives the wealth. Note that the language of 6:2 parallels, almost word for word, 5:19. In 6:2, however, it is a negation. The negation lies in the fact that God does *not* give the individual the ability to master or to enjoy the prosperity (*wĕlō' yašlîṭennû*) that the deity has bestowed upon individuals.

Readers of both the Proverbs and Ecclesiastes know well the motif of losing wealth to either a foreigner or simply to another. One of the threats of the "'other' woman" in Proverbs 5:1-14 is that all of one's substance could eventually be taken over by someone else. Further, the sage here has already brought to the reader's attention kings turning their thrones over to others (4:13-16) and wealth for which ordinary citizens have toiled being turned over to others (2:18-23). These verses address human failure to realize fully the wealth, prosperity, status, or whatever one has worked for as the defining feature of God's withholding the ability to enjoy.

Verses 3-6 take up in a different way the disaster of the inability to enjoy prosperity. There is no separate formula for "seeing," implying that vv. 3-6 are not to be read independently from vv. 1-2, although v. 2 does conclude with the assertion of "vanity."

Readers will recognize the reemergence of the question of the birth of offspring. The context of 6:1-6 makes the situation somewhat different than its occurrence in 5:14, however. In 6:3-6 having children as well as long life is another blessing indicating prosperity. However, one's inability to be satisfied with it all, like one's lack of a proper burial, leads one to loathe all of those things. [Burial Practices] The allusion further evokes thoughts of stillborn children and the advantage they have over those who must face life and endure the

---

Burial Practices

The reference to burial in the context of a hypothetical situation on the inability to enjoy life seems abrupt to modern readers (Eccl 6:3). Admittedly, there are textual problems. R. N. Whybray believes the text has been damaged and is thus impossible to understand fully. J. Crenshaw believes the image is not referring to the unhappiness of the wealthy person, but to the stillborn child in the ensuing verse (6:4). The sage discusses improper burials elsewhere in the book and thus makes more plausible here the reference as one of the disappointments of the wealthy man (see 8:10) (thus, Fox). Seow understands the term

Artist rendering of the
Calaphas Family Burial Chamber.

qĕbûrâ, translated in NRSV as "burial," as a reference to a "burial site." As a burial site, the reference is to advance preparation for death, something only the very rich would make, and thus represents a ridiculous complaint, highlighting the wealthy person's inability to enjoy all that he has.

What is as important as the textual difficulties is some knowledge of the ancient cultural influences. Proper burial in antiquity is a mark of prosperity and wealth. Concern about proper burial gives evidence of a worldview remarkably different from that of most readers. Moreover, it allows readers to understand how improper burial could be considered a threat.

Ancient Hebrews did not make a distinction between the body and the soul (*nepeš*), in either life or death. The body in life or death was still a soul (*nepeš*) and continued in some sense to be viable. Thus, proper care for a body after death was essential since the connection between the body and soul remained. Failure to do so was considered a curse (1 Kgs 14:11; Jer 16:4; Ezek 29:5). Proper care for deceased bodies was given through the building of tombs, chambers dug out of rock, generally, or caves. However, burial was expensive and the biblical literature does recognize a distinction between the tombs of the wealthy and those of the poor (e.g., Job 3:14; Isa 22:16).

For further reading, see Everett Ferguson, *Backgrounds of Early Christianity* (Grand Rapids: Eerdmans, 1987); and Amnon Ben-Tor, *The Archaeology of Ancient Israel* (New Haven & London: Yale University Press, 1992).

James L. Crenshaw, *Ecclesiastes*, OTL (Philadelphia: Westminster, 1987), 126.

Michael V. Fox, *A Time to Tear Down & A Time to Build Up* (Grand Rapids: Eerdmans, 1999), 220.

Choon-Leong Seow, *Ecclesiastes*, AB 18C (New York: Doubleday, 1997), 225-26.

R. N. Whybray, *Ecclesiastes*, NCB (Grand Rapids: Eerdmans, 1989), 105.

inability to enjoy the manifold possessions they have (cf. Job 3:11-19). The closing thought in v. 6 returns to the idea first set forth in Ecclesiastes 3:20. When people are not given the ability to enjoy what they toil for, there is no difference between the living and those already dead.

The Conclusion—The Insatiable Appetite, 6:7-9

The final three verses of the first half of the book provide some closure by returning to the familiar language of toil, vanity, and wind. The only likely connection with the preceding concern about the possibility of enjoyment comes in the imagery of the appetite. The connection between the appetite and toil may be familiar from Proverbs 16:26. In Ecclesiastes the sage turns the meaning into a statement of insatiability: "the appetite is not satisfied."

Verse 8 raises doubt, therefore, about the value of wisdom over foolishness. The translation of 8b by NRSV implies that there is not any advantage for the poor in their understanding of "how to conduct themselves before the living." The meaning of this latter phrase is unclear, although it parallels 8a broadly in its assertion that there is no advantage for anyone. The concluding phrase in 9a, the "sight of the eyes" is better than the "wandering of the eyes," is an assertion of the priority of immediate gratification over delayed gratification. The sage states in 9b that stressing the immediate gratification over delayed gratification is "vanity and a chasing after wind." Nevertheless, in light of the general inability to enjoy one's toil, the tyranny of the immediate seems preferable.

CONNECTIONS

"The Want Bone"

"On their [*sic*] deathbed, no one ever said, 'I wish I had spent more time with my business, . . .'" wrote former United States senator Paul Tsongas as he resigned from office in 1984 in order to pursue cancer treatment and spend time with family.[6] Both his affirmation and his action reflect the kind of insight few people will ever achieve. Most people spend their lives toiling for prosperity and success only to find that time and circumstances get in the way of satisfying enjoyment. Such is the message of the sage in these verses; behind the endless toil is the presumption that somehow it will all be worth it in the end, that successes will endure, that prosperity makes one invincible. How does one overcome such presumption?

Robert Pensky's poem, "The Want Bone," perhaps provides an image that will remind readers of how tenuous life is. In a prosaic, sing-song way, the image created by the poem is one of perpetual desire and eternal frustration. It pictures the sun-dried skeleton of a shark's jaws gaping open on a beach. The skeleton, or "mouthbone," is frozen into the shape of an "O" symbolizing its erstwhile power to consume, to conquer, to evoke fear and dread in its prey. But in the present, the once powerful jaws are baked by the sun into a sardonic grin that mocks every passerby who believes in the inevitability and perpetuity of enjoyment, satisfaction, power, even life. "But where was the limber grin, the gash of pleasure? Infinitesimal mouths bore it away, The beach scrubbed and etched and pickled it clean."[7] ["The Want Bone"]

The sage is struggling to encourage readers to learn the lesson of the "want bone." Individuals must find something that will remind them that life comes and goes, and it is a rare gift if anyone can find enjoyment in it. When that gift of enjoyment comes, individuals must savor every moment of it as though it were the most precious of gifts. Even God's gifts do not last forever, and especially the gift of being able to enjoy one's toil.

"The Want Bone"

The tongue of the waves tolled in the earth's bell
Blue rippled and soaked in the fire of blue.
The dried mouthbones of a shark in the hot swale
Gaped on nothing but sand on either side.

The bone tasted of nothing and smelled of nothing,
A scalded toothless harp, uncrushed, unstrung.
The joined arcs made the shape of birth and craving
And the welded-open shape kept mouthing O.

Ossified cords held the corners together
In groined spirals pleated like a summer dress.
But where was the limber grin, the gash of pleasure?
Infinitesimal mouths bore it away,

The beach scrubbed and etched and pickled it clean.
But O I love you it sings, my little my country
My food my parent my child I want you my own
My flower my fin my life my lightness my O.

Robert Pensky, "The Want Bone," in *The Norton Anthology: American Literature*, vol. 2, 5th ed., ed. Nina Baym (New York & London: W. W. Norton & Co., 1998), 2784.

NOTES

[1] R. N. Whybray, *Ecclesiastes* (NCB; Grand Rapids: Eerdmans, 1989), 97-111; note Murphy's assortment of themes in 5:1-6:9; 46-56 (*Ecclesiastes* [WBC 23A; Waco: Word, 1992]).

[2] James L. Crenshaw, *Ecclesiastes* (OTL; Philadelphia: Westminster, 1987), 119-130; but compare Michael V. Fox, *A Time to Tear Down & A Time to Build Up* (Grand Rapids: Eerdmans, 1999), 213, with Choon-Leong Seow, *Ecclesiastes* (AB 18C; New York: Doubleday, 1997), 215-17.

[3] Seow, *Ecclesiastes*, 204, 218.

[4] Thus Crenshaw, *Ecclesiastes,* 125.

[5] Seow, *Ecclesiastes,* 209, 224.

[6] Paul Tsongas, *Heading Home* (New York: Knopf, distributed by Random House, 1984), quoted in "Statement of Senator Carl Levin in Memory of Paul E. Tsongas," *Congressional Record* (21 January, 1997) 105th Congress, 1st Session <http://levin.senate.gov/floor/012197>.

[7] Robert Pensky, "The Want Bone," in *The Norton Anthology: American Literature*, vol. 2, 5th ed., ed. Nina Baym (New York & London: W. W. Norton & Co., 1998), 2784.

RESTATING THE PROBLEM: WHAT IS GOOD?

Ecclesiastes 6:10–7:14

Things Could Always Be Worse, 6:10–12:14

At Ecclesiastes 6:9 readers arrive at the Masoretic midpoint of the book. [Masoretic Midpoint] The notation of this detail in the margins of the Hebrew text was not added until long after the book was written. Nevertheless, one of the challenges to readers is how this division reflects either structure or meaning in the text (see [The Problem of Structure in Ecclesiastes]). Since 6:9 concludes with the refrain of "vanity" (*hebel*) and "a chasing after wind" (*reʿût rûaḥ*), the familiar thematic boundary markers utilized extensively in the preceding chapters, it is likely that a new section begins in 6:10.

An overall two-part structure, such as that implied by the supposed midpoint of the book, should be especially amenable to readers who have made their way through the Proverbs. The poetic parallelism of each individual saying establishes a manner of describing reality that is responsive: evaluation follows assertion; response follows claim; qualification supports, modifies, or refutes intimation. Readers might therefore think of the second half of Ecclesiastes as a parallelistic response to the first half of the book.

Does the second half of the book advance the findings or the argument

Masoretic Midpoint

The Masoretes—those medieval scribes responsible for adding to the Hebrew consonantal text an apparatus to assist vocalization of the text—were careful in preserving the text of the Hebrew Bible. One technique was to count each letter. The purpose of such counting was apparently to prevent copyists from either adding (through dittography) or deleting (through haplography) any letter that was a part of the text. Then, the tally was made and entered at the end of books.

They also noted the midpoint of sacred texts. Such entries were made in the margins of the texts, and the notation for the midpoint of Ecclesiastes comes between 6:9 and 10. One implication is that something new begins with 6:10. While this is not necessarily so, as midpoints could come in the middle of sentences, readers should nevertheless consider the possibility. What is perhaps of greatest interest is the care given in the process of passing on the sacred text to the next generation of faithful.

Further reading, see Emanuel Tov, *Textual Criticism of the Bible* (Minneapolis: Fortress; Aasen/Maastricht: Van Gorcum, 1992); Reinhard Wonnenberger, *Understanding BHS: A Manual for the Users of Biblia Hebraica Stuttgartensia* (Roma: Editrice Pontificio Istituto Biblico, 1990); and Israel Yeivin, *Introduction to the Tiberian Masorah,* trans. E. J. Revell (United States of America: Scholars Press, 1980).

of the first half of the book? Not especially. In fact, the second half of the book looks similar to the first in its return to the themes of the deity's determination of everything and the elusiveness of wisdom and righteousness. The assertion that everything is in the hand of God (9:1) is at once an affirmation of certain order and inescapable monotony. As the first half of the book concludes with a consideration of the possibility of enjoyment (5:8–6:9), so the second half concludes with enjoyment (11:7–12:8). The two halves of the book are complementary in that the second half reasserts the statement of the first half.

Restating the Problem: What Is Good? 6:10–7:14

While it is impossible to be certain whether there is any kind of clear beginning in 6:10, readers will nevertheless recognize that the language of v. 10 parallels thematically 1:9; v. 11 parallels 1:14; and v. 12 parallels 3:21. Verses 10-12 could therefore be read as a kind of recapitulation of the most dominant themes of chapters 1–6 and thereby offering a sort of introduction to the statements that follow. [Structure at a Glance: Ecclesiastes 6:10–7:14]

Structure at a Glance: Ecclesiastes 6:10–7:14

AΩ Alternatively, many read 6:10-12 as an independent unit functioning more in reference to what precedes than to what follows (Whybray; Fox). Choon-Leong Seow reads 6:10-12 as a theological introduction balancing a theological conclusion in 7:13-14, creating a framing device for the sayings within. He notes that there are strong verbal correspondences between the language of 6:10-12 and 7:10-14, implying a kind of framework. His taxonomy is as follows:

6:10-12	7:10-14
mah-šehāyâ (6:10, whatever has been)	*meh hāyâ* (7:10, why were)
lō' yûkal (6:10, are not able)	*mî yûkal* (7:13, who is able)
yōtēr (6:11, better)	*yōtēr* (7:11, advantage)
kaṣṣēl (6:12, like a shadow)	*bĕṣēl* (7:12, in the shadow)
'aḥărāyw (6:12, after them)	*'aḥărāyw* (7:14, after them)

We might therefore envision a structural arrangement in three parts, set out as follows:

Vv. 6:10-12: Transition and Prospect
Vv. 7:1-12: "Better than" Sayings
   Vv. 1-7: Death and Life, Wisdom and Foolishness
   Vv. 8-12: The Advantage of Wisdom
Vv. 13-14: Conclusion and Retrospect

Michael V. Fox, *A Time to Tear Down & A Time to Build Up* (Grand Rapids: Eerdmans, 1989), 213-25. In Fox's case, the unit is itself a part of a larger structure beginning with 5:9 and concluding with 6:12.

Choon-Leong Seow, *Ecclesiastes* (AB 18C; New York: Doubleday, 1997), 241.

R. N. Whybray, *Ecclesiastes* (NCB; Grand Rapids: Eerdmans, 1989),109-11.

The central section, 7:1-12, is a collection of "better than" statements. There does not seem to be any consistent thematic unity among them as a collection. Rather, there are recurring terms that may serve to link one saying to the next. The dominant word is "good" (*tôb*), which, conjoined in the sentence with the comparative particle, *min*, may be translated "better." There are eleven occurrences of the comparative *min*; translated "better"; six occurrences of "wise/wisdom"; five occurrences of "heart"; four occurrences of "fool"; three occurrences of "sorrow/anger"; and two occurrences each of "laughter and house of mourning."

COMMENTARY

What Has Been Named Already, 6:10-12

Naming establishes character, and the opening verse of part two reminds readers of the character of the present investigation as well as the naming of humankind at creation (Gen 2:19). In the former instance, one recalls that the sage believes there to be nothing new under the sun (1:10-11). Life is a series of endless and inescapable cycles (1:3-9; 3:1-9), there is no way to prosper since all toil is quickly consumed (4:4; 6:7), enjoyment is an unpredictable gift of an unknowable deity (6:1-2), and were it not for the relative good, there would be no good at all (5:17-19).

In a larger sense, the naming of humankind (cf. 7:1) recalls the creation story and the affinities between *ʾādām* ("humankind") and *ʾādāmâ* ("the dust"). [The Name *ʾādām*] The stark reminder that the

---

The Name *ʾādām*

AΩ Readers may recall the paradise story in Gen 2:4b–3:24 and the play on the word *ʾādām* that develops within the narrative. The term designates the man whom Yahweh forms, as well as his affinities with the earth out of which he is fashioned (Gen 2:7). The term given for "humankind" is *ʾādām*; that for "earth" is the related term, *ʾādāmâ*. The implication is that human nature is determined by the substance out of which humanity is fashioned. Thus, humans always go back to the earth when they die. Moreover, the animals themselves are also fashioned from the earth (Gen 2:19), connoting a shared nature between humankind and the beasts.

The claims of v. 10 are interesting in their connections to earlier parts of Ecclesiastes as well as the larger ancient Near Eastern background. The act of naming is only just one of signification, but one of creation itself. The Babylonian creation epic, *Enuma Elish*, opens as follows. Readers should observe the use of the word *name* as a verb of creation.

When on high the heaven had not been named,
Firm ground below had not been called by name,
Naught but primordial *Apsu*, their begetter
(And) *Mumu-Tiamat*, she who bore them all,
Their waters commingling as a single body;
No reed hut had been matted, no marsh land had appeared,
When no gods whatever had been brought into being,
Uncalled by name, their destinies undetermined—

ANET, 60-61.

name given to humans is one of ephemerality, dust, casts a gloomy shadow on creation. Verse 11 reminds readers that words, too, are futile (*hebel*), a theme asserted several times in the first half of the book (e.g., 1:8; 5:2, 6). God is the one who set this overwhelmingly meaningless struggle in motion and has made it so that humankind cannot dispute with one who is mightier than they are. Even the most vociferous contender, Job, was only able to evoke a response from the deity shrouded in riddles and mystery (Job 38–41).

Verse 12 opens with a familiar rhetorical question, "who knows what is good." While the sage's skepticism is made unambiguously evident in this question, as readers have already seen (e.g., 2:19; 3:21), the question about what is good foreshadows what is to come in the ensuing collection of "better than" sayings in 7:1-12. There may be no absolute good, all things being qualified by human ignorance, divine hiddenness, and an immutable, impenetrable universe, but there may be relative good. Such relativity is not so dissimilar from the conclusion of the book of Job. In Job there are no absolute answers, only answers that make Job's situation relatively better.

What Is Good—Relatively Speaking, 7:1-12

The reader of the English text misses the elegance of the first half of the opening saying. There is an alliterative play between the sound of the word "name" (*šēm*) and the word for "ointment" (*šemen*). Four words combine to create a chiasm: *ṭôb šēm miššemen ṭôb*, "a good name is better than precious ointment." Notice the identical outer words and the alliterative words in the middle of the line. The idea sets up the ensuing theme of death in vv. 2-4 and alludes to a proverbial saying about having a good name (Prov 10:7; 22:1). The theme implies that as a good name, or a lasting reputation, is better than ointment, so one's death is better than the day of one's birth (see Sir 41:12-13). The irony, of course, is that with death all that is left is one's reputation. What is more, in death one's reputation tends to improve. Some tantalizing evidence of this is the Chronicler's treatment of King David. Although the treatment of the Bathsheba affair and cover-up sets in motion an extraordinary sequence of events that shapes the succession of Solomon (2 Sam 11–1 Kgs 2), the Chronicler simply leaves the entire episode out altogether (1 Chr 20:1-3). Readers can only speculate that the Chronicler's larger purposes in writing the history necessitated the rehabilitation of the royal reputation.

Verse 2 contrasts celebration and mourning by opposing references to the wedding and the wake. [Houses of Mourning and Feasting] One possible implication is that death, and one's reputation that extends beyond death, is actually more desirable than life. The irony that one might find happiness only in death provides a certain perverse rationale for giving more attention to one's death. The living "lay to heart" the inexorability of death, perhaps in the sense implied in Psalm 90:12 where the supplication is for instruction on how to "number one's days."[1] When individuals "number" their days, they acknowledge that their lives are finite and that an endpoint is inevitable.

Verse 3 raises the provocative connection between sadness of face and gladness of heart. However, the contrast only continues the implications of the two preceding sayings. Readers recall that in Ecclesiastes 1:18 knowledge is associated with vexation. Alternatively, readers are invited to speculate as to the related question of human appearances in the midst of pain. The assertion in Proverbs 14:13 implies the possibility that even those who appear happy are sad and that ultimately all joy ends in sorrow. Thus what it means to be wise is to be aware of all of life's possibilities. Verse 4 implies that the wise person does not forget life's mix nor life's unpredictability. What is more, at any moment one can find both joy and sadness.

The statement in v. 4 about the wise connects with the following statement in v. 5 contrasting the wise and the foolish. On the one hand, wisdom requires a complex state of awareness that joy and sadness are inextricably bound; on the other, wisdom, with all of its complexity and apparent inconsistency, is still better than folly. This relative goodness of wisdom is not new. Readers have encountered the idea in several wisdom books, including the Proverbs (e.g., 1:33; 3:11; 6:23; 13:24; 22:15; Job 15:17-18; Sir 22:6). The theme of the rebuke of the foolish is not new either (e.g., Prov 28:23; 27:6). However, readers are not to think that there is any absolute good in wisdom. It, too, is still vanity.

The image of the sound of a fool's laughter (v. 6) is anticipated in v. 5 with the alliteration on the word *sir*, "song." In v. 6 the words translated "thorns," *hassîrîm*, and "pot," *hassîr*, form an entertaining sound as well as a clear link to v. 5. The final formula, "this

Houses of Mourning and Feasting

AΩ The "house of mourning" is a metaphor for the home of mourners. There is no other biblical evidence for its occurrence, although it is used frequently in rabbinic literature. As to a literal house for funerary ceremony, Jer 6:5 and 8 refer to a "house of mourning," *bēt mārzeh*, which is also a place of revelry and drinking. [Choon-Leong Seow, *Ecclesiastes*, AB 18C (New York: Doubleday, 1997), 235-36.] The "house of feasting" is similarly a metaphor for the home of merrymakers and is conveyed with two apparently synonymous terms: *bēt mišteh* in v. 2 and *bēt śimḥâ* in v. 4. Fox urges that readers find the same synonymy between *śimḥâ* (joy) and *miśteh* (drinking) in Esth 9:17, 18, 19, 22, and in the fragment of Eccl 7:2 from Qumran (Fox).

Further reading, see T. J. Lewis, *Cults of the Dead in Ancient Israel and Ugarit,* HSM 39 (Atlanta: Scholars Press, 1989).

Michael V. Fox, *A Time to Tear Down & A Time to Build Up* (Grand Rapids: Eerdmans, 1999), 227-28.

also is vanity," implies the meaninglessness of foolishness as well as wisdom. It must be remembered that the good is only relative. The ensuing statement in v. 7, for instance, offers an example where the wise are no longer distinct from the foolish. The verse opens with the particle *kî*, "for," which usually functions to introduce a causative phrase in reference to what precedes. Since v. 6 concludes with the *hebel* ("vanity") formula, it is seen as a conclusion to the cluster of vv. 5 and 6. Some scholars believe that a saying such as that in Proverbs 16:8 has inadvertently been left out ("Better is a little with righteousness than large income with injustice").[2] Without an intervening verse, however, v. 7 functions as an explanation for the conclusion of v. 6.

With the statement that the end of a thing is better than its beginning, readers are left searching for some way of linking the sage's stream of consciousness. However, v. 8a reads more like a new beginning, paralleling v. 1 more than it does connecting with the ideas of vv. 5, 6, or 7. Proverbs 14:29 offers a more helpful connection with v. 8b, which deals with the importance of patience. Finding a connection between the "end of a thing" and the "patient in spirit" is the challenge for the reader's reflection. The idiom for patience utilizes a term (*ʾārēk*) that also occurs in collocations denoting the prolongation of life (e.g., Deut 4:26, 40; Prov 28:16). The play on words implies that patience is also a prolongation of life, even if the end of life is better than the beginning (as v. 1 states).

The negative admonitions of vv. 9 and 10 seem to be linked to the statement in v. 8 concerning patience. The relativity of anger and vexation is illustrated by comparing v. 9 with v. 3. In v. 3, anger (translated as "sorrow") is better than laughter. The admonition is nevertheless not to hasten to such emotion. Such emotional responses are the sure indications of foolishness. While the admonition in v. 10 is not necessarily an example of anger, it could be a result of an emotional, perhaps even sentimental, veneration of the past. Since there is nothing new under the sun, it is ridiculous to think that the past could be any better, or even different, from the present moment. Wise people take the present as it comes, without any undue sentiment for past or future. However, this view could also subvert the sage's own regard for the wisdom that was passed on to him.

Such subversion of traditional wisdom, and the traditionally high regard for wisdom may be implied in the saying in v. 11. NRSV takes v. 11 as an equation of wisdom with the value of an inheritance. The significance is left to the reader as to whether this is an affirmation or a subversion. Nevertheless, the assertion is quite a turn-around from the statements in Proverbs 3:14; 8:19; and 16:16, where wisdom is far and away much better than wealth. The translation depends upon the meaning of the Hebrew term *ʿim*. The term means "with" or "like," and functions in 2:16 to imply equation. In the context of a "better than" statement, readers would expect the particle to be the comparative *min*. In that case the statement would say that wisdom was better than an inheritance. However, this is not the case. Wisdom is simply equated with an inheritance.

The statement in v. 12 reiterates the notion of wisdom's benefits by invoking the image of the "shadow" as one of "protection" (NRSV). The real textual difficulty grows from the parallel use of the Hebrew preposition meaning "in, with, or by" (*bě*). A literal translation would be, "For in the shadow of wisdom, in the shadow of money."[3] Readers have encountered the same word in 6:12, where the word "shadow" (*ṣēl*) is a metaphor of ephemerality. In 7:12 it functions as an image of safety as in Numbers 14:9, Isaiah 30:2, and Jeremiah 48:45. Thus the safety of wisdom is counterpoised with the safety of wealth.

What God Has Made Crooked, 7:13-14

The questions concerning what is good in the opening verses, 6:10-12, are now balanced with the response that ultimately God determines what is good. The relativity that is built into creation stems from the frank acknowledgment that God has "hard-wired" into the universe things that cannot be straightened. What good there is comes only because of its relationship to phenomena that are worse.

Verse 13 suddenly breaks from the rhetoric of vv. 1-12 by opening with an imperative. This new mode of address signals the conclusion of the unit of thought and the invitation to reflect upon what precedes. Any thought the reader might have entertained about the absolute benefits of wisdom based upon vv. 12-13 are here subverted. No matter how beneficial wisdom is, it is impossible to undo what God has twisted.

The language of v. 14 parallels that language concluding the earlier collection of sayings in 3:1-15 in its assertion that mortals may not find anything out. Not only is it impossible to undo something God has set into the universe, it is impossible to have understanding of God's universe. Ultimately, one's only alternative is to reflect upon God's mystery. One may enjoy what good comes his way, when it comes. But that good is only a relative good. One is never allowed to enjoy the good without also being fully aware of what is twisted.

CONNECTIONS

Numbering One's Days: Reflecting upon Relativity

The thrust of the sage in these verses concerns relativity. Finding the good is only an experience of the relative good for Qoheleth: it depends upon one's point of view. Perhaps Psalm 90:12 helps us understand the nature of this relativity. The psalmist importunes the deity, "Teach us to count our days," thereby making a tacit acknowledgment that there is at least one thing certain: life comes to an end eventually. "Counting" one's days may be more aptly understood as reflection based upon those clear boundaries that circumscribe humans' lives ("You turn us back to dust, . . ." v. 3). The prayer might rather be, "Teach us to be aware of the brevity of human life," because such awareness of those limitations (numbering one's days) yields a "wise heart" (v. 12b). And yet, the brevity of human life is to be lived out with the consciousness of God's infinity. The psalmist has extolled the deity's perspective over against that of humanity's: "You turn us back to dust, and say, 'Turn back you mortals.' For a thousand years in your sight are like yesterday when it is past, or like a watch in the night" (vv. 3-4). The human point of view is forged between the eternal and the temporal, between the bounded and the boundless.

Annie Dillard captures this relativity with extraordinary imagery in *Pilgrim at Tinker Creek*. In the chapter titled "Fecundity," she sets out the enormous extravagance of nature in selecting the few that are needed from all creatures to perpetuate their species. [Natural Selection] Nature's extravagance is indicated in the production of billions and billions of cells and eggs, only a small percentage of which are ever fertilized; of those, only the smallest proportion even survive.[4] From barnacles, to muskrats, to preying mantises to water bugs, only a relative few survive. What right does the human species have to claim the survival of all its members, much less the happiness and prosperity of all those members? From a larger perspective, one that relegates humanity to a relatively less central place in the universe, death pervades this existence more than life. Death surrounds us, penetrates us, defines our natural existence. It is humanity's emotional attachment to life that gives humanity a

Natural Selection

The language of selection reflects Dillard's assumption of natural selection, that process by which natural processes determine which species survive and which do not. In Charles Darwin's theory of evolution, there are two stages involved in the process of survival. The first is a somewhat random distribution and realignment of genetic materials. The second is not random at all; rather, the natural environment "selects" those species most likely to survive their particular environment. Interestingly, Dillard uses this language of natural selection without abandoning the language of religious faith. Ultimately, the deity's purposes would be behind the process of natural selection.

For further reading, see Ernst Mayr, "Darwin's Contributions to Modern Thought," SA 283/1 (July 2000): 69-74.

sense that the world is "twisted." Ours is the false consciousness of reality that somehow one may have life without death. What appears as twisted to such people so enamored with their own notions of life is simply the way God does it.

Those who can count their days understand that no one can say "what is good for mortals while they live the few days of their vain life, which they pass like a shadow." Those who can count their days understand that "In the day of prosperity be joyful, and in the day of adversity consider; God has made the one as well as the other, so that mortals may not find out anything that will come after them."

NOTES

[1] Thus James L. Crenshaw, *Ecclesiastes* (OTL; Philadelphia: Westminster, 1987), 134.

[2] Thus Michael V. Fox, *A Time to Tear Down & A Time to Build Up* (Grand Rapids: Eerdmans, 1999), 229, who notes also that the Qumran fragment has a lacuna with space for fifteen to twenty letters between 7:6 and 7:7. But compare Choon-Leong Seow's more doubtful comments, *Ecclesiastes* (AB 18C; New York: Doubleday, 1997), 237.

[3] See Roland Murphy, *Ecclesiastes* (WBC 23A; Dallas: Word, 1992), 61, for a fuller explanation of the textual difficulties.

[4] Annie Dillard, *Pilgrim at Tinker Creek* (San Francisco: Harper Perennial, 1974), ch. 9.

RESPONSE TO HUMAN NATURE

Ecclesiastes 7:15-29

The sage turns to consider human righteousness and wickedness against the larger backdrop of human nature generally. Stymied by the fact that humans cannot know God, and that the deity's creation is unyielding to human attempts to understand (7:13), the sage puts forward righteousness as another example of what is impossible to achieve. Readers have already encountered Qoheleth's skepticism about human righteousness (3:16-17; 4:1-3). Here he takes it up again perhaps with a view to subverting the traditional view of its central importance. More likely, his aim is to balance the high ideals of righteousness with the realities of human nature. The sage asks how human righteousness may be held up as a goal of moral action when human nature so readily undercuts it (7:29).

The sage recognizes that humans are capable of both goodness and evil; they are simultaneously just and unjust. The traditional equation between righteousness and wisdom, so characteristic of the Proverbs (e.g., 1:7; 14:16; 15:28; 16:22), is challenged through the recognition that individuals are required to moderate their extreme notions of these two poles.

[Structure at a Glance: Ecclesiastes 7:15-29]

Structure at a Glance: Ecclesiastes 7:15-29

ΑΩ The organization of the unit turns upon thematic concerns. Readers may find helpful the following outline of thoughts for this section:

7:15-16 Contradictions on righteousness and wickedness
Vv. 17-22 Contradictions that call for balance
Vv. 23-28 Observations of human nature
7:29 Contradictions based on human nature

The conclusion in v. 29 parallels the final thought of the preceding unit in its return to reflections upon what the deity has established in creation. The implication is that the reflections beginning in v. 15 are to be read as a unit. The concern with human "straightforwardness" (*yāšār*) in v. 29 provides a thematic connection with the concern for righteousness and wickedness in vv. 15-16. Most scholars subdivide these verses into at least two different and unrelated sections, beginning with vv. 15-22 and concluding with vv. 23-29 (Crenshaw; Murphy). The reader is invited to consider how the opening concerns for the traditional views of righteousness and wickedness are to be read against the ensuing concerns for wickedness and folly (Seow).

James L. Crenshaw, *Ecclesiastes* (OTL; Philadelphia: Westminster, 1987), 140-44, treats 7:15-22 and vv. 23-29 under separate headings.
Roland Murphy, *Ecclesiastes* (WBC 23A; Waco: Word, 1992), 68-73, likewise treats vv. 15-24 as a unit and 25-29 as a unit.
Choon-Leong Seow, *Ecclesiastes*, AB 18C (New York: Doubleday, 1997), 251-76.

COMMENTARY

Contradictions that Call for Balance, 7:15-22

The sage opens with a familiar experiential formula: "I have seen everything." The phrase may provide a connection between the preceding observations about the relative good and the ensuing observations on relativity. To the extent that the phrase translated "everything" (*hakōl*) anticipates what follows, the sage prepares to discuss two examples of contradictory reality. He also uses the familiar term *hebel* to describe his life. The term is used here to denote ephemerality.[1]

The observation that sets up the ensuing series of instructions is one that disconfirms the retributionary model of reality so characteristic of Deuteronomic and Priestly theology: the righteous ones "perish in their righteousness," and the wicked ones "prolong their life in their evil-doing." The statement is not emotional and thus quite different from the vitriolic accusations of Job (e.g., 21:7-26) or the angry complaints of Jeremiah (cf. 12:1). The sage asserts as a matter of fact that he has seen the righteous suffer and the wicked prosper (cf. Ps 37:25), and this becomes a basis for his advice. He knows he cannot change the situation; arguing with God or fretting about the way things work is pointless. Thus his advice stresses balance. The notion of balance is fitting both thematically and pragmatically. Thematically, his concern with righteousness follows the concern with what is good in 7:1-14. Readers might even wonder why the topic was not treated in the first half of the chapter. Pragmatically, it continues to offer advice based upon the mode of living that seeks the relative good.

Verses 16 and 17 are set up structurally as balancing ideas (see diagram below). They create the effect of balance through their formation of a chiasm. In v. 16 the parallel topics of righteousness and wisdom are set out; in v. 17 the parallel topics of wickedness and foolishness are set out. However, in v. 16 the two parallel topics are expressed in different ways: the former with a negative particle and verb of being plus a noun (*ʾal-těhî ṣaddîq,* "do not be too righteous"), the latter with a negative particle plus verb form only (*ʾal- tithakkam,* "do not act too wise"). The chiasm is completed in v. 17 when this use of forms reverses sequence; the first phrase consists of negative particle plus verb form only (*ʾal-tiršaʿ,* "do not be too wicked"), followed by negative particle and verb of being plus noun (*ʾal-tehî sākāl,* "do not be a fool"). Both sentences conclude with rhetorical questions introduced with the interrogative *lammâ,* "why?" Taken together they seem to be advising individuals not to be *too* righteous and wise, nor *too* wicked or foolish.

Verse 16	Verse 17
ʾal-tĕhî ṣaddîq	al-tiršaʿ harbēh
wĕ ʾal-tithakkam yōter	wĕ ʾal-tĕhî sākāl

NRSV's translation of the rhetorical question in v. 16 implies that being overly righteous and wise will lead to one's self-destruction (*tiššômēm*). While this idea provides a good parallelism with the following rhetorical question in v. 17, which concerns death (*tāmût*), it is an admittedly extreme statement of possible results of too much righteousness and wisdom. Still, it is not unrelated to the observation in v. 15 that the righteous "perish" (*ʾōbēd*) in their righteousness. Perhaps the NRSV translation "destroy yourself" should be understood more metaphorically, in the sense of shock or extreme disappointment. [Can Too Much Righteousness Destroy?]

Verse 18 seems to have the admonitions of vv. 16-17 in mind and takes the rationalization further by implying that both righteousness and wickedness are equally a part of human social existence. The concluding statement urges that the ones who "fear God" maintain a balance between righteousness and wickedness. Is the sage being ironic, subverting traditional views of the meaning of the fear of God? Perhaps, but more likely he simply recognizes that piety is a struggle between both equally real aspects of human nature. This point anticipates the concluding affirmation in v. 29:

Can Too Much Righteousness Destroy?

AΩ The NRSV translates V. 16c as "why should you destroy yourself," implying that excessive righteousness and wisdom lead to ruin. The idea is thought to be similar to the conventional wisdom notion that overconfidence leads to destruction (Prov 16:18)(Whybray; Crenshaw). In this case it is not a literal destruction that is intended, but a more metaphorical application of the idea.

Ordinarily the root *šāmam* does mean "to destroy." But the word is in a particular Hebrew stem, the hithpolel (*tiššōmēm*), which denotes a "reflexive" meaning; that is, the action of the verb has the actor as its object, thus "destroy yourself." The word is usually parsed as a hithpolel of the root *šmm* with an assimilated -t- instead of the metathesis (see Murphy; Gordis; Seow; but Crenshaw, n. 106, takes as a Hithpoel; Fox takes as a Hithpael). In other contexts the same form of the verb does not mean "destroy," but to be shocked or dumbfounded, referring to some emotional or psychological effect of the reflexive action (e.g., Ps 143:4; Isa 59:16; 63:5; Dan 8:27). With this larger context of usage in view, we may suppose the sage to be saying that wisdom and righteousness are potentially sources for emotional trouble. In comparison, zeal for wickedness, discussed in the following verse (v. 17), may indeed be a source of untimely death and destruction.

James L. Crenshaw, *Ecclesiastes* (OTL; Philadelphia: Westminster, 1987), 141.

Michael V. Fox, *A Time to Tear Down & A Time to Build Up* (Grand Rapids: Eerdmans, 1999), 235.

Robert Gordis, *Koheleth – The Man and His World* (New York: Schocken, 1968), 277.

Roland Murphy, *Ecclesiastes* (WBC 23A; Waco: Word, 1992), 68.

Choon-Leong Seow, *Ecclesiastes* (AB 18C; New York: Doubleday, 1997), 254.

R. N. Whybray, *Ecclesiastes* (NCB; Grand Rapids: Eerdmans, 1989), 121.

Does Wisdom "Strengthen"?

AΩ NRSV's translation of v. 19 implies that wisdom "gives strength" to wise people more than anyone else. This seems awkward, and even earlier readers emended the text from a verbal root of *'āzaz* to *'āzar*, which means to "help" (Fox). With such an emendation, wisdom's rendering "help" would not seem uncommon at all. However, even though the root *'āzaz* usually means "be strong," it may have other nuances of meaning.

Seow notes that the noun form *'ōz*, which usually means "strength," occurs frequently in apposition to words like "honor," "glory," and "majesty" (cf. Prov 31:25; Pss 29:1; 63:2; 68:35) Further, he argues, the adjective *'izzûz*, also usually translated "strong," may mean majestic or glorious. The point is that the verb *tā'ōz* may not itself only mean strong, but could mean to be esteemed or highly valued. Thus, wisdom is the tool of choice for the wise persons, over against the implied choice of strength of ten rulers of a city (Seow). Wisdom brings honor and glory.

Michael V. Fox, *A Time to Tear Down & A Time to Build Up* (Grand Rapids: Eerdmans, 1999), 257, goes with this translation based upon LXX and 4QQoh.

Choon-Leong Seow, *Ecclesiastes* (AB 18C; New York: Doubleday, 1997), 256.

God has made humans upright, but humans have devised many schemes.

Verses 19-22 follow on these assertions with important opposing statements. As the NRSV translation reads, v. 19 poses a stark contrast with the conclusions of vv. 16-18 by insisting that wisdom "gives strength" to the wise beyond that of ten rulers. The idea is conventional (e.g., Prov 21:22; 24:5) and occurs again in Ecclesiastes 9:16. If this is the proper translation, Qoheleth could simply be quoting it in order to place it in juxtaposition with his assertions in v. 16. It may be that the translation "gives strength" should rather be translated "is valued," or "esteemed," in which case the saying may be directed at the wise themselves who overvalue wisdom. The saying is therefore consonant with the preceding observations that moderate the significance of wisdom. [Does Wisdom "Strengthen"?] In any event, the statement concerning the wise and wisdom follows well with the statement concerning the "fear of God." This complex of ideas—wise, wisdom, fear of God—is another reminder of how the sage juxtaposes conventional wisdom with his own observations.

Verse 20 more directly challenges the conventional assumptions regarding the possibility of human piety. The Deuteronomic theologians urged that national unrighteousness had contributed to the fall of Judah and Jerusalem. Job's friends, further, are depicted as taking the notion of personal piety to an unrealistic extreme (cf. Job 4:7; 8:1-7; 11:1-6). The possibility of such righteousness is called into question here by simply asserting that no one can do good without sinning. Thus, on the topics of wisdom and righteousness, both vv. 19 and 20 provide points of reflection on the observations of vv. 16-18. The entire system of retribution is made relative in these verses.

In view of the unreliability of retribution, and the general imperfection of people, Qoheleth admonishes not to "give heed" to everything that people say. One could easily infer that the reference to "your servant" (*'abdĕkā*) implies the people addressed were the wealthy only. However, the term "servant" need not only mean "slave," but could simply mean a subordinate. Even slaves could have slaves in antiquity.[2] The advice seems to be a call for grace or tolerance in full view of human imperfection. The high ideals of human and social righteousness must be balanced with the realistic understanding of human imperfection relative to such standards. Tolerance allows for such balance to exist.

Observations of Human Nature, 7:23-29

Readers may feel that vv. 23-29 stand as a separate unit of thought unrelated to vv. 15-22. The recurring idea of "finding" (*māṣâ*) wisdom dominates the section and strongly implies some new concern.[3] However, v. 29 returns to the theme of human imperfection, and the internal examples of misogyny (vv. 26 and 28) seem to make more sense in view of the sage's concession of such imperfection and his call for tolerance and grace.

We are reminded in v. 23 of the task Qoheleth began, that is, to test all things *by* wisdom (1:13). Actually, his investigation has been as much a test *of* wisdom as it has been utilizing wisdom. It is nevertheless a provocative thought that wisdom, the very utility necessary for Qoheleth's investigation, is the thing that is impossible to obtain. The investigation to obtain wisdom has only revealed that wisdom is inaccessible. The sage, like Job (28:12-22), Sirach (24:19-29), and Baruch (3:15-23), has found that wisdom was far from him, thus eluding his grasp.

The rhetorical question punctuating v. 24 and its assertions of wisdom's remoteness and depth—"who can find it?"—is really an assertion that no one can find wisdom. Just as the sage's frequent question "who knows" implies that no one does, so the question "who can find wisdom" implies that no one can. He recalls in v. 25 that his assumptions going into the investigation were that wickedness was folly and foolishness was madness. He is no longer certain of those assumptions, especially in view of his discoveries that the system of retribution does not always work (7:15).

What the sage found is equally troublesome: the adulterous woman. NRSV understands v. 26 to be an expression of the

Malleus Malleficarum ("The Witch Hammer")

Carole Fontaine notes that "the woman who brings death" is a familiar figure in Scripture and reappears in 7:26-29, or at least so it was thought by medieval interpreters. Apparently, Qoheleth's remarks were thought to be so virulent toward the "evil woman" that they were quoted in the 15th century inquisitors' witch-hunting manual, *Malleus Maleficarum* ("Ecclesiastes").

The text was first published in 1486 to aid inquisitors in their "identification, prosecution, and dispatching of witches," under the authority of a papal bull from Pope Innocent VII. Heinrich Kramer and James Sprenger, both professors of theology in the Dominican order, plied this demonic quest in northern Germany. In Part I, Question VI of the text the authors are trying to answer the question "Why . . . women are chiefly addicted to Evil superstition." They utilize the verse from Ecclesiastes 7:26 that suggests women to be "more bitter than death."

For further reading, see *Malleus Maleficarum*
<http://paganteahouse.com/malleus_maleficarum/>.

"Ecclesiastes," in *Women's Bible Commentary*, ed. Carol A. Newsom and Sharon H. Ringe (Louisville: Westminster John Knox Press, 1998), 162.

conventional wisdom readers encounter in Proverbs concerning the adulterous woman who ensnares unsuspecting men (e.g., 2:16-19; 5:3-6; 6:24-26; 7:5-27; 22:14; 23:27-28). If the verse is taken in this way, clearly the sage is not addressing his remarks against all women, only a particular kind of woman. [Malleus Maleficarum ("The Witch Hammer")] The sage's later remarks about the happiness obtained in relationship to one's wife, for instance, seem to ameliorate the possible misogyny of 7:26 (cf. 9:9-10). The fact that this woman is described with imagery recalling that of the seductress—"snares," "nets," and "fetters"—further implies the particularity of her identity rather than that of all women.

Readers are reminded in v. 27 of Qoheleth's inductive method: moving from the particular bits of evidence to formulate a generalizing hypothesis, or the "sum." More perplexing is the accompanying third person reference to the sage. This is the only such reference outside 1:12 and its "I Qoheleth." The editor evidently thought it important to remind readers not only of Qoheleth's method, but of his *own* conclusions as well. This would be especially important in a potentially controversial perspective on women, as in the case of the ensuing verse, v. 28.[4] There is no question that the sage places greater value upon men than women. Out of a thousand, he has found only one righteous man, and no women. The reference to "a thousand" may be an attempt to conjure affinities with the Solomonic tradition: "700 wives and 300 concubines" (1 Kgs 11:3).[5] Nevertheless, the difference between the sage's regard for males over females is marginal. The observation will not allow males any real superiority. Humanity, both male and female virtually alike, are unrighteous.

The concluding verse reminds readers of the puzzles in Qoheleth's journey. He has searched for the "sum" of all things (*ḥešbôn*) and has found that humankind have devised many "schemes" (*ḥiššĕbōnôt*). The similarities between the two words playfully characterize the disappointing results of the sage's assessment of human nature. To be sure, he asserts that God made humankind upright. However, readers must not forget that God must also take responsibility for whatever else has been placed in the human heart (cf. 1:13 and 3:11).

CONNECTIONS

Frankenstein

One commentator has observed that a person is *simul iustus et peccator*, "at once a just one and sinner."[6] It may well be that the virtue of wisdom is in acknowledging both aspects as part of the human experience. One cannot be embraced apart from the other. However, this may be the most important struggle humankind faces in its attempt to create some meaningful identity of faith.

Mary Shelley's *Frankenstein* is an extraordinarily insightful nineteenth-century investigation of some very modern psychological verities, not the least of which is the development of self-awareness. [Mary Wollstonecraft Shelley and Her Gothic Novel] After the death of Justine for the murder of William, the full weight of the implications of being a creator of life come to bear on Victor Frankenstein. At that time, his own creature, now having become a murderer, tracks him down at a cottage in the Alps and relates to him the story of his

---

Mary Wollstonecraft Shelley and Her Gothic Novel

Mary Shelley (1797–1851) is interesting for her life as a woman in a misogynistic, late 18th century environment, as well as for her bizarre novel, *Frankenstein.* She was the daughter of the radical feminist, Mary Wollstonecraft; she eloped with the well-known romantic poet Percy Bysshe Shelley at the age of seventeen, when Shelley was a married man. After Shelley's accidental drowning in 1822, eight years after their marriage, Mary Shelley gave herself to the support of her son and her father through her literary output.

Her most well-known novel, *Frankenstein*, is a type of gothic romance. The genre was beginning to be popular in the 18th century and is considered a forerunner of today's science fiction and thriller novels. Because she was a woman, it was originally published anonymously. What is interesting for a female writer, though, is the absence of mothers in the plot. Not only is the monster of the novel born motherless—the creation of Victor Frankenstein—but Victor's mother, like Mary Shelley's own mother, dies when the children are very young.

For further reading, see Harold Bloom, ed., *Mary Shelley's Frankenstein* (New York: Chelsea House, 1987); Anne K. Mellor, *Mary Shelley: Her Life, Her Fiction, Her Monsters* (New York: Routledge, 1988); and Johanna M. Smith, *Mary Shelley: Frankenstein* (Boston: St. Martin's Press, 1992).

Frankenstein's Monster

growth, education, and developing self-awareness after being abandoned by the doctor who created him, the very one to whom he is speaking.

The creature's story includes the details of his own remarkable education and intellectual growth at the hands of some cottagers whom he encountered in a forest. He had for a long time observed them at work and in relationship. Day after day he secretly listened to them discussing great works of art and literature. Yet, the creature was unable to participate fully in their society because, as he discovered, he is different. His frightening size and ugliness and his own awareness of that condition prevent him from the kinds of full relationships he desires. He describes his self-awareness to the doctor in a lengthy speech, excerpted here:

Of what a strange nature is knowledge! It clings to the mind, when it has once seized on it, like a lichen on the rock. I wished sometimes to shake off all thought and feeling; but I learned that there was but one means to overcome the sensation of pain and that was death—a state I feared yet did not understand. I admired virtue and good feelings, and loved the gentle manners and amiable qualities of my cottagers; but I was shut out from intercourse with them, except through means which I obtained by stealth, when I was unseen and unknown, and which rather increased than satisfied the desire I had of becoming one of my fellows.[7]

The agony of Frankenstein's creature is his discovery of a multidimensional nature. On the one hand, he discovers himself as an individual, with awareness, feelings, thoughts, ideas, and a will. And yet he is so different from others that he is alone and must remain alone. On the other hand, he longs for an "other." He cannot bear his loneliness and inability to find a place in society. He is both an individual and a social being; the hell he must live through is the inability to satisfy both aspects of his being. The creature ultimately holds his creator responsible for his own misery. The doctor had made him incomplete and unsuitable for full and appropriate social interaction, and then abandoned him with no direction or instruction on how to survive the competing impulses within.

The agony of Qoheleth is a similar awareness of human nature. It is good and evil at once for both women and men. Ironically, the human struggle is to elevate one over the other. But, the sage remonstrates, this is impossible. Using the traditional values of male and female, for righteousness and wickedness, neither can be elevated over the other. They are both present and valid parts of human individuality and society.

People of faith, like the Frankenstein creature, are in a struggle for self-discovery and awareness. They too often find that there are things about them they do not like and seek to cover them up. The sage here urges a kind of disarming honesty about who we are: both righteous and unrighteous. However, he offers little help with how to cope.

NOTES

[1] See Michael V. Fox, *A Time to Tear Down & A Time to Build Up* (Grand Rapids: Eerdmans, 1999), 35-42; Choon-Leong Seow, *Ecclesiastes* (AB 18C; New York: Doubleday, 1997), 252.

[2] Seow, *Ecclesiastes,* 258.

[3] R. N. Whybray, *Ecclesiastes* (NCB; Grand Rapids: Eerdmans, 1989), 123, for instance, notes the eightfold occurrence of "to find" (*māṣâ'*) and urges that its occurrence in 8:1 actually creates the inclusio marking the boundaries of the unit. Likewise, Fox, *A Time to Tear Down,* 237.

[4] Whybray, *Ecclesiastes,* 126.

[5] James L. Crenshaw, *Ecclesiastes* (OTL; Philadelphia: Westminster, 1987), 148-49, notes that the idiom of "a thousand" occurs elsewhere in wisdom contexts not concerned with wives (e.g., Job 9:3).

[6] Seow, *Ecclesiastes,* 268.

[7] Mary Shelley, *Frankenstein,* in *The Mary Shelley Reader*, vol. 2, ed. Betty T. Bennett and Charles E. Robinson (Oxford: Oxford University Press, 1990), 89.

THE TASK OF RESTRAINING
THE WIND

Ecclesiastes 8:1-17

The sage continues his perilous trek near the edge of the precipice of meaning, peering for a prolonged time down deep into the darkness of the chasm. He sees no bottom, no end to the blackness. Readers who walk with him must wrestle with the hypnotic effect of his lulling imagery: the trouble of the mortal realm is heavy, no one can restrain the wind, no one knows the day of death. All of that is true. Yet, only as people resist this sense of life as a bottomless pit will they experience the effect of yet another commendation of enjoyment (v. 15). Only at the conclusions of the sage's observations does he pull his readers back, inviting them to consider again the possibility that there can really be joy, that some experiences are better than others. In a life characterized by arbitrary use of power (vv. 1-8) and reversals of justice (vv. 9-17), readers are invited to reconsider how tenuous and momentary, and therefore how precious and rare, their enjoyment is.

Two statements concerning the wisdom and the wise frame the observations in this unit. The opening statement concerns wisdom and the wise (v. 1); the closing statement concerns the inability to find wisdom (v. 17). A familiar question that readers recognize from as recently as 7:24—who can find wisdom?—functions as a thematic touchstone and is made ironic by the two topics within. Inside the framework, which serves to reinforce the general sense of skepticism that pervades the unit, claims that even those who are wise must submit to arbitrary power. Even those with wisdom must submit to the inexorable arbitrariness of inequity. Even the powerful people cannot control such arbitrariness. [Structure at a Glance: Ecclesiastes 8:1-17]

However, both verbal and thematic links, such as that between v. 1 and v. 17 concerning the inability of finding wisdom, encourage readers to examine the chapter with an overall structure in mind. The conclusion in v. 9, "one person exercises authority over another to the other's hurt," is an effective introduction to the topic in v. 14, "there are righteous people who are treated according to the conduct of the wicked." The phrase "applying my mind" in vv. 9 and 16 further provides a parallelism that connects the two units.

Structure at a Glance: Ecclesiastes 8:1-17

AΩ The following outline suggests a possible way of organizing the meaningful elements of the chapter.

Vv. 1-9 Power, not wisdom, rules
    V. 1 Can anyone know wisdom?
    Vv. 2-4 The power of a king
    V. 5 Can humans resist the arbitrariness of life?
    Vv. 6-9 Inexorable realities of life
Vv. 10-17 Arbitrariness, not order, rules
    Vv. 10-13 Arbitrariness of retribution: case of the wicked
    V. 14 Arbitrariness of retribution: case of the righteous
    Vv. 15-17 Impossibility of understanding

It is not uncommon for some scholars to treat 8:1 as though it were the conclusion to the preceding unit, 7:23-29. Its concern with wisdom provides an effective inclusion with 7:23-24 on the inability to find wisdom (Fox; Whybray). Neither is it uncommon for scholars to read ch. 8 in its entirety as only a loosely connected collection of miscellaneous observations and assertions (Murphy).

Michael V. Fox , *A Time to Tear Down & A Time to Build Up* (Grand Rapids: Eerdmans, 1999), 272-73.
Roland Murphy, *Ecclesiastes* (WBC 23A; Dallas: Word, 1993), 79-87.
R. N. Whybray, *Ecclesiastes* (Grand Rapids: Eerdmans, 1989), 123-29.

COMMENTARY

Power, Not Wisdom, Rules, 8:1-9

The initial challenge is to determine how 8:1 relates to the ensuing observations on relations with a king. The two rhetorical questions introduced with the interrogative, "who," remind readers of similar questions previously in the book of Ecclesiastes. The ensuing assertion that "wisdom makes one's face shine . . ." is subverted by the preceding introductory claim that no one really knows the interpretation of a thing.[1]

The term translated "interpretation" in v. 1, *pēšer*, occurs here in Hebrew and in Aramaic in Daniel 2:4, 5, 6, 7, 9, 16, 24, and in Qumran literature. Clearly, it is late terminology. However, its cognate, *pitrôn*, occurs in Genesis 40:5 and 8, in the narrative context where one wise individual offers a king an interpretation. In the context of Genesis 40, Joseph is a wise man who knew the "interpretation," *pitrôn,* of a dream. Whether the sage here intends the allusion to the Joseph story is not clear, but the allusiveness of the opening rhetorical question forms a provocative connection to the ensuing concern on the whims of a king.

The observation in v. 2 opens a series of reflections that culminate in the idea that there are occasions when everyone has to yield to arbitrary power, as though one were bound by a sacred oath. The king is the central symbol, although as the sage expands his observations, it is clear that he is not simply concerned about obedience to a king. The troubles of mortals are much more expansive than mere political power (v. 6). The problem of determining which Israelite king a Jewish sage might be referring to in the late Persian or Hellenistic period is therefore alleviated. That is, if the book was written in the Persian or the early Hellenistic era, there was not a time when Israel had its own king. The better strategy is to recognize the symbolic significance of the image of the king. Since the sages have traditionally admonished that both obedience (Prov 24:21) and avoidance of royal displeasure were things to take seriously (Prov 14:35; 16:14; 19:12; 20:26), it is clear that these traditional views become a basis for evoking thought about still larger, more threatening matters to which individuals are on occasion called to submit.

The line of reasoning seems clearer in v. 3b regarding the matter that is translated by NRSV as "unpleasant" (*bĕdābār rā*). It is difficult to know whether the sage has anything in particular in mind, such as "cursing the king" as in 10:20. Verse 5 also refers to an "evil thing" (*dābār rā*) and in a context that clearly indicates such an evil thing to be the result of one's failure to obey the command of the king. The point of v. 2 is then reiterated in v. 3. It is better to yield to overwhelming power than to suffer; the king always gets his way.

Verse 4 continues the thought on the power of the king, urging here that his "word" is "powerful." No one can question the will of the king. Reflections upon the idea of unquestionable power are not new with the book of Ecclesiastes. Traditional wisdom knew that one took one's own life into his hands when he provoked the king's anger (Prov 20:2). Moreover, the specific question of 4b, "Who can say to him, 'What are you doing?'" is certainly reminiscent of Job's description of the unyielding power of God (Job 9:12). In Job's case this statement functions as a basis for mistrusting the deity. For Qoheleth it is a basis for admonishing the individual to take care in the presence of the king. [Persian Kings]

While v. 5 corroborates the admonition to surrender to incomprehensible power, the latter half of the verse is a transition to a broader application of the principle: "the wise mind will know the time and way." The word NRSV translates "way," *mišpāṭ*, is more typically translated as "judgment." The present translation probably stems from an understanding of *mišpāṭ* as a legal procedure or process.[2] The contextual emphasis upon the king's ability to

Persian Kings

The titularies in Old Persian inscriptions reveal the ancient Persian understanding of the status of kingship. Samuel Eddy wrote, "The texts almost without exception begin with the formula, 'I am X, Great King, King of Kings, son of Y, and Achaemenid.'" Usually there was also language that indicated the king's office was bestowed by Ahura Mazdah, the Persian deity.

Persian religion was henotheistic in ways not dissimilar to the Hebrews. There were many gods, but only one was to be worshiped. In Persian theology this deity was Ahura Mazdah. All history was moving toward an eschatological battle with Ahura Mazdah's chief rival, Ahuman. Victory was assured in the end, and the cosmic victory motif provided a theological grounding for the earthly kings' defeat of their enemies. This defeating of enemies motif shows up often in the imperial art that characterizes their reigns.

For further reading, see Jim Hicks, ed., *The Persians* (New York: Time Life Books, 1975).

Samuel Eddy, *The King is Dead* (Lincoln: University of Nebraska Press, 1961), 41.

A detail of a relief in the Treasury of the Palace at Persepolis, the capital city of Persia, illustrates the power of King Darius (550–486 BC). Note the relative size of the attendant and the king (seated) indicating the view of Persian royalty.

Darius the Great. Stone relief. 491–486 BC. Persia, Achaemenid Period. Persepolis, Iran.

determine one's destiny suggests that "judgment" is appropriate and that the wise person is one who understands its inevitability.

Verses 6-8 offer a series of observations, most of which readers have already encountered in the book of Ecclesiastes, that function as motivations for caution in the presence of a king. They appeal to the general arguments stemming from both the created order and human nature. In this way Qoheleth moves from his particular example of the impossibility of escaping the arbitrary commands of a king to the impossibility of controlling the phenomena and events that shape one's life generally. [Chiasm on Human Concessions]

Verse 6 is introduced with the explanatory particle *kî*, "for." The implication is that v. 5 draws its conclusions based upon the reality of the claim in v. 6. The phrase "time and way" recurs in v. 6 and recalls 3:1 and its claim that all things have a time. In the present context, even submission to power has its proper time. Knowing the appropriateness of something, even surrender, does not diminish the fact that troubles are heavy, however. The allusion to

---

Chiasm on Human Concessions

AΩ Verses 6-8 move readers thematically from the particular example of arbitrary power to general statements of equal arbitrariness, which readers have already encountered, e.g., the assertion of a time for judgment (3:17); no one knows one's destiny (2:19); the pain of human toil (2:23); and so on. What is of even more interest is the poetic nature of vv. 6-8. Vv. 6-7 consist of a series of four statements introduced with the Hebrew particle, *kî*. V. 8 consists of a series of statements introduced with the negative particle, *ʾên*.

Verses 6-8 stand together to form an intriguing chiasm. There is already an implied symmetry in that the four *kî* clauses of vv. 6-7 (translated as "for," "although," "Indeed," and "for") are balanced with four negative clauses introduced with *ʾên* and *lōʾ*. The thematic relationships between vv. 6-7 and v. 8 mirror the response to the consideration of resisting a king's power.

Chiasm in vv. 6-8

Hebrew Transliteration	NRSV Translation
a. *kî lēkol-ḥēpeṣ yēš ʿet ûmišpāṭ*	For every matter has its time and way
b. *kî rāʿat hāʾ ādām rabbâʿ ālāyw*	although the troubles of mortals lie heavy upon them
c. *kî ʾênennû yōdēaʿ mâ-šeyyihyeh*	Indeed, they do not know what is to be,
d. *kî kaʾăšer yihyeh mî yaggîd lô*	for who can tell them how it will be?
d[1] *ʾên ʾādām šallît bārûaḥ liklôʾ ʾet hārîuaḥ*	No one has power over the wind to restrain the wind,
c[1] *wēʾ ên šiltôn bēyôm hammāwet*	or power over the day of death;
b[1] *wēʾ ên mišlaḥat bammilḥāmâ*	there is no discharge from the battle,
a[1] *wēlōʾ-yēmallēṭ rešaʾ ʾet bēʿ ālāyw*	nor does wickedness deliver those who practice it.

The two outer claims (a:a[1]) correspond in that the first concerns the inevitability of judgment and the latter the impossibility of deliverance from death by wickedness, a concrete example of judgment. The next two assertions (b:b[1]) correspond in that the former concerns the heaviness of evil upon human life and the latter the impossibility of escape from warfare. The latter again offers a concrete example of the former. The two central pairs function in tandem; both c and d reiterate each other in the assertion that the future cannot be known and c[1] and d[1] likewise reiterate each other in their response that death like wind is irrepressible. The latter pair, furthermore, offer a response to the unknowability of the future: death is as certain as the wind.

---

the troubled human existence in v. 6b introduces another explanatory clause in v. 7, opening with the particle *kî*.

Verse 7 develops further another theme encountered already, that no one can know the future. This inability to predict is part of the heaviness that weighs upon humans and is a further illustration of a phenomenon to which humans must submit. Verse 8 proceeds to illustrate the impossibility of knowledge of the future by offering four examples: the impossibility of restraining the wind, of escaping from death, of being released from war, and of deliverance from the punishment for wickedness for those who practice it.

The concluding verse in this section (v. 9) appeals to the authority of the sage's own personal experience. His examples and advice are based upon his examination and deliberation over their significance.

Arbitrariness, Not Order, Rules All, 8:10-17

Reading chapter 8 as a single unit, vv. 10-17 may conceivably be read as a response to the verses that precede them. The observations in vv. 1-9 begin with a specific example of senseless power and move to general observations about the futility of resistance. The observations in v. 10 begin with the related theme of the suffering of the righteous and the prosperity of the wicked, then move beyond such observations to the individual's response to such injustices.

Verse 10 illustrates the absolute lack of human control by appealing to the traditional crux of retribution. The sage begins his remarks with the familiar language of personal experience, indicated by language of "seeing." The sense seems to be that the wicked receive honorable burials due in part because they participated in public worship in the city. The clear implication is that, despite the public adulation for their piety, the wicked have not received their just rewards. This, the sage calls vanity, *hebel*.

The absurdity of such injustice evokes further exploration into the question of injustice. Qoheleth attempts to account for the behavior of the wicked by noting the lack of immediate punishment, or sentence, *pitgām*. There may be some ambiguity in this verse over whether it is God or the king who is slow to offer punishment. The word translated "sentence," *pitgām*, is a Persian loan word and occurs also in Esther 1:20 in reference to a royal decree. [Persian Loan Words] Earlier in the chapter we saw discussions of the king's powerful and arbitrary word (8:3-4). Whether the slowness to punish stems from the king or from God, the sage is offering an explanation for the existence of such evil. The result is that human hearts are set on doing evil, an echo of a conclusion already reached in 7:29.

Verse 12 seems to be putting forward two competing assertions. On the one hand, sinners commit evil deeds and prolong their lives thereby. There is no denying this phenomenon based upon Qoheleth's observations. On the other hand, the sage knows that it will be well with those who fear God. This is equally true. He has already asserted that God's justice is eventual and inexorable (3:17).

Persian Loan Words

AΩ There are two words in the book of Ecclesiastes that are borrowed from the Persian language: "parks" (*pardēsîm*) in 2:5 and "sentence" (*pitgām*) in 8:11. These are not to be confused with Aramisms, words that are directly from Aramaic or have syntactical features like Aramaic. Although Aramaic became the vernacular in the administration and commerce of the Persian empire, Persian is not the same language. It is an Indo-European language, whereas Aramaic is Semitic.

Because of the relative lateness of the Persian empire (539–333 BC), biblical books that contain Persian words in addition to Ecclesiastes are dated very late. These include Chronicles, Ezra, Nehemiah, Esther, and Daniel. The books of Haggai, Zechariah, and Malachi concern matters that reflect an awareness of the Persian Empire, but they do not contain Persian words.

For further reading, see R. Bianchi, "The Language of Qohelet: A Bibliographical Survey," *ZAW* 105 (1993): 210-23; F. C. Burkitt, "Is Ecclesiastes a Translation?" *JTS* 23 (1922): 22-28; and A Schoors, "The Use of Vowel Letters in Qoheleth," *UF* 20 (1988): 277-86.

The concluding thought on the arbitrary judgment of the wicked evokes again the image of the ones who "fear God." Readers encounter this image several times in the book of Ecclesiastes (cf. 3:14; 5:16; and 7:18) as well as in the Proverbs (e.g., 12:13; 13:2, 13; 14:2). It may well be that the sage uses the phrase either to mean "dread of the awesome" or "religious devotion" in this book.[3] While it would be convenient to correlate wickedness with the absence of religious devotion, this would seem to contradict the thrust of v. 10. There the wicked are afforded proper burial because of their public religious devotion. What is missing from the religious devotion of the wicked is some sense of dread that underlies their public devotion. They are merely going through the motions for the public show. That is because they have no real sense of dread, and this may be due to the problem that judgment upon their wickedness is not passed quickly. Therefore, the wicked doubt any real connection between their actions and some moral order.

The arbitrariness of response to wickedness is further elaborated by asserting the converse: the righteous ones are treated with equal arbitrariness. Verse 14 offers yet another example of vanity, *hebel*. The righteous are treated as though they were wicked. Following v. 13, where the sage observes that eventually it will not be well with the wicked, v. 14 seems to be a contradiction. It seems to be that Qoheleth has returned to v. 10 and to the observation that the wicked are actually treated as though they were righteous. In the end, readers may simply have to allow the conclusion that there are exceptions to every rule.

In the face of such arbitrariness, v. 15 returns to the theme encountered in 5:18: experiencing enjoyment is the central human impulse. Readers recall that enjoyment is a gift from God, and if God allows one to have enjoyment, one should take it gratefully. Arbitrary pleasure is the only antidote to the paradoxes of an impenetrably absurd existence.

Verses 16-17, which conclude the section, return to the question concerning wisdom that opens the chapter in 8:1. The difference in these later verses is they are autobiographical. The sage speaks of his own struggle to know wisdom and to understand the ways of God. His conclusion is that it is arduous work and only results in a loss of sleep. He states again for his readers that God's ways cannot be known (see 3:10-15). Those people who claim to have wisdom and therefore claim to understand God's ways really cannot find out themselves. Ultimately, understanding God is as impossible as restraining the wind.

CONNECTIONS

Naming Arbitrary Power and Restraining Wind

No matter how we modern readers try, it is difficult to imagine the arbitrariness of power in terms of kingship. For most who read this book, being subjects to one who has the kind of absolute political power depicted in biblical texts is far from their reality. It may be easier to conceive of arbitrariness, therefore, in symbolic terms such as retribution for the righteousness and the wicked. However, our world is not totally devoid of either such real power as that of a king, or of the arbitrary application of such power. We don't have to look that far in order to understand such use of power.

Mary Pipher's book *Reviving Ophelia* (1994) is one example. Dr. Pipher, a clinical psychologist, documents through case studies the oppressive effects that American culture is having on adolescent girls. She summarizes in her preface that girls are growing up in a more dangerous, "sexualized and media-saturated culture." She calls it a "girl-poisoning" culture. Girls "face incredible pressures to be beautiful and sophisticated, which in junior high means using chemicals and being sexual. As they navigate a more dangerous world, girls are less protected."[4] The purpose of the book is to isolate the nature of the unnamed problem and provide ways of strengthening adolescent girls as they move through this time of life.

What seems most powerful, though, is Pipher's description of one of the most influential forces in her own life, her father. She describes him as "the best and worst of fathers." On the one hand, he wanted to see her excel and to accomplish her goals. He maintained an unwavering confidence in her abilities. On the other hand, Pipher says, "he had a double standard about sex and rigid views about women," creating the complexities and bewildering ambiguities that make it difficult for adolescent girls to gain their own voice and identity.[5] This seems to be a close parallel to the kind of arbitrary power described by Qoheleth. The difference is that the sage encourages submission to the power while the psychologist, first, strategizes about ways to diminish the existence of such arbitrary power and, second, encourages the discovery of approaches to strengthen adolescent girls to overcome such power.

Readers may pause here to remember that the sage does not believe it possible to straighten what is crooked. His advice, especially concerning the inevitability of submission to power, is not offered as an acknowledgment that power is good or its use changeable. Rather, arbitrary power simply is. Submission to such power is a temporary strategy made necessary by the overwhelming impossibility of making any real change. By contrast, Pipher is far more optimistic. She believes, even in the face of an endless stream of adolescent victimization, that it is possible to change both culture and individuals' responses to culture. Qoheleth might smile, perhaps entertaining the thought that she is naive, maybe even a Pollyanna. Pipher would respond to Qoheleth that he does not have the advantage of a modern, scientific worldview that now understands individuals no longer to have to wait for God to give them enjoyment.

NOTES

[1] Michael V. Fox , *A Time to Tear Down & A Time to Build Up* (Grand Rapids: Eerdmans, 1999), 272, asserts that *mî*, "who," occurs seventeen times in the book, sixteen of which occur in rhetorical questions that expect the response "no one."

[2] Robert Gordis, *Koheleth: The Man and His World* (New York: Schocken, 1968), 182 and 289, translates the term as "procedure."

[3] James L. Crenshaw, *Ecclesiastes* (OTL; Philadelphia: Westminster, 1987),156, explains that "fear of Yahweh" may mean either dread of some impersonal force or behavior that is a rational response to such feelings.

[4] Mary Pipher, *Reviving Ophelia* (New York: Ballentine Books, 1994), 12.

[5] Ibid., 116.

LIVE LIFE IN THE PRESENT, BECAUSE DEATH STALKS

Ecclesiastes 9:1-10

Live Life Now, 9:1–12:8

The concluding section of the book conveys a tone of admonition, paralleling the section contained by 5:1–6:9. The language betrays an attempt to offer advice, especially in connection with the individual's response to a world in which one may not expect to get ahead, to benefit from one's toil, or to find meaning that is self-evident. The opening reflection and admonition acknowledge the pervasiveness of death and the importance of living for the moment (9:1-10). The conclusion recaps the importance of the present and the tragedy of failing to act in the present while youthfulness allows enjoyment (11:7–12:8). Together the opening and closing instructions frame internal instructions on wisdom and folly. The effect of the framework is to relativize any claim that wisdom provides individuals more than a marginal advantage in life. The urgency about placing in a proper perspective any notion of gaining some advantage thus continues throughout this concluding section.

Four subsections comprise the closing section of the book, plus at least two epilogues. Ecclesiastes 9:1-10 asserts the importance of living life in the immediate present. Ecclesiastes 9:11–10:15 offers a series of instructions asserting the marginal benefits of wisdom over folly. The element of risk is evoked in 11:1-6 as a transition into the final statement on youth and old age, 11:8–12:7. Ecclesiastes 12:8 closes the sage's instructions by returning to the theme set out at the beginning of the book: that all is vanity, *hebel*.

Live Life in the Present, Because Death Stalks, 9:1-10

Much like the first half of the book (1:1–6:9), the second half observes that life is bound by the inexorable realities of a hidden deity, an impenetrable universe, and a certain fate. Within those boundaries humankind must discover a way to enjoy what God has given to be enjoyed. In these opening observations of the final section

Structure at a Glance: Ecclesiastes 9:1-10

AΩ There is little scholarly consensus on how to distribute the verses into clusters. The following outline is suggestive of an approach to structure.

Vv. 1-6: Death Comes to All
  V. 1 All in the hand of God
  Vv. 2-3 Couplet on "one fate"
  Vv. 4-5 Couplet on "advantage of life"
  V. 6 All perish
Vv. 7-10: The Call to Life
  V. 7 Imperative to live
  V. 8 Injunction to dress festively
  V. 9 Imperative to love one's wife
  V. 10. Imperative to do what one is skilled at doing

The NRSV does not translate the particle *kî*, "for," in v. 1. As the introduction to a motive or explanatory clause, the particle could imply that v. 1 serves as the conclusion to 8:1-17 (Fox). As the beginning of a new unit of thought (so NRSV), the particle functions asseveratively. The *kî* would indicate that there is a break between ideas, and might well be translated "indeed" or "see." This latter possibility is reinforced when we compare the language in 8:9, which concludes the section in vv. 1-9, with the language in 9:1. There is linguistic similarity between the two verses. However, 8:9 concludes the preceding ideas and does not begin with the Hebrew word *kî*.

Michael V. Fox, *A Time to Tear Down & A Time to Build Up* (Grand Rapids: Eerdmans, 1999), 290-91, for instance, sees 9:1 as connected to 8:17 within a larger framework concluding in 9:6.

---

of the book, the sage again reminds his students that the time to take action is in the present.

Verses 1-10 divide into two sections. Verses 1-6 reflect explicitly upon the common human fate of death. Verse 6 concludes the subsection by noting those things the dead do not have and are not able to experience. The second section, vv. 7-10, offers the familiar call to enjoy life in the present. It concludes with an admonition to use one's own strength in doing what one is skilled at doing. This admonition is motivated by the reality of what one cannot do in the realm of the dead. In this way v. 10 parallels v. 6 and thus unifies the thought of the opening ten verses.

The rhetoric changes within this unit from inferences drawn from observation to imperative instruction. This leads Seow to conclude that here begins the latter section of part 2 of the book on ethical implications of the observations that have preceded.[1]
[Structure at a Glance: Ecclesiastes 9:1-10]

COMMENTARY

The Same Fate Comes to All, 9:1-6

The topic of death is prevalent in the book of Ecclesiastes (e.g., 2:16; 3:19-21; 4:2-3). In fact, it seems as though the sage values death over life in certain circumstances (e.g., 4:2-3). As readers turn from the immediate topic in 8:16-17 concerning the impossibility of understanding how God's universe operates, the reference to death's inexorability seems especially foreboding, although not surprising.

The thrust of 9:1 is that the deeds of the righteous and wise alike, whether "love or hate," come before the deity. It is possible to interpret this phrase as a reference to either the deity's love or hate,[2] thus a reference to the unpredictability of God's attitude toward the righteous and wise. Since v. 6 returns to this identical language of "their" love and hate, however, it seems more likely that the phrase in v. 1 renames the "deeds"[3] of the righteous and wise rather than those of God. Thus, the statement is an assertion that all things are in God's control, including those deeds of the righteous and the wise, whether of love or hatred. [Redistribution and Emendation of *hakkōl*]

Verses 2 and 3 stand together as a combined illustration of the claim in v. 1 regarding the all-pervading reality of death. Both verses illustrate the same point: "the same fate comes to all." The illustrative material within the verses consists of a list of all the people the sage's readers might possibly think had a chance to avoid the fate of death. The list comprises a series of pairs that states the positive idea first, then the negative. The "righteous" occurs first, paired with the "wicked"; the "good" is followed by the "evil,"[4] and so on. The same positive-negative pattern applies to "those who sacrifice" and "those who do not sacrifice." The implication is that the sage regards sacrifice as good, thus suggesting his sympathy with cultic activity.

Redistribution and Emendation of *hakkōl*

ΑΩ NRSV emends the Hebrew text of v. 1 in its translation of the word *hakkōl*, "everything" to *hebel*, "vanity." NRSV does not, however, change the versification, retaining the "vanity" at the beginning of v. 2 as the MT has it. The implication is nevertheless that the emended word, *hebel*, actually concludes the sense of v. 1 rather than begins v. 2. Thus, some confusion results over the need for a redistribution of the words in the verse. This emendation reflects the translation of LXX, which has *mataiotēs en tois pasin*, "all is vanity," and actually makes good sense of the text.

However, the MT also provides satisfactory sense without the emendation. First, the concluding phrase of v. 1 is "humans who know what is before them," taking the Hebrew phrase, *lipnêhem*, in either a temporal sense—what is to happen—or in a spatial sense—what is before their eyes. The point of the phrase reiterates the general state of ignorance that characterizes the human situation.

The phrase beginning v. 2, *hakkōl ka' ăšer lakōl*, may be translated something like, "everything is as for everyone." The point is, the same things come to all people. The idea fits well with the preceding claim about human ignorance, which introduces the ensuing discussion of "one fate for all" (see Murphy; Fox; Seow).

Michael V. Fox, *A Time to Tear Down & A Time to Build* (Grand Rapids: Eerdmans, 1999), 256-57.

Roland Murphy, *Ecclesiastes*, WBC 23A (Dallas: Word, 1993), 91.

Choon-Leong Seow, *Ecclesiastes* (AB 18C; New York: Doubleday, 1997), 299.

Taking Oaths

The references in v. 2 to those who take oaths and those who do not are offered as examples of contemporary piety for the sages' day. Taking oaths was frowned upon. Readers should not confuse this activity, however, with that of making a vow, as in 5:3. The two activities are not the same.

The oath was a curse upon oneself, ensured by the deity as a test of the validity of one's claims to innocence. In the case of a wife whose husband accuses her of adultery, the oath was a test of her innocence (Num 5:11-31). The implication was that, if guilty, the deity would activate the curse. Such contributes to the irony of Job's invocation of an oath in Job 31. If he does not die after invoking the deity's intervention, the tacit implication is that Job is innocent and God is guilty.

A vow, by contrast, is a conditional promise to give or to consecrate to God a person or a thing. Such is common practice throughout the ancient Near East, and witnessed frequently throughout the biblical story. Individuals promise a tithe (Gen 28:20-22), a sacrifice (2 Sam 15:8), plunder taken in war (Num 21:2), or a person (Judg 11:30-31; 1 Sam 1:11). The vow is associated with one of three different kinds of offerings that fall into the category of "communion sacrifices," or *šĕlāmîm*. There is the sacrifice of praise (*tôdâ*) as in Lev 7:12-15; 22:29-30; then the voluntary sacrifice (*nĕdābâ*) as in Lev 7:16-17; 22:18-23; and finally the votive sacrifice to which suppliants bound themselves by a vow.

For further reading, see Sheldon H. Blank, "The Curse, Blasphemy, the Spell, and the Oath," *HUCA* 23/1 (1950): 73-95; and K. Joines, "Vow in the Old Testament" *MDB*, 950.

The final pair, "those who swear" and those "who shun an oath," reflects a reversed sequence for the purpose of ending on a positive rather than a negative. [Taking Oaths] Verse 3 echoes 7:25, where the sage recalled his opening assumption: folly is madness. In 9:3 the sage seems not only to assume that folly is madness, but that as madness folly lives in the hearts of all. The madness seems to be that of thinking that one can actually defy the exigencies of existence, especially death. Whereas once death was presented as that which awaited the foolish, now it comes to all.

Verse 4 continues with the claim that life is better than death, and this affirmation stands out in relief against the opposite assertion in 4:2. The NRSV translation of v. 4, "whoever is joined with," seems an odd way of referring to the people who are living. It translates the *qĕrē'* tradition of the text rather than the *kĕtîb*, that is, the way tradition "read" the text rather than the way tradition "wrote" the text. The same word translated here as "hope," *biṭṭāḥôn*, also occurs in 2 Kings 18:19 and is there translated as confidence. The word "hope" may convey a more positive outlook than is actually intended in this context. Readers should remember the preceding introduction on the inevitability of death. It may well be that the only confidence one may have, ironically, is that one will die. Perhaps the ensuing image of the dog versus the lion illustrates the sense of confidence envisioned. Nonexistence, which results from death, cannot be compared favorably with even the miserable life of a dog.

In v. 5 that existence is admittedly made even more miserable by the fact that the living know they are going to die. By contrast, the dead know nothing. Still, the dog has the better of the two options. The juxtaposition of "reward" (*śākār*) and "memory" (*zākār*) unfortunately does not convey in English the assonance of the two terms. In Hebrew the two words sound similar: *śākār* and *zākār*. Both reward and memory have vanished for the dead, a view the sage has put forward previously (see 2:16 and 7:1). The words' similarity in sound implies the similarity in effect: if one's memory is the only reward one asks for, then it, too, will vanish.

Verse 6 concludes that all of life's passions—love, hate, and envy—perish with people when they die. Qoheleth observed in 4:4 that jealousy or envy is what actually drives human life. These passions nevertheless represent the potential for enjoyment in life, but all of that potential is lost for the righteous and the wise as well as for the unrighteous and the fool. [Sound and Sense]

Sound and Sense

Verse 6 offers a good illustration of the ancient poet's craft. The convention of using language to imitate the sense of a thing or an action is called onomatopoeia. Although such a term was not known to the poet sage who authored the Hebrew of the book, v. 6 reflects this poetic convention. Not only does the verse provide closure on the thought of the opening six verses by returning to the topics of love and hate, first introduced in v. 1, it also creates the sense of inevitability through the sound of its poetic cadence. The successive repetition of the particle *gam*, usually rendered as "also," attached to nouns with the third masculine plural suffix, creates a cadence that reinforces the idea of the one fate that inevitably comes for all (Crenshaw).

For further reading, see Robert Alter, *The Art of Hebrew Poetry* (New York: Basic Books, 1985); and C. Hugh Holman, "Onomatopoeia," in *A Handbook to Literature*, 3rd ed. (New York, Indianapolis: Bob Merrill, 1972), 367-68.

James L. Crenshaw, *Ecclesiastes* (OTL; Philadelphia: Westminster, 1987), 162.

Dog's Life? 9:7-10a

The topic of enjoyment has been raised several times already in the sage's reflections (e.g., 2:24-26; 3:12-13, 22; 5:17-19; 8:15). This instance stands out from the others in that it is dominated by imperatives: "go," "eat," "drink," "see life," "do with all your might." Commentators typically note the similarities between this set of admonitions and the similar set of admonitions in the ancient Mesopotamian epic poem Gilgamesh (see the Introduction and [The Gilgamesh Epic]). Siduri, the tavern keeper who encounters Gilgamesh before his journey into the underworld, offers advice that stresses eating, clothing in fine garments, washing one's head, and the long-lasting embrace of one's wife.[5]

> Let thy garments be sparkling fresh,
> Thy head be washed; bathe thou in water.
> Pay heed to the little one that holds on to thy hand,
> Let thy spouse delight in thy bosom!
> For this is the task of [mankind].[6]

Ninsum
Image of Ninsum, mother of Gilgamesh. Another royal mother gives advice to her son, a king. In a dream she alerts Gilgamesh of the approach of Enkidu, his companion.

The Goddess Ninsum. Seated steatite figure, bas-relief from Tello. 2150 BC. Louvre. Paris, France.

There is no way to prove that Qoheleth knew of or drew upon the ancient epic poem in formulating his advice. However, the view that humankind is not in control of life, and that ultimately all must surrender to this lack of control, is not only shared between the book of Ecclesiastes and the Gilgamesh Epic. Egyptian texts (for citation of a Harpers Song, see the Introduction) and Greek texts are typically cited as offering the same kind of advice.[7] The implication is that such ideas were common property across the intellectual world of the ancient Near East.

As in previous instances, Qoheleth praises God for the possibility of enjoyment. It is God's gift. This does not mean that enjoyment is something one can anticipate or strategize to obtain. One can only conclude that, if God extends to one the possibility of enjoyment, one should take it and enjoy life to the fullest. The admonition to "enjoy life" in v. 9 translates the idiom "see life," *rĕʾēh ḥayyîm*. Readers have encountered the similar use of the word "to see" in 2:1 regarding "the good" (see also Jer 5:12; Job 7:7). One is to enjoy life with the wife one loves, or at least with a woman taken for the purpose of marriage (see Prov 5:18-19).[8] For readers familiar with Paul's advice against marriage due to an impending eschatological reality (see 1 Cor 7:8-9), Qoheleth provides an interesting contrast. In the face of a certain death, the sage nevertheless admonishes the enjoyment of life to the fullest. Individuals should occupy themselves with what they are able to do. There will be no such ability or activity in Sheol, where all humankind are going.

CONNECTIONS

"The Slow, Smokeless Burning of Decay"

The height of wisdom would seem to be a quiet understanding of the human situation, vividly portrayed here by Qoheleth as a counterposition of enjoyment and death. Real enjoyment is that experienced in the unflinching knowledge of the inexorable realities of existence. One is certain of only one thing: there is finally an end to all, and it is more likely to come sooner than later. Life from a human point of view may take on the appearance of progress and increasing control over circumstances. But in actuality, all things pass away, leaving little trace of humanity's input. One must find enjoyment while one may.

Such a feeling is likewise provoked in reflection on the progress of science over disease. Though the present generation boasts of the elimination of deadly viruses, in actuality humanity's confidence should be tempered with the humility brought on by scientific

This stone relief from ancient Egypt depicts women gathering and carrying lotus blossoms to be pressed. It is uncertain whether the lotus will be used for perfume or medicine.

Preparation of Lotus Flowers. Egyptian. Relief. Museo Egizio. Turin, Italy.

Medicine in the Bible

The broader question of health in the ancient Near East would require inclusion of such categories as public hygiene, beliefs about causes of illness, and the involvement of governments in the prevention of disease. Archaeological evidence from Syria-Palestine indicates that as far back as Neolithic times (10,000–4000 BC) there was specialized medical care. Liver models found at Late Bronze Hazor and Megiddo (1550–1200 BC) imply medical consultation and hepatoscopy (examination of animal organs for divining purposes). The Amarna tablets from 14th century BC describe epidemics and the work of physicians.

In the Bible healing is understood as Yahweh's work. In the Hellenistic period (333–60 BC) there were physicians, but they were merely agents of the Lord (cf. Sir 38:1-15). Earlier biblical texts are not so tolerant as Sirach. The Chronicler criticizes Asa for seeking the help of physicians instead of Yahweh (2 Chr 16:12). Use of physicians and their medicines are the bases of bitter sarcasm directed against the faithless people who seek to avoid God's judgment (Jer 46:11; 51:8). By contrast, 9th century prophets are portrayed as the agents of healing. Elijah resuscitates a child from death (1 Kgs 17:17-23); Elisha heals Naaman of his leprosy (2 Kgs 5:1-14). Both events, however, come by the word of Yahweh.

For further reading, see Hector Ignacio Avalos, "Medicine," in *Oxford Encyclopedia of Archaeology in the Near East*, vol. 3, ed. Eric M. Myers (New York & Oxford: OUP, 1997), 451-59; and Howard Clark Kee, "Medicine and Healing," *ABD* 4:659-64.

reality. Reports of the devastating effects of the 1793 yellow fever outbreak in Philadelphia, for instance, leave readers appalled at the power and indiscriminate taking of life of such horrific viruses.[9] The present generation scornfully celebrates the passing of such medical practices as bloodletting, the height of the conventional medical wisdom in the midst of the Philadelphia outbreak. Talk of yellow fever vaccination allows a buoyant confidence in human dominion over the world of threatening microbes.

Yet scientists patiently remind us that large quantities of the actual virus that causes yellow fever ("A. aegypti") are still in existence. The virus, spread by mosquitoes—another pest thought to be controlled by human technology and ingenuity—is an ever-present threat.[10] Readers might think of the situation in comparison to Yahweh's rule over the chaos of the sea. The evil sea is portrayed as being in check, but not defeated altogether (Job 38:8-11)[11] Clearly, the status of the so-called defeat of deadly microorganisms is one that invites humility from those who speak so confidently about human superiority and dominion over nature.
[Medicine in the Bible]

Robert Frost's poem "The Woodpile" offers a compelling image of the tension between life's activity of accomplishment and that activity's ultimate yield. The poem describes a neatly measured, cut, and stacked cord of maple standing unused for some time deep in a swamp. Human toil and technology that surely went into cutting the wood and stacking it in preparation for some future use offer little guarantee against the forgotten realities of time and circumstance. The narrator, having wandered into the woods and discovered this woodpile several years old, sees so much potential. He turns to muse, however, at the great quantity of energy having been expended to prepare fuel for warmth. The woodpile still sits, unused by any human, yet being consumed inexorably by time and the elements.

> . . . I thought that only
> Someone who lived in turning to fresh tasks
> Could so forget his handiwork on which
> He spent himself, the labor of his ax,
> And leave it there far from a useful fireplace
> To warm the frozen swamp as best it could
> With the slow smokeless burning of decay.[12]

NOTES

[1] Choon-Leong Seow, *Ecclesiastes* (AB 18C; New York: Doubleday, 1997), 38-46, 302.

[2] So Michael V. Fox, *A Time to Tear Down & A Time to Build Up* (Grand Rapids; Cambridge: Eerdmans, 1999), 291.

[3] The word translated "deeds," *ʿăbādehem*, is an Aramaic word that is equivalent to the Hebrew word typically used by the writer, *maʿăśehem*. Fox, *A Time to Tear Down*, 291, comments that such occurrences of Aramaic words make the theory of Aramaic origins of the text most persuasive.

[4] NRSV follows the LXX translation adding "the evil," *lārāʿ*, which is lacking in the MT. The word was most likely inadvertently left out. See Seow, *Ecclesiastes*, 299.

[5] See James L. Crenshaw, *Ecclesiastes* (OTL; Philadelphia: Westminster, 1987), 162; Seow, *Ecclesiastes*, 305, both of whom quote text from Gilgamesh. Also see *ANET*, 90.

[6] *ANET*, 90.

[7] R. N. Whybray, *Ecclesiastes* (Grand Rapids: Eerdmans, 1989), 143, stresses this point.

[8] Even though the term *ʾiššâ* lacks the article and thus leaves open the possibility that the sage is referring simply to any woman rather than one's wife, it seems unlikely that he would advocate the wanton pursuit of sexual desire outside of any relationship. See Crenshaw, *Ecclesiastes*, 163.

[9] See, for instance, the article by Kenneth R. Foster, Mary F. Jenkins, and Anna Coxe Toogood, "The Philadelphia Yellow Fever Epidemic of 1793," SA 279/2 (August 1998): 88-93.

[10] Ibid., 93.

[11] See Jon Levenson, *Creation and the Persistence of Evil* (San Francisco: Harper & Row, 1988) for this interpretation.

[12] Robert Frost, "The Wood-Pile," in *The Norton Anthology of American Literature* 5th ed., vol. 2 (Nina Baym, Ed.; New York and London: W. W. Norton and Co., 1998), 1128.

LIFE TURNS ON
UNRECOGNIZABLE DETAIL

Ecclesiastes 9:11–10:15

As readers have discovered in previous passages within the book of Ecclesiastes, there is no definitive method of setting out the thematic and literary structure of the verses. Most scholars tend to separate the materials in these verses into smaller units of thought. Readers who have encountered similar difficulties in the Proverbs know that the task of reading includes puzzling over possible thematic and literary relationships of the ideas contained within these ancient collections of instruction. It is the possible combinations of ideas that may be of more use for readers than the actual linear sequencing of the ideas within a collection (see "syndesis" in Connections: 12:9-14).

The opening of the second half of the book of Ecclesiastes, 6:10–7:14, is subdivided into three sections: two theological reflections frame an internal collection of better-than sayings. The present collection of materials seems to parallel that pattern and may be suggestively subdivided into three units: 9:11-12, "Time and Chance"; 9:13–10:4, "Attention to Small Things"; and 10:5-15, "Reversals of the Real World."[1] [Structure at a Glance: Ecclesiastes 9:11–10:15]

> **Structure at a Glance: Ecclesiastes 9:11–10:15**
>
> AΩ The outline set out below provides organization for the discussion that follows.
>
> 9:11-12 Time and Chance
> 9:13–10:4 Attention to Small Things
>   Vv. 13-15 Illustrative parable
>   V. 16 Reflection on the parable
>   9:17–10:4 Reversals due to small things
> 10:5-15 Real-world Reversals
>   Vv. 5-7 Autobiographical observations
>   Vv. 8-11 Reversals in tradition
>   Vv. 12-15 Contrasts evoke fear of further reversals

The opening section, 9:11-12, may be read as an introduction to the themes of reversal and subversion by less significant things. The unit stands apart from the larger context by its introductory formula, "Again I saw." Likewise, vv. 13-15 are separated out by the introductory formula, "I have also seen," which introduces the parable of the city under siege. This parable functions as an example of the principles set out in vv. 11-12. The parable invites the sage's reflections in v. 16, which then introduces a series of reflections in 9:17–10:4 upon the various reversals that might take place as a result of lesser things subverting greater.

The concluding collection develops the notion of subversion by returning to the traditional contrast between the wise and the foolish. Verses 8-11 remind readers that some reversals are matters of traditional wisdom. But, in view of the larger context, vv. 8-11 consider the possibility of foolishness subverting and even dominating wisdom.

The dominant theme seems to be the contrast of the foolish and the wise. A tendency to couch this contrast in examples where the more weighty or influential phenomenon is subverted by the weaker or lesser pervades the unit. Ultimately this entire series of reflections implicitly admonishes readers to remember that it is not superior skills, strength, wealth, etc. that lead to success; it is not the superior forces that save the besieged city; it is not the loudness or confidence of words that cause them to be heeded; it is not even the most honorable people who attract attention. Rather, there is more likely a subversion of those expectations: the weaker win out over the strong; the poor take the position of the rich; even the foolish and silly put to shame the knowledge of the wise. Those things one takes for granted as small and insignificant are the things that make all the difference.

The dominant form in this unit—the saying—invites readers to reflect upon the possible interrelationships among these many ideas. The entire unit is clearly ended when in 10:16 the theme turns to matters of kingship and government.

COMMENTARY

Time and Chance, 9:11-12

Verse 11 abandons the admonitory style of 9:1-10. In vv. 11-12 we recognize the familiar language of observation: "Again, I saw." Following the admonition to work at whatever one is able to do, the observation of vv. 11-12 provides the balance Qoheleth is accustomed to providing. Though one may indeed be skilled in several areas, ultimately skill is not necessarily enough to provide success. One's diligent work may therefore not achieve the desired outcomes.

We have already seen how Qoheleth challenges the traditional wisdom view that work pays off in the end (e.g., 1:3; 3:9; 4:4).

Time and Chance

AΩ The phrase "time and chance" in 9:11 risks being interpreted modernistically, that is, from the perspective of a worldview shaped by a quantum theory of the universe. Actually, what is intended here seems far more basic.

The phrase is actually a *hendiadys*, that is, a rhetorical convention of using two words to imply a single idea (Seow; Fox; Murphy). One of the two words here is "time," *ʿēt*, the same word used so extensively in 3:1-11 to set out the view that all things have an appropriate place in time. The second word is *pegaʿ*, translated "chance," though probably better translated as "event" or "incident." This noun occurs only one other place in the Hebrew Bible, 1 Kgs 5:18, and functions there to denote an evil incident (the modifier is *raʿ*, "evil").

The verbal root of the noun simply means "to meet" or "encounter" and occurs in both negative contexts (e.g., Josh 2:16; Judg 8:21) and in neutral contexts (e.g., 1 Sam 10:5; Gen 32:2). In the present context of Ecclesiastes, the hendiadys is better translated "timely event" or "timely incident." The context simply implies that whatever the particular incident might be, it makes the advantage due to skill, such as that of an athlete or warrior, much less advantageous.

For further reading, see Luis Alonso Schökel, *A Manual of Hebrew Poetics* (Rome: Editrice Pontificio Istituto Biblico, 1988).

Michael V. Fox, *A Time to Tear Down & A Time to Build Up* (Grand Rapids: Eerdmans, 1999), 296.
Roland E. Murphy, *Ecclesiastes* (WBC 23A; Waco: Word, 1992), 94.
Choon-Leong Seow, *Ecclesiastes* (AB 18C; New York: Doubleday, 1997), 308.

This traditional view is one that the book of Proverbs puts forward consistently throughout its various collections (e.g., 10:1-5; 11:25; 12:2, 14). For such a reason, the child is admonished not to spend time in too much sleep (e.g., Prov 20:13). But in v. 11 Qoheleth offers five different examples where one's work does not necessarily pay off: athletics, warfare, agriculture, prosperity, and success. The emphasis upon "time and chance" in v. 11 alludes to the sages' own concerns earlier in the book. [Time and Chance] In 3:1-11, for instance, Qoheleth states that all things have a proper time. The timeliness of all events, even success at skilled activities, is therefore a part of the hiddenness and unpredictability of even the most certain outcomes. Even death, as certain as it is, is unpredictable (v. 12).

Death's unpredictability underscores the need for humility in matters of one's own work and skill. For the sage, the specter of death provokes further reflection upon the cruelty of life. Humans are like animals caught in snares and traps. Such imagery is encountered in both the Proverbs (e.g., 1:17-19; 7:23) and Job (e.g., 19:6). Job's lament comes across rather as an accusation: God is the hunter and Job has been ensnared in his net. The "time of disaster" in v. 12 translates the word *ʿittô*, "his time." The phrase "evil calamity" of v. 12 translates the Hebrew *lĕʿēt raʿâ*, "time of disaster." Whether death or some other unpredictable calamity is intended (e.g., 5:13), the point is that people are at the mercy of events they cannot foresee. It is a forgone conclusion that God bears ultimate responsibility by making everything "suitable for its time" and choosing to keep humankind uninformed (3:9-11).

Attention to Small Things, 9:13–10:4

Compared to the great skills manifested in the five activities mentioned in v. 11, timeliness must seem like a minor thing. And yet, things that happen at the inappropriate time can undo much good and subvert the outcomes of great skill. After setting out a parable that illustrates the power of small things in vv. 13-15, and then reflecting upon it (v. 16), 9:17–10:4 offer a series of sayings that, in one way or another, assert the power of small things like timeliness, illustrating that those things one might tend to overlook should be taken very seriously.

The opening parable presents wisdom itself as that which tends to be taken for granted. The parable functions to elevate the importance of wisdom against much greater military power. In this sense, the claims of v. 11 are vindicated. The parable is narrated as though it were a part of the sage's own autobiographical experience: "I have also seen this example of wisdom under the sun" (v. 13). Such autobiographical language lends to the observation the weight of the teacher's authority. The same pedagogical technique occurs in Ecclesiastes 4:13-16 and Proverbs 7:6-23. Verses 14-15 assert that it is the poor wise man in the parable who, by his wisdom, subverts the power and military skill of the attacking king. This familiar theme occurs in Proverbs 21:22. The contrast between great and small is clear in this passage through the contrasting language: "little city" and "great king." [Siegeworks] The fact that the wise person is designated "poor" (*miskēn*) may intensify the unlikelihood that such a one would even have the social status to have allowed his being consulted.[2]

Verse 15b extends even further the irony that a poor person might even be consulted in a matter of strategy. NRSV translates as though the wise person "delivered" the city and afterward no one remembered him. It is also possible to read the entire parable as an example of "wasted wisdom."[3] Instead of reading in 15b that "he by his wisdom delivered the city," one might read, "he could have delivered the town by his wisdom." In this case the deliverance of the city is only hypothetical. The city actually falls due to the forgetfulness of the townspeople (v. 16) that wisdom is more powerful than military strategists and their overpowering armies. Either way, the point is that the deed, or its potentiality, is forgotten. The

Siegeworks

AΩ The NRSV translates 9:14b as "building great siegeworks against it [the city]." The Hebrew text has the word *mĕṣôdîm*, which is actually the masculine plural of the feminine noun *mĕṣôdâ* or *mĕṣûdâ*, "net" or "prey." The word also occurs in Job 9:6 and Eccl 7:26. BDB indicates that the form *mĕṣûdâ* may indeed mean "stronghold," or "fortification." But in that case, what is described is a defensive structure instead of an offensive tower, which is required of our present context. NRSV therefore likely emends the text from *mĕṣôdîm* to *mĕṣûrîm*, taken from the masculine noun *māṣôr*, which more properly denotes an offensive strategy or deployment for laying siege to a city.

For further reading, see Roland DeVaux, *Ancient Israel,* trans. John McHugh (London: Darton, Longman, Todd, 1961), 241-44; and Yigael Yadin, *The Art of Warfare in Biblical Lands,* vol. 2 (New York: McGraw-Hill, 1963), 309-93.

The image of the siege of Lachish by Sennacherib depicts the siegeworks against which the ancient city of Lachish had to defend itself. After Lachish fell in 587, Jerusalem followed shortly.

Tower with Defenders. Assyrians attack the Jewish fortified town of Lachish. 701BC. Detail of a relief from the palace of Sennacherib at Nineveh, Mesopotamia. British Museum, London.

forgottenness of wisdom serves to underscore its insignificance vis-à-vis military might.

The concluding observation in v. 16 consists of two thoughts, not one. The first thought affirms that wisdom is "better than might." The second is the more serious. The sage does not fail to recognize the real implications of the poor man's social situation: "wisdom is despised, and his words are not heeded." It is difficult to reconcile that such extraordinary deliverance should be forgotten. Yet forgetfulness seems also to be at work in a more positive sense in 5:20, where God causes people not "to brood over the days of their lives." The forgottenness of wisdom in vv. 13-15 may simply be a matter of overlooking potential because of the outward appearance of a poor person. The sage is driving at this contradiction: the small thing is more powerful, but precisely because it is small, it is overlooked in significance.

Verses 17 and 18 are both "better than" statements. Verse 17 is only implicitly so since it lacks the Hebrew word *ṭôb*. The comparative particle *mem* in the second half of the verse signifies the comparison. The semantic correspondences between vv. 17 and 16 imply a connection between the two, even though the thought of v. 17 could stand on its own. Precisely who the "shouting" ruler is in the saying is unclear. Perhaps he is the one who, in all of the confusion within the city under siege, forgot to ask advice from the wise person. Verse 18, by contrast, returns explicitly to the thematic concerns of the parable in vv. 13-15 by opening with the conclusion stated in v. 16a: "wisdom is better than weapons of war." The thought of 18b recaptures the meaning of v. 16b by asserting that "one bungler" (*ḥôṭeʾ*)[4] subverts much good. Readers could easily identify this "bungler" with the shouting ruler of v. 17, or the one responsible in v. 16b for forgetting the wise person so that his words were not heeded.

In the final four verses of the unit, 10:1-4, the motif of the small subverting the great is kept constantly before the reader. The contrast between the wise and the foolish serves as a recurring reminder of the failures in the parable in vv. 13-15. How foolish it would be either to fail to ask or to heed the words of one who could deliver a city from military siege. How foolish to forget such words of salvation.

The thrust of the saying in 10:1 is that wisdom and honor are themselves subject to stupidity, no matter how small or insignificant the stupid act. Yet the translation in v. 1 is only an approximation. There is no definitive way of understanding the phrase translated in NRSV as "dead flies," or the words rendered by NRSV as "give off a foul odor."[5] Nevertheless, the general meaning seems clear, and it continues the thought of subversion begun in 9:11. A very small thing, a fly that dies, corrupts something that serves the purpose of bringing sweet odor. Likewise, folly is of more significance than wisdom and honor.

The thought is continued in v. 2 with a more direct comparison of the wise and the foolish. Interestingly, there is no verb "to incline" within the verse as readers might suppose based upon the NRSV translation. Two sets of nouns and adjectives are juxtaposed: the heart of the wise and the right; the heart of a fool and the left. The right stands for goodness, the left, for what is evil. It may be that the implications are not only moral, but also intellectual. Jonah 4:11 states that not knowing the difference between "right and left" reflects a lack of responsibility, or maturity, and thus a basis upon which the deity refuses to destroy Nineveh.

The MT of v. 3 implies that fools are people who consider all other people to be fools. We are invited thereby to reflect upon the general question concerning the recognition of a fool: how does one know a fool? The occurrence in v. 3 of the word "heart," translated "sense" (*lēb*), clearly connects v. 3 to v. 2, which also reflects upon the "heart" of both the wise and the fool. However, NRSV translates v. 3 in such a way that there is ambiguity as to whether fools reveal their own foolishness or whether they simply regard all others to be foolish. The word "they" in the phrase "and show to everyone that they are fools" requires a clear antecedent. Does this refer to fools or to others who pass by on the road? It may well be that such ambiguity is intentional, and with the double meaning, the answer to the question about recognizing a fool is implicitly answered: people who think all are foolish but themselves, are themselves fools.[6]

Verse 4 closes the second subsection of this unit by returning to the subject matter of behavior in the presence of a king. Within the confines of the subject Qoheleth reflects upon a previous theme: that of deference in the presence of the king (e.g., 8:23), and reiterates the matter at hand: that of the smaller or weaker thing having greater influence over more powerful things. Similar observations are made in Proverbs 14:30; 15:4; 16:14; and 25:6-7. Not only is a calm spirit recommended for long life, but it is always better to soothe the king's anger because he is much more powerful. In the present context, "calmness" soothes great wrongs. Such response to power is certainly more virtuous and efficacious, but, again, because calmness does not nearly attract as much attention to itself, is likely to be forgotten.

Real-world Reversals, 10:5-15

The observations concerning the subversion of great things by smaller things provoke yet another line of investigation: that of reversals of expectation generally. The final subsection is introduced by another observation of reversal, this time role reversals. As in 9:13-15, these reversals are set out autobiographically. The sage introduces the narrative as what he has seen. The role reversals articulated in vv. 5-7 then call for a series of reflections upon more predictable kinds of reversals, the kinds of reversals that seem to be a part of the ordered world, vv. 8-11. Even though it is impossible to predict the future (v. 14), there are yet certain reversals of order that are quite predictable.

The shift from sayings to autobiographical narrative as well as a return to an explicit example of reversal signals to readers the beginning of a new subsection. Yet, by following on v. 4 and its reflection upon kingship, readers may infer not only that such role reversals as described in vv. 5-6 stem from the hand of the king ("as if it proceeded from the ruler"), but that such a "great error" (v. 5) is an example of what happens when kings make decisions in anger. As in previous references to kingship in Ecclesiastes, however, readers need not conclude that these words were written during the literal time of the reign of an Israelite king. This functions well as a hypothetical example, and readers make the applications to their own settings.[7] The "evil" thing mentioned in v. 5 is not necessarily that there is reversal, but the nature of the reversal.

Verse 6 creates the impression that there was class bias on the part of the sage writing these words. While we would likely agree that "folly," meaning a fool's, obtaining a high leadership position is undesirable, we would not so readily agree that people of wealth are necessarily people of wisdom who should themselves fill those positions of leadership. While a generous reading would grant that the sage is simply assuming a direct connection between social class and wisdom (social class being the result of wisdom), a less generous reading simply recognizes that this sage was not himself free from such unwarranted generalizations. Either way, wisdom itself has been subverted since folly, anathema to wisdom (though not necessarily to wealth), has been placed in the authoritative position (see Prov 30:21-23).

The image in v. 7 of slaves on horseback and princes walking in the road reiterates the topsy-turvy situation imagined by Qoheleth. Horses were the trappings of the wealthy nobles in antiquity. Slaves walked alongside. [Horses in Ancient Israel] It is not merely a question of violating order, but one of creating situations of gross incompetence in demanding situations. The king, who has the responsibility to preserve justice and integrity, cannot do so when incompetence thwarts him at every turn.

Horses in Ancient Israel

The extremity of the reversal described in 10:7 is perhaps not appreciated without some awareness of the use of horses in ancient Israel. Horses were not native to the land of Israel. Thus the biblical stories of monarchy report their being purchased from foreign countries for use in chariotry and trade (1 Kgs 10:28-29). The extent of royal chariotry seems nevertheless small and the existence of a cavalry nonexistent. It is significant, therefore, that the Rabshakeh taunts Hezekiah that even if Sennacherib were to provide 2000 horses, there would not be riders for them in Jerusalem (2 Kgs 18:23). The other references to horses in the Bible are mainly to those of foreigners (2 Kgs 9:17; Zech 1:8-11; Ezek 23:6; Ezra 8:22; Neh 2:9). Likewise, Job's description of the war horse (Job 39:19-25) is likely based upon impressions of non-Israelite armies.

All of this is simply to say that, given the scarcity of horses in Judah and Israel, and their main use by nobles and warriors, the sight of a servant astride a horse, while a nobleman walked alongside, would be shocking indeed.

For further reading: Roland DeVaux, *Ancient Israel*, trans. John McHugh (London: Darton, Longman, Todd, 1961), 222-25, 278.

The four observations in vv. 8-11 appeal to well-recognized reversals of expectation. The four statements are in two pairs. Verses 8 and 9 open with participles; vv. 10 and 11 open with conditions. All four reflect variously upon the problems of reversals of expectations and subversion of order. As they occur in tradition, they function to affirm the sure retribution of the Lord upon the wicked (see Ps 7:16-17; Amos 5:19; Jer 8:17).[8] However, in the present context, wherein the matter of reversal seems to be the actual order of things, the sage's observation creates doubt as to whether these are unfortunate reversals or matters of course in the real world. If one digs a pit, that one will unexpectedly fall into it. Similarly, one who breaks into a wall, despite any resolve to watch for snakes, will be bitten. In other words, injury from such activity is almost an inevitable course, according to Qoheleth.

The statement in v. 10 may be the only statement with which readers will readily agree. A dull ax creates more work, not less. The implicit application is made in 10b. Wisdom, like a sharpened blade, helps one to succeed. ["That Ax Won't Cut"] This statement of the obvious implies that the sage takes the preceding statements to be equally obvious, even though they are not necessarily. It is simply not true, for instance, that whoever digs a pit will fall into it. Only in the sage's dark and topsy-turvy world can such statements be true. Nor is it necessary that persons will be bitten by a snake when they are breaking through a wall. Again, the exception to readers' common sense is the sage's view of reality. We have to grant the validity of his world in order to grant the validity of his claims.

Following upon v. 10, wherein wisdom is to success as a sharp blade is to cutting wood, the idea of a failure to charm the snake focuses upon the charmer's skill. The failure to charm the snake not only denies success, but it can be quite deadly.

The concluding four verses, vv. 12-15, join together as a single reflection upon the fool. Verse 12 opens the subsection with a saying that reflects the traditional contrast between the wise and the foolish, focusing upon the contrast in the effectiveness of their speech. The words of the wise yield "favor"; those of fools turn

---

"That Ax Won't Cut"

AΩ Whybray notes that v. 10 has been considered "the most difficult in the book" linguistically. While there are many difficulties, commentators nevertheless roughly agree on the meaning: wisdom is to success what a sharp ax-blade is to cutting wood. NRSV never uses the word "cut," and does not specify a cutting tool in 10a. The difficulty of the translation "blunt" is that its verb form is Piel, *qēhâ*, yet in the contexts where it occurs with that meaning in the Bible (Ezek 28:2), it is in the Qal stem. Thus, "blunt" is an anomalous meaning for that Piel verb form. The indefinite subject, "one," assumes that the antecedent of the pronoun *hû'* is the one cutting trees in v. 9. The translation "edge" for the word *pānîm*, which ordinarily means face, derives from such usage in Ezek 21:21. The word "to sharpen" is derived from the Pilpel form of the word *qal*, to be "light" or "quick," perhaps referring to the strokes of the whetting stone rather than the blade or face itself.

The concluding phrase translated "but wisdom helps one to succeed" is more literally rendered "and the advantage of making succeed is wisdom." Readers can see that interpreters take a great deal of latitude in providing the present translation.

R. N. Whybray, *Ecclesiastes* (Grand Rapids: Eerdmans, 1989), 153.

back upon them and consume them. Verses 13 and 14 provide two examples of how this happens. First, v. 13 contrasts the beginning and ending of the fool's speech. This saying assumes the anteceding subject of 12b, the fool. The beginning of the fool's speech is folly. Its result or end is "wicked madness."

Verse 14a continues by saying that the fool multiplies words. Qoheleth has already referred to such multiplication as vanity (Eccl 6:11). The next half verse, 14b, actually restates themes Qoheleth himself has already offered regarding the impossibility of predicting what will happen (e.g., 6:12; 7:14; 8:7). Readers may pause to reflect upon Qoheleth's implication that fools are those who try to predict the future. Not only will fools multiply words (like so many wisdom teachers?), they will also fail to accept the reality that such predictions cannot be made. In the present context where the predictable order of things is subverted by a timely incident (9:11), wherein even wisdom itself is subverted (10:5-7), the implication is that the truly wise know when to keep quiet. Verse 15 implicitly urges that confidence in ordinarily predictable things is tantamount to a fool's inability even to walk into the city.

CONNECTIONS

The Inexplicability of Success

Older pianists who remember him say that Artur Schnabel was no technician at the keyboard. Even so, his playing, though full of technical flaws, was some of the most musical ever heard. He was the first pianist to record (in the pre-LP days of the last century) all thirty-two of the Beethoven piano sonatas. It was not until his 1930 tour of the United States, after failed tours in 1921 and 1922, that Schnabel finally achieved success. In the years between 1931 and 1935 Schnabel recorded extensively, so that by 1935 he was a recognized master worldwide. However, his colleagues wondered how someone who suffered such embarrassing technical gaps could have attained such notoriety.[9]

It is easy to construe our sage as becoming so focused upon the small things that subvert the great that he has forgotten life's tapestry is made up of so much more than the individual strands woven together. In fact, readers are invited to argue with Qoheleth at this point. No one doubts that timely incidents can subvert the predictable order of things. But does this really mean there is no

reliable order? And isn't there a danger that follows such an observation, which privileges a kind of resignation that failure and
unpredictability rule? Artur Schnabel's failure to attend to technical
details in his playing, though embarrassing for many of his knowledgeable peers, only caused others to look for some other factor
that explained his significant contribution to piano playing and
piano pedagogy. One of his students, for instance, commented that
she gained "freedom and assuredness through his inflexible literal
interpretation [of the music of Beethoven, Bach, Mozart, and
Schubert]."[10] She goes on to make an important distinction
between technique and mechanics. She quotes Leopold Godowsky,
another significant nineteenth century pianist, "Speed, fingerwork,
octaves, according to him, fall into the latter category; they are separate problems, tools, while technique is all-inclusive. Technique
implies complete mastery of the keyboard, including the ability to
produce beautiful tone, to use the pedal sensitively, to
memorize."[11]

Should we not disagree with Qoheleth? The sage's perspective is
one that emphasizes the inexplicable failures; but what about the
inexplicable successes? Probably every person can relate a story
similar to that of Artur Schnabel. Lapses in mechanics do not necessarily undermine pianistic technique (because technique is
actually much larger than mere mechanics). Similarly, the occurrences of certain kinds of subversions of expectation do not
undermine ordered reality. Nature sports. There are intrusions of
the unique and the truly diverse. One response is to search for a
larger principle that unifies and holds every detail together in some
kind of predictable order. Another response is to remember that
sometimes the observable details, such as pianistic mechanics or
one's skill, do not necessarily add up to success. Nor do they therefore explain entirely why things fail. The best advice Qoheleth
offers is that fools multiply words of explanation.

NOTES

[1] This treatment of structure is an adaptation of Choon-Leong Seow's summary of the structure of these passages, *Ecclesiastes* (AB 18C; New York: Doubleday, 1997), 306, 320.

[2] Ibid., 311. Seow explains that although the *miskēn* was not necessarily a poor person, he was surely not a nobleman. He was definitely someone whose social status would have made it very unlikely that he should have been consulted.

[3] So James L. Crenshaw, *Ecclesiastes* (OTL; Philadelphia: Westminster, 1987), 165.

[4] The Hebrew word *hôteʾ* usually is translated "sinner," implying a religious or moral significance. Here it means more "to miss or fall short." See Eccl 2:26; 7:20, 26; 8:12; and 9:2.

[5] Readers should consult Seow, *Ecclesiastes,* 311-12, and Michael V. Fox, *A Time to Tear Down & A Time to Build Up* (Grand Rapids: Eerdmans, 1999), 264-65, for thorough treatments of the difficulties and proposed solutions.

[6] Both Seow, *Ecclesiastes,* 313, and Crenshaw, *Ecclesiastes,* 170, preserve this ambiguity in their translations.

[7] R. N. Whybray, *Ecclesiastes* (Grand Rapids: Eerdmans, 1989), 151.

[8] Crenshaw, *Ecclesiastes,* 172, takes v. 8 as a statement of the belief in retribution.

[9] Harold C. Schonberg, *The Great Pianists from Mozart to the Present* (New York: Simon and Schuster, 1963), 401-408.

[10] Ruth Slenczynska, *Music at Your Fingertips* (New York: Doubleday, 1968), 12.

[11] Ibid., 35.

THE REALITIES
OF HUMAN SOCIETY

Ecclesiastes 10:16–11:6

This penultimate section of the book returns to a concern with kingship. There have been several allusions to kings or kingship throughout the book (e.g., 8:2-5; 9:14-15; 10:5). The theme of kingship seems intriguing since it is unlikely that the book's audience would have known anything about being subject to a king. However, the topic provides for readers a sense of closure by echoing the book's opening testimonial that also came from the lips of a royal figure (cf. 1:12–2:26). The sayings comprising the first half of this section (vv. 16-20) reflect upon the risks and benefits of kingship. The concluding section (11:1-6) consists of admonitions that address principles of the economy of success, which may have far ranging economic significance for the kingdom. These admonitions may also be just as relevant to the household.

The entire section, 10:16–11:6, stands out rhetorically from the sayings that begin in 9:17. There is a decisive shift from observations

---

Structure at a Glance: Ecclesiastes 10:16–11:6

AΩ Structurally, the passage might be organized as follows:

10:16-20 The Realities of Kingship
    Vv. 16-17 Servants vs. noblemen
      V. 18 The kingdom as a house
      V. 19 Observation of court life
    V. 20 The royal presence
11:1-6 Economic Principles
    Vv. 1-2 Speculating on the future
    Vv. 3-6 Admonitions about the rules of prosperity

The opening subsection reflects an inclusio formed by an opening couplet, vv. 16-17, contrasting a good king and a bad king and a concluding reminder of the inescapable presence of a king, v. 20. Within are two observations about money and laziness. The challenge of reading the section is then in understanding the relationship between the inner sayings—on money and laziness—and the outer—on kingship.

The concluding subsection, 11:1-6, contains admonitions whose meaning and relevance are not so accessible. This is especially true in the cases of vv. 1-3, which challenge readers even to grasp what they are saying, let alone their application to concrete reality. The only clear admonitions are in vv. 4-6 concerning the sage's certainty about conducting one's agricultural business.

and inferences to direct address and imperative commands (e.g. 10:16, 20; 11:1, 6). The two subsections, 10:16-20 and 11:1-6, are distinguished by their thematic differences. The materials in vv. 16-20 are contained within an inclusio on kingship; the materials in 11:1-6 are concerned about economic or commercial prosperity. [Structure at a Glance: Ecclesiastes 10:16–11:6]

COMMENTARY

The Realities of Kingship, 10:16-20

Nobles

AΩ The parallelism of vv. 16a and 17a juxtapose the terms "servant" (v. 16a) and "nobles" (v. 17a). The term translated servant is peculiar, however, since in most contexts it means "youth." It is the latter parallel term for nobles (*ben-ḥôrîm*) that leads translators to understand that more is implied in the former term than simply the relative youthfulness of the king. There is a social appropriateness that also attaches itself to the king's office.

The word *ḥôrîm* is late, occurring in the biblical literature thought by most scholars to derive from post-exilic contexts (e.g., Neh 2:16; 4:8, 13). Etymologically the term is related to *ḥārar*, meaning "to be, or become free." The term's designation of nobility seems certain given the literary contexts in which it is used. In the present context *ben-ḥôrîm* stands in parallel with *śārayik*, "your princes." The same kind of parallel relationship exists in Isa 34:12 where *ben-ḥôrîm* is used synonymously with "princes."

For further reading, see Roland DeVaux, *Ancient Israel*, trans. John McHugh (London: Darton, Longman, and Todd, 1961), 69-70.

The opening word, "alas," in NRSV's translation is a malediction. That is, it is a pronouncement of ill or woe. It should not be confused with a word of resignation or acceptance. The sage is concerned to state to his audience that the land is in trouble when its king is "a servant." The Hebrew term translated servant is actually *nā'ar*, which more typically means "child" or "youth." Perhaps the translation of "servant" is warranted by the parallel phrase in v. 17, "a nobleman," *ben-ḥorîm*, which implies that social status, not youth, is the critical issue in determining the effectiveness of a king. If the king is a servant, then a reversal such as that pictured in 10:7 has taken place. [Nobles] The second half of the pronouncement of woe is the assertion concerning a lack of leadership among the princes. There is an appropriate time for feasting, and an appropriate purpose—for gaining strength and not for getting drunk (v. 17). Such inappropriate behavior fits well into the larger context that acknowledges the reality of reversals. Again, the observations of the sage in 10:5-7 concerning slaves astride horses while princes walk alongside become relevant. This opening verse makes unambiguous the sage's feelings about such reversals of leadership. They put the state at risk.

Verse 17 is a "blessed" (*'ašrê*) statement. The verse begins with the assertion of "happiness" or "blessedness" and pictures the proper state of government: the king is a nobleman and the princes know

Palestinian Flat Roofs

The observation in 10:17 is illuminated by the knowledge that roofs of houses in ancient Palestine were flat. Usually their construction consisted of crossbeams overlaid with smaller tree branches, then covered with a mud, straw, and chaff mixture to make a kind of plaster. For larger roof spans, a house might have one central beam that rested on the walls of the house. That beam was supported with intermediate posts situated into sockets in the floor of the house.

The Bible describes the flat roofs as places of much activity, not the least of which was worship (2 Kgs 23:12; Jer 19:13; Acts 10:9). It was on the roof that the booth was constructed for *sukkôt*, one of the three major annual Jewish festivals, and concerning which the Deuteronomists legislated the building of a parapet or railing for safety's sake (Deut 22:8). To this date no houses have preserved to the roofline, so the actual existence of such parapets is not confirmed archaeologically.

For further reading, see John S. Holladay, Jr., "House, Israelite," *ABD*, 308-18.

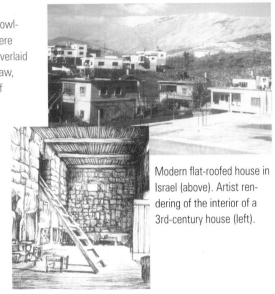

Modern flat-roofed house in Israel (above). Artist rendering of the interior of a 3rd-century house (left).

the appropriate time to feast. This majestic image provides the counterpoint to the woe statement in v. 16.

Verse 18 contains a saying that reflects a traditional wisdom work ethic. Laziness always leads to ruin (Prov 6:6-11; 12:11; 18:9). The reference to houses reiterates the point since roofs in Palestine were in need of regular attention and repair (Prov 19:13; 27:15-16),[1] thus laziness led to a leaky roof. [Palestinian Flat Roofs] The reference to houses invites yet another connection, especially in the context of kingship. The king's house also was his dynasty (e.g., 2 Sam 7:4-17). As a house that is not tended leaks in the rain, so a royal dynasty that is run by impostors and drunkards will not last.

Verse 19 likewise gives readers pause to consider the larger context of kingship, even though it is most likely singularly concerned with the benefits of money. The saying has three parts; the first two stand in a chiastic relationship: "feasts" and "laughter" are paralleled by "gladdens" and "wine." The third phrase is the punch line. It asserts that money meets every need. The term translated "meets" is the Hebrew word *ʿānâ,* "to answer." However, this word has already occurred in key arguments with the meaning of "to be busy with," in the sense of preoccupation (e.g., 1:13). Here, if the word has the meaning of "answer," the meaning of the proverb affirms the importance of money. If the word is in the Hiphil stem, it could easily be a comment upon money's ability to cause all to be preoccupied with it.[2] The idea here is to evoke the readers' reflections upon the multiple meanings of this saying in the present context. Money is efficacious, indeed, even though the sage has already commented upon its ineffectiveness in providing happiness (e.g., 4:7-8; 5:10-17). Qoheleth has also admonished those who may find enjoyment to do so (e.g., 2:24; 3:12-13; 5:18-20). Money can certainly provide such enjoyment, but such enjoyment may also put the state at risk.

The admonition in v. 20 advises against cursing the king. The reason is one of pure pragmatics: the king is more powerful than any individual and grave consequences could follow should he hear of one cursing him. The sage has demonstrated similar concerns for pragmatism in 8:2-6 and 10:4 regarding proper submission to authority and the king's anger.

The real puzzle in v. 20 concerns the meanings of the phrases "even in your thoughts" and "a bird of the air." Regarding the first phrase, the word "thoughts" translates the Hebrew word *běmaddā'ăkā*, the plural noun for "knowledge." Only by extension does the term for knowledge become "thoughts," a meaning attested at Qumran.[3] However, one should not read the verse literally; it is unlikely that anyone, even a king, could detect one's thoughts without their being put into words first. We would therefore have to read this as a hyperbolic statement, an exaggeration to emphasize the severity of cursing a king. The second phrase, a "bird of the air," only makes hyperbolic sense on the assumption that one's thoughts have been given voice. But even then, there could be no literal truth to the image.

Seow suggests that the sexual connotations of the root *yāda*, "to know," may be the key to interpretation. The noun form of *yāda'* is *madā'* (translated as "thoughts"). The word literally denotes "a place of knowledge." The parallelism with the word "bedroom" (*běḥadrê miškābĕkā*) provides an image of "intimacy. The admonition is then to avoid cursing the king in the presence of a person with whom one is intimately related. Then the hyperbole "bird of the air" makes more sense. Something spoken even to an intimate companion may inexplicably ("a little bird," "the walls") make its way to the king, whose response may be costly indeed.[4]

Economic Principles, 11:1-6

The second subsection to the unit returns to the broad line of thinking set out in 10:18 regarding the connection between prosperity and work. While this is most clear in vv. 4-6, only through some imaginative interpretation does it become so in references to vv. 1-2. The interpretations of these verses have historically ranged far. Although scholars favor interpretations that point toward commercial implications, due largely to the much clearer implications of vv. 4-6, such interpretations need not be the only possible alternatives. In fact, Fox sets out four possible meanings of the opening two verses: (a) overseas commerce; (b) risk-taking in commercial activity; (c) deeds of charity without expectation of any return; (d) the unpredictability of actions.[5]

It may be more helpful to read vv. 1 and 2 together. Certainly, they have suggestive parallels: both opening clauses are imperatives; both concluding clauses are motive clauses. The meaning of the phrase "Send out your bread upon the waters" is challenging. A literal interpretation seems not to make any sense. Bread scattered upon water simply disintegrates within a matter of minutes. Thus, some figurative meaning seems more appropriate.

That the verse concerns commerce is suggested by its use of the terms "send," *šalaḥ*, and "upon the waters," *ʿal-pĕnê hammāyim*. This language is used in Isaiah 18:2 in reference to the travel of ambassadors by sea, thus the possible connection to international commerce. In Proverbs 31:14 the term for bread, *leḥem*, occurs in a context that clearly implies commercial activity. Still, the traditional understanding of the verse had to do with the giving of alms to the poor.[6] The conclusion of v. 2 certainly inserts the element of the unknown into the two verses. Since one does not know what will happen, this unknown element could serve as a basis for admonishing one to save one's money. Alternatively, the saying could simply be an admonition to share one's possessions in several ways.

Verses 3-6 illustrate again the pragmatism of the sage in his recognition of a causal universe, as well as his equally strong conviction that effects demand more attention than causes. In contrast with the opening two verses, where cause and effect are uncertain, vv. 3-4 guide the reader's reflection upon the conclusions that may be drawn from things that are predictable. When rain clouds are full, there will be rain; whether a tree falls toward the north or south, it remains in the place it falls. However, is the implication that just as nature is predictable, the claims in vv. 1-2 are equally predictable? Readers' reflections upon this question are related to their particular interpretation of vv. 1-2.

Verse 4 qualifies the predictability implied in v. 3. The reference in v. 4 to the wind invites reflection upon the causes of the falling tree in v. 3. While wind is observable by its results (falling trees), watching the wind (as a sign of the weather) does not guarantee one's recognizing the proper time to plant. The implication of 4a is exactly the opposite from that in v. 3: one will watch forever and not plant. Similarly, 4b alludes to the implied causality between clouds and rain, yet watching the clouds does not guarantee that one knows when to harvest. Even though there are signs of order and predictability, even cause and effect, these signs do not necessarily mean that one knows enough about that order to benefit from it.

The series of observations about the relativity of knowledge comes to a climax in v. 5 with one final observation. NRSV translates as though there is only one example of limited knowledge: one does not know how breath comes to bones, that is, to a fetus developing in a mother's womb. The motif of wind continues, only here, clearly, the sage is using the term with its other possible significance, breath or spirit. Nevertheless, both vv. 4 and 5 contain the word for "wind" or "breath," *rûaḥ*, and v. 3 may imply its presence. The point of the verse is that, again, even though certain effects are quite observable, knowledge is still limited.

The concluding verse in this section, v. 6, returns to the sowing imagery mentioned in v. 4. It is the basis of a concluding admonition that grows from the recognition of the uncertainty argued in the preceding verses. The premise is that, even though there are observable causes of successful farming, these do not guarantee sowing at the optimal time for a great harvest. So, the sage concludes, one should know that there is a right time, but continue sowing from morning to evening anyway whether one knows the right time or not. Commercial success, if that is what these concluding verses address, is not a matter of chance. However, individuals do not really control all of the elements that contribute to success. Therefore, individuals should work as though they did and leave the results to the unknown.

CONNECTIONS

The Individual and the Government

It is fitting for this section to return to matters of kingship. The sage recognizes both the importance of government to the life of the individual and the threat it poses. Reading Ecclesiastes 5:9 with NRSV seems to urge that it is better to have a king than not. These

concluding remarks in 10:16-20 allow one to consider this perspective, especially given the possibility of a bad king or of inferior
government. It is perhaps even more significant that the book itself
began with the reflections of a king who sought to use wisdom to
find out what is good. Such remarks may evoke connections with
Plato's conviction that kings in the ideal republic should be
philosophers.[7] More likely, readers will seek for ways to construe
the sage's concern with kingship as a basis to reflect upon their own
government and personal citizenship. Obviously, kingship is not
the issue in the western world. For Christians, furthermore, there is
a yet more complicated problem: that of owing allegiance both to
the state (e.g., Rom 13:1-7) and to God's kingdom. To put a finer
point on it, readers have to wonder about the sage's assumptions of
individual liberty over against the power of the state.

Glen Tinder probes the conflict between the Christian emphasis
upon the preeminent value of individual liberty and the state's use
of power to ensure the continued existence of that liberty. True
community only exists for Tinder when there is individual
freedom, but the government must use its power to maintain that
freedom for all. The problem is the use of power. Power is inherently evil and leads to a coercive denial of individual liberty and
ultimately to violence. Tinder argues, however, that coercion may
be minimized constitutionally and that the state is a lesser evil than
the alternative of pure anarchy. In an anarchic situation only the
strong are able to exercise their liberty; the weak and helpless are
not. Thus, Tinder concludes, "Without the systematic use of power
and violence, by public authorities and according to established
procedures and safeguards, there would be no common liberty and
hence no community."[8]

More importantly, the individual must understand that liberty is
the recognition that the individual's life is grounded in a reality
beyond the state. It is there that individuals may find their destiny.
For Christians, that destiny lies in their redemption through
Christ. It is a redemption that calls them beyond mere society into
a community that is moving toward that ultimate redemption.
Thus, politically, Christians are not only concerned about the
state's workings. They must be concerned about what lies beyond.
Their allegiance to the state must be real, thoughtful, and sincere.
At the same time, the state is not the end of such allegiance. It
exists under God for the purpose of ensuring the existence of
various communities of the redeemed.

When the sage, operating within a completely different political
reality, nevertheless pronounces woe upon a land whose king is not

---

The Proper Rule of Kings

Ernst Cassirer writes of Niccolò Machiavelli's *The Prince* (1513–1514): "The book describes, with complete indifference, the ways and means by which political power is to be acquired and maintained. About the *right use* of political power it does not say a word" (Cassirer). Machiavelli's manual on government was shocking in its day, although it probably would have a certain appeal today. He opens his ch. 18 on the ruler's integrity as follows:

How praiseworthy it is for a prince to keep his word and live with integrity than by craftiness, everyone understands; yet we see from recent experience that those princes have accomplished most who paid little heed to keeping their promises, but who know how craftily to manipulate the minds of men. In the end, they won out over those who tried to act honestly. [*The Prince*, 49.]

How differently the inscription of Yehimilk, king of Byblos and contemporary of Solomon, reads at one point:

May Ba'lshamem and the Lord of Byblos and the Assembly of the Holy Gods of Byblos prolong the days and years of Yehimilk in Byblos for [he is] a righteous and an upright king before the holy gods of Byblos! [Taken from Gaalyah Cornfeld, *Archaeology of the Bible Book by Book* (San Francisco: Harper & Row, 1976), 112.]

The view that kings were to use power to maintain justice is also binding upon Israelite kings. Ps 72 reflects such an attitude in the following words:

Give the king your justice, O God,
and your righteousness to a king's son.
May he judge your people with righteousness,
and your poor with justice.

What is more, ancient Israel idealized kingship but recognized the need to hold the king's power in check. Thus, the Deuteronomic law makes clear that kings, too, had to keep covenant with Yahweh as did all other citizens of the nation (Deut 17:14-20). Resting upon this assumption, Israelite prophets brought withering rebukes to the kings concerning the way they exercised their power and failed to maintain justice (e.g., 1 Kgs 17–19; Isa 7–8; Amos 7).

Ernst Cassirer, "Implications of the New Theory of State," in *The Prince*, trans. & ed. Robert M. Adams (New York & London: W. W. Norton, 1977), 168.

---

appropriate for the task, readers may immediately connect that to their situations. Political leaders must understand the delicate balances involved between the value of free individuals and the value of the state's power. [The Proper Rule of Kings] Neither value may be taken for granted. What is more, the rather pragmatic admonition not to curse the king (v. 20) may be pragmatic for different reasons. It is not only that the king will hear, but that kingship is ordained by the creator. It is a means by which God ensures the delicate balances that must exist between individual liberties and obligations for the common good.

NOTES

[1] This is Roland E. Murphy's observation about the flat roofs of Palestine, *Ecclesiastes* (WBC 23A; Waco: Word, 1992), 105.

[2] Choon-Leong Seow, *Ecclesiastes* (AB 18C; New York: Doubleday, 1997), 333.

[3] Michael V. Fox, *A Time to Tear Down & A Time to Build Up* (Grand Rapids: Eerdmans, 1999), 310-11.

[4] Seow, *Ecclesiastes,* 333.

[5] Fox, *A Time to Tear Down,* 311-12.

[6] Robert Gordis, *Koheleth: The Man and His World* (New York: Schocken, 1968), 329; Murphy, *Ecclesiastes,* 106.

[7] Plato, *The Republic,* book 5.

[8] Glen Tinder, *The Political Meaning of Christianity* (San Francisco: Harper Collins, 1991), 142-43.

CONCLUSION:
ON HUMAN DESTINY

Ecclesiastes 11:7–12:8

It may be useful for readers to reread the opening sections of Ecclesiastes again; there we see the sage's concern with the cycles that pervade all of his reality (1:4-11). The conclusion of the book returns to that motif of life's cyclical nature by juxtaposing images of youth and death. Interestingly, this appeal to life's cycles follows a treatment of kingship and its realities (10:15-20). This further extends the parallel with the book's opening in that the reflections upon cycles in 1:2-11 is followed by the words of a king in 1:12–2:26. The images of government and the individual enveloped by the realities of life's cycles to which all must ultimately yield—nature, youth, and death—form the overall framework for the sage's wisdom that is perhaps meaningfully discernible only at this point in the reader's experience of the book.

The overall unit is in two parts. The first part concerns youth and the familiar theme of seizing opportunities for enjoyment (11:7-10). The second part concerns old age and death, the inevitable consequence of the human life cycle (12:1-8). [Structure at a Glance: Ecclesiastes 11:7–12:8]

Structure at a Glance: Ecclesiastes 11:7–12:8

AΩ The following outline captures the structure of the ideas within the passage.

11:7-10 Act Now
    V. 7 Thematic statement of life's goodness
    V. 8 Motive clause
    Vv. 9-10 Imperatives of response
12:1-7 Death Is Inevitable
    V. 1 Thematic statement with first temporal clause
    Vv. 2-5 Images of advancing end with second temporal clause
    Vv. 6-7 Emblem of the end with third temporal clause
    V. 8 Thematic statement of the book

The theme of light in 11:7 anticipates a similar concern in 12:2. Likewise, the theme of youth in 11:9 anticipates the treatment in 12:1. However, the opening section reflects the attitude of *carpe diem*, "seize the day," while the second half reflects on the ultimate human destiny.

Within this unit are three temporal clauses that separate the thoughts of the poem. Verse 1b denotes the urgency of doing things "before the days of trouble come"; v. 2a cautions "before the sun, light, moon and stars are darkened"; v. 6a appeals to students to work "before the silver cord is snapped. . . ." The central unit, vv. 2-5, contains a series of images introduced by a general and well-known eschatological figure: the darkening of the cosmos. Verses 3-5 are contained by images of the house, *bayit.*

Perhaps the most important aspect of the overall section concerns the way to read the second half, and in particular, 12:3-5. Traditionally, this short passage has been read as allegory, a form of symbolism that pairs a metaphor with a single concrete significance. Jesus' parable of the sower in Matthew 13:3-8, for instance, is allegorized by Matthew in 13:18-23. That is, the potential meanings of the original (metaphoric) images are frozen in their correspondence to a single domain of alternate meaningful ideas. While older interpreters relied upon allegory to interpret 12:3-5, modern readers are less satisfied with the inconsistent application of allegory required to make the unit meaningful.[1] Generally, there is a recognition among scholars that readers must be open to several different modes of interpretation for these concluding verses.

Readers ordinarily have little difficulty with literal language. In that mode of reading the word or idea is the very thing that is named. The only problem this could pose is in the understanding of antiquated phenomena that no longer exist in a modern cultural context. Various kinds of non-literal language further invite readers to puzzle over what exactly is being depicted by words and phrases. So, for instance, when Qoheleth states that humans "are but animals" (3:18), is he speaking literally? We have suggested that the sage is using this hyperbolic language to make the distinction between God and human. He is therefore not speaking literally, but non-literally. Further, there is an implied comparison within the phrase. In some sense humans are *like* animals. Such implied comparison is perhaps illustrated more clearly in the sage's use of phrases such as "chasing after wind" to describe what he considers to be a nonbeneficial or productive activity (e.g., 1:14; 2:17; 2:26; 4:4; 6:9). But readers do not attempt to interpret the image in any literal sense, that is, by imagining a person trying to catch wind. Rather, they understand that there is an implied comparison. In the case of 12:3-5, the more fixed and less implied the comparison, the closer readers are to allegory.[2] Unfortunately, the more fixed those comparisons are, the more likely they are to be exclusively held by readers who have inside knowledge of those comparisons. Inside knowledge makes it even less likely that readers will grasp the intended implications of the images. We do not have access to the "code," as it were.

COMMENTARY

Act While You Are Able, 11:7-10

Qoheleth's instructions are interspersed at several points with the sage's admonitions to "act now," "enjoy life if possible" (e.g., 3:12-13; 5:18-19; 8:15; 9:7-8). In this concluding admonition the sage offers the same advice. Light is an image of life and sweetness an image for goodness. The notion of seeing implies life, thus the statement in v. 7 seems to be implying that no matter how bewildering, life is better than death (see 6:5 and 7:11). Commentators frequently cite a passage in Euripides, "it is sweet to see the light," to imply the commonality of the idea. Such commonality does not necessarily imply any direct borrowing, however.[3]

Verses 7 and 8 set out the contrast that will be exploited in the ensuing verses on the topics of life and death. The sense of v. 8 is probably more forcefully captured in a conditional introductory phrase: "if one's years are many." Upon that condition the sage offers a forceful word. The NRSV translation of "should" in v. 8 captures the polite imperative form, the *jussive* form, of the words "rejoice" and "remember." If days are long, rejoice, but also remember that dark days are coming. The recognition that life is fleeting makes enjoyment all the more dear.

There is some question about the meaning of the imagery of "darkness" in v. 8. Is it a reference to old age, to death, or to both? Whatever the case may be, the reference to dark days anticipates the language in 12:2. Whether the concern is for death or old age, it is clear there is an eschatological urgency about this awareness. The phrase "all that comes" need not refer only to death. It can simply mean "all," anything and everything. All is vanity in light of the inescapable and inexorable cycle of human existence. Moreover, Qoheleth has already indicated that no one knows exactly what is coming (e.g., 6:11; 10:14)

The force of the jussive forms in v. 8, the third person imperatives, gives way to the second person imperative forms in vv. 9 and 10. There is therefore a rhetorical intensification as the sage now

"The Desire of the Eyes"

AΩ The instruction in 11:9 was regarded as questionable to ancient interpreters, even though there was an established tradition in the maxims of ancient Egypt of associating enjoyment of one's wealth with its attainment (Murphy).

LXX translators added *mē*, "not," and *amomos*, "without sin," after "heart" in order to ensure the understanding that the admonition was not

An outdoor banquet scene depicts the delights of privilege and position. Those enthroned are enjoying the service of others.

Banquet. 7th C. BC. Relief from Ashurbanipal's palace in Nineveh. British Museum, London, Great Britain.

toward a lifestyle or life practices antagonistic to piety. Midrash Rabbah on Qohelet quotes Num 15:39 as an objection to the sage's imperative. That passage explains the admonition to make fringes on the corners of garments as reminders to follow the commandments of the Lord and not the desires of the heart and eyes.

Even more significantly, the hedonistic character of 11:9 contributed to rabbinical disputes over the inclusion of Qoheleth in the biblical canon. Along with the internal contradictions of the book of Ecclesiastes, the instructions contained within were thought to have a "heretical tendency," which was illustrated in some respect by this verse.

For further reading, see Roger Beckwith, *The Old Testament Canon of the New Testament Church* (Grand Rapids: Eerdmans, 1985), 284, 287; and J. P. Lewis, "What do we mean by Jabneh?" *JBR* 32 (1964): 125-32.

Roland E. Murphy, *Ecclesiastes* (WBC 23A; Waco: Word, 1992), 116.

moves in v. 9 to the three imperatives that contain his advice: rejoice, walk, and know. The sage is suggesting that youth itself is a gift from God to be enjoyed. One should therefore rejoice that the opportunity for enjoyment is there. Such rejoicing is one's heart taking the lead. The NRSV accurately reflects the Hiphil stem of the verb, which implies that one's heart is doing the cheering up and not being cheered up. That only leaves one to respond by "following," or to "walk in the way of" one's heart. The idea of following one's heart is not new with this passage. A kind of personification of the heart occurs in 2:1-3, where the sage's heart was spying out what was good. ["The Desire of the Eyes"] The verse concludes by admonishing a simultaneous awareness, "know" that God brings all things into judgment. Some scholars believe this final phrase to be a gloss by a later reader, perhaps one who failed to accept the notion that all things are "vanity."[4] However, this is not necessary given that the sage has frequently navigated a precipitous path between apparently opposing realities (e.g., 5:2 and 9:7) and has furthermore incorporated a sense of judgment throughout his instructions (e.g., 2:14b; 3:19-20; 9:10-12). On the one hand, youth enables individuals to have enjoyment; on the other, there is a time of reckoning for all things.

Verse 10 closes the opening section on youth with two further imperatives: "banish anxiety" and "put away pain." Since v. 9 admonishes rejoicing, this advice in v. 10 seems consistent. How can people rejoice when they are distracted by anxiety and pain? The sage suggests that both youth and the dawn of life are vanity. The phrase translated "dawn of life" is most interesting. In Hebrew the word is "blackness," *šaḥărût*. The LXX translates the term with the word *anoia*, or "lack of understanding." This is understandable since the same word has that meaning in Proverbs 1:28 and 8:17. However, it is more likely that the term "blackness" is a circumlocution for "blackness of hair." Blackness of hair is an attribute of youth that is used to refer to youth itself. This is a metaphoric convention called metonymy: a technique of evoking an idea by using a term that is associated with the idea.

The Puzzle of Growing Old, 12:1-8

Readers may pause to question the appropriateness of Qoheleth's sudden jump to one's "creator," *bôrĕêkā*, when in preceding verses he has admonished youths to banish anxiety. What could create more anxiety than the thought of God's judgment (e.g. 3:7; 5:4; 8:11-13)? For that reason, scholars have suggested other readings of the Hebrew letters. With minor emendations the term could be "wellspring" (*bĕʾērĕkā*), which could be an image for "your wife." Such an image would be consonant with the look backward in view of the future the sage is preparing to describe. Likewise, the term could mean "the pit" (*bôrĕkā*), an image for death anticipating the ensuing treatment of the destiny of all humankind.[5] [Your Creator] Possibly all three images are intended and the audience is understood to be *hearing* the term, not *reading*. Through an aural medium the term evokes at least these three images related to the overall context of 11:7–12:8.[6]

The overall function of v. 1 is to confront readers with a sense of urgency. While it is unclear to what "days of trouble" refers exactly,

Your Creator

AΩ To a Hebrew auditor, as opposed to a Hebrew reader, the sound of the word translated in NRSV as "creator" forms a homophone with at least two other Hebrew words. These words could just as reasonably be substituted as the intended words in v. 1 since remembering the creator seems an unlikely admonition in view of the preceding admonition to follow the desires of heart and eyes. It may well be that all three are indeed possible and further contribute, at an *aural* level, to the development of thought in 12:1-7. To remember one's *bôrĕkā*, one's "cistern," one might read Prov 5:15, 18, where one's cistern is a cipher for one's wife, thus "enjoyment." To think of one's *bôrĕkā* is also to think of one's "pit" or "grave," thus also to think of death.

The single homophone evokes at least three ideas—one's wife, one's approaching death, and one's creator, God. As hearers progress through the poem, they think of enjoyment, of death, and of God (Seow).

For further reading, see Michael V. Fox, "Aging and Death in Qohelet 12," *JSOT* 42 (1988): 55-77; M. Leahy, "The Meaning of Ecclesiastes 12:1-5," *ITQ* 19 (1952): 297-300; and Graham Ogden, "Qoheleth XI 7-XII 8: Qoheleth's Summons to Enjoyment and Reflection," *VT* 34 (1984): 27-38.

Choon-Leong Seow, *Ecclesiastes* (AB 18C; New York: Doubleday, 1997), 352.

whether death or old age, the time phrase in 1b is significant. It governs the images that follow by evoking the feeling that the days of youth (11:7-10) are fleeting.

The phrase translated "before" in v. 1, *'ad 'ăšer*, recurs at the beginning of v. 2, signaling the beginning of something new. The sage now elaborates on the phrase "days of trouble" of v. 1 in non-literal language. The imagery of darkening sun, light, moon, and stars calls to mind prophetic eschatological passages concerned with life's end (Isa 5:30; 13:10; Ezek 32:7-8; Joel 2:2; Job 3:6). Interestingly, this sage makes a distinction between sun and light in much the same way as Genesis 1:4. In the creation story of Genesis 1, the light that exists apart from the sun and moon is of a special nature. Readers will recall that in the opening of Qoheleth's instruction the sun rises endlessly. At the conclusion of the sage's book of instructions, the sun is finally darkening. Clouds cover the luminaries and may therefore also function as eschatological imagery.[7]

The real challenge of interpretation comes in vv. 3-5. Are these metaphors that evoke reflection upon old age, or death, or an approaching storm? Could the language possibly connote a funeral procession? Do these metaphors join together to create a sustained allegory? All these possibilities have been suggested to various degrees.[8] Verse 3 opens the unit with an image of the house, *habbayit*, and v. 5 concludes with the same image, *bêt 'ôlāmô*. In the latter case it is clear that the allusion is to death. It is not so clear in v. 3, however. Four images govern v. 3: "the guards of the house tremble," "the strong men are bent," the women who grind cease," and "those who look through the windows see dimly." The traditional allegorical meanings assign the following meanings: the guards are the aged and trembling hands, the strong men are legs, the grinding women are teeth, and the women looking through windows are eyes. Yet the uncertainty of these significances and the inability to sustain the transference of meaning throughout the poem makes such interpretations open to possible alternative meanings.

The images may simply refer to those who occupy a household and cease their work for a very auspicious day. Fox argues that a funeral procession is the governing metaphor, which provides a reason for people to stop their work, join the mourning, close doors, desist from talking so that the sounds of birds rise.[9] There is a balance between two masculine images in v. 3a and two feminine images in v. 3b. The phrase "guards of the house" occurs also in 2 Samuel 15:16, 16:21, and 20:3 and simply refer to those in charge of a household. The approaching procession causes them to be afraid. That phrase stands in parallel with "strong men," which justifies the understanding that these are guards and not mere housekeepers. The maidservants who cease their grinding because there are few is clear enough. What is not clear is the connection between the approaching day and their diminishment. If these are the effects of a funeral procession, then it may be that their numbers diminish because of the need to participate in mourning. The women who look out windows may well be the well-to-do who observe. Likewise, they could be the women whose hopes are dashed (e.g., Judg 5:28; 2 Sam 6:16; Prov. 7:6).[10]

Verse 4 does not consistently allegorize the decrepit human body. If the funeral procession in the street is the governing image, then in v. 4 the point of view changes from those inside houses to those out of doors who perhaps participate in the procession. The closing of doors causes the sounds inside houses to diminish on the street, especially the sound of work in the mills. NRSV's translation of 4b there clearly assumes that the governing metaphor is the old person. The implication is that an old person's sleep is easily disturbed. If the governing image is that of a funeral procession, then the statement may be translated as the increase of the sound of a bird. The increased sound to people on the street—the sound of a bird—is a result of closing doors to competing sounds such as the mills indoors. Likewise, the "daughters of song" could be mourning women. In parallel with the image of birds, "daughters of song" could also refer to some kind of bird associated with death and mourning.[11]

Five images dominate v. 5. In the first two images NRSV maintains the allegory of an individual's experiences of old age by continuing the indefinite subject, "one." The translation "afraid" rests on multiple manuscripts, although there is greater manuscript evidence for reading the Hebrew word as "they see." The reading of "fear" is probably due to the parallel in 5ab concerning "terrors" in the road. This is perhaps fitting with a certain view of old age. However, the plural "they see" might have as its antecedent subject "the daughters of song" of v. 4. Taken as some kind of bird, the "daughters of song" are the ones who see from on high, and become observers of this funeral procession.

Verse 5b continues with three images that invite speculation as to their significance: the blossoming of the almond tree, the dragging along of a grasshopper, and the failure of desire. Since the almond blossom is white, the image privileges the NRSV reading of another allusion to the white hair of an old person. The rabbinic readings of the burdened grasshopper saw in it an allusion to the inability of sexual arousal that accompanies old age. The translation "failure of desire" renders a Hebrew word (*hāʾăbîyônâ*) that might otherwise refer to a plant called the caper berry. Capers were used as flavoring to stimulate the appetite. Thus, it is perhaps a reference to the loss of appetite.

Alternatively, blossoming of almonds, breaking open of the caper, and the engorged grasshopper could also be images of springtime.

In such a case they would function to provide a contrast between the fate of nature and that of humans. Natural images opened the sage's discussion (e.g. 1:2-9) and now the sage draws conclusions on the basis of nature's cycles: "there is nothing new under the sun." Job makes a similar assumption about nature's cycles when he asks about the fate of a tree: "For there is hope for a tree, if it is cut down, that it will sprout again, and that its shoots will not cease." "But mortals die, and are laid low; humans expire, and where are they?" (Job 14:7,10). The sage's conclusion in v. 5 seems related. Unlike the cycles in nature, humans go to their eternal home: death.[12]

The third and final unit of the poem is marked by the third temporal clause, translated "before" (cf. 12:1 and 2). The imagery that follows seems clearly to concern death without having to appeal to allegory. The first two images should be understood as two parts of the same thing: a lamp. The silver cord is very likely the stand and the golden bowl the container that holds the oil. The image is one of breaking a lamp so that the light is extinguished. ["Is Snapped"] Since light has been a common metaphor for life in the sage's instructions (e.g. 11:7; 4:3), the image signifies the loss of one's life. The image is fitting for the context whether it is an allegory for old age or a series of metaphors depicting a funeral procession.

The image of light connects well with images of fountains and cisterns since, as sources of water, they, too, may function as imagery of life. If the images refer to broken pulleys with which to draw water,[13] then clearly in their larger sense, they also refer to the end of life. However, Seow is not so certain that water was drawn from cisterns with "wheels," or pulleys. He notes that the words

"Is Snapped"

AΩ The phrase in 12:6 translated by NRSV as "is snapped" poses an interesting challenge for translators. The *kĕtîb* tradition has *yērāḥēq*, "to be distant" or "to be removed." This makes no sense in the context, so most scholars adopt the *qĕrēʾ* tradition, which is *yērātēq*, substituting the Hebrew *taw* for the *ḥet*. The meaning of the word in reference to the "silver cord" is that it is "not bound or joined." It is possible to make further substitution by suggesting that the word is *yēnātēq*, supplying a *nun* for the *reš*, meaning "snapped." This term is thought to be the original word since it appears to be reflected in the LXX translation with the word *anatrapei*, "to be overthrown," a term implying a sudden cataclysmic event. NRSV's translation "is snapped" seems to follow such a chain of emendations.

Seow argues that the appeal to the verb *yēnātēq* is unnecessary, since in various uses of the root *rātaq* (thus *yēnātēq*) in Aramaic, the meaning "to be broken" or "to be crushed" is derived. Thus the *qĕrēʾ* tradition suffices to convey a single cataclysmic event in the metaphor of the silver cord and golden bowl.

Choon-Leong Seow, *Ecclesiastes* (AB 18C; New York: Doubleday, 1997), 365.

translated as fountain and cistern also may refer to the grave or the pit. The image may actually be one of smashing pots at the graveside as a funerary practice.[14]

Verse 7 solidifies the references to death by using two familiar biblical images: "dust," *'āpār*, and "breath" or "spirit," *rûaḥ*. That the dust returns to the earth recalls both Genesis 2:7 and 3:19; (cf. Eccl 3:20). In the Genesis 3:19 it stands as the symbol of humanness: humans are made of dust and to dust they return. Readers may also remember that Abraham denigrates himself by applying the symbol (Gen 18:27). Job's friends also denigrate humankind using the imagery of dust as a symbol of inferiority (Job 4:19; cf. 8:9). The breath that returns to God is a conventional reference to "death." The fact that Qoheleth alludes to the breath's return to God in v. 7 does not diminish the literal questioning of whether it actually returns in 3:21.

With v. 8 readers have come again to the thematic phrase that introduced the book. Here it functions as the conclusion to the discussion, and may well have been the original ending to the book, before the various epilogues were added in vv. 9-14.

CONNECTIONS

Fraying into the Future

Archaeological excavations in 1978 in an area of Northern Tanzania called Laetoli revealed an extraordinary discovery: a double pair of footprints in a layer of volcanic rock. Radiometric dating of the sets of footprints suggested they were between 3.4 and 3.8 million years old. As well as being the crowning achievement of archaeologist Mary Leakey, the footprints have proven that early hominids had erect posture and thus were fully bipedal.[15]

The footprints provoke further reflections, not the least of which concerns the trajectory of human evolution over an unfathomable amount of time. Could it be that these hominids were what humanity looked like millions of years ago? Readers cannot help but wonder about who these two individuals were. Where they were going that required their walking in cooling volcanic ash? Was it a husband and wife, a father and son? Why the leisurely pace, and why the two sets so close together? In retrospect, it is furthermore a reality that they, like modern humans, faced the reality of life's end. Did they reflect upon life's meaning? Did they share their reflections with each other? The millions of years of evolution have been composed of cycles upon trillions of cycles of birth, youth, old age, and death. On the one hand, the preservation of these very ancient footprints permanently reminds us of the antiquity of human presence on this tiny planet. At the same time, the footprints trail off, leaving no trace, and remind us of human destiny. All must die.

Qoheleth is caught in this kind of reflection upon the significance of birth, youth, old age, and ultimately death. The endless cycles of repetition cause him to realize that enjoyment of life is the only lot for humanity, and that lot has been with us forever. It is in enjoyment that meaning must be sought. Thus, if it is possible, humans must strive to enjoy. These cycles are not out of God's sight, either. They are, rather, God's way. They testify to God's immensity and unfathomability. It is therefore not that God does not act, but that God acts slowly, almost imperceptibly, through these endless cycles.

Richard Wilbur's poem "Years-End" captures something of the significance of such cycles in its reflection upon the seasons, both of the year and of a human life. Peering into houses from a street, the poet's voice observes the quiet unawareness of time's passage. Winter's snow provides the comforting down of the year's death. Humans never cease to expect yet another sunrise, never think that the plans they had made might suddenly be unattainable. In the poignant final stanza, the poem reads:

> These sudden ends of time must give us pause.
> We fray into the future, rarely wrought
> Save in the tapestries of afterthought.
> More time, more time. Barrages of applause
> Come muffled from a buried radio.
> The New-year bells are wrangling with the snow.[16]

To be sure the future is rarely wrought; but so are we, except as we look backward and realize how quickly time has passed and how many things there were to do that we let pass. The sage looks back and says, "Remember your creator in the days of your youth," knowing the inescapable truth that time's passage unravels the best of intentions.

NOTES

[1] Choon-Leong Seow, *Ecclesiastes* (AB 18C; New York: Doubleday, 1997), 372; Michael V. Fox, *A Time to Tear Down & A Time to Build Up* (Grand Rapids: Eerdmans, 1999), 343-49. The discussion that follows relies extensively upon Seow and Fox.

[2] Fox's excursus on aging and death, *A Time to Tear Down,* 343-49, in which he discusses modes of literal, figurative, and allegorical meaning, is helpful and influential (see other contemporary commentaries). However, it is itself probably too rigid a taxonomy to be of use to non-specialists. George B. Caird's *The Language and Imagery of the Bible* (London: Duckworth, 1980), 131-71, continues to be a helpful introduction.

[3] See James L. Crenshaw, *Ecclesiastes* (OTL; Philadelphia: Westminster, 1987), 183; and Roland E. Murphy, *Ecclesiastes* (WBC 23A; Waco: Word, 1992), 116; but compare Seow, *Ecclesiastes,* 347.

[4] Crenshaw, *Ecclesiastes,* 184.

[5] See Murphy, *Ecclesiastes,* 113, for a summary of other proposals.

[6] Seow, *Ecclesiastes,* 352.

[7] Ibid., 353. Seow notes that clouds are associated with divine warrior language and thus become eschatologically significant. See 2 Sam 22:12; Ps 18:12; Judg 5:4; Isa 9:1; Job 36:29.

[8] Fox, *A Time to Tear Down,* 333-36.

[9] Ibid., 325.

[10] Seow, *Ecclesiastes,* 356.

[11] Fox, *A Time to Tear Down,* 326; Seow, *Ecclesiastes,* 359.

[12] See Tobit 3:6 for the same image and its reference to death.

[13] Crenshaw, *Ecclesiastes,* 188.

[14] Seow, *Ecclesiastes,* 366-67.

[15] Neville Agnew and Martha Demas, "Preserving the Laetoli Footprints," SA 279 (September 1998): 44-55.

[16] Richard Wilbur, "Years-End," in *The Norton Anthology of American Literature,* vol. 2, 5th ed., ed. Nina Baym (New York and London: W. W. Norton Co., 1997), 2571.

DISTANCE MAKES THE DIFFERENCE

Ecclesiastes 12:9-14

Most scholars regard the closing six verses of Ecclesiastes as an epilogue, that is, an addition to the text not originally written by the author of the main part of the book. The most convincing evidence is the sudden shift in narrative voice. Qoheleth is no longer speaking; rather, he is being spoken of by another voice. These verses are therefore taken as the response of one (or possibly more) of the earliest readers of the book. The central questions readers should bear in mind concern whether this closing word helps them to assimilate the difficult teachings of the book: (1) How does the narrator's voice in the epilogue create distance from the speaker in the body of the book?[1] (2) How does the personal information (vv. 9-11) affect a reader's understanding of the person who wrote the words of the book? (3) What new and different significance might be attached to "wisdom" and the notion of "the fear of God" after having read the contents of the body of the book, and indeed, the contents of Proverbs?

COMMENTARY

Ecclesiastes a Sage, 12:9-11

A more positive attitude toward Ecclesiastes characterizes these first three verses and provides a recognizable criterion of differentiation from the latter three verses. In vv. 12-14 readers encounter a cautionary warning about the pointlessness of such intellectual pursuits described in vv. 9-11, in addition to an admonition to fear God and keep the commandments. While it is likely that vv. 12-14 actually comprise a second epilogue deriving from yet another reader, in the present form, these verses provide a concluding word that, though different from vv. 9-11, is nevertheless put forward in the same narrative voice as those verses.

"Teaching, Weighing, Studying, Arranging"

AΩ The language of v. 9 originates with one who can look at Qoheleth from some distance and give readers insight into the professional work of at least one sage. The many references to the words of the wise (e.g., 12:11; Prov 1:6; 22:17; 24:23) are illuminated in this description of the activities in which this sage is involved.

The overall task of the wise is to teach the people knowledge. The process includes "weighing," "studying," and then "arranging" the proverbs that are taught. The word translated "weighing" is *'izzēn*, a term most usually associated with the noun *'ōzen*, ear. The implication is that the task of "weighing" is one of listening and evaluating in some respect. Alternatively, another form

The position of scribe was one of great importance in antiquity. Scribes were among the very few persons who could read, write, and thus record the data that would become history.

Scribes. Bas-relief. 18th Dynasty. Egyptian. Museo Archeologico. Florence, Italy.

of the same consonantal root creates another related noun, "scales." From this noun likely comes the verbal idea of "to weigh." Weighing is thus a more metaphorical way of noting the listening activities that accompany the sage's teaching.

The following word, translated "studying," is *ḥiqqēr,* from *ḥāqar,* "to spy out, search out, or examine" (Prov 25:2; Job 5:27). Both these words, *'āzan* and *ḥāqar,* occur in different forms in Job 32:11 as Elihu describes his patient listening while Job searches for words. Describing the sage's activity as chiefly "listening" and "studying" implies that the gathering of information is a more important component than disseminating information.

The final term, *tiqqēn,* is translated as "arranging," implying some kind of editorial activity with reference to proverbs. The LXX translates with *kosmion,* implying a task of "bringing order to," perhaps an activity involving collecting and writing sayings. Perhaps this final term is informed by the occurrence of *tiqqēn* in Eccl 1:15 and 7:13 where it means to straighten something that is crooked. In a sense, teaching is a task that may be thought of as straightening that which is crooked.

For further reading, see James L. Crenshaw, *Education in Ancient Israel* (New York: Doubleday, 1998); and Roland E. Murphy, "The Sage in Ecclesiastes and Qoheleth the Sage," in *The Sage in Israel and the Ancient Near East,* ed. J. G. Gammie and Leo G. Perdue (Winona Lake IN: Eisenbrauns, 1990).

A clear progression of thought is evident in vv. 9-11: v. 9 describes the specific activities of Ecclesiastes; v. 10 elaborates the activities by offering a more general statement describing his criteria; v. 11 concludes with a saying on the efficacy of the words of the wise. Interestingly, vv. 9-10 abandon the image of Qoheleth as a king and portray his work as that of a wise man, *ḥākām.* He taught knowledge, *da'at* (see Prov 1:2, 4); he "weighed," "studied," and "arranged" many proverbs, *měšālîm.* These latter three activities, as translated by NRSV, probably do not quite capture the breadth of possible meaning implied by the Hebrew words themselves. The task of "weighing" might also include the activity of "listening" to proverbs, while the word of "arranging" might also include the "writing" of his own proverbs, some of which readers have undoubtedly read in the preceding chapters. ["Teaching, Weighing, Studying, Arranging"]

Two further aspects of the sage's scholarly work provide depth to the activities depicted in v. 9. Verse 10 elaborates by saying that he sought to find "pleasing words." This implies an aesthetic dimension to his work. That he sought to write "words of truth plainly" implies his integrity. The adverb "plainly" translates the noun *yōšer,* "uprightness" or "honesty," which suggests more than mere clarity of communication, but integrity in handling truth. An interesting chiasm develops between the public and private activities portrayed in the two verses: teaching people, searching proverbs, seeking delightful words, writing the words of truth:

- Teaching people
  - Searching proverbs
  - Seeking delightful words
- Writing the words of truth

The activities of teaching and writing are the results of the sage's personal creative activities of investigation and reflection. Verse 11 is likely a proverb on the value of wisdom instruction, "the words of the wise" generally, functioning to reiterate the value of the teaching of Qoheleth. Even though this phrase, "the words of the wise," occurs throughout the Proverbs (e.g., Prov 1:6; 24:23; 30:31; 31:1), it is likely a reference to a wisdom tradition. The comparison of instruction to "goads," *kaddārĕbōnôt* ("cattle prods") and "nails firmly fixed," *kĕmaśmĕrôt,* implies that, although wisdom teaching may be harsh, it nevertheless has a constructive effect. ["The Collected Sayings"]

"The Collected Sayings"

ΑΩ The term translated "collected sayings" in v. 11, *ba'ălê 'ăsuppôt,* is taken by NRSV to refer to a collection of sayings. That the term is paralleled with "words of the wise" in the same verse suggests some kind of collection like that in the biblical Proverbs, perhaps even Proverbs itself.

Alternate meanings are possible, however. The term *'ăsuppôt* can be translated as "assemblies," not of sayings necessarily, but of people. This is the meaning of the term in the Talmud where members of the Sanhedrin, the Jewish ruling council, is denoted. In this case the words of the wise may not be written collections, but the words of those who sit as masters in the assembly or council.

For further reading, see G. Wilson, "'The Words of the Wise': The Intent and Significance of Qoheleth 12:9-14," *JBL* 103/2 (1984): 175-92.

Piety before Wisdom, 12:12-14

The concluding three verses offer pragmatic advice for ones who are sympathetic with the wisdom tradition as well as more traditional Yahwistic expressions of piety. Verse 12 opens with the same adverbial phrase that begins v. 9: *wĕyōtēr,* "of anything beyond . . . ." The problem is recognizing the possible referents of the plural demonstrative pronoun, which is the object of the adverb *mēhēmmâ,* "these things." Is the reference to the advice immediately following in v. 12,[2] or a reference to the advice immediately preceding, in which case the phrase concerns the "words of the wise" in v. 11?[3] The stronger case recognizes that the word "these" in v. 12 requires an antecedent, and the most immediate for the reader is "the words of the wise." The warning to the pupil, here addressed as "my son," is to avoid teachings that are not officially sanctioned, in this case, anything that goes beyond "the words of the wise." A proverb ensues in v. 12 and reiterates the preceding warning, especially if one understands the phrase "there is no end" to mean "there is no point or purpose." Obviously, the making and studying of many books, the word of the sage Qoheleth, has no point if these books are not sanctioned as "the words of the wise." The question is, should readers understand this statement as an implicit warning against the book to which it is attached?

Most translations of v. 13 take the Hebrew word *nišmāʿ* as either a finite verb in the perfect state, "all has been heard" (NRSV), or as a participle, "when all has been heard" (NAS). The vocalization in the MT would also support an imperative, "hear all." The LXX reads the word *nišmāʿ* in this latter fashion, *akoue,* "listen." In this case, the conclusion put forward in v. 13 offers a trio of imperatives: "hear all," "fear God," and "keep the commandments." While the admonition to "hear all" probably appeals to modern democratic, individualistic biases, it seems a weak reading in view of what precedes immediately in v. 12. The words admonish the student concerning the pointlessness of too much study, especially of material beyond "the words of the wise," the traditional teachings of the wise. Why then should one "hear all" if anything beyond the "words of the wise" is superfluous? It is more likely that the "all" is related to the immediate context in which it occurs and therefore concerns what has been put forward in the book; the immediately ensuing verb, then, reflects action completed, "all has been heard."

Readers have previously encountered references to "the fear of God" in the book (e.g., 3:14; 5:7; 7:18; 8:12). Far from being surprised that the epilogist should return to this theme, readers find a clear connection with earlier arguments in the book. What is genuinely new, however, is the accompanying admonition to "keep the commandments," *miṣwotāyw.* This kind of language, which has not occurred previously in the book of Ecclesiastes, is far more characteristic of the Deuteronomic concern with the adherence to Yahweh's covenant law and command. While there are numerous studies recognizing the linguistic and conceptual affinities between the Wisdom and the Deuteronomic traditions,[4] it remains a point of debate as to whether this expression in Ecclesiastes reflects "a movement afoot to understand the wisdom statements as, in some sense, the very commandments of God."[5] A more cautious stance would admit that only in the much later wisdom book of Jesus ben Sirach does one encounter such an identification between wisdom and law.[6]

The concluding verse is a clear allusion to 11:9 where the youth is admonished both to pursue his desires and to keep fully in mind the unavoidable fate of God's judgment. The same certainty of the deity's judgment upon all things, including secret things, whether good or evil, closes the book. More importantly, this assertion provides a stark contrast to the statements throughout the preceding body of the book that claim death to be the only sure fate for humanity (3.20-22; 6:3-6; 9:5, 10). Moreover, the sage has insisted throughout that God is far less involved with humankind than one might suppose (e.g., 7:14; 8:17). One not only stands in awe of such a bold affirmation of piety, but has some clear indication of how this later reader understood the main thrust of the book of Ecclesiastes. Such an affirmation of piety is warranted to the later reader if he perceives that the teaching, in the words of Job's friends, "does away with the fear of God, and hinders meditation before God" (Job 15:4).

CONNECTIONS

Synthesis or Relationship that Seeks the Truth?

David Robertson suggested that cultures past and present know at least two different ways of creating meaning: synthetically and syndetically. The most familiar is the former, where meaning is created through progressive resolution of opposites, and thus where successive phases of thought grow from preceding ones. "Aristotelian plots and Hegelian logic are paradigmatic examples."[7] Alternatively, syndesis creates meaning through repetition, accretion, and proliferation. There is not necessarily any resolution of opposites and no synthesis of ideas. Like the book of Proverbs, there is an "additive list without a sum."[8] The epilogue to the book

Ancient Interpretation of Scripture

Whatever the meaning of the epilogue in relationship to the words of Qoheleth, it is certain that the epilogue is evidence of the ancient process of scriptural interpretation. The fact that appended to the work Ecclesiastes itself are verses suggesting a way of making the work more meaningful to readers gives modern readers some understanding of the role of interpretation in the origins of Scripture.

We see similar signs of interpretation throughout many of the Bible's documents. One clear instance is where one reader of 1 Sam 9:9 has provided illumination on the meaning of an obscure term. It seems that the word "seer" (*rō'eh*) had lost meaning. The interpreter of that text explains that the equivalent term is "prophet" (*nabî*). Other instances might be cited where Deuteronomy makes textual references to materials in the Covenant Code, sometimes indicating this through a formal citation ("which he commanded"), and sometimes without citation. Prophetic proclamation reveals interpretative expansions of legal cases, such as Jer 2:26 and 34, which offer an interpretation of the law of the thief caught in the act, Exod 21:1-2a (for these and other such examples see Fishbane).

The epilogue in Ecclesiastes calls readers' attention to yet another matter they must attend to in interpreting the book. They must pay attention to the interpretations of those who passed the materials on.

For further reading, see J. Bradley Chance and Milton P. Horne, *Rereading the Bible* (Upper Saddle River NJ: Prentice Hall, 2000); Dana Nolan Fewell, ed., *Reading Between Texts* (Louisville: Westminster John Knox Press, 1992); and Michael Fishbane, *The Garments of Torah* (Bloomington: Indiana University Press, 1989).

Michael Fishbane, *Biblical Interpretation in Ancient Israel* (Oxford: Clarendon, 1985), 163-64, 312.

---

of Ecclesiastes is clearly an addition. The question is whether it is an attempt to resolve the contradictions that precede, or only another addition that proliferates the riddles. [Ancient Interpretation of Scripture]

One who reads Ecclesiastes carefully and in its entirety for the first time probably does not actually come to the so-called epilogue and immediately think of later readers who have appended these concluding words to the book. More likely one recognizes the shift in narrative voice and infers an attempt to put what precedes in perspective. Whose perspectives are readers reminded of, though? First, we are reminded of the author's perspective (the one writing the book, who may indeed be different from the narrator's voice); second, the narrator's (the one in the book telling about Qoheleth, 1:1-2; 12:9-14); and finally, Qoheleth himself (who talks about his experiences in his youth from the perspective of an old man).[9] Readers should therefore conclude that "the essential function of the epilogue is to mediate Qohelet's words to the reader in a way that makes them more plausible and more tolerable."[10] In these closing words, readers see that Qoheleth is himself a sage, participating in a longstanding tradition of instruction, one that we have already discovered to be full of multiple significances and meanings, buried in metaphor and delightful rhetorical-verbal play. This makes readers believe that Qoheleth only has their best interests in mind. He was himself a practitioner of a more pious faith, and the author and his narrator are inviting readers into Qoheleth's world. It is a difficult world to be sure, but a world where one is not alone.

Marsha Norman's play *Traveler in the Dark* seems to have been written with Qoheleth's struggles well in view.[11] The play's setting is the funeral of a woman, Mavis, who has died unexpectedly from a sudden illness. The conflict stems from the attempts of various friends and family to find some meaning in her death. Everett, an aging Evangelical preacher and longtime friend, finds comfort by interpreting Mavis's death within the framework of his religious convictions. He believes that God uses such events to "get our attention." Sam, Everett's son and a successful surgeon—on whose operating table Mavis died—rejects his father's religion and renounces any possibility of meaningful assimilation or synthesis of this tragic event through traditional belief systems. Sam's wife, Glory, remembers Mavis as both a rival for Sam's attention and as a friend. She struggles after Mavis's death to comprehend the internal conflict she feels over the loss of one who played such conflicting and confusing roles. The focal point of these many emotions is Stephen, the twelve-year-old son of Sam and Glory, who is caught within the three-way interpretive struggles of father, mother, and grandfather. These three represent for Stephen competing ways of responding to Mavis's death and to death in general. As each character discovers his or her systems of belief to be inadequate, the anger that results threatens to sever their relationships. The play's solution is not, however, any synthetic explanation of why the tragedy happened, but a resolution of the relational conflicts through forgiveness. With the relationships restored, the family can at least face together their doubts and anger over Mavis's death. They do not have to assimilate her unexpected death into any artificial framework of meaning. They can face it honestly without letting it destroy what is the beginning point of meaning: relationships.

The epilogue to the book of Ecclesiastes is not a synthesis, but rather an invitation into a relationship with the sage's perspective on things. These closing words reflect upon a world of hard and often unbalanced truth that does not necessarily synthesize well into one's pious framework of meaning. The relationship is not with Qoheleth alone, though. It is also with wisdom herself. Wisdom, readers now recall, is that woman who calls all those who pass by to turn aside and learn from her.

NOTES

[1] Michael V. Fox, *A Time to Tear Down & A Time to Build Up* (Grand Rapids: Eerdmans, 1999), 350-62; see also his "Frame-narrative and Composition in the Book of Qohelet," *HUCA* 48 (1977): 83-106.

[2] R. N. Whybray, *Ecclesiastes* (Grand Rapids: Eerdmans, 1989), 169-74.

[3] James L. Crenshaw, *Ecclesiastes* (OTL; Philadelphia: Westminster, 1987), 34-35, 192; Fox, *A Time to Tear Down,* 353.

[4] See, for instance, R. N. Whybray, *The Intellectual Tradition in the Old Testament* (BZAW 135; Berlin & New York: Walter de Gruyter, 1974); Moshe Weinfeld, *Deuteronomy and the Deuteronomic School* (Oxford: Clarendon Press, 1972); and Calum Carmichael, *The Laws of Deuteronomy* (Ithaca NY: Cornell University Press, 1978).

[5] Gerald H. Wilson, "'The Words of the Wise': The Intent and Significance of Qohelet 12:9-14," *JBL* 103/2 (1984): 183; in opposition see Fox, *A Time to Tear Down,* 375-77.

[6] See Gerald T. Sheppard, *Wisdom as a Hermeneutical Construct* (BZAW 151; Berlin & New York: Walter de Gruyter, 1980), 120-29.

[7] David Robertson, "Job and Ecclesiastes," *Soundings* 73/2-3 (Summer/Fall 1990): 258.

[8] Ibid., 259.

[9] Fox, *A Time to Tear Down,* 371-74.

[10] Ibid., 371.

[11] Marsha Norman, *Traveler in the Dark* (U.S.: Dramatist's Play Service, Inc., 1988).

BIBLIOGRAPHY

Proverbs

Barton, John. "Understanding Old Testament Ethics." *Journal for the Study of the Old Testament* 9 (1978): 44-64.

Blenkinsopp, Joseph. *Wisdom and Law in the Old Testament: The Ordering of Life in Israel and Early Judaism.* Revised edition. Oxford: Oxford University Press, 1995.

Brenner, Athalya, ed. *A Feminist Companion to Wisdom Literature.* Sheffield: Sheffield Academic Press, 1995.

Brown, William P. *Character in Crisis: A Fresh Approach to the Wisdom Literature of the Old Testament.* Grand Rapids: Eerdmans, 1996.

Camp, Claudia V. *Wisdom and the Feminine in the Book of Proverbs.* Sheffield: JSOT/Almond Press, 1985.

Clifford, Richard J. *Proverbs.* Old Testament Library. Louisville: Westminster John Knox Press, 1999.

Crenshaw, J. "The Concept of God in Old Testament Wisdom." *In Search of Wisdom: Essays in Memory of John G. Gammie,* ed. Leo G. Perdue, Bernard B. Scott, and William J. Wiseman. Louisville: Westminster John Knox Press, 1993.

———. *Old Testament Wisdom: An Introduction.* Revised and enlarged. Louisville: Westminster John Knox Press, 1998.

———, ed. "Prolegomenon." *Studies in Ancient Israelite Wisdom.* New York: Ktav, 1976, 1-45.

———. "The Sage in Proverbs." *The Sage in Israel and the Ancient Near East,* ed. J. G. Gammie and L. G. Perdue. Winona Lake IN: Eisenbrauns, 1990, 205-16.

———. "Wisdom." *Old Testament Form Criticism,* ed. John Hayes. San Antonio: Trinity University Press, 1974, 225-64.

Day, John, et al., eds. *Wisdom in Ancient Israel: Essays in Honour of J. A. Emerton.* Cambridge: Cambridge University Press, 1995.

Fontaine, Carol R., and Sharon H. Ringe, eds. *Woman's Bible Commentary.* Louisville: Westminster John Knox, 1998.

Garrett, Duane A. *Proverbs, Ecclesiastes, Song of Songs.* New American Commentary 14. Nashville: Broadman Press, 1993.

———. *Wisdom and Creation: The Theology of Wisdom Literature.* Nashville: Abingdon, 1994.

Hildebrandt, Ted. "Proverbial Pairs: Compositional Units in Proverbs 10–29." *Journal of Biblical Literature* 107 (1988): 207-24.

McKane, William. *Proverbs: A New Approach.* Old Testament Library. London: SCM Press, 1970.

McCreesh, T. P. "Wisdom as Wife: Proverbs 31:10-31." *Revue Biblique* 92 (1985): 25-46.

Murphy, Roland E. *Proverbs*. Word Biblical Commentary 22. Dallas: Word, 1998.

————. *The Tree of Life: An Exploration of Biblical Wisdom Literature.* Grand Rapids: Eerdmans, 1996.

————. "Wisdom and Creation." *Journal of Biblical Literature* 104 (1985): 3-11.

Newsom, Carol A. "Woman and the Discourse of Patriarchal Wisdom." *Gender and Difference in Ancient Israel,* ed. P. L. Day. Minneapolis: Fortress Press, 1989, 142-60.

Perdue, Leo G. *Proverbs*. Interpretation. Louisville: Westminster John Knox Press, 2000.

————. "Liminality as a Social Setting for Wisdom Instructions." *Zeitschrift für die alttestamentliche Wissenschaft* 93 (1981): 114-26.

Plöger, O. *Sprüche Salomos (Proverbia).* Biblischer Kommentar 17. Neukirchen-Vluyn: Neukirchener Verlag, 1984.

Rad, Gerhard von. *Wisdom in Israel.* London: SCM Press, 1972.

Scott, R. B. Y. *Proverbs, Ecclesiastes.* Anchor Bible C18. New York: Doubleday, 1965.

Van Leeuwen, Raymond C. "The Book of Proverbs." Vol. 5, *New Interpreter's Bible.* Nashville: Abingdon Press, 1997.

————. "Liminality and Worldview in Proverbs 1–9." *Semeia* 50 (1990): 111-44.

Washington, Harold C. *Wealth and Poverty in the Instruction of Amenemope and the Hebrew Proverbs.* Ann Arbor: University of Michigan, 1994.

Weeks, S. *Early Israelite Wisdom.* Oxford: Clarendon Press, 1994.

Westermann, Claus. *Roots of Wisdom: The Oldest Proverbs of Israel and Other Peoples.* Trans. J. Daryl Charles. Louisville: Westminster John Knox Press, 1995.

Whybray, R. N. *Proverbs*. New Century Bible Commentary. Grand Rapids: Eerdmans, 1989.

————. *The Book of Proverbs: A Survey of Modern Study.* Leiden and New York: Brill, 1995.

————. *The Composition of the Book of Proverbs.* Journal for the Study of the Old Testament Supplement Series 168. Sheffield: JSOT Press, 1994.

————. *Wealth and Poverty in the Book of Proverbs.* Sheffield: JSOT Press, 1990.

Williams, James G. *Those Who Ponder Proverbs.* Sheffield: JSOT Press, 1981.

Yee, Gale. "I Have Perfumed My Bed with Myrrh': The Foreign Woman (*issah zarah*) in Proverbs 1–9." *Journal for the Study of the Old Testament* 43 (1989): 53-68.

Ecclesiastes

Brown, William P. *Ecclesiastes*. Interpretation. Louisville: Westminster John Knox Press, 2000.

Crenshaw, James L. *Ecclesiastes*. Old Testament Library. Philadelphia: Westminster, 1987.

————. "The Expression *mi yodea* in the Hebrew Bible." *Vetus Testamentum* 36 (1986): 274-88.

————. "Youth and Old Age in Qoheleth." *Harvard Annual Review* 11 (1987): 1-13.

Dell, Katherine J. "Ecclesiastes as Wisdom: Consulting Early Interpreters." *Vetus Testamentum* 44 (1994): 301-29.

Fox, Michael V. "Frame-Narrative and Composition in the Book of Qohelet," *Hebrew Union College Annual* 48 (1968): 83-106.

————. "The Identification of Quotations in Biblical Literature." *Zeitschrift für die alttestestamentlich Wissenschaft* 92 (1980): 416-31.

————. *A Time to Tear Down & A Time to Build Up: A Rereading of Ecclesiastes.* Grand Rapids/Cambridge U.K.: Eerdmans, 1999.

Gordis, Robert. *Koheleth—The Man and His World.* New York: Schocken, 1968.

————. "Quotations in Wisdom Literature." *Jewish Quarterly Review* 30 (1939/1940): 123-47.

————. "Virtual Quotations in Job, Sumer and Qumran." *Vetus Testamentum* 31 (1981): 410-27.

Kugel, James. "Qohelet and Money." *Catholic Biblical Quarterly* 51 (1989): 32-49.

Loader, J. A. "Polar Structures in the Book of Qohelet." Beihefte zur Zeitschrift für die alttestamentliche Wissenschaft 152. Berlin and New York: De Greuyter, 1979.

Longman III, Trempor. *The Book of Ecclesiastes.* New International Commentary on the Old Testament. Grand Rapids: Eerdmans, 1998.

Murphy, Roland E. *Ecclesiastes.* Word Biblical Commentary 19a. Dallas: Word, 1992.

————. "The Faith of Qoheleth." *Word and World* 7 (1987): 253-60.

————. "Qoheleth and Theology?" *Biblical Theology Bulletin* 21 (1991): 30-33.

Ogden, Graham S. "The 'Better'-Proverb (Tob-Spruch), Rhetorical Criticism, and Qoheleth." *Journal of Biblical Literature* 96 (1977): 489-505.

Perry, T. A. *Dialogues with Kohelet.* University Park: Pennsylvania State University, 1993.

Priest, J. "Humanism, Skepticism, and Pessimism in Israel." *Journal of the American Academy of Religion* 36 (1968): 311-26.

Seow, Choon-Leong. *Ecclesiastes.* Anchor Bible 18C. New York: Doubleday, 1997.

Short, Robert L. *A Time to Be Born—A Time to Die: The Images and Insights of Ecclesiastes for Today.* New York: Harper & Row, 1973.

Towner, Sibley. "Ecclesiastes." Vol. 5, *New Interpreters Bible.* Nashville: Abingdon, 1997.

Trible, Phyllis. "Wisdom Builds a Poem: The Architecture of Proverbs 1:20-33." *Journal of Biblical Literature* 94 (1975): 509-18.

Whybray, R. N. *Ecclesiastes.* New Century Bible Commentary. Grand Rapids: Eerdmans, 1989.

————. *Two Jewish Theologies: Job and Ecclesiastes.* Great Britain: University of Hull, 1980.

———. "Qoheleth, Preacher of Joy." *Journal for the Study of the Old Testament* 23 (1982): 87-98.

Williams, James G. "What Does It Profit a Man?: The Wisdom of Koheleth." *Judaism* 20 (1971): 179-93.

Wilson, Gerald H. "'The Words of the Wise': The Intent and Significance of Qohelet 12:9-14." *Journal of Biblical Literature* 103 (1984): 175-92.

Wright, Addison D. G. "The Riddle of the Sphinx: The Structure of the Book of Qoheleth." *Catholic Biblical Quarterly* 30 (1968): 313-34.

———. "The Riddle of the Sphinx Revisited: Numerical Patterns in the Book of Qoheleth." *Catholic Biblical Quarterly* 42 (1980): 35-51.

———."Additional Numerical Patterns in Qoheleth." *Catholic Biblical Quarterly* 45 (1983): 32-43.

INDEX OF MODERN AUTHORS

INDEX OF SIDEBARS
FOR PROVERBS

ILLUSTRATION SIDEBARS

INDEX OF SIDEBARS
FOR ECCLESIASTES

ILLUSTRATION SIDEBARS

INDEX OF SCRIPTURES

INDEX OF TOPICS

ILLUSTRATION CREDITS

Qumran © Tony W. Cartledge

Egyptian Scribe © Giraduon / Art Resource, NY

Jaws of Death © Smyth & Helwys / Barclay Burns

Servants Netting Wild Geese © Erich Lessing / Art Resource, NY

Ancient City Gate © Smyth & Helwys / Barclay Burns

The School of Athens © Scala / Art Resource, NY

Sacred Trees © Smyth & Helwys / Barclay Burns

The Vision of Christ © The Pierpont Morgan Library / Art Resource, NY

Sisyphus Sleeping © Michael Bergt

Wine and Bread © Smyth & Helwys / Barclay Burns

Weighing of the Souls © Alinari / Art Resource, NY

Guardian Lion © Scala / Art Resource, NY

Fertility and Harvest © Erich Lessing / Art Resource, NY

Tetradrichm with Bee © Erich Lessing / Art Resource, NY

Cuneiform Tablet © Erich Lessing / Art Resource, NY

Moses and the Tablets of Law © Snark / Art Resource, NY

In the Salon at Rue des Moulins © Erich Lessing / Art Resource, NY

Gilgamesh Cuneiform © Erich Lessing / Art Resource, NY

Heliopolitan Ennead © Smyth & Helwys / Barclay Burns

Boethius, Consolation of Philosophy © Giraudon / Art Resource, NY

Ritual Slaughter of Oxen © Erich Lessing / Art Resource, NY

Judgment of Solomon © Erich Lessing / Art Resource, NY

Waiting for Godot © Steve Gilliam

Goldworking © Smyth & Helwys / Barclay Burns

The Dead Sea © Brewton-Parker

Burnt Offering © Smyth & Helwys / Barclay Burns

Praying Priest © Erich Lessing / Art Resource, NY

Hittite God with King © Smyth & Helwys / Barclay Burns

Copper Smelting © Smyth & Helwys / Barclay Burns

The Crossing of the Red Sea © Scala / Art Resource, NY

Megiddo © Smyth & Helwys / Barclay Burns

Lion and Bull © Giraudon / Art Resource, NY

Eye Idols © Smyth & Helwys / Barclay Burns

The Drunkeness of Noah © Nicolo Orsi Battaglini / Art Resource, NY

The Wine Harvest © Réunion des Musées Nationaux / Art Resource, NY / Photo: J. G. Berizzi

Wine Press © Mitchell Reddish

Mount Hermon © Brewton-Parker

David © Scala / Art Resource, NY

Two Potters at the Kiln © Borromeo / Art Resource, NY

Tear Bottles © Erich Lessing / Art Resource, NY

Team of Plowing Oxen © Scala / Art Resource, NY

Pharoh Seti I © Smyth & Helwys / Barclay Burns

Texitle Making © Smyth & Helwys / Barclay Burns

Goddess Maat © Scala / Art Resource, NY

Sisyphus © Smyth & Helwys / Jim Burt

Re, the Sun God © Smyth & Helwys / Barclay Burns

Mother Theresa © Smyth & Helwys / Barclay Burns

Hanging Gardens of Babylon © Réunion des Musées Nationaux/ Art Resource, NY / Photo: J. G. Berizzi

Sukkot © The Jewish Museum, NY / Art Resource, NY: Photo: Joseph Parnell

Amphora © Scala / Art Resource, NY

Dancing Maenad © Scala / Art Resource, NY

Grave Stele © Scott Nash

Herodian Temple © Erich Lessing / Art Resource, NY

Burial Chamber © Smyth & Helwys / Barclay Burns

Darwin © Smyth & Helwys / Barclay Burns

Frankestein Monster © Smyth & Helwys / Barclay Burns

Darius the Great © SEF / Art Resource, NY

The Goddess Ninsum © Erich Lessing / Art Resource, NY

Preparation of the Lotus Flowers © Alinari / Art Resource, NY

Tower with Defenders © Erich Lessing / Art Resource, NY

Flat Roofed Houses © Scott Nash (photo); Smyth & Helwys / Barclay Burns (illustration)

Banquet © The British Museum

Scribes © Scala / Art Resource, NY